The Plains of Talavera

the Hills of Busaco.

Martin McDowell

Published in 2016 by FeedARead.com Publishing – Arts Council funded

First Edition

A CIP catalogue record for this title is available from the British Library.

Dedication

To my wife, Doreen, and children, Amy and Steven,
who are so indulgent of my unfathomable
Napoleonic obsession!

Also to David Richard Wood, my good friend and
colleague, who always appeared interested, for which
encouragement I am eternally grateful

Acknowledgments

The History of the Peninsular War-
Volumes II and III

Sir Charles Oman

Talavera -
Andrew W. Field

Talavera –
Peter Edwards

Waterloo
Mark Adkin

An Atlas of the Peninsular War
Ian Robertson

During the Campaigns described in this volume:-
-   Oporto and the pursuit – 105th are in the place of the
29th Foot, Worcestershire, 'The Two and a Hook', 6th
Brigade.

- Talavera – the 105th are in the place of the 2/31st Foot, Huntingdonshire, Mackenzie's Brigade, 'The Young Buffs'. The 2/31st were one of the three heroic Battalions that held the British centre until the 48th arrived.
- Busaco – the 105th are in the place of the 45th Foot, Nottinghamshire, 'The Old Stubborns' Mackinnon's Brigade. It was a Wing of the 45th that joined the 88th for their charge against Merle's column.
- Defence and advance of the Lines of Torres Vedras – the 105th are in the place of the 71st Foot, Glasgow Highland, Erskine's Brigade. It was the 71st that repulsed the attack out of Sobral

Books by the same author.
105th Series
- Worth Their Colours
- Close to the Colours

A Question of Duty.

Cover picture
1st Regiment of Foot Guards at Waterloo by Brian Palmer.
The light company of the 1st Foot Guards commanded by
Lord Saltoun, defending the hollow way, behind
Hougoumont

Chapter One

Between Two Cities

They had come and they had conquered, surmounting all walls and defences, brushing aside defenders who had earlier marched through so assuredly to man the parapets and bastions of the ancient city. However, now were heard within the well-appointed streets, not shouts of relief, but the cries of a thousand anguished voices as the news spread. To these wails of despair were soon added the crackle of flames engorging treasured landmarks and edifices, all of which had stood the test of time, war and pestilence but were now engulfed in the tragedy of military conquest. What few spaces there were within the cacophony of this tumult were filled by the noises of conflict; cannon, bugles, muskets, frightened horses, shouts of triumph and cries of defeat. Oporto had fallen, all defences taken, all defenders now falling back. All this came to the eyes and ears of the Capucin-Franciscan Friar, Juan Delica as he set foot on the first planking that carried the bridge of boats over the wide River Douro, now the only escape for almost all of the people of the city. Merely minutes earlier he had done his best to quell the chaos of the main street which led down to the bridge, but all was to no avail, for then came cavalry, of his own countrymen, riding at full speed down the main street, trampling hundreds in their own efforts to escape by using the crossing, only to be halted by the sheer press that itself was vainly attempting a place on the precious bridge. The best that could be done by him now was to help the weak and infirm remain upright in the stream of panicked humanity that continued to add to the river of distress that inched its way down to the banks of the Douro and the bridge that was their only means of escape from the rapacious incoming French army.

6

The panic had been intensified by the sudden collapse in high confidence that all had placed in their own defences and soldiers, but these had stood for mere minutes before the oncoming invader and, now, those same soldiers of Portugal were mixed in the throng, the presence of their uniforms giving testimony that their city was now lost. Juan Delica stood on the first yards of the bridge, the planking now echoing the sound of hundreds of feet beating upon it, adding to the sounds of the chaos. He could do little but support here and guide there and soon he had little choice but to allow himself to be carried on, to cross with the fleeing multitude of the terrified to the far bank. At mid-way he came to the drawbridge in the centre of the pontoon where the horror that was great within him now descended to new depths. Many Portuguese soldiers, over 50 each side, were pulling the ropes to raise the drawbridge, with thousands yet to cross. Juan Delica also had heard the new sounds of conflict along the quayside and saw what could only be French troops advancing to the end of the bridge. This is what had caused the Officer to give the order to raise the drawbridge, but the effect could only be an obvious disaster. He fought his way through to the Officer to plead for the vital woodwork to remain in place, but the result was a pistol thrust into his face and the order to get himself over to the far bank.

The drawbridge continued to lift, the soldiers straining to left both the bridge and the mass of fugitives stood upon it. As the gap grew many flung themselves at the ascending edge, some to cling on for safety, some to fall into the receding tide. Then came the full horror, for those further back on the bridge continued to push forward, not knowing that there now existed a forty-foot gap in the centre. Loud and despairing were the cries of those, of all ages and classes, that were pushed over the edge to join the stream of the drowning that was being carried out to sea. The numbers falling were added to when firing erupted all along the quay, for the French, seeing so many Portuguese

7

uniforms amongst the crowd opened fire on the now static crowd helpless upon the narrow causeway. The citizens on the safe side of the gap moved on quickly, but not quick enough, for even some of these fell from musket fire. Juan Delica remained with the soldiers as they now pulled up the strongest whose strength had taken them across the gap by clinging to the bridge or even swimming, Delica not to help up those alive but to give the last rites to those on his own side hit mortally by the assault from the gathering French now pouring musket fire into the whole mass of humanity trapped on the bridge. The horror grew, for the gap was now bridged, not with stout timber, but by the sunken bodies of the drowned, and so the strongest were able to wade and scramble their way across to safety over the noisome and writhing causeway.

Mercifully, the firing from the quayside ceased and the French soldiers, seeing that almost all upon the bridge were civilians, were at last showing mercy and were pulling and pushing, mostly by using their musket butts, all those remaining on the bridge, back into the city. Juan Delica now joined the Portuguese soldiers as they finally completed their crossing of the now hideous river to the village of Villa Nova de Gaia, to then climb the Serra hill above the South bank and from there to witness yet more horror, albeit from a distance, as the final garrisons of Portuguese taking false refuge in palaces and bastions, were finally overcome and the survivors bayoneted. Then the city was sacked in an orgy of plunder, murder and rapine that occupied the rest of the day. Juan Delica heard much more than he was able to see whilst remaining there for some hours in the remote hope of providing some help, but no opportunity presented itself, nothing came but the morose sight of bodies floating back on the incoming tide. Finally, he removed his Friar's robe and threw it over the cliff at his feet.

oOo

On the same day, a scene of stark contrast was playing out on the quaysides of Lisbon, a scene of hope and no little joy. Yet more Battalions of the newly arrived British army were disembarking, filing patiently from their transports to form up on the stonework, now both warmed and cheered by the early April sunshine. An endless stream of Redcoats, or so it seemed, filed through the disembarkation ports of their vessels and onto the several gangplanks that led to the quayside, all welcomed by band music, speeches, flowers and coloured bunting fluttering in the cheerful breeze. On top, came the applause and greetings from the grateful population of the capital of Portugal, a crowd that had maintained its size all through the days of the British arrival. The unloading was to be done quickly; many more ships remained out in the harbour, all filled with Redcoats and their Followers eager to be quit of shipboard life, after 10 days at sea across a turbulent Bay of Biscay.

Jed Deakin, Colour Sergeant, First Battalion, 105th Wessex Foot, Prince of Wales Own, placed his first foot on the gangplank, followed by his good companion of more years than they could remember, Corporal Toby Halfway. Whilst Deakin secured the precious Regimental Colour under his arm, Halfway hitched both his musket and pack into a more comfortable alignment.

"Don't expect much change in this place, Jed. Not since we was here last August, don't seem much more'n yesterday."

"Can't say you'm wrong, Tobe, but I can't see us gettin' lucky like last time and beddin' down in that castle up there".

He pointed with his free arm to the imposing and extensive castle that was Fort St. George, high on its hill, but the statement was too obviously correct to extract a reply from his good friend Halfway as they made their way confidently over the firm woodwork. Soon all ten Companies of the Battalion were formed on the quayside and expectancy grew that soon they would march off. They made a fine sight, all uniforms were new, as were all items of kit and footwear, but all was far from uniform in the expression on their faces. For most, veterans like Deakin and Halfway, this was far from new, but for many the anxiety showed. This was not safe England, this was a foreign land and any that explored the thought of the distance that a three days march would take them, then pursued the idea further, found their thoughts inevitably at the notion of facing the French in open battle, a very perilous idea indeed. The 105th had lost over a quarter of its strength during December and January past, being part of the Corunna retreat and then the battle that had followed. Therefore many new recruits stood anxious and uneasy, for this was now reality, they were on campaign and with cause to be fearful, because certain conflict lay in the future. Typical of these were Privates Nathaniel Solomon and George Tucker, both plainly agile and durable men, the former very powerful, therefore both stood within the ranks of the Light Company on the far left, but their thoughts dwelt little on the sights and sounds around them, more on the feel of foreign ground beneath their feet and the alien language of the crowd behind them, mostly meaningless shouts of "Viva Inglese".

But one "company" now remained to disembark and gather, that of the 'Followers', the few wives and children of those allowed by their Commander in Chief, one General Arthur Wellesley, to accompany their husbands, joined either by Church or Common Law. He had dictated that only those who could add to the effectiveness of his army could accompany their men, and so there had been no lottery to choose who should be with their men and thus swell the numbers of those that 'followed'. Wellesley was only too well aware of the encumbrance that had hampered Moore's army during its retreat to Corunna, fully adding to the horrors that had befallen all of Moore's command on that dreadful Winter retreat, for, in many ways, the experience of the families was worse than that endured by the soldiers. Soon the Followers had joined on the end of the column, a much smaller number than was traditional and usual, but all were prepared for the march, as were their men, each woman with a wooden cross, not unlike that of an itinerant tinker, on which to carry the pots, pans and spoons that enabled them to cook the family rations as they progressed through the too often bleak and barren countryside.

As all finally gathered, Lieutenant-Colonel Bertram Lacey, the Lieutenant Colonel of the 105th, accompanied by his Senior Major Padraigh O'Hare, were deep in conversation with another Officer of higher rank, him being Brigadier Richard Stewart, now giving orders for the 105th to leave the quayside. The subject of the conversation had been a map, but this was now lowered from sight, accompanied by much nodding of heads and then salutes as Stewart left to consult with another of his Brigade Colonels. Thrusting the map into a pocket, Lacey hurried but yards to the awaiting Regimental Sergeant Major Cyrus Gibney, one imposing and engulfing figure not least caused by the effect of his prominent moustache and sideburns which swooped up under his shako to add to the impression of great height, which was actually so, for there were few that cast a longer shadow, nor broader, than that of Cyrus Gibney.

"Sar Major!"

"Sir"

This accompanied by a perfect and punctilious salute.

"March the men off. I will lead. We are in camp, someone on the outskirts, alongside the Grand Trunk. Their main road."

Gibney took one pace back, saluted and spun on his heel. He marched to the centre of the long column of Redcoats, and sucked in one enormous breath.

"Paraaaade!"

The sound echoed from the warehouse walls and even the hulls of the moored ships nearby. All in the ranks came to 'order arms', their musket held alongside their right leg. After more bellowing the 105th were marching away, in ranks of four, muskets now across shoulders, all in perfect step, but their footfalls were drowned by the cheering crowds, unintelligible to most English ears, "Bravo Inglese!"

Their route was to the North and soon they were in sight of the Campos, the wild and untilled region above Lisbon, but its nature was wholly altered by the ranks and battalions of white tents that marched and spilled over the slopes and hills. Merely a few minutes more and they were off the road and onto already beaten and trodden earth to then come to a halt before their own ranks of the pale, crude, triangular structures. The Officers left the tedium of the allocation of tents to the Sergeants of each Company and here Company Sergeant Ethan Ellis came into his own. He was the embodiment of a grim, uncompromising, veteran soldier, liked by few, but certainly respected and always obeyed. Ellis marched his Company, 82 strong along their rank of tents, allocating ten to each, eleven to the last two. The final group included the men he had most and least time for; the most being John Davey and Ezekiel Saunders, both a Chosen Man, the former even though once a poacher condemned to serve by the Courts. Also the huge Saunders, solid, dependable and a very good man in any type of conflict, for he was once, and still could be, a wrestling champion. The least, was Tom Miles, complaining, argumentative and often neglectful of his uniform, sometimes deliberately in the opinion of Ellis. However, Ellis knew his worth, for Miles ill-temper made him as potent a soldier as any in the Battalion, but he would never allow this to be known to Miles. Both exchanged ill looks as Miles ducked under the tent flap to join a group that was one more than the tent was designed for, which Miles immediately commented on.

"Bit overcrowded, b'ain't this crib?"

Already inside were the other members of their mess, John Byford, the intellectual "Gentleman Ranker" of the Company, Joe Pike, a young volunteer, but now a campaign veteran; Len Bailey, a housebreaker and also a "King's Hard Bargain" similar to Davey. Ellis had included the two new recruits; Solomon and Tucker, in the hope that these experienced veterans would soon mould the newcomers into something like capable soldiers. The remaining four were all experienced Light Company infantrymen. Within minutes these had established themselves and were preparing to cook their rations, Bailey was sent to the supplies wagon, Byford to gather wood for their fire. Within the hour all were contentedly eating and drinking, with the inevitable exception of Tom Miles.

"How come we ain't put up in some decent building somewer'? 'Stead of rolling about out yer in the mud!"

The reply came from Davey, one of the few who could bandy insults with Miles, without the conversation descending into a fight.

"Who'd want you as a neighbour?"

The constructive reply was provided by Byford.

"This is a sizeable army, Tom. No room in the city, especially for the sort that contains me and thee. Besides, rumour is that Wellesley's due in soon, so don't expect to have to put up with this for too long. He'll be eager to get us out and up against the Johnnies."

The last addition did nothing to ease the feelings of Solomon and Tucker.

oOo

The decent buildings, as Miles would describe them, that held any vacant space were the preserve of the Officers, and two of these were now exiting their billets, having partaken of a very decent meal, as cooked for them by their servant. These were Major Henry George Carr, the

13

Junior Major of the 105th and Captain Nathan Jameson Drake, Captain of the Light Company. Since coming together in the Battalion over a year earlier, the two had formed a firm friendship, although Carr was always of the senior rank. The two were very different in character, Drake's rook to Carr's raven. Drake's head and eyes always seemed to be on the move, looking, enquiring, absorbing, and sending information to an active mind that always needed something to comment on. Carr, in contrast, seemed sedate, almost detached, seemingly there, right enough, if not taking part, but captured in indolence. However, as Drake knew, in battle his character totally changed, converting him into one of the most capable Officers in the Battalion, the equal, at least, of both Lacey and O'Hare. Carr had once commanded the Light Company as a Captain, with Drake as his Senior Lieutenant, which is what had brought them together as friends. Now both had risen in rank after the Corunna retreat.

It was Drake who was doing all the talking, but this time the topic dwelt at home, mostly about his beloved wife, Cecily, now left behind in England and now pregnant. They had married almost as soon as they had returned to England from Spain. Carr was "sort of" or "practically the same as" engaged to Cecily's cousin, Jane Perry, but the final nuptials were far from certain. Jane's father, General Edmond Perry, was violently opposed to the match. The same General was on campaign with them, commanding a fine Brigade comprising four Battalions of Kings German Legion, German troops from the lands of Hanover, fighting for their Ruler, the King of England.

The pair ambled down the road, avoiding wherever possible the effusive greetings of the locals. Drake continued to voice his anxieties about Cecily, to which came a reply chosen from one of three possibilities, "I'm sure it'll be fine", or "She's in good hands", or "She's a strong and healthy young lady". Soon they were in the main square of Lisbon, a large expanse, 100 yards by 200, but all was movement, a scene more in keeping with the hour after a passing carnival, with the orange light from the Westering sun, adding a cheerful glint to the windows on the South and East facades. The refined and the gentrified citizens of the city were filling the square, engaging in their evening perambulations, an essential of their social round. The scarlet of British uniforms stood out, especially against the sombre black of the men, but even more against the more colourful apparel of the women. Inevitably it was Drake who first remarked on the scene.

"Henry, I say, this could be Pall Mall, or Bond Street, or some such, on a summer's evening. You'd not think these people were at war, it's all so….. so…… at ease and casual."

Carr nodded, and let out a deep breath, seemingly of exasperation.

"Yes, as you say, at ease and casual. A people at peace, I'd go so far to say, or at least, very, very confident of what lies between them and Soult's army. What's up North is way down South within their minds!"

"Oh, I don't know, Henry. Don't be too hard, keeping this up, helps them to face up. If you see what I mean."

Carr nodded again as they passed on, a smile of pleasure remaining on the face of Drake as they moved between the conversing groups of Lisbonese high society. Whatever they came to, to distract Drake, did nothing for Carr, his thoughts were elsewhere, dwelling on the teasing anxieties of what lay ahead, would the 105th live up to their reputation, the "Rag and Bone Boys" of Corunna? Yet his confidence in his own abilities did not enter the question. However, strolling around the beautiful square, beneath the buildings that had been added during a more opulent and successful age, was pleasant and distracting enough and his concerns did not surface sufficiently to mar the occasion, until an unpleasant nasal drawl came to his ears from behind.

"Ah! Major Carr! Thought it was you. Surprised to find you here!"

The justification of the final remark, with the accent heavy on both the 'find' and the 'you', was not forthcoming, whatever it may have been, but then Carr and Drake turned, during the sound of another utterance, this also spoken in the same dismissive tone.

"And Captain Drake, the inevitable accompaniment!"

Carr and Drake were confronted by two obvious society Officers dressed in the most gorgeous and expensive Officer of Cavalry uniforms, a dark blue, not navy but just light enough to be elegantly sober, the facings were a deep red, whilst the whole was shot both across and upward from knee to shoulder with white cords and arrows. Across one shoulder, suspended by its white cord hung the standard Light Cavalry pelisse, as short jacket, worn as a cloak. The sleeves were rarely filled by the arms of the owner.

The gentlemen were Captains of Horse Lord Frederick Templemere and Lucius Tavender, neither any kind of friend to Henry Carr, because some time ago, Carr had threatened to kill Lord Templemere after meeting him in two duels, both of which he had won, but illegally. Lucius Tavender was the preferred match for Jane Perry in the mind of her Father General and also, Carr had rendered generous help to Tavender twice, during the campaign of the previous year, but Tavender's attitude towards him had not moved one step from open animosity. Drake was immediately on his guard; years of society training had taught him that this would be no pleasant conversation, whilst a look of wearisome contempt spread across the face of Carr. He had noted immediately that he outranked both, but to "pull rank" in order to dismiss the pair and send them on their way, would simply be too close to a form of surrender, as he saw it. Confrontation was his natural reaction when faced with these two, but for the moment he'd give both their chance to keep the encounter polite and

16

social, in which manner he would behave himself. He nodded once, determined to be terse but civil.

"Tavender. My Lord."

Both infantrymen stood waiting, neither wishing to initiate any form of social conversation, much preferring to pass on. Both cavalrymen had noticed Carr's badge of rank, a purple sash around his waist and the single gold epaulette on his left shoulder. It was Templemere who spoke first, the inevitable disdainful tone watching the mocking grin.

"Congratulations on your promotion, Carr. I do hope that you are not going to insist on us both calling you 'Sir'?

A quizzical look came across Carr's face, as though such were an idiotic question, but his tone was jocular.

"Oh no! I do think that such can be dispensed with, especially amongst established acquaintances such as ourselves."

He allowed a pause to include the slightly disrespectful smile that he regularly employed what dealing with people that he little or no respect for, his head on one side.

"Was there something that you wished to say?"

It was Templemere who spoke again, whilst Tavender retained a blank look; stony, with a total absence of warmth.

"Why no, not especially. Merely wishing to renew…. er……. relationships."

He turned to Drake.

"Captain. I trust your new wife is well. She is with child, I believe."

Drake allowed his shoulders to dip slightly forward, but he had no idea how Templemere could have knowledge of such.

"Thank you for your enquiry, my Lord. She is quite well."

"Not here with you."

A statement, more than a question.

"Why no. For fairly obvious reasons."

Templemere nodded.

"Just so."

This time Tavender spoke up, a question directed at Carr.

"I understand Miss Jane Perry remains an acquaintance of yours?"

It was Drake who immediately answered.

"More than that, as I suspect you well know. Letters are exchanged regularly and I think you'll find she wears a ring now, as given to her by Major Carr here."

Templemere grinned conspiratorially, as though possessed of exclusive knowledge.

"That may have changed!"

"If so we would have heard"

A frosty pause, finally broken by Carr.

"The last time I saw you two was on the stairs of the Pump Room at Bath, you had purchased Captaincies in the 20th Light Dragoons, if memory serves. Does that still pertain?"

This time Tavender answered.

"No. We've transferred. Done an exchange, if you understand. We're now in the 16th Light Dags."

Carr allowed the insult to pass, that perhaps he had no awareness of Officers exchanging Regiments, but Tavender continued after a pause.

"We're both on General Perry's Staff. Jane Perry's Father. He's a Brigadier here, in case you are unaware. In command of some rather good Battalions of King's German Legion. Four to be exact, making his the largest Brigade in the army."

Carr laughed.

"Yes, I am aware of the General's presence. Army lists do reach us, down in the infantry."

He looked carefully into the face of each.

"I'm sure you'll all make a good combination. But now, I think we must pass on. Whole Battalion business and

Major's paperwork to attend to, you see. But, on the subject of proper form, I do think a salute is called for. To set an example to the Junior Officers hereabouts. Good discipline makes an army, you'd agree?"

Anger came into the faces of both, but Carr looked fully into the eyes of each. Captains saluted Majors and eventually they came, sloppily from both. Carr responded, both with a salute and a rebuke.

"You'll need to come up sharper than that, if Wellesley comes near you. He's totally one for the fully correct, so I hear. Also as I remember, when having him ride up to my picket before Vimeiro."

With that, both Carr and Drake diverted left and walked on. They made good time back to their billet, with the evening now somewhat soured.

There was a far more convivial atmosphere outside the tent of Jed Deakin, amongst the Third Company. Many gathered there after having eaten, to go about their evening business; to check and clean equipment, listen to the musical instruments being played all around or simply to sit and talk. Deakin, before being made a Colour Sergeant had been a long time comrade of Tom Miles, John Byford and Zeke Saunders and was one of the very few who could give Tom Miles orders and instructions that were immediately obeyed. Deakin had also formed a very respectful relationship with John Davey whilst Davey was being marched to Taunton from Devizes gaol. It now made no difference to the veteran soldiers that they were now in the company of common criminals. 'There but for fortune' was their attitude as long as these did what was asked of them, which very much included holding their place in the firing line.

Deakin's common-law wife, Bridie, always had tea, hot and available, as did her good friend Nelly Nicholls, the legal church wife of Sergeant Henry Nicholls of the Third Company, this being the Colour Company in the 105th. Joe Pike came along with Davey and Miles, for he was married to Mary, nee' O'Keefe, Bridie's younger sister. All three 'wives' were Irish. Adding to the family atmosphere were the children of Bridie, these being Eirin, Patrick, Kevin and Sinead, Eirin being the eldest, an Irish beauty in her late teens, down to Sinead who was now twelve. All could perform duties around camp and on the march, as also could the three daughters of Nelly Nicholls, these being Sally, Trudie and Violet, aged 15, 13 and 11 respectively. Bridie had accompanied the 105th as a privilege to Jed Deakin, him being a Colour Sergeant, whilst Henry Nicholls had no such high status, but his wife did. If there was a Captain amongst the Followers, it was she and Colonel Lacey knew this full well and therefore she was 'required', he had decreed, something above merely being "allowed".

If there was ever any discord within this happy group, it was between Tom Miles and Nelly Nicholls. Nelly disliked Tom Miles for being a misery, Miles disliked her for telling him so, but tonight a truce pertained and besides, Tom Miles was sat some way away, talking with Davey, Byford, Saunders and Pike. All were trying to comfort Joe Pike, clearly saddened and morose and all knew why. John Byford was doing most of the talking.

"She'll be fine, Joe, your Mary. Especially being pregnant means she's well out of what could be waiting for us in the next few months".

He looked at John Davey.

"She's with your Molly, John, is she not?"

Davey nodded.

"Sright. Mother'll and family and whatnot will take care of the pair, both bein' in the family way. Could be they'n well out of it, 'specially if we gets a repeat of what happened under Moore".

He turned to Joe Pike.

"And that's another cheerful side of it Joe. They b'ain't moulderin' in some barracks someplace, waitin' to catch gaol fever. That smallholding of ours is a fair good spot. She'll be fine."

20

A ghost of a smile passed across the face of Joe Pike as Tom Miles chipped in, somewhat cheerfully for him.

"You two be knockin' out sprogs like pots from a chinaworks! This'll be your third, b'ain't it John."

Davey laughed.

"Molly's third. My second."

The group turned to reminiscing and laughing at memories from the previous time they were in Lisbon, but Miles was now indulging in pleasant memories of his own whilst looking at the St. George's Fort, silhouetted in the dying light of the evening sky.

"Wonder if that good looker is still livin' down under that castle?"

It was Saunders who answered.

"You mean the one as did your washing?"

"That's the one."

Miles twirled his bayonet in the dust.

"T'as only been a few months."

It was Davey who replied.

"A few months, true, but long enough to get herself hitched up to some good looking Don".

Miles nodded whimsically.

"You'm right, true, but that don't mean I wouldn't like to see her again. Consuela was her name."

More nodding and twirling.

"I think she liked me."

At this point, the coquettish Eirin joined in, an insolent grin bright on her face.

"I always thought you was sweet on me! Tom Miles!"

Both anger and embarrassment competed across the face of Tom Miles, as all within hearing laughed, but he made no reply, for all the Redcoats in the group were springing to their feet. The Captain of their Third Company had arrived, making his evening rounds, this being Joshua Heaviside, a stocky and thickset figure, though not short and always in need of a shave. He was deeply religious and more often than not the first words that came from his mouth was a quote from the Bible. This evening was no exception, although, more often than not, his men had not the faintest idea what he was trying to convey.

"Delight yourself in the Lord, and he will give you the desires of your heart. Psalms 37. Verse 4"

Being Senior, it was Deakin who answered, giving his stock reply.

"Yes Sir. I'm sure all the lads sees it that way, Sir."

Heaviside nodded gravely.

"Have you everything you need? He hath given meat unto them that fear Him. Psalms 111. Verse 5."

"Yes Sir, thank you Sir. We are well provided for. Rations is near and plentiful."

Heaviside nodded and passed on in the dying light, to dispense the same to the next tent. Within a minute came the four notes of Lights Out and all made ready for sleep.

oOo

The houses, bridges and even the trees could now be predicted from memory, both for the going out and the coming back. On each day when they were not needed for Guard Duty or such duties, Lacey marched his men out into the Campos to the North of the city, there to run, jog, and form into, at the greatest possible speed, every tactical formation from every other tactical formation. However, what mattered most to Lacey and O'Hare was their rate of fire when formed in line and, on most days, the men marched back with an empty cartridge pouch, having fired all fifty. It was much to the satisfaction of both that each Company could manage seven rounds in two minutes, whilst the standard for the army was six.

On the days when the Line Companies of the Battalion was taken for Guard Duty, Carr and Drake took the Light Company out to practice their drills and this day

22

emerged from the area of the Seminary. However, what did now emerge were the citizens of Oporto, crudely armed and bent on revenge, born of the memory of what happened when their city was sacked back in March. They came from the back gardens and alleyways and were already clubbing to death the first French wounded that they found. Carr was incensed.

"Fire over their heads!"

His men who were loaded did so, then Carr led his men down onto the road, scrambled past the horse-teams and up onto the field beyond. Carr shouted at Fearnley as they ran over.

"Sergeant, get them back against those walls!"

There was no need to elaborate on who "them" were and Fearnley himself fixed his bayonet and forced back several of the vengeful citizens, then he was joined by the rest of the Section following his example. Carr looked around. He could hear screaming from further down the slope where the French had come from, but he could only see Ellis.

"Sergeant Ellis! You and Captain Drake take charge here. I'm going further down with Captain Shakeshaft's."

Ellis screamed his orders as Carr ran off. Soon the French wounded were gathered in one row, guarded by angry and protective Redcoats. Ellis saw Miles, eyeing the dead French and knew immediately his hopes and intentions. However, he was well aware that they were both on campaign and every help could make a difference, especially if they were required to march on before nightfall. It could make the difference in the days ahead between living or dying.

"All right, Miles! But packs, pockets and knapsacks. Nothing gets cut! Y'hear? Understood?"

Miles nodded. Whatever their personal animosity, he had his own code that was not so dissimilar to that of Ellis. Miles ran over to the French dead, followed by many others.

Carr, meanwhile, was leading Shakeshaft's Two Section down the slope to meet, or so he hoped, the back wall of the Seminary. The screaming had stopped, which could mean one of two things, either the civilians had murdered every wounded Frenchman, or some Redcoats had put a stop to it. The answer turned out to be the latter, because they passed wounded French still alive and guarded by Redcoats. Hill had left a Company of the Buffs in the Seminary and they had come out to protect the wounded remaining from the conflict now just ended at their back wall. Carr easily identified their Regiment as he approached a Captain nearby, because his facings were indeed Buff, with the Roman numeral III on his crossbelt. The Captain brought his sword up in salute, which Carr acknowledged.

"Captain. I take it you are here to protect the French wounded?"

"Yes Sir. Just so, Sir."

"Very well. Carry on. I'll take mine on further and try to find my Battalion."

Then Carr noticed, just further down the slope, what was indeed the back wall of the Seminary, with the space before it covered in a French dead, often one on top of another. He looked at the Captain.

"Tough fight!"

The Captain shook his head.

"Not so bad, Sir, in truth. We had the wall and plenty of men. No contest, really."

Carr nodded.

"Right. I take my leave. Good luck, Captain."

"And to you, Sir."

Salutes were exchanged and Carr led his men past the Seminary and down, and then, with Shakeshaft now beside him, they came onto the road alongside the river. This was an utter charnel house, covered in French dead, sometimes two, sometimes three deep. Each body was shattered; all wounds having been caused by the one-inch grape shot fired from the batteries in the Convent. Both

"Both right files. In line, follow me."

The two right files cantered after Tavender, leaving Templemere with the two left files, but now he understood, having been taught by example He turned in his saddle.

"With me."

The two files, over 100 Troopers each, followed him and soon, down both sides of the Spanish supply column, stood a fixed guard of Light Dragoons, two ranks deep. The leading Spanish horseman, an Officer, now plainly hugely concerned and also wholly offended, halted just yards before Stapleton Cotton. He rose up in his stirrups, the better able to swing back his arm towards the mules

"Estas disposiciones son para el ejército español!"

Stapleton Cotton did not take his eyes from the man.

"Anybody any idea what he said?"

It was Johnson who spoke.

"Not exactly, Sir, but I can hazard a good guess. He's saying that these are for the Spanish Army."

A dismissive growl came from deep within Stapleton Cotton's chest. He turned to Johnson.

"Give me pencil and paper."

Johnson opened his sabretache and withdrew the writing materials requested. Once receiving them, Stapleton Cotton, wrote, speaking out loud.

"These supplies have been sequestered on behalf of the British Government. Any payment due can be collected from the British Representative in Cadiz."

He signed the paper with a flourish, rode forward, and thrust it against the chest of the astonished Officer, who took it and read it, but, of course with no understanding. Stapleton Cotton then spoke to the nearest Trooper on either side, who happened to be Sergeants of Horse.

"Pass this on. Ride in and collect the reins of the pack mules."

The word was passed on down the line and soon the

reins of the mules were being removed from the hands of the drovers whilst the Spanish Dragoons looked on, bereft of orders and very much intimidated by the numbers around them. Stapleton Cotton watched proceedings until he was satisfied.

"Right. Were going back."

With that, he wheeled his horse, as did Withers and Johnson and the whole column turned back, British Light Dragoons in escort, with the pack mules in between. Soon, there was nothing left on the road, bar hoof prints, two dozen bemused Spanish Dragoons, the same number of drovers, one Officer incandescent with rage and Stapleton Cotton's note a screwed up bundle on the road.

That evening the British army had bread, and enough flour for bread again the following day, and so over those two days, with food inside them in some form, they gained Miajades, where they made camp, but all in Wellesley's command remained close to starvation. As the day finished, Carr walked with Heaviside around the 105th camp.

"What do you think, Joshua? Will they hang together?"

Heaviside began with his own question.

"Ours or the whole army?"

"I speak of ours."

"Well, Merida, Montijo and Badajoz. They are all in the Guadiana valley, are they not?"

"Yes."

"And Merida is the first and two days march away?"

"About!"

"It is not unreasonable to suppose, I should say, that in the Guadiana valley, a rich region, we should be able to obtain supplies. Perhaps even be met by a supply column of our own."

Carr took this as a statement, not a question.

"I'm inclined to agree."

was one such. Drake had ordered Ellis to break up the established file teams of three men to train the new recruits and so Davey and Miles had George Tucker with them, whilst the other newcomer, Nat Solomon, was with Byford and Saunders. They were practicing retreating by files and Tom Miles wasn't happy. Tucker had fired off his round and then ran back to take his position behind Davey, leaving Miles now at the front. Miles fired his, and then retreated back behind Tucker, leaving Davey at the front. Davey fired and then fell back. By now Tucker should have reloaded, but he was still returning the ramrod to its guides, whilst Miles was already half way through reloading.

"Bloody Hell, Tucker! What if some Frencher was close on up, or a bugger on a horse or somesuch? 'Tis your job to bring'n down, not be still soddin' about, pockin' a ball down the spout!"

However, Ellis has heard and ran over.

"That's enough Miles! What goes wrong is my worry, you get loaded and face up!"

Miles was not one to keep quiet.

"Tis my worry too, if I gets a Dragoon on top of I!"

Ellis turned on him.

"I said you shuts your gob and face up! We're here to practice and spend time gettin' it right. Now you finish loadin' and come to the "make ready."

Miles did now hold his tongue and he held his weapon directly vertical, the trigger just level with his chin, ready to bring the rifle down the firing position. Ellis went over to Tucker.

"His right. When you leading filemate runs back, puttin' you at point, you've got to be ready. 'Tis you that then has to down any oncoming Johnnies. Your filemate's lives depends on it, besides your own."

Then he smiled, rare for him.

"But you'n not far off. Another second or two and you'd have given him no cause. But you've got to be there!"

Tucker nodded.

"'Tis but a dose of nerves, Sergeant. I was fine back in Somerset, but here, well, within days, this could be the actual."

Ellis said no more but ran off, exchanging stoney looks with Miles as he passed.

Thus it went on, all under the critical eyes of Drake and Carr, until darkness gathered across the dark heathland. Then they formed up and marched back, Miles again complaining to Ellis.

"An' tomorrow I s'pose we'n back up yer in Battalion?"

"S'right Miles and I'll be checkin' your flint, pan and touchhole."

Miles scowled.

"What about buttons?"

"Them too! Shiney! And shako plate. And crossbelt plate!"

The last was shouted and Saunders grinned behind Miles.

"Want to borrow some brickdust, then? Tom?"

Low chuckles from all around, the discomfiture of the grumpy Miles was always a source of certain amusement, but little more was said, as the first houses of Lisbon approached.

Simultaneously, in a well-appointed room, deep with Lisbon, humour and bonhomie was also much prevalent. Lord Templemere had invited a long acquaintance of his to supper, this being Captain Lord Charles Carravoy, along with Captain Lucius Tavender and Lieutenant The Honourable Royston D'Villiers. The families of Templemere, Carravoy and D'Villiers were neighbours in Gloucestershire and all friends of long standing. Both Carravoy and D'Villiers were of the 105th and both were Officers of the Grenadier Company. It was Tavender who was footing the bill for this occasion, having engaged a local hotelier to provide the meal and each dish had indeed been sumptuous, accompanied with just the correct wine. Whilst his fellow diners were all of noble birth, he came from a family of probably greater wealth than the families of his fellow three combined. The talk had been standard for men of their social class, ranging across tailors, horses, saddles, gunsmiths, hunting, racing at Ascot and now Wellesley. The final topic was initiated by Templemere, a simple question.

"This Wellesley. What's he like?"

D'Villiers was a mere Lieutenant in the company of Captains, two of whom were Lords. He had an opinion, which was generally favourable towards their General, but he knew Carravoy's opinion and it was probably shared by Tavender. In the event, it was Carravoy who provided an answer, confirming D'Villiers' suspicions.

"Irish! And mostly served in India. Sepoy General some call him. I'll grant the victories of Rolica and Vimeiro, but the French played right into his hands. Marching right up for us to blow them all to Hell. My complaint is that he has no respect, nor any understanding, of the needs or standing of his Officers. On a whim he'll strip you of your servants and necessaries. You'll be no more than a plain ranker. And end up looking like one!"

Tavender nodded.

"On top, he's total infantry. Little idea of how to handle cavalry. Look at that shambles at Vimeiro. A total mess! With that, I rest my case."

D'Villiers was in a quandary. He had the firm opinion that it was Wellesley Generalship that had gained the victories aforementioned and the cavalry shambles at Vimeiro had been their own entire making, running completely out of control and too far into the French lines. Should be speak up? He was outranked both militarily and socially, but then came the bombshell from Templemere, totally changing the subject and raising what was most likely the whole point of the evening.

"What are we going to do about Carr?"

Both Templemere and Tavender looked steadily at the two opposite, but Templemere continued.

"I'd say I'm right in thinking that we all have a score to settle there."

He pointed to the scars on his right cheekbone, where fragments of bone had to be removed before the hole was trepanned. Carr had smashed the pommel of his sword into the spot during their first duel. D'Villiers had no such grudge and was aghast at the thought of becoming engaged in some conspiracy against a fellow Officer of his Regiment, but he managed not to show it. Carravoy, on the other hand was deep in thought. A strong rivalry existed in his own mind between himself and Carr, especially as Carr had been promoted Major over him, at a time when he was the Captain of the Senior Company, the Grenadiers. That rankled greatly and it was Carravoy who answered.

"What can be done? He's now a gazetted Major."

Templemere twirled a knife, making a hole in the tablecloth, then threw a nut into his mouth. His chewing of it did not affect what came next.

"We are about to go on campaign. Things inevitably go wrong and blame must be lodged, wherever it may fall. If Carr was around at the time, part of the whole and on the scene, as it were, I'm sure something can be constructed. It may not need to be too much of a………."
He paused.

"……..work of fiction, if you take my meaning."
Tavender leaned forward, determined.

"All we have to do, Gentlemen, is to keep our eyes and ears open and see what coincides between the presence of our Major Carr and the ups and downs of our fighting the French. On top, we have a General who'll back us up, our own General Perry. We're on his Staff."

Templemere immediately filled each glass, the gleam in his eyes matching that of the fine crystal.

"A toast to that!"

Each raised their glass and drank, but D'Villiers took merely a sip.

oOo

It was in merely a backroom in a backstreet house, but Lacey and O'Hare knew why they were there even before they entered, as they ascended the stairs through the gloom and dank air, somehow chillier within these confines than the late morning breeze outside. Each found a chair as more Officers arrived to put themselves in the presence of their Brigadier, one Robert Stewart. He sat his own chair, awaiting the last arrivals, himself every inch a Highland Commander. Apart from sideburns that descended to his collar, he was clean-shaven, exposing cheeks ruddy from the blasting wind of the moorland. His far seeing eyes were shaded by his Highland bonnet which sported a huge badge at the front and his left hand flexed endlessly on the pommel of his claymore, whilst his right was rock steady holding a glass of scotch. This had just been provided by his servant, in full Highland uniform, standing behind his left shoulder. As the last Colonel and Major arrived, glasses were passed around and the servant moved forward to provide a more than generous measure in each. For Stewart, first things first, which was to swallow the scotch.

"Slange!"

His spirit disappeared in one gulp, requiring his guests to do the same. He then came straight to business.

"I doubt ye've met each other, whilst I've met ye all, so I'll do the introductions."

He concerned himself solely with the Colonels, starting on his right, and pointing to each.

"Burns, First Sixteenth Portuguese Line. Lacey, Hundred and Fifth Foot, Ruskin, First Detachments."

All nodded and smiled as the names came forth, but Stewart was onto the main business.

"Wellesley arrived yesterday. He's divided us into Brigades, with a Portuguese Battalion in each, as now trained up by Beresford and mostly Officered by ours."

He nodded in the direction of Colonel Burns and received one back.

"He briefed us in the evening and now ah'm includin' you. Soult's still at Oporto and Wellesley wants onto him immediately. Mackenzie's left during the night, us all to assemble at Coimbra, halfway there. Today's the 23rd, we leave on the 25th. Get your men on the Grand Trunk at Noon. Dismiss."

He turned himself around for another gill of scotch, paying no more attention to the six Officers now exiting through the door. On the stairs, Lacey half turned to O'Hare, following close behind

"What shape are we in?"

"Good enough as we speak, with us marching to the Campo most days. The spare day will take out the last wrinkles."

"You check with the Company Captains, give Carr responsibility for supplies, medical and Followers."

Thus, within hours Henry Carr was presenting himself at Commissariat Headquarters and joined the queue before the Quartermaster Sergeant who suddenly had more to cope with than could easily be achieved. He left the building with a requisition for three days supplies for 722 men and Followers. This meant that replenishment would occur en route after the three days. He had already visited Nelly Nicholls who already knew, probably before he did, and she had spread the word. Then Surgeon Pearce, a less than cheerful man, but experienced and plainly competent and he was found in a permanent state of readiness because his skills could be required at any time. Now there remained but the Battalion Chaplain, a man whom he had little to do with so far, not since he had joined the Regiment back in February. This was the Reverend Thomas Albright, an uplifting name for a Man of the Cloth and hopefully for someone of a sensible and constructive disposition. The Chaplain's Assistant he did know, Private Percival Sedgwicke, a thief, de-frocked from the Priesthood as a consequence and condemned to serve in the Army for the duration. He was a fish-out-of-water, being an educated man, down in the ranks, but he was undoubtedly popular with the men, despite being an utterly hopeless soldier in a firing line. However, he had spent a great deal of his time in the army as a Storesman and, being highly literate and numerate, he was possessed of good organizational sense and could see his way through most organizational challenges.

Carr found Albright, beside his wagon and at his midday meal, a plain combination of bread, fish and fruit. Albright spoke first, recognising Carr as one of the Majors of the Battalion. He was at once welcoming and cheerful.

"Major Carr! Good-day, Sir, you are most welcome."

He rose from his chair and extended his hand, which Carr took, to receive a warm handshake, but Carr had no time for any further pleasantries.

"Good-day Reverend. I'll come straight to the point. We march day after tomorrow. North, to meet the French. You'll need to be ready."

Carr was treated to a beaming smile.

"As we will be, Major. As we will be, be most assured of it."

Somehow Carr was not convinced, but the comforting words had been spoken and so he saluted, this being to a Reverend, and then left. Albright finished his final mouthfuls and hurried around the wagon in the hope of finding Sedgwicke, but failing. What he knew was that his Assistant was of the habit of visiting the Followers and so he began to move in that direction, but, as luck would have it, Sedgwicke immediately appeared around the corner of a wall. Albright greeted him with a look of deep concern.

"Sedgwicke, we are due to march out of here within 24 hours."

He paused to allow that to sink in.

"What does that mean?"

Sedgwicke, for all his sheltered upbringing and tender calling was a veteran of two campaigns, not least the retreat to Corunna and, with justification, he regarded both of the immediate superiors he had 'assisted unto' so far, as being wholly less than what they should be. His first Chaplain had made not one good decision and had then deserted before the battle of Corunna. This one, having just landed, had no notion of what could come their way during the rigours of a campaign and here he was, asking what it meant to begin a march. He sucked in a deep breath and let it out as a barely audible sigh.

"Well, Sir, it means that all that we need to sustain us whilst traveling and will enable us to perform our ministrations must be loaded into that wagon. Sir."

Albright looked at the wagon as though seeing it for the first time. It was not the wagon for a carrier, more a light cart, with an awning, it being a vehicle small and undemanding for a team of two mules.

"That wagon? Alone? I thought it for my own personal use."

"It is, Sir, for your own personal use, for your effects and mine, although mine all go into a pack and a haversack."

Albright looked incredulous, as Sedgwicke continued.

"What we must do, Sir, is discard anything not essential. If feed for our mules is unavailable, they starve and what then moves the wagon? If they are weak, which is often the end result, the lighter the load the more likely they are to keep going. Sir."

Albright continued to stare.

"We will be on campaign, Sir. Against the French, who march faster than we do. We may be without food, yet still required to move quickly. Sir."

Astonishment now overtook his superior, but Sedgwicke had interpreted the look.

"Yes Sir. There may be much that we have to leave behind. We can include a few luxuries, Sir, but a few. Weight is paramount."

No reply.

"I'll see to the selection, Sir then I'll make a list for your final appraisal."

A resigned nod was the response. Sedgwicke saluted and left, not to his duties but back to the fireside of Nellie Nicholls and Bridie Deakin. The wagon was already packed, all that remained outside were his Reverend's bits for camp. Besides, Albright had eaten, he would not need feeding again for sometime and the two good women, in whose high esteem Sedgwicke dwelt, had always tea and doughcakes ready for the hungry.

The day came and all were standing in their place, the last notes of the band who were leading out an earlier Brigade echoing but dying between the tall buildings. Although this was the third day of the army marching North, there was still a good crowd, ready to cheer any departing soldiery, but especially those of their own Portuguese army, a Battalion in every Brigade. The men were stood easy in their marching ranks, some being fussed over by Followers, helping with straps and buckles, easing as best as possible the 30lbs weight of full kit, with rations on top. However, in many cases, the rations issued to the men were now back with the Followers. Easing their load was one thing, but them being killed with a full haversack to be pillaged by the French would be a disaster, therefore, the children of Bridie and Nellie carried the rations of single men such as Byford and Saunders and the lovelorn Joe Pike.

Lacey and O'Hare were mounted, alongside Stewart, him equally mounted and now passing a hip-flask across to the pair. He was the picture of a bucolic Highland Laird, passing a fatherly eye over some festival of highland dancing taking place on his estate. Thus he was wholly relaxed over the whole affair, for the times of marching out to war were numbered beyond memory for a veteran such as he. Carr had no mount, but preferred to march anyway, at the rear if the column. Someone of his rank may be needed in that part of the Battalion. Lacey turned his mount around for him to walk back to the Honour Guard. He had seen the Portuguese 16th break out their Colours, them having been given the honour to lead out the Brigade. They had two Colours, as had British Infantry Regiments, their King's Colour was an intricate accumulation of red and blue rectangles, a yellow diagonal cross, then with the Royal Arms of Braganza large in the centre. Their Regimental Colour, in the case of the 16th, was almost all white, with a red border, and with a much smaller Arms of Braganza in the centre. Their appearance at the head of their men had caused a bout of wild cheering from the Lisbonese all crowded along the roadside. Lacey looked at Ensign Barnaby Rushby the senior of the two, who carried the King's Colour. Ensign Trenton Neape carried the Regimental.

"Break out the Colours Rushby. I think a bit of a show is called for."

Although the order was addressed to Rushby, it was the two Colour Sergeants who obeyed it, Deakin drawing the King's Colour from its leather casing, Harry Bennet the Regimental. That done they were handed to their respective Ensigns and the huge Union Flag of the King's Colour and the lurid green of the 105th Regimental Colour added their gaiety to that of the Portuguese. At first silently, this being nothing more than a nod from Stewart to Burns at the head of the Portuguese, the process began to enable them to move, this starting with the Portuguese being brought to 'shoulder arms'. Lacey took this as his signal and gave the nod to Gibney who bellowed his men through the same process, him then followed by the NCO's of the 1st Detachments behind. They all began to march off, to the intense cheering of the civilians either side. At the head of the column, in Number Three Company, the men took their lead from Heaviside, his order to march being inevitably prefaced by a Bible quote.

"For I know the plans I have for you, declares the Lord, plans for welfare and not for evil, to give you a future and a hope. Jeremiah 29. 11."

At the rear, in the Light Company, the men picked up the step, with the friendship group close up to each other, Miles, Byford, Pike and Davey in one rank, with Saunders, Bailey, Tucker and Solomon behind in the next.

Even Miles, marching on the left, felt uplifted by the endless lines of cheering and smiling faces, then came one he knew, it was his 'washer girl', laughing and waving at the 105th Redcoats as they passed by. He raised his voice above the din.

"Consuela! Consuela!"

Bailey spoke to Saunders marching beside him

"What's he shouting about? Daft bugger!"

"I think he's seen his washer-girl."

She heard her name and turned to see him as he approached. He pointed to his chest.

"Tom! Tom!"

Recognition came into her face. She said something, but it was drowned. Miles turned to Byford beside him.

"Byfe. What's 'good luck?"

"Boa sortay."

Miles turned to Consuela, now almost passed.

"Boa sortay, Consuela! Boa sortay!"

She waved and so did he, but it was clear that she was heavily pregnant. Also there was a man stood behind her with his hands on her shoulders. She said something to him and he gave Miles a friendly salute as they finally passed by, but Ellis, having seen all, was incensed.

"Miles! You keeps your arms swingin' at your sides. This is a parade, not some pub crawl jaunt!"

But Miles, in uplifted mood, was in no frame of mind to be quiet.

"Just buildin' good relations with our civilian allies, S'aren't. That's all!"

Ellis may have replied, but it was Saunders that was heard.

"Looks like she's found that beau we was talkin' about, Tom. An' got well spliced!"

Miles nodded and actually grinned, good white teeth in brown face.

"Ah well. She remembered me and it looks like she's happy. That's all to the good."

Saunders, from behind, gave him a consoling pat on the shoulder.

oOo

The army was less than campaign fit, a sea voyage, then weeks in Lisbon had taken its toll on their capacity to march at the pace Wellesley demanded. Over the first days, several could be seen at the roadside having fallen out with blisters or muscle cramp. However, it was much to the satisfaction of the Senior Officers of the 105th that not one man left their ranks. Lacey allowed a nod of congratulation to himself; the days of drill up in the Campo had been much to the good, his men were as good as any, better than most. However, what also helped was the veteran experience of the likes of Jed Deakin, Tom Miles and even Joe Pike. It was but the third day that found Tucker and Solomons suffering. The frame of their pack cut into the small of their backs and the cross-strap of it that connected the two shoulder straps was tight across their chests, making breathing difficult. Deakin told them to undo the buttons of their jacket and open it up, so that the thick wool and thick green facing bars were no longer beneath the cross-strap, thus making space. Pike told them to put the pack's shoulder straps above their shoulder tabs, not under them, to give more thickness between their shoulders and the weight. Tom Miles gave them the benefit of his experience that night in camp.

"Get a 'Frencher pack' first chance you gets. Theirs is made out of good strong cowhide and don't come apart in the rain. On top, theirs don't have no cross-strap and rides higher on yer back."

The problem with the frame was solved by Deakin.

"On parade your blanket has to be a neat roll on top. Out yer, that's as much use as your stock."

He pointed to his neck, now bare. The stiff leather collar that had held his head correctly in place whilst stood on parade was now at the bottom of his own pack.

"Roll your blanket into a thin roll to run between the straps at the bottom. That'll keep the wood away from your back. An' keep yer blanket dry."

The next day saw all as advised on the persons of Tucker and Solomons. Sergeant Ellis made no comment about the irregularities. He was marching using exactly the same modifications.

Stewart's Battalion was managing a good fifteen miles each day and Wellesley's orders that his army marches North with a time gap of often a day between Brigades was also producing dividends. An army marching through provides good business for the local population and the 12 or 24 hours gap gave the locals in the towns time to replenish their stocks, of whatever they may have to sell, it being a huge variety ranging from fresh fruit to horse fodder. They had reached Leiria, the main town between Coimbra and Lisbon and the 105th, as for the other two Battalions, had been allowed to fall out and were lounging in the shade. Spring had arrived, significantly warm.

The filemates, Miles, Davey and Pike had obtained permission to visit the market stalls speedily put up on their arrival. Miles and Davey had been examining useful items, such as knives and small axes, while Pike concerned himself with more feminine items. He picked up a bracelet.

"Do you think she'd like that, John?"

Davey examined the workmanship, but it was Miles who spoke up.

"Save yer money, boy. There'll be plenty of such you'll be pickin' up for free if this jaunt goes right. Civilians is always quick to go and they always leaves behind what they can't carry."

"But that's stealing Tom!"

Then from Davey.

"More like lootin', Tom. They'll stretch your neck!"

"I don't see it as such, more like findin' a good home for what's been abandoned. 'Sides, I don't take nothin' as won't go in my pack and won't need chuckin' away as bein' too bulky. On top, 'tis we as is clearin' the Frogs out of 'ere, so I looks upon the odd ornament or whatnot as fair payment."

Meanwhile Davey had fixed upon a large knife and a handy sized axe. After much finger raising to indicate price, a bargain was struck and they returned to their companions, the axe to go into Davey's backpack, the knife into that of Miles. Now it was time for food and all the group, which included Toby Halfway as Jed Deakin's closest friend, were content to give over their rations to the wives of Jed Deakin and Henry Nicholls. This was because Bridie could work miracles with the indigestible saltbeef that was their ration. Few could match her knowledge of the herbs to be found along the wayside and Nelly's doughcakes were unmatched within any one's experience.

However, this occasion saw renewed hostilities between Tom Miles and Nelly Nicholls. The stew of beef, potatoes and peas, was ladled from the pot by Bridie, but the doughcakes given out by Nelly. Tom Miles received one that was significantly smaller than most others, three inches instead of four. He pointed to one of decent size.

"Why can't I have that one?"

Nelly took instant umbrage, never far from the surface in the presence of Tom Miles, and Nelly had had a tiring day. Henry Nicholls looked up from his place amongst the group to judge whether or not his wife required his support, but, as usual, there was no need. The repost was fierce with the serving spoon not far from Miles' nose.

"First, because that's the one as've come first to hand, and second 'cos a gobshite like you don't deserve no more than the next man!"

Miles was about to hit her, but luckily Zeke Saunders, who towered over both, was next in line. His hand on Miles' forearm was enough to prevent any blow, but Miles was livid.

"You baggage! What the bloody Hell would you know about bein' fair? Fair's what's best for thee an' none other. Savin' the best for last and thyself and they husband, you old ......"

Henry Nicholls did now stand up.

"Miles! You got a problem, you takes it up with me!"

However, Saunders had pulled him away and was now in front of Nelly. He wore a stern look, unusual for him.

"Which for me?"

The question was full of undertone and even menace. Nelly gave him the biggest.

"Well, such a size as y'are, I do suppose that ye should have a good one."

She felt under suspicion and thus felt the need to justify herself.

"Sure, when you're makin' them up, 'tis impossible to tell how they'll turn out! None'll be equal!"

The last shouted at Tom Miles, but it was Saunders who answered.

"I believe you, Mother. I'm sure you're right."

The generous doughcake fell onto his plate and Saunders turned away, to then break off a piece and give it to Miles, who wasted no time in showing his plate to Nelly with the extra now on it, but Saunders ushered him away before any more could be said. When Miles sat down, a stern look from Jed Deakin was enough to signal the end of this particular argument. A long look from Sergeant Henry Nicholls also prevented any further outbreak of hostilities.

Mayday saw the 105th march into Coimbra, a town of learning and culture, but there was little of such in evidence, for, although the buildings were open, there were precious few students nor many of their mentors. The allied army simply marched in and made the best of what was available, for there were no tents now, all remained in Lisbon, and so all had to shift for themselves, finding shelter in doorways, sheds, outbuildings, or simply in a narrow alleyway. Not so for most Officers who were found billets of various degrees of comfort, but at least they were under a roof. Carr and Drake, with Coimbra wholly unknown to them, after a decent supper, decided to leave their abode, which was merely a well appointed coach-house, to take a walk and a look at the town in the warm evening air, leaving Lieutenants Maltby and Shakeshaft in charge of the Company. They walked the narrow streets, as bordered by elegant buildings and, on passing one of the more imposing, found themselves confronted by Private Byford of the Light Company, exiting the building. He was well known as an educated man, yet none knew his history, but, him knowing that Coimbra was a University town with many libraries, he had decided to visit the nearest, this being but a few streets from where the Light Company were at their ease. Byford sprang to the attention, staring over Carr's left shoulder, and saluted. The reply from both Officers was an airy wave of their hand, but Drake was less than pleased.

"What are you doing here, Private?"

"Visiting this library, Sir, Taking the opportunity to obtain some reading, Sir."

"Who gave you permission?"

"My Section Commander. Sir, Lieutenant Shakeshaft."

This gave both Officers pause. Permission had been given and so, unless he was lying, there could be no disciplinary offence, other than the possibility of theft.

Drake continued.

"And did you? Obtain some reading?"

Byford remained at attention.

"With your permission, Sir."

Drake nodded and so Byford reached into his haversack and drew out a thickish leather bound book, which he held vertical, face to the Officers. The cover was blank, bar the picture of a Roman Legionary. Drake remained curious.

"And this is a book of what?"

Byford turned the book so that Drake could see the spine, but it was too small.

"You read it."

Byford did not need to.

"History of Tertium Bellum Servile, Sir. "

No response from either Officer and so Byford explained further.

"It's Roman History, Sir."

Drake got to the point.

"Did you steal it?"

Byford was incensed

"No indeed not, Sir! I was lucky enough to meet a Latin Professor who engaged me in conversation, Sir. He generously gave me this copy. They have several. Sir."

He paused for reaction, but none came.

"He's just inside, at a desk. Sir."

The reply was a stony look from both Officers, but it was Carr who terminated the conversation. He knew

Byford when he commanded the Light Company and knew that what he spoke was almost certainly the truth.

"Byford. You know what this looks like. You, a ranker, coming out of a building such as this, for which you have little or no business in."

"Sir!"

"You're lucky it's us and not a bunch of Provosts. If you want to visit academia, see me first, and I'll give you a note. That's how things are and that's something that should be well known to a man such as you."

He paused, but nothing more from Byford.

"Back to your Section."

Byford returned the book to his haversack, sprang to attention and saluted. He did not wait for a response, but skirted around the two and made off. Drake looked at Carr.

"Rum cove that!"

They watched him disappear.

"Any idea what the book was?"

"Haven't a clue! History of some war of some sort."

Byford soon arrived back at their camp, to find a mood of misery. There was no firewood to be had anywhere, even with such as Davey, Miles, Bailey and Saunders as the search party. Supper was water and biscuits dipped in salt. Meanwhile, Carr and Drake wandered on to drink two glasses of wine at an open tavern, the both of which were given without charge. The good people of Coimbra well knew that all to the North of them was French territory and they knew who would be attempting to keep them at bay, therefore they felt obliged to be more than merely accommodating.

French existing off to the North was a fact not unknown to Colonel Lacey. The order at dawn was for parade and inspection, to be undertaken by both Officers and Sergeants. Ellis, perhaps to maintain at least the merest of passable of relations with Miles paid no more attention to his kit than to any other member of the Light Company, but, inspection done, Lacey marched them off to a large open space with a pair of posts at each end of some ground covered in hoof marks. A polo field concluded his Officers and all were incredulous that it was played in Portugal, but here the Battalion practiced again moving from column to line and then to defensive square, then back again. This entertainment soon attracted an audience who cheered and applauded each change, accompanied to the sound of the drums, as beaten out by the Battalion Drummerboys.

That evening there was wood. Foraging parties, Officer led, had gone out far and wide to gather from the wooded hills. Fresh wood was obligatory, for the order came that any wood taken from houses or any building would be regarded as looting. Wellesley was taking no chances with offending the local population, who would not have begrudged a few sticks of old furniture anyway, what with the town prospering immensely from the presence of so much hungry and moneyed soldiery. Thus, was much of the army occupied for the next three days, largely taking their ease. In the Deakin group, to maintain the peace, he himself made sure that where Nelly Nicholls was, Tom Miles was not.

On the 5th May Lacey called his Officers for a meeting, using the floor of Carr and Drake's coach-house. He wasted no time.

"There are rumours of the French having evacuated Oporto. Ignore them! They are not true and I want the men in a state of mind as if they were going to meet the French this afternoon. The Johnnies are still in Oporto and all reports confirm that they are some way South, if only to monitor our progress and perhaps do us some damage, if we make a mistake, or at least delay us, whilst they fortify Oporto. We are manoeuvring to retake the city. Mackenzie's Brigade, reinforced by Portuguese, have been sent back to Abrantes to hold off any French that may appear behind us. Tomorrow, General Beresford marches inland with two Brigades of British and Portuguese to get around the city that way if he can cross the Douro, or at

41

least give Soult a headache if he learns of their presence. The day after tomorrow, we march out. Wellesley has put our Stewart's Brigade and General Perry's KGL into a Division under General Paget. I'm sure we remember him from the stroll we had back to Coruna !"

Many smiled, not at the memory of Coruna nor even being commanded by the very able Paget, merely the absurd description of the Coruna retreat.

"Ensure your men are ready!"

oOo

A similar military meeting was taking place away to the North, inland at the small town of Lamego, in the mountains above the River Douro. Fray Juan Delica had wandered inland after Oporto, deciding within himself what should be his response, whilst being fed and sheltered by the local population who knew his as a Man of God. Amongst his flock, talking, eating and listening, he had learned of the depravations of the French around Oporto as they gathered their food and supplies. A French army lived off the land, taking whatever they needed from the local population, and he now knew the consequences. He had heard of small bands resisting the French and the brutal reprisals exacted by their French occupiers. Gradually the conclusion grew within him that this invading army must be fought, it was almost a Crusade to do so, and that if those willing to fight could be brought together and led, then, as a co-ordinated force they could do far more damage than acting as little more than separate bands of brigands picking off the odd Frenchman.

Thus, as he roamed he spread the word, for all those ready to fight to meet at Lamego Church on the evening of the 5th and so now he stood, as he so often had before, at the meeting of the transepts, the aisle and the chancel, but this time, very much not as a man of peace. Men were filing in and not a few women, all taking their place in the pews and up in the gallery above, but there was little talking; the habit of waiting silently for guided worship was too strong in such a place. When no more had entered for three minutes, and their number was approaching two hundred, Juan Delica threw up his hands and there was instant silence. He then spoke, not of patriotism, or love of their King, merely of the need to defend their homes and families and to make the French fearful of venturing out of Oporto in nothing less than serious strength. This would give time to prepare for their arrival, which meant hiding their food, women and children, and to fight and harass the French all the way. He spoke of a 'guerrilla', a little war, to be fought by them in aid of their own King's army.

This last brought forth rousing cheers and many cries of "Conduzir nos!", but he did not want to become their leader, he had no military experience at all, not even from books. He asked if any there were ever in the army, but none came forward. There was total silence as he looked around, then he slowly nodded and smiled as the cheering as renewed. What choice did he have? So, the first sensible task was to see who had weapons and who had horses. The former was done inside the Church, the latter outside. Fray Juan Delica's guerrilla band had been formed.

oOo

The 105th led the infantry column that marched North on the Grand Trunk, but they were not in the lead for the whole army. This was undertaken by the Light Cavalry led by General Stapleton-Cotton and behind them came the Light Infantry screen composed of the three Companies of Stewart's Brigade. All had been on the march for two days and all were in good spirits even if now apprehension was growing as they came nearer by the hour to the awaiting French. At the front of the Battalion on the road came the Colour Party and, as usual, the less experienced Ensigns were hoping for answers and predictions from the three veterans alongside, these being Colour Sergeants Deakin and Bennet and RSM Gibney, although most questions were directed at Deakin and came mostly from Rushby.

"What happens if we encounter the French, say, in the next hour, Sergeant."

Deakin manipulated his chinstrap with his jaw.

"We'll stop, Sir, an' await orders."

A poor answer, thought Rushby.

"And then?"

"We'll wait what the cavalry have to say, Sir. 'Twill be them as've spied the Johnnies, an' so a parcel of they will come back to report. Then 'tis up to the General. Sir."

"What would you hope?"

"That we sees them, afore they sees us, Sir. Then we can do what's best for us, without no hindrance from them."

"Do you think there will be a battle?"

"Oh, there'll be somethin', Sir. Afore long."

Rushby leaned forward in order to view the giant figure of Gibney.

"What do you think, Sergeant Major?"

Gibney flexed his chin and twisted his mouth, movements emphasised by his magnificent whiskers. He was a man of few words and this occasion was no different, nor was his broad Yorkshire accent.

"Aye Sir. Ah'd say that Deakin here, has just about the raht of it!"

Behind them came the Grenadiers, led by Carravoy and D'Villiers. The third and final Officer of the Grenadier Company, Lieutenant Simon Ameshurst, was back with his Section to the rear. Both somewhat morose, both Carravoy and D'Villiers maintained a gait somewhat between a plod and a trudge, Carravoy, because he was tired and much of him below the waist ached, D'Villiers because he was very apprehensive, anxiously gazing ahead at the cavalry far beyond the infantry screen. Although a veteran, now, of four battles, his memory of his own conduct in each did not fill him with much confidence. Carravoy was speaking of the campaign so far, in none too complimentary a tone, much of it sourced from his own aching legs.

"Too quick! He's pushing us out too quick. We'll outrun our supplies and what then? Another pull back like at Coruna!"

D'Villiers knew that much of what was said was untrue. He himself had supervised the issue of another three days rations and he fully appreciated the virtues of taking the French unawares.

"We may catch them on the hop."

Carravoy snorted.

"Catch out Johnny Frog! His cavalry are the best in the world. They'll see us first more like."

D'Villiers changed the subject.

"Well, if we do have to pull back, at least it's in Spring weather!"

Carravoy was in no mood to be mollified.

"Small mercy!"

In the Light Infantry screen, life was utter tedium, required to advance thirty yards apart with all conversation barred and not even allowed to puff their pipes. If there was any conversation it was with a patrolling Officer, roaming up the ranks and usually admonishing someone for failing to maintain the correct distance. For Miles and Saunders nothing of such came, for them maintaining distance was pure instinct, but Tucker and Solomon often heard the rough edge of the tongue of their Sergeant, the formidable Ellis, or even the usually more forgiving George Fearnley, second Sergeant of the Light Company. However, even for Miles and Saunders, carrying their Baker rifle across their chest and at the ready, was beginning to make their arms ache severely. It was not long before they used the rifle sling over their left shoulders. Ellis said nothing.

Further out, within the cavalry so directly spoken of by both Deakin and Carravoy, Captains Tavender and Templemere were thoroughly enjoying themselves. Their mounts were of the best and each had huge confidence that both stallions would have enough speed to propel them out of any possible trouble. The only cloud of the day had been their Commander, Colonel Withers, damning the pair of them for sitting their horses outside of cover, which was a very convenient spinney of trees. However, status quo had been somewhat repaired when Withers asked to borrow Tavender's telescope, a most splendid four draw instrument. Through it Tavender had seen blue uniforms withdrawing and now Withers could do the same. He rode off to tell Stapleton-Cotton, their Brigade Commander, whilst Tavender scoured the hills through the fine lenses, for French uniforms. None could be seen and so the squadron trotted forward, Tavender now de facto leader.

Furthest back for the 105th came their Followers, behind even the supply wagons, mules and the light cart of the Reverend Albright. From these people came more noise than any other part of the whole, the incessant timpano of pots and spoons colliding together and their chatting, shouting and laughter. However, as usually transpired, beside Sedgwicke, as driver of the Chaplain's cart, walked Nelly Nicholls, Bridie Deakin and the children of both. The question most commonly asked up into the cart came from Nelly Nicholls, directed at Sedgwicke

"Sure now, Parson darlin', how long d'ye think before the next stop?"

Sedgwicke sucked in a deep breath. He had registered the beginning of this stage at 2.30 and so he consulted his watch which read 4.00. If he said what he thought, he would be saying one and a half hours, but, that would mean little to Nelly, her never having owned a watch in her life, nor having any understanding of fractions. Instead he looked ahead and fixed on a far hill.

"Can you see that hill, up there? The one with trees running down the right."

Nelly craned her neck.

"Sure! Yes, I can."

Sedgwicke smiled down.

"I'd say just over the other side. We could well be there for the night."

Albright felt the need to say something; this was, after all, his flock. He came upon a combination that would apply both to walking and to his calling.

"God will carry us forward, my good woman. Are we not, after all, about his Good Purpose?"

Sedgwicke gave an irritated sigh and slapped the reins, whilst Nelly barely heard, for Bridie had tapped her on the shoulder.

"Where's Patrick? Sure I've not seen him for much of this day."

Nelly looked around.

"Nor I. The scamp! Sure, he'll be up to something."

The something was discovered when they made camp that evening on the far side of the hill, which had been identified by Sedgwicke. Patrick came marching into their area wearing the full uniform of a Drummerboy, white facings all over the front, the collar and the shoulder wings, with a black symbol similar to a fleur-de-lys every two inches. His sleeves were covered in rings of the same design. He carried his drum slung by its strap over his shoulder, sticks in his belt. Bridie shrieked, not at her son, more at Jed Deakin.

"Jed! He's joined up! He's a Drummerboy! Look! Look!"

Deakin barely moved.

"That was always on the cards, Ma. He's old enough and tough enough."

Hearing no support from her husband, she burst into tears and lifted her apron to her face. Deakin sighed, he loved Bridie dearly and was always upset with any upset in her, so he rose and put his hands on her shoulders.

"Bridie, he's a good strong lad. Sooner or later they'd have made him join, either the Drummers now, or the firing line later."

He allowed the fearful idea of the firing line to sink in.

"'Sides, he'll get paid now and it'll keep him out of mischief."

He paused again.

"'Tis not so bad a thing".

Bridie leaned against him for a second or two and then went over to embrace her eldest son, who, once released from her arms, waved a companion into the light of the fire.

"Ma, I've got a mate. His names Henri. He's French!"

Henri walked forward, nervous and unsure, but Deakin was cudgelling his memory. He looked at Davey.

"B'ain't this the boy that you dug out of Elvina, after Coruna?"

Davey examined the boy in the firelight.

"Looks like. Can't be sure."

He turned to Byford.

"Ask him, Byfe."

Byford came forward to stand before the boy.

"Êtes-vous le garçon nous avons trouvé de Elvina?"

The boy looked up, re-assured to be spoken to in his own language.

"Oui, je suis."

All understood that reply and so Byford sat down, but Deakin had noticed something.

"Byfe. Ask if we can see his drum?"

Byford rose and spoke again.

"Puissions-nous voir votre tambour?"

The drum was swung around on its strap and Deakin's suspicions were confirmed.

"I bloody knew it! He's still got the same drum as we found him with. That bloody French thing what he wouldn't let go of."

Deakin's tone alarmed the boy, but Byford was still near.

"Il est très bien. Tout est bien."

Nelly Nicholls had memories also, of a starving, wasted and terrified youngster, captured by his enemy after a dreadful march and an appalling battle. She did now, what she did then, to hold up a welcoming hand.

"You come on here now, honey, and lets see what we can get ye t'eat."

As he came within reach she laid the welcoming hand on his shoulder, then send an admonishing look all around the camp.

"Fine welcome ye've all given the lad. Youse! Spalpeens, the lot of ye!"

The boy was pushed onto a log, given a dish and then some stew was ladled into it. Nothing more was heard from the boy, but Bridie was greatly concerned.

"What of his Mother, Jed? She'll be beside herself with worry, his body not found after the battle and no word from nowhere!"

Deakin looked over at her, exasperated and astonished.

"What can I do? There's none too many letters as moves between home an' France, never mind between the rankers of armies."

However, Davey had been listening.

"I reckon something can be done, Jed. But not just now and only if we can get pencil and paper. Byford here can put something together."

Byford looked up, something between a sarcastic thanks and astonishment on his face.

oOo

Everything had changed at the end of that day. The dying light of the day gave significance to the distant pop of cavalry carbines, which meant that they were up on the French and that the French knew of their arrival. Stewart was riding with Lacey and O'Hare and, with the sound of conflict, Stewart said but one sentence.

"Wellesley's up with us. We've a meet this evening, then you after that. My tent at 10.00."

With that they parted company until the stated time when all seven senior Officers of the Brigade squeezed in, only three able to sit. Stewart did not depart from his standard routine and the prelude was the usual gulping of near tankards of scotch whisky. That done he came straight to the point.

"Our General likes to use his flanks, and so to that end, Hill and Cameron have taken their Brigades to Aviero, just over from us at the coast, to get into boats and then go up the coast aways and get behind the Johnnies. We will be supporting a night attack of cavalry and guns at the end of tomorrow. Wellesley hopes to force the crossings of the River Vouga and push all opposition back to Oporto, doing as much damage as we can."

A pause.

"See to your men!"

They all filed out as Stewart partook of his final, pre-bed, swig of scotch.

The following day was spent with inspections, then rest, but only the most experienced managed any form of beneficial sleep. For many this was their first combat and for many others, thinking of the last time they had faced the French, it had been in a battle won only by extreme effort and courage.

For Templemere and Tavender life had suddenly become extremely arduous. They had spent the day maintaining a cavalry screen in the hills above the River Vouga and had barely had time to eat before they were called to form up and trot forward again. Little was said as both set out with their squadrons, side by side, Tavender more than a little nervous, he knew the success rate of night exercises, whilst Templemere was in a state of near terror! Their General, Stapleton-Cotton, commanded the leading squadrons, all being from the 14th Light Dragoons, whilst, Tavender, as a Senior Captain, commanded three squadrons at the very rear of the 16th, and he now well realised just how much they relied on their guide, an unknown Portuguese, who arrived in the night, called Godofredo and could only communicate by sign language. After crossing the Vouga at a ford and it wasn't long before he was unseen, lost ahead in the dark and the mist, which was growing thicker by the minute. Tavender asked the obvious question.

"Where's Fredo?"

Templemere had no answer and so the answer came from Tavender.

"Damn traitor! Damn all Portuguese idiots!"

Thus, it wasn't long before they had a choice between two narrow gullies, which to take and Tavender took the one directly forward, but soon it turned disconcertingly rightwards, inland. Tavender called a halt.

"Can you hear any firing?"

"Not in this slot in the earth!"

"We have to bear left."

In this haphazard manner they took their decisions to bear left, bear right, or even countermarch, until dawn cracked the sky. They had not fired a shot, nor attacked any Frenchman, however, someone's luck was in, for as the day lightened, they saw Stapleton-Cotton's squadron's drawn up on a ridge and so they silently led their men over to extend his line from the right. There came no messenger from the General and a nearby Cornet in the 14th told them that their night advance had not gone at all well either. Plainly Stapleton-Cotton was examining his options. They were looking at a village across a valley whose length both left and right was hidden in the mist, across the valley were drawn up an array of French cavalry, well in excess of 1,000 sabres, with infantry to the side and cannon in front. By this force they were outnumbered and the situation became yet more anxious when these began to advance, and then bugles sounded, British calls not French, which told them that

Stapleton-Cotton was ordering a retreat and so all turned their horses heads to the rear to quickly fall back.

Meanwhile, the Light Company was advancing forward, in a close column, led by Carr and Drake, with their guide Leandro close at hand. A mist hung heavy in their ravine and a shape grew out of the gloom to reveal itself as a field-gun stuck behind rocks. Drake, ever ready for any act of kindness, spoke up.

"Should we help?"

Carr shook his head.

"There's beefy Grenadiers right up close behind."

With that dismissal they moved on, to then see even more threatening shapes appear. Carr took no chances.

"Halt! Repulse cavalry."

His column immediately adopted formation, front rank kneeling with bayonets extended, the two ranks behind at the 'make ready'. Drake yelled into the mist.

"Identify yourselves!"

The call came back in the positive.

"16th Light Dragoons!"

As Drake commanded his men to reform into column, Carr walked forward, so find a group of Light Dragoons.

"Do you have an Officer?"

The reply came from a Sergeant.

"Yes Sir, off to the right, Captain Tavender."

"Are you sure he's there?"

"No Sir."

Carr let that drop.

"Weren't you supposed to clear the way?"

"Yes, Sir, but the Johnnies are in strength up ahead, Sir, and've all come on, so we've fallen back."

"Are they behind you?"

"Can't say, Sir."

Carr was instantly livid. This was what cavalry were there for, to find intelligence and these knew nothing.

"Right. You turn around and you go back and find out exactly what Johnny's up to. Then come back here and report to me. Take all these with you and keep together."

Such a clear order from a Major had to be obeyed and the Sergeant turned his horse again and rode back, taking his men with him. Drake came up to Carr, who turned to meet him.

"Keep the men together, Nat. This is a God-awful shambles and who knows what's coming our way. Last report was Johnny advancing, as cavalry!"

At that moment there came the sound of galloping, but from behind and of but a few in number, three as it turned out, being Stewart, Lacey and O'Hare. Carr came to the attention and saluted. The reply was to be handed a whisky flask.

"Report, Major."

"Our cavalry have pulled back, Sir. I have sent some to return forward to find out what is happening. Other than that, I'm in the dark, Sir."

Stewart looked down at him whilst fixing the top onto the flask and sliding it into his pocket. He had not drunk from it.

"Your name?"

"Carr, Sir. 105th."

Stewart peered forward through the thinning mist, then another Officer appeared, a full Colonel.

"Sir, are you General Stewart?"

Stewart nodded.

"Good, Sir, glad I've found you. General Stapleton-Cotton has gathered his men and is about to attack. The French have seen your men here and the Portuguese 16th and have pulled back. You are to push your Light Companies forward as skirmishers whilst keeping the remainder of your three Battalions in column, two side by side, one in reserve. You will be following cavalry, Sir."

Stewart peered forward some more, then turned to the messenger, clearly an Aide-de-Camp.

"And your orders come from whom?"

"General Wellesley, Sir. He's with your 1st Detachments."

Stewart nodded, then turned to Lacey.

"Your Lights have Bakers, do they not?"

"Sir."

"I want yours in the centre. The Portuguese Lights will be on your right, those of the Detachments on your left."

He then looked down at Carr.

"You're in command of the screen. Don't move until your supports arrive either side."

Drake had been listening and called his Company forward.

"Skirmish order! Files of three."

Stewart nodded, but with no mirth on his face, as the 105th Lights ran forward, adopting formation as they ran. It was not long before they found themselves looking at a long line of horses tails, many swishing to and fro with impatience.

Relieved of the mist, Tavender and Templemere were again looking across the same valley of a little earlier, at the same village, but now with only a single Regiment of cavalry before it. Both were positioned on the right of their line, with Stapleton-Cotton out in front of them and the 14th on their left. Stapleton-Cotton turned in his saddle.

"16th! Draw sabres!"

The eerie scrape of swords leaving scabbards came to all ears. He lifted his own.

"Advance!"

The pair immediately behind him did not like the odds. They were nothing like their full strength of 700 Dragoons, with so many still lost, and they were about to charge a whole Regiment. Stapleton-Cotton led them down the slope at a walk, to splash through the small stream at the bottom and then walk up the far slope. Lacey and O'Hare, with Stewart now gone, both shared the same thought, spoken by O'Hare.

"At least Cotton knows his business, keeping his horses fresh, but he's taking the risk of being charged down the slope."

Lacey nodded.

"Perhaps, but I think he's pushing at an open door. They won't stand, not with us coming up behind Cotton and his men."

The 16th reached the crest in good order and continued their walk forward. With the good daylight aiding them another whole squadron of the 16th, once lost, now galloped over to join the line, which re-assured Tavender, whilst Templemere had eyes only for the static French, now but 300 yards away. The order came.

"Trot!"

Then, soon after.

"Canter!"

Templemere's heart came into his mouth, but then he could have shouted for joy. The whole French regiment were turning their horses and disappearing back to a line of trees. His whole emotion somersaulted — "Surely we should charge?" He heard a bugle sound but it did not register, until he realised that the line of troopers was now significantly back behind him and he reined in his own horse. Stapleton-Cotton had slowed his men back to a walk, then an Officer galloped across their front to him and he ordered a halt. They sat their mounts for a few minutes and then the infantry screen came up to them and passed through. Carr was in the lead and passed close to Tavender, but gave him barely a glance, for he walked straight to Stapleton-Cotton.

"Sir. Major Carr. 105th Foot. General Wellesley has sent us forward as a screen, Sir, with General Stewart's three Battalions following in column."

Stapleton-Cotton nodded.

"Right. I'll stay out front between you and them. Watch for a messenger from me, I'm sure I'll discover something you'll need to know."

He ordered his troopers forward and they soon passed through the Light Infantry files. During the interim, whilst both sides had stood idle and close to each other, Zeke Saunders and the ex-thief Len Bailey had used the remains of the mist to exchange a flask of French wine for a quantity of British tobacco.

With the cavalry screen out before, Carr led his men on, following. For Templemere all anxieties returned. They were once again in the lead as they entered the trees, but mercifully for his nerves, it was but a rank of thin specimens bordering a field and no French could be seen beyond. For an hour they walked on, slowly climbing a shallow incline. Templemere and Tavender were now side by side, and the former, now moderately re-assured by the knowledge that he had almost their full 700 Light Dragoons at his back, felt distracted enough to look around and over to the left where saw, by the naked eye, what looked like a brown and green smudge, about half a mile distant. He turned to his companion.

"What's that? There?"

He pointed and soon Tavender had his telescope focused.

"Peasants! On horses. Mounted peasants."

"Should we not tell Stapleton-Cotton?"

"I think not. They've probably come to watch the show."

Whatever Tavender's opinion, within 15 minutes, one of the mounted peasants had galloped over to accost their General and communicate, possibly by speech but also with much gesturing and pointing. They saw Stapleton-Cotton turn in his saddle and wave for someone to come forward. Tavender decided who.

"Fred. You'd better go forward. He wants someone."

Templemere spurred his horse forward to reach his Commander, who wasted no time.

"Do you speak Portuguese?"

"No Sir."

"Fair enough, but as best I can work out the French are drawn up at, or at least near, a place called Grijon."

"Yes Sir."

At this point the messenger spoke up, recognizing the place name, which inspired a repeat of his message.

"Os Franceses estão em Grijon."

Stapleton Cotton looked at Templemere.

"There. I gather from that, that the French are at Grijon. How far that is, I can't say, but we must assume close. Find General Wellesley and tell him. Tell him that I am advancing with caution."

He looked full in the face of Templemere, making no small challenge.

"Got that?"

Templemere nodded, more than a little irritated at being spoken to in such a manner, but he turned and rode off to pass through his own line, to see then Carr coming up from behind. Being unable to resist the temptation to exercise his superior knowledge he set a course to pass by at a walk.

"Carr! Major Sir!"

Carr turned towards him as Templemere spoke further, a dismissive half smile on his face.

"Our General says that the French are up at a place called Grijon."

He grinned fully.

"You'll be in action soon."

Carr managed an indulgent smile and made a reply which brought just a shadow of discomfiture back across Templemere's face.

"So will you!"

A pause.

"I take it you've been sent to find Wellesley?"

Templemere nodded.

"Then perhaps your first utterance should have been: where is Wellesley?"

No reply. Carr was absolutely correct and he continued.

"You see the brown column behind us, with a red one to your right of them?"

Templemere rose on his stirrups and looked, but said nothing.

"He's between the two."

A pause for a triumphant grin.

"It's always a good military axiom that an Officer should know where his Superiors are. And a walk is a wholly unsatisfactory speed for delivering a message to our Commanding Officer!"

They parted, Templemere now much put out and Carr's Light Infantry marching on, always upward, always on a rocky plain. Carr looked around to see, re-assuringly, several teams of field guns picking their way through the rocks. Then came Templemere, riding back to his Dragoons, at some distance from them and then Stewart came cantering up, accompanied by four Dragoons of the 14th.

"Major Carr. The Johnnies are up ahead. Formed up, we must assume, at a place called Grijon, it's but yards ahead, less than half a mile. Cotton has been ordered to attack if the situation is favourable, you are to push on and skirmish against the place, but frontally. Behind you, your 105th are coming up with the Detachments. The 16th Portuguese will advance on your right and over to the left, Wellesley has sent the whole of Perry's Brigade, four KGL."

He looked down, in almost fatherly fashion.

"Good luck, Carr."

Carr saluted.

"Thank you, Sir."

Carr drew his sword; a straight, solid, blade of shiny steel but a dull metal bell-guard to protect his hand. He then looked to left and right to see that his men at least, of the three Light Companies, were in perfect formation.

By now Templemere was alongside Tavender, all anxieties firmly uppermost. His mouth was dry and something was not quite right with his stomach. Things did not improve when Stapleton-Cotton called "Draw sabres." Again the scrape that stretched nerves and soon all both to left and right carried a sword erect in their right hand. All was happening all too quickly. The order came, "Trot", then soon after "Canter". At some speed they were moving forward, his stallion needing to be held back, being caught up in the excitement. He was comforted to see Tavender just ahead and even more so to have Troopers come up on either side. From no order, or at least one unheard by him, the line broke into a gallop. Then he saw the French, a blue and maroon line, if static or moving forward he could not tell. The men either side of him were howling, an animal moan heard above the pounding hooves. Then the blue and maroon line turned into individual men, but seconds away, and they were Hussars it seemed, some subconscious memory told him, because they had no breastplate. The two lines crashed together with an unearthly crash, almost like a huge wave carrying rocks spending itself on a rocky shore. He would soon be passing a French Hussar who had his sabre raised to land a blow. Terrified as he was, Templemere was no dunce with a blade and parried the blow to allow it to slide down to his hand guard. A shriek behind told him that someone had felt the edge of a sword, but whom he knew not.

The conflict was now a melee, but being mounted on horses, this held the combatants away from landing many telling blows. Whether for seconds or minutes, Templemere could not tell how long it lasted, whilst his horse pirouetted around, Templemere trying to land blows, whilst his back and neck cringed at the arrival of a blow from behind, but then the French broke and galloped away. A shout of triumph came from the Dragoons and the pursuit began, Templemere, so well mounted, was now in the van. His horse overtook a French Hussar, who heard the noise of the overtaking hooves to turn his head round and give a terrified look before Templemere stood up in his stirrups and brought his sabre down across the man's neck. He fell behind and someone shouted, "Well done, Sir." Then it became easy. His superb mount overtook Frenchman after Frenchman and all were dealt a telling blow. Templemere was intoxicated, here he was leisurely dealing out death to the men whose presence but minutes earlier had reduced him to a state of terror. He downed another Frenchman, but then the situation changed.

The French had ridden back upon supports and his horse was brought to a halt by a solid group in his path. Instinctively, he turned his horse and he found that he was terrifyingly alone, for either he had outrun his comrades or they had stopped once the French were routed. He spurred his horse on, back towards safety, but his mount was now tired, almost blown, from the charge and the fight and the pursuit. He looked over his shoulder to see at least three vengeful faces beneath French Hussars caps. They were going to pursue him as far as was prudent, this murdering British cavalryman, at least as they saw it. Suddenly, the situation changed again, now he was surrounded by the mounted peasants seen earlier and the French were gone. One, clad in brown homespun, seized his bridle just behind the bit and led him back to the now static British, like an incapable child, but Templemere was too relieved to object. His rescuer turned and grinned through brown stained teeth, before releasing the bridle.

"Lá você é inglês. Está seguro agora.."

Then his rescuer turned his mount, as had his companions and was gone; they had other business. Their leader Juan Delica, had soon deduced what their best tactic was, that his men were more effective against scattered and broken troops and so, watching from the distance and seeing the French cavalry turn from the fight, beaten and broken, he led his men forward to hit the retreating French from the side. They had inflicted several casualties, but then his men had stopped, well taught to go no-where near formed troops, but just at the moment when Templemere needed a rescue, they decided to do the extra and take the chance to save this 'loco Inglês'. The same, now chastened and realising that he had had a very fortunate escape, turned his horse and sat in front of the ranks, beside Tavender.

"You were lucky there, Fred! Still, you must have downed several."

He turned to look at him.

"No-one can condemn you for that."

Templemere was examining his sword, but seeing nothing. The fear had yet to subside.

oOo

Carr led his men on, across the high, rocky plain that, with midday approaching was becoming warm and he was becoming thirsty. He looked behind to the right to see Sergeant Ellis, once of his Company.

"Sergeant! A drop from your canteen, if you please!"

Such was tantamount to an order and so Ellis unslung his canteen, caught up with his Major, pulled out the cork stopper and handed it over. Carr took one long pull, then handed it back, for Ellis to return the cork, but Carr had more on his mind. They were now "in the presence of the enemy" and all convention of rank was irrelevant as they walked on.

"What d'you think?"

Ellis had his opinion and gave it.

"There's French cavalry about and I don't like it. Not with us out front as skirmishers."

He looked both left and right, but re-assuringly he could see no-one on any horse, nor wearing any colour of uniform.

"Looks like that one charge was about all our cavalry had in 'em. Sir."

Carr nodded.

"Pass the word. Any sight of French horsemen, shout and holler!"

"Sir."

Ellis dropped back and the message began, circulating outwards from him. Then, once again, Carr heard hooves behind, to, once again see Stewart with his escort. Carr halted and saluted. The result was the same, a whisky flask. Stewart spoke as Carr took a sip, but he would have preferred water. With Carr, their Officer, now halted, so did his men and all listened who could, to their Brigadier elaborating on what he had said earlier.

"Grijon's just beyond those trees and the French are drawn up, either side, in strength. Your 105th and the Detachments are in column behind you, but Wellesley wants them held in reserve. On your right the Portuguese will attack in open order and on your left the whole of Perry's KGL Brigade are going in. That's the main attack, to come in on their flank. You penetrate that wood and distract them from the front. Assume it's full of French, which is very likely. It's you that Wellesley wants to open the ball! Good luck."

With that he wheeled his horse around and cantered off.

Carr looked at the trees, 300 yards distant. It was his decision, they could walk up, in skirmish order, and see what happened, which would mean taking some casualties, but that would make possible an advance according to their drill, which would mean fewer casualties as they entered the wood. Or they could close up into a line and rush the trees, hoping that there was much less than a whole French battalion in there. Carr had about 240 men. He decided that they would rush the tree line in open order, in no formation at all. He looked for his bugler Arthur Bates, well known as 'Bugle Bates', unsurprisingly.

"Bates. Sound advance on my word."

He drew his sword and walked forward, the signal for all to advance with him. Staring at the trees and certain that he was a prime target at the fore, his own apprehension grew. On his left was Richard Shakeshaft's section with the Lights of the Detachments beyond them. On his right was Drake's section, with the Lights of the Portuguese beyond them. The file of Miles, Davey and Pike were the furthest right, and so they were next to the Portuguese, which did not please Miles one jot, holding his place in the middle of their file, with Davey before and Pike behind. It was Davey that received Miles' opinion.

"How much can we count on these Portugee? I ain't never heard of one yet as could stand up to what the French can throw at 'em!"

The reply came from amongst the brown uniformed ranks to his right.

"You look to yourself, Inglese! Where you go, so will we!"

Davey gave himself the luxury of a look back and a grin at the discomfited Miles.

"There's your answer! Perhaps these is more eager for this fight than you"

Miles sucked in breath for a reply, but the bugle notes of "double forward" came and so he used the breath to run. The Portuguese were yelling "Ataque! Ataque!", encouraged by their Officers at the front, waving their swords. The distance lessened to one hundred yards and then the firing came from the trees before them. Men fell, uniformed in both red and brown, but then they were onto the last yards. The French had fired one volley and as Davey entered, closely followed by Miles, they found no French at the edge, they had fallen back to contest the deeper recesses of the wood. Drake was as relieved as any Officer, for he too had realised the possibility of the wood being held in great strength, but what they were opposed by, they could cope with.

"Advance! In files."

Davey moved forward, from tree to tree, staring forward when he could, feinting one way then the next, always changing whether or not he emerged left or right from behind a tree. Musket balls began to sing past him, smacking into the heavy bark. He looked right, never directly forward, which would cause him to move too far out of cover. He saw a blue uniform, raised his Baker and fired. The Frenchman slumped down and Davey reloaded, for Miles to run to the next tree forward and find his own target. In the centre, armed only with a sword, Carr could do nothing, until one of his men was badly wounded, then he picked up the Baker rifle and added his own fire to that of his men. The sound of the musketry was continuous, the fighting ferocious, but his men, armed with the accurate Baker rifle were making progress, picking off the French at longer range. Their light infantry drill was pushing the French back, each man taking targets off to the side, half to fire across left, half to the right, so that they remained in cover, but clearing the way for their comrades off to the flanks, as they were doing for them. The tactic was devastating for the French, picked off from the side, where they could be seen, whilst not from the front. As their casualties mounted, the French began to give ground. Miles and Davey had fought their way forward to the first French casualty, a wounded man, gasping for breath, but Miles simply kicked away his musket as he passed by.

"Who be these, John? These b'ain't those tassel swingin' bastards, nor be they decked out in blue and red!"

Davey gave no answer as he reloaded, the fact that his opponents were neither assault Voltiguers nor trained sharpshooter Tirailleurs, was all to the good. In his eyes, who they actually were counted for nothing.

However, the sounds of combat were fiercest on the right. The Portuguese, almost heedless of casualties were pushing forward, indicating that something very different was happening on that side; perhaps their whole battalion

64

had caught up. Close to them, Joe Pike was kneeling behind a stump, looking for a target to his left when across his front came a rush of brown uniforms; many more than had entered the wood with him. The Portuguese had been reinforced from somewhere and were now advancing in strength, all enemy in blue falling back before them. After checking that all in blue were gone, Pike stood up, to soon be joined by his two filemates. Davey looked at Miles.

"Now what was you saying about the Portuguese?"

However, Miles had other things on his mind, clear ideas about his own comfort.

"These Frogs is gone. I'm for what's in their packs and a French one of they for me, afore Carr sends us forward again."

With that he walked to the nearest French body, whilst the Officer that he spoke of, this being Carr, was indeed leading his men forward cautiously, always keeping a tree to his front, giving Miles very little time for his pillaging. Soon the gloom of the centre of the wood was broken by light from the far edge and, when Carr came to the last tree, he called a halt. Grijon was in view, with no French in the fields before, but what looked like three whole Battalions were drawn up in the fields beyond. Either side of the small village, retreating French infantry were streaming past and on either side of Carr's position he could see, coming in from the left, the red uniforms of the King's German Legion pressing forward and over on the right the brown of the 16th Portuguese charged forward with their two Colours in the van, bright and clear. 'A good day for them', Carr thought. He led his men out of the woods and into the fields, across the short stubble. Some cattle and pigs, utterly panicked, ran across their front and firing began again, to which Carr turned a blind eye, deciding his men deserved some boiled pork. They had fought well and casualties seemed light. With that thought put aside he watched events beyond the village, because the three French battalions, in good order, were breaking from line into column and then, at double speed, forming on the road that could be seen disappearing over the ridgeline behind the village. French soldiers were joining them from both sides and soon there were none to be seen. Then some British cavalry came in from the left, led by a lone Officer, galloping directly onto the road which forced Carr's command into their own narrow column by the side of the road. The horsemen then galloped over the ridge, presumably in pursuit of the retreating French and then Drake appeared at Carr's side, providing an audience for Carr's thoughts on the headlong cavalry charge forward, which they had just witnessed.

"Good luck to them with that!"

Drake nodded.

"Rather them than me!"

Carr smiled, the euphoria of a successful combat still within him.

"I'd rather them than you! I can ride better than you!"

Drake made no reply. The judgment was probably true! Then, not now to Carr's surprise, Stewart arrived and again came the whisky flask, but Carr felt able to refuse.

"I'd prefer water, Sir!"

Stewart motioned one of his Dragoons forward and he passed down his flask, another doing the same for Drake. As both pulled deeply from the flasks, Stewart spoke.

"Get your men into the village, Carr, and await your Colonel. He's coming up shortly. Tell him that the 16th Portuguese will be advancing on his right, the KGL on his left. The Detachments in reserve. Wellesley wants us pushing straight on to Oporto."

He leaned forward, his forearms on the pommel of his saddle.

"Ye've done well! Best of all, the Portuguese, I'm riding over to tell them, but Johnny made no stand anywhere. The KGL pushed them back like an open door!"

Carr nodded, the flask now back with its owner.

"They're hoping to stop us at Oporto, Sir."

Stewart was already moving.

"I don't doubt that, laddie. Not for a second."

Carr led his men into the village, but saw no dead French. The only life that arrived were civilians, crawling up out of cellars and other holes in the ground, grateful that their village had not been fought over. Carr led his men through and waited in the field beyond to take stock and estimate casualties, and it wasn't long before his Regiment came up, Lacey and O'Hare in the lead. Carr saluted, as did Lacey and O'Hare, then Carr reported.

"Two dead, Sir. Six wounded, three severely.

Lacey nodded.

"Leave them with the Surgeon. Meanwhile, we are in the centre for the next advance, so Stewart has told me. You're in the rear, Carr. Yours have done enough."

Carr saluted.

"Sir."

But Lacey had gone, leaving the two Majors alone and sharing a water flask, Lacey was making straight for Carravoy.

"Captain! Get yours on a company front, two lines. We are advancing forward in column to see if Johnny has anything left in him today."

He stared into Carravoy's face.

"Five minutes!"

That was clearly an order and so Carravoy ran off, to find his Lieutenants and Sergeants. His Grenadiers looked almost pristine having endured nothing bar a march up from Lisbon and, due to the efforts of his Sergeants, they were soon in a two deep line, 40 men across and all the remaining nine Companies in the same formation, drawn up close behind. When Lacey was satisfied, he looked over to his right to see the column of the 16th Portuguese, then behind to see the Detachments also with a 40 man front. A turn to his left saw a column of the KGL already in place, probably one of the four Battalions that had seen no combat so far. Lacey had only to wait for orders and they came from the highest level. Wellesley himself came galloping up, accompanied by his Staff, his escort and Brigadier Stewart. At the sight of the bi-corn hat, worn 'fore and aft", Lacey ordered Gibney to bring the whole column to 'present arms' which was in process by the time Wellesley arrived and he seemed to fully appreciate, lifting his hat as he passed the first rank. He recognized Lacey.

"Afternoon Lacey! Pleased to see you are well."

Lacey saluted, which was acknowledged.

"Afternoon, Sir."

"Move your men on, the rest will follow. There is a cavalry screen out in front of you, but I don't expect Johnny to stand again, at least not this side of the river. He'll be over his bridge at Oporto and then set about feeling more secure, probably by exploding the damn thing."

He sat upright in his saddle and looked at Stewart, then back to Lacey.

"Can't be helped."

He smiled down.

"Two hours marching and you'll be there."

He turned his horse.

"Good to see you again, Lacey. And your men!"

With that he was gone, leaving Stewart with Lacey and O'Hare.

"Best march on then, Colonel."

The orders were given and they set off and soon they came to the results of the cavalry charge down the narrow road. All three men wordlessly passed the sight of rows of dead, both French and British, and several horses, now dead, having been shot because of broken legs caused when their riders had presumably attempted to clear the walls either side, the better to attack their enemy. Wellesley was correct with all his predictions, for they saw no sign of a retreating army, no equipment discarded, only a few French too wounded to continue. Within two hours they were at Villa Nova on their side of the Douro and almost at the exact moment when they caught sight of the wooden bridge of boats, it was blown up, sending a mushroom of white smoke and dark wood up into the sky. The last of the French were now on the quayside, having trodden upon the bridge but minutes before. There was nothing left for the Allies to do, but to make camp and await their Commander's wishes. However, the last act of the day was for the energetic Colonel Waters, Wellesley's Senior Intelligence Officer, Wellesley's eyes and ears for any advance into unknown territory, to visit Juan Delica. By dawn three wagons of supplies, weapons and munitions were being shared out amongst his followers. Juan Delica and his followers were now truly in the war.

oOo

Chapter Two

But One River to Cross

Lacey and O'Hare sat their chairs, each purloined from a nearby abandoned house and both men perched high on the Serra Heights, but close to the walls of the Convent built on that significant summit. The solid sanctuary rose high to their right, somehow lowering over them; Holy walls, tall and white, with jutting parapet and Catholic crosses described in bis relief every ten yards, religiously ornate in black and gold. They each cupped a glass of brandy in their hands, the better to warm up the enlivening spirit before taking a grateful sip, now that night was fully fallen and the chill sea breeze fully woken. O'Hare was of full Irish descent, softly spoken and kindly to all in both English and Gaelic and few Officers dwelt as highly in the affections of their men as Padraigh O'Hare, except perhaps Captain Joshua Heaviside and their own Colonel. Despite the difference in rank, they were firm friends, a friendship born of respect and confidence, each in the other, and now, on their third campaign together, they sat and watched the last embers of the bridge burn themselves out, the aftermath of the late afternoon explosion. Also, close to the opposite bank, burned the last boats of Oporto, those that could not be drawn up out of the water, and so they burned down to the waterline, the crackle of the bursting boats timbers across from them adding to the sound of rumbling artillery wheels behind.

It was O'Hare who spoke the question that each was thinking.

"So, how to cross that?"

The wide waters of the Douro showed shiny black against the dancing flames, but the power of both the river and tide were clear in the turbulence that showed both on the dark surface and in the sound of the outgoing current surging against the remains of the bridge of boats, this now

70

merely shattered uprights protruding from the black surface. Both men were slowly shaking their heads, but Lacey began at least a train of thought.

"An assault in boats directly across that doesn't bear thinking about. M'sieu would line up his guns on the far bank and that would be that."

O'Hare wasn't so sure.

"We'd have our own guns up here, giving strong support. From up here!"

"We would, but you saw what I saw. Fascines all along that bank opposite to give his guns cover from our fire. I can't see how any number of batteries up here could make much difference."

O'Hare changed tack.

"What about fording down stream at low tide?"

Lacey had that covered.

"We'd have to wait for a very low one and again, you saw what I saw, Soult has marched almost all his force seawards. He has most of his strength between the bridge here and the beach."

Both took a drink of brandy, before O'Hare spoke again.

"So what then?"

But he answered his own question.

"Outflank inland, where Beresford's been sent?"

Lacey replied, somewhat sorrowfully.

"Yes, but he has only one Brigade, some cavalry and a few Rifles. Soult could hold us on this side of the river with but a quarter of his force, six men, a boy and a dog, and march out to crush Beresford or at least send him running back!"

Both drank again, before O'Hare voiced the conclusion lodged within the minds of both.

"Glad I'm not a General!"

Such ideas were far from the thoughts of his own men, now spending the last two hours between their evening meal and bedding down for the night on the back slopes of the Serra Hill, hidden there from the French. The children were snug inside a lean-to shelter which they could all now make up, as instructed by ex-poacher Chosen Man Davey. The tasks at hand were mostly concerned with cleaning, especially their Baker rifles, and repair, but little of the latter. The day's fighting had taken only slight toll on their equipment, but many in the group were considering how to use a French pack in place of their own. Did any there know anyone in the Battalion baggage train who could be bribed to store their King George issue in an odd space? Len Bailey thought he did. Thus, in the main, the group were in good heart, they had eaten a good meal and there was much French booty to be made good use of, but suddenly the mood changed as Deakin sprang to his feet followed by all the others. It was not Heaviside, he had come and gone with a mug of tea inside him; this was new, a visit from Reverend Albright, accompanied by Private Sedgwicke. The Reverend saw the end of this particular day as a perfect opportunity to visit 'his flock', despite the advice from Sedgwicke, that the men would all be busy making good after the long march and combat. The reply had been both stern and dismissive.

"When, Private, is there not a good time to say a Prayer to the Lord?"

Being deeply religious himself, Sedgwicke could fashion no appropriate answer and so around they went on their hopeless task of visiting each mess group before 'lights out' and each soldier wrapped themselves in their blankets to sleep. However, such mathematical considerations dwelt not in the ecumenical concerns of the good Albright and thus Deakin's group were the fifth visited in the all encompassing dark, each identified by their bright campfires. The Battalion Chaplain came into the centre of the light and began as though he were bestowing the most uplifting and vital service to all within hearing, filling the gap that existed in the centre of all their requirements.

"Men, I have come amongst you to lead you in a prayer of thanks. Please stand and bow your heads."

All already were, for an Officer had come amongst them, and all knew that the Reverend's words were tantamount to an order.

"Oh Dear Lord, we lift our hands and our hearts to give thanks to You for your granting that we be chosen to survive this day of trial and that we all meet here now in good fellowship and gratitude for the success of our arms."

He stopped, which all took as a good end to a short prayer, so they began to sit down, Miles being the most lithe and wiry actually achieving a sitting position, but the Reverend was just getting into his stride and so Miles had to regain his feet, which did not help his mood.

"In the name of our Dear Lord and your Dear Son, Jesus Christ, we beseech you to keep us safe and to grant us victory over the Godless foe who do stretch their wicked hands across this Christian land. Grant, oh Lord, that we march always in strong Faith in thee and that our deeds and thoughts lie in righteous harmony with the teachings of our Lord and Saviour, Jesus Christ."

Another pause, but no-one moved.

"Amen."

The response came from all around, some sincere, but some reluctant and with ill grace, but the Reverend still had not finished, although all were now sat as if he had. He stood his ground, hands clasped together before his chest, slightly leaning forward, his wide brimmed priestly hat tilting and rising as he spoke.

"I trust that you all are in good heart and fine spirits after this excellent day for our cause?"

He beamed around, the firelight red on his shaven cheeks and bright on his many buttons. It was Miles who answered.

"Yes, Reverend. We'n all well fed. Now! None of us is hungry. Nor cold, not tonight, anyhow."

The irony and lack of spiritual content in Miles reply were lost on the good Reverend, but not on Sedgwicke. He knew that his superior had interrupted the only free time the men had and he knew that they now should move on.

"I think we can manage one or two more before sleep, Sir. There is a camp just over here, Sir, if you'd like to follow me!"

Still beaming and still holding the same pose and feeling well satisfied with his work, Albright followed Sedgwicke out of the firelight and into the intervening dark. Within a minute all of his prior congregation were wrapped in their blankets and a minute after that, fast asleep. The last light on the Allied bank to be extinguished was in the Convent as a meeting between Wellesley and his Brigadiers broke up. They had asked just the same questions as had Lacey and O'Hare and voiced just the same, unhelpful answers.

The following dawn broke mild and overcast and began with no more military activity than opposing Officers studying each other through telescopes. When the light grew, Wellesley, up on his hill, even picked out Soult, and vice versa, Soult obvious on a balcony opposite. What purposeful activity there was, happened somewhat upstream and was centred around Colonel Waters, Wellesley's Senior Intelligence Officer and now well established as a compatriot of Juan Delica. Waters and three others, in the growing light within the valley, were lying down atop a ridge, which descended to the riverbank. The three with him were Juan Delica, a barber from Oporto and a dockside foreman, the last used to dealing with English ships. He could speak some English and now belonged to Delica's guerrillas. The barber had crossed the Douro during the night in a hidden skiff and found Delica, who had then sought out Waters for inclusion in their own discussion late the previous night. This had now resulted in the four staring intently across the busy brown/green waters. The barber now pointed forward.

"Está vendo ali, quatro barcaças de vinho."

No translation was needed. Waters could see the four large wine barges, plainly used to ferry a wine cargo out to vessels too large to enter the harbour. Each was moored against the far bank and, as Waters studied further, the barber continued.

"Não há nenhum francês aqui. Eles estão todos dentro da cidade."

Waters looked at the docks foreman, for interpretation.

"He says that there are no French this far up. They are all in the city."

Waters continued looking over the river, this time studying a large, high walled compound with an imposing building within. Close alongside the river, it was also isolated by some way from the Oporto quayside by a wide, empty space, which was open to the river. A road ran up from the quayside, whilst on the far side there was nothing. Almost hidden by the walls and building, a scattered group of houses came down the slope to meet the very back wall. Waters pointed across the river, then addressed their translator.

"What is that?"

The reply arrived back, after translation.

"The Seminary of our Bishop."

One more question.

"Can you see the Serra Convent and the Bridge of Boats from the Seminary?"

After translation, the reply from the barber was quick.

"Si senhor. Muito claramente."

Waters needed no translation and slid backwards to leave, but he was stopped by the hand of Juan Delica on his arm.

"Senor. Não há mais."

He looked at the interpreter.

"He says there is more!"

Juan Delica began talking rapidly and Waters listened and translated for himself as best he could, but he needed confirmation from the interpreter, and so he listened intently to what became vital information.

"There is a ferry one and a half leguas upstream at Barca D'Avintas. It is being repaired and baled out by the people there."

"A working ferry?"

The interpreter nodded his head.

"Si, senhor."

Waters slid back with his companions, shook hands with the three and was gone, soon after to be admitted into the Convent and Wellesley's quarters.

At the same moment, Brigadier General Edmond Perry was sat in his own quarters picking over the lunch that he had been given, wondering which sections of the pork joint on his plate were fit to eat. Perry was a man who permanently had the appearance of someone wrestling with some disagreeable issue and this time that issue was manifest and on his plate. Around him were his Staff, Colonel Withers and Major Johnson of the 16th and his two family acquaintances, also of the 16th, Tavender and Templemere. The latter two had abandoned the food itself and were indulging in the wine, which both had judged as "agreeable". However, Perry was suddenly relieved from the problem on his plate, because a messenger entered, a full Colonel Aide-de-Camp, his shako respectfully under his arm, and he addressed himself to Perry.

"Sir. General Wellesley, requests your attendance at the Convent."

Perry looked up. He didn't like his meal, but he objected to it being interrupted.

"Now? Immediately?"

The Aide-de-Camp remained at attention.

"Yes Sir. Immediately."

Perry stood up, followed by his Staff, but their Brigadier addressed himself only to his Colonel.

"Withers. You're with me!"

Three hours later, Perry was mounted and at the head of his command, albeit smaller than he would have wished, in this case two battalions of his King's German Legion, two guns and two squadrons of the 14th Light Dragoons. Tavender and Templemere, both unaware of what they were there for, being 16th, sat their own horses just behind, both with heads still befuddled by the 'agreeable' wine. Through this alcoholic fog, they were making enquiries of the Colonel assigned to the cavalry force, their Colonel Withers. The reply was clear and somewhat disturbing.

"We are to get up to a place called Barca D'Avintas, about four miles up. Get onto the ferry there, cross and establish a bridgehead."

He saw the concern cross the face of Templemere, but he ignored it.

"If no resistance, then push on until we make contact."

There was no reply, merely a blank look from widening eyes.

"We are to grab Johnny's attention. And keep it!"

Suddenly sober, both Tavender and Templemere spurred their horses forward as the order came to march.

Simultaneously, a far more perilous undertaking was in progress. Waters, Juan Delica, the barber, and two men were crowded into the small skiff and rowing upstream, far enough upstream to be hidden by the bend in the river above the barges. Some of Juan Delica's guerrillas had watched the far bank and found that a French picket passed each half hour and he had now passed. The row over was hard and slow, for they were towing a doubled rope, attached to a tree on their bank, but they came under the French bank and the tide, carefully timed, was now fully turning and so they were drifting down alongside the reeds, barely using the oars. Around the bend, the first barge appeared and, needing no guidance, their skiff bumped into the high, blunt bow and Waters scrambled up the salt stained side, four foot above them. He slowly stood to examine the bank, but saw nothing; neither soldier nor peasant. He motioned his companions to follow him and he helped up the first. Then they moved rapidly to implement the scheme as worked out by their dockside longshoreman, that of lashing all four barges together, stern to bow, and also their own double cable to the bow of the barge uppermost in the stream, the first that had been boarded by Waters. That done, all four were cast off from the bank and, with agonising slowness, the barges were caught by the rapidly quickening tide and moved downstream. Their double cable began to take the strain and with a groan and fountains of water issuing from the tightening fibres, the tide began to swing all four over to the Allied side, the vessels now suspended from the anchor point on that far bank. The more the barges entered the tide, the more rapid their swing across, until the man on each was able to throw ropes over to their bank, where stood waiting guerrillas. The barges were then pulled fully across so that all four could be securely moored against the Allied side. The whole had taken merely minutes and no sentry had been seen. Waters, now much relieved, as were his companions, quickly mounted his horse and galloped off to the Convent.

oOo

Orders were arriving rapidly, troopers of the 20th Light Dragoons riding hither and thither on horses that were tiring rapidly from being asked to ride up and down the Serra Hill. Stewart, with concerns of his own, had simply sent his harassed messenger on to find his three Colonels, the first being Lacey. The trooper handed down the note before saluting, whilst Lacey read it, his hand then falling down to his side, whilst he looked around for O'Hare, but this gave the trooper some concern.

"Can I have the note back, please Sir? It is the only copy and I have to get on."

Lacey, trying to collect his thoughts, handed it back.

"Of course!"

The trooper saluted before taking the note, then rode off to find either Colonel Burns and his Portuguese or Ruskin and his Detachments. O'Hare had sensed the sudden activity, not least seeing a long column of field guns begin to tackle the steep road up to the Convent and he immediately had deduced that his place should now be with his Colonel and so Lacey soon saw him running up, whilst buckling on his sword. His arrival, at the run and also armed, asked its own question, 'What's going on,' which Lacey answered.

"Stewart wants us on the road, in column. He received an order from Wellesley, which he sent around. He has added, 1st-105, 2nd-16th, 3rd-Det."

O'Hare was still adjusting his scabbard slings.

"So us first?"

"Looks like."

"To do what?"

O'Hare raised both his eyebrows and his hands.

"As yet, unknown."

O'Hare took a deep breath.

"So who first in the column? Lights or Grenadiers?"

It was Lacey's turn to breathe deeply.

"If it's an assault, then Grenadiers."

Unusual for him, O'Hare slightly raised his voice.

"Across that bridge! With a big hole in the middle!"

Lacey nodded.

"Assume that."

O'Hare's face twisted in bemusement.

"I'll get Carravoy. See him first"

At that moment Captain Lord Charles Carravoy was enjoying a good chicken lunch, with some sort of green vegetable which Binns, their servant, had called calabrese. The wine was good and Carravoy was just taking a swallow, when his table companion, Captain D'Villiers, looked out of the window, as he was seated so to do.

"I say! Seems a lot of hustle and bustle out there. Do you think there might be something afoot?"

Carravoy turned to look for himself, to see shakoes and muskets passing at a pace. The door then opened and in came their third Officer of Grenadiers, Lieutenant Simon Ameshurst. He looked directly at Carravoy.

"Sir. The whole Battalion has been ordered to form up on the road. Six across, Sir, with us in the van."

Carravoy swallowed the mouthful he had been chewing.

"Advance or retreat."

Amehurst's brows narrowed.

"Advance, Sir. Seems something has happened and we're going to try to cross."

At that, both his fellow Officers took one final gulp of wine. Then Carravoy spoke.

"What of our Company?"

"Sergeant Ridgway is forming them up now, Sir. At the front, as I say."

Both Carravoy and D'Villiers stood up, for Carravoy to then raise his voice.

"Binns!"

Their servant, Private Arthur Binns, put his head around the kitchen door.

"Sir?"

"Swords and pistols. Now!"

Meanwhile, Lacey, with his two Majors, Carr and O'Hare, were stood at the head of their column, but deep within the houses of Villa Nova and unable to see anything significant of Oporto across the river. Their men were formed up, in a column six across, so there was little they could do but wait. However, they did not have long to wait before Stewart rode up and immediately began talking, the absence of the whisky flask telling its own tale of urgency.

"Wellesley going to attempt a crossing! We've got four barges over to our side and he's loading in the Buffs and sending them over, led by Paget. There's some big building on the other side, a Seminary or somesuch, that's unguarded and a distance from the town. Seize that and we have a bridgehead!"

He paused for breath.

"He's put three full batteries into the Convent to see off any French attack from the town to this place. The Seminary!"

Now Stewart did pull out his flask and take a drink, to then pass it down. The spirit perhaps loosened his tongue, at least to give vent to his own thoughts.

"Damn risky. These barges are the most unwieldy damn hoys you could ever lay your squints on, so, it'll be no swift crossing, but Johnny's asleep! None to be seen! Therefore, Wellesley's taking the chance that's there. If he loses half a Battalion from failure, well, that we can swallow. If this takes the town, well, that speaks for itself."

Lacey handed back the flask.

"What of us, Sir?"

Stewart shook his head.

"Stand by. You may get your own turn to get across in those clumsy hulks."

He allowed that to sink in before turning his horse.

"Good luck to us all!"

With that he was gone, on to convey the same to Burns and Ruskin. Carr turned around to see the small portion of the Douro that was visible.

"Is there no way we can get ourselves over, Sir, to support the Buffs?"

Lacey scratched his forehead.

"Don't know. Let's go down and take a look!"

Leaving Carravoy and D'Villiers at the head of their Grenadiers, the three walked into the town, all three pulling out their telescopes. They came to the last building on the road before it reached the crossroads that marked the beginning of the bridge of boats, and they knocked on the door. It was unoccupied and so the three entered, climbed the stairs and Lacey and O'Hare went to the nearest window, looking directly over the surging waters of the Douro. Carr went to a side window that gave a view upstream. Stood at their window, Lacey and O'Hare shook their heads. There were several boats, perhaps twenty, drawn up on the shingle opposite, out of the tide, but the gap in the bridge of boats remained imposing, jagged and impossible. Along the quayside at their end of the bridge and taking their ease, mostly sat or lying down, was a whole Battalion of French soldiers, with perhaps two more Battalions, equally at ease, downstream to the left of the bridge. Then Carr spoke.

"Sir. You should come take a look at this."

Both did come over to his window and what they saw upstream was enough to tighten their throats and stomachs. The four barges, all indeed patently very unwieldy, were crossing the river, all not yet halfway, filled with recoated soldiers and propelled by nothing other than two huge sweeps each side, manned by the labouring men of the Buffs. For two minutes, five, then ten, the vessels inched forward, the tension rising within every observer along the Allied bank. Each minute one of the three at their window raised their telescope to examine the streets beyond the river that led down to the quayside and the road that ran upstream to the Seminary, but no blue uniforms were seen. More importantly, there was no movement from the French troops directly opposite. Finally, after what had seemed an age, the first barge grounded and about 25 men leapt into the water to splash up to the bank and disappear around the far wall of the Seminary. Within a minute the iron gate that allowed access from the road to the town was shut. The other three barges shed their compliment of men and they also followed the same route around the back wall. All three observers exhaled a sigh of relief, then the barges returned, only after some brown clad figures had run up the bank carrying rope, which they attached to any anchor point. The barges were now to cross, back and forth, as ferry boats attached to a cable secured to both banks. The four barges left the bank, moving much quicker as they were pulled back. They disappeared behind the bend and the scene resumed it's tranquillity, as before, with not a Redcoat to be seen.

The three watched another crossing, with no reaction from the French, then another, but, as the barges began their third return, at last there came some reaction from the French. An hour had lapsed since the first embarkation and the Seminary was now held by more than three Companies of the 3rd East Kent Foot. However, now a cloud of French Tirailleurs followed by three Battalions in column were on the quayside and doubling up to the Seminary. Then came a battery of field guns, which immediately began to unlimber on the quayside, for their crews to point them at the four wine barges. At that moment came the bark of a howitzer from above the three watchers and a shell burst over the leading French field-gun to kill or disable every man and horse belonging to it. Then the remaining guns in the Convent opened fire to cut swathes through the three French Battalions with grapeshot. The survivors reeled back including the gun crews, leaving their guns forlorn on the bank, pointing uselessly across the river. Several times the French attempted to creep forward in groups to fire at the barges, perhaps thinking this to be more important than to attack the Seminary, but each time the fearsome discharges of the eighteen guns on the heights sent them back into the cover of the houses, leaving the road covered with the gruesome remains of all three Battalions of a whole French Regiment.

From their upstairs window, the three Officers watched the French attacks fail, then musketry was heard, continuously, from the side of the Seminary furthest up from the river, the uppermost wall that did border the scattered houses. Plainly an attack was coming from that direction, down the slope from the town, using the houses as cover, but the barges were plying to and fro and, now that two hours had lapsed, close on three British Battalions were holding the Seminary. Lacey turned away.

"We'd better get back. We're going to be needed, in one way or another."

He turned to Carr.

"You stay here. I'll send you a runner or two. Any developments, send word back."

Carr heard them exit the room and descend the stairs, then minutes later appeared two Grenadier Corporals, who both came to 'order arms', their muskets grounded beside their right leg. Carr waved them forward.

"Come and see this, both of you. The crossing of the Douro! Something to tell your Grandchildren."

The pair chose their own window as another volley from the guns of the hill sent smoke and grapeshot across the intervening river to shatter yet another French attempt against the gates of the Seminary. As a professional soldier, Carr was appalled, condemning the French performance as totally incompetent. To leave as potent a foe as the British, who had beaten them everywhere on the Peninsula, totally unobserved when separated by merely a river, was the worst dereliction of military judgment he had ever heard of, akin to treason! A concluding thought entered his mind, "You may give us trouble, but you aren't going to beat us, Johnny. Not anywhere, if you can't do better than this!" He continued to watch upstream, when one of the Corporals, at a front window, called for his attention.

"Sir, I think something's happening."

Carr hurried to the window and saw the development. The three Battalions opposite had been ordered to their feet and assembled into column. They were, as he looked now, leaving the bridge and making their way upstream to join in the attack on the Seminary. Carr spoke to the Corporal next to him.

"Back to the Colonel. Tell him what you've seen."

The man saluted and left, leaving Carr at that window, continuing to look over the ebbing waters of the Douro, thinking of the thoughts of the soldiers opposite, many of whom were going to certain death. All marched on, leaving the bridge and quayside unoccupied and for minutes nothing changed, but then figures appeared from the streets and buildings behind the quayside. Furtively at first, in one's and two's, then a crowd and then a throng. Their purpose soon became clear, when, in their tens and twenties, they jumped down onto the shingle and launched all the boats, for their crews to then row, with frantic energy, across the river. Carr needed no messenger.

"With me!"

They both exited the building with a clatter and Carr, just before turning away to leave the river looked over to see the first boats already halfway across. At that point he heard the British batteries beat the attack of the three Battalions into yet more bloody ruin. He ran the final hundred yards to confront Lacey and O'Hare.

"Sir. The French have abandoned the quayside opposite. The people of the town have launched the boats there and are coming over to us. They will have crossed within minutes."

Lacey looked at Carr, then at O'Hare, then back to his Regiment.

"Carravoy! Forward!"

With the three in the lead, the column started forward. They ran over the bank and down to the shingle just as the first boat was touching. Lacey gave his orders.

"Padraigh. Over with the first boat and push up the main road with the Grenadiers. Carr, I'm sending the Light Company over next. Go over now and take command when they arrive. Penetrate up between the houses upstream of Carravoy. I'll be over with the rest, but only after I've told Burns and Ruskin."

There were now enough boats at the shoreline for a whole Company and in climbed the Grenadiers, their three

Officers and Carr and O'Hare. The Grenadiers doubled at the oars with the Portuguese and the nimble boats sped forth. Carr was sat in the stern of the lead boat, facing a straining Portuguese oarsman, who felt the need to give some encouragement.

"Viva Inglese. Luta bem. A morte da francesa!"

Carr nodded and smiled encouragingly, without having a clue what the man had said, bar the first two words. Then he looked at O'Hare.

"Any ideas what he said?"

O'Hare adopted his clearly nonplussed look.

"Long live us and death to the French is in there somewhere!"

He then looked at the Portuguese.

"Viva Portugal."

The oarsman grinned, but they were soon over, for O'Hare to immediately lead them across shingle and up the steps to the quayside, then to the entrance of the main street, which ran up the slight hill. He took one look up the road, wide for a town street, but narrow for a firing line. He made a rapid calculation, then found the nearest Grenadier Officer; Simon Ameshurst.

"Simon. Get your men across the road. Three deep. Hold there."

He next found D'Villiers and Carravoy, close together.

"Charles, get Royston's Section behind Ameshurst's. In support. Expect to file through when they've given a volley."

He ran back to Ameshurst's Section, now across the High Street, placed himself in front and drew his sword.

"Come on!"

Filling the road, they advanced forward. The people of Oporto, now arriving from all over, and then seeing so intimidating a sight as a whole line of Redcoat Grenadiers advancing towards them, fled into the sidestreets to avoid the inevitable conflict. For this O'Hare was wholly grateful, when, 100 yards up, he saw a disorganised band of French running down the street, nevertheless in some strength and led by what looked like a Senior Officer. O'Hare held up his sword.

"Three rank volley!"

Well drilled on the Campos, the Grenadiers halted. The front rank kneeling, the back two standing, but the third, 'locked on' between the heads of the middle rank.

"Make ready!"

All muskets were raised in the air, triggers besides their chins, thumbs pulling back the hammer.

"Present!"

All muskets came level as the French came on, with the slope in their favour.

"Fire!"

A full volley for the 105th in three ranks meant each rank counting three before delivering its fire in turn, 'What's the point of hitting the first man with three bullets? Give 'em time to fall over and expose the next', as Lacey had drilled into them. Therefore, three separate hideous crashes echoed between the buildings, beginning with those kneeling. Then all was obscured in smoke and what had happened to the French could not be seen. O'Hare filled his lungs.

"File through!"

What came next gave O'Hare no small amount of grim satisfaction. Every alternate file of Ameshursts Section ran forward to create a gap in their ranks for D'Villiers men to then advance through. It was perfectly done and soon D'Villiers' Section was under his command.

"Three rank volley!"

Again the men formed up and O'Hare peered through the clearing smoke. The ground was covered in French dead, but more were coming on behind. He ordered the volley and then repeated the file through. Now, with Ameshurst's Section leading, he advanced further up the

High Street, but the French were pulling back, in full retreat, at least in this part of the city. Carravoy was with him.

"Hold here. The rest of the Battalion are coming up to you."

With that he turned and jogged back down the High Street, to see the Colour Company advancing up, led by Lacey and Heaviside, both Colours flying, the whole parade being cheered and clapped by the re-emerging populace.

Meanwhile, Carr and the Light Company were advancing in their files through the upstream suburbs of the city, followed by three Line Companies of the 105th, sent after them by Lacey. The sounds of the fighting at the upper wall of the Seminary were growing louder with each street they entered as they eased rightwards. Carr knew that the city was carried and the French would now pull back, so he was determined not to risk many lives as he cautiously advanced on. Miles, Davey and Pike were just ahead, filing up, each running into a doorway or alleyway to cover the advance further of the next. Miles, in the lead, peering intently ahead, saw a blue uniform, just over 100 yards ahead, shouting into an opening. He was waving a sword, which was enough for Miles. He pulled back the hammer of his Baker rifle, braced the barrel against his doorway and fired. When the smoke cleared the Frenchman was on the ground to roll over once, move an arm, then lay still. Davey came up as Miles reloaded.

"Officer bastard! That'll be a few silver buttons for later!"

Davey moved past, saying nothing, followed by Pike and then Major Carr. Nothing was said and by that time, Miles had reloaded and was moving up to file past Davey, but Carr now took the lead. The conflict at the Seminary was as fierce as ever and, moving up and to the right, they would soon meet it. He quickly reasoned that they must get above the French and come in on their flank and rear. He had four Companies with him, almost half the

Battalion and he soon decided what to do. He looked for Drake and motioned him over.

"Nat. Stay here. I'm taking the Lights up to the top of the town. Tell the following Captains to come up towards me a bit further, but not to join. They are to choose a street and advance right. The four of our Companies should come in on the French flank and relieve those lads holding the Seminary."

Drake looked puzzled and so Carr came to his aid.

"That bloody great religious building, upstream, on the edge of town. The first we took."

Then humour came forth, unusual for Carr.

"If you get in, say a prayer for me!"

But Drake was more sombre.

"And for Jane and Cecily!"

Carr's mood sobered.

"Yes. Now I'd better get on."

With that he ran up the street, calling for Lieutenants Stuart Maltby and Richard Shakeshaft. With these two beside him, he led the whole Light Company upwards, in column, until the city thinned into scattered smallholdings. They looked over to see the smoke from the fighting at the Seminary, this rising thick and white, as was the sound of the fighting.

"Right. Stuart, take yours straight ahead, soon you'll meet the French. You've got three Companies of ours on your right. Go."

He turned to Shakeshaft.

"Dick, we're going further up, then over."

As Maltby's Section ran forward, Carr led Shakeshaft's 100 yards further up the slope, then swung right. Carr immediately changed formation, yelling both left and right.

"Open order! Ten yards."

The files of three spread out to a ten-yard gap as they advanced. There was a hedge of what looked like tall reeds and the noise of some activity beyond it and also down towards the town, this told by shouts and orders in French. Carr doubled forward, his men copying. Immediately beyond the hedge there was a narrow lane and, galloping up it, was a whole French battery, trying to make their escape.

"Open fire!"

At 50 yards distance his men opened fire to bring the lead gun to a tangled and bloody halt, dead and dying men falling down amongst dead and dying horses. The lane was now totally blocked and so the remaining gunners, with the potent arrival of Redcoats above them, abandoned their pieces and ran off over the fields, joined by their Officer on a very rapid horse. Carr's men had captured a whole French battery, but Carr ran screaming along the top of the lane; a retreating battery would be followed by Battalions of men, far outnumbering one Section.

"Take cover. Reload. We hold here!"

His men took cover and reloaded, whilst, incongruously, the horse-teams below waited patiently in their harness. Carr sent down two men to despatch two wounded horses and, as they climbed back up the bank, what must be Maltby's Section and the supporting Companies joined the fight on their right. Within two minutes retreating French from the Seminary began to arrive, running through the fields on the other side of the road. They were in their hundreds and Carr feared that they may come his way or even try to rescue the battery.

"Open fire!"

His men loosed a full volley, to bring down several retreating French, but the mass veered away; they had no idea if the far side of the road was held in force or not. The horse-teams below, trained to remain calm during the sound of conflict, ignored the reports occurring merely feet above their heads. The firing intensified to his right, it would seem Maltby had joined, which was all to the good. Carr allowed his men to continue firing, the more brought down now, he reasoned, the fewer they would have to face later, until one word came from Shakeshaft's Sergeant, George Fearnley.

"Sir?"

Fearnley could see that what they were doing and, to his mind, continuing to shoot at fleeing men was little short of murder. Carr heard the tone of his word, both accusing and questioning, and he reluctantly agreed.

"Cease fire."

The last of the fleeing French were crossing before them and they continued unmolested, passing between or jumping over the fallen bodies of their comrades, which littered their path. Some 200 yards behind came the pursuing British, led by an odd figure on a horse, somewhat portly and perhaps old before his time, wearing a worn out British Uniform, but he was plainly a Senior Officer, identified by his sword and sash. He rode over to Carr, who was now standing on the bank above the road, and Carr began to identify the features of this Officer as he came nearer, a sad, down turned mouth, set below far seeing, but equally gloomy eyes, and a nose perhaps a little too long. Carr came to the attention, bringing his sword up to his own nose. The Officer was now directly opposite above the road and looking down into it.

"What's all this, Major?"

Carr lowered his sword.

"A French battery, Sir. All six, that we prevented from escaping."

The cheerless mouth then broke into a delighted smile.

"Six guns! Ha!"

The delight continued.

"A whole battery! Wellesley will be cock-a-hoop!"

More delight.

"Six!"

He looked at Carr.

"Who are you?"

"Major Carr, Sir. 105th Foot. Prince of Wales Own Wessex."

The face became cheerful.

"Ah! The "Rag and Bone Boys!""

Carr was more than a little incensed.

"Some call us that!"

A pause.

"Sir."

There came a slight, almost sympathetic smile.

"I think you'll find most people say that not too unkindly. Certainly not Wellesley."

However, the Officer was immediately back to the business in hand.

"Now, Carr. If you find a Senior Officer, tell them that I am pursuing, with the 3rd, 66th and 48th. A mile or so, then I will halt where I can counter any French return. Got that?"

"Sir. Who should I say sent the message?"

"General Hill! That's me. Paget's probably lost his arm. To a musket ball."

"Sorry to hear that, Sir."

"Can't be helped. That's the game we're in."

He gathered the reins of his horse.

"I'm trusting you, Major. See that Wellesley is informed."

"I will Sir. You may count on it."

"Be certain of it, but I'm away. Good luck Major."

Carr brought his sword up in salute as Hill rode off, leading the men that had gathered around him, and talking to them as though about to lead a group of infants out of a nursery.

"Now, men. See to your effects and such. We're off on a long chase, to who knows where, on Johnny's coat-tails."

Every face around him broke into a smile as he led his men off to join the pursuit already gone past. Hill's group were the last of his Brigade, for no more Redcoats

British and Portuguese, aided by French prisoners, were doing their best to give what help they could, but most often it was only water to wet the lips of a dying man. Carr could not help but think that 'A few French sentries in the proper place would have saved them all this.' However, they progressed on to reach the bridge, Carr very mindful of the need to pass on Hill's message, but then the problem was solved. Wellesley was about to disembark from one of the boats still ferrying Redcoats over the Douro. Carr hurried over and came to the attention at a respectful distance, but still within hearing, and so, as Wellesley passed, he spoke.

"Sir, if I may, Sir. I have a message from General Hill."

Wellesley diverted his course and came over. Carr saluted with his sword, which his Commanding General acknowledged, but Carr wasted no time.

"General Hill is pursuing the French, Sir, with the 3rd, 66th, and 48th. For a mile, he said, then he will halt at a position where he can resist any French return."

Wellesley studied him for a second.

"You saw the French, Major?"

"Yes Sir. They passed across my front before General Hill came up."

"And what would your assessment be of the condition the French were in?"

Carr paused, in order to choose his words carefully.

"In full retreat, Sir. Not a rabble, but certainly disorganised."

Then Carr took a deep breath and smiled.

"We captured a full battery, Sir. Six guns!"

Wellesley shared in the mirth, but not quite laughing.

"All six!"

He turned to an accompanying Brigadier in full Scots uniform.

"You hear that Campbell? All six!"

Campbell nodded, a smile illuminating the gloom beneath the peak of his enormous bonnet. Then Carr continued.

"I'm afraid I have some bad news, Sir, in case you are as yet unaware."

Wellesley frowned.

"I'm afraid General Paget is wounded, Sir. He may have lost an arm."

Wellesley nodded, his face resigned.

"Thank you, Major. I'm grateful for your information."

Carr stepped back and saluted, then Wellesley looked at him more carefully.

"Am I correct in thinking that it was you that I saw atop a bank of shingle when we landed at Mondego last summer. Commanding a Company of Light Infantry as I recall."

Carr smiled.

"Yes Sir. That was me. Kind of you to remember, Sir."

Wellesley smiled and walked on, but saying one more thing over his shoulder.

"The 105th! The Prince's Wessex Own."

"Sir."

At that point, with Wellesley gone, Saunders came running up.

"Sir, I've found the Colonel, Sir. He's in the High Street, about half way up. This way Sir."

Carr waved his hand, signalling 'lead on' and soon they were in the High Street, but they had to push their way through a crowd of Portuguese, all yelling abuse at a group of French prisoners. There was no need to guard the prisoners; they cowered against a wall, far back behind the cordon of Redcoats holding back the vengeful population. Carr saw Lacey up ahead and hurried on, leaving Shakeshaft with his Section. Then the stones began to arrive, in a shower, landing on both French prisoners and wounded and so he immediately slowed his walk up to Lacey.

"Richard! Use you men and any others, to push those back. Right back!"

Hearing only the obedience of his orders, this shouts from the Redcoats, Carr had arrived within earshot of Lacey.

"Sir. I've left half the Lights and the three Companies above the Seminary."

"Casualties?"

"Two wounded. Slightly. Here, Sir?"

"Same."

Both smiled, both relieved.

"Any orders, Sir?"

"No, and I doubt there will be. At least, not for some time, we have a whole army to get across the Douro, so we'll get the men settled here. I'll find Burns and Ruskin and we'll get ourselves into a camp beside the river, downstream. Make it easy for our Followers to find us and there we're assembled as a Brigade, which Stewart will appreciate. Go back up and bring down the Companies you left. We're at least a day here, probably two."

oOo

The sounds of the conflict downstream came on the wind, rising and falling, either with the power of the gusts or with the ebb and flow of the fighting. The crossing using the ferry had been slow, but the only danger had come from the spatchcock nature of the repairs to its hull affected by the Portuguese, who had stood to cheer every Allied group of soldiers either marching aboard or marching off. With all his men over, Perry had felt it prudent to simply hold the section of bank now gained, but Withers had reminded him of the requirement to make contact and then make their presence felt. Now, with a visibly anxious Perry at their head, the column was advancing seawards along the North riverbank of the Douro, using the main road which they had found two miles after leaving the ferry. Immediately behind Perry and his Staff, came the two Squadrons of 14th Light Dragoons, followed by two field-guns and two Battalions of Kings German Legion infantry. Beside Perry, but just behind him, came Colonel Withers, Major Johnson, Tavender and Templemere. Portuguese civilians came out of their houses to clap and cheer, but this did nothing to ease Perry's mind, especially when the sounds of fighting died away, finally to nothing. Perry's anxieties heightened.

"Halt!"

The column halted behind him, which caused Withers to ride up, followed by Major Johnson, but it was Withers who spoke.

"Sir! We should push on and make contact."

Perry turned to look at him, then he resumed his stare towards Oporto.

"What if Wellesley's scheme has been an utter failure? What if we are the only Allied force on this bank? What if we were seen at the ferry and there is an overwhelming part of Soult's army coming for us, now?"

"Agreed Sir. That is possible, but our orders are clear."

Silence, and so Withers continued with an idea that may appeal to the doubly anxious Perry.

"Sir, if I may take our two Captains here, I'll scout forward. Then you can proceed on, if circumstances allow."

He knew that he needed to say something encouraging, even mollifying.

"Cautiously. I can give early warning if we are about to be attacked in force, then we can make a rapid withdrawal. Sir."

Perry could not argue with the good sense in Withers suggestion, so whilst his anxiety waned, that within Tavender and Templemere waxed, but they had no choice as Withers turned to them.

"You two. With me."

They walked their horses forward, but then Withers broke into a canter along the good road, a pace seemingly altogether too incautious for the pair. Withers then turned right to gain the top of a small hill and there he stopped. Across the valley, less than a mile beyond, could be seen a long blue ribbon, evidently on a road of its own. Withers drew his own telescope and studied the column, but it was too far to discern the detail he needed. However, he noticed that Tavender was using his and he hoped that he could see more.

"What can you see?"

Tavender waited a second.

"One long column, Sir."

"Tell me. Are they in marching in Battalions? Blocks of infantry?"

"No Sir, it's one long column."

"Are their guns mixed up in the column?"

Tavender paused and studied.

"Yes Sir. I'd say so."

Withers leaned over to him, holding out his hand.

"If I may?"

Tavender handed over the instrument and Withers focused for his own eyesight. Tavender was right, the infantry were in one long stream, with guns here and there, mixed in. He handed back the instrument.

"You're right! And that's a retreat, after a defeat. They're pulling back and they're all over the place. In no shape to do much to anyone."

With no more words, he turned his horse and galloped back to the road, where the column had just come up to the point where they had left the road to surmount the hill. Breathless, they came up to Perry, where Withers immediately reported.

"Sir. The French are in full retreat, with no organisation at all."

Perry's brow became furrowed, but he said nothing, therefore Withers continued.

"If we get onto that ridge, Sir, we can cross the valley in column, then get into a firing line alongside their road, deploy our guns and cut off their retreat, Sir. We could capture thousands. There must be a pursuit behind them of some kind. They'll soon reinforce us."

Perry eased himself in his saddle. He had collected his thoughts.

"You recommend that we attack a whole army!"

It was not a question, it was a dismissal. Withers fell back onto his, safer, alternative.

"Sir. We should at least show ourselves to hurry them along and perhaps change their mind about attempting a rearguard. At least to deploy on that ridge up there, Sir. It's a strong position for our infantry."

He pointed to the hilltop that they had just left. Perry looked at him, but he had to agree.

"Agreed. But we remain in column. From the left, cavalry, guns, then our two KGL."

He turned to Johnson.

"See to it, Major."

As Johnson galloped off, Perry, followed immediately by the Light Dragoons, swung off the road and ascended the hill, the cavalrymen to soon become the leftward point of Perry's deployment. There they waited for a good fifteen minutes, watching the French retreat through their telescopes, when Johnson spoke up.

"Sir. Someone's coming, Sir, up from the road."

All turned to see one rider in the lead, with a cavalry escort. The rider made straight for Perry's group, but, by the time he arrived and had looked over the valley, he was visibly angry. He turned, face red and brow furrowed.

"Are you General Perry?"

Perry nodded.

"I am! And you are?"

"Stewart! Major General. And why are you not attacking that column?"

Perry realised that he was outranked.

"Because, Sir, I am vastly outnumbered. I had reason to believe that those over there are the whole of Soult's force."

The anger grew in Stewart's face, but he wasted no time on argument, merely giving Perry a thunderous look, somewhere between contempt and astonishment.

"I'm taking one of your Squadrons."

He looked at Tavender and Templemere as he rode forward, having noticed their distinctive Light Dragoon uniforms.

"You're Cavalry aren't you?"

The two nodded.

"Sir."

"Then with me."

It was Templemere who objected.

"But we're 16th! Sir."

The reply was dismissive and plainly brooked no argument.

"With me."

They joined on the rear of Stewart's escort and followed him as he rode up to the Commander of the first Squadron of the 14th that he came to.

"Name!"

"Captain Hervey, Sir."

"How many men?"

"Just over 100, Sir, 110 to be exact."

"We're going to attack."

Attack who was patently obvious, then Stewart rose in his stirrups and addressed the Troopers forming the line.

"Men of the 14th! Time to make our presence felt. There's a French column over there who think they can wander off in their own time. Well, I've a mind to change their minds!"

He looked across the valley, then turned back to Hervey.

"Column of threes!"

As Hervey called back the order, Stewart drew his sabre, which was followed by all of the Squadron, without an order. Stewart spoke one word, heard by few, but the sweep of his sabre forward carried all the instruction needed.

"Forward!"

Forming a column three broad as they advanced, they crossed the valley. For Templemere this was a time of mounting disquiet, growing into outright fear. As the distance lessened, so the details grew, of individual men, guns, and Officers, these evidently taking charge to meet the threat coming their way. Stewart was leading them towards a gap in the column, which would give them access onto the road, but then any further prediction failed. Would he cross the road to attack those beyond in the fields, or strike directly along the road? For the Troopers within the column, all was dust and thundering hooves, no orders being given, simply to follow the man in front. For Templemere, effectively in Stewart's retinue at the front, all was revealed only too clearly, especially the consequences of what Stewart's decision was; he was on the road and leading them up it, to hit the rear of the group of French now marching along it. As they galloped up the road, Templemere saw that the wall on his left was lined with French, two and three deep, with their muskets levelled over it, but luck was with him. The French Officers preferred to wait until the main body of Dragoons, three deep and in close ranks, came up to them, whilst he and Tavender were merely in ones and two. However, as he passed, the Officer levelled a pistol at him and fired, but he was down over his horse's neck and the ball went wide, passing unheard. The crash of the French volley came immediately, followed by the thinner crack of Dragoon pistols making a reply, but both Templemere and Tavender had other worries. The rearguard on the road were fully prepared for cavalry, all standing with bayonets fixed. From behind the pair came the same unearthly howl that they had heard at Grijon, but the French remained ready to receive the attack. Templemere's mount baulked at the obstacle and slithered to a halt, but, by some miracle for both, the hedge of bayonets dissolved and then Templemere was caught in a torrent of horses that plunged him forward into the mass of fleeing Frenchmen.

All foes were scattering off the road, but Templemere was struggling to retrieve his sword, the cord of which had somehow worked up to the crook of his elbow. For him all was total confusion, but suddenly there was Tavender at his side.

"Come on Fred, this way!"

Forgetting his sword for the moment, Templemere followed Tavender over a low part of the wall, then into the fields beyond. There the scene was mostly of French lying on the ground, some stood motionless with their hands in the air, and of Troopers attempting to round up still more fleeing French or trying to subdue groups who were fighting back and edging their way to safety. Again, suddenly, it was Stewart at his side.

"You! Captain! Get some men and hit that group there."

He pointed with his sword at a group of determined veterans who had formed a rallying square of about 30 men and were making progress towards an escape, fighting off with their bayonets any Dragoon who came too near. Templemere recovered his sword, but he was at a loss. There were only individual Dragoons around, all very busy and eager to attack any infantryman who was close at hand, rather than to stop, reform with others and then mount a disciplined attack. He soon decided that the order was impossible to carry out and instead he rode at a Frenchman who was running to join the group. He came up and noticed first, ridiculously, the bobbing blanket roll on the man's back as he ran, but the pair had been noticed by the rallying group and so, at the perfect moment, some in the group called out, "Tomber! Maintenant!" The man fell and rolled to the right, out of reach of Templemere's curving sabre and then the sight of several muskets levelled at him caused him to spur his horse away, but the fight all around was already ebbing away. The Dragoons, now barely 100, could do little more than had already been done. The French rearguard had been scattered, but the main body had escaped unmolested. Templemere then found Tavender, him having a bayonet wound in his leg attended to. A Trooper of the 14th had rolled up the trouser leg and was now applying a bandage. That done, and with no thanks given, Tavender kicked his horse into a trot to join Templemere, who was riding to join Stewart. They arrived at the same time as one of his Staff, who had a pertinent question.

"Sir. Men are arriving up from Oporto. Ours, Sir. To which should we hand over our prisoners? Those coming or General Perry, back there?"

Stewart looked in both directions, at Perry's command, remaining back on their ridge and then at the arriving footsoldiers, led by an Officer, who approached Stewart immediately, but it was Stewart who spoke first.

"Who are you?"

The Officer saluted.

"Badgworth, Sir, Captain, 3rd Foot Guards."

"Who's your Brigadier?"

"General H. Campell, Sir."

"Sherbrook's Division!"

"Sir."

"Very good! Badgworth, I'm passing these prisoners over to you, and I also expect you to look after my dead and wounded, 35 of both. My compliments to General Campbell. Tell him that, I, General Stewart, am ordering General Perry over there……"

A dismissive wave of his arm.

"……… to follow the French and keep them under observation."

Badgworth saluted and Stewart and his staff watched as the French were transferred from the malignant gaze of the Light Dragoons to the more understanding attentions of the Guards, which mostly began with the trade of tobacco for brandy. Stewart then bade his bugler sound recall and his Dragoons fell in behind him as they all returned to Perry, him and his Command remaining at a standstill across the valley. Once within speaking distance, Stewart was the soul of brevity.

"These are your orders. I'm sending your Brigade after the French. Keep out of trouble but keep them under observation. I'll inform Wellesley."

He barely waited for any form of reply, but none came and so he terminated the meeting himself, most perfunctorily.

"We took two hundred prisoners and killed or wounded about 30 more. So! Good day to you Sir. And be damned!"

oOo

All through the evening and into the night, the army's baggage train was ferried over, on and on, until the dawn of the next day, when by then the bridge of boats was repaired by a full mixture of craft of all sizes and the planking was restored, albeit with a variety of humps and gradients. Only now, with the whole army fully across could now come over those with the lowest priority, the Followers. Once on the North bank they immediately set up full camp, firstly because it was well into morning and no-one had eaten whilst they waited to cross, and secondly because an unwritten communication had filtered out of Headquarters that they would not be moving that day, but very probably the next. Supplies came over the bridge and cooking began, but much did not go into English mouths. The French, following their practice of living off the land, had picked Oporto clean of almost all food and provender, therefore the whole population was close to starving. It was not long before children especially, arrived at the British campfires and were given their first good meal in weeks. Then began a day of entertainment and jollity, mostly provided by the ecstatic population of the town, but not to the full amusement of the Redcoats, for they preferred to prepare for the pursuit, which they knew was to come and also to get some sleep. There was not a soldier in Wellesley's army who did not appreciate the enormity of crossing the Douro and retaking Oporto with so low a 'butcher's bill'. Thus was spent a tranquil day of contented respite.

Not so for Perry and his men. He could only move at the pace of his infantry, slogging on in the footsteps of the French, him only knowing that they were on the correct road because of the amount of discarded booty strewn around, thrown to lighten French packs, and also the occasional dead Frenchman. Some had plainly succumbed to their wounds, but some had been obviously murdered, with their heads smashed in or their throats cut. Perry was in almost constant conversation with Colonel Withers riding beside him, whom, it was now known, was a veteran of Wellesley's campaign of the summer of the previous year, therefore, not surprisingly, Perry relied heavily on his experience. Withers was reassuring, mostly making full use of the words, "The French will not stand. Wellesley will be relying on us to keep in touch and relay information back." Tavender and Templemere, riding behind with Major Johnson, particularly latched onto the final phrase, hoping for just such a mission, but so far none came. It was Noon and the force was eating on the move, as advised by Withers, eating biscuits, fruit and any other kind of food which was portable and did not require cooking. Both were chewing on biscuits, when from ahead, but distant, there came a muffled explosion. Templemere looked at his companion.

"What was that?"

Tavender shook his head.

"Johnny blowing something up. Probably a bridge; which will severely curtail our close pursuit. Perhaps even end it!"

The last delivered with a smile, but further progress, which included several bridges, continued at the same pace. Then they came to the first buildings and houses, which soon grew in density along the roadside, the more they rode on.

"Penafiel."

Major Johnson spoke, in answer to no-one's question, but he thought he should impart it all the same, for it was he, after all, who was custodian of the map. However, their entry into the town revealed a most extraordinary sight; on the hillside people were dousing large fires and pulling salvage from the black and sodden piles, but, when they entered the town proper, most of the population were all in the streets that surrounded the main square, not just on the ground but on the roofs and in the gardens around. As they rode closer, the purpose could be seen, for the people of the town were finding and picking up coins which were scattered all around. The black burn mark in the centre of the square explained the explosion and the eager, even frantic, people explained the reason for the explosion; this spoken by Johnson.

"Well damn me if he hasn't blown up his army's treasure. Too heavy to lug along. They're in a mess. Desperate I'd say!"

Now Withers had turned his horse from Perry and was back with them. He knew, even if Perry did not, that the prospect of treasure could destroy the whole column, men falling out to secure as much as five years pay, which required but a small amount of effort in this case. However, he did not know whom he trusted most to act as guards to keep their men on the road; the Light Dragoons or the King's German Legion. He decided that being mounted gave most chance of being effective, and so he gave orders to Johnson, Tavender and Templemere.

"You three. Pull out four men each and ride the length of the column. Keep all in their place."

Simply by pointing, the three chose their men and rode back. In the event, they were superfluous. The superb discipline of the King's German Legion was immediately evident as the two Battalions marched on, in step and in good order. However, the temptation was too much for two of Templemere's escort. The Dragoons arrived at the rear of the second KGL Battalion and found themselves alone, amongst the now significantly richer Portuguese. The two reined in, having seen large purses in the hands of two middle-aged civilians, and both quickly dismounted. One Dragoon ran up to citizen and punched the astonished townsman, then he took his purse, whilst the other needed to do no more than draw his sword and raise it for the bag of coins to be handed over. Then both re-mounted and rode off, to the shouted curses of the men and also those who had witnessed. Templemere caught up with the pair, to receive challenging looks. Their options were clear in their minds, to kill him and then speak of his sad death at the hands of stragglers, or even to desert, but they were in a mood to bargain, the nearest opening negotiations.

"What'll it take, Sir, for you to forget about what you've just seen?"

Their heavy Dragoon pistols, very visible on each saddle, conveyed a threat that had no need to be spoken, their challenging looks conveyed it well enough. Besides, there was profit here for everyone.

"Eight from each of you, for me, and we'll say no more!"

The coins were handed over from each and the three parted company, Templemere now the richer by sixteen Gold Napoleons.

oOo

All through that day, the guerrilla band of Juan Delica tracked the French, always keeping the last of their retreating column in sight. Thus was the day occupied in despatching Frenchmen who could march no longer and lay helpless at the roadside, but Delica would countenance neither torture nor bestiality. Death was to be dealt out swiftly. Now he was lying in some trees above the French column, their army now on the desperate roads over the Serra de Santa Catalina. He was examining the sight below him, where the last of the French were crossing a bridge over a ravine. With so many of them now over it and so few to come, perhaps they could capture the bridge and cut off those yet to cross? He looked at the French. All still carried their muskets and accoutrements, meaning that his men would have to fight back against capable veterans, who would show no mercy. So far he had not lost a man. He slid back into the trees, deciding to keep it that way, for they had done well, by his measure, because they had already despatched over 30 of their enemy who had fallen out from the retreating column. Therefore, that night, they kept watch on the French campfires, both sleeping and keeping vigil by turns. His men were in good spirits, they were doing harm to the French, no-matter how small in the grand design of things, but they were doing much to put fear into their enemy, so that for these, all around and anywhere beyond the road was decidedly hostile and deadly. There was not one man who did not harbour the deepest hatred of the French within himself and tomorrow would bring the same, when the peaks of the Serra would defeat the energy of even more of these detested and vicious invaders. Thus, sunrise found the Delica band riding the goat tracks high above the French column, within sight, but out of musket range. They did not leave their vantage point, but remained watching, knowing that their very presence created fear and that those of their band following on the road would end the life of any Frenchman who fell behind.

The same sunrise saw the 105th on the road leading out of Oporto and ready to march. Lacey, O'Hare and Carr were at their head, but standing, not mounted, as was their

Brigadier Stewart. All stood together and all were drinking, but not of the contents of Stewart's flask, at least not directly, for some of its contents had been poured into the coffee mug of each and each relished the taste of the warming liquid. Little was said, once Stewart had said his piece.

"Wellesley wants the French pushed to the borders. He knows we'll not catch them, but perhaps all these guerrillas, or their militia 'Ordenanza', who have sprung up all around, can delay them awhile. Then we'll see."

The companionable silence that came next was terminated by an order to march, delivered by an Aide-de-Camp. The last of the coffee was thrown into the gutter and the pursuit began, but the 105th were in good heart. Knapsacks were full of supplies and French packs and French boots were about the persons of those who wanted them, including Tom Miles, whose only issued clothing was his British tunic and shako and his British crossbelts supporting his knapsack, bayonet, cartridge box and water flask. All was well in the mind of Miles, especially when they were able to spend that night as occupiers of a decent village, which they had reached, Villa Nova de Famelioccao, so Byford told them, but no-one took much notice.

For Perry and his command, their lot was another night on the hillside, beneath hedges and walls, although Perry and his Staff were able to commandeer an abandoned barn, which smelled appallingly of mouldy straw and generations of sheep droppings. However, it was paradise compared to what was endured by their men outside, who, when not soaked by frequent rainstorms, were required to cope with a chilling and eerie fog. All woke cold and in low spirits and what little wood there was would not kindle and so, on Withers advice, they gave up and mounted their horses or formed their columns, everyone cold and hungry. The knowledge that on that day they would rejoin the main army, almost certainly at Braga, did little to boost morale,

110

nor did a view, across a rain swept valley, of the retreating French, a large body, so Tavender, through his superior telescope, told them. Were they in a position to know it, they had seen the rearmost columns of the main French army.

Such a view put some urgency into the onward progress of General Perry, suddenly feeling himself to be a vital cog in the Allied military machine.

"Wellesley must be informed. I will convey the same myself."

To that end he quit the company of his two Battalions of infantry, leaving Withers as their Commander and, with an escort of 20 from the 14th Light Dragoons and Major Johnson he galloped into Braga as the light was fading and the shadows darkened even more from those remaining the dismal day. Here, as expected, the main army were resting and Wellesley had presumably set up his Headquarters so he roamed the town for some time in his attempt to find the necessary building, until it was identified by Major Johnson.

"Sir. That building there looks to be the centre of activity. At least they should know, Sir."

Without a word, Perry spurred his horse into a canter and dismounted, flinging the reins at a nearby sentry. He entered and took himself straight up to a Major, sat behind a desk, attended by several 'runners', these being private soldiers.

"Major! I have some important information, which I must convey to General Wellesley immediately."

In languid fashion, the Major looked up.

"May I have your name, Sir?"

"Perry. General Perry."

"And your information, Sir, briefly, if you please. It may help you to gain an early appointment."

Perry's temper was rising, but the Major was talking sense.

"The whereabouts of the French."

The Major nodded, and scribbled a note, which he handed to one of his waiting soldiers, who hurried off. Perry left the table, his left hand flexing on the hilt of his sword, showing his impatience. The building was run-down shabby, but at least there was a good fire in the grate, of large, spitting logs. He stalked over to stand before the marble mantelpiece, pock marked and chipped from misuse, some of the damage plainly of recent origin. Above was a large gloomy picture of some local worthy, a civilian, and Perry read the first word of the title beneath; "Don Emilio….." but then the tangle of 'y's 'g's and 'h's defeated him. 'No-matter', he thought for he was being approached by the messenger soldier.

"Sir. If you'd care to follow me."

The soldier led him up a bare staircase of dirty pine timber on which both their boots clumped and scraped. Then along the landing to the final door, which the soldier opened for Perry to enter. There, behind a plain table sat General Wellesley, writing despatches. He paid Perry the courtesy of immediately ceasing to write, on hearing his entrance and he lifted his head, to regard Perry with a pair of wide, challenging, eyes that seemed to immediately convey disbelief, even shock. Fixed by those eyes, Perry walked forward and stood still. Wellesley leaned back, with the quill pen still between his fingers.

"General Perry. I'm told that you have something useful for me. You've seen the French, or at least the back of them."

Perry straightened, self-importance rising all the while.

"Yes Sir. On my way here, back to rejoin you."

Wellesley stood, the ghost of a smile passing across a mouth somewhat small, compared to the size of the nose above.

"I'm glad to hear it. Could you show me?"

Wellesley walked over to a large map pinned to the wall and then stood aside to give Perry his opportunity. He walked forward, suddenly very unsure of himself. The map showed the few existing roads and a few villages and towns, the rest were rivers and valleys. Perry found Penafiel and Braga, then he vaguely worked the route of his sweep around from the former to the latter, but which valley the French were marching up was a mystery. Johnson, his map reader, had made an educated guess at the time of the sighting, but even that memory was now less than clear, especially when faced with a map of such detail. All that Perry could do was pass his hand over a portion of the map.

"In this area, Sir. Heading North."

Then a thought.

"Or perhaps North-East."

Wellesley nodded again.

"And some cavalry of your command are following them, yes? Those you saw?"

There was sarcasm contained in the voice. Perry cleared his throat.

"No Sir. I brought my men in."

The eyebrows above the eyes were raised.

"All!"

"Yes Sir. My men have been out for three days. Our rations are exhausted and they are very tired!"

The challenge came.

"And the French are not?"

Wellesley allowed the words to sink in.

"I would have thought, General, that you could have gathered together enough rations from amongst your force to provision half a squadron, especially as you knew you were about to join the main road to here, where you could re-supply?"

Perry trawled his mind for a reply and found one, albeit plainly weak.

"I was not certain that I would find you. Sir."

The eyes bored into him, then Wellesley raised his own hand to the map.

"I suspect, General, that the French you saw were here."

He placed a finger on a specific point.

"Labouring up this valley, the valley of the Cavado, to Guimaraens just further up, where Loison will almost certainly join them, having been pushed back by Beresford. Both will then probably go on to Salamonde and try to cross the river. My own Dragoons are following and a message came back this Noon. To that effect."

Perry had recovered.

"I'm pleased that I can confirm that. Sir."

Wellesley was returning to his desk, where he sat down and again picked up the quill pen. Perry walked over to regain his original position, but now Wellesley was looking at him, plainly there was more to be said and the silence was held until Wellesley dropped the quill pen.

"Post Oporto, General, I am informed by Major General Stewart that your conduct against the retreating French must be called into question."

Wellesley leaned forward, his hands on the edge of the desk as though he were about to stand and deliver a ferocious tirade. Perry's confidence fell a significant measure in expectation, but Wellesley remained seated and continued.

"You had an opportunity, General, of doing the French a great deal of harm, in fact, of possibly cutting off half his army, if you had placed your men across their path."

A pause, for Wellesley to allow emphasis to build within the rebuke and for Perry to think up an excuse, but Wellesley had his next phrase thoroughly ready and his voice up a decibel.

"A risk, I would agree, but a risk worth taking if it could take out half the French army of Portugal! Which we will have to face at some time in the future. Your Germans didn't fire a shot! And you had two strong Battalions! And two squadrons of cavalry!"

This delivered by a voice barely raised, but thick with disapproval. Perry replied the only way he could.

"I was concerned that your attack across the river, Sir, had failed and mine was the only force on the North bank. Sir."

He took a deep breath.

"Also, I felt myself very outnumbered. Sir."

Wellesley gave no reaction, but his words were measured.

"A modicum of thought, General, would have led you to the conclusion that my attack had succeeded, for why else would the French be in full retreat? As to outnumbered, with my men plainly across the river, you could have counted on reinforcements! Sooner or later. We must have been pursuing, or did that not occur to you?"

The words echoed around Perry's head, but there was nothing more to be said, other than the final words of Wellesley, conveying all the condemnation required.

"You are lucky that there is not enough time for a Court Martial."

Again the dreadful silence, but there had been no words conveying Wellesley's dismal opinion, merely a systematic deconstruction of all Perry's excuses, an expose' of opportunity wasted, and the consequences thereof. Wellesley lowered his head to his despatches.

"Now, good night."

Perry gave the salute he thought was required. It was not acknowledged and so he walked out of the room and the building and into the night.

For Juan Delica and his men, that night was as abominable as the previous, with soaking rain carried painfully on a howling wind, as they remained mobile and watchful, following a goat track along a mountainside. However, they remained in good spirits. Now well informed by Waters, who saw Delica as a most useful ally, Delica had told his men that another French army, which had been operating in the South-East and had been out-manoeuvred by an Allied force sent against them, was also retreating and liable to concentrate at Guimaraens. This was commanded, or so was believed, by the hated Loison, 'The One Armed Assassin', the butcher of Evora, a massacre during the first French invasion of Portugal during the previous Spring, yet now the French were being forced out of their country and Delica impressed upon his men that they must play their part.

Their guide told them that Guimaraens was just over the next ridge, further on in the inky black of the pre-dawn, so Delica allowed his men some sleep and awaited the light, but, as both the rain and wind lessened he could hear the clear sounds of a marching army; most telling the rumble of hundreds of wheels over stone and gravel. He allowed himself no sleep, but crept forward with his guide to the ridge. There could be seen hundreds of campfires, for it was the main French army from Oporto taking what rest they could. Delica knew that Soult had two choices, to take the trunk road out of Portugal from Oporto and through Braga, or again a very difficult road over the mountains to Salamode. The growing dawn gave him Soult's answer, told by huge explosions and fires, as baggage was destroyed and guns were wrecked. From this, he knew that the French were destroying what was brought to Guimaraens by this newly joined force, destroying what they could not carry or pull over a mountain road. Therefore, he concluded, they were going to Salamonde, which meant crossing the bridge just after that village over the Cavado, at Ponte Nova. Such a bridge could be held by 50 men against thousands! He roused his men and headed off, along the most direct mountain track.

He hurried his men on, all mounted on decent horses. Soon they were able to descend to the road, all the marching French having been left behind, and they made better progress on the road's easier route, but not a better surface, for there was nothing significantly different between this mountain road and the high track they had descended from. It began to rain again, but his men were covered in good British cavalry cloaks and so they pushed on, speed undiminished. At Salamonde, Delica gave the Mayor one simple warning and one simple instruction; that the French were coming, so take to the hills and muster your Ordenanza. Within minutes the small town was in uproar, with the old, the women and the children taking the paths up the hillside, whilst the Ordenanza Militia paraded, for the want of a better word, along the main road. Any firearms they possessed were utterly ancient and would probably harm the user as much as any enemy. Their most potent weapons were their axes and pitchforks. Nevertheless, they marched out with Delica and just before Noon they were riding over the bridge with the torrent of the swollen Cavado beneath. Beyond was the small village of Ponte Nova, so Delica led his men in and found the leader of the Village Council; it was too small to have a Mayor. The immediate knowledge that the French Army of Portugal was on its way and that tools were needed to destroy the bridge, reduced the man to a state of near despair. He wanted to leave the bridge, let the French through at their best speed and for the village population to take to the hills. He knew that to hinder the French meant reprisals, but Delica was incensed and yelled at the man.

"Haverá represálias de qualquer forma quando você não dá-lhes comida suficiente!"

Many within earshot nodded in agreement, and the man could not argue. Reprisals would be inflicted anyway if insufficient food was handed over He led them to the blacksmith's and indicated the best tools they could provide for the job of demolishing the bridge. Delica indicated for his own guerrillas to gather them, which they did, and then they returned to the bridge to begin stripping away the surface planks, beginning from the far side, while the Ordenanza demolished the easier balustrades. When all was done that could be and only the main crossing beams remained in place, Delica led the Ordenanza to a group of

117

huts above the bridge and allowed them to shelter from the rain, but pressing two men as sentries, pushing them in misery to the point where the bridge was overlooked. Then what to do? The French would be there before dark, but the bridge surface and the balustrades were already in the Cavado, bar the remaining main beams which spanned the chasm. Without explosives, these were impossible to remove, but, three feet wide, they would provide a crossing for desperate men, and the French would certainly be just that, with Wellesley coming on as fast as he could in pursuit. More men were needed to hold their side, so he again ordered the Ordenanza to keep a continuous watch on the remains of the bridge, all through the night, then he gathered half his men and rode further up the valley, hoping to find another village to gather more Ordenanza.

Placed in the middle of Wellesley's army, the 105th slogged on, now 20 miles behind Delica and 10 behind Soult. The pursuit had begun before dawn, all parading on the road in slanting rain, blown in on a cold wind chilled by the sea. All were tired, the cold and the wet both taking their toll on men who were part of an army that was outreaching its supplies and consequently hunger was growing amongst them. No French dead nor badly wounded had been seen for hours, which gave no encouragement that they were overtaking the fleeing French army. Miles had an even more fundamental question, which he flung in the direction of Ellis.

"Can we be sure, even, that we'n on the right road?"

Ellis was in an even worse mood than his questioner.

"Shut your mouth and keep movin', Miles. This'll finish, sometime soon, either in a fight or us just callin' off the chasin'. One or t'other!"

All within earshot heard the reply and pulled their heads further down into their greatcoat collars, but the rain trickled in anyway. Then Gibney arrived, him feeling the need for some disciplined encouragement.

"Pick up the step!"

Wholly unnecessary, they were all automatically in step anyway, but they all pushed the soles of their boots a little harder into the soft earth of the road to increase the pace, each man but a small part in a much greater whole, this set upon a much greater purpose than simply to keep dry and ignore the hunger.

Night fell, and with it the rain, now in torrents. Juan Delica at last returned to Ponte Nova, after an almost fruitless quest. Half a dozen extra men were on their way in a farm cart. He tethered his horse and went to the bridge, rain beating on his cloak and water running in rivulets down the street to join the now raging Cavado. He hoped for a sentry, but was not surprised to find none. The rain beat upon the two cross members that still spanned the river, the splashing of the drops on the soaking timber somehow creating points of light in the inky black of the all-encompassing night. The cross-members were wide enough to be walked over for anyone with normal balance and the French could be on the other side, just across that chasm and, if quiet, there at that moment, unknown and unseen. The rain turned to sleet and the wind picked up, almost matching the sound of the Cavado beneath his feet. His mind returned to the matter of a sentry, but who could blame anyone for not wishing to stand out, on guard, throughout such a night? However, one was unquestionably needed. He stood for some minutes more, hoping to see or hoping to hear, but it was hopeless with the flooding torrent and the beating rain. However, there must be a sentry, if only for half an hour each, to warn of any attempted crossing, so who? His men were hardier, all volunteers, now resting further back in the village, so the guard would best come from them. He walked back up the slight slope, passing the group of huts that contained the local Ordenanza and entered the first house beyond that contained his men.

He roused one, a man made thoroughly reliable through his often demonstrated hatred of the French. They left the building and began their return to the bridge. They had not made any more than a dozen steps, when suddenly, from the area of the bridge, there was uproar, shouts and screams. The street was filling with dark shapes of men running in panic, and when the first arrived, he was a member of the Ordenanza. He pointed back down the street, breathless from panic rather than his run.

"Os franceses estão aqui. Eles estão matando todo mundo!."

The French had crossed the bridge and were slaughtering the Ordenanza in their huts. Delica turned to his fellow guerrilla.

"Obter os cavalos."

The horses would be needed for a quick escape, but first the French must be delayed. He ran into both houses to rouse his men.

"Tudo lá fora. Formem uma linha."

His men emerged, many carrying what should be draped around them, but they formed a line across the road. The last of the lucky escapees of the Ordenanza were passing through, but no French. Perhaps they were now too busy at the vital bridge, content for now of having either despatched or put to flight the Ordenanza guardians. He waited for some minutes, until he saw no point in beginning a hopeless fight against a whole army.

"Monte os cavalos. Hora de ir."

The line dissolved as his men turned to run back to their mounts. Soon they were leaving the village and then they slowed their horses to a walk because the road was too bad to even trot in the dark. At the first building, a barn, Delica dismounted, kept two men with him and ordered the rest to ride on to the next bridge. He slept till dawn, guarded by his two companions, a deep sleep, but terminated by both the light and his underlying concern of the oncoming French. His companions were a little way down the road, where they could see some way back to the village, so Delica joined them and bid them go back to bring the horses down. Then he climbed a small hill, carrying his telescope and, as a blessing, the rain had stopped and visibility became adequate, so he focused the instrument back on the village and saw what he had feared. The French were tearing the houses apart, partly to look for food but mostly to provide material to repair the bridge, sufficient for an army to cross, albeit footsoldiers and horses only. The continuous stream of men going down to the river and carrying materials told him that work was now ongoing, with some urgency. There were some guards at the top end of the village, but none beyond; however, through his telescope he could see the dense column of the French army, still held on the far side of the river. There was no point in remaining, his companions were beneath him with the three horses, so he descended, mounted and they all rode on.

All serious work for the pursuing British force during the main hours of daylight remaining was undertaken by Cavalry, not least the two squadrons of the 14th Light Dragoons, commanded by their Brigadier, General Perry. They were in the lead of Wellesley's force, scouting to find the French and, within minutes, after a miserable and late lunch of water, army biscuit and hideous Spanish cheese, they rounded a corner of the road to immediately see the French rearguard, a very substantial force. Tavender used his glass to count a whole Brigade of infantry of three, perhaps four battalions and two Regiments of Cavalry. Perry used his own telescope to study their formation, to conclude that they were well positioned, using a valley that crossed at right-angles the defile they had just ridden up. He turned to Templemere

"I want you to ride back and tell Wellesley that we are in contact with the French rearguard."

Now the lesson learned but days earlier was put into practice.

"Johnson! Show me where we are."

The Major walked his horse up to Perry and offered the map, whilst pointing with his finger.

"Here Sir. We have passed Salamonde and we are coming up to the Cavado, at a point close to this bridge shown here, I would say."

Perry turned to Templemere.

"Got that? Between Salamonde and the river."

Templemere nodded and turned his horse to canter back. Perry looked again at the French.

"We stay here."

However, Withers, further losing faith in his Commander, felt the need to speak out.

"Sir, we should engage them, if only as skirmishers. To keep them here, Sir, to let them know that we are up to them and that they cannot easily pull back. We can use our carbines."

Perry looked at Tavender for support, posing the question to him that remained unsaid. Was that right?

"Colonel Withers is correct, Sir, if I may be permitted to say. We have to let them know that we have caught up."

Perry nodded, somewhat reluctantly.

"Right. You two, lead the men forward."

The Dragoons dismounted and carrying their carbines they crept forward, led by Withers and Johnson. The first shot came from the French, then a bickering fire began all across the narrow valley. For half an hour this continued, with Johnson organising his men to repulse a French sally, then counter-attacking to push them back further. It was the main event of the conflict, but then it began to rain and the firing died away to almost nothing. There had been minimal casualties on either side in over two hours fighting.

Meanwhile, Juan Delica was now buoyed up with rekindled hope. Ten miles back from the Ponte Nova he came to another bridge, over a tributary of the Cavado, the

Misarella, with its bridge of a single span making a spectacular leap over a deep chasm. However, what had caused his hopes to rise so markedly was the fact that the far side of the Misarella was held by what was evidently several hundred Ordenanza. He rode over the bridge, passing men destroying the balustrade. The bridge was of very solid stone and this was all that could be done, then he rode around an abattis of stakes before completing his crossing. Once over, he found his own men, who came down to him and they pointed out an Officer, obviously British by his red uniform. Delica approached him with his interpreter, the one who had done duty at Oporto. Each introduced himself, Major Warre and Juan Delica simultaneously shaking hands, but Delica felt the need to make it clear that he was more than just another partisan, that he was a leader of men, but more than that, his band needed a name, so he quickly thought of one.

"Eu sou o líder da Guerrilha do Porto"

Hearing the translation, Major Warre, congratulated him, before asking what he really needed to know.

"Where have you come from?"

The reply came.

"Ponte Nova. De onde vieram?"

Warre replied. It was fair that this Guerrilla leader should know where he had sprung from.

"General Beresford's force."

That translated, he asked his own question.

"Are the French across?"

"Si."

"How far are the French behind you?"

"Dez legua."

Warre needed no translation for any answer. About ten miles, less than three hours marching and the French may have already started. One more thing.

"Will your men stay to help?"

Delica looked at the interpreter as the question was relayed, then back to Warre.

"Si."

"Muito obrigado."

Delica was pleased at the reply in Portuguese and they shook hands, before Warre left to inspect what had been done. The abattis was in place, there were no parapets on either side of the bridge and the earthworks either side of the exit were almost complete. Thus satisfied, he set about deploying his men. The best armed he put in the earthworks, the rest on the hillside beyond. Delica's men he wanted in reserve but Delica wanted no part of being in reserve.

"Não! Uma linha para defender a estrada."

Warre could not argue with that. Delica's men were well armed with British muskets. A firing line across the bridge from behind the abattis would provide a good first offering to the inevitable attack. Delica departed to order his men to clean and check their firearms, whilst Warre climbed to a vantage point. It was probably during the 30th time that he raised his telescope that he saw the oncoming French vanguard and through his telescope he saw that they did not look like beaten men, they were formed up and in step. Within a minute they had halted and a General came to their head, identified as such by his gorgeous uniform and massive, almost ridiculous, hat and identified as General Loison by the fact that he had no left arm. Another Officer soon joined him and they consulted for some minutes. Meanwhile, all of Warre's force was in position, with Delica stood behind his men, but after looking at the terrified faces of the Ordenanza on either side behind the earthworks, he tapped one of his men on the shoulder and gave his order.

"Certifique-se que os cavalos estão prontos para partir."

It was clear that this would not last long. He was determined to do what damage he could, but not sacrifice the lives of his men in a massacre, as had happened at Ponte Nova. He would have the horses ready. From where he was he could see some way beyond the bridge and he knew that

124

it was a forlorn hope to expect these men to hold back the French. These Ordenanza would have no stomach for the hand-to-hand combat that would be needed to even delay the French and it needed little deduction to conclude that Soult would happily lose a thousand men if it allowed his army to escape. This was soon confirmed, for, led by a single Officer, came forward one huge column, something like 1500 men, running towards the bridge. The Officer reached the end of the bridge, yelled something as he held his sword aloft and ran onto the bridge's surface. Delica knew his moment.

"Primeiro lugar. Disparar!"

His first rank fired, covering all with smoke, which quickly cleared in the breeze. Many French were down, but it had made no difference to the number still charging across the bridge.

"Segundo lugar. Disparar!"

Again the noise and smoke, and again, when it cleared, there were several more dead and injured Frenchmen, but it had made no difference, a dense crowd of blue uniforms were charging across the bridge. In seconds they were at the abattis, some trying to pull it away or tear it apart whilst others thrust with their bayonets through the woodwork to keep Delica's men away. His men fought back with their own bayonets and musket butts, some even managing to reload and fire a third time, but the French were down on the banks at either side and storming the earthworks. One Ordenanza, either berserk or doubly vengeful or both, climbed onto the top of the earthwork, screaming defiance, but he was hit by two bullets, whilst the rest were already melting away. Some fired their weapons, but soon there were no Ordenanza in either earthwork. Delica waited no more. Any more delay and they would be encircled.

"Cai para trás. Chegar a seus cavalos."

His men ran back up the hillside to their horses, where hundreds of Ordenanza were scattered around, running to the valley sides to then climb up to some form of refuge. He could not see Warre, so he mounted his own horse and led his men away. They had left one man behind, dead, hopefully, he told himself, rather than wounded and left there for the oncoming French. At a vantage point he reined in his horse to take a last look back. The French were despatching the few wounded who could not run mercifully with musketfire, whilst the vanguard, with Loison at the head, poured across the bridge. It was at that point that Delica heard the sound of cannonfire from some way back, probably at the Ponte Nova.

Merely minutes earlier, and a mile on the far side of the Ponte Nova, Perry remained sitting his horse, satisfied that he was engaging the enemy, but dissatisfied at the desultory nature of the conflict. Whilst pondering such, he was notified of Wellesley approaching and so Perry turned in his saddle as his Commander approached. Perry was now unsure, whether to speak or wait to be spoken to, but the latter came from Wellesley as he came up level.

"I see you've got your men into action, General!"

The sarcasm was evident, but Wellesley was now studying the French and asking a question at the same time.

"What do you know?"

Perry took a deep breath.

"We have seen three, perhaps four, Battalions of infantry, Sir, with strong Cavalry support, perhaps two Regiments."

Wellesley nodded, but during the act of studying the French for a minute further, he looked not again at Perry, but instead for the Commander of his lead Brigade, and he quickly found him. It had taken but minutes to formulate his plan.

"General Campbell! Get your Lights off to the left and skirmish against their right flank."

General H. Campbell saluted and rode off to find his two Light Companies of Guards and the single of the

60th Rifles. Wellesley was looking next for his Divisional Commander.

"Sherbrook! What's your nearest battery?"

"Lawson's Sir, three pounders."

"Get two up. Either side of the road."

At last Wellesley gave Perry some attention, but speaking as he once again used his telescope.

"General Perry. Be so good as to recall your men."

Perry turned to Johnson, who rode off and, within a minute the bugle notes rang out, and the Light Dragoons edged their way back.

Meanwhile, Wellesley had fixed upon a Guards' Colonel who was part of his Staff, this the Colonel of the Coldstream Guards Battalion halted just behind, with the 3rd Foot Guards to the rear of them. The three Light Companies were already detached and running over to the left.

"Mackinnon!"

"Sir."

"Get both yours and the 3rd ready to advance. In column, then forming a company front as you come within range."

As Mackinnon departed, so the guns arrived and, knowing that they were under the gaze of their Commanding General, the guns were rapidly unlimbered, sited, directed and charged, but not yet the type of shot. Lawson approached Wellesley.

"Grapeshot Sir?"

Wellesley nodded.

"Indeed."

Lawson's gunners had heard the confirmation and the heavy canvas bags were loaded into the waiting muzzles. Lawson himself directed each gun and as he left the gun on the right, to then cross the road and train that on the left, the first gun opened fire. The three pounder exploded with a sharp bark, then all was smoke, which quickly cleared. The French line was unharmed.

"Down ten!"

The left hand gun fired and, when the smoke cleared there was a gap in the French line, marked by prone figures and writhing wounded. Both guns then commenced loading and firing at their best speed, whilst Wellesley studied the ground over to the left. By the naked eye the two Guards Light Companies could be seen advancing with the green, less conspicuous, uniforms of the 60th Rifles in the lead. Soon they were fully engaged when Wellesley turned to find that Campbell had returned.

"That'll do Lawson. Your turn, Campbell!"

Still on his horse, Campbell walked forward to be followed by the two Battalions of Guards in column, four men wide across the road as Lawson's guns gave one last discharge. However, once clear of Wellesley, each Guards Battalion immediately formed a Company wide column and the 3rd Foot Guards caught up with the Coldstreams whilst changing formation to make one long line. The speed and precision was well noted by all behind and also by those in front. The French facing them, knowing that they were the rearguard of a beaten army and facing the obviously very capable vanguard of a victorious and formidable one, almost immediately broke formation and hurried to the rear. As this happened, keeping formation, and with Campbell and Mackinnon in the lead, the Guards hurried after them, but not sooner than the 60th who were onto the last of the French immediately, bringing down both men and horses. Wellesley and his Staff walked their horses forward in slow pursuit, but Perry felt the need to be included, somehow.

"General Wellesley, Sir. What for me and my men?"

There was no reply.

With little hope of drying out after a night and most of the day spent in the rain, Lacey, O'Hare and Carr were now halted someway back from the conflict, amongst the 105th. They had heard the same discharges of Lawson's battery as Juan Delica, but all knew the likely reason, spoken by O'Hare.

"Rearguard being pushed back."

Within minutes of the last of the cannonfire, the 105th were marching again, soon to come up to the evidence of combat, French dead being stripped by civilians who had come from no-where and the few British dead and wounded, lying in rows, the latter being attended to. Another half mile and the unbroken sounds of conflict intensified, made more so by the noise of a full battery in action, however, with the onset of darkness the fighting ended, and the order came to halt and make camp. In the narrow defile, crowded between the steep slope and the road, the men of the 105th made a meal from what was in their haversacks, meagre as it was. However, as a third blessing, the rain held off, for all were warmed by good fires burning as much wood as they wished gathered from the nearby forests, and, even if a little hungry, the men of the 105th Light slept warm and dry under their 'Davey' lean-to shelters. Nevertheless, it was a sleep punctuated with the groans and cries of wounded coming to them through the heavy air of the still, damp night, which reluctantly changed into a grey, sickly dawn. Ellis was around rousing all and moving on quickly to the next group, even before Miles could engage in any argument, not that Ellis felt the need to avoid Miles, simply that he wanted his Company to be first up and ready. The three considered their breakfast, Miles looking at Pike.

"What've you got, Joe?"

Pike tipped out the contents of his haversack and studied the result.

"Three biscuits, a bit of bread, some kind of fruit and a bit of dried beef."

The other two did the same and the food was spread around, but not all consumed. All had learned only to eat the minimum when they were unsure as to when the next issue of rations would arrive. Soon they were back on the road and marching forward to almost immediately see the source of the mournful sounds that had come during the night. The

129

French rearguard had been overtaken at Ponte Nova and casualties amongst them had been severe, their dead now dragged off the road and also about 50 prisoners, sat cold, forlorn and mournful at the roadside. However, this sight, gruesome enough as it was, did not prepare them for what was to come at the bridge. Both the cross beams and the makeshift surface were splintered and torn, evidently by the continuous blast of grapeshot. All was red with blood, evident as the 105th approached, but even the most veteran winced at the sight below, markedly stemming the river torrent, fierce as it was. Joe Pike was on the outside of the file as they made their way across the torn collection of doors, table tops and window shutters.

"John! Look at that."

Davey peered over to see what was in effect, a damn of bodies, human, horse and mule, with the water made bright pink as it flowed through and over the hideous mound. The cannonfire in the dying light of the previous evening had wreaked appalling slaughter on the French rearguard attempting to escape the two oncoming Guards Battalions. Evidently, they had been held up by the perilous bridge and, crowded together, they had made an easy target which Lawson's guns had taken full advantage of. However, what thoroughly annoyed Tom Miles was not so much the evidence of such a loss of life, as the sight of both the Light and Grenadier Companies of the both Guards Regiments, taking full advantage of the French dead. The pack mules themselves, left abandoned by the escaping French were left unmolested by the plunderers, evidently under the protection of 'officers' orders', they were not to be killed for food. However, the French rearguard had carried all their looted booty from Oporto with them and so the packs and haversacks of both the men and the mules all contained valuables of all kinds, including gold and silver plate and cups stolen from both churches and houses. Thus, on the banks of the Cavado, rifling through the packs and panniers which they had rescued from the noisome pile, sat these men of the Guards, joyfully pulling out both food, drink and plunder.

"Lucky Guards bastards! Walkin' off with booty like that. Wouldn't say no to meetin' one of they on a dark night an' relievin' 'em of some of that!"

Davey looked carefully at his aggrieved companion.

"Our turn'll come, Tom. Somewhere, sometime! Meanwhile, I'm happy that I'm in one piece and that supplies'll soon come up."

Tom Miles continued to look enviously at the gleeful Guardsmen, him not at all mollified to any promise of supplies. They marched on, now in the van as part of Campbell's Brigade. Under an hour's hard marching saw them cross the spectacular arch over the Misarella, which showed no record of the recent conflict, bar the absence of balustrades either side of the bridge The dead Portuguese had been given a Christian burial by their own local people and, from a small mass grave, French bodies being exhumed by the locals in the hope of some gain, perhaps good boots and breeches. At that moment the sun thoroughly cleared the clouds and the day became hotter and more airless, continuing to wear down the pursuing men of Wellesley's army, but, as the evidence of a French retreat grew less and less, it was clear that they were falling behind.

Marching at the head of the 105th column were the Colour Guard and so it was they who first entered the village of Ruivaens as the day thankfully ended, to be greeted by an ecstatic population, who pressed upon them a share of whatever they had been able to carry away into the hills, to keep out of French hands. Soon the four, these being Deakin, Bennet, Rushby and Neape were sharing bread, wine and sausage amongst themselves. Heaviside, accepting what was thrust upon him, for plainly there was little choice but to accept, summed up the feelings of all, because, all over the small square were men and women on their knees praying thanks for their deliverance and all others, except those bestowing gifts, were dancing and cavorting with glee.

"In every way and everywhere we accept this with all gratitude. Act 24. Three."

However, their habitual messmates from the Light Company, at the rear of the column, saw none of the results of this gift bestowing from grateful civilians until they made their camp in the fields outside, because all had been given to those arriving before by the time they finally entered the village. Yet even Tom Miles could not complain as he and the others received their share saved for them out of the villagers' generosity by Lacey and O'Hare and, in addition, at last rations came up, carried by a string of mules towed around by Chaplain's Assistant Sedgwicke. Still surprisingly to Sedgwicke, he was greeted warmly, first by Jed Deakin.

"Hello Old Parson. Be these rations?"

Sedgwicke found himself smiling at the warm greeting, but somewhere deep within him the total familiarity slightly irritated, it remained something that he had some difficulty coming to terms with, to be greeted as an equal by such as these, but another part of him fully appreciated their warmth and kindness.

"Yes, these are your rations."

He counted the men before him.

"Eleven men. How many families?"

Deakin answered.

"Two, Parson. Wives and seven childs."

Then he had a thought.

"Does that mean the Followers is soon to come up?"

Sedgwicke nodded.

"It does. They are on their way, but probably arriving tomorrow."

Sedgwicke produced the parcels from the mules' panniers and laid them on the ground. Saunders found cause to be cheerful.

"No prayers this time, Parson. Where's your Vicar?"

The possessive word grated in Sedgwicke for he once had been one, but he answered.

"Asleep! But expect him at sometime. Prayers are always a help in times like these!"

"Amen, Old Parson."

Sedgwicke moved on and all sat around their fire to eat and perform their maintenance rituals before sleep. However, they were not roused early. It was obvious that Wellesley had given up the chase when, with the sun by then high and warming, Gibney came around to order them to assemble by the roadside, prior to taking their place as part of the whole Brigade. Opposite them, on the far side of the road, were the 16th Portuguese Line, with the British 1st Detachments further off to the right. As if to confirm that the pursuit had ended, Wellesley himself cantered back between them, with his Staff. Immediately, at the sight of their Commanding General, all the Portuguese took off their shakoes and put them on the muzzle end of their muskets. Then the shout went up from all stood within their ranks

"Douro! Douro! Douro!"

The 105th and 1st Detachments did nothing as spectacular or informal, merely to present arms at Gibney's command, but Wellesley was obviously pleased at the reception and took off his hat which he held before him as he rode through. When Wellesley came to the Light Company at the end of the 105th line, the Portuguese were still shouting the single word, which aroused Drake's curiousity, him stood with Carr.

"So that's their name for him?"

Carr nodded.

"Seems so. The man who got them over the Douro! And sent the French packing."

"What are ours calling him? Any idea?"

"Nosey! But I've heard Atty."

"Atty!"

"Yes. His first name's Arthur."

Now it was Drake's turn to nod and laconically agree.

"Makes sense."

However, if any more was to come from that conversation, it was interrupted by Gibney forming the Battalion on the road, and soon Lacey himself marched them off along a side road to camp alongside a small hamlet, where they rested for that day and occupied themselves with their usual equipment and uniform routines. The conversation revolved around speculation as to when they would get back to Oporto and when their Followers would get to them. On top discussing deals of barter with the local farmers, trading food for French clothing and equipment.

For Wellesley and his army, the Oporto campaign was done, but not for Juan Delica. He and his men continued to harry the French army with what form skirmishes, however small, they could manage and even when Soult's men entered Spain, they spent two days carrying out as vicious a farewell as they could create, before returning to Montalegre where they, themselves, used the opportunity to take their ease amongst their own respectful and admiring people. This admiration significantly intensified by the many tales of hazardous exploits against the departed French, all told in the bars and at the family tables of their now tranquil homes. Also, another nickname was bestowed, for his people had not forgotten that Delica had once been a Capucin Monk, therefore now, all around, he was known as that brave guerrilla leader, El Capucino!

For the 105th, the Followers came up to them the day after their arrival at Ruivaens. No sooner had they marched in than they scattered to find their loved ones and the noise level and general good cheer increased throughout the camp as families were rejoined. Joe Pike and John Davey, although with no Followers, were as pleased as anyone, but for a different reason, this spoken by John Davey.

"Well! At least quality at mealtimes will be going up a notch."

This provocation was overheard by Tom Miles, who most often did the cooking when there were no Followers.

"And my cooking is what? Like?"

Both Pike and Davey looked at him, but Davey spoke, in quiet understatement, more worthy of Byford.

"Well, lacking a certain quality in both flavour and …… structure!"

Miles' brows knitted together, but Davey continued.

"An' don't tell me that you don't fully enjoy what Bridie serves up, neither!"

Miles' temper subsided and they wandered over to where Bridie and Nelly were greeting their 'husbands', but Bridie was soon giving most attention to her reunion with her Drummerboy son, Patrick, never taking her hands off the sleeves of his elaborate uniform and speaking to him in tones both admonishing and affectionate at the same time, until ordered by Deakin to 'give the lad some peace.'

The days became weeks and the whole army settled in. Within a day extra lean-to shelters had been built for their newly arrived Followers and, two days later, matters improved further, with Saunders and Bailey entering the camp. It was Miles who saw them first and, in his astonishment, blurted the question to which the answer was obvious.

"What's that?"

The giant Saunders looked down in mock bemusement.

"So, you Bristol boys have never seen one afore. 'Tis a cow!"

"What for?"

"Something else you don't know. You gets milk out of it!"

Miles gave up the argument, then looked at Bailey. The burden he carried was also obvious, a crate of chickens.

"What's them for? Eatin' or layin'?"

"Both. An' don't you go lookin' for more'n your fair share. These is for special days."

"Like what?"

However, the business brain inside Miles quickly gained prominence.

"How'd you pay?"

"Frog Officer buttons!"

Miles nodded. He had provided several of the silver articles himself for the community fund.

Thus were the days spent, in something as close to bliss as could be for any army on campaign. May became June and the heat grew, but supplies were regular and the surplus could be traded for extra luxuries such as wine, dried meats and fruit. The only cloud on their horizon was that Lacey had them back on manoeuvres, now that they were well rested, and Drake took the Light Company out into the woods and fields to practice their drills. A Portuguese Light Company came with them and performed well, once taught and drilled by both Carr and Ellis. Then, on the 9th, came the order to break camp and ready themselves for a long march and so rumours abounded, 'they were going East into Spain, back to Madrid', no, 'they were going North, back to Astorga'. Finally, the truth filtered down, they were marching South, past Oporto, even past Coimbra, to Abrantes, less than 100 miles from Lisbon. Something had happened, events were on the wing, but few knew where, or in what form.

oOo

Chapter Three

More of Spain.

General Jean Baptiste Marie Franceschi-Delonne, although he only ever used the first and fourth of his queue of names, sat a tired horse, between two half squadrons of the 1st Chasseurs a Cheval, their green uniforms covered in dust, their crowned helmets similarly dulled in the high June sunshine. He was tired himself, as were his escort, and he was annoyed that it required such a force, moving with little rest and needing to be commanded by such a rank as his own, to deliver any French message around this area of Spain. His route was from Zamorra, North of Salamanca, to Madrid, bearing a letter from Marshall Soult for King Joseph Napoleon in Madrid. He felt belittled; despatched by Soult to carry a despatch, the contents of which he was unaware, but he sustained himself with pleasant memories, of amorous encounters and also of his being promoted General on the field of Austerlitz. They had made good progress and in thus manner he allowed his horse to trot on, the reins slack, as the good mount, snorting from the dust, followed in the hoof-prints of those Chasseurs before.

All at once he was jolted out of his sojourn by an anxious awareness of where they were and where this execrable road was taking them, for now they were in a steep gully, which widened ahead, but not for the better, for the easier slope had allowed trees to grow and they came right down to the roadside, their thick new season leaves arching over to almost meet above the darkened road. The hair on the back of his neck stood up as the troopers up ahead entered the deep shade. A count of twenty and he was in the gloom himself, then it happened, a volley of shots, then another and many of his men were down. Then came the attack out of the trees, not on foot but mounted, 50 or 60 brown-green figures charging into the Chasseurs, many of whom had not yet had time to draw their sabres. He turned to urge forward his rear escort, to spur to the aid of those before, but before the words could clear his mouth he saw that they had their own problems, there was pandemonium at the very rear of his column, for they had received volleys of musket fire at the same time, from above and now, from what he could make out, they were being charged from behind, along the road.

He heard the Officers back there screaming to their men to turn and meet the threat, then he looked ahead, to see to his horror that it was all over, all that remained of that conflict were the few Chasseurs left alive and not prisoner, forcing their horses up through the trees, the better to make their escape. One guerrilla was screaming at his men and immediately those unoccupied with guarding prisoners were riding past Franceschi to finish the last French resistance back in the gully. The Chief Guerrilla, if that description was correct, followed his men, but stopped at Franceschi to then seize his bridle, grin malevolently and fix him with a look of pure hatred before speaking, the words coming as a soft hiss.

"Juan Delica, em seu serviço, Senor."

The sarcasm was obvious and, before Franceschi could make any reply, the dispatch bag was cut from his shoulders by another guerrilla and tossed across to who must be, Franceschi reasoned, the damnable bandit El Capucino, distinctive by his upper body being covered in a poncho made from a cut down Capucin monk's robe, hood still in place. This brigand unfastened the leather flap to the satchel and looked inside, to then bring out a bundle of papers, which he soon returned to the depths of the bag. He then looked at the waiting guerrilla.

"Llevarlo con nosotros!"

The guerrilla moved his horse up to Franceschi and pulled the reins from his relaxing grip. He was then led forward into the trees where, spread around were the results of the recent combat, dead Chasseurs being stripped down to nakedness, a few dead and wounded guerrillas, and the last of his command, wounded or whole, being despatched at the roadside with a single axe blow to the back of their heads.

oOo

The 105th had been three days on the march before Lacey received any knowledge as to why, with all speed, they were marching South. It came in the form of Brigadier Stewart, who reined in his horse besides Lacey and O'Hare, to turn his mount and ride along beside them. He came straight to the point.

"Wellesley's received a captured dispatch. Soult's abandoning Galicia, seems he's in nae shape to continue there. Staying there, he'll just be bound up in various strongholds doing nothing, penned in by guerrillas and eventually starving. He's all out of supplies of all sorts and has tae move towards Salamanca."

He allowed the words to sink in, before continuing.

"Seems we did him a lot more harm than we thought."

Another pause, but the pair that were his audience were listening intently.

"So, with nothing to the North of us, he's taking us back down South, with a view to co-operating with that grand old man La Cuesta. Good luck to him with that! Seems we'll be back in Spain again before long and he wants us in tae Spain before Soult can get himself back together."

With that information, now Lacey had his own question.

"How far down does he want to go, Sir. We've heard Abrantes."

"Ye've heard aright."

"That's a fair stretch, Sir. The men are feeling the pace already."

Stewart now spurred his horse forward to leave, at the same time making his final comment, this practically an order.

"Can't be helped! Keep them going, push them on."

The pair rode on through the dust of Stewart's departure, O'Hare thinking logistics more than Lacey was.

"Which is the next main town? Do you know?"

Lacey's mouth slewed sideways in thought.

"Must be Oporto!"

O'Hare sighed deeply.

"And there'll be damn all for us there!"

Thankfully, O'Hare was wrong. Oporto had been turned into a supply base, but veterans like Jed Deakins were not beguiled when they were issued double rations. Himself and Toby Halfway were together occupied with finding space for provisions in packs and knapsacks and any other hole, which could receive a portion, however small.

"You know what this means, Tobe?"

Halfway did not need it to be explained.

"I do. No other issue for a long time down. Lucky we have the families to carry extra."

A return to the Deakin and Nicholls families found a similar scene, all trying to find additional places for the extra rations, such that even the smallest, Sinead Mulcahy and Violet Nicholls were weighed down with bags of food. For the three man messes of the 105th, there was nothing for it but to recover their King George backpacks from their supply train and somehow drape these about their persons, prepared to bear the burden of the extra food. Thus, in this most incongruous and unmilitary form, the march continued.

It was now the second week of June, with the sun almost at its zenith and each day it eased its way painfully across the roaring blue of the continuous arch of sky, taking its time, the better to deal wearying heat onto the plodding column of humanity below. Three days and then half a night brought them to Coimbra, which they entered as a town just waking up, but at least much recovered from the fear of the French invasion merely weeks ago. Although it was the dawn of a new day, the whole army, their Followers and baggage all simply found a space and slumped down to sleep and then wake later in the heat of the Noon sun. Food and water were the only concerns they had and they were nearing desperation, especially the issue of water. For this reason did RSM Gibney take himself to the encampment of the Battalion Chaplain, but it was Sedgwicke that he wished to find and he did, the good ex-Cleric just rousing himself from under his small cart. He bent down from his great height to seize the shoulder tab of the half conscious Sedgwicke.

"Percy. Hast tha' a jug and a bucket?"

Sedgwicke nodded.

"Yes Sergeant Major."

"Fetch uns. Then with me!"

By doubling his normal walking pace to maintain station alongside the marching Gibney, Sedgwicke found himself beside the only well within reach of the 105th, where a near riot was taking place to get at the water that came up in the single bucket. In consequence more was spilt than found its way into the containers, which both the soldiers and Followers carried. Gibney expanded his chest.

"Enough! That'll do! Not one of you moves, not one!"

At the familiar voice all stood stock still as Gibney shouldered his way through, with Sedgwicke in his wake. He came to the well and glowered all around before delivering his edict.

"Canteens gets one jug. Cooking pots gets two."

He allowed that to sink in.

"As doled out by our trusted man Sedgwicke here."

The word 'trusted' was not used lightly and was the reason why Gibney had selected Sedgwicke, because two years past Sedgwicke had uncovered a plot to steal the men's rum and this was one of the reasons why the ex-

Cleric was so well liked and treated so familiarly, even if it grated somewhat on his own self-esteem and the requirement for natural respect.

Gibney had more to say and a role to play for himself.

"I'll keep a full bucket up here, now us've got two, and thee, Percy, uses the jug."

Thus it began, Gibney maintaining a full bucket on the rim of the well, while Sedgwicke gave the issue. Soon Gibney found himself looking at Zeke Saunders.

"Saunders. Get tha' water an' then fetch Deakin an' Halfway up to this place."

Saunders soon departed and soon returned to the well with the two trusted NCO's.

"Halfway. Take over with t'buckets. Deakin, take charge."

Only now did Gibney march away, military order having been restored.

As a consequence, now well watered, Miles, Pike and Davey were considering extra food. The double rations had run out on the previous day, bar the standard issue of flour and this they had handed to Bridie Deakin. Davey asked the first question of Miles.

"How many buttons we got left?"

Miles did not need to look.

"Four!"

Miles then pondered the question not asked, his mouth working with each calculating thought.

"Dried fish, bread, some beans."

Davey nodded.

"Give two to the boy. He's better lookin' than you and some old dear at the market might take a fancy to'n an' chuck in a bit extra."

Miles nodded at the wisdom, but he had thoughts of his own.

"Better some doe-eyed girly. Try to find one and try your luck, Joe."

The buttons were produced and given to Joe Pike, the blond Adonis, who departed without a word.

As chance would have it, those three ingredients were exactly the combination that Lacey, O'Hare and Carr were dining on, albeit accompanied with some local red wine. In between combining some fish, beans and bread on his fork, Lacey asked the key question of O'Hare.

"How are the men bearing up?"

O'Hare finished his own mouthful.

"So far, quite well, but there was a bit of a set to at the well a while ago, dealt with by Gibney."

He paused for thought.

"I'd match the discipline of ours against any in the army, including the Guards, but this is a forced march and we're only just over halfway. On top, it's my bet he'll take us over the Sierra on the direct route to Abrantes. That, will be nothing less than arduous. It'll take its toll, on strength and discipline."

Both then looked at Henry Carr, but it was Lacey who spoke.

"What do you think, Henry?"

"Can our Commissariat keep us fed, Sir? I don't see what else can be said. If yes, we'll get there as an army, if no, then as a rabble. We all remember Coruna."

More thoughts took place within Carr, before he spoke again.

"However, once fed we came back together again well enough. So there's hope there."

Both nodded and Lacey poured more wine. Meanwhile, Pike had returned almost empty handed, to sit miserably before his two messmates and produce some bread and cheese, but, at least, one remaining button.

"Stalls were almost empty. Hardly anything anywhere."

Despondently, Davey took up the bread and began ripping it apart, using his Baker bayonet. However, Miles had thoughts.

"This town is well set. Where is it all? Nothin' hardly left as can be seen, an' they needs feedin' too, those as lives 'ere."

The question was answered with the dying of the day. Whilst what was available in the market had all been bought up by the Officers, also Wellesley's Commissariat had previously gone around the whole city, buying at top price whatever was available in the stores and warehouses. So, in the gathering darkness came an issue of flour, dried fish and dried beans, both green and red, but this small blessing was immediately counterpointed by the order that they were to be ready to march out at dawn of the next day.

Lacey had been only half right concerning the crossing of the Sierra between Coimbra and Abrantes, for the 105th like the rest of the army, were only called upon to add their weight to the gun and wagon teams on one occasion, when they crossed a pass into the valley of the River Zezere. Four times each Company hauled a gun up through the narrow streets of some impossibly remote village, to then descend back down to take up the rope of another gun or wagon. However, once in the valley, water was plentiful and the height of the valley head reduced the June heat, but food was once again a problem for both men and animals, to the extent that marauding began against the local farms and settlements. It was Stewart who delivered the warning, delivered perfunctorily as usual, as they descended the valley, marching besides the clear Zezere.

"Wellesley's sending the Provosts out, Lacey. He wants nae ill feeling 'tween us and the populace caused by villainy. Keep your men in hand."

Such brevity gave weight to his words, making them an order, and Lacey saluted as Stewart rode away. He then looked at O'Hare.

"Warn Gibney."

O'Hare turned his horse to ride back down the line and find their Sergeant Major.

However, that evening in the drawn out dusk of the long summer day, there was a serious discussion in the mess of Miles, Pike and Davey, Miles looking at Davey.

"What we going to do, John? We've eaten damn all for the past two days and this Abrantes place is two more away."

He paused, to gather yet more weighty words.

"You was the poacher! How'd you get food in times like these?"

Davey looked at him, but it was Pike who spoke.

"They catch you out roaming and scavenging, then you're for the rope. You know that Tom."

Davey gave a thoughtful poke to the fire.

"Well, we all knows that from a farm you can get animals, hens and eggs. But, like Joe says, get caught carrying any of that back, gets you hauled up."

More thought.

"How far's the river?"

Miles pointed with his thumb over his shoulder.

"Half mile. That way."

Davey stood up.

"Best go now. It looks better in the dusk than the full night."

Within the hour they were beside the Zezere and in the full moonlight, all three were using 'scoops' made from thin branches to Davey's design, this well suited to trawling beneath the banks, even though requiring over an hour to make. Their fishing proved fruitful, four each for Miles and Pike, but seven for the more experienced Davey. Then, with their catch strung together over their shoulders they set off back, but the moonlight which had aided their fishing now caused their undoing as they crossed an open field. In the stark white light they stood out like rocks on a beach and, almost immediately, they heard galloping horses from their right. Miles, most often involved with the Provosts, gave immediate advice.

"Walk on, nice and steady. Look innocent, like you was about your common business an' expect them to ride on past, them goin' about theirs."

But, of course, they did not ride past, instead pulled up in their path, large men on huge horses, their almost ridiculous helmet crowns adding to their height. The three under suspicion stopped, but it was the Provost Sergeant who spoke first.

"Out plunderin'."

Davey, the Chosen Man replied first.

"No, Sarn't. Out fishing."

"Caught where?"

"In the river back yonder."

This seemed to place the NCO in a quandary. Fish were no-one's property, yet here were three men, out of the lines, in the full dark of night. However, just then an Officer came galloping up, to rein in between the two groups.

"Three? Sarn't?"

"Not sure, Sir. These has fish. From the river, so they say."

The Officer turned to carefully examine their three captives. As if to help the decision, Miles held up one of his catch, on its string, to emphasise the point. The Officer was evidently very put out, but as much at a loss as to what to do as was his Sergeant.

"You are out of your lines!"

However, Davey was growing in confidence.

"Yes Sir, but we've just made camp and now we're lookin' to catch our dinner. Sir."

The Officer sat back in his saddle, patience quickly evaporating, but this was plainly no hanging matter.

"Back to your camp. And stay there! If we find you out again, it's your neck!"

All three saluted, the fish swinging with the motion of their arms, all three speaking in unison.

"Sir!"

The Provosts rode off and the gap between the two groups grew, each yard adding to the ease in the chests of the three. They continued, the moonlight guiding every step, then the crossing of a field boundary brought a change in the ground beneath their feet, something was growing there, evidenced by green haulms all around. Joe Pike voiced his curiousity.

"John. What're all these ridges. What're they for?"

"I was askin' myself the same question, Joe, and I think I knows the answer."

He removed his fish from around his neck and laid them on the ground.

"Get out your brummagem. You too, Tom."

Within a minute both were digging in the ridges with their bayonets and soon they had unearthed pale tubers, shining almost white in the moonlight.

"Tatties!"

Miles looked up.

"Wher' be they Provosts?"

All three stood and looked, but mostly listened. There was nothing, not even receding hoof beats.

"Right!"

Miles had decided and all three dug further and then they filled every pocket that had any space to receive such a bounty. Finally, Joe Pike was stood up, his fish draped around his neck and his hands cupped before him. These received a few more of the fresh tubers, then Davey did the same for Miles. That done, and crouching low, they hurried back to their camp.   Within the hour the fish were gutted and boned and the potatoes peeled and chopped, as the main ingredients in a good fish stew, all lovingly created by Bridie Mulcahy, adding herbs and a few army biscuits. That night they were late to sleep, their bellies being too full, but the next dawn found them well into marching in their place in the ranks of the 105th, making good progress along the good road. Wellesley wanted some distance behind them before the heat of the day arrived and that was not the only method by which he demonstrated his concern for his men. A supply train had left Abrantes to meet them, containing not only plentiful food, but also new boots and breeches. However that evening came the counter from Wellesley, delivered by RSM Gibney, on his way around every mess, delivered perfunctorily and broking no argument, except inevitably from Miles.

"Stocks! Sar' Major. We 'as to wear stocks!"

Gibney regarded Miles as if he were a cockroach in his favourite stew, his outrage deepened by the firelight that flickered over his kitted brows.

"Tha' heard me, Miles, an' make sure that thine is up high and laced up tight. I'll be lookin' for thee, count on't!"

That evening several from their mess took themselves to the baggage train where their banished King George backpacks were, containing their hated leather stocks. Then in the morning, after eating, because the stiff leather restricted even swallowing, each tied the loathed object around the neck of another, to finally force their heads high, erect and immobile to either side. On that day, they marched into Abrantes, looking as smart an army as those good people had ever seen.

oOo

As part of Stewart's Brigade, the 105th marched straight through Abrantes to camp in the fields beyond, and soon, all around the ancient and picturesque town, the fields were filled with the constituent parts of Wellesley's army, his battalions, his artillery and his supply train. However, for Deakin and his companions the days that followed were marked by the return of hunger. The supply wagons that had arrived on the final days of their march proved to be a 'one-off' event and Abrantes was too small to have enough stocks of food for a whole army. Soon the complaints began, each to another, such as Carravoy complaining about

148

being served horse-meat of wholly suspect provenance, but the complaints that mattered were those that reached Wellesley's ears from the local Junta, complaining about robbery and theft. The next day saw the return of the Provosts, their numbers swelled by men from the 3rd Dragoon Guards, five Dragoons under the command of one of the Provosts, this measure intended to reduce the risk of bribery within the less trusted Dragoon Guards.

However, within three days supplies did appear, arriving by the almost unique method of being hauled up the Tagus on flat bottomed barges. The complaints of the local Juntas lessened in direct proportion to the reducing hunger felt by the army and supplies arrived regularly by this very reliable method of river transport. In fact, each day a full variety of materiel arrived, evidently the supplies for a forthcoming campaign. One evening, Stewart invited his three Colonels and their Senior Majors to dinner at the Casa of a local merchant. This local worthy had complained as loudly as anyone during the time of theft, but he knew full well the value of this Allied army keeping the French away from his home, also from his warehouses, albeit the fact that they were now empty and that he had been paid top price to make it so. Thus all the hospitality was at his expense.

O'Hare had made his excuses, some kind of fever, 'had it on and off since Africa with Abercrombie', and so Carr attended in his stead. The room was classic Portuguese, low ceiling, mostly of blackened beams, thick white walls, their expanse broken just correctly by shallow alcoves, the whole deep within the house to escape the summer heat, which even at that time of the evening was felt in the deep and narrow streets outside. The evening was relaxed but flat, all with minds still subdued by the relief of the hard march just ended and their arrival into the town. However, with the arrival of the nuts and port the talk turned to military matters but the topic did not last long, Carr delivering the one telling phrase that seemed to both begin and end the discussion concerning the merits of their French opponents.

"They've not stood well against us! Not once, from Rolica 'till now. It's only numbers that prevents us from pushing them right back to Madrid and beyond."

No-one could gainsay such an opinion and so Stewart finished the evening by speaking of the main reason why they were there.

"Wellesley's re-organised his army and we're parting company."

He looked at Ruskin.

"You're going back to Portugal. All Portuguese troops are being trained and re-armed and such as yours will be the backbone of a new Portuguese Army."

Next, to Burns.

"You're staying with me, but yours, Lacey, are now in Mackenzie's Brigade. Donkin's Brigade is with you in your Division, but Mackenzie's the Divisional Commander."

He reached for the port.

"Not that this stuff quite fits the bill as would guid scotch, but it'll have tae do."

He filled each glass to the brim, seven, including his own, then he raised the fine, cut glass containing the dark red liquid to shoulder height, circling his hand around the table in the direction of them all.

"Guid luck! Slange."

All drank and then quickly left into the warm night, Lacey and Carr with the most to ponder.

"Have you heard of him, Henry?"

"No, Sir, other than his name, Alexander Mackenzie. He wasn't at Oporto; his Division was sent to here and so stayed out of it. As to the sort of person he is Sir, I've little idea."

The next day, early, they found out, Mackenzie riding alone up to Lacey's tent and requiring Sergeant Bryce, Lacey's secretary, to enter the tent and request his

Colonel to come out. What Lacey saw was a cadaverous face, lantern jawed, staring down from beneath, in his case, a modest Highland bonnet, his eyes stark, just outside its shade. Mackenzie's words were acerbically brief, spoken in a flat, but profound Highland accent.

"Ah want to inspect yorr men, Colonel. One hour."

Lacey looked around at the crowded tents.

"Where Sir?"

"You find a place, Colonel and I'll find you. Never fear."

With that he turned his horse and required it to walk off, presumably to the next battalion, to order a parade for two hours time. Lacey turned to Bryce.

"Get around the camp! Tell every Officer and Sergeant that you see to ready the men for General's inspection. Where, they'll be told in good time."

By now, Bryce had turned away, but Lacey had another thought.

"Is Major O'Hare still indisposed?"

"Yes Sir, last I saw him."

"Right. If you see Major Carr, ask him to find me."

Bryce continued his way in one direction, Lacey in another, but both with the same intent, to stir the camp for a Major General's inspection and within ten minutes Carr came running up to him, somewhat breathless.

"Sir. You asked for me."

Lacey, equally breathless from his own exertions, gave a brief reply.

"We need a space for the parade inspection. Find one."

Lacey looked around, trying to be helpful.

"I'd say over there, that way, there seems to be a little more room between us and the 88th. Look there first."

Carr saluted and ran off to find that Lacey was correct, almost, because the striking of two tents was required, then there would be a long run of space, in fact all of the 150 yards that were needed. He found the first tent full of Grenadiers, who came to the attention the second he entered.

"Are you all now ready for the inspection?"

A Corporal answered.

"Yes Sir. We were the first to be told."

"Right! Your tent needs to be moved to give us the run long enough for the parade. Strike your tent now, then store it somewhere in the lines. After, you can bring it back to here."

With that he was gone, but the Grenadiers were exiting after him to pull out the tent pegs and then carry their canvas home the necessary yards out of the way. In the second tent he found Captain Lord Carravoy and Captain The Honourable Royston D'Villiers. He began in much the same fashion as he had with the Grenadiers.

"I assume you've heard of the inspection?"

A nod from both.

"I'm afraid I've bad news, your tent is in the way of the only possible parade ground. I'm afraid it will have to be moved. Temporarily."

This was no easy affair. In the case of the Grenadiers, their tent contained but blankets and their equipment, but for the two Officers it was practically a furnished room, with beds, tables, a desk, collapsible chairs and two lanterns, even, hanging from the apex. Carravoy was immediately incensed.

"And this choice of ground? Yours presumably?"

Carr immediately recognised the acid tone of the reply.

"Yes and no. The Colonel sent me over here and I recognised the possibility. With the removal of your tent and the one of your men, then we will have our parade ground."

He felt the need to be conciliatory, for these were, after all, brother Officers.

"I'm sorry for the huge inconvenience, but there it is; an order from our new Divisional Commander to hold a parade."

Carravoy was not mollified, not least because of the inconvenience but also because the instruction came from Carr.

"Why can you not extend the parade the other way and have our tent just off the end, not involved, as it were?"

Carr was losing patience, knowing that time was passing and had already passed.

"Not possible, Charles. That would take us into the lines of the 88th. Not possible!"

The reply from Carravoy was wordless, in as much as he went red in the face with anger, but Carr was not far behind.

"Charles! I'll make it an order if I have to. I'll not have the Regiment humiliated in the face of our Division. However many men you need to take this damn thing down and then put it back up, with all as was, I'll arrange. But this has to happen!"

D'Villiers did not like how this was developing and decided to intervene in the best way he could.

"Yes Sir. Thank you for that offer, which we appreciate. Also, if you see our servant, Binns, he should be just outside, if you could send him in, Sir, we would appreciate that, whilst we are packing things up."

A pause.

"Sir."

Carr had the reply that he needed, so he nodded his acknowledgment and left, almost colliding with Binns, who had heard all from the other side of the canvas.

"I'm Binns, Sir. I'll make a start from here."

With Binns now inside, Carr looked around to see several Grenadiers.

"Attention!"

All within earshot responded and Carr began to point.

"You, you, you and you. Report to your Captain's tent. He has a job for you."

A little later, chivvied on by Gibney, the final redcoats had just taken their place in the long line, when Mackenzie appeared, on his horse, from an odd space within the tent lines. He was accompanied by a single Major, as an Aide-de-camp and one Orderly, him on foot. With his appearance, Gibney took over, at more than usual volume.

"Paraaaade!"

All came to order arms, their musket butts tight beside their right leg.

"Parade. Present. Arms."

In perfect unison the whole 736 men lifted their weapons for the butt to be cupped in their left hand, their right to go below the trigger guard, their left to then go above it and the weapon to be moved in front of their chins and lowered so that their left forearm was parallel to the ground. In unison with their men, the 35 Officers moved their swords to the salute. All was then rigidly still and silent, but for the occasional snap of the two Colours in the gusting breeze. Mackenzie rode up to Lacey and saluted. Lacey, in response, moved his sabre out to the right and then returned it. The General then dismounted and handed the reins of his horse to the Orderly and his Major did the same. Mackenzie now stood before Lacey, which showed that he was a little shorter, but still above average height.

"Morning, Colonel. If ye'll accompany me, we'll take a walk."

With that, he walked briskly to his left, followed by Lacey and the Major Aide-de-Camp, to start with the Grenadiers. On reaching their ranks on the far right, he began a slow walk back, neither halting nor speaking. Thus, he soon came to the Colours and then spoke for the first time, but to Heaviside.

"Captain! May I see the Regimental Colour?"

This was odd. A General of his rank would normally do as he liked, but this was clearly a request which acknowledged the practically sacred status of a Battalion's Colours.

"As you choose, Sir."

He slightly raised his voice.

"Ensign Neape. Please to lower the Regimental Colour."

Neape allowed the staff that had been pressed against his nose to tilt forward to the extent that the huge bright green square hung straight down, but not touching the trodden grass. Mackenzie stooped slightly and angled his head, pulling the Colour straight enough with his right hand to read what was there.

"Maida. Vimeiro. Coruna."

He straightened himself.

"Thank ye, Captain."

He looked at Heaviside.

"Tough fights, all, ye'd say?"

"Sir. But perhaps not Vimeiro. At least not so much as the other two."

Then came the inevitable.

"To him that knocketh it shall be opened. Matthew Seven, verse eight."

Lacey sighed, but Mackenzie smiled.

"There'll be a few more hard knocks afore we're done here, Captain. We are not of them who draw back unto perdition; but of them that believe to the saving of the soul."

"Amen Sir. Hebrews, 10, 39."

"Just so. Good luck, Captain."

"Thank you, Sir."

Mackenzie passed on, again neither speaking nor stopping, until he came to the first of the Light Company, this being the giant Saunders, at his place on the end of the rank as a Corporal. Mackenzie first looked up, then down, to see that Saunder's weapon was not standard. He turned to Lacey.

"That's a Baker!"

"Yes Sir."

Mackenzie looked further along the Light Company.

"They all have Bakers!"

"Yes Sir. Since Maida."

"How come?"

"I bought them myself, Sir, for the Light Company. Every third man, back then."

Mackenzie eyes narrowed, for what reason, he did not say, then he turned to Saunders.

"And your opinion?"

Saunders swallowed hard, choosing carefully the words he was about to use to the highest-ranking Officer he had ever spoken to in his entire life.

"'Tis good to have a piece as'll give us a better chance of downin' who we aims at, Sir. The more we hits of them, the less there is to send back at us. Sir."

"So it's accurate? More so than a musket?"

"Yes Sir. Without a doubt, Sir. We can put 'em down out of their range for accuracy, Sir."

Saunders grew in confidence with the progress of the informal conversation and smiled.

"It gives you a better feelin', Sir, when you'n out there, between the lines. Sort of thing."

Mackenzie nodded.

"One thing more. Why aren't ye a Grenadier? Man of yorr size."

Saunders stock reply to this frequent question was, 'too intelligent', but now he used a word he had learned from Byford.

"It was where I was assigned, Sir."

"But why the Lights?"

"Can't say Sir. Perhaps the Grenadiers was all full. Sir."

Lacey intervened.

"He was in the 9th Foot, Sir, the East Norfolks, but they were shipwrecked back in the year five and only 200 survived. They were added to the Provisional Battalion that we were then. He came as a Light. Sir, and no-one thought to change."

Mackenzie nodded and walked on, perhaps a little more briskly. Soon he was at the end of the ranks, where he saluted Carr, who acknowledged with his sword. Within three more minutes, he was back on his horse, but not yet done, for then he sat forward in his saddle, to draw himself up and raise his voice.

"Men of the 105th !"

He rocked back and forth in his saddle.

"Ye're guid lads all, I can see that. So too, from what I've read on your Colours."

He paused.

"Ye're lads for a fight, that's certain, an' when it comes, ah'll be callin' on ye, be sure, in the days ahead."

He sat back in his saddle, but still was not finished.

"An' your pays come up!"

He did not wait to watch the grins and smiles spread across the faces of the front rank, but turned his mount to make his departure.

oOo

The next day saw the promised issue. The two months of January and February were owed prior to leaving England and they had been in Spain a total of 92 days, each day worth one shilling and so, all day, the queue of 'other ranks' progressed past the paymaster and almost all day he spoke the same words to each man, unless he were an NCO.

"Seven pounds, eleven shillings, no pence. Less deductions, four pounds, eight shillings and seven pence."

The coins were scooped up and carefully tipped into a tunic pocket or an upturned shako, before the recipient marched off. That night, the dice began to roll and Joe Pike was carefully shepherded as he watched the dice players throw the treacherous, as they undoubtedly were for some, cubes of ivory onto a blanket. Thankfully, he made no effort to join in.

Even though monied as they now were, for the 105th, firewood was a more pressing issue. With a whole army, numbers now much increased from Lisbon and in the vicinity of what was little more than a market town, the most frequent sound beyond its low, white buildings, was the chopping of axes in the woods, each day further and further away. All foraging parties passed anxious locals, anxious for their precious olive trees, but none had been touched, because Wellesley still maintained the Provost patrols, well up to strength, still reinforced by the 3rd Dragoon Guards.

It was on just such a trip, late morning, that the six of Davey, Miles, Pike, Saunders, Byford and Bailey encountered their near Battalion neighbours, both parties blessedly not heading for the same tree, but two that were adjacent. As their axes bit in, begun by Pike and Saunders, one of the neighbouring party wandered over and it was immediately obvious that he was Irish, but more Northern than Southern.

"And what Regiment would youse lads be part of, now? You must be Irish, with that shade of green?"

His own collars and cuffs were a pale yellow, this quickly noted by John Davey as he stood to meet the visitor, whilst waiting his turn with the axe.

"No! We're English. 105th Wessex."

He allowed a pause.

"And you?"

"88th Connaughts! At your service."

Davey almost smiled, but he was wary. He had had many dealings with Irish tinkers and diddykites in his previous life and never once had he felt that he had the edge on any deal that he had ever made with them, but he felt the need to be at least welcoming, so he nodded.

"Just come up? From Lisbon?"

"Ah no, they threw us off at a place called Figueira, and we humped it from there to here."

As Davey nodded, the Connaught extended his hand.

"Michael O'Donnell, all the way from Castlebar."

Davey took the hand.

"John Davey. Backhole place near Gloucester. You'll have heard of neither."

Byford was stood near and O'Donnell naming his hometown, jogged a historical memory.

"Castlebar! There was a bad affair there in '98."

O'Donnell seemed just a little embarrassed by the statement, but he quickly recovered.

"Ah that! Sure now, we was never part. Way overseas were the Rangers, all of us. None of us even part of the put down that came after."

He changed the subject.

"So what's this Spain like. Well set, are they, these Spaniards?"

The implication was obvious, what did they have which could be traded, stolen or even plundered if the chance came? Davey immediately answered.

"Don't expect much. They'n as poor as Church mice, mostly, especially after a French army's gone through. Johnny Frog lives off the land and takes all, includin' anythin' what can be carried away. When you think of a French army, remember that. They picks the place clean!"

O'Donnell was plainly set back by the information, but changed the subject again, perhaps to the one which was his purpose all along.

"Well, that's a shame, so it is, but, now, would youse boys be up for a bit of sport, sort of thing?"

Davey was instantly suspicious.

"You've got something in mind?"

O'Donnell screwed up his face and swung his head from side to side, as though he had but a vague idea of the answer.

"Well, if I'm thinkin' of the sort of happenings back home, what was horse-racin' an' what we calls hurling, but there's neither place nor room for such as that out here."

A pause.

"No. I was thinkin' perhaps of some kind of wrestlin', of a type. For a wager, like, just to add some spice, y'see. I'm told you've just been paid."

Davey folded his arms and sighed. All was revealed.

"Wrestling! For a wager."

O'Donnell brightened considerably. His suggestion had not been rejected outright.

"You've got it! I'm lookin' at that lad y'have there. Sure, couldn't he put up some kind of a show? 'Twould take some lad to get the best of him!"

Saunders, overhearing all, gave the tree a final push, which sent it crashing to the ground and then handed the axe to Bailey. He walked over to Davey and O'Donnell.

"So you'm talkin' about some kind of match. What purse you puttin' up?"

O'Donnell was again silenced by the direct questions, but Saunders continued.

"An' style? Plain Folk? No punchin', gougin', nor head buttin'?"

Such knowledgeable questions from someone who could very well be a genuine wrestler and an experienced one, caused O'Donnell to pause and think.

"Plain Folk! That's the one. And as to purse, well, 'tis you as've just been paid."

Saunders looked at him astonished.

"If you puts up a man to win our money, you matches our purse. You risks what we do! That's how it is!"

Now, in silence, both Davey and Saunders stood looking at O'Donnell. The silence spoke the challenge, 'Take the terms, or walk away'.

"Am I right in thinkin' that 'tis youse as'll be steppin' up?"

Both nodded and O'Donnell seemed to think, for a long second, then an ingratiating smile spread across his face, making it Davey's and Saunders' turn to feel uneasy.

"Done!"

Again the smile.

"Let's say three days, back here. Three days to work up our man. An' you yourself, you'll want some time to put some agility into those muscles, eh?"

With that he turned to walk away, but Saunders had not finished.

"And the purse?"

O'Donnell stopped and his eyes narrowed.

"Twenty pounds sounds good!"

Saunders nodded and so the Connaught Ranger turned and walked away, but not before speaking over his shoulder.

"Three days, then. This time, back here. Noon."

Davey looked up at Saunders.

"Zeke! What've we done?"

Saunders shrugged.

"Arranged a wrestling match, is all. B'ain't no different to the hundred or so others I bin part of."

With that he walked back to the felled tree and began lashing branches together until he had a bundle that he swung up onto his shoulders.

That evening, the shako went around, carried by Tom Miles and John Davey, but the record of contributors was kept by Percy Sedgwicke, who logged the contribution of each man, even though simultaneously thoroughly disapproving of the idea of making wagers. When the £20 was raised, they returned to their messfire and talked tactics, Tom Miles with the first cunning thoughts.

"Whilst you're trainin', we needs to get a look at the man they're putting up. 'Tis important, but how're we goin' to do that? Anyone tryin' to get out of our lines and not in uniform will end up on a charge and anyone wearin' our jacket, with all the green, through theirs, will get theirselves scragged!"

Jed Deakin drew in a deep breath.

"I think I knows how it can be done, but first, I needs to see Bert Bryce."

At the end of the following morning, Bridie and Nelly Nicholls were ready for their mission, but not before Jed Deakin was thoroughly assured of their knowledge of the 88th Connaught Rangers, as he read from the information written out for him by Lacey's Sergeant Clerk, Herbert Bryce.

"Right, now their Colonel is who?"

Both women answered in unison.

"Alexander Wallace!"

"And he's English?"

This time Bridie alone answered, annoyed by the trick question.

"He is not! He's Irish, as much as I am."

Deakin nodded and then continued, again to Bridie's annoyance.

"And he's got black hair."

This time Bridie hit him.

"He has not! 'Tis ginger, like Nellie's there."

Deakin flexed his now painful arm.

"And their Senior Major is?"

"Beatson."

"And he is, what?"

This time in unison.

"English!"

Deakin nodded, satisfied.

"Now, talk to no-one. Just wander about, 'till you finds someone doin' what looks like some kind of preparation for a wrestlin' match."

He allowed that to sink in, but it already had, several times the previous evening.

"An' when you finds him, just ask if he's the lad as will be fightin' in two days time. That's all!"

162

A pause.

"Get a good look, watch for a minute or so, then come back! Come back, no jawin' nor chin waggin' with any old Irish biddy as wants to pass the time of day. Come straight back!"

There was no reply, simply impatient faces.

"Right, off you go! An' keep your scarves close around your heads, like you was shadin' your eyes from this sun."

The two women departed and were soon out of the lines of the 105th and into those of the 88th. All was utterly familiar and similar to what they had just left, the tent lines containing the Followers all going about their domestic chores and their men cleaning and checking their equipment. They wandered around, for some minutes, ten, then twenty, attracting no attention, but seeing nothing that could be in any way connected with wrestling. Then they were approached by a Sergeant, his eyes fixed on Bridie, smiling broadly from a brown face, much decorated by cavalry whiskers. He looked to be mid-forties and his bearing and manner conveyed clearly that he regarded himself, with justification, as being very much 'one for the ladies'. Plainly, he had noticed their apparently aimless perambulations, taking it to be promenading for some social reason.

"Well now ladies, for what reason might you be a walkin' up and down the lines? Perhaps there's someone you're lookin' for? Someone you'd like to meet? Perhaps I'm your man? Or at least one who can help."

Nellie instantly recognised the potential, but it had to be constructed carefully.

"And why, now, should we both be thinkin' that? Is it that you have some special powers around here?"

Whilst listening to Nellie, he had been looking at Bridie, a glint in his eye and a knowing smile on his face. He ignored the question, at least for now.

"Sidney O"Rourke's my name."

More smiling and eye twinkling in Bridie's direction.

"So what might your ladies names be?"

However, Nellie saw no reason to co-operate, at least not yet.

"Sure now, isn't Sidney an odd name for an Irishman?"

He managed to take his eyes off Bridie.

"But wasn't my mother English and her father called Sidney. So I got that from her. But I'm as Irish as you. A true son of Eirann!"

He struck his chest and bowed.

"Now, sure, from goodness, I'd like to know who it is I'm talkin' to."

Nellie made the introductions.

"I'm Nellie and this is Mary."

Total concentration on 'Mary'. He even took her hand.

"Well now, Mary. 'Tis overjoyed that I am to meet you."

As he stared down at her, Nellie developed her scheme.

"Sure, now, you might just be the one to cheer her up, some. Sure, now, haven't I tried."

O'Rourke turned to look at Nellie, so she continued.

"Now wasn't her man taken by the Provo's! An' like to be hanged, for stealin', almost the day that we landed up in this gombeen place. For a few turnips, was he not? And weren't they all a pokin' up through the ground, just askin' to be picked up!"

O'Rourke's face registered the possibilities, suddenly showing thoughtful, rather than merely amorous. Here was a very handsome woman, but a Follower, almost widowed, therefore with no man, in the middle of a foreign campaign. Being single himself, he reasoned, this could work out very well. He looked down at Bridie, his face a picture of concern, still holding her hand.

"Sure, now Mary, 'tis very sorry that I am to hear that."

Bridie had by now realised the Nellie had some scheme afoot, albeit unknown to her as yet. She quickly adopted her part, looking back up at O'Rourke, in as sorrowful, bereft and forlorn a manner as she could manage.

"I thank you for that, Sir. For those very comforting words."

However, then the conversation took a dangerous turn. O'Rourke was a Sergeant and knew much of the Battalion's affairs.

"What was his name?"

Bridie paused, as if summoning the fortitude to speak his name, but her mind was working furiously. She had noticed the red wings on the shoulders of O'Rourke's uniform.

"Connor. Brian Connor."

O'Rourke's brows came together,

"Connor? We've Connors a plenty, but, sure, I can't recall anyone being taken called Connor."

Bridie adopted her best weepie look before replying.

"Sure now, why would you? He was not a Grenadier, like yourself. He was but a line sodjer."

She dreaded the question which could now come, asking for the company number, or even its Captain, but Nellie was intent on moving the scheme forward.

"Now we was just takin' a bit of air, what with the tents getting' so close an' stiflin', an' us now hopin' to see somethin' of this wrestlin' what we hear is afoot. Back home, we never missed a contest, if we could get to it easy, an' some even if we couldn't. Now, wouldn't that be the main reason why we're both out wanderin', like."

Bridie immediately saw into Nellie's scheme and looked invitingly up into the face of the Connaught Grenadier.

"That's right! Always partial to a bout of wrestlin', weren't we both?"

Her best smile poured into the world of Sergeant Sidney O'Rourke. He had not released Bridie's hand.

"Well now, isn't it so that ye're right? There is to be a spot of wrestlin' day after next, Thursday, between one of our lads an' someone out of that bunch of Heathen Protestants next camp over."

More beaming down.

"Perhaps you'd let me escort you there, ladies, to the match that is, when the time comes. Meanwhile........"

He had created a meaningful silence, but it was Nellie who filled it.

"To be escorted there by you would be an honour indeed, Sir. You can take Mary, here, an I'll go with my man, Pat Jameson. Same company as Brian, every good luck to him."

For O'Rourke this was triumph, but Nellie continued.

"But, for us, the trainin' what we saw, back home, that is, was as good as the fight. I used to watch me father, makin' his moves. Now, wasn't he a handy lad in the circle."

The last two words spoke of enough knowledge to convince O'Rourke, and Bridie was still gazing fondly up at him. Time for O'Rourke to build on what had been done so far.

"Well, I can't see the harm in a stroll up into the woods, to take a bit of a look. We keep him up there, away from pryin' eyes, y'see. Sure, a bit of a surprise before the fight always gives any man a bit of an edge."

Both were now bathing him in beaming smiles. He made up his mind.

"No harm, no harm at all. This way, ladies."

He took Bridie's arm and looped it through his, then he lead them uphill, through two lines of tents, all filled with busy members of the Battalion, then over a short stretch of grass, through some scattered trees, and finally into a clearing. There was already an audience, but O'Rourke, being a Sergeant, made space for them. There, in the centre of the clearing and practicing throws with some Grenadiers, was a figure that looked barely human. He was almost as broad as he was tall, a body shaped like a barrel, no change being discernible for waist, chest, nor shoulders. He was practicing a throw whereby, as his opponent came forward, he would drop to the ground, seize his opponent's leg, then, using his great strength, which was vital for such a move, lift him, with his shoulder in the groin, to topple him back and then fall on top. That after jumping as high as his bulk would allow. The unfortunate Grenadier was rendered hors de combat for some time, until hauled to his feet by a trainer and then encouraged.

"Sure, now, Michael, is it all not in a good cause? You'll be right, soon enough."

Bridie gave O'Rourke's arm a tug, whilst speaking loudly.

"We've not seen that before, have we now Nellie?"

Nellie was in no small way intimidated and spoke with a hesitant voice.

"That's the truth there, Mary. No, not anywhere."

O'Rourke saw the opportunity to impress.

"Ah now, that's his speciality. If it doesn't end the fight there, the end soon comes. Few have much fight left in them after a fall like that."

They watched as the Connaught wrestler lumbered around. He was evidently not quick, but not slow either and was stable enough on his immense legs to resist the charge of two Grenadiers, bringing them both to a standstill. They watched for some minutes as the wrestler and his trainers executed a variety of moves, but soon after that Nellie had seen enough.

"We thank you for this, Sergeant, but, much as we'd like to stay, I must be on and away for me good husband's dinner. We thank you once again."

167

With that she turned to go, but O'Rourke still had hold of Bridie's arm and, as he spoke, his voice was laced with hopeful intent.

"Now Mary, you've not got to go, surely."

He waved his free arm in the direction of the training still in progress.

"There's much more still to see and you can be sure I'll see you safe back. Which Company was it now?"

Nellie had the situation well in hand.

"Ah well now, Sidney, she has to come, for the drawing of rations, y'see. Her with four children, one but a babe, that bein' Brian's. An' 'tis my eldest as is carin' for all four, an' that can't go on for much longer. She has not the milk!"

She let the words sink in.

"Will y'not see us back down?"

However, it was Bridie who finally cast them loose, first by extricating her arm and then walking, to be quickly joined by Nellie. O'Rourke had little choice but to follow, but Bridie remained cheerful and encouraging.

"But the contest, Sidney. When shall we find ye? To get there, where it's to be?"

O'Rourke was only just recovering from the shock. Four children! And one a suckling babe. However, this Mary was a most comely woman. Perhaps, yet, even so?

"Same place as we met. That'll be the place. At Noon, day after tomorrow."

There were no more awkward questions as they soon reached the tent lines and Bridie and Nellie turned right, but not before Bridie had made everything sweet and unsuspicious by kissing him on the cheek.

"Noon then, here. God Bless You, Sergeant."

O'Rourke was much encouraged and eager to part on the best of terms.

"God Bless You Both. Has it not been a real pleasure? So, Noon, Thursday. I'll see you both then."

With much smiling and hand waving both left and hurried back through the 88th's camp and, with a final wave back to O'Rourke, they turned between two tents, for appearance sake, then they crossed the ditch and hedge which divided the two Battalions. Wasting no time they hurried back to their tent to find Jed Deakin sat with all comrades around. He looked up as they both hurried in, each more than a little flustered with their close encounter with the Sergeant of the 88th.

"Where have you been? Nigh on two hours nor more."

He allowed them to sit.

"You've been natterin'!"

Bridie took instant umbrage.

"We have not! You wouldn't believe what we had to go through, nor had to say, to get a sight of their man. Didn't we have some Sergeant slaverin' all over us? And, did we not have to kid him along, just to get taken up to where their man was rehearsin' his moves?"

All the while Nellie was nodding furiously.

"That's right. That's the truth of it, an' one wrong word would've got us scragged, an' lucky to come out alive."

Now Bridie was nodding, with even more energy.

"An' sure, was it not us, as've risked our necks to give youse all a better chance with this eejit fight that you've all fixed up?"

There was no argument against that, and so Jed changed the subject to the object of the visit.

"So what did you see?"

Bridie looked at Nellie, as if asking who should start and what to say, so Nellie began.

"He's huge! Not tall, but huge. I've never seen a man his shape. He's like the front end of an ox. No neck and a head like a bucket, turned upside down!"

Bride joined in.

"With no ears! None that you could see. But we saw him lift a Grenadier right off the ground, throw him, then jump on top."

Both were now nodding.

"If he'd told us that he was the Champion of all Ireland, we'd have no cause but to believe him."

Deakin was now more than curious, over a subject of his own.

"Who's this you were taking to?"

Nellie answered.

"This Sergeant that we had to butter up. O'Rourke. But I'll say that he was a decent sort of fellow and expects to escort us both to the fight this Thursday."

Deakin was less than pleased, but it was undeniable that both had found out what they went for and both were back safe, albeit with the full use of feminine wiles and Bridie's handsome looks. He turned to Zeke Saunders.

"What do you think, Zeke?"

"I've heard of such a man. And he is Irish."

His face was thoughtful, as Deakin asked the next question.

"Has he been beaten?"

Saunders shook his head.

"Not that I've heard. I've only heard of how he's won his fights, with a throw just like Bridie here described."

Davey now joined in.

"So you think what? Can you wear him down? He's just come off a ship!"

Saunders nodded.

"That's the hope. Sound's like he has a lot of weight to shift around."

He turned to the two women.

"Did you see him charge at his opponents at all?"

Both women shook their heads, but Nellie answered.

"No, not once. He waited for them to come onto him."

Saunders nodded.

"Not more than one, surely?"

Nellie nodded.

"He held off two. Grenadiers, I'd say, by the size of 'em."

Saunders looked around at his messmates.

"This has to be all science, but I wouldn't like to bet on it, either way."

With that, all went to the parade ground space to work out some moves and tactics, but confidence was not in abundance!

The following day saw an order circulate for equipment inspection and a parade after Noon meal. Saunders, Davey and Miles gave their kit to Byford, Pike and Bailey to check, and so they continued to practice throughout the morning. On parade they all passed the inspection and so the rest of the day was spent on tactics designed to tire the Connaught. At days end came a good meal and then quiet talk by the campfire, before sleep.

Dawn came, with no orders and so, after a simple meal of porridge, Saunders spent the time in his tent, resting or flexing and stretching. At 11.00 Miles came in for some final words and to massage his shoulders and then they left the tent, with Saunders wearing only breeches and his tunic draped around his shoulders. Both joined the throng heading for the site of the contest, seeming to come from all around, not just from the camps of the two contestants. The word had evidently circulated of a match between two prime wrestlers. However, Miles and Saunders were just nearing the ring, its whitewash clear on the grass, when suddenly bugles sounded from all directions and everyone stopped. The call was 'warning for parade'. Many looked at each other, but there could be no doubt. In five minutes would come 'quarter call' and five minutes after that 'fall in'. The sound of the bugle carried the same weight as a direct order from an Officer, so all had no choice but to turn and hurry back the way they had come. To fail to arrive on parade could mean fifty lashes, even being hung for desertion with some Colonels. All thoughts of wrestling contests died with the last notes of the bugle and within two minutes all that remained at the contest ground was downtrodden grass around an incongruous white circle. The Battalion parades were then formed up, throughout each Brigade of Wellesley's army, for all to be told that within the hour they would be marching East, into Spain.

oOo

Carr and Drake were leaning on the parapet of the bridge over the River Elga, the heat in the stone penetrating the cloth of their tunics and the sun hot on their necks beneath warm collars and hot shakos. They were staring North placing Portugal to their left and Spain to their right, therefore, to mark the occasion each was holding a small pewter tankard of red wine, almost as warm as the water in their flasks. On the Spanish side of the pair stood Shakeshaft and Maltby, each with their own tankard. Carr raised his drink for a toast.

"Here's to another dose of Spain. More palatable than the last time, we can only hope!"

His audience did not repeat the toast, but drank instead of the blood hot liquid. However, Shakeshaft made reply.

"I think, Sir, that this time our problems will be somewhat different. At least not caused by the cold."

Carr could only nod in agreement and he made no reply, as all four now made better use of the break from their march, by turning to sit on the parapet until the heat became unbearable, forcing them to return to leaning on it, whilst watching the sluggish and turgid water trickle its way through the many runnels and channels of the winter wide stream bed. Some men of the Light Company came to the riverside to fill their canteens, but Carr sent them back.

"Not from here! You can't trust it. At the next village, I'll commandeer the well and you can fill from there. It'll not be too far."

The men saluted and returned to the shade of the olive trees and scrub that they had been using as shelter, all carefully corking their canteens, because the water contained therein had suddenly become very precious. The notes sounded for 'fall in' and the whole Battalion of the 105th emerged from the undergrowth to fill the road. From the front, the Grenadiers began to march and the following Companies joined on, to march through the lingering dust thrown up by the whole army, both before and after. The cloud remained in the hollows of the road, but thankfully was usually shoed away by the light breeze that wafted over the more open stretches of the light brown strip of dirt that masqueraded as a road.

The village did not come until late afternoon and Carr was as good as his word, finding a well amongst the low white houses and holding it for Gibney and Sedgwicke to perform their organizational scheme and carefully share out the good water. As the evening meal was being cleared away, there came a real surprise, as usual delivered by Bugle Bates. The clear, sharp notes of Post Call! After fifteen minutes all Company Sergeants were making their way back to their Companies, Ellis in the case of the Light Company. When coming to the mess of Deakin and his companions, Ellis threw a letter in the direction of John Davey, this perfunctory act accompanied by no words, as he then progressed on to the next mess ground. Davey looked at the names on the cover, recognizing his own, but also that of Joe Pike.

"'Tis for me an' thee, Joe."

Joe Pike hurried over, soon to be joined by the whole group, including the Followers. Davey looked around at his growing audience, before breaking the seal and opening the paper, which was, surprisingly, of good quality.

He scanned down, speaking aloud any words that he recognised.

"Molly. Mary. Well. Cows. Now. Sold."

Deakin's patience collapsed and he took hold of the letter to find the content beyond him.

"Wer's Byford?"

The answer came from Saunders.

"Sentry go."

By good chance Deakin looked up to see Sedgwicke passing by, having finished his duties at the well and now carrying his own filled bucket.

"Parson!"

The word gained Sedgwicke's attention, and Deakin waved him over.

"Yer."

The simple, almost brutal, summons from one such as Deakin again rankled, but Deakin had always been more than welcoming and helpful, and besides, and perhaps more importantly, Deakin was a Colour Sergeant and he the merest Private. Whatever, his arrival at their fire soon mollified any anguish within the self-esteem of the good Sedgwicke as Nellie thrust a mug of tea and a dough-cake into his hand. He sat down on a box.

"Parson. We got a letter yer from Molly and Mary an' our reader is on sentry."

He handed the letter across and Sedgwicke turned it towards the fire. All around stopped what they were doing and silence fell.

"It was written by Tilly."

Tilly was Molly's first child by a 'husband' before Davey and Sedgwicke had begun her teaching when they were all in barracks together in 1806. Sounds and gestures of great satisfaction came from all around, as Sedgwicke began to read.

"Dear John and Joe. Both Molly and Mary are doing well and we can pay for a Doctor to come and see both from time to time. He is very happy with how they are.

174

The farm is making money for us all and we can add to the small cottage that was on the land when we bought it. Eggs and pigs are best for making money, but we can keep three cows for milk which always gets sold. We are thinking of renting extra land to grow our own feed, probably turnips as they keep through the winter to keep the animals going. Your Mother is well and your sister, but your Mother's leg gives her a bit of pain, but she still works around the animals, particularly the pigs. I go to school each day, paid for by our local Parson, the Reverend Blackmore, who is also the Squire. He is a good kind man. We would like it if you could get a letter back if you can. We hope that this gets to you and you are both alive and well. All the best of our affections to you both, and Uncle Jed and the others. Love to you all, Tilly."

Sedgwicke handed back the letter to Deakin and began the pleasurable business of eating his cake and drinking his tea. Meanwhile, all around came words on two subjects, first, how well the smallholding was doing and, second, what a wonderful letter Tilly had written. As one of their own, they all took great pride in her learning and advancement, Sergeant Henry Nicholls speaking the thoughts of many.

"That girl's a real credit to you, John."

It needed Tom Miles to slightly change the subject, looking at Davey and Pike sat together.

"Them two sprogs of yourn is like enough to be raised as twins, when they'n born, bein' as you both did the business at the same time."

Nellie Nicholls seized her spoon and waved it in front of his face.

"Now that's enough from you, Tom Miles! Such talk! What a married man and his good wife gets up to is no concern of yours. No concern at all!"

Miles immediately took umbrage.

"John an' Molly b'ain't married! Mary an' Joe, but not they two!"

Nellie was deflated somewhat, but soon regained her ground.

"They are according to what we looks upon as married! Didn't he take the rope, back there in Taunton? An' that does well enough for the likes of us, an' that includes you!"

A pause, before she withdrew, being now a little more content at having countered the harsh words of Tom Miles.

"John and Molly is two good people as've started out together and are bringing up a family. God'll not condemn them for that, would he now, Parson?"

Sedgwicke took time to swallow a mouthful in order to gain time. This called for the most careful of diplomacy.

"Well, it has to be said that, for a union between a man and a woman to be recognised as a marriage, the union should be made in a Church before an Ordained Priest."

Tom Miles began to smile, then the expression died on his face.

"On the other hand, I am wholly sure that our kind and forgiving Lord God will not condemn two God Fearing people who come together in a manner of good intent as would any Church wed husband and wife and then raise their children in a God Fearing manner."

He paused, but all were listening.

"Is it not the case that, in the ancient times before the coming of the Church of Our Lord Jesus Christ, many marriages were made and acknowledged in all kinds of different ways and held good till death did them part?"

Nellie was triumphant.

"There, Tom Miles. Pick the bones out of that!"

Tom Miles was far from subdued.

"You can pick out of that whatever you like!"

Jed Deakin smiled and nodded and gave Sedgwicke two hearty slaps on his back.

"Well said, Old Parson. I'd say that was about the truth of it. Now ...."

He looked up and all around.

"We've twenty more miles on the morrow. Make sure you're all up together."

Deakin had spoken and the discussion ended as all eased away from the fire to attend to their kit and with that, Sedgwicke lifted his bucket and went on his own way, but Davey called to him as he left.

"Come next evenin', Parson, if you will, an' we'll get a reply letter started."

Sedgwicke waved his agreement and continued on his way.

Simultaneously, in another part of the camp, two Officers were engaged in their own reading, each with their own letter of huge significance from their own lady. Of the two, Drake finished first, his being from his wife Cecily and he looked up to begin his questioning, but Carr was still thoroughly absorbed with that from his fiancé Jane. Forced by the silence, Drake began reading again, until Carr looked up, and then Drake spoke.

"Any news? Of great import, at all?"

Carr let fall the hand holding the letter, took a deep breath and sighed.

"None as such. With Father away, here with us, she's living in the family home, but Lady Constance is a great support, managing her income from the money invested for her and making good use of what I send back. She mentions your Cecily as a great comfort and support."

He paused.

"But she speaks nothing of our wedding, you know, such as 'looking forward to the time, when we'll be together', that sort of thing."

It was now Drake's turn to sigh.

"And, of course, you put all that in your letters to her!"

The sarcasm in his voice was patent and it showed on Carr's face that the words had some traction, but he said nothing. As far as Drake was concerned, he didn't need to.

"Right! Next letter, you'll fill the thing up with all that sort of stuff. Starting tomorrow night's camp."

He looked quizzically at his good friend.

"You do keep a sort of journal, each day, adding a few lines 'till you've enough for a letter, finished off with highly ornate language about missing her most terribly."

He paused for a reply, but none came.

"You know they love all that sort of daily doings thing, like when the heel came off your shoe and whatnot. That little domestic stuff, besides the big story, that we're marching into Spain to tackle the French once more!"

Carr changed the subject.

"So how's Cecily?"

Drake perked up, considerably.

"Well! Very well. She's settled into our home, employed two servants, a cook and a gardener. And sprucing up the place is coming along very well, just two rooms to go."

He sat up beaming with satisfaction.

"All is very well. The Doctors are very pleased with her."

More beaming.

"I really am the luckiest of men!"

Carr nodded and genuinely smiled.

"You are. Indeed you are."

Then he changed he subject back.

"But, you know, I cannot dislodge the thought that she wants her Father's blessing. He's her one remaining parent, you know."

It was now Drake's turn to nod knowingly.

"You may be right, but I'd say that, if you show enough push behind the affair, then she'll still go through with it. Especially if you can get home, with Father still out here."

He paused.

"He's in disgrace, by the way. His KGL are now under Sherbrook and he's been whizzed back to the Commissariat. Hopefully he'll make a better job of commanding wagon loads of flour and biscuit than he did of troops and cavalry at Oporto."

Carr grinned openly.

"Can't say I have any regrets about that. Ridiculous man! But our food and supplies depending on the likes of him. That's not reassuring."

Another thought occurred.

"Which must leave the twin-like two out on a limb, just a bit. Remember Templemere and Tavender, speaking in grand terms about them being on his Staff. Wonder if they still are?"

Drake grinned.

"Hope not. Neither of those two would know a side of bacon from the side of a barn!"

Both laughed as their servant, Henry Morrison, brought them their supper of cheese and fruit. Soon came the bugle call for 'Lights Out'.

Both voicing concern over supplies proved to be disturbingly prescient, because six dry and dusty days later, the whole army halted at the small town of Plasencia, making camp in the hills and fields all around. In their camp, two miles out, Carr, Drake, Maltby and Shakeshaft were sat awaiting their evening meal, which was eventually ladled out by a very sheepish Morrison. Drake took a spoon, dipped it in and held it up to examine the result.

"Enlighten me, Morrison. What exactly am I required to dine on, this evening?"

Morrison was wholly ill at ease.

"Well Sir, the green is dried beans, the long sort, the white is potato, and the red is them Spanish beans, Sir. The seedlike sort!"

"And the liquid?"

"Water, Sir. With some biscuit stirred in. An' some sage, Sir, there's plenty of that all over."

"Two days ago there was some fish and before that some beef, albeit of the army sort."

"Yes Sir, but supplies have failed, Sir, an' all the dried fish an' beef have all gone off in this heat, Sir."

"Gone off?"

"Yes Sir. Smelled terrible. I even had to throw the bag away. Couldn't put nothin' more in there, Sir. Such as is perishable has to come up and then be ate quick, Sir, and hope for more to arrive. As soon as they opens the barrels for the givin' out, well the clock's tickin', Sir."

Carr interrupted, he had some sympathy for Morrison, who had always preformed at his best for them.

"Eat up, Nat. This is all we have, so this is all there is."

He looked up at their distraught servant.

"Thank you, Morrison. I have no doubt that you have done your best."

Morrison brightened somewhat.

"Thank you, Sir. There is a bit of sage in that, Sir."

"Good man, Morrison. You've done your best."

The same subject, but on a more universal scale, was being discussed in Mackenzie's Divisional Headquarters, this being no more than a different tent shaded by a different tree, but it included Colonel Rufane Donkin, Colonel of the 2/87th Foot and acting Brigadier of Mackenzie's second Brigade and all the latter's Divisional Colonels, including Lacey, and Wallace of the 88th. The meeting had been called to discuss defaulters, of which there were a growing number, but it was Wallace who brought up the subject that concerned the Colonels most and was very much linked to the discipline problems that they were having.

"The men have next to nothing to eat, Sir, and we've precious little to give them. As we speak, mine are eating army biscuit and weak tea. It is no wonder that they are out roaming, looking for whatever, found or stolen."

Mackenzie nodded, exasperation writ large on his face, there was little he could say, other than to shift blame.

"Wellesley's been made promises by the Spanish which have nae more substance, as we now know, as smoke in the wind. The Central Junta promised us food and transport to campaign here and they have provided neither. All gone to Cuesta, our Spanish ally, ah'd guess. What's more, this part of Spain's been picked clean by everyone, both French and Spanish. Go into Plasencia and you'll find no one thing, in fact the Spanish hate their own armies as much as they hate the French! Both steal and sequester, without so much as a brass coin."

He slumped back into the chair, demonstrating a depression of his own.

"Wellesley would never have come, had he known the state of supply. Our bases are too far back for the transport available, money and reserve ammunition are stuck back in Abrantes, with no wheels tae move them anywhere and what's been promised by the Spanish has gone elsewhere."

He looked up and all around.

"We're stuck, lads! Nae moving anywhere, fore nor back, until there's something in our bellies to march on."

Lacey now spoke up.

"We hear that, Sir, but what's to be done? We're not so far off the level of starvation that'll cause the army to fall apart. Without firing a shot!"

"I know Lacey and ye're right. The Provosts are out, but ah've given orders than any men who come back carrying a few rabbits, crows or even fish are nae to be bothered. Farm livestock, now that's a different kettle o' fish. We cannot afford to stir up the locals! That'll get us nae place, they'd not even allow us the hire of a few mules and carts."

Donkin now spoke, him of erect bearing and an immaculate uniform.

"What of the defaulters? Wellesley would normally hang the lot!"

Mackenzie nodded.

"Go easy! Lashes for farm stock, stoppage of rum for crops, but turn a blind eye tae the rest."

He looked around, to then sum up his feelings.

"I've a strong yen that this campaign will be dogged by little food and transport. We'll hit the French when we can, then come back out. No army our size can sustain itself here, but I'll tell ye now, as soon as anything arrives, flour, beans or anything, he's marching on. The promise has been made to link with Cuesta, somewhere by Oropesa and Talavera, and he'll do it. Mark my words."

Thus discouraged, all filed out, to walk back to their respective Battalions. Lacey walked with Donkin, even though they would be together but a short while and they exchanged few words, mostly Donkin questioning Lacey.

"You were in the Coruna campaign, were you not?"

"Yes I was, and that army fell apart for nothing much more than want of food! They were as willing to fight as any army I've been part of, but we lost more to starvation and the weather than we did to the French. Dead from cold and starvation, and loss from desertion!"

Donkin spoke, out of the gloom, before they parted.

"Keep on keeping on, then!"

"What else?"

"Good luck, Lacey."

"You too, Donkin."

The following day was a grim day all round, the army eating whatever could be shot, gathered or fished, but the Rio Jerte, which circled the South of Plasencia was little more than a trickle in the June heat and the almost stagnant pools, which could at least provide eels and small fry, were quickly cleared out by Noon. John Davey and Tom Miles had other ideas, rather than fishing, for both sat throughout the morning using their clasp knives to carve lead bullets into small pieces of shot, then, with enough for a dozen shots each, they set off with their Bakers to try their luck in the woods to the North. They found themselves amongst many others with the same idea, for musketry was ringing out for almost all parts of the wood.

"This place sounds like a right set-to is goin' on all over, John."

Davey nodded his agreement. The sounds from the wood equalled that of a serious skirmish before a major battle, because as many soldiers had entered the trees to try their luck for wildfowl, rabbits or any other edible creature. He looked up at the sky, shading his eyes from the now fierce Midday sun.

"Look, all that commotion is drivin' birds out, but not so many as if they was bein' beaten out for a shoot, clearin' it, sort of thing. There's still plenty birds in they trees an' they takes their leave when the noise eventually gets on their nerves, like!"

He looked again at the trees and the flight of the escaping birds.

"Let's go right. Get the sun at our backs an' see what flies out."

They took their position and Davey was right. All kinds of flying fowl emerged in twos and threes and so, between them, both being excellent shots and with their special ammunition, they bagged well over a dozen. Their shot now used up, they tied their haul together and set off back to camp, with Miles voicing a thought that had been in his subconscious all along.

"Be this poachin'?"

Davey replied, in very philosophical vein.

"Well, 'tis much the same as poachin'. 'Tis someone else's farmed land, or much the same as, but you takes the chance, or you starves. With the last, you'm certain for to die!"

Both grinned and increased their pace, neither concerned, both even content, at the carcasses colliding with each other and swinging into their own bodies as they walked, but it was the far-sighted Davey who ended their cheerful sojourn.

"Horsemen! Comin' this way."

"Provosts?

"No, I'd say not. Can't make out their ludicrous helmets."

Miles changed the subject.

"Where'd you learn a word like that?"

"Too long round Byford!"

Miles laughed, but the horsemen were nearing and Davey could pick out more detail.

"Looks like Officers, with Dragoons up behind."

Davey was proved right as the group came closer. The ploy they adopted for the Provosts the night of the potatoes was adopted again, to simply walk on, as though about ordinary business, only in this case they would need to add a salute. However, as in the case of the Provosts, the tactic was in vain, for the group reined in their horses some five yards in front of them and the pair had no choice but to spring to attention and salute, just after a judgment from Miles.

"Here's trouble!"

The order 'At ease' accompanied by a raising of a riding crop came from the central figure, a man distinguished not in the least by his clothes, these being a bi-corn hat, worn fore and aft, a plain blue frock coat, white breeches much discoloured by dust, and high black leather boots, also dusty. However, the questions came from a full Colonel, who had urged his horse slightly forward.

"And what have you there, men?"

It was Davey, as Chosen Man, who answered.

"Rooks and crows and some kind of game bird, Sir."

The last said whilst pointing to a plump bird with striking red legs, which Davey knew full well to be a red-legged partridge, which he could identify at 100 yards distance, but ignorance seemed the safest course. The Officer folded his arms on the pommel of his horse and leaned forward.

"That's a partridge."

Davey nodded.

"As you say, Sir."

"Whose is it?"

Davey put on his most querulous face

"Whose, Sir? Can't say, Sir. I've no idea who owns this land, if anyone. Sir. 'Tall looks a bit barren an' unfarmed to me. Sir. More wasteland, like."

"If someone owns it, then you are poaching!"

Davey took a deep breath.

"Well, Sir, seein' as we brought these down whilst they was flyin' through the air, then 'tis hard to say who they belongs to. Again, if anyone. Sir."

Another Officer, with even more gold-braid, then spoke.

"So, you brought them down with your muskets?"

"Sir."

"Having cut up the ball into birdshot."

This was stated as a fact, to which Davey gave no reply.

"Destroying King George's property! If I dug into one of those birds I'd not find a complete ball. Would I?"

However, now, mercifully the central figure intervened.

"Let it go, Stapleford. You too, De Lancey."

This frock coated Officer, just spoken, looked down upon the pair, not unkindly, but with no warmth.

"I'll give you a guinea for a brace of those partridge."

With this, Miles could keep silent no longer, but he knew perfectly the words to use.

"Beg pardon, Sir, but right now, here, any food has be much more important to us than any coin. Our mess nor Followers b'ain't had no decent meal in days. Sir."

However, Davey knew that they were caught and what the charge could be and so he was already loosening the tie on two of his birds, but Miles words had thoroughly incensed the first Officer who had questioned them.

"You impudent scoundrel! Don't you know I can have you flogged for this, even hanged!"

The frock coated Officer again intervened.

"De Lancey! Enough. I'll call this honest foraging, such as keeps us all going, even at the cost of a few cartridges."

By now Davey was walking forward, holding out the two birds and the Officer took them, tested them for plumpness, then passed them back to what must be a servant until now fully at the rear. He then felt into his pocket for the guinea, which he handed to Davey, who took two steps back and saluted. Again the acknowledgement came via a nod of his head and a wave of the riding crop, then all spurred their horses forward, leaving the pair richer in coin, but poorer in provender. Davey looked at Miles.

"Who'd you think that was?"

Miles turned his head to look back at the receding group.

"Well, I can't see no reason to say that that weren't Nosey hisself."

Davey's eyes widened.

"You mean Wellesley?"

Miles nodded

"I do. Remember when they 'ad us on parade on the quayside at Lisbon after Vimeiro, when he took ship for back 'ome. 'Tis the same, I'd swear."

Davey now laughed.

"And you told him that our food was more important to us than his coin!"

Miles scowled

"Yes. They all knows how scarce food is, but they comes ridin' up, still, an' happily uses their money and King's Regs to get what's the only thing as is keepin' us this side of Death's Door. I'd 've took a floggin' to get that in."

Davey chuckled.

"Right. Well. We'd best get these back, afore another parcel of Officers rides up and demands their share."

They both hurried forward and were soon back at their tents, where the birds were pounced on by Bridie and Nellie to be plucked and boned and for every piece of edible flesh and innards to by tossed into the pot. Soon the story was all around the Battalion that Tom Miles had told "Nosey" that everyone was starving and that take some birds took fairly, off men as was so hungry was wholly against natural law!

oOo

Chapter Four

Over the Alberche

The four who had, some days back, stood on the bridge over the Spanish border river, the Elga, now found themselves leaning on another parapet looking down at the clear flowing waters of another river. Drake now addressed the Senior Officer present

"And what river is this?"

Carr did not turn his head but instead rejoiced in the cooling sight of the waters below.

"This is the Tietar."

Now he did raise his head to look right.

"And that sorry collection of hovels, over there, is called Bazagona."

All four looked over to see a collection of tiled roofs, the number of which could be counted on the fingers of both hands. Drake passed judgment.

"Nothing to be had here!"

"No indeed!"

"Then why did he come forward?"

Carr turned towards him, leaned his forearm on the hot stone and pointed down to the flowing stream.

"Well, not being privileged to be amongst those consulted by our noble Commander, I can only pass on what I have heard. Water! All are, or rather were, running low."

He then pointed to the horizon of the hills to their right.

"And to keep faith with our Spanish allies. Somewhere over there….."

He swept his arm round in a short arc.

"…….. are about 25,000 under Cuesta, which our 20,000 odd are about to join."

He removed his forearm, now too hot.

"To meet Victor's army, which rumour has it could be pushing 50,000!"

The impact of that fact on the faces of his companions immediately became apparent and he nodded.

"Yes! There's going to be a battle. A big one. And not too far into the future. He, Cuesta, is now in touch with the French advanced guard, so we are told."

At this, Shakeshaft made a stern face and turned to place both hands on the parapet, ignoring the heat, at least for now.

"Well. Let them come, I say. Let them come. We smashed them at Vimeiro and Coruna and their performance at Oporto was the sorriest shambles I've ever heard of. Let them come. Whatever the odds."

All smiled and Drake slapped him on his shoulder.

"Well said, Richard. We'll face up to them. Whatever."

Carr, meanwhile, bit back what would have spoiled the moment, this being that, properly led, the same French troops had stormed all across Europe, and were probably burning for revenge, but he contented himself by changing the subject.

"Come on, let's see what Morrison's cooked up. Now with fresh water. I sure it'll be better than army biscuit porridge, which we've been dining on for the last three days."

Maltby now spoke up.

"Yes. You know I'm sure I saw him coming back with rabbits, just as we left."

Drake looked at him.

"Rabbits! Then perhaps a bottle or two would be appropriate. Claret, would you not say, should go well with such rich meat as that."

All laughed at the absurdity of such an impossibility being available and Shakeshaft pointed to the river again.

"I'll settle for clean, fresh water."

The four walked on, much contented.

Such a mood was universal throughout the army. Although food remained scarce, all could now wash and bathe below the bridge, and gather fresh water above it. A canvas screen was set up for the women Followers and another for the few Officers' wives who were present. Rocks were thrown at Tom Miles when some felt that he was in danger of swimming too near the enclosure of the former. The day's rest and clean hose and underwear made all the difference for the march the following day, which saw the whole army march into Oropesa. However, here the mood ended. The British were met with sullen looks from people already half starved. The British were greeted with doors being slammed and backs turned. The men of the 105th, halfway down the column, set their heads further down into their collars and picked up the step, urged on by Gibney.

"Up straight, now boys. Show 'em oose come! British army, never been beat."

Arms perhaps swung a little higher, but soon it was clear why the population were so resentful of their presence. Cuesta's Spanish army had arrived some days earlier and had practically stripped the place bare, right down to window frames and floorboards. In fact, it was Cuesta's men who provided the only significant audience for the British arrival and they lined the main streets as Wellesley's men marched in and through. At the sight of the watching Spanish standing and sitting idle at the roadside, backs did then straighten and arms swing a little higher.

Wisely, the cantonments allocated kept the two armies apart, the Spanish to the North and West, the British to the South and East, but there were inevitably some points where they were near neighbours, and at one point there was a well, neither wholly Spanish nor wholly British. However, in the minds of the Spanish battalion beside it, there was a de facto boundary at that point, which placed the well within their camp. Their British neighbours were the 105th and the first to be repulsed were Nellie and Bridie. Such was not easily done and the resultant shouting and screaming brought Heaviside to the well. His Spanish was limited, but enough to impose himself on a Spanish NCO with simple words.

"Official. A qui!"

The NCO resentfully scuttled off, leaving Heaviside, accompanied by Nellie, Bridie and a few others facing up to a rank of Spanish soldiery, whose uniform sported a large and prominent III on either collar. He turned to Nellie.

"Is there no other well?"

"No, your honour. Sure there is not. Even the river down over is almost dry."

Heaviside nodded.

"Can the rush grow up without mire? Can the iris grow without water? Job 8, verse 11"

"Sure now, your honour, isn't that the truth of it?"

A Spanish Officer duly arrived, mercifully with a reasonable command of English. His rank was uncertain, but Heaviside began in the correct formal manner and at full attention he saluted.

"Captain Joshua Heaviside. 105th Foot."

The Spanish Officer responded, if with a somewhat haughty manner.

"Capitan Don Manuel de Portago. Tercer Regimiento de Infantería Sevilla."

Heaviside nodded his acknowledgment, then came immediately to the point.

"Our people need to use that well, if you'd be so kind. We have no water."

The Spanish Officer flexed his hand on the hilt of his sword and shifted his stance.

"Is our well."

Heaviside came straight back, forcefully.

"No such thing. We all need water, if we are to fight the French. No water, no fight!"

More shifting and flexing.

"The well is not much water."

Heaviside pushed forward, picking up a stone. He was unopposed as he marched through to drop the stone into the well to then hear a loud and succulent splash. He then looked at the Spanish Officer, who had trailed in his wake.

"Much water. Mucho agua!"

He motioned the two women forward, who by now were escorted by the likes of Sergeants Obediah Hill and Henry Nicholls, Ezekiel Saunders, Nat Solomon and George Tucker, neither of these last pair being lightweights. Now intimidated, the Spanish gave way and Bridie lowered the well's bucket to draw up and provide the fill for her own, then Nellie did the same, before turning to Heaviside.

"The Lord's blessing on you Sir, for the Good you did just now."

"The Lord's Blessing upon you also, Mrs Nicholls. With joy you will draw water from the wells of salvation. Isaiah 12, verse 3."

He then turned to Hill and Nicholls.

"Keep guard. Stop no-one, but let no-one be prevented. Come, everyone who thirsts, come to the waters. Isaiah 55, verse 1."

Hill came to the full attention and circled a blistering salute, as much for the impression it would create with the Spanish audience as to convey his respects to Heaviside, considerable as they were.

"Sir."

Trouble between the two armies occurred elsewhere, also in a market set up by the locals, but prices were exorbitant. On the following day, with the dying of the light, Mackenzie called a meeting of his Colonels in his tent, for two reasons, or possibly three; to enjoy a halfway decent meal, to convey Wellesley and Cuesta's plans and to drink some whisky. Mackenzie began with the latter and three glasses later they sat down to what appeared to be dried fish, potatoes and some beans, but the food was overshadowed by what their Divisional Commander had to tell them.

"Victor's over the Alberche, the river to the far side of Talavera with some units occupying the town. Cuesta's in touch and, as we speak, he's riding off, or more like being held vertical on his horse, he's so decrepit, so that he can take a look at some of his Spanish who have just arrived to boost his strength. Riding off to them, from just now inspecting Campbell's Guards Brigade and Fane's Dragoons."

Mackenzie took a mouthful of fish and needed to spend time extracting a bone, but none of his audience felt inclined to fill the silence, he plainly had more to say.

"We're all on half rations. Nothing's arrived for us, bar some new boots, breeches, shirts and underwear. Why they did not fill those wagons with food and nothing else escapes me, but there it is. We're going forward on the morrow, the Spanish using the main road, us using the paths in the hills above. Expect to move soon after daybreak."

Now his audience did contribute, in the form of Wallace of the 88th.

"So where is Victor now, Sir? I mean, do we know any more, beyond that some of his are in Talavera. Is he fully over the Alberche, Sir, or just some units?"

"Mostly still on the far side, so latest reports say, but his cavalry are well up to us. Expect some action somewhere, 'though unlikely to include the likes of us."

He then scanned the faces of all his Colonels.

"Are you men up to the mark? Tomorrow's the 22nd, we could be in action on the 23rd. What ah can say, is that Wellesley information on the doings and whereabouts of the French is superb. It seems Spanish ruffians, guerrillas they call themselves, are forever in and out of his Headquarters. So we'll not be surprised, more like us surprising Johnny, which is why ah say we could be fighting on the 23rd. Only time will tell."

By now all had finished their meagre meal, but Mackenzie was not yet done.

"Afore ye go!"

The whiskey bottle again made its appearance on the table and, by the time the seven Commanders of his Division had left him, after at least two more measures, the night was full dark.

The notes of Reveille had barely died away before Lacey ordered full inspection. Breakfast would have to wait, short and paltry as it was. In the Light Company Miles barely had time to flex some movement into his new boots before Ellis was about his person checking all that should be checked and more besides, including pulling at the straps of the French pack Miles was using. However, Miles bore it stoically, he could not expect Ellis to treat him any differently than any other member of One Section and he did not.

After their hurried meal, the 105th were paraded along their side of the main road, whilst the Spanish marched onto it. The British had to wait for their Allies to clear the town, for now the Spanish were to the South, the British to the North. In the centre of the 105th ranks, with the Colour Party, Deakin turned to look at his companion stood behind, Toby Halfway.

"Remember they Spanish we saw march into Salamancee back last November time? Sorry looking and diseased crew they was. At least these looks a shade better."

"Better perhaps, but many of these looks not much more'n boys."

Deakin nodded. This was a fact he had noted for himself and more besides. He had, many times, seen men walking to their execution and many of the Spanish soldiers now passing by him had much the same dejected bearing and downcast eyes.

With the last of the Spanish now gone, Mackenzie's Division took the lead, with Donkin's Brigade first. The reason being that his contained five Companies of the 60th Rifles, who were soon out as a skirmish line, in their green uniforms almost invisible as they trudged forward behind the 14th and 16th Light Dragoon cavalry screen of Cotton's

Brigade. This included Templemere and Tavender and both were out on the left, higher than most, as they followed the hill tracks Eastwards. More than once they were thoroughly discomfited to see horsemen emerging from the trees both above and before, but each time they quickly recognised these as mounted guerrillas making their way on to Wellesley with reports. One even called out to them, "Batalla mucho antes. Inglés. Sí?" From whom these intimidating figures received their orders, the two knew not, but on one occasion they saw a group emerge from the trees with a prominent figure in the centre wearing what looked like a cut down monk's robe, in a distinctive light fawn. It was this figure who, from the high vantage point he had chosen, studied the two formations, one British, the other Spanish. After mere minutes the group turned their horses and were gone, off in the direction of Talavera.

For the infantry, behind and below, the march along the winding tracks and over dusty fields was one of the worse since Oporto. The wind from the South-East picked up the dust from the marching feet, including whatever else was loose and carried it, on hot gusts, across the line of the British advance. There were few who did not voice their envy or frustration at the Spanish on the good trunk road whilst they slogged past every turn and obstacle, the dust as fine as flour that penetrated all gaps in boots and clothing. Soon all were coated brown-red down their right side. The Followers, trailing along through the now disturbed and churned up dirt suffered the worst, but Sedgwicke again grew in the affections of all, suggesting that the children walk in the lee of his wagon, to best be sheltered from the blown mire. However, this was a march to a battlefield, either this day or the next or the next, but it would be soon, and this thought crowded in often enough for all to forget the heat and the dust and thus to think often on the possible events of the morrow.

The morning wore on towards Noon with the sun still climbing and bright in the sky, when the unmistakable sounds of conflict came from the direction of their Spanish allies, but far ahead. Soon it became general and even included artillery. Templemere looked at Tavender, the more experienced of the two.

"Do you think it's starting?"

Tavender shook his head.

"No. We're feeling each other out. Not much more than saying hello. But we can say goodbye to taking them by surprise."

That evening, taking shelter in what was no more than a stand of trees, the Officers of Cotton's Brigade were sharing their meagre food and passing around the bottles of rough red wine, when August Shaumann, the Commisary of the 14th Light Dragoons, rode in and, after passing his horse to a servant, took a seat on a log. Then, after taking a long pull from a bottle handed to him, pronounced on the days proceedings.

"Not good!"

He drank again from the bottle, pulling a face at the rough edge of he wine, but his audience had gathered. All were silent, wishing to know what justified such a pronouncement.

"I followed our Spanish Allies as they moved forward into today's fighting. All I can say is, that if you have them on your flank, count it as open. About 15,000 infantry and 3,000 of their cavalry couldn't push out 3,000 Frog Dragoons, who stood them up for four hours. It was only when Anson's Lights showed up that Johnny did the right-about and shot off for Talavera. Then, and this is worse, Stewart put himself at the head of their noble 3,000 horse and could not get them to charge two small columns of no more than 500 foot combined. They didn't close far enough to even discharge their pistols. Several times Stewart tried, riding in the van himself, all to no avail, any fire from the French sent our Dons on another turn-about, but that didn't stop the cowardly bastards murdering a few French wounded, left on the road from our artillery.

"Not good, boys. Not good at all."

His depressing judgment ended when a servant handed him some food. From then on silence reigned as the hungry man wolfed down the meal, the ingredients of which could well have come from the feedbag of his horse. Templemere and Tavender opened another bottle, each, and drank heavily from such. Confidence was not of the highest, but then Shaumann gave one final opinion.

"Whatever it is, boys, rumour is we've got them outnumbered if you put us and the Spanish together. So give yourselves a lift from that."

Unknown to Cotton's cavalry, despite the growing dark, the British infantry were still moving forward, Mackenzie riding beside Lacey and O'Hare, the latter two on foot, with all three moving purposefully along the Madrid highway through Talavera. The Spanish army was now camped for the night down the side roads, but, judging by the sound of music and celebration, there was little sleeping. However, Lacey and O'Hare had ears only for what Mackenzie was saying.

"Victor's now entirely back over the Alberche, every man on his side. We're 55,000 whilst he can be little more than 20,000, or so our Spanish irregulars tell us. As we speak, Wellesley's trying to persuade Cuesta tae attack at dawn afore Victors reinforcements come up. The Alberche has the main road bridge over it and can be forded in several places. We could beat them piecemeal, first him, before his supports arrive, then his supports after. So, take your men on and stop at the river and man the bank. It's about two miles beyond the town. The 24th will be on your right, holding from you down tae where the river goes into the Tagus. The 45th will be in reserve. Don't worry about noise on your left. That'll be Donkin moving up alongside you, upstream of the bridge, beside the river like yourselves."

The whisky flask was passed down and, on its return, Mackenzie spoke his final words to them.

"If Cuesta can be persuaded tae join us, we attack at dawn. We go over and form again on the far side as we were. The Spanish will come over and be on our right, tae cross by the bridge and the fords alongside. Out of the mist."

Lacey laughed.

"What mist is that, Sir?"

"Spanish mist!"

"Not Scotch!"

"Would that it were!"

With that he turned his horse and was gone into the gloom, this pierced only by a few lanterns from the surrounding houses on the outskirts of Talavera. Lacey turned to O'Hare.

"Get Carr up here and a few Lights who can find their way about in the dark"

Within fifteen minutes Carr was up to his Colonel with half of Maltby's One Section.

"You need me, Sir?"

"Yes. Double on ahead with these and get over the river. We will be on this side with the 24th on our right below us, closer to the Tagus. It could be that we will be attacking at dawn. The men sleep in position, but I want pickets on the far bank and someway beyond. Don't use the bridge, find the fords and use them. That may be useful knowledge."

If there was weariness or even dismay in Carr's reply, Lacey did not hear it. Whatever, within the hour, Miles, Davey and Pike, with Sergeant Ellis in command of the half section, were waist deep in the Alberche until finally splashing up the far bank. Ellis motioned all forward until they could hear nothing of the moving waters, nor the soldiers moving into position on the far bank. He motioned all to kneel and listen. There was nothing, bar the sound of the wind through the rye grass, nor any light ahead, such as a significant campfire. Satisfied, Ellis gave his orders to his 12 files of three; each man on watch for two hours, asleep for four. That done he returned to Davey, where he took the time to eat what he had in his haversack, in the surly company of Miles, while Pike kept first watch. Unsurprisingly, Miles, once his food was consumed, did not join in with any social pleasantries, but rolled himself in his blanket and fell immediately asleep, but not before a usual comment.

"Wer's they bloody Rifles? Shouldn't they be doin' this sort of job?"

Dawn came and with it came Lieutenant Maltby, calling them back over the river. On the far side they saw their whole Battalion drawn up in line, with the 24th to their right. To their left, beyond the bridge, Donkin's two Irish Regiments the 87th and the 88th were drawn up in equal readiness. His Brigade's Riflemen were now over the river and remained there, as the Lights of the 105th passed through and then waded the river to take their place on the left of the 105th line. There they stood and waited whilst the sun climbed higher and hotter. Lacey walked, strode, stormed and fumed up and down his line, replying to the frequent question, "Can we cook something, Sir?" with the same answer, "We daren't. We may be sent forward any minute." However, with each minute that passed this seemed more and more remote. He could see the bridge that carried the Madrid trunk road over the Alberche and its emptiness spoke of Spanish tardiness at least, if not outright refusal. Nothing could be seen of any Spanish force at all, not even using a study through a telescope back to Talavera, but his 105th were under Wellesley's orders.

In the end Lacey relented. His men were already in a state of hunger from the last week's marching and now they were famished with no breakfast, apart from what was in their haversacks, which had been very little for all the past weeks. He turned to O'Hare.

"Where are our Followers?"

"A good mile back, Sir. They didn't cross the Portina, that little brook that runs into Talavera down from the North."

Lacey nodded, his face grim.

"Ride back. See what you can get up here, if only water and biscuit."

Within minutes O'Hare was back amongst the Followers and immediately sought out Nellie Nicholls, who was busy at her cooking pot, with Bridie alongside.

"Mrs Nicholls! If you can, we need to get something up to the men. They're about a mile up and a bit more. I'd be obliged if you could pass the word and gather anyone who can carry water or biscuit up to them. Meet at the Commissary, which is where I am going now."

Nellie looked up, nodding her head, whilst still holding her spoon.

"Sure, we can do that, Major O'Hare, your Honour, but I'll go and see Parson as well. Sure, in his little cart he'll be able to take up a good portion. Water, mostly, I'm thinkin', plus a bit of whatever."

O'Hare smiled and nodded himself at the good sense and so, within the hour, water, biscuit and salt was arriving at the 105th line. For her men, which included Deakin, Davey, Pike and Miles, besides her husband, she had a portion of the bean stew she had been cooking. Such a gesture brought acknowledgment from Tom Miles, now dried out from his soaking, even though it was doled out with the usual challenging look from Nellie.

"This is a well thing, Mrs. Nicholls. We're all much obliged."

The usual look of animosity for Tom Miles died on her face, instead turning to one of great satisfaction as she looked around to see her men gratefully eating. The other battalions were being serviced in much the same way and, on the return journey; Nellie, Bridie and Sedgwicke were passed by Wellesley and his Staff, all going up to the line. On their arrival, Mackenzie broke off from the group to visit his Colonels, Lacey being the first.

"Cuesta won't move. He's changed his mind. The

Reek says the bridge will nae carry his artillery and, on top, 'tis Sunday. Wars don't happen on a Sunday, in his Spain."

He saw the astonishment grow on Lacey's face.

"Ah know, ah know! Say nothing, what can be said? Ah'm onto my other men, but Wellesley wants ye here, still. Nae withdrawal. Victor's still near, so Wellesley's going tae try again, tae go forward with this Don, late afternoon. Ah'll get rations sent up, such as ah can find, so at least ye can cook a halfway decent meal if ye have to stay the night. But nae cooking 'till ah say so."

He gave a fierce nod of his head.

"Rheet, ah'm awa!"

He wheeled his horse around to leave Lacey in a state of bewilderment, but he did not dwell long in his confused state. He was pleasantly distracted by his Sergeant Clerk, Bert Bryce, him carrying a mug of tea and a lump of bread, with something in between that looked as though it once had scales.

An hour passed, then two. The men of the 105th were allowed to sit and many were cooling their feet in the river, when, Carravoy, being on the right and having a better view of the road from the side, looked over to see what could only be described as a small pageant approaching, from the direction of Talavera. Red uniforms were outnumbered four to one, by the gorgeous blue and gold of many Spanish Staff. Carravoy turned to his two Lieutenants, D'Villiers and Ameshurst.

"Now what do you think that portends?"

The two shook their heads as the cavalcade came to the bridge, when Ameshurst passed the only comment that could be made.

"Staff conference! High level discussions of strategy."

One figure in the lead was evidently Wellesley, whilst another was probably Cuesta just visible amongst a group of Spanish Dragoons holding him upright on his horse. The group stopped at the bridge and the Dragoons drew back, leaving Wellesley and Cuesta alone. The former made many gestures in the direction across the river, whilst Cuesta remained motionless. After some minutes, the Dragoons came forward, carefully turned Cuesta's horse, and then escorted him back. Red uniforms broke off from the group, one being worn by Mackenzie. He merely slowed his horse to a trot as he passed by Lacey.

"Cook your meal, Lacey, when rations arrive. We're nae movin' today. His Honour says there's too many Johnnies over yonder, though none of us could see nary a one!"

Lacey shouted after him.

"But Sir! Do we stay?"

Mackenzie turned in his saddle.

"Oh aye. Ye sleep here."

Lacey looked at Carr, who had been stood listening.

"So, let's see what tomorrow brings."

What the morrow brought was the whole Spanish army marching over the bridge, out to meet the French, followed by a very long train of carts, wagons, mules, Followers and herds of sheep, pigs and cattle. There was not one soldier of the British army who could not see the cavalcade tailing the Spaniards and did not look angrily and enviously at the evident full extent of their army's supplies. It was Mackenzie again who provided the answers, concerned to keep his Colonels well informed, but this time all grouped together back in a peasant's hovel, where at least there was shade and with benches for seating and an opportunity for glasses of whisky.

"Victor's gone! Pulled back thirty miles, and so, our valourous Don, ardour now much rekindled, is marching after him."

The bottle again circulated.

"Relations are at a new low. Wellesley's refusing to cross the Alberche unless he's given transport and supplies and, as ah'm sure ye saw, Cuesta's got the lot!"

Then he paused.

"But it's worse. Reports are that three French Corps are marching on Salamanca, from the North. That's about 60 miles North of Plasenia, our road back to Portugal. So, with Victor's two and those three, things are getting tight. Expect a battle, aye, but then a quick back out, win or lose. We could find ourselves in the middle of 100,000 men, so he's more concerned to keep us intact, than crash into the Johnnies. He'll fight defensive."

He began pouring again.

"It's Wellesley's opinion, an' ah think he's dead right, that Victor, when he knows that 'tis only the Dons as're chasin' him, will turn on Cuesta."

All had a glass at least half charged and so Mackenzie raised his.

"So, tomorrow we cross the Alberche, us an' Sherbrook's, to cover the Don's certain withdrawal. We're to go five miles over."

He lifted his glass further.

"Slange! An' guid luck to us all!"

oOo

Miles and Davey, standing amongst the Light Company on the left of the 105th line, were nearest the road, kerchiefs over their mouths and noses to resist the stifling dust thrown up by the progress of a whole Spanish army, plus two squadrons of King's German Legion Hussars, sent, or so Carr and others concluded, to help cover the Spanish withdrawal. However, for Miles and Davey the passing of soldiery carried but little interest. Their attention was centered on the memory of the herds of animals, which had accompanied the Spanish advance forward. Two hours passed before came the livestock, when Miles looked around for Spanish Officers, but none could be seen, such as they saw no need to share the choking dust. The 105th stood their place as rearguard, there to see the Spanish safely back over the Alberche, now five miles behind them. In his hand, Miles had a musket cartridge with a small length of fuse,

203

this filched from their Divisional artillery lines. Davey had the pan of his musket full of powder, Bailey was alongside with a fully loaded musket. Pike wanted nothing to do with what was about to happen.

When the sheep came, Davey sparked the powder which Miles used to light the fuse of the cartridge, which was then tossed in amongst the sheep. The explosion caused them to scatter in all directions and Bailey shot one as it passed, for Davey to immediately bring his musket down onto the leg of the carcass, breaking it with a loud crack. By now sheep were all over the British lines and it took some time for them to be re-gathered, but one herder soon spotted the bloodstained carcass and ran over, to stand pointing at the remains of one of his herd.

"Muderers! Has matado a uno de mis ovejas!"

Saunders could not help but grin.

"Must have been his favourite! Give him the button, Tom."

A silver button, a large one, cut from the uniform of the Officer that Miles had downed in Oporto, had been readied for just such an eventuality and Miles immediately held up the button, by its sewing ring, inches before the face of the herder. His eyes moved inwards towards each other as he focused and then took the button between grubby thumb and forefinger. Large, yellow teeth bit into it, to leave a mark in the soft silver. With its value now established, the button was thrust into a pocket and the man left, with not even a backward glance at the 'murderers of one of his sheep'.

With the last of the Spanish baggage train now past, the 105th were formed up on the road, but within the ranks of the Light Company, at the rear, was the carcass of the sheep suspended on a pole. Drake was incensed and pushed into the ranks to confront Saunders and Tucker who were shouldering the pole.

"What the Hell is this, Saunders?"

However it was Miles who answered.

"Back a while, Sir, somethin' worried the sheep as was with the Spanish, an' they was all over, Sir, in a panic, like. This 'un broke his leg, an' we 'ad to shoot'n, Sir. They Spanish herders just left'n, Sir. Too anxious to get away from the Johnnies followin' up!"

For emphasis, Saunders reached forwards and flexed the broken leg back and forth.

"Couldn't leave'n for the French, Sir!"

Drake was silenced. To leave the carcass behind was absurd, but villainy had taken place, of that he was sure, but he had no option.

"Right. Bring it along. But something's not right."

No-one spoke as Drake left the ranks and the 105th marched off, to undertake the five miles back to the Alberche and there they saw the whole Spanish army camped along its banks, on the near side, exposed to the oncoming French. They had made a full camp with tents all erected; therefore they evidently had no intention of crossing to the safe side before nightfall. Lacey was appalled and halted his men on the road, and soon Sykes, Colonel of the 24th rode up to join him.

"What do you think, Lacey? It's not just our two and the 45th, but the whole of Sherbrook's, behind us, who are still on this side."

Lacey nodded in agreement, then he shook his head, consternation now write large on his face.

"We can afford to wait awhile. For orders! Mackenzie cannot be far."

He looked from Sykes to the Spanish army, now well established around their campfires and busy cooking their rations. He shook his head.

"This is appalling!"

Just then came rescue. Mackenzie did come riding up accompanied by Sherbrook. Both reigned in and dismounted. There were no introductions as Mackenzie came straight to the point.

"Wellesley thinks these will have crossed by now.

Ah've just sent a messenger to tell him otherwise."

He turned to Sherbrook.

"Ah've agreed with Sherbrook, here, that we all should cross and he should then march on to Talavera. We, and that includes Donkin with his Rifles, will hold a line on the far bank here. We'll deny the bridge, at least, and cover the Spanish coming over, when that happens."

Just then came another rider, but from the direction of Talavera. He rode straight up to Mackenzie and Sherbrook. He was evidently an Aide-de-Camp of Wellesley's

"Sirs, I have order from the General."

He handed down a piece of paper, with a seal, which Mackenzie quickly broke to read out loud the single line.

"First and Third Divisions to remain East of the Alberche to act as cover of the Spanish withdrawal to Talavera, which will take place at daybreak tomorrow."

Mackenzie lowered the letter.

"How does he know that's goin' tae happen? Cuesta's here, not in Talavera! The Old Jock cannae move no more than one mile at a time. Who's spoken to him? But East of this damn cessditch!"

Mackenzie looked at Sherbrook, who seemed to have made up his mind.

"I'll put mine across the road, between the Spanish and any oncoming French. When they're all across, I'll use the bridge."

He paused for breath.

"Yours, Mackenzie, I suggest you deploy to the North, for the same purpose and use the fords up at Cazalas, when the Dons are all safely over."

He let out a long breath, resignedly.

"We've had our orders."

Mackenzie nodded and mounted his horse, to then look down at Lacey.

"Go upstream. I'll see Dunford and get him to

follow with his 45th. Then Donkin. Take up a position to cover Cazalas and the fords."

Salutes were exchanged, then both Divisional Generals mounted and rode off. Sykes left them to return to his 24th and Lacey swung his men off the road to march North and along the edge of the Spanish camp. His men looked over at the carefree scene as they passed, cheery campfires heating large cooking pots, all the men around sat at their ease. The 105th marched on, to be passed by O'Hare, sent forward to establish the Northern limit of their line. He passed the Light Company and could not fail to notice the sheep being carried in their ranks. He reigned in.

"Where'd that come from, now?"

The reply came from someone unseen.

"It died, Sir. Takin' it for a decent burial."

"Not of old age, I'll warrant!"

With that he spurred his horse on and soon he had established the end of his line and waited for the whole Battalion to arrive, which happened within the hour and soon cooking fires were burning. Soon Lacey rode up to him, whilst his men further established some form of camp, but still remaining in line.

"Get the men to check those fords. Are they practical?"

O'Hare grinned.

"No need, Sir. All the firewood you see burning now came from the other side, those olive groves and cork trees. It's all pretty dense over there. Better wood than this scrubby stuff on our side."

Lacey looked over, then pulled out his telescope to focus it at a point over the river.

"There's some building in the woods or beyond. I can see a sort of pinnacle, but no more."

He lowered the telescope.

"Do we have a map, of any kind?"

O'Hare shook his head.

"Not that I've seen."

Lacey returned his telescope to its place on his saddle, then dismounted for an Orderly to lead his horse away. He stood for a while, plainly concerned, looking around, but their own camp items were arriving and soon he sank gratefully into the collapsible chain provided by Bryce and another soon arrived for O'Hare. Next came a mug of tea for each, but Lacey had taken but one sip, before returning to the subject which most concerned him.

"This is dire! Where are the French? They can outmarch us, never mind the Spanish. They could be out there amongst all that scrub and bushes!"

Then a hurried thought.

"Are our pickets out?"

O'Hare nodded.

"Number Two Company. I considered that our Lights had done their share when we first came up."

However, Lacey was not satisfied.

"Get them further out, then I want a screen between them and our line. Carravoy's Grenadiers can do that. Add on Number Four."

"I'll see to it."

"Drink your tea first. Catch your breath."

They sat in silence, until there came another horseman, a Captain, whom they recognised as part of Mackenzie's Staff, but there was no note.

"Sir. Tomorrow, when all the Spanish are over, you are to cross and hold the Casa de Salinas, Sir, following the 45th and 24th. They go over first, then the 24th will be on your right, the 45th in reserve. Colonel Donkin's Brigade will be on your left, holding the wood to the North of the Casa."

Lacey looked up at him.

"This Casa de Salinas. It's where?"

The Captain rose in his stirrups.

"You can just see its roof, Sir. From here. It's about three-quarters of a mile back from the river."

Lacey nodded. He now knew what he had been

looking at through his telescope.

"For how long do we hold there?"

"That I do not know, Sir."

"How do we know that the Spanish will cross?"

"General Wellesley's with General Cuesta now, Sir, we believe trying to persuade him to do so. General Mackenzie is assuming that they will. If not, we hold here, Sir. Until they do."

Lacey nodded.

"Thank you, Captain. That's understood."

The messenger was about to leave when he halted and turned in his saddle.

"Oh yes, Sir. One more thing. General Mackenzie says to burn those huts to the North. They were built by the French when they occupied this ground some days back. Why leave them to be re-occupied, he considers?"

Lacey nodded.

"Tell the General it will be done."

The Captain saluted and rode off. O'Hare finished his tea and then left to send out a very peeved Carravoy and his Grenadiers, accompanied by Number Four Line Company, to form a screen inside the pickets, which he sent further out. Thus, an anxious night was spent by all, guarding the Spanish army, which had sent out no pickets of their own. However, perhaps the night was somewhat more tolerable for some members of the Light Company and their friends in the Colour Guard, chewing on roast mutton.

Dawn came and the Spanish camp began to slowly break up. Lacey met with O'Hare and Carr.

"Plainly the meeting between Wellesley and Cuesta has been fruitful. Wonder what he needed to say to get the old so-in-so to move?"

Carr shook his head.

"Impossible to say, Sir. But they are moving, albeit at Spanish pace."

Lacey looked at O'Hare.

"What's today?"

O'Hare shook his head, so Lacey turned to Bryce, his Sergeant Clerk.

"Bryce! What's today?"

The reply came back from inside their tent.

"Wednesday, Sir. 27th."

Lacey nodded.

"Not that it matters. Right. Carravoy can fire those huts. After the 24th and 45th, we cross in Company order, Two up to Nine, then the Grenadiers last. O'Hare, you go over first, lead Two up to the Casa and mark out our line, Two furthest and leaving enough room for the Grenadiers between the end of Nine and the Casa. Lights fill in around the Casa when they arrive. Carr, you to remain till last and see Drake's Lights across. Donkin should already be holding those woods above us by the time you come in. Johnny can't be far off, so........."

Lacey looked at the Spanish camp. The only change had been the disappearance of the Officer's tents.

"Christ Almighty!"

O'Hare crossed himself.

"Apologies, Padraigh, but have they no sense of urgency at all?"

"I think we can assume that they move at the same speed as their General, Sir."

"Yes, like cold treacle! Now, Carr! Get the Lights out and Number Two in. Get Carravoy to burn the huts."

The staccato nature of Lacey's speech told of his anxiety at the danger he knew they were in. The three went in different directions, Carr off to where the Light Company were. He did not fail to notice bones and a sheep's fleece scattered on the ground. He stopped near Ellis, who had also noticed.

"Seems a good meal was taken here last night."

"Yes Sir. Seems there was. One of the Spanish sheep had a bad accident, Sir."

"Did he fall or was he pushed?"

"Can't say, Sir."

"So, yes, seeing as they're well fed and rested, get them out on picket. Number Two are coming in. Soon, I hope, we will cross, but only after the 24th and 45th and them only after the Spanish. I'll leave you to inform Captain Drake."

"Yes Sir."

Carr acknowledged the salute and walked off, out to where he could see Carravoy and D'Villiers sitting in their own collapsible chairs, taking some food. His approach caused them to rise, it evidently meant developments of some sort.

"Charles! Royston. Good morning. I hope you got some sleep."

The grim and hangdog look that he was treated to by Carravoy gave him his answer, but he continued, in what he hoped was the same cheerful tone.

"Well, once over, I think we can get some rest and perhaps something to eat, and on the Talavera side of the river. Meanwhile, yours are to fire those huts over there, no point leaving them for the French, then get over the river. Line Companies will be crossing first, then you, then the Lights, but all after the others in our Brigade and the Spanish, of course."

They all looked back to the river.

"Who seem at last to be moving, but meanwhile we stand in readiness. So, get your men going to begin the burning, I'll stay with the Lights."

Carravoy was in no good mood.

"My men have just begun eating. What should I do?"

"Give them five minutes. Even with our Lights out there, this scrub could hide an army, and a French one is on its way."

Carr looked directly at Carravoy.

"Five minutes, Charles, then things must happen. You get yourselves ready to move. Once over, you follow the Line Companies up to some building called the Casa de

Salinas, where Drake's will be holding the building itself, you immediately to his right, between him and Nine. Major O'Hare's in charge."

He took and released a deep breath.

"It's just under a mile beyond the river. I'll feel much better when we're all over. And soon, I hope."

Carravoy had only been half listening, relying on D'Villiers.

"What's that village on the other side and someway up?"

"Cazalas. But don't go near it, too far from the fords. Just get yourselves ready!"

With that he walked off, leaving the two to finish their coffee and a bread roll, and Carravoy to mumble, "Damn jumped up!", but from a standing position, for Binns had heard all and was gathering up their few camp items including the chairs. Carravoy, looked at the huts in the distance, but spoke to D'Villiers.

"What's the time?"

D'Villier's dragged out his modern, yet ornate, watch.

"A little before seven."

Carravoy looked back to the river.

"Are the Dons moving? I do believe they are."

His evidence were some dark blue columns marching in the direction of the bridge, but others, in white and light blue still seemed to be taking their ease. D'Villiers looked over.

"Some, yes. But expect all only within two hours, at best."

Carravoy nodded, then thought.

"Where's the wind blowing?"

D'Villiers, not too well versed in such rustic skills, took a look at the trees over the river and gave his best estimation.

"Our way."

"Right. Leave the hut firing until the last. What's

the point in hanging around here, chewing on smoke. Tell off Ridgway, for the job. He fires, then follows us, clear?"

"Absolutely Charles!"

"Very good. Now, form ours up, ready to cross."

There were many intervening consultations of D'Villiers' watch before the last reading showed 10.30 and the last of the white Spanish uniforms entered the fords. Then came the 45th and 24th, showing much more urgency and they were quickly through the ford. D'Villiers looked over to Sergeant Ridgway, stood waiting with 20 men.

"Off you go, Sergeant. Then follow us over."

All of the Grenadiers were in the water, when the smoke of the burning huts began to blow across the fords and the woods, but Carravoy took no notice, him being carried over by one of his men, one of the largest, even amongst Grenadiers. However, this lasted but a few yards, for Mackenzie was on the far bank and highly incensed.

"Get off, Sir. Off. What your men endure, so should you. Off, ah say."

However, the Grenadier plodded on, until Mackenzie spoke directly to him.

"Let go, laddie. Release your Officer. This instant."

It was done, but carefully, giving Carravoy the chance to find his feet, albeit under three feet of water, but he remained in touch with his soldier, lest the unseen large and slippery stones forming the riverbed should prove too treacherous. Carravoy had not long emptied his boots before the Light Company came splashing across, the men filing either side of his rather humourous figure sat on a patch of grass, feet bare and him wringing out his less than white hose. Last to cross was Carr, acknowledging the salute of Sergeant Obediah Hill, commanding the pickets at the ford.

"Keep a good watch, Sergeant. They could be anywhere in that scrub."

"Yes Sir. But I don't like this smoke, Sir."

It was blowing thickly downriver from the burning huts, sometimes obscuring even the far bank of the river.

"I agree Sergeant. But, can't be helped. Orders from on high to set fire to an old French camp. Hold here. When we're positioned and ready, I'll send back your Relief."

"Sir."

Carr padded up the wet bank and noticed Carravoy.

"Are you all right, Charles? Need any help?"

The answer was Carravoy standing up, then reaching out for Carr's left shoulder to steady himself whilst he pulled on his second boot. Carr had tucked his footwear into his belt and so now he availed himself of help of the same type from Carravoy, as he pulled on both boots.

"Right! Properly shod. Time to get on with the war!"

They walked on together, following the Light Company.

"You know where your position is?"

Carravoy's fragile temper almost broke at such a question.

"Of course! Wasn't it you that told me?"

"Yes Charles, indeed, it's just that I assume you have not been in these woods. They're I bit 'as of England', if you take my meaning. Denser than Spanish."

He drew a deep breath, giving enough time to change the subject.

"Donkin's Brigade should already be over, in the woods above this Casa place. Best I check, I think, when we get there, to establish their state, as it were. They will hold our left in any action, if Johnny comes over sooner rather than later."

He looked at Carravoy, hoping for some comradely word or even expression, but none came, merely a curt nod of his head.

"I'd best get up to my Grenadiers."

Carr watched him increase his pace to overtake the Light Company. Soon they came to the Casa to find it a tall ruin, but with an intact tower significantly higher than the crumbling walls. Now within sight of it, he turned right to explore the woodland. Soon, he came upon the 87th of Donkin's Brigade and what he saw set off alarms in his head, because the 87th were at camp, cooking, sleeping or just sitting and lounging. What was in many ways worse, was the fact that all the men had divested themselves of their equipment, with their muskets piled together in stacks of five or six. He hurried through their lines and the first soldier of any status that he came to was a Colour Sergeant, who immediately sprang to attention on being approached by this unknown Officer. Carr wasted no time.

"Where is your nearest Officer?"

The Colour Sergeant turned and pointed.

"There, Sir. Stood with his back to us. Captain Bryant."

Carr hurried away to tap Bryant on the shoulder. He immediately turned around, saw that he was dealing with a Major and came to attention. Carr spoke first.

"Morning. Carr, 105th Foot."

The Captain saluted.

"Bryant, Sir. 87th."

Carr looked around to confirm his anxiety, before speaking

"I must get back to my own men, but, please query this with your Colonel. We know, when perhaps you do not, that the French could be right up to us. So, is this wise, for your men to be in such a state of unreadiness? You are like us, you cannot see much further beyond your front than fifty yards, through this wood! And your pickets are up on the river bank itself, close to half a mile away."

Bryant looked back towards the river, but inevitably it could not be seen. Then he looked at the men around, all in a state such as described by Carr.

"I'll pass it on, Sir. I suspect that you may be right."

"Very good. That is my strongest advice."

Carr returned Bryant's salute, then hurried away. It required mere minutes before the haggard walls of the Casa de Salinas emerged from the trees and there he found the

Light Company, these also at the beginnings of taking their ease and lighting fires. The first Officer of any description he found was Ellis.

"Sergeant!"

Ellis sprung to attention and saluted.

"Allow the men to take food, such as they have, but they remain equipped and formed up with muskets loaded. We are the front line. Our pickets are out, but unseen, back at the river."

"Sir."

Carr made to walk off, to pass on his order further on, but Ellis had more to say.

"Beg pardon Sir! Something you should know, Sir."

Carr turned and pulled his eyebrows together as Ellis continued.

"General Wellesley, Sir. He's up above, in tower of the Casa here. Lookin' for the French. Sir."

Carr's eyebrows came even further together, before hurrying off to the far side of the building. There in the courtyard he found three riderless horses, in the custody of six Dragoons. The thought came hurrying in, "If Johnny arrives now, with Donkin's half asleep and Nosey at the top of a long staircase, there could be the Devil to pay!"

It was at that exact moment that there came a crash of musketry from the direction of Donkin's men and the sound, to Carr's experienced ears, was definitely the shriller bark of French Charleville muskets, then came the uproar of shouts and screams. He raced out of the courtyard and back to the Light Company, where he found men already scrambling to their feet and forming a line, muskets at "Order Arms."

"Stand to! Stand to! Face left. Fix bayonets."

Face left was not a good order, for at that moment his own pickets came running back directly at their front, with French Voltiguers practically alongside them, Hill and others fighting for their lives fending off blows as they ran. The Voltiguers must have waded over even below the ford to advance unseen and surprise Hill and his men. Carr drew his sword and felt, more than saw, men from the Light Company beside and behind, he heard Ellis yelling, then he was in the midst of frantic combat. A Voltiguer came at him with his bayonet levelled at his throat. Carr took the bayonet on the join between his blade and the bell-guard which gave him all the leverage he needed to push the bayonet aside, and his sword in the best position to send a back-handed swipe into the neck of the French soldier, who fell clutching a spouting jugular, but more French were coming and, what was worse, formed up French infantry, following their own Light troops. Carr could only hope, so he drew a deep breath.

"Make ready!"

A pause.

"Present!"

Some bayonets came down alongside him.

"Fire!"

A volley, of sorts, crashed out either side of him, but it was hopeless, there were too many French, all steady and in proper formation. The best contribution of the volley had been to fill the area with smoke. Then the thought occurred, 'what is happening on the far side of the Casa? If the French are there, then they are all cut off and will soon be prisoners.'

"Fall back! Fall back!"

His men paced backwards, bayonets still menacing the advancing French. One Frenchman came out of the smoke to encounter Saunders, who brushed aside the bayonet, before sending the butt of his musket up and into the man's chin. Then they heard "Tire!" and a French volley whistled amongst them, fortunately a little high, but many of Carr's men grunted and screamed as the French balls found their mark. Many were down, prone and making no move, whilst others writhed in agony and some, less wounded, dragged themselves back or were dragged back by their comrades. Some more 105th arrived and fired into the smoke but the effect could not even be described as temporary, for the smoke was thinning and the French were coming on, in numbers and in full line formation.

There was no option but to continue back and quickly. The 105th had been surprised and broken, and so also, Carr suspected, had the 87th and 88th. Then the situation became even worse when Carr looked into the courtyard at the rear. Their Commander had not yet emerged, it was clear, for the riderless horses still remained with the Dragoons, but, some 30 yards beyond to the far wall, French Voltiguers were pouring through the far gate.

"Ellis! Saunders! Hill! Anyone! To me!"

Carr led a collection of men through the gate and indicated the line he wanted, with his sword. To his great relief, at that moment, Wellesley came hurtling out of the back door, with his Staff and his three-foot telescope bobbing alarmingly on the back of an Orderly. Within seconds all were in the saddle, but the French were using them as a target and a Dragoon slumped forward, to be held momentarily in the saddle by his comrades, but to no avail. He slipped sideways and slumped to the cobblestones. Carr's line was no obstacle to the riders and they galloped through as Carr gave his orders to fire. The thin volley downed some French and halted their forward momentum, but they had no time to congratulate themselves. Instead, they could only to run back out of the gate where they found the main French assault line, mere yards from enveloping the Casa on all sides. They ran at their best speed, through a line of Grenadiers, commanded by Ameshurst, who sent a volley into the oncoming French, but then he inevitably turned his men back to also join the headlong retreat.

Relief came some 100 yards further back in the form of the 45th, steady as a wall, muskets loaded and stood at the 'make ready'. Needing to push through the two deep line did not cause any break in their speed, but once through, Carr saw O'Hare, Lacey, and even Wellesley himself, with Heaviside and the other Captains, doing their best to rally the retreating men. Carr immediately joined in.

"Halt! Form up! Form up! Two deep. Support the 45th."

Yet many still continued to run, many of his own Regiment and many with the facings of the 88th and 87th, confirming Carr's suspicions that Donkin's Brigade had also been broken. Carr screamed at the top of his lungs.

"Stand, you bastards, stand! Form on the 45th!"

Some halted, some continued on, but the 105th were now in a firing line, albeit much shortened, mixed Companies and all disheveled and breathless. However, as Carr yelled, pulled and prodded, the half-Company volleys of the 45th began to ring out, the non-stop crash of muskets telling their story, which was that the advancing French were being met with the usual devastating firepower of a British firing line. The 45th took not one backward step and the French attack had been halted, but not withdrawn, nor silent. The French had brought some artillery across the river and soon cannonballs began to plough up the dry earth. The line of the 105th was now growing apace and so Wellesley rode off to rally the 87th and 88th, now each forming a ragged shape, but at least an expanding one.

The word was now spreading down the line of the 105th, 'Form Fours'. This was quickly done from their firing line and they marched off, at the pace of 'quick time'. Carr stood and watched the column pass by and the faces of the men told its own story of the past minutes, a near panic that had lasted not even beyond half an hour. There was shock on the face of many, these still breathing hard from the sudden terror. Many were bloodied, from their own wounds or from those of their wounded companions; of which there were many, some limping, some nursing upper body wounds and some being supported, even carried, by their comrades. It was a sad sight, defeat writ large, but the continuing French artillery fire hurried them along. At last it fell silent as they emerged out of range and Lacey called a halt and spoke to all Officers within earshot, knowing that it would be passed along.

"Re-form Companies."

The Captains of each took their positions and their men soon joined them for the column to reform as Companies and continue their retreat. Off to their left was the re-assuring sight of the steady columns of the 45th and the 24th, whilst to their right and equally re-assuring, were of the two Battalions of Donkin's with his Rifle Companies spread behind as a rearguard. With them were two squadrons of Cotton's cavalry, which included a squadron of the 16th Light Dragoons, which included Captains Tavender and Templemere. Both eased their horses across to come within earshot of the 87th, now reformed but supporting many wounded. Tavender called across to an 87th Captain.

"What happened?"

"We were taken by surprise. He got over the river, unbeknown to us and came at us through the woods. We were making camp."

Tavender's interest grew.

"Where were the 105th?"

"On our right. They were surprised, too, and broke as well."

The Captain took a drink from his flask.

"And I'll tell you another thing. They nearly got The General. He was up the tower of that big house and just got away, before the Frogs took the place."

"Who was holding the house?"

"The 105th. Their Lights, of that I'm sure. They came alongside us as we pulled back."

Tavender wheeled his horse away, saying no more to the Captain, but much more to Templemere.

"105th Lights nearly allowed Wellesley to be captured. I bet Carr was there."

Tavender allowed that to sink in.

"I feel that this, may have some potential!"

The 105th slogged on, over the hot, dry, plain,

watching the town of Talavera grow in detail, but not quickly enough. Wellesley was long gone, but Mackenzie rode up with his Staff, having seen his other two Colonels.

"Bad business, Lacey!"

Lacey nodded wearily. The hectic rout had taken its toll on him.

"We were surprised, Sir."

Mackenzie continued.

"How many have ye lost?"

"Too early to tell, Sir, but I'd gauge 40 or 50. We have many wounded."

Mackenzie looked down the column.

"Aye, ah can see that."

He looked again, then addressed Lacey further.

"Ah'm leavin' Dunn here to guide ye to our Division's position. 'Tis beyond the Portina, up a ways from a funny little hump they call the Pajar. Ye cannae miss it and Dunn'll see you to ye're place. Ye're behind Cameron's, up from Campbell's Guards, and in reserve, ye'll be relieved to know. So, when ye've passed the Guards, ye're aboot there. Anyway, Dunn'll show ye."

He turned his horse and gave his parting words.

"Expect a battle on the morrow, Lacey. Expect it. An' it'll be a big one!"

Their paths parted as Mackenzie moved on. The sun remained bright and hot, the flat plain shimmering as the heat rose from the honey coloured grass and stubble and, almost unbelievably, birds rose and fell, looking for food. All in the columns suffered in the stifling heat but it soon became clear where the Allied line was, because running North from Talavera was a wooden palisade of obviously huge strength, solid tree-trunks which even artillery would struggle to penetrate, and it gave few openings for hostile musket-fire. The whole ran for a mile at shoulder height beginning at the North wall of Talavera and ending at the slight rise which Mackenzie had called the Pajar with its farm atop. Lacey turned to Dunn whilst pointing in the direction of the formidable construction.

"That is for whom?"

Dunn studied it himself and then looked down at the walking Colonel.

"It's for the Spanish, Sir. General Wellesley had it built yesterday and finished today. The Spanish are behind it now."

"As we speak?"

"Yes Sir. There now."

"General Wellesley feels more confident in the Spanish if they have something such as that to defend. Sir."

"And for us?"

"I'm afraid the open plain, Sir, mostly, but our line terminates at a hill called the Medellin. That's a good defensive position."

"But not for us!"

"No Sir. General Hill is there."

Lacey nodded, resignedly.

"Right. Lead on."

oOo

Bridie and Nellie turned from their laundry at the sound of the commotion. One of the Followers was running back into their camp, waving an empty basket, the contents of which had fallen out but a minute before when she heard the news herself.

"The men! They've been broken! Up ahead."

Both women dropped their washing into their buckets and joined the rapidly gathering group of women, all yelling questions at their new arrival, but she could only blurt out what she knew and not in the order of the questions.

"Broken up by the river! Prisoners. Dead. I don't know. A Cavalryman told me. All our Regiments up there guarding the river have been broken."

Bridie lifted her pinafore to her mouth and began

sobbing with deep breaths, now with growing panic.

"My Patrick! He's just a boy. With a drum. And Jed!"

She fully broke down and fell to her knees. Nellie sucked in a deep breath. Her Henry was in the centre, with the Colour Company, where there was always fighting. She fought back her own tears of worry, before kneeling beside Bridie, who was kneeling in the dust in the middle of a growing group of Followers all milling around hoping for extra information.

"Now, Bridie. These things always sound worse than they are. Ye're not to despair. There's always hope. Lots of it."

She lifted her friend up and they both clung together, but Nellie could now see Chaplain's Assistant Sedgwicke approaching. He too had heard of some kind of disaster and then Nellie released Bridie.

"Parson! Have ye heard?"

Sedgwicke nodded, but Nellie had a plan.

"Parson! Do you think you could go up and see what you can find out? Nobody knows a thing."

Sedgwicke nodded and began to fully button his tunic.

"I'll go now."

Then a sudden thought, spoken out loud.

"I'd better go fully equipped."

However, before he could move Bridie had seized his arm.

"Patrick! My Patrick. He's with the Drummerboys."

Sedgwicke needed no more explanation. He ran back to his small cart and spent many frustrating minutes donning the full equipment of a line soldier. Much burdened, his slight frame hurried on, in the direction 'forward', to soon come up against the Spanish defensive palisade and find that there was no easy way over. He looked at the grinning Spanish soldiers, amused at his confusion, but Sedgwicke was unperturbed and his Spanish was by now perfectly adequate for the task.

"El inglés, que forma?

Several pointed and one spoke.

"Esa ruta."

Sedgwicke started North and, after a march of many minutes, came to the Pajar. There he saw his first Redcoats and he approached the nearest Officer, him with numeral XL on his crossbelts. Sedgwicke came to "order arms" and saluted.

"Beg pardon, Sir. But I am trying to find the 105th, Sir. Part of General Mackenzie's Division."

Sedgwicke paused while the Officer studied him.

"I was hoping that you could help, Sir. Their Followers have just heard that they have been broken, Sir, the 105th, and this has caused a great deal of distress. I'm trying find out what has happened, Sir, at least to enable me to pass on a more accurate picture, Sir."

The lucidity of Sedgwicke's speech came as a surprise to the Officer and it made him sympathetic. This was evidently an educated man on a kindly mission and he should, in all humanity, be helped.

"Well, soldier. All I can say is that Mackenzie's just marched across our front. I have to say that they carried many wounded. They will have been positioned somewhere beyond us, further North, where Mackenzie's are. That's the best I can say."

Sedgwicke took a step back and saluted.

"Thank you, Sir. I'm very grateful for your help."

Sedgwicke carried on through the lines of Redcoats. Every 50 yards he asked, "105th?", but each request received a shake of the head, until the question gained the response, "Over there." Sedgwicke instantly recognised the lurid green of their facings and ran over to their lines to then run along it to find the man whom he knew could tell the most. He found him, sat on the ground, adding fuel to a fire.

"Sergeant Deakin!"

Deakin looked up to see a fully equipped and

breathless Parson now standing over him.

"Parson! Why be so far up?"

Sedgwicke took a deep breath.

"The women have just heard about what happened up at the river. They've been told that you were broken and now there are wild rumours of huge casualties and many prisoners and wounded. What can I tell them?"

Deakin stood and placed his hand on Sedgwicke's left shoulder.

"'Tis good of you Parson, to come up and find out for 'em. There's no other way they'll get to know, an' that's certain."

He released a breath.

"We'n all well, here. Me, Toby an' Henry."

He allowed that to sink in before continuing.

"As for the Lights. Well, they passed me by a while back and asked after me an' Tobe. I asked after them and they said all are well, part from cuts and bruises. One 'as a slight bayonet hole, one called Tucker, and him I don't know."

He allowed that to be absorbed.

"Go back an' tell 'em all that we'n all up here, an' making camp. So a bit of grub, if they has any, would be more than welcome. I surely can't see the Colonel stoppin' the women from comin' up. We are in reserve, so I'm told."

Sedgwicke grinned and lifted his musket from the ground.

"Best I return, then."

"That's so, Parson. Be certain that we'n all grateful."

But he did not remove his hand.

"Now, Bridie'll be anxious over Patrick."

He paused.

"Of him I don't know, but they'n just behind us a piece."

He pointed back, releasing Sedgwicke's shoulder.

"Thereabouts."

Sedgwicke turned and walked through the traffic of passing soldiers. The sight of drums painted with a generous contribution of 105th green told him that he had arrived and there he picked out the largest Drummerboy.

"Patrick Mulcahey."

Amazingly the reply came in French.

"Ah oui. Il est mon ami. Mais il est blessé."

Sedgwicke wiped the shock from his face at being replied to in French.

"Où est-il?"

"La!"

The Drummerboy pointed to a group sat around a fire. He went over.

"I am looking for Patrick Mulcahey."

A ring of bandage turned upwards to reveal a grinning face. Blood had seeped through to the outside layer that circled the top of his head.

"Your Mother is worried about you. You've been hit. How bad?"

The grinning continued. To his mind he was a wounded hero.

"Not bad tell her. Not bad. But I'm hungry. That's for sure."

With that, Sedgwicke turned and hurried back through the British lines, hurrying as much as the many pounds of equipment would allow. On his return he was pounced on and questioned from all sides, but, above the din, he shouted the best general answer he could give.

"It's my opinion that you can go to your men. They are in reserve by the first stand of trees you come to. Up left."

This removed at least two-thirds of the crowd who left immediately, leaving Nellie and Bridie amongst the remainder, their anxious faces beseeching more information.

"Jed and Henry are unhurt, but Patrick seems to have a slight wound."

With those words, Bridie nearly swooned again, but both caught her.

"It's not bad. Not bad at all. He say's he's hungry."

With that Nellie took charge.

"I'll stay, now I know my Henry's all right. Parson, you take Bridie back up there now. I'll stay and come up with the pots of food when 'tis ready."

The day was dying, but not quite yet the conflict. As the Followers of the 105th were running up, with those of Mackenzie's other Regiments, cannon-fire began from the hill opposite the British occupied Medellin, but nothing came their way. All hurried on, to either find their men or discover the worse. Their arrival was seen by Carr and O'Hare, who, at that moment were studying the French artillery line, but they immediately returned to their telescopes.

"Does that hill have a name?"

O'Hare replied instantly.

"The Cascajal."

However, it was then that the Followers were around them, which immediately changed the subject. Carr looked around at the anxious faces, but his worry came from military concerns, not from sympathy.

"Will the Colonel allow this?"

O'Hare nodded.

"I'm sure, yes. Let it go, we are in reserve. By now they'll have heard about what happened up at the Alberche. They'll want to know and it'll surely be a cruelty not to let them find out."

They resumed studying the Cascajal, obviously ringed with a huge French battery. British guns were ineffectually replying from the Medellin, but their fire only added to the din, not reducing that of the French. Nellie looked up at the sound, but then returned to stirring both pots, hers and Bridie's. However, what came next caused equal consternation to all, these being Nellie, Carr, O'Hare and every soldier and Officer in the British army. From the

Spanish line there crashed out a huge volley, seemingly every man in the Spanish Army firing their muskets together, but then what happened to Nellie went beyond mere curiousity, for within minutes of the sky splitting sound, she was deluged by running Spanish soldiers. The first, merely ran past, but the next, perhaps not quite so panicked and running through the British camp, took the time to study what was around and their eyes lighted on Nellie's two cooking pots, both full. One Spanish soldier seized the handle but then quickly released it, for it was so hot from the fire, but others were taking whatever could be picked up, blankets, haversacks, whatever was portable. The Spanish soldier, still at the pot, was on the point of dipping in his hand, when he was practically laid out by a blow from Nellie using the heavy iron ladle that she used for sharing portions. Then, with this medieval weapon, and the almost as heavy stirring spoon, she defended her patch, swinging either implement at any that came close enough to threaten, accompanied by one of two phrases; "Filthy, thieving, Spanish tripehounds!" or "You cowardly Spanish gobshites!"

Within minutes all had passed, but much was missing from her camp and she set about restoring order to what remained, albeit much scattered. However, during the remaining hour of the day, the fugitives returned, having been rounded up by their Officers, but all within her view were treated to a look that would have frozen molten rock and a threatening gesture from the ladle. At the sound of the volley and the commotion, Bridie, much to Patrick's relief, broke off from the finer adjustments of his bandage and, with Deakin and Halfway, they hurried all back to the camp. They took charge of the cooking pots, which needed to be taken up to the lines, but Nellie would not leave, still needing to vent her anger on any Spaniard within earshot. Miles also, on returning to their camp when their turn came, vowed dire revenge.

"Them Don bastards can expect no charity nor

228

square deal from me! Not after this. Not never!"

It was Mackenzie, inevitably, who brought the story to the 105th, speaking to Lacey as he rode by.

"Nae good, Lacey. Some French Dragoons rode within sight, in sight mind ye, that's all, nae near at all, and fired their pistols. The whole Don army loosed off their muskets and ran. Ah dinnae ken it at all, and like it even less."

Wellesley's army was still assembling at about 8 o' clock and two KGL Brigades marched between the 105th and those at their front; the 2/83rd of Cameron's Brigade of Sherbrook's Division. Lacey, recognising the KGL facings of royal-blue, dredged up the German from his past to exchange greetings as they marched on, all evidently very tired, on towards the valley between the Medellin and the Cascajal. Then Mackenzie returned, with orders from Wellesley.

"I know ye're in reserve Lacey, but Himself wants a skirmish line out there on picket. What with us an' Johnny bein' so close. So, get some men out to support the 83rd, at your front. They're already there."

Lacey went himself to find Heaviside, who sent out a Section, half the Colour Company's strength, but then not trusting merely what he had been told, as a precaution, he sent out Carr to check that all was well and in place.

Carr walked forward in the fast fading light of the late July evening, and found Captain Heaviside out amongst his men, dispensing rum and morale boosting Bible quotes. Even in the growing gloom, each quickly recognised the other as Carr approached

"Joshua."

"Henry."

Each had the deepest respect for the other and had served together as Captains, especially during the difficult assault at Rolica, and so the two, out of comradeship and shared past danger, could seen no reason to make any change in how they addressed each other, even after Carr's promotion. The thought never occurred to either.

"All well?"

"All's well."

At that moment a flame sparked up, in the gloom somewhere between the lines. Evidently, some trading was taking place between the pickets, almost certainly involving brandy and tobacco.

Carr chuckled.

"Nothing new here."

"No. The first law of picketing."

But it was Carr who finished off.

"Leave well enough alone!"

Both laughed.

"Have you had any sleep?"

"Not much!"

"Well I have, so get some rest. I have a feeling that tomorrow will be as bad a day as any we've ever been through."

"I doubt many will sleep tonight, even if the French allow it. A little sleep, a little slumber, a little folding of the hands to rest. Proverbs 6, verse 10."

"Amen to that, Joshua."

Heaviside walked back to leave Carr alone in the rapidly enveloping dusk, but he stood in nothing like night-time silence, instead hearing the rumbling of yet more French artillery being moved into position opposite his picket line and in the distance behind, the chilling sound of their own Battalion Surgeon, Charles Pearce, administering crude medical help to the wounded of that day. Visually there was also a distraction, just under a mile up from where Carr stood, this from the Cascajal, from where French howitzers fired their shells into the night, their fuses fizzing in a long white arc across the darkening sky, to land amongst the British lines. In the distance was another kind of light, that of burning wheat fields, the smoke drifting towards him, sometimes but a smell to his nostrils, sometimes chokingly thick. The French horse-artillery continued their leisurely pounding of the British line opposite for several more minutes, but then suddenly, perhaps mercifully, it stopped. Carr estimated the time to be ten o' clock.

oOo

Chapter Five

The Plains of Talavera.

Historians have argued over the official beginning to the Battle of Talavera on 28th July 1809, but for Carr it began well before midnight of the previous day, although he was but minimally engaged. After the 10.00pm cessation of French artillery, and with but the merest of light remaining to guide any footsteps and himself out amongst the pickets, Carr was certain that he heard an extra sound, that of thousands of marching feet. Faint on the wind, in the distance and up at the Cascajal, but it was unmistakable and never-ending. He looked around to find the soldier he wanted, and saw merely a shape, but it was the unmistakable bulk of Sergeant Henry Nicholls of the Third Company.

"Sergeant!"

"Sir."

"Alert the men. Keep them on their toes. Something's happening, starting up North."

As a shock to both, Nicholl's reply was drowned by several blasts of musketry, in ragged volleys, but obviously between the two hills to the North. The sounds of combat died down but did not end completely, such that, within minutes, he could see the flame of musket fire moving right to left, all between the two hills. If the fight was moving that way, then the French were advancing in a night attack which others could also plainly see and, in response, shouts and orders echoed through the darkness, as, all along the British line, the Battalions 'stood to'.

"Nicholls! Are you still there?"

"Sir."

"How many 83rd are still out here?"

"Plenty, Sir."

"Right. Tell our men, face their front, but close in to me."

"Sir."

Nicholls ran off and Carr turned, to now see a sight which caused him the deepest anxiety, that the flame of combat was now ascending the Medellin and then it reached the summit, this discerned by its silhouette in the last of the Western sunset. Evidently, the French were on, and may even have won, the key to the British position. At the same time came the sound of another clash, only this being nearer, perhaps only half a mile further North up the Portina, but Carr's mind and sight were fixed on the Medellin, where the flash of musketry could still be seen, continuous but disordered. However, what was worse for Carr was the arrival of an Officer of the 83rd, calling in his pickets. As they closed up to their Officer, Carr ran over to him. There were no introductions and Carr asked his question, anxiety giving pace to his words.

"What's happened? What do you know?"

The reply was spoken with equal rapidity as the 83rd pickets arrived and formed up around their Officer.

"I know very little. We've been pulled out of the line to get onto the Medellin. Seems the Frogs have attacked with two columns and broken the Germans. One is now on the Medellin, but the other, the nearest, seems to have been stopped somewhere. For now!"

He looked at his men, gathered into but a shape in the dark.

"Must get back."

The 83rd Officer ran off, as did Carr, but back to his own men still out on picket and, having found them, he shouted his orders.

"Spread out, but keep in touch, by sight. Face your front and wait. Anything you don't like, shout."

However, again his words were interrupted by sounds of conflict from the Medellin, but this was the sound of a controlled volley, at a volume matching the crack of thunder, seemingly up in the sky, but the height was gained from it coming from the top of the Medellin. "That's

British", he thought, then came another to the left of the first, then another to the right of the first. He was reassured, "That's a firing line," he thought, "They'll be pushed back," which impression was confirmed by the flame of the continuous musket fire moving now rightwards and down, back towards the French Cascajal. Another minute passed, then another volley, but, reassuringly, further down the slope of the Medellin, giving birth to another comforting thought, "They have been pushed back." Now he was looking upon individual musket flashes, now appearing and moving left to right. Three or four minutes passed of what must be confused fighting, then all died away into complete darkness. The only sound of conflict now was the second combat which had started, that further up the Portina and nearer, but soon that also ceased.

Carr released a sigh of deep relief. He knew, that,had the attack succeeded, then the battle was over, the French would have held the dominating high ground and the British would have no choice but to withdraw the following day, but the return of near silence meant, surely, that the conflict up there, at least for now, was ended. Were the French still on the Medellin, there would still be sounds of combat. He returned to his men, to come first to Sergeant Nicholls.

"No sleep for us now Sergeant. Now we'll all be worrying about night attacks, both them and us."

"Right Sir. Just stay alert, then Sir. What else?"

"What else indeed, Sergeant, but let's hope the 83rd come back."

"Sir. But I'll get off round the men, Sir."

"Yes Sergeant. Carry on."

The tension in the air was palpable and it affected both the French and British. For the next hour all could hear frequent 'Qui vive!', from the French piquets, disconcertingly within earshot, as they challenged their own patrolling Officers. The rumble of gun carriage wheels and the jingle of their harness could also be heard clearly,

234

adding to the apprehension for the following day. All on the British side could follow the movement of French artillery into position, because it was accomplished by the light of myriad flambeau torches, which built the tension still further. Eerie to look upon, all moving seemingly disembodied in the thick darkness as though at the behest of some malevolent sorcerer weaving his malignant minions into place, using fire conjured from another world.

After the fraught first hour had passed, Sergeant Nicholls reappeared out of the darkness.

"Sir. I've made contact with the Guards, Sir. Their pickets are out, beyond ours, to our right."

"Very good, Sergeant. Carry on. Keep the men alert."

"Sir."

Then he was gone, this known only by his running footsteps across the crackling grass and stubble. Carr stood still, using only sound to guide his thoughts and decisions, or lack of them, for nothing had changed, bar the tension that was building for the following day, its dawn now but three hours away. Condemning as useless the idea of standing still at one spot, improving the lot of no one, least of all himself, he walked the 300 yards or so covered by his own pickets, responding to each softly spoken challenge with the simple words, 'Major Carr.' Beside each man he stood to exchange a few words, usually concerned with the proximity of their equivalent French picquets and usually parting to words from his own men, "Don't like 'em this close, Sir!" He walked on to eventually meet a fiercer challenge, which told him that he had reached The Guards. The challenge and the answer brought over their Officer, but it was Carr who managed to discern the human shape, the Guards Officer not being against the black of the Medellin, unlike himself.

"Carr. 105th."

"Felsham. Coldstreams."

However, the conversation did not last long, the first words coming from the Coldstream Officer.

"Anything new?"

Unconsciously, Carr shook his head.

"No, nothing, other than the obvious. Johnny's building some force over there."

The Coldstreamer's voice became more uncertain.

"We understand that there are rather more than we had hoped."

"Judging by the noise from over there and that they are happy to waste men in a risky night attack, I'd say that was true."

With that, both turned to patrol again behind their line, and nothing more was said. Then, after what seemed another interminable hour, Carr heard shouting, from the direction of the Medellin, which continued for but a minute before Carr was brought stock-still from horror. From the top of the British line, but obviously below the Medellin, there began sporadic firing, which was soon taken up further down the line. From the muzzle flashes the British miscreants thought they were aiming at the French, but, crucially, this was in his direction and that of his men. Carr took a deep breath.

"Down! Everybody down. Lie down!"

To what extent Carr's order was obeyed he did not know, for within the next seconds he was forced to concern himself solely with his own preservation, which meant lying flat on the ground, his cheek feeling the still warm earth, his hands grasping handfuls of stubble. The firing was progressing all down the British line, and soon he could hear the soft buzz of musket balls passing just above his prone figure. Soon Officers could be heard screaming to cease-fire and, when he was certain that the firing was not going to be repeated from any part of the British line, only then did Carr stand up.

"Sergeant Nicholls!"

From some distance he heard the reply and Carr ran in its direction.

"Anyone hit?"

"Not that I know of, Sir. Your shout probably saved many of the lads, Sir."

Carr nodded.

"Right, but no change. Keep a watch as before, but now get the men to call their names to the next man, let's see if anyone has been knocked over."

In the still inky darkness, he heard the naming begin and, to his huge relief, the word came back, via Sergeant Nicholls, that all were sound and unwounded.

"All's well, Sir. But I think the Guards, on down, may have lost a man or two."

"Very good, Sergeant. Give thanks."

"Sir."

It must have been in the last hours of the night, when they heard cannon-fire from the Spanish lines and Carr whirled around to, thankfully, see no more volleys rippling down the British lines. The sound, coming from the town area, echoed away to create the return of a silence which, somehow, was not silent but spoke of a lingering threat, dire and patient, out beyond the Portina. The final event of the night was Nicholls bringing to Carr a French deserter, him with no shako and plainly wet and dishevelled.

"We heard'n splashing through the Portina, Sir, then crawlin' to us on his knees, speakin' "Mez amees. Dez soldats anglaze," or some such."

Carr allowed himself a small laugh.

"Your pronunciation does you much credit, Sergeant."

"Done a lot of tradin', Sir."

At that point the cowering deserter, still being held by his epaulette by the meaty hand of Nicholls, repeated the phrase, but Carr asked his own question.

"De nombreux Français derrière vous, oui?"

"Oui, Monsieur. De nombreux soldats."

Carr turned to Nicholls.

"Take him back, Sergeant. Make sure he gets to the Colonel or Major O'Hare and does not run off, which is what he wants to do. One of our Generals will want to question him."

"What did he say, Sir. Beg pardon."

"He said, yes. Lots of soldiers behind me."

Nicholls departed, almost dragging the Frenchman along, as Carr turned towards the French lines, where the first cracks of dawn were appearing in the Eastern sky. As the light strengthened, one by one the French flambeau were extinguished. The rumble of artillery wheels had long ceased. They had made their preparations.

oOo

There was just enough light for Carr to see between the lines of the 61st and 83rd as he brought his pickets back in, using this gap between the two Battalions holding the front line. His first destination was behind his own line, to the fire kept burning by Morrison, where he drank coffee, ate some bread and shaved, all at the same time. Then he closed his eyes, hoping for an hour of sleep. Close by, as the daylight strengthened, Lacey and O'Hare, were both stood together on a cart, behind the Colour Company, each with a telescope trained on the Cascajal. Lacey brought his down whilst O'Hare continued to study.

"What can you see? My eyes aren't what they used to be."

"What I don't like. I'd put the number of French guns up there above 20. I can see a mass of troops above his gun-line, as you must have, but I swear to a huge mass below it, almost in the valley."

He lowered his own telescope and turned to Lacey.

"Let me borrow yours. Mine's a family hand-me-down."

He focused Lacey's superior instrument onto the point of the forward slope of the Cascajal that he wanted and, after ten seconds of study, he made his pronouncement.

"A big attack. He's going to have another stab at the Medellin."

Lacey retrieved his telescope and tried again, this time seeing more.

"I think you're right. He's going for another mass attack, up that slope, and against a formed firing line! Wellesley will be holding his men back, behind the skyline, just as at Vimeiro."

He lowered the telescope but continued to look North to the Medellin, now with no Redcoat line to be seen.

"This French General, whoever's running it up there, must have his brains in his boots!"

He turned to O'Hare and spoke more in sadness than in any form of satisfaction.

"Haven't these damned Frogs learned one thing about fighting us?"

O'Hare gave a short laugh.

"Sure, now! Let them remain in ignorance, so long as they get thrown back."

At that moment a single gun fired from the centre of the Cascajal, this being the signal for every French gun either on the Cascajal or near it, to begin firing, at a range that was almost point blank, across the Portina Valley. Within a minute the space between the two hills was filled with smoke, the thick cloud hanging in the valley and this being added to by their own British guns replying from the Medellin or just below, but it was a counter bombardment that was paltry in comparison to what was being sent their way from the Cascajal and also from the next French battery down on the plain.

Lacey's face became apprehensive, him more listening than looking. Within half a minute he had come to his conclusion.

"Nothing for us!"

O'Hare was again using his telescope and, even at that distance, he could see the deluge of iron throwing up obvious gouts of rock and earth from the summit and upper slopes of the Medellin.

"No! The whole lot's onto the Medellin. Pray he's pulled them back."

"He will have. If not Wellesley, then Daddy Hill will have brought them back out of harm's way."

A sudden thought.

"So, when did the Ball open?"

O'Hare dragged out his watch, huge and ancient, another family heirloom. It took some effort to manoeuvre it into a position from which he could read the hands.

"Five o' clock."

O'Hare nodded.

"God preserve us all!"

"Mostly those up on that hill."

Both resumed using their telescopes, but Lacey spoke first.

"Here we go!"

Throughout the Battalions of Mackenzie's Division and also Sherbrook's in the line before them, all eyes were on the Medellin, either naked, or with the use of the telescope. Stood in the centre of the Colour Company, Jed Deakin leaned on his musket, with a very agitated Ensign Rushby by his left arm and an equally wound up Ensign Neape one place beyond, against Rushby's left arm. As usual it was Rushby who began the questioning, Neape's mind being in a turmoil of thoughts, worries and contradictions.

"What do you think will happen, Sergeant? Up there, I mean?"

Deakin adjusted his chinstrap by flexing his chin.

"The Frogs'll get thrown back down, Sir. They've got as much chance as a snowball in a kettle!"

Rushby turned his head away from the Medellin to look at Deakin, his face full of astonishment.

"How can you be so sure?"

"Well, Sir. Them lads up there is no better nor no worse than us. If we was up there, we'd throw 'em back, just like at Vimeiro. 'Specially with them havin' to slog their way up a slope like that 'un."

At that point, those with good eyes or a telescope could see the red of General Hill's Light Companies mixed with his green uniformed Riflemen emerging from the smoke of the French bombardment and reaching the top of the Medellin slope as they retired before the French attack. Their skirmish line down in the valley has done its work and within a minute emerging from the smoke could be seen what looked like a blue wave reaching for the top of a steep beach. At that point the French cannonfire ceased and, moments later, the lines of Redcoats came into sight along the summit. The sound of the first volley, which they delivered into the heads of the French columns, could be heard even by those beyond the 105th, towards Talavera, and then it became one continuous crash as the Company volleys ran along the British line. After studying what could be seen, which was mostly smoke, for two or three minutes, Deakin looked away and took a drink from his water flask, for the day was already becoming insufferably hot. When he looked again the Redcoat line had charged forward and blue-coated mass fell back rapidly. From somewhere in the valley the sound of musketry sprang up, but it was unlikely to have come from the Redcoats descending the Medellin. Even though they continued to press forward, these were no longer firing in any controlled way, Deakin surmised to himself, but most likely using the bayonet. The controlled volleys in the valley continued.

"I bet that's they Germans, givin' Johnny the good-bye as they passes across their front."

Some ten minutes more came the last act; the Redcoats re-ascending the slope of the Medellin, in seemingly casual manner, evidently unhindered, either by a counter-attack, or French cavalry. Deakin took off his shako and mopped his brow.

"That's that then! But 'twill be us as they tries for next. That hill's a no go, as it always was. It'll be down 'ere next."

Behind him, O'Hare had again hauled out his watch and agreed with Deakin, albeit out of his hearing.

"Ten to six. A good start for us, but that's all. He'll be trying here at some time."

Lacey nodded, but looked down from the cart to where Bryce was stood, waiting patiently.

"Bryce! Get us a drink of something will you?"

Bryce saluted and made off, to return ten minutes later with a mug of tea for each. The pair now used the cart as a bench and they sat, taking their ease and drinking their tea. It was in this state that they were found by Mackenzie.

"Johnny's been smashed up on the hill! The slopes are covered in his dead and wounded. Thrown back like slops intae a pig trough!"

Lacey and O'Hare conjured up the image described, then Lacey offered his mug to Mackenzie who took a drink, then returned it with only a nod of thanks. His thoughts were elsewhere.

"He'll try down here next. When, cannae say, but he's plenty reserves back over the stream. He'll come, sooner or later."

He took a deep breath.

"One fact to cheer ye up. There's nary one French musket opposite the Dons. He's sending his whole damn army against us. Five, six, to one, easy, I'd say. An' in his favour, I dinnae need to tell ye."

As his words died and he rode away, leaving the two to finish their tea, the guns began again an exchange between the Cascajal and the Medellin, started by the French, as though needing to make a repost to their thorough defeat of barely an hour previous. However, within the next hour the firing died away and the eerie silence that had ruled the night settled in again. The two stood again on their cart to study the French dispositions directly opposite their line, but, even using their telescopes, all that could be seen was merely a blue and white line, shimmering in the heat that rose up from the ground. Time went on, with nothing happening, bar the movement of men between the two hills either side of the Portina, carrying wounded from the recent conflict up the slope of their respective hills, back to their own lines.

Then Lacey took a glance at the Cascajal and immediately raised his telescope.

"Tactical conference occurring opposite."

O'Hare raised his own glass to see an array of glittering uniforms, all mounted on horses covered in equal finery. A gun spoke on the British side of the valley, it may not have been loaded or the shot flew over, but the warning was clear, 'Approach too far at your peril.' The group rode back behind a line of their own infantry and remained there for the next hour or more. Eventually, O'Hare pronounced judgement.

"Seems like a bit of an argument's going on up there!"

Lacey used his own glass.

"If all that arm waving shows such, then I agree."

He then lowered his telescope and pulled out his own watch.

"10 o' clock. We've been idle these four hours and it'll take them up there another hour to decide their next move, at least."

"I'd say three, before anything happens."

What did happen was a column appearing behind them, made up of Spanish infantry, cavalry and guns, moving up towards the Medellin. Lacey gave this event barely a thought, unlike Miles who spoke his thoughts out loud.

"'Bout time they thievin' Spanish muckrakes took a turn!"

Lacey's thoughts were elsewhere. He was as conscious as any Officer above the rank of Captain, that the whole British army was remaining at 'stand to', in line, awaiting what they thought was the inevitable, and imminent French attack. Both Lacey and O'Hare used their telescopes again to look for French movement opposite, but there was none and the waiting continued. Lacey gave an order which allowed his men to sit down, but remain in line. Sometime before 11 o' clock, Carr arrived and spoke to Lacey.

"Sir. Water is very scarce and the men have had very little food."

O'Hare added his agreement.

"He's right. We've all been drinking water and the men have had no time to cook anything, having to stand to, then stand down, up and down, all through the night."

Lacey nodded agreement.

"Water at least, but where from?"

Carr spoke next.

"It seems that there is some kind of truce holding between the two hills and just below. A Captain on Mackenzie Staff told me. It came about whilst the wounded were being gathered and it's holding still, such that both sides are obtaining water from the Portina."

"You're sure."

"Yes Sir."

Lacey nodded.

"Right, by Companies, starting with the Lights. One man with five canteens. We'll assume one canteen can be shared between two when they get back. We'll start with that."

He looked at O'Hare, who nodded his agreement, for Lacey to then look down at Carr.

"Right. See to it."

He looked at O'Hare.

"Could the Followers come up, d'you think?"

"I'd say yes, and that I'll see to myself."

He jumped down to turn right, whilst Carr felt the need to take a look first at the Portina and only then he walked forward to pass between the 61st and the 83rd, to there find a Major of the former.

"Carr. 105th."

"Russell. 61st."

"We've a mind to send some men forward to the stream to get some water. Seems there's some kind of an agreement further up."

Russell nodded.

"Our thoughts entirely, but Johnny's got his Tirailleurs out just beyond the brook. If we send our men out there in two's and three's they're just as likely to get bagged."

Carr sighed.

"True. So?"

Russell paused for thought.

"If we both send ours out as whole Companies and only a little way forward in skirmish order but within reach of the stream should anything flare up, then that may get them to hold off and we both get a drink, them and us."

"Good idea. I'll get mine out, but not far enough to be an obvious threat."

"Right! See you are the bar!"

Carr laughed and they both returned to their men, Carr going straight to Drake, the first Company on the left.

"Nat. Take yours out, beyond the 61st, as a skirmish line. Then, ten men with five canteens each to go up to the stream and get them filled. Do that about five times or so to get water to your whole Company, sharing each canteen between two. There seems to be an informal truce all up and down that seems to be holding. Johnny's not moved these past five hours."

Within minutes, the Light Company were spread before the British line, in the company of the 61st Lights. Amongst the first ten, Drake had chosen Saunders, Miles and Byford, the latter because he could speak more than

245

halfway decent French. Their Baker rifles were slung behind them, across their backs, as insurance. Anxiously, the three approached the Portina, even Saunders craning his neck to try to see beyond the reeds. Just then, to their great relief, a French Tirailleur pushed through the reeds, carrying several canteens himself, soon to be followed by four more. The three looked at the five for several seemingly eternal seconds, before Miles pushed forward.

"Come on. These is after the same as us!"

Seeing Miles walk forward, so did the Frenchmen and soon all were busy filling canteens. By chance, one slipped from the grasp of a Frenchman and the eddy around a stone sent it over to the British side, but within the reach of Saunders. He pulled it out and tossed it back over to the same Frenchman, who nodded in return, but did not smile.

"Merci!"

Saunders nodded, then replied with a growl. Tirailleurs were their most often opponents during the Retreat to Coruna.

"Think nothing of it."

Byford translated.

"C'est rien!"

At this, the Tirailleur did smile, but if there was any thinking happening, it was taking place behind the ferretlike eyes of Tom Miles.

"Zeke! How much tobacco you got?"

Saunders did not look up from thrusting a canteen beneath the waters.

"Full pouch. Nearly."

Miles turned to Byford.

"An' you, you're full, I knows! You don't bloody well smoke!"

Miles looked across to study the Frenchmen.

"These looks like good lads, who knows how things work. Give us 'em yer!"

The tobacco pouches were passed to him from both sides and then, with his own, he displayed the three open pouches on a rock. The invitation was obvious and it soon attracted the attention of the French opposite.

"Byfe. Do the speaking."

Byford took a deep breath.

"Vous aimeriez au commerce du tabac de brandy ?"

The Frenchmen heard and plainly understood, but at first they only looked at each other. Then, one pulled out from his own haversack a flask of brandy, to be followed by the others. Miles reached into his own haversack to pull out the flask he used but Byford stopped him before it could emerge.

"Leave it there. It's loot, it came off a dead Frenchman. They'll probably take offence. Use my additional canteen."

Byford pulled out of his own haversack the extra canteen, which he had brought to obtain extra water for himself, and handed it to Miles. He took out the stopper and, using a central rock for purchase, he reached across the stream, holding out the canteen, obviously inviting his customers to pour in some brandy. Each did and each time Miles shook the canteen to gauge the depth of the contents. He only needed to shake his head once to obtain the extra required for a fair swap, before he then pointed to a French haversack hanging from the shoulder of the nearest Frenchman, but he clearly failed to understand, until Byford intervened.

"Votre havresac, s'il vous plait, pour le tabac."

The haversack was passed across and the three tobacco pouches emptied into it, then it was closed and passed back. The last of the canteens were being filled with water, when one of the Frenchmen pointed at Saunders.

"Votre fusil. Puis-je voir?"

Byford looked at the Frenchman, trying to make a judgment.

"He wants to see your Baker."

The three British looked at each other, before Byford spoke.

"Don't take it off, Zeke. Just slide it around to your front."

Warily, Saunders did as suggested and he then twisted it so that the firelock could be seen, but the Frenchman broke into a wide grin.

"Une arme très fine."

It was Saunders who answered, the words needing no translation.

"Yes. Bloody good!"

However, Miles had the last word as they rose to leave, but spoken in a low tone, as the wet canteens slopped against them, staining wet their coats and trousers.

"Bloody fine, yes, an' it may be the one as puts a bullet through your kisser!"

However, if that was heard, it made no difference, as they parted with a slight wave of their hands and half smiles, but all well content.

oOo

The watering parties continued apace from both sides and the Followers arrived, with kettles of food, such as they could create with the meagre provisions and, with the men stood in line, the stew had to be given out in tin mugs. Little was said, bar "Thanks. Take care, now", as the men took the food and ate where they sat or lay, but still in line.

Carr, being more of a free agent than O'Hare, took the time to wander towards the Medellin, where a battery of field-guns had just arrived to position themselves between the 83rd in the front line and the most Southerly Battalion of the King's German Legion, the 1st KGL. Whilst they unlimbered and wheeled their pieces forward into line, Carr, trying to occupy the idle hours, introduced himself to the Battery Captain.

"Good afternoon. Carr 105th."

The Captain saluted.

"Good afternoon, Sir. Sillery, Royal Horse Artillery."

Carr nodded.

"Pleased to have you alongside. I'm sure you'll make a difference."

"Oh we will, Sir. Count on that."

"You've come from the hill."

"Yes, Sir. We supported the repulse of the morning attack. Now we've been sent down here."

He swallowed hard.

"I have to say, Sir, that there are thousands of the Johnnies opposite. You don't have to be a genius nor need a crystal ball to work out that they will be trying here next."

Sillery paused before pointing at the Cascajal.

"And he has batteries all down his line, not just up there on his hill. I counted 25 up there alone, Sir."

Carr nodded.

"Well, we can but trust to our own firepower, you'd agree, but don't let me keep you, you must have much to attend to."

"Yes sir. Thank you. I must see to our line."

He saluted and trotted forward, to where his gunners were already arranging the six guns.

Meanwhile, Lacey and O'Hare were making observations of their own, although slightly more frivolous. Lacey looked across from the height of their cart at their hurrying water parties and those of the French opposite, each largely ignoring the other.

"Have you ever seen the like?"

O'Hare grinned and shook his head.

"No, nor even heard."

Lacey looked up at the Cascajal.

"Our glitterati have not reappeared. Gone since Noon."

He took a deep breath.

"This is absurd! And cannot go on for much longer. Remember what Mackenzie said about French armies closing in behind us. Wellesley won't advance, he's happy on the defensive, but we'll have to get out sooner or later. Even out of Spain altogether!"

It was at that moment that an Aide-de-Camp galloped up to rein his horse to a halt before the pair.

"Sir! Orders from General Wellesley, Sir, get your men back to their positions. Significant movement opposite you can be seen from up on the Medellin."

He saluted and rode off. He did no need for him to say where the 'significant movement' was and Lacey was grateful to see Cyrus Gibney stood nearby.

"Gibney! Get them in."

Gibney ran forward to shepherd the current watering party back to their lines, accompanied by Officers of the 83rd and 61st, all obeying the same order. O'Hare now pulled out his own watch and he was not alone, almost every Officer in the British army did the same, to note the resumption.

"2 o' clock! How nice of him to choose the hottest part of the day to resume this particular quadrille!"

At the same time, close behind the line, the Followers had finished handing out what food there was, Bridie kneeling beside Jed Deakin, him sat on the dry earth.

"'Twas not much, Jed, but a few beans in a mug. We'll try again later, if the flour comes up."

Deakin turned and smiled as he handed the mug back.

"You did your best, Bridie. You did your best."

It was at that moment that all the cannon on the French side opened fire with an ear-splitting crash, this time the ball and grape showering amongst the British occupying the plain. Screaming began and not just amongst the soldiers. Followers were hit also.

"Get out Bridie! Get back!"

She needed no further bidding, as did the other Followers, but she did pause just enough to kiss him quickly before running off, spoon and cooking-pot in either hand. Lacey and O'Hare jumped off their cart just as it was wrecked by a cannon-ball, but they gave themselves no time to reflect on their lucky escape. Instead, they ran along the line, giving the only order they could.

"Stay down! Lie flat."

It was not long before that order had been obeyed along the full length of the British line, from the Medellin in the North down to the Pajar in the South. On the Medellin, Hill pulled his men back behind the crest and into shelter, but for the three Divisions on the Talavera plain, Mackenzie's, Sherbrook's, and Campbell's there was no shelter, merely hope, as they flattened themselves as best they could against the unyielding earth. Thus, their trial began and those who survived spoke of it later as the worst hour endured throughout the whole Peninsular Campaign. The fire from eighty French cannon, many firing at the rate of six rounds per minute, rained down upon them, many with the advantage of the height of the Cascajal. Men called to each other, to discover who was still alive, for none dared to lift any part of themselves more than an inch from the greater safety of the hard ground. Deakin found himself lying beside Ensign Rushby who seemed to be enduring the cannonade as well as could be expected, but Ensign Neape was chattering with fear and Deakin could hear Colour Sergeant Bennet doing his best to comfort the terrified youngster, him in his mid teens. With Rushby still settled, Deakin called out for Halfway.

"Tobe! You still alive?"

The reply came, barely audible above the sound of the cannon and the passing of the shot.

"Yes, I be. But somethin' hit my foot, took off the heel, but only in passin', like."

Deakin gave a small smile in relief.

"There'll be plenty of spare shoes afore this day's done!"

All along the line could be heard the screaming of the wounded and those newly hit, a sound as continuous as the bombardment itself. Lacey, O'Hare and Carr crawled amongst their men, encouraging or consoling. Carr found himself rolling into Heaviside, him speaking encouraging words to his own men.

"Well done, Joshua. We'll get through this."

Heaviside did no more than pat Carr on the arm, before crawling onward to a group of his own men, where he heard again the common question.

"Sir! What's to be done?"

"Endure! What else? When they come, and they will, there will be a reckoning. For judgment is without mercy, to one who has shown no mercy. James 2. Verse 13."

From somewhere came the beginnings of a reply, but this was soon lost in the screams of someone newly wounded. Still close by, Carr found himself crawling next to Carravoy.

"Charles! Should you not be with your men?"

"Doing my best to get there! I was at my tent when it all started. Now struggling to get back."

Carravoy crawled on a little further, even raising himself a little.

"Is it lessening, do you think?"

Carr rolled onto his back and pulled out his watch.

"I've got 2.55. An hour would be about right for any kind of softening up."

He lay on his back, watching the white smoke drift across from the French side, but now more listening than seeing.

"You're right, Charles. It is, tailing off."

He turned to face him, seeing Carravoy's tailored uniform covered in dust, dirt and scraps of stubble.

"Give it another minute or two, then probably you can walk back to your men."

Carravoy crawled on.

"Minute or ten, more like."

Carr raised himself up onto his elbows. The cannonade was no longer a continuous roar; rather it was only the report of individual guns which could now be heard, some clearly from the French battery immediately opposite them. The bombardment lessened further, so that the moments of silence grew and became more frequent. Carr heard drums and trumpets, unquestionably from over the Portina. He sprang to his feet.

"Up! Up. Stand to and face your front. Johnny's on his way."

All along the line of the 105th men were obeying the order, so too were those of the 61st and the 83rd in the line before them, as were every British Battalion on the plain. At their feet, all along the line, remained the evidence of what they had just endured; prone figures remaining stretched or contorted on the dry ground.

Carr ran along the front rank.

"Check your flints! Check your priming!"

Few needed reminding, most had already done so. Bennet was helping Neape to his feet. His legs would not work.

"Lean on the flagstaff, Sir. It won't be needed for a while."

Neape grasped the warm wood and pulled himself up, then he tried his legs, one at a time. Both still shook, but each would take some weight off his clutching hands that were now around the leather casing of the Regimental Colour.

"That's it, Sir. Give the lads a bit of a show, those around The Colours, like!"

The sudden sound of musket volleys down at the Pajar, caused Neape's legs to give way again.

"Come on now Sir. We'n goin' to need you soon enough. Wavin' the Old Bits of Rag in the Frog's faces. That's where they looks, you see. They wants to see our Colours waverin', even runnin'!"

A larger crash was heard, from the same direction.

"That's our lads, Sir. Dishin' it out. 'Twill spread up to us soon enough."

From the distance came the sound of continuous musketry exchanges, then came the roar of cannon, soon continuous, as their crews sponged and loaded at their maximum possible speed. Then the cannonfire ceased and there came the unmistakable sound of a cheer.

"That's us, Sir. Frogs don't cheer like that. 'Tis all drums an' 'Old Trousers', from them. I d'reckon that the lads've seen 'em away!"

Neape managed a weak smile and straightened and, thankfully, Bennet noted, he was no longer leaning on the Colour staff. On the other side, alongside Rushby, Deakin was looking between the 83rd and the 61st.

"Time to get the cases off, Sirs. The monsewrs is on their way."

He could see the lines of blue now visible, but still many yards beyond the far side of the Portina. Rushby pulled off the stiff leather case from his King's Colour and handed it to Deakin, then he hoisted it and set the but end of the staff into the holder slung around his shoulder. It took some seconds before Neape did the same with the Regimental Colour, but all along the British line, both front line and reserve, the huge Colours stretched out their defiance into the steady breeze. To the right front of the 105th the King's Colour and buff Regimental of the 61st and, more over on their left, the King's Colour and, the pale yellow Regimental of the 83rd. All down Mackenzie's front, his Battalions formed a solid line, all stood steady at 'Order Arms". From further down line the order 'lock on" could be heard and the second ranks of 61st and 83rd moved slightly to their right to reveal the heads of the first rank. This meant that combat was imminent and men took a last swallow of precious water and gripped the wood of their muskets, now sticky with sweat, brought on not only by the fierce heat of the mid-afternoon but by the heavy anxiety of the forthcoming combat.

Stood forward of their own line between the 83rd and the 61st, Carr and Heaviside watched the French cross

254

the Portina. The British skirmish line crackled with musket fire, but they were soon running back before the oncoming French formations. They were advancing in their customary columns, but there were so many that the French front appeared to be one continuous line covering something like three-quarters of a mile; this distance before the Divisions of Sherbrook and Campbell, the many Eagles above their heads, but set far back. This aroused some disdain in the mind of Major Carr.

"You know, Joshua, it's only a small point, but I do think it significant that our Colours are plain to see, in the centre of what is only a two deep line, sort of an honest challenge, as it were, 'here they are, come and take, if you can'. Whilst theirs are held back, deep within their ranks, at their least vulnerable point."

Heaviside nodded.

"For we aim at what is honourable not only in the Lord's sight, but also in the sight of man. Two Corinthians. 8. Verse 21."

"Amen, Joshua, but I do believe it is time to get back."

The pair turned and trotted back to their positions, Carr off to the left, Heaviside to the centre, just as Sillery's battery opened fire on the approaching French. The 105th could only stand, wait, and watch as Sherbrook's men in the front line made their preparations to receive the French onslaught. This began with the order, unheard above the roar of Sillery's guns, for the muskets of the 83rd to be raised to the "make ready." In the spaces between the crash of the guns could be heard the standard sound of a French attack, the drums, 'dum dadadum dadadum dum', repeated endlessly and the equally endless shout of "Vive l'Empereur." The French bombardment had not ceased entirely and shot still found targets amongst the British line, but the concentration of all stood in the line was on the approaching French.

Sillery's guncrews were straining every sinew, but

the impact of their fire was hidden from most of the 105th by the line of the 83rd. It was also hidden from Carr on the left, but in his case by the smoke from the guns themselves. However, not for Carravoy and D'Villiers, stood with their Grenadiers on the far right. They could see much between the 83rd and the 61st and it was plain that Sherbrook was holding his fire until the very last moment. Anxiety grew within the pair, for, even back in the reserve line, they could pick out every detail of the first rank of the French column which they could now plainly see; the wide cross-belts, the bucket shaped shako, the heavy brass chinstrap and the epaulettes of each man, even if some sported a fine moustache. The French were within 50 yards when, finally, came the order, "Present", obeyed by both the 61st and 83rd. Almost immediately they heard "Fire!" and the two lines fired, with the standard three second gap between front and rear. Carravoy and D'Villiers saw the French go down in swathes, but, oddly, there had been no sound of any musketfire from the Guards, further down to the right. Carravoy walked forward to where he was just in time to see the whole of the Guards Brigade charge forward, without firing a shot. Within a minute the 83rd and 61st, also charged forward into the smoke, following The Guards. There was nothing left to be seen of the British first line, but the dead and wounded of the previous hour's bombardment.

Lacey and O'Hare, in the centre before The Colours, looked at each other, but it was Lacey who voiced the deep concern of both.

"This I don't like!"

The sounds of great tumult and mayhem came to them from beyond the curling smoke of the British volleys, but then it cleared. The 83rd and 61st were advancing steadily, their Brigadier clearly visible, mounted and leading them on, but of The Guards to their right nothing could be seen, and of the King's German Legion to their left all that could be seen of them, were clumps of Germans pursuing the blue coated French before them to the slopes of the

Cascajal. Sillery's guns had ceased to fire, but Carr's anxiety was as great as that of Lacey and O'Hare. He ran across and soon found Sillery, peering ahead, equally aghast at what he saw.

"This will end badly! Get your guns loaded. There are too many oncoming French, they'll soon push ours back and then be onto us again."

Sillery saluted and ran along his gun-line giving orders. Carr returned to his position where he found Drake, also in an agitated state of mind.

"Henry! That was too soon. They'll be damnably mauled."

"Yes! Count on it."

He looked around at the chaos, with even the 83rd and 61st now crossing the Portina.

"And when it comes, it'll be us in the way."

There was not one Officer in Mackenzie's own Brigade that did not share the same sentiment. D'Villiers, looking anxiously all around, was only slightly relieved to see General Mackenzie with the 24th down to the right, moving the whole Battalion up towards them, to where The Guards had once been, also, some cavalry were moving forward into the place vacated by the 24th. However, what was now happening before him soon outweighed that slight relief, because away in the distance could be seen cavalry sabres rising and falling, almost certainly at the point where The Guards would have arrived after their headlong advance. For Carr, on the other flank, it was worse. Using his telescope he could see the King's German Legion now on the slopes of the Cascajal but being terribly mauled by cannonfire from the same slopes above them and to their left. Worse again, masses of formed French troops were already pushing them back. Within minutes, the four fine Battalions of KGL were little more than a disorganised rabble, streaming back, a few groups holding momentarily as a rearguard, but standing for little more than the time for one volley. Carr spoke out loud, now very seriously worried.

"They won't rally! We're done!"

He realised that there was now a huge gap between themselves and the 88th of Donkin's Brigade far up on the slope of the Medellin. It was at that moment that Mackenzie came riding up and Carr automatically saluted.

"Carr, isn't it?"

"Yes Sir."

"Dragoons, two squadrons, will be up on your left, behind Sillery."

"Yes Sir."

"We have to hold, and hope that he sends somethin' down from the Medellin. If we can hold and be reinforced, we may yet see them awa!"

He leaned forward in his saddle.

"We're in for a bad scrap, laddie! There's just ma three Battalions! Do yere best and stand fast. Encourage yere men!"

Carr saluted as Mackenzie rode off, but not far, soon to halt before The Colours of the 105th. He stood up in his stirrups, his fervour accentuating his Scottish accent.

"One Hundred and Fifth! Ah said to youse lads awhile back that ah'll be callin' on ye, an' the time has come."

He pointed over his shoulder.

"Thone daft Reeks have gone after the Johnnies and they'll be back soon, in no shape to do damn all, leavin' the whole thing to us. Us bein, you, the 45th and the 24th. Just us. We hold here or we're all off to Perdition or some French jail. Move forward an' hold 'em off lads! Ah told ye back then ye're lads for a fight. Remember who ye are! The lads of the One-Oh-Five. Maida an' Coruna!"

Someone, somewhere caught Mackenzie's mood.

"Three cheers for old Jock Mackenzie!"

The huzzas broke out and Mackenzie's face broke out into a broad grin. He turned his horse to ride down to deliver the same to the 45th and then the 24th and, as he passed, each Officer of the 105th brought his sword up in salute.

However, what all had feared was now happening. Even the 83rd and 61st were running back in some disorder, carried back by the headlong flight of The Guards and the King's German Legion. Both Battalions would soon reach the 105th line, causing utmost confusion if they were not easily allowed through. Lacey filled his lungs.

"Open by Companies!"

The order ran down the line and, with complete steadiness, each Company swung back from the left to open their line. The 83rd and 61st ran through the gaps and not a few Guardsmen of the Scots Fusiliers. The looks of derision which they received in their passing were withering, not least those from RSM Gibney, contorting his face into his very best scowl of contempt at all who passed, including Officers. Choosing his moment Lacey again took a very deep breath.

"Close the line!"

The Companies swung around, even though some Guardsmen remained in their front, but the time had come to form a line, which these last few Guardsmen would have to push through. On the far left, Carr was looking left, remembering Mackenzie's words that they could perhaps expect help from up on the Medellin and he could see it on its way, thus came hope but this soon ebbed.

"One Battalion! He's sending one Battalion."

He watched as the red column, formed in two's, descended the slope at the double to arrive down on the plain where he could no longer see them. Clearly they would soon be in position, but he had already calculated that this one Battalion was to hold a line once held by four of the King's German Legion. Then the sound of jingling horse harness distracted him, at which he turned to see two squadrons of Light Dragoons moving up behind Sillery's guns, but there remained a huge gap beyond the six field-guns, that flank was exposed and 'in the air' unless the reinforcement he had seen descending arrived in time and came this far down.

The two cavalry Squadrons were from the 14th and 16th Light Dragoons, the 16th including Tavender and Templemere. For the latter it seemed as though he were looking into a scene from Hell, all was noise, smoke, explosions from bursting howitzer shells, passing shot and the cries of badly wounded men. He leaned forward to lower himself a little more behind his horse's neck, this providing a little more protection, then he looked across to Tavender.

"What the Hell are we doing here?"

Tavender was equally horrified at what he saw, but it was made worse, because he understood their role.

"Filling a gap!"

He said no more, expecting Templemere to work out the importance for himself.

Meanwhile, Lacey had more immediate and pressing matters than those facing Carr, to bring his men into Mackenzie's line. Placing himself before The Colours, he raised his sword.

"The One Hundred and Fifth will advance!"

He led his men forward to the position so recently abandoned by the 83rd, this now marked by the prone bodies of their dead, and there he raised his sword to halt. They were now on the front line, level with Sillery's guns and the line at the Pajar, which had come under renewed attack and was again wreathed in smoke and din, but Lacey could see that the 45th had also advanced between themselves and the 24th, with Cavalry filling the last gap to the Pajar. However, he was anything but re-assured for all that stood between this huge French attack and victory were Mackenzie's three battalions; his own, the 45th and the 24th. He turned to look at the French, crossing the Portina, and advancing in distinct columns, possibly a dozen in number. He turned to his men.

"Men! You heard the General. It's just us and the lads down to our right."

He took another deep breath.

"This'll be toe to toe, boys. Toe to toe. Who can take it, as well as give it out. But we, we, don't give best too easily."

He raised his sword high in the air.

"We are the fighting One Oh Five!"

Cheers rang out and many brandished their muskets high in the air, then the order rang out from the Captains and all was as if on parade.

"Lock on."

The heads moved in the rear rank.

"Make ready!"

All muskets were raised in the air.

Lacey moved back to stand beside The Colours, between Deakin and Rushby. Lacey was breathing hard, something noticed by Deakin.

"Are you alright, Sir?"

Lacey turned his head to face him.

"Yes, thank you, but perhaps a bit too old for this caper."

Deakin grinned.

"You said that at Coruna, Sir."

This time he laughed.

"Ah yes, so I did. I remember now."

He turned back to watch the oncoming French advancing steadily, accompanied by the same drumming and their upright Eagle Standards, now clear and prominent above their heads. Lacey immediately knew that these were veterans, not just by the campaign medals that could now be seen on the chests of the front rank, but by their steady, inexorable tramp forward to the beat of the drums, and the steady, levelled bayonets. Lacey had one more thing to say.

"They think it's going to be easy, boys! But they'll find nothing easy about me!"

Replies came back from all around.

"Nor me, Sir!"

"We can take this lot! Sir!"

"Nothin' diffrent from Vimeero, Sir."

At that moment Sillery's guns opened up, firing the probable double charge of grapeshot loaded after ball, this ploughing lanes through the oncoming columns, but the gaps were closed and the columns came on.

Carr took no notice of the advancing French; he had his own concerns and began running up towards the Medellin, hoping to meet the reinforcing Battalion. His running behind Sillery's guns was noticed by Tavender, remaining on his horse with the 16th. He shouted across to Templemere.

"That's Carr! Running off! Where's he off to?"

Templemere was about to answer when he felt a burning pain along the outside of his right thigh. His hand went down to feel before he dared look and the first thing he felt was the opened cloth of his trouser, but, re-assuringly, his leg was still there. He looked down to see that his leg had been cut almost from knee to hip, a deep cut now bleeding profusely. Unsurprisingly, Tavender's question was ignored. Instead, his words were solely concerned with his own plight.

"I've been hit. I'm bleeding! Get me some help."

The help soon arrived in the shape of a Trooper who dismounted and ran over, although him not immediately too concerned for his Officer's life, because Templemere remained sat on his horse.

"It's a cut, Sir. Not too bad, some ...."

Templemere raged above the unfortunate.

"I can see it's a cut, damn you! What happens now?"

"Bandage it up, Sir, wrapped around, until we can get you some more attention. Do you want to come out of the line, Sir?"

Templemere remained enraged.

"Of course. What do you think I can do, with all this happening?"

The Trooper looked up.

"Right Sir. I'll get the bandage on and then you can get yourself back. If you could take your foot out of the stirrup, Sir."

Templemere gingerly required his leg to work and disengage the stirrup. With his leg straight out, the bandage was wrapped around and Templemere gratefully wheeled his horse and rode to the rear.

Meanwhile, Carr was still running on at his best speed and he soon met the descending Battalion, these still on the move and, wholly breathless, he ran to the leading Officer.

"Carr. 105th."

The Officer replied, him also almost as breathless, as they jogged on together.

"Wilson, Sir. Grenadier Company, 1st 48th."

"Captain! If your orders allow, you should lead your men further down. Otherwise there will be a large gap, between yours and mine, about 200 or 300 yards further."

"Yes Sir. I can go a little further, but not too much."

Carr took a deep breath.

"Good. Do what you can. We must have a continuous line, or the next best to it."

They jogged on together, until Wilson stopped.

"It must be here, Sir. I can go no further."

"Very well. It will have to do. Good luck to you, Captain."

"And to you, Sir."

Carr ran on, soon to see Sillery's guns through the smoke, but he was only marginally reassured. He knew, although he could not see, that on the plain down beyond the guns and facing the renewed attack, they had but the merest simulation of a continuous firing line, merely three Battalions. Passing along the rear of the gunline, Carr could say no more to Sillery than a few words, as he ran on.

"Well done, Sillery. We can do this!"

Back in the centre Lacey now realised that conflict was but moments away. He looked over to see Heaviside, stood next to Colour Sergeant Bennet.

"You're first, Heaviside."

Heaviside raised his sword, but he had something to impart first.

"Let no man's heart fail because of him; thy servant will go and fight with this Philistine. One Samuel. 17 verse 32."

A pause.

"Front rank. Present!"

The muskets reached out beyond and around Lacey and the order was repeated out from the centre to the flank Companies. Lacey let them come on until they came up to the French dead of the previous encounter.

"Fire!"

The muskets crashed out and all was smoke as the muskets came down for Heaviside's front rank to make a rapid reload. Then, at this signal and all along the front rank, moving both left and right, half Company volleys crashed out. Lacey stood and waited for the smoke to clear, as did Heaviside, now choosing his moment. As the smoke thinned in the breeze, he called 'Present' and the muzzles of the second line came down beside Lacey. There was just time enough for Lacey to see that the French front rank before them had been demolished, almost all prone on the ground, before Heaviside, with the smoke now almost gone, called out 'Fire' and again came the blast of noise and choking smoke. Lacey now turned to pass through the ranks and he emerged out of the second rank just as Heaviside ordered the front rank to fire again. There was nothing more that Lacey could do now, other than to encourage his men. The half Company volleys were incessant, the noise itself deeply intimidating besides the non-stop assault of the bullets against the French ranks, but it was plain that his own men were now taking casualties, as bodies slumped down between the feet of their comrades and the men from the second rank stepped forward to fill the gap. The French were standing; like the veterans they were, to make a firefight of it, their Officers knowing that they outnumbered their enemies by over five to one.

For those of the Light Company on the left, life was suddenly an experience of noise, smoke and the closing of their minds to all but the automatic motions of loading, waiting and firing. Joe Pike was in the front rank, with Tom Miles to his left and John Davey locked on behind. At the first discharge all was dense smoke as they reloaded, but, with that done, Joe Pike raised his Baker to the 'make ready' and looked forward, which caused him near panic.

"Tom! I can't see anything! What do I aim at? Tom. What do I do?"

Miles was also at the 'make ready'.

"Wait for Drake's order. If you can't see nuthin, then just aim a bit down from level and pull the trigger. Anything blue, aim at it. If you sees a shako, two foot below."

The smoke was clearing and Pike saw a row of shakoes, around 40 yards distant. Drake also could now also see enough.

"Present!"

Pike aimed his Baker just below a shako that was a little higher than the others.

"Fire!"

The Baker kicked back and Pike began an automatic reload.

"I think that worked, Tom."

He turned his head slightly to bite the cartridge, but not to see Miles there, instead a space that was soon filled by Nat Solomon. Tom Miles was rolling on the ground, holding his leg and cursing. Pike stopped his reload and reached down to him, which was noticed by Ellis.

"Keep firing, damn you! The more bullets you sends into those bastards yonder, the less of us gets knocked over like that."

Shocked at the fierce rebuke, Pike drew out his ramrod and continued to reload. As he finished there came a yelp from Captain Drake and Ellis took over giving the orders.

Over on the right, O'Hare came to the Grenadiers, and began shouting encouragements, however, mostly useless above the din. He was there because his trust of Carravoy and D'Villiers was not of the fullest, but there could be no cause for concern, the Grenadiers were punishing the French as hard as any Company of the 105th. Both Ameshurst and D'Villiers were obviously controlling their half-Company volleys as well as any other Officer in the line, Ameshurst, in between using a whole stream of words wholly unbecoming of an Officer, mostly centered around the dubious parentage of the French. D'Villiers, in contrast, was stood in a dreamlike state which translated into a nightmare inside his head, but, as far as his men and O'Hare were concerned, he was stood in the front rank, sword erect, controlling their fire. His narrowed mind dutifully watched for the French shakoes through the smoke, which would bring about another half-Company volley. However, it should be their Captain who was controlling the fire of the Grenadiers and what O'Hare did not like was to see Carravoy behind the second rank, albeit encouraging his men vociferously. He angered instantly.

"You should be alongside your far right file. Get there now!"

This place was near enough for O'Hare to point at and Carravoy, the shock of the order coming on top of his fear of the mind numbing conflict, ran off to comply; he was in no condition to argue. At that moment, O'Hare saw Mackenzie, still mounted and riding along the back of his line, shouting encouragements, mostly unheard above the incessant crash of his men's reply to the French onslaught. Mackenzie stopped.

"O'Hare, is it not?"

O'Hare saluted.

"Yes Sir."

"We're holding them, tell Lacey. The Guards have

266

come back, what's left of them, an' there somethin' come down off the hill, sent by Himself, so ah've bin told."

O'Hare nodded.

"Yes Sir, we're holding here, and should………."

O'Hare stopped in mid sentence. At that moment a hole appeared in Mackenzie's tunic just below his left collarbone. He toppled forward and would have hit the ground had O'Hare not caught him and eased him to the ground, to then loosen his collar. That done, he shouted at Carravoy, now stood near and in the correct place.

"Carravoy! Get two men to carry the General back!"

However, the General raised his hand to seize O'Hare's left epaulette. His words came between gasps for air.

"No, lad. No! Ah'm done, ah can feel it. The lads are holdin', guid lads all. Tell 'em so, an' keep 'em goin'. Tell Lacey…….."

But the sentence was chocked off by a huge gobbet of blood emerging from his mouth and Mackenzie's head fell back. The two soldiers had arrived and O'Hare gave his order.

"Carry the General back, to our old line. Then back to your places."

O'Hare was overcome as he watched them carry the body back, but then he set his teeth and rose, needing to find Lacey. Holding his sword safely away from his feet, he ran to the centre, noting with grim satisfaction the smooth, non-stop movement of his men re-loading, readying their weapons and firing to orders. The rhythm of their defence was being maintained; the punishment being given to the French must be appalling. He found Lacey, giving water to a wounded man and he ran up and knelt beside him.

"Mackenzie's dead. Just now. You're the Brigadier!"

Lacey showed no reaction, but lowered the canteen to place it beside the man's hand.

"What orders to give? If we hold, the thing's done. There'll be no more after this, we've fought each other to a standstill."

O'Hare nodded.

"Right. Then I'm for the front rank! Where else? Try to do some good."

He picked up a discarded musket and pulled an ammunition pouch from the body of a dead soldier. With that he filled one of the many gaps in the second rank and began to load.

"Mind if I join you, boys? I fancy a go at these unwelcome Johnnies!"

Ironic laughter came from either side and soon he was at the 'make ready' and under Heaviside's orders. He well knew the Hell of the firing line, but if his joining them put extra spirit into the men stood close, then he would do it. All around was noise, smoke, the flash from the flintlocks and the blast from muzzles so close as to make any head dizzy from the repeated explosions. The Colour Company were behaving perfectly, their muskets going through the motions to enable them to respond to Heaviside's orders and O'Hare was confident that the same was happening all along their line, but that was much thinned, the second rank being less then half what it was. He had little idea of how long he stood there amongst the common Privates manning the firing line, for the uproar was incessant and he envied the soldiers who had tied a rag across their ears. All too soon, he also had a raging thirst from biting the cartridges and he took the time for a swallow of water from the canteen of the man next to him. On extracting the next cartridge from the box, he noticed that it was over half empty, so he must have fired almost thirty shots, this confirmed by the fearsome recoil of his musket, which told him that the barrel was now badly fouled. He must have been in the line for nearly ten minutes. Then came a call, which brought him out of his automatic work with the musket.

"Sir! An Ensign's down."

He looked over, but The Colour still remained upright. A Colour Sergeant must be holding it. O'Hare bit into the cartridge, then tipped a little into the priming pan.

"Then grab some Drummerboy. Anyone will do."

He then poured the rest of the powder into the barrel, stuffed in the paper with the bullet and pulled out the ramrod from its guides, giving no further thought to the Ensign as he finished his reloading.

Lacey was in need of re-assurance. What was happening with the combat between his men and the French? He found a gap in the second rank and looked between the heads of his men standing before. What he heard from the Private stood to his left re-assured him greatly.

"We're holding these, Sir. They've stopped an' come no nearer. We're spinnin' 'em, soon as they steps forward."

He ran to another gap and was further relieved to see the same. His half Company volleys were bringing down whole sections of the column's front rank. What this was doing to the French was not hard to calculate, even though veterans, victors all over Europe, they were not expecting this, the fiercest resistance they had even encountered. Lacey felt inspired, immeasurably proud of his men, all stood loading and firing, all holding to their Officer's commands. He filled his lungs.

"Well done, lads. Stand fast. They can't take much more! Close up to them, boys. Get right in their faces."

As if in obedience his men edged closer to the still solid blue line.

On the left, Carr was doing the same as O'Hare, only him with a Baker rifle, which he used to accurately bring down any Officer or NCO that he could see. Beyond Sillery, he was sure that the 48th were performing heroics to hold back their columns, but it was the guns that were doing more damage to the French than the musketry, all six now definitely firing canister into the columns. This Carr knew, as a glance left showed the gunners loading into the muzzles of their busy guns the canvas bags full of musket balls. Being on the left of the 105th, he could not fail to notice that they had been edging right, to close to the centre and fill the gaps left by casualties, but this lengthened the gap between him and Sillery. There was no change in the intensity of the fighting, because the French, still in vast numbers, were filling the casualties in their front from the numerous ranks behind, but their dead and wounded were now in a three deep pile before them. Suddenly came hope, when an Irish voice came onto his left shoulder and it was not O'Hare.

"Metcalf. 83rd. I'm bringing mine back into the line, either side of the guns. We'll make a better job of it this time."

Carr could do nothing but nod before the Officer was gone. If a Colonel or Major, he knew not, but within a minute Carr had the 83rd's Grenadiers within touching distance and their volleys joined his own.

Simultaneously, Lacey, as acting Brigadier, was giving orders to bring the reformed 61st back into the line. The immediate concern was the gap between his 105th and the reformed Guards, caused by both closing in to their centre, leaving gaps on their flanks. The Guards had returned to a place between his 105th and the 45th He was talking to a Major of the 61st, their Colonel having been wounded.

"Get one wing in there. I'll lead your other between the 45th and 24th."

The Major reached his men first and yelled his order.

"Lights, Nine to Six, with me! Grenadiers and Two to Five. With the Colonel."

Lacey ran on behind The Guards and then the 45th, hoping that the Companies numbered would follow, they did. It was evident from the crash of their volleys that The Guards and the 45th were dealing out a dreadful mauling,

270

but when he came to the 24th he was shocked. There was hardly any line left at all, no second rank and several gaps in the front rank. They had suffered severely, their dead and wounded at their feet, but their Colours remained upright and those still standing maintained their fire into the French ranks before them. Whilst Lacey stood in disbelief, his five Companies of the 61st formed their line in the space and soon began their own half Company volleys against those opposite. Lacey ran back to his own Command to find O'Hare where he had placed himself in the line close to The Colours. There Lacey noticed that his own firing line had been edging forward to close the range, this evidenced by the trail of dead and wounded now behind them, no longer at their feet. Peering through the thinning smoke of another volley he could see that the range was down to closer than 20 yards, which meant that every shot from the thinning ranks of his own men, all still maintaining their fire discipline, was finding a mark.

The space behind the fighting line of the 105th was a scene of nightmare. The number of dead was bad enough, but much worse was the fate of the wounded, many too badly injured and condemned as too likely to die, therefore left to their fate where they had fallen. Equally dreadful were the screams and suffering of those dragged back from danger, hauled over the ground by whoever came, Waggoners, Orderlies, Bandsman and Followers, many of whom now lay dead and wounded themselves. Where they were taken was a scene of almost total despair, as Medical Orderlies ran back and forth doing their best to staunch the flow of blood from almost who arrived, whilst Surgeon Pearce worked ceaselessly at his blood drenched table. Whilst Sedgwicke hurried around with water and bandages, his superior Albright stood in a state of shock and stupor, stood amidst a scene that he could barely take in. Men were screaming before, behind and to either side, making it impossible to choose who to give succour to, either medical help or the Last Rites. By instinct he knelt beside one, but his choice was the poorest, the wound was severe but not life threatening, if the blood could be staunched. He saw this, but remained helpless, until Eirin Mulcahy came to the far side of the soldier, pulled out the man's belt and used it as a tourniquet. She looked at his distraught and bemused face.

"It's alright, Father, I'll take care of this. There's plenty of other men needing the final words from such as yourself."

Then Sedgwicke arrived, having overheard.

"This way, Sir. The men needing you are over here."

Still in the midst of the conflict, for Carr, on the left, hope was growing further. The French were edging back, leaving the bank of their dead now clear before them. The incessant and overlapping volleys had taken their toll throughout a firefight that had lasted for what seemed an hour, but was actually only 20 minutes. Then hope turned to certainty. From somewhere on the left, seemingly from the 48th, beyond the 83rd, there came a cheer. It was taken up by the 83rd and, like a wave it carried on, picked up hoarsely by his own Regiment and then continuing on, seemingly down to the Pajar. The sound acted like a final devastating volley such as to cause the French to finally lose heart and to fall back and so they did, still facing the British line, but leaving their ground covered in their dead and wounded, many piled one onto the other. Carr's wing of the 105th made to advance forward, but he ran in front of them.

"Stay! Hold here. The things done. Hold here."

For many it was as though the strings holding them up had been cut and they fell to their knees, clutching for water-bottles. For others it was sheer relief, leaning on their muskets and shaking hands with messmates still standing. All over the battlefield the musket firing died away. There came some sounds of some form of conflict beyond the Medellin, faint sounds to those stood in the centre, but the battle was done, what remained to be coped with was the aftermath, spread shockingly, both at their feet and out before them.

oOo

Jed Deakin and Toby Halfway were stood together, both leaning forward, both supported by their muskets, both too hot to hold, they could but lean on the muzzles protected by the thick cloth of their tunics.

"I ain't never seen the likes of this before, Tobe, an' I never wants to again."

Halfway made no reply, he was too appalled at what stretched out before him. It mirrored the scene of a massacre, bodies lay side by side and piled up, and the scene was not quiet, hundreds of the wounded cried out for help and succour. Before them was the desolation of the battle's aftermath, immediate, with the smoke not yet cleared and the now pointless cacophony of the final cannon exchange between the Cascajal and Medellin. The gunsmoke from this final and ultimately insignificant chapter of the day's events drifted like a shroud down towards the town, as if to draw a merciful veil over an event utterly ghastly and tragic. As if the final French attack of the battle was not catastrophe enough, acrid smoke blew back into the faces of the British lines, smoke from grass fires, started by the final cannonading. Deakin knew what it meant.

"There's wounded out there, as is goin' to get burned, burnt to death even."

However, this was spoken as he attended to his first concern, the Regimental Colour, which should now be rolled up and stored. He took it from Rushby and began the process, but found it to be almost impossible. The green silk was full of holes, both large from cannonballs and also small, from grapeshot and musketballs. The shaft was also severely damaged in several places. He sighed.

"Bridie's goin' to have a fine time repairing this

273

lot!"

The same observation regarding the spreading fires had not escaped Lacey, now acting as Brigadier, but the French were still in sight, which placed him in a quandary, 'Should I send out parties to gather the wounded, or hold my line? They may try again.' However, two things enabled him to make up his mind, firstly, that the French were collecting their own wounded and, secondly, he could also see that the fires were spreading, the dry stubble and trodden down corn burning fiercely. Soon came the sound of flat musketry, a dull subdued popping, accompanied by renewed screams. The cartridge boxes, still on the bodies of the wounded, were exploding in the heat, causing additional appalling injuries. He needed no further thought and ran up to the ranks of the 83rd, to find their Colonel, whom he knew.

"Davison, pleased to see you still here. Mackenzie's dead, so I'm acting Brigadier. We must send men forward to get the wounded out of those fires, or put them out or do something. Are you in any shape to provide men? I'm sending mine, four Companies. We must do something."

Davison nodded and answered as he turned away to carry out his own promise.

"I'll send the same, assuming Johnny doesn't start another show."

Lacey looked at the French, now in the far distance, but Davison had gone and Lacey felt safe enough to now send out his own men. He ran back to Carr, still on the left.

"Henry. Get out there with four Companies, the Lights, seven, eight and nine. Do what you can about those fires and get the wounded back in, theirs as well as ours."

Carr gathered his men and led them forward, but it was a hopeless task, the severely wounded were everywhere and any measure of command was impossible. His men were soon scattered across the area, doing what could inadequately be done, but at least the fires were soon extinguished. Within an hour almost the whole British army was out towards the Portina and beyond, carrying wounded back to their lines. Lacey was as horrified as anyone on seeing the line upon line of wounded, both French and British, now building up on what had once been the 105th firing line. He saw Surgeon George Pearce, moving down the line, instructing his Orderlies and he ran towards him, coming up to him soon enough to hear him say one of three things to his men as he came to examine each patient.

"Beyond help. On the table. Can wait."

Lacey kept pace with him

"George. Have you enough men?"

Pearce looked at him.

"To carry to the table those I may be able to save; yes. To perform the operations, no! There's just me."

Lacey nodded, his face full of pity, not just for all the wounded, but also for Surgeon Pearce himself, whom he knew was now utterly overwhelmed.

Out towards the Portina, Sedgwicke and Reverend Albright were walking amongst the wounded, giving a last drink of precious water and saying the last Rites to both friend and foe. Incongruously, a French Priest appeared, having ridden on a donkey to the scene of conflict from the French lines, which were now a half-mile back in the middle distance. He saw Albright and recognised the Vestments that were part of his uniform.

"Ah, M'sieu. C'est mal. C'est tres mal!"

It was Sedgwicke who replied, Albright having no French.

"Oui, M'sieu Le Cure'. C'est mal, très certainement, très mal."

The Cure' walked around the small area, soon in a helpless daze and then reduced to merely kneeling and wringing his hands whilst chanting prayers.

Meanwhile, Pike, Davey, Byford and Saunders were out with the Light Company, under Carr's orders, but hoping to get themselves back to their lines, under any pretext. It was Davey who spoke the reason.

"We've got to get back. Find out where they took Tom. We've spent enough time out here to keep Carr happy. If we pick up another and get him back, then we can find Tom."

Davey looked around, but he was spoilt for choice as to severely wounded, before he finally choose a KGL Sergeant, him with a wound of unknown severity, but it had made a wide rent in his tunic.

"He'll do."

They gave him some water from a French canteen and then, despite his screaming, they rolled him onto their blanket, by now wet with blood, and each to a corner, they carried him back. Their burden, now in less pain, spoke to them, between gasps.

"Danke, meine Kameraden. Vielen danke."

Saunders looked down, wincing from a wound of his own in the top of his left arm.

"Just doin' what we can, mate, but you may not thank us so much when the Surgeon gets hold of you."

Soon they could drop their patient at the end of yet another extending row, and then Davey looked around, for wounded that had their own 105th facings, the bright green. These were five rows back and so they picked their way over. Joe Pike soon began calling.

"Tom! Tom! Are you here, Tom?"

A tunic rose up, its wearer leaning on his elbows.

"Yer! Yer! I'm yer."

They soon came to him and Byford examined his wound, first by cutting open his left trousers leg around a hole in the cloth that was much stained with blood, above his knee. A rope had been wound tight around his upper thigh. Byford carefully pulled back the cloth to reveal a bullet hole, some nine inches above his knee. Joe looked at the wound, then at Miles.

"Does it hurt, Tom?"

Miles gave him a look somewhere between rage

and impatience.

"Course it bloody well hurts, you soft sod! Even more if that rope was took off, so leave'n be!"

However, Saunders was looking around, realising that they could take advantage of all the confusion.

"We can't leave him here. The Surgeon will just take his leg off! 'Tis quicker than fishin' about for a bullet."

Miles heard all

"Well, ain't you the sort of cove as is just needed to cheer a body up!"

However, Saunders was ignoring him.

"We have to get him to where he just looks like minor wounded. Them as has no need for the Surgeon, at least for a while. Try to get the ball out ourselves."

Davey nodded.

"Right. You're right. An' that's back to our mess. Bridie an' Molly will look after him, at least till we can see what can be done."

Davey looked at Miles then at Saunders.

"Pick 'im up and over your shoulder. Then back to Bridie an' Nellie. Then we'd better get back out, afore Carr sees us."

Then he looked at Miles.

"An' you needs to keep your gob shut, like it was just a scratch or suchlike."

Miles looked daggers at him, but his face grimaced with pain as Saunders dragged him to his feet and slung him over his right shoulder, then set off to cover the few hundred yards back to their camp. However, after but a minute Saunders was challenged by an Officer of the 45th.

"You! What are you doing with that man? The lines for the wounded are back there. Take him back and then get yourself back out to bring in the other wounded."

However, Saunders had a reply.

"This uns just had a whack on his head, Sir. A ball passed a bit close. I'm gettin' him back to our Followers, Sir. They can deal with this, an' not bother the Surgeon. Sir.

He'll be right in a day or so."

The Officer took a step sideways, still looking, but not enough for any kind of serious examination and he soon gave up. He had his own urgent concerns.

"Right, but then back out. There's plenty more wounded that need to be brought in."

"Yes Sir, As you say Sir."

As Saunders jogged on, the Officer noticed the tourniquet, but was too pre-occupied with his own 45th wounded to call Saunders back. He soon reached the camp where Bridie and Nellie were trying to conjure a meal out of biscuit, meat bones and some herbs, but that soon stopped when Saunders lay Miles down close by the fire.

"He's took a bullet in his leg, but we hopes to dig it out and save his leg. Sometime this evening, so can you look after him, 'till we can get back to you?"

Both women nodded and Saunders ran off. Bridie then brought some hot water, Nellie found a cloth and both then set about cleaning the wound. Eirin also arrived and she continued the cleaning, whilst Bridie held his hand and wiped his face, while doing her best to be comforting.

"We'll get Jed. He'll know what to do."

Nellie than gave him some brandy mixed with water, which did most to improve his state of mind.

Meanwhile, Lacey continued to think about the whole Brigade. Water was the biggest concern after the wounded, who were being brought back in, now by the whole army, or so it appeared. Lacey saw Carr.

"Henry. Can we get any water from the stream?"

Carr shook his head.

"No Sir. All the to and fro across it, theirs and ours has turned it into slush."

Lacey frowned.

"Any ideas?"

"Only a hope, Sir. Those houses behind us, they may have wells."

Lacey nodded.

"Right. Go and see."

Carr pointed to three Grenadiers.

"You! With me."

In this manner was the rest of the afternoon and the evening spent, obtaining water from a handful of wells at the rear of their lines and the bringing in of the wounded of both sides, but to these poor wretches simply being moved made little difference. No one came to ease their suffering, but at least they were now amongst the living and those about to die, rather than being out with those already dead.

Carr had found a well and had left RSM Gibney to supervise the carrying of buckets to the lines of wounded, where the water was passed to one of Surgeon Pearce's Orderlies for the precious liquid to be poured, via a cast iron ladle, into the parched mouths of those awaiting the Surgeon's attentions. As the light faded, Carr was stood with Lacey and O'Hare, but it was the Irishman who voiced their next concern.

"With night the locals will be out, murdering both theirs and ours. There are still hundreds out there."

Lacey shook his head.

"The men are exhausted. And starving. And few got any sleep last night. I can't ask them to mount picket throughout another night."

He stood, in sorrow, but still thinking.

"We can ask Donkin. He's Division Commander now, and his Brigade were barely engaged."

Then he released a deep sigh.

"And food! We've only had half rations today and the day before."

O'Hare nodded his head.

"Quarter more like, but let's get a message to Donkin."

He looked around and found a Lieutenant of 4 Company.

"Gerald. Take a message up to the Medellin, will you?"

oOo

Through the growing dark the wounded continued to be found and brought back. Out amongst the casualties, Davey, Pike, Saunders, Solomon and Byford now listened more than heard, but it was Davey who stood up to see a new development, that the French had lit fires all along their lines.

"Well, Johnny's still around, but 'twouldn't do no harm if they did their bit to get their wounded out of this."

It was Saunders who answered, out of the gloom.

"Don't speak too soon, keep 'em here. You look through the haversacks of some of these dead Frenchers. They've been given, or stole, a good portion of rations. We should try to get some of it back."

He shook a French canteen

"They got water, too."

Davey agreed.

"Right. Injured back in, then, in the dark, same time, we gets rations off the French. Worry most about the injured, 'tis easier to find a full haversack in the dark than tryin' to discover if another poor sod's half dead or close to dying."

He released a deep sigh.

"On top, an' I don't know about you, but I needs to sleep. I can't manage this for much longer."

There came no disagreement, but, nevertheless, for the next hour and in the full darkness they examined the bodies still covering the ground, the only light coming from the distant French bonfires and the waxing moon for the coming August, but that shrouded in some thin cloud. Some lanterns were moving around, but they added nothing by way of light that could help. Many French haversacks were simply removed and hung around their own shoulders, or the contents stuffed into one, but often they took the time to give one last drink of water to a dying man. They left many where they were, because, Davey reasoned, that if they could last the night out there, then they could be saved next morning. The too badly injured would die anyway. The Humanitarian Byford objected, but Davey replied harshly.

"We've no food, John. The whole damn army! Come two or three days we'll be marchin' out of here, still with no food, an' then we starves or drops out to be done in by the French or the peasants. We can't leave this food on the battlefield. It may be all what keeps us all alive!"

Byford knew he was right, so held his peace. Davey had spoken the brutal reality of their predicament, but, on their return back they did agree to carry one more in. They let Byford choose and he was doing so, when they heard a scream but yards away. They all ran over to find a peasant who was going through the pockets of a wounded French soldier. Saunders kicked him to the ground, then drew out his bayonet to place the point up under the man's jaw, at which point he began pleading.

"Por favor, Senores. Por favor. Sólo tomo de soldados franceses. No Inglese. No Inglese."

"What's he sayin', Byfe?"

"He says that he only takes from French soldiers. Not ours."

"We should kill the murderin' bastard."

Davey intervened.

"No! We don't murder, an' we don't know that he has. An' we knows full well what the French does to peasants who don't give up their food."

He now spoke to Byford, anxious that they finish their time away from their lines.

"You made up your mind yet?"

Byford walked off, but then Davey noticed the sack tied around the Spaniard's shoulders.

"What's in that sack?"

Saunders pulled off the sack and felt inside. All inside were hard objects.

"Plunder! Valuables of one sort or another."

"Any rings? With blood?"

"Some, but too dark to see."

Davey had now made his decision.

"Benefit of the doubt! Haul him up, kick his arse and send 'im off."

Saunders did just that and the man uttered his deepest thanks, even as Saunders boot lifted him off the ground to send him on his way.

"What to do with this, John? You can bet 'tis worth a bit of coin."

In the darkness, Davey shook his head.

"We can't carry that back in. Food is one thing, booty is another. If we'n caught 'twill mean a floggin', maybe even the rope."

A pause.

"Best leave it here. We've enough to carry."

Nat Solomon then spoke up, somewhat appalled.

"Hang on, hang on! To carry back a sack full of loot is one thing, but a few bits hid in our pockets, like out of sight. Now that's another."

With that obvious statement, all dipped their hand into the sack and pulled out several articles each, which went into their pockets. That done, the sack was depleted, but still substantially heavy.

Saunders lifted his head. Had Byford made his selection of their final wounded man?

"John! You found one?"

"Yes! And some kind of French Priest, too. Mumbling prayers. Probably what they call a Curé."

At which point, Pike had a thought.

"We could give the sack to him. It's from the French after all."

Davey was running out of patience.

"Right. To the Vicar. Then we'n back."

He turned towards the direction from which they had heard Byford.

"John. We got a sack of booty here, off that Don.

Give it to their Vicar.'

They all picked their way to where Byford had found a wounded Guardsman, with Pike carrying the sack, which he handed to Byford.

"John says give it to the Priest you found."

Byford took the sack and placed it under the arm of the Curé, him still kneeling and still praying.

"Monsieur le Curé. Pour les pauvres, de soldats français."

The words brought the Curé out of his trancelike state. He looked up at Byford, seeing only his silhouette against the few stars.

"Merci M'sieu. Merci beaucoup."

Byford patted his shoulder and then left to take his corner of the blanket, which now contained a grateful Guardsman, who said little, lapsing in and out of consciousness, despite being given some water and French brandy. It was not long before they passed through an orderly line of Redcoats, obviously moving towards the French to form a picket line and no words were exchanged, everyone was simply too tired. However, Carr still sent them out again, twice more and, thus, it was past Midnight when their own particular wounded man could receive any attention, but this came in the form of a simple, blunt verdict from Jed Deakin, himself just come in from collecting wounded.

"Get George Fernley. He's medical for the Lights an' the one I'd trust. Get George."

Toby Halfway climbed wearily to his feet and trudged off, but, within ten minutes George Fearnley was kneeling over the leg of Tom Miles, to then shake his head.

"Can't do nuthin' till mornin'. Better light, for one thing, and, if I'm to go pokin' about for a ball, a few hours will let the swellin' go down some."

No-one felt able to argue and so Miles was given some food and some French brandy, for all around to then fall to the ground and immediately sleep, all too tired even to remove their kit, bar Joe Pike who half removed his backpack before succumbing to deep sleep himself.

However, not so for Carr, and also for many other Officers of Wellesley's army. He returned to where his tent should be, expected to be stood welcoming and erect, to find all a wrecked shambles, with Morrison trying to restore some order by the inadequate light of a lantern.

"Morrison. What's happened?"

His servant was almost in tears.

"Well, Sir, as much as I can gather from the Followers around, Spanish deserters plundered all during the battle, 'cos no-one was around, Sir. I was in the firing line. The tents were deserted."

Carr stood aghast, then came another question.

"Where's Captain Drake?"

"He's up on the Medellin, Sir. With the Officer wounded. He was hit in the foot, Sir, so got took up there."

Carr was immediately concerned. A hit in the foot could mean amputation.

"How bad?"

"Oh, not bad, Sir. He may have lost a toe perhaps, but he stayed with his Company until all was finished. Then he hobbled off, Sir."

Carr felt much reassured but then he returned to the subject of their wrecked camp and he looked around at the scattered remains of many Officers' belongings, not just his own.

"Spanish, you say?"

"Yes, Sir, so the Followers said. They didn't bother them, just went for the tents, where they knew some valuables would be."

He let out a quick sigh.

"I'm afraid they smashed open your chest, Sir, along with that of Mr. Drake, Mr. Maltby and Mr. Shakeshaft. I can pull out your cot, Sir, they did nothing to that, and I can get much of the tent back up, Sir."

Carr let out his own sigh. He was utterly tired, so

much so that he could barely think.

"No need. Drag it out and I'll sleep outside. Get some sleep yourself. Tomorrow will be a long day."

oOo

The next day dawned for yet another burning sun to climb into the arching blue of a Spanish July and, under it, Wellesley's army again dragged themselves to their feet. Lacey, O'Hare and Carr immediately found each other in order to plan the day, for which they sat at a small table, purloined from a nearby building and hoping to begin with some breakfast, but all that was placed in front of them was a mug of coffee and some army biscuits. Lacey looked over his shoulder at Bryce, his Sergeant Clerk and servant.

"What's this Bryce? I was hoping for some bread rolls, at least."

Bryce's face showed all the anxiety and disappointment that he felt.

"Sorry, Sir, but those Spanish as deserted during the fight and plundered the Officer's tents, did the same to a supply train further back, Sir, an' took all the flour."

Resignedly, Lacey picked up a biscuit and dipped it into his coffee, this being black and bitter. All the sugar was now gone.

O'Hare picked up the theme.

"We can't ask too much of the men. They aren't getting much more than four or five mouthfuls to last them all day."

He took a sip from his own mug.

"And, soon, in a couple of days, we will be marching away in full retreat."

Lacey nodded.

"I'll talk to Donkin. He's Division now, perhaps he can get something out of Wellesley."

He paused, but had to push away his own black thoughts in order to sound positive.

"Right. To business. What's to be done today?"

However, before either of his two companions could answer, they heard cheering building from the direction of the Pajar and then, when the cheering reached them, they could see the reason. First, came the fierce and dour countenance of General Robert Crauford, on a huge horse, then followed by the three battalions of his Light Brigade. However, Deakin was not convinced.

"What's the good of these? 'Tis just more mouths to feed."

However, events of the late morning was to prove him wrong. Crauford had abandoned his baggage to increase the speed of his forced march, but late morning it arrived and the whole army could be given some rations, albeit very meagre, it being enough for three Battalions but now having to be shared over 36, somewhat deleted Battalions. However, the messes of Deakin, Davey et al, gratefully received the rations, although merely flour and biscuit, but these could be hoarded for later, because breakfast consisted of what had been gleaned from the French dead. Although it was mostly biscuit, garlic and chopped up cheese, it did included some sausage and plenty of French brandy, to accentuate or hide the taste, depending on your palate.

Soon, the results of their Officers' deliberations around coffee and biscuits were soon being spread around the Battalion and Sergeant Ellis arrived at the mess of Davey and Saunders, all in close proximity to that of Jed Deakin. Ellis went immediately to his Light Infantrymen, but stopped himself from speaking when he saw Tom Miles. The antipathy between the two men was deep, but Ellis knew the value of a soldier like Tom Miles, vicious and reliable in a fight and almost as good a marksman as John Davey.

"How bad?"

Miles pulled open the long slit in his trouser leg.

"Bullet."

"Still in?"

"Yes."

"You should be with the Surgeon."

Miles angered immediately.

"An' what will he bloody well do? Leg off and bugger off!"

Jed Deakin had heard all and now intervened. He and Ellis were different kind of NCO's entirely, but they shared no dislike between them and each saw the other as steady and capable.

"We've got George Fearnley comin' over, to see if he can fish out the bullet. Then we can only hope."

Ellis saw the sense. Keeping Tom Miles within the Company was worth the effort and trouble.

"Right. But you'll need lads to hold him down whilst all that is going on, and I've orders to get everyone out; collecting wounded and then burying the dead."

"I hear that, Ethan, and soon as 'tis done, I'll send them out. Carr nor Drake will complain if two or three lads is kept back awhile to save the leg of Tom Miles, awkward sod as he may be."

Most laughed, save Miles, who looked much pained and aggrieved, but then Deakin offered himself.

"I'll be one."

However, as fate would have it, Fearnley arrived at that moment and Ellis immediately asked him.

"How many will you need to keep him still? You've got Jed and Zeke here, who else?"

"Two should do it. 'Tain't that bad. Zeke and Jed can do his shoulders and leg. Nellie and Bridie the other leg. Twill be easier what we gets him drunk!"

Miles was immediately incensed.

"You ain't wastin' good brandy on that! I'll hold still. B'ain't no need to make I three sheets to the wind for such as this!"

Ellis permitted himself a smile, then grinned malevolently at Miles.

"Well, there we are then. An' I hope that it don't hurt much more than full agony!"

"Sod off, Ellis!"

This Ellis ignored, but he then led his men away and all wished good luck to Miles as they passed, leaving Saunders now kneeling at his head. Fearnley gave his instructions.

"Zeke, hold down his shoulders, Jed, the leg."

He looked at Bridie and Nellie, stood nearby and waiting. Eirin was there also.

"You three, each an arm and the other leg."

The five positioned themselves, at which point Nellie and Miles shared a look, not of dislike, but one which showed that a truce had been struck, at least for now. Fearnley arranged his instruments; a sharp blade and two more, but square and flat, and a pair of forceps.

"I need clean water."

Bridie reached across for the bucket and Fearnley matched the two edges together of Miles trouser. His face became grim, the two edges did not match.

"Looks like the ball took in some cloth, Tom. That'll have to come out too."

Miles remained incensed.

"Just do what you've bloody well got to do."

Then Fearnley cut apart the trouser leg, from the bottom to almost the top, almost up to Miles' groin. He produced a flask of brandy, both French, and tipped it over the hole. Miles winced.

"Never mind wastin' my trousers, on top you'n wastin' good brandy too."

"There'll be plenty of both around here, to replace any used up. These trousers is French, b'ain't they?"

Miles nodded.

"S'right. Got at Oporto."

But while Miles was talking, Fearnley had cut into the flesh either side of the bullet hole, deep and almost three inches either way.

Miles' fists clenched together, but Fearnley had only just begun.

"This is going to hurt now, Tom!"

"Oh yes! Like that didn't!"

Fearnley took out a piece of wood with a leather thong at each end. It was covered in teeth marks and it went into Miles mouth, between his teeth, to be secured behind his head by the leather attached. Fearnley looked at his companions.

"Hold him."

Each took a firm grip and Fearnley inserted the forceps into the cut and Miles arched his back and gave out a stifled scream but he held himself steady. For a minute Fearnley searched down through the bullet hole and twice closed the forceps, but to no avail. Blood welled up which Bridie wiped away, but finally Fearnley close the forceps for the handles not to meet and he brought out the ball, which he placed on Miles chest.

"Keepsake!"

Even more anger arrived in Miles' eyes and he spoke something unintelligible over the gag. Bridie took the bullet and dropped it into a skillet lid.

"Zeke. Give 'im a drink. Brandy."

The gag was removed and Miles given a good swallow. Then the gag was replaced and Eirin was given a small stick with clean rag tied around it.

"Eirin. I needs you to wipe away the blood, while I tries to find the bit of cloth."

He took his two flat blades and eased the cut apart causing blood to flow immediately. He searched with his knife, whilst Eirin did her best to mop up the blood. Miles was tensed but lying still, with Zeke still holding down his shoulders.

"Well done, Tom. The worst is over. The ball's out, so not long now."

However, Fearnley was still searching and the full flow of blood caused Eirin to pull out her wiper.

"This is soaked. Have you another?"

Fearnley reached into his bag and found one, but then Eirin looked carefully at the first.

"What's this, stuck to the side?"

Fearnley took the stick and examined it. Amongst all the clotted blood he could see what they were looking for, a shred of cloth. He offered it to the edge of the trouser that had not matched its opposite and it fitted. He grinned mockingly at Miles as he removed the gag.

"There Tom. Eirin fished it out for you!"

Eirin laughed and leant right over Miles' face.

"Yes Tom. And for that you owe me a big kiss!"

It was of benefit that Eirin distracted the patient at that point, because Fearnley was pouring brandy into the wound which he had again prised apart. Miles screamed, but no-one was sure of the cause, either from pain or more probably the non-permitted use of the brandy. That over, he raised his head and, with the gag removed, he gave vent to his feelings.

"When this is done, I'll be bloody well up and punch you senseless, Fearnley!"

Fearnley laughed.

"You'll be up no where for some time, never mind the punchin', Tom Miles."

He returned to his task.

"Right, now for stitchin'."

Again from his medical kit, he found needle and clean cotton. Miles had no need to be held as seven stitches were inserted. The wound was washed and more brandy tipped over, to Miles continued annoyance. Fearley then bandaged the leg, before giving two more bandages to Miles.

"Change the bandage, every day. Which means washin' what's fouled."

Then he stared Miles full in the face.

"An' use the brandy. Infection now is your worst worry. It could mortify and that'll be you gone, never mind the leg!"

All nodded, including Miles, then to everyone's surprise, incongruously Miles offered his hand to Fearnley.

"Thanks, George. I'll not forget."

Fearnley nodded and took the hand, then he replied, but not unkindly.

"Sergeant to you!"

Deakin stood up as Fearnley left

"Right, Zeke. You'd better get out, like I promised Ellis."

Saunders departed and Deakin made to follow but first he gave a clear order to Miles.

"Keep that leg still, or 'twill start bleedin'."

The reply from Miles was a long pull on the brandy flask. Deakin looked at Nellie and Bridie.

"Find a long pole and bind it to his leg, so's he can't bend it. An' keep him still, but if he wants to drink himself out of this world, well, that's his affair!"

oOo

Lacey and O'Hare were watching the last of the wounded being brought in, but most were now very near to death. O'Hare spoke the obvious.

"We bring them here, but then what. The track down to Talavera is covered in wounded, the streets are full and the population, curse them, will not allow any wounded of any army, into their homes. On top, every Doctor and Surgeon has now been working for over 24 hours, with no break."

Lacey nodded, his face as much a picture of helpless despair as O'Hare's.

"I know. It's hopeless, and we'll be marching soon. How do we take them with us? We can leave the French, they'll be back once we've gone, but our own?"

He paused.

"What's our 'Butcher's Bill'? Any idea?"

O'Hare shook his head.

"Not yet. Not until we call The Roll, but it'll be bad?"

"Bad as Coruna?"

O'Hare nodded.

"About. But we can't parade the men to find out until all this work's done. We'll be burying soon."

"What about Officers?"

"Three wounded. One Captain, two Lieutenants. One Ensign dead, Trenton Neape. Through the head, he was dead before he hit the ground."

At that moment Rufane Donkin arrived, having ridden down from the Medellin. He dismounted wearily from an equally weary horse. He nodded his greetings to the pair and began his enquiries, his own fatigue making him terse and impatient.

"What's your situation?"

Lacey answered.

"We've many casualties, many more wounded than dead. The biggest problem is water and food. The men are practically starving and, as we speak, we are still bringing in wounded, from both sides."

Donkin nodded, but his comments remained terse.

"Regarding water, the Portina's running better, now it's been cleared of dead and channeled through the mud. Wellesley tells me that some food is on its way from both our own supplies and the Spanish, but the latter is just a promise that will be broken, I feel sure. Cuesta will prioritise his own army. We're now onto burying the dead, ours first, so get your men onto that. As for the wounded, that's the tragedy of this battle, many will have to be abandoned. We'll be marching back, probably in two days time, the day after tomorrow, or at least the day after that. Why, because the French are moving in behind us, which will place them between us and Portugal. The retreat won't be easy and I can tell you now that there will be nothing like adequate transport for our wounded. There are over 4,000 just from our army. Try to make your own arrangements for your own wounded, I can probably find you some transport from our baggage train."

His face became even more dour.

"I don't need to tell you to take only those that can travel and have a more than even chance of surviving the march. And rejoining the ranks."

The last was spoken with emphasis, but then he paused, giving time for any comment or question, but none came.

"Right, I'm on to the 45th and 24th. Expect to see me tomorrow, I'll have more news."

He remounted and rode off, for Lacey to then speak his next question to O'Hare.

"What of our wounded? How many?"

"A hundred give or take, at a guess. Pearce is working his way through them. The man hasn't stopped since we pulled back from the Alberche."

Lacey sighed.

"We must give him what help we can. There's a Sergeant with some medical training in each Company. Get them to him, then perhaps he can sleep for a couple of hours."

He paused to suck in a sorrowful breath and sigh again.

"Meanwhile, you heard what Donkin said, we're now burying our dead. Get that organised."

O'Hare looked fully at him.

"And tools? What do we use?"

Lacey pointed over his shoulder.

"There are farms up behind us, beyond the houses. Get some from there. Get Carr onto it and, if we're now burying, we'll need Albright and that odd cove Sedgwicke, he can say a word or two. And Heaviside will fill the gaps, I'm sure."

As a consequence, close to Noon, Carr was leading a Section of the Light Company to the farms beyond the houses where he had previously found the vital well and at the nearest, he saw some sheds and barns beside a well appointed house. He noticed a face at an upstairs window, before he knocked on the door, and it took a minute for a man to open it.

"¿Qué quieres?"

Carr had no idea what the man had said but immediately motioned for him to follow. The man came out of the door and followed Carr to the barn, where Carr's men had found various farm tools, all of which could help dig graves and were now in their possession. Carr pointed to the tools and then pointed back to the battlefield. If the man understood at that moment Carr knew not, but he did not care and he pointed with is thumb.

"Back!"

As Carr's men began to move, the man then clearly understood what was about to happen and barred their way out of the barn. The burly Nat Solomon and the even bigger Saunders brushed him aside and they left, at which point the man began screaming.

"Son ladrones! Le están robando mis herramientas. Mis herramientas!"

Not understanding one word, and short of patience, Carr turned to him and spoke, whilst prodding a finger into the man's chest, which intimidated him into silence.

"We've just bloody well kept the French out of your parlour, so you can lend us your tools to bury our dead and, like as not, you'll get most of them back."

The farmer stood aghast, helpless, there was nothing more that he could say and with that Carr started back, following his men. After their return and for the rest of the day, the task was to clear the battlefield of the British dead and bury them. Saunders, in charge of a burial party, began the task, but found it far from easy, the soil being rocky and none too deep. The dead could only be laid out in shallow graves and, after a few words from whoever was available, the earth was shovelled back over. The three

294

'clerics' named by Lacey, did as required, but it was only Sedgwicke and Heaviside who helped to place the bodies into the shallow trench, Albright stood and muttered pre-prayers before the closing of the grave. This being his first battle, he was clearly in a state of almost permanent shock, a kind of mental denial at the appalling consequences of the previous day's battle. Some British wounded were still being found, dreadfully sunburned and almost dead either from their wounds or dehydration, but these were almost all hopeless cases and were brought back to die at least amongst those who could speak the last words that they would hear in their own language and administer water to help their raging thirst.

Night approached again and this time the men of Crauford's Light Brigade went out into the growing dark on picket to discourage marauding locals still hoping to rob the thousands of bodies. The British trudged back after another exhausting day in the heat, back to sleep rather than to eat, for there remained little by way of rations. Carr, however, did not go straight to their re-erected tent, but instead to the Officer Hospital set up at the foot of the Medellin, conveniently off the track used by the 48th the previous day for their run down from that hill to help Mackenzie. Remembering what Morrison had told him and where Drake had been taken, he decided that the time had come to find out how severely his friend had been wounded. He soon saw many wounded Officers at the open-air hospital, each lying on their own blanket, or some on a straw-filled paliasse. Each Officer's jacket was hung on a support of all types but mainly a musket stuck into the ground by a bayonet. He found a Surgeon.

"I'm looking for an Officer of my Battalion, the 105th."

"Which Division?"

"Mackenzie's."

The surgeon smiled ironically.

"We've plenty of them, but try over that way."

He pointed in a direction further up the slope, and Carr walked on. He spoke the word 'Mackenzie's' several times to various Orderlies and each time was advised to walk on, but each time he was given good direction. With relief he saw the green facings on some jackets and one had Drake lying beneath it, but propped on one elbow and then, with equal relief, Carr saw that Drake had nothing missing. All that was different was a heavily bandaged right foot.

"Nat!"

Drake looked up.

"Henry! Good of you to show. You must be busy."

Carr nodded.

"Yes. Things are pretty grim. But how're you? Your foot, I take it?"

"Yes, but a bit of luck really."

He raised the bandaged limb, as if that would help with his explanation.

"Bullet hit the toe of my boot. It went between two toes and lodged there, splitting them apart. The sawbones says there is nothing broken, but there's an odd sort of cut down between the two, what's left after he pulled the bullet out."

Carr sat down, then looked from Drake to the bandage and back again, but Drake was now engaged in humour.

"Must mention this to my boot maker. The good leather and construction saved my foot, so I've been told. Do you think he'll give me another pair, this time on the cheap, if I spread the word about? Do you think?"

Carr laughed.

"You can only try and perhaps if you give him the boot to hang up somewhere, in full view, with a note something like 'Saved a customer's foot at Talavera' pinned to it."

Drake smiled.

"You think!"

He reached behind him.

"Well here it is."

He thrust his hand down through the boot for his finger to appear through a neat hole. Carr took the boot and studied the damage.

"Well, keep out of the water, when we come to any."

"True, but I'll be on horseback, at least for a week."

He leaned forward.

"Talking of sustenance. What's the food situation? Nothing's arrived and I do mean nothing. Can you get Morrison to bring anything up?

Carr shook his head.

"I'll try, but I can promise nothing. There are rumours of supplies coming from the Spanish, but that is utter stuff. We've had nothing from them since we crossed the border and that'll not change. All I can say is, that we will be pulling back soon, we have to. If we stay here we'll starve and be cut off by the French on top. Day after tomorrow, I'd say."

He saw Drake's face fall and he felt the need to be somewhat more encouraging.

"The men have found rations on the French dead. That's what's keeping them going. Johnny was better supplied than we were, so I'll get them to share a bit with you, if only a bit of French cheese and a clove of garlic!"

"Sounds dreadful, but I'll be grateful even for that."

He suddenly sat up.

"By the way, did you know that Templemere's here?"

"Here? He's been wounded?"

Drake grinned and nodded.

"Yes. Got a cut up his leg whilst sat with the 16th Dragoons behind Sillery's guns. Got it while still sat on his horse."

Drake ran his finger up his own leg to show the line of the cut.

"How'd you know?"

"Cornet from the 16th told me. When I saw the Lord Fred carried past, I made enquiries."

Drake then guffawed, almost in disgust.

"He screamed blue murder when a Medical Orderly tried to stitch him up. Said it had to be a proper Surgeon, and when one didn't come, that for obvious reasons, he lay there fuming, for a long time, until the Orderly did it anyway."

He pointed further up the hill.

"He's up over there, should you wish to pay your respects."

Carr breathed out something between a laugh and an ironic sigh.

"I think not! What I do think is that I need to get back."

He patted his arm.

"And I will try to get you some food."

Carr then stood up.

"Right. Best get back before it gets too dark and I get lost."

The following day, early, Carr took it upon himself to find Sergeant Ellis, finding him in the camping grounds of the Light Company. Ellis was sat with Fearnley and, on Carr's approach both sprang to attention.

"Sergeant Ellis."

"Sir."

"Your Captain is up at the Officer's Hospital."

"Yes Sir. We know."

"No food is arriving up there. I understand that several of your Company have gathered food from the French dead."

There was a pause, whilst Ellis pondered if that was a question or a statement.

"That seems to be so, Sir. Yes."

"Right. I want you to get around your various messes and gather something for him. He is your Company Captain, after all."

"As you say, Sir."

Carr nodded in satisfaction.

"Can I leave that with you, and you will take it up to him?"

"Yes Sir. I'll see to it, Sir."

Carr walked off and Ellis looked at Fearnley and sighed in annoyance.

"You hear that? Take some food off the lads. An' what have Shakeshaft 'n' Maltby thrown into the pot?"

Not in the best of humour, he picked up a spare haversack and began his rounds, which soon brought him to the mess of Davey, Saunders, and the rest.

"The Captain's wounded and up on the hill. Major Carr wants a bit of food sent up."

He sniffed loudly, indicating that what he was about to say he did not believe.

"Seems they're starving up there."

He opened the haversack.

"So, what can you throw in? Don't need to be much, so long as this is half filled."

Jed Deakin was sat nearby.

"Be you tellin' us, Ethan, that no rations is reachin' the Officer's Hospital?"

Ellis looked at him.

"That's pretty much what Major Carr said and that Captain Drake is very hungry."

"So he's takin' off of us! I'm not sure that's legal! There'll be nothing on that in King's Regs as says that men has to give up food when Officers is feelin' hungry. What if we'd paid for the provender out of our own coin?"

"I know, an' you may be right, but a bit thrown in from each mess won't hurt anyone too much an' then Carr's happy. You want to make a fuss, Jed, well that's up to you, but a bit of French cheese, an onion, an' some of their bread, that hard stuff, won't be too much missed, an' then the things over an' we won't have no Officers down on us."

He paused, whilst Deakin frowned, unconvinced.

"An' Drake's not a bad stick. You know that, an' we've both 'ad worse. Remember Bishop, when we was in the Ninth?"

Deakin nodded, memories of a brutal, almost sadistic, Officer coming vividly back.

"Alright. Just to keep the peace."

He looked around.

"Find something an 'throw it in. It doesn't need to be much, 'tis just for one man."

The items were produced, all being much as Ellis had described. The contents of the bag were sufficiently increased and Ellis peered in, satisfied, but there were no thanks, instead orders.

"Right. Now, out. There's burying to be done. And a few more lads to find, perhaps still alive.

In similar manner was that day also spent, again in the morbid collection of the dead and with these the sorrowful, almost pointless, collection of more wounded. Their Noon meal was their best, consuming French rations, but that for evening was no more than three biscuits and some thin coffee. However, by then all were too tired to care, both from hunger and the physical effort of digging and carrying bodies, both dead and nearly so.

Dawn saw the arrival of Lieutenant Shakeshaft, now Acting Company Captain. All sprang to their feet, bar the Followers. He addressed himself to Saunders, as a Corporal and to Davey, a Chosen Man.

"Orders for today are to continue with the burying; of ours, that is. Spanish are being employed to bury the French."

He paused to look more carefully. He was genuinely concerned.

"Have you anything to eat?"

No-one answered, at least not immediately, but Saunders felt the need to give at least some answer.

"No more than anyone else, Sir."

Shakeshaft nodded sadly.

"Well, we can only hope for some supplies to come up."

Davey now spoke.

"Sir. Rumours are that we will soon be marching back to Portugal. How true is that, Sir?"

Shakeshaft smiled, pleased with the change of subject.

"Pure truth is hard to define, Davey, but I'd say that it is very likely."

"Yes Sir. Very good, Sir."

Shakeshaft passed on and they all picked up the tools which they had used the previous day and again took themselves out onto the noisome battlefield. After the heat of the previous three days, the stench was appalling, for the French dead had barely been touched and there were hundreds more French bodies than there had been British, who were now almost all gone. Scavenging crows now hopped and circled all over the battlefield and no dead body was without some extra injury from their sharp beaks. Davey, Saunders and their companions worked till Noon, digging two more graves, at which point Donkin did a tour of their area and pronounced the burial of the British dead to be complete. They walked back to their lines, watching the Spanish gather up the French bodies and throw them into farm carts. Joe Pike was intrigued and asked of their most experienced soldier.

"What happens to them, Zeke?"

Saunders did not need to turn his head.

"They won't bother with diggin' holes. They'll be burnt, or chucked down some crevice or whatnot. Don't pay it no mind."

Saunders was right. Soon fires began all over the battlefield, the funeral pyres for those who were once proud French soldiers. However, the number of fires decreased when the supply of wood was exhausted, but the carts continued to leave the battlefield for areas beyond, all day and into the evening, only to cease with the full dark.

Saunders' prediction was coming true.

However, the respite caused by the final clearing of the battlefield now gave time for the feared calling of the Roll. The Battalion was paraded in the last light of the evening and the list of names of those that had been present at the beginning of 28th July in each Company Section, was given to their Sergeant. Although barely able to see the names in the poor light of candle lanterns, the names were read out to receive one of four answers, "Present, wounded, dead, or not seen." For several minutes, after the mournful reading, the Company Captains merged both lists and found their totals. These were handed to Major Carr, who then made his own calculations from the ten pieces of paper he received and these were then merged into two groups, one for Officers killed, wounded and missing, which Lacey already knew, and one for 'other ranks'. The numbers for 'other ranks' read; killed 21, wounded 102, missing 5. Lacey gave a sigh of relief, he had expected much worse, but the number of wounded immediately replaced the dread of calling The Roll with the deepest concern for these; 'Where were they all now, could they be cared for?'.

Shakeshaft's prediction of the previous day seemed to be accurate. Over a short and meagre breakfast, Lacey was looking at a note which had arrived by mounted messenger from Donkin, a simple, one sentence missive, 'Likelihood of retreat tomorrow'. This blunt warning brought Lacey into a state of anguish, which O'Hare was equally helpless to alleviate. No word had come from anywhere that transport for their wounded would be available.

"Our own are in Talavera?"

"Most likely on the road to it, or lying in one of the streets."

"How many are with Pearce? Do you know?"

"About thirty."

Lacey thought for a few seconds.

"We could use travois, like we did on the Corunna

302

retreat."

O'Hare nodded.

"I'll get some men off and around for the poles."

"Yes, do that. When we know what we are to be given to carry them and how many, only then can we go around and make a selection."

The thought mortified him.

"Leaving them behind will be a death sentence!"

O'Hare nodded and walked off, as did Lacey, the latter back to their tent, hoping for something to eat or drink. He passed the site of Deakin's small camp and felt the need to enquire, albeit to gain but a small impression of what his Regiment's situation may be. All of the usual members were there and all sprang to their feet at the presence of their Colonel and saluted.

"Hello, men. I was wondering how things are with you."

It was Deakin who answered.

"Things could be better, Sir, but then again a lot worse."

Lacey looked around and saw Miles.

"I see you have some wounded of your own."

Lacey looked at the prone figure.

"Miles, isn't it? And you're old Ninth?"

Miles brought himself up onto his elbows.

"Yes Sir."

"Not too bad I hope."

"Bullet, Sir. But it was dug out."

Lacey nodded.

"Well, I do hope you recover. We'll be needing good men, especially old Ninth. At least you seem to have something to eat."

"Yes Sir. Took off the French."

At this point, Bridie intervened.

"We've a bit spare, Colonel Lacey, your honour, if you don't mind a bit of a mixture."

The only one within hearing who was pleased with

her offer was Lacey himself, but all held their peace, and their intemperate looks.

"Well yes, Mrs. Mulcahey. If it is spare. I cannot remember what I've had beyond raw coffee and biscuits for some days now."

She spooned out a portion from their pot into a skillet lid and handed it up, with a spoon. Lacey took the lid, then the spoon and began to eat. He was surprised.

"You know, Mrs Mulcahey, this is rather good!"

Bridie smiled and curtsied.

"That's kind of you to say, your honour, but 'tis Nellie here, as is the one with the herbs."

Nellie Nicholls, now on her feet, smiled and curtsied, but by now Lacey had finished the few spoonfuls.

"That was most generous, and I am duly grateful. So now, I can tell you. We leave tomorrow and we will try to put together some travois. Any wheeled transport will be for the wounded. You remember travois from the march to Corunna?"

Nellie now answered.

"Yes, indeed we do, Sir, and very workable they was too."

Lacey smiled in reply.

"Let's hope that they serve equally well now."

With that, he left and all looked daggers at Bridie, but saying nothing whilst Lacey was in earshot. However, Nellie the Formidable immediately leapt to the defence of her friend. She knew what was coming.

"And sure, now, wasn't that no more than a kind Christian thing to do, for a kind Christian gentleman. Sure, didn't he look as starved as any of us? And isn't he doin' his best to find ways for us all to get out of here?"

This finished any argument before it started and all there, all now knowing what was coming tomorrow, began to prepare for the march, which would probably begin at dawn. Back at his tent, Lacey had a visitor, himself taking the opportunity to sit, rest and drink something hot. It was

Donkin and he had some news, particular to the subject uppermost in the mind of Lacey.

"I can give you four carts, Lacey, and about a dozen horses. Ex cavalry, from that shambles in the valley at the end of the battle. You heard?"

"Yes I have. The 23rd and some KGL ended up in a ravine the other side of the Medellin and others were roughly handled by a French column."

Donkin nodded.

"The same. Now we are using their mounts as draught animals, and food later on, I shouldn't wonder."

"That's a help."

Lacey took a deep sorrowful breath.

"So now I have to select whom I take."

Donkin nodded again, his face grim.

"Yes."

With that single word he swallowed the last of his coffee and was gone, for Lacey to sit down and begin his calculations. Each cart could take eight wounded, that was 32, and four carts used up eight horses and two wounded could sit on each of the remaining four horses, adding another eight. That meant 40 wounded, not even half of what was needed. At which point, Carr arrived and it needed only one look at his Colonel to see that something was wrong.

"Sir?"

Lacey looked up.

"We've transport for only 40 wounded!"

Carr sighed, but he had his own thoughts on the matter.

"Sir. Have we any money?"

Lacey was hugely puzzled.

"Some, yes, but we are going to need it, for buying food on the march back. There'll be nothing from the Spanish. Why?"

"The farmer I got the tools from. He had two carts in his barn, much worn out, but still serviceable."

"I wish I could give the money to buy them. I could give a crown or two, but with no money to buy the extra food we'll need, we'll lose many more from dropping out on the march from hunger. We're in a parlous state now, before we leave."

Carr's face was set.

"Understood, Sir, but I think I know where I can gather a few items that would add up to the value we need if our Purser could manage one crown."

Lacey nodded his agreement and Carr marched off in a particular direction. He had been the Captain of the Light Company and he knew just where all the villainy lay. He soon marched into the camp of Saunders and Davey where all sprang up and saluted. Carr came straight to the point.

"Saunders, where are the tools we took from the farmer?"

Saunders pointed.

"There, Sir, an' none missing"

"Right. That will help."

He looked around, giving a stern look to all.

"This is the thing. We have over a hundred wounded and only transport for forty. The farmer that we took the tools from had two old carts in his barn, old, but workable. And bigger than those we use."

He looked around.

"I cannot go in and haul them out and off. That's robbery and Wellesley would hang us all, but I can buy and that will mean two dozen more of our wounded coming with us."

He took off his shako, found two crowns from his own pocket and then dropped them in. The gesture was obvious, but for a good few seconds no-one moved, then all went to their possessions and pulled from their valuables what they would give. Soon the bottom of the shako was covered in silver buttons and buckles, and gold rings and earrings. Carr looked around at each there, but said nothing and this hiatus lasted for a few seconds, while they looked at him and he stared back.

"Right. All of you, those that can walk that is, follow me. Bring the tools."

He had eight men with him and they hurried to the farmer's house. Carr hammered on the door and the same farmer appeared. The tools were shown, all in the hands of Carr's companions, which evidently pleased the farmer. Carr pointed to the tools, then to the barn. The farmer understood.

"Si. Volver a la granja."

However, Carr motioned for the farmer to follow, which he did. Once in the barn, Carr found a sack and tipped the contents of the shako onto the cloth. The farmer looked pleased but puzzled and remained so, even when Carr went and placed his hand on the two carts. Both were old and plainly had not been moved for years. Perhaps non-comprehending, the farmer shrugged his shoulders, but Byford now intervened.

"Perhaps I can help, Sir."

He placed a hand on one cart and then pointed to the other.

"Compramos estas dos."

The farmer shook his head. Carr was incensed. The carts had plainly not been used for anything for years, but he still wanted to bargain.

"To Hell with him!"

Carr re-wrapped the valuables and thrust the sack into the farmer's arms, taking no time to see the look of shock on the man's face.

"Get these out and back to our lines."

The eight spread themselves over the two carts and began to haul them out of their long time resting places. Both carts creaked and protested, but they moved. Carr looked back at the farmer, who was examining the contents of the sack, not looking at what was happening to his vehicles. Carr was the last to leave the barn.

"Done deal. Mucho gracias, Senor."

The farmer merely glanced up and quickly nodded in brief reply before returning to his absorbed examination of a ring. Carr followed his men back to their camp and, once back, he gave his orders.

"Get these clean. Fit for wounded."

The eight began gathering tufts of grass and hay, there was nothing else available for such a task, and with that they began to remove the dust of years. Carr went back to Lacey at his tent.

"Sir. I've two more carts. Farm carts, Sir, a bit bigger."

Lacey looked up and smiled.

"Two more! That's sixteen more that we can take with us. Well done."

"More like two dozen, Sir. They are large, as I said."

However, Lacey then sighed heavily.

"That's 54. Now I have to choose. We load them at first light."

He sighed again.

"How do I choose?"

Carr took a deep breath.

"If you want my advice, Sir, you choose those that are still conscious. Those that are not will just drift off, and it's best for that to happen with them in that state. Choose the least wounded that are still conscious. That's where you start."

Lacey nodded resignedly.

"That's sense. Brutal, but sense. I'll start with those with Surgeon Pearce."

He stood up.

"Time to make the choice. The day's ending. Please come with me."

They soon arrived at Pearce's hospital and were guided by him. Pearce chose 22 out of his wounded that had a good chance of recovering sufficiently so that they could rejoin the ranks. Those that would never fight again or would not survive, were omitted from his list. Lacey and Carr then walked towards Talavera where the scene was utterly heart-rending, where wounded of both armies were strewn, largely unattended for three days, all along the road and in the streets of the town. Lacey looked at Carr.

"Do you think ours were taken to a special place?"

"That I doubt, Sir."

"So do I. Go back and get some men. Two Companies. Those that go with us tomorrow, we get out of here now, with 32 more."

Lacey walked back to the road, where he found 16 whose wounds were minor enough to meet Pearce's judgment. There he waited until Carr returned and the wounded were helped or carried back to where the carts were assembled. That done, Carr and Lacey progressed into the town, to be met with a scene of unrelenting misery; dead, dying and suffering wounded, all of whom could be helped were there the time and the resources. Lacey was aghast.

"These are all good men. From both sides. They deserve better than this."

Carr, not a man who could ever be called overly warm hearted, was as lost for words as his Colonel was distraught, at the sights and sounds from every street and courtyard.

"We'll have to call out, Sir. That will help us decide who to take. If they can hear and answer, they could be well enough to recover."

Lacey nodded, and the two patrolled the streets of wounded, calling 'One Hundred and Fifth!' Answers came from all around and these were carried back to the road, until they had over 60, more than Lacey had calculated. Pearce came to examine each.

"They're all fit to travel, Sir. What will you do? Draw lots?"

Lacey had had enough.

"No. They all come. Given time some will be fit enough to walk, if we can feed them, or they can take turns in the cart if able to walk for a short time. They all come."

Pearce saluted.

"Very good, Sir. But what of my wounded that are not going?"

"Get them into the town. Or on the road into it. What else?"

He turned to Carr.

"Get that done. Before dawn. And use proper stretchers, no carrying in a blanket."

Across the early hours the job was done, with, mercifully, most now too unconscious to know what was happening, as they were laid on a blanket in a Talavera street. For those conscious, there was but a comforting word, delivered by a fellow line soldier. "We've got to leave you, mate. We can't take all, but you'll be alright. The Spanish will care for you, an' the French too. The Johnnies aren't so bad." Finally, Lacey and O'Hare toured the dark and sorrowful streets by lantern-light, to say a last word to those able to listen, always speaking what seemed to be the only thing that could be said; thanking them for their service and re-assuring them, even if they were only too well aware that it was wholly unlikely, that all would be well in the care of the Spanish or French.

With the first sign of dawn in the East, Wellesley's army formed up and began their retreat Westwards, back to Portugal. Tom Miles' kit and equipment had been wordlessly shouldered by his messmates and he now hobbled beside them, a wooden pole bound tight to his leg to take the weight on that side and a crudely fashioned crutch helping with the same. Shakeshaft looked suspiciously at him but said nothing, whilst their Captain Drake saw nothing, because he was riding at the back with the wounded, on a horse. Deakin had but one thing to say, marching alongside Toby Halfway.

"Bugger off, Spain! Next time can be as long a time

in comin' as never, is all I've got to say!"

oOo

Chapter Six

A Collection of Armies

"Pyrrhic victory, that!"

"You've lost me."

Drake looked at his marching companion and spoke, his voice heavy with sarcasm.

"No Latin, was there, in your evidently lamentable education?"

Carr let out a noise something between a sneeze and a laugh.

"I take it that your reference has something to do with Roman history."

"Indeed yes, it has. In short, King Pyrrhus of Egypt lost so many men beating the Romans that he was almost knocked out of the Pyrrhic War, as it was called. He beat them twice."

Carr looked at him.

"Very good. Now, wishing to fend off a tedious lesson in Roman history, I take it that, in your opinion, this obscure term applies to us, at this very time? More to the point, I find your levity to be somewhat off the mark. That was as dreadful a 'toe to toe', as I've ever heard of, never mind been part of! No subject for any joke, however academically astute."

Drake sensed the tetchiness in Carr's reply, and so conciliation crept into his. He was now somewhat inclined to be more serious, now that they were leaving the dreadful plain of Talavera, for with the passing of time, more sober reflection had come upon them all.

"No disrespect intended and, yes, no argument there, but what will they say back home? It is, after all, we who are retreating."

Carr sighed and nodded his head.

"The papers will say whatever massages public opinion towards their own political inclinations. Although, so we are told, we are marching to confront yet another French army, which is on its way down from Salamanca, but, I'll grant you, that is being done in order to secure our retreat."

Now it was Drake's turn to be argumentative.

"Well, is that quite so? I mean, if we get supplies from the Spanish, then we can stay in Spain. Stay and confront the Johnnies once more."

Carr sighed in exasperation.

"You know as well as I do, that any promise from the Dons is a sculpture in smoke, gone after the first puff of wind. We'll be back in Portugal next month; I'd put a hundred guineas on it. If we stay in Spain, relying on Spanish promises and generosity, we'll fall apart."

Drake's brows came together.

"So what about our own Commissariat? We'll be close up to the Portuguese border. Surely supplies could come up?"

Carr repeated the odd noise from his nose and mouth together, this time dismissively.

"Our good General Perry's part of that, so there's your answer."

Drake looked at him indulgently.

"Plainly optimism wasn't part of your wardrobe this morning!"

This time Carr did laugh, genuinely, but it did nothing to change his mood.

"We fought a veteran French army to a standstill. Gave them the bloodiest nose they've had since all this began. Outnumbered six to one, we just about wrecked their whole army."

He sucked in a deep breath.

"And what's happening? We are retreating. And why, because we are starving, beaten not by the damnable Frogs, but by simple lack of food. I know we could be about to fight another army of theirs and doubtless win, but its only purpose would be to hold open the door back into Portugal."

He paused, for another breath and somewhat changed the subject.

"Then there's all those wounded that we had to leave behind. In the care of the Dons!"

The dismissive noise through nose and throat was repeated, but Drake had more sympathy for their Allies.

"You may be right and probably are, but don't forget that this country has been in a total shambles for three years. No effective Government or anything. No one should be surprised that they cannot supply their own armies, never mind ours. And also take from us, when faced with the stark choice and starvation the only alternative!"

Drake looked at Carr, who was staring back, somewhat taken aback, but Drake continued.

"Yes! But still they keep raising armies all over that always get smashed by the French, but they still come back for more, to keep the fight going. Also, this guerrilla war thing must be worth some credit, civilians rising up all over and having a joust at the French. And if they're caught, it's the firing squad or the rope. No status as a prisoner of war, like with us, but that hasn't stopped them. Credit where credit's due, I say."

Carr looked away, across the burnt brown fields.

"No argument there. What you say is true, but we're here, marching back, because of the false reliance that we placed upon them. That's my point. And I remember that long supply train that they crossed the Alberche with, when we were living on coffee and biscuits!"

"And no argument from me on that, but such as that is for Generals and politicians, way beyond the remit of the likes of us."

Carr returned his gaze to the road and reached for his water bottle. He lifted it up and gave it a shake, enough to gauge how much was in there and how much he could dare to take as a swallow.

Simultaneously, at the front of the 105th column, Senior Major O'Hare was doing the same to his canteen, only with less optimism, even though he was shaking it next to his ear, the better to make a judgement, which turned out to be somewhat depressing. He brought up a subject which he hoped would distract him from his thirst and needed the opinion of his marching companion, Colonel Lacey.

"We need another Ensign."

"Who did we lose? Neape wasn't it? Regimental Colour?"

"Correct."

"Who's carrying it now?"

Lacey turned around to look and answer his own question. The Colour Party were immediately behind and his brows came together in shock.

"Is that a drummer boy?"

O'Hare did not need to look.

"Yes. Called forward during the thick of it."

He looked at his Colonel.

"And didn't flinch once!"

This time Lacey's eyebrows went skyward.

"Is that so, now?"

He paused for thought.

"A new Ensign?"

More thought

"What about a subaltern or somesuch? Do we have?"

"No! Only Lieutenants, each with their own Sections and four of those are wounded. Marching with us, but wounded."

"A new and bona fide Ensign should come from our Militia, back in England, if we follow the proper form. Someone of the correct background. You know how it is!"

O'Hare sighed.

"Only too well."

"What's his name, the drummer boy?"

"Patrick Mulcahey."

Lacey was surprised and looked at O'Hare.

"Son of the Mulcahey we lost at Maida?"

"The same!"

Lacey sucked in a deep breath. He was thinking the unthinkable.

"Is there such a thing as 'Brevet Ensign' do you think?"

O'Hare laughed.

"It'll be a new one on me, but we cannot demote anyone down to the lowest Officer rank, and we need someone to carry the thing, at least back to Portugal. Then, who knows?"

He looked at Lacey, conspiratorially.

"We still have Neape's uniform."

"Right! Stick him in it. From what I hear, we could be in for another set-to with M'sieu before too long and going into that with just one Colour is, well, not to be contemplated."

O'Hare nodded and broke into a broad grin.

"Right. Consider it done."

They fell to silence, but only after each had taken the smallest sip of water from their canteens, the discussion had added to their thirst. It was similarly so throughout the whole of the 105th column, for much of the time marching in silence, conserving water, sucking a pebble, trying to ignore their additional hunger. However, for one, silence gave no vent to his ill temper. Tom Miles shifted the pebble in his mouth just enough to speak, yet to no one in particular.

"How long we been on this plod?"

Marching behind, Zeke Saunders was the first to reply, him still carrying Miles pack, whilst Solomon carried his Baker and Pike the rest.

"That French brandy you've been soakin' onto your bandage now gone to your head? So's you've lost track of time?"

Miles swivelled on his makeshift splint and gave him an evil look.

"No surprise if I have, sloggin' down this Godforsaken dirt track. What's a body to do?"

He took a glance to the far horizon, now with a column silhouetted against the burning sky as they climbed the slope and crossed the horizon. He waved his unoccupied left arm for emphasis.

"An' what's it like when we comes to a village, what do we get there? Evil looks, like we was the ones as got beat. You gets a load of Spanish jabberin' even when you tries to fill your canteen at their well. Or even their muddy brook!"

Wry grins arrived all around. Tom Miles was recovering, but his question needed answering and this came from John Byford.

"Six hours! Six hours we have been marching."

Miles looked around at his informant.

"An' how come we'n on our own? If the Spanish was alongside, there's a better chance of a bit more provender. From tradin' like."

It was Zeke Saunders who again answered.

"Tell you what, Tom. The next time we sees Wellesley, we'll call 'im over and get a full and good answer, just for you!"

Despite their thirst, laughter broke out all around, except from Tom Miles who adopted his habitual scowl, whilst all fell to listening to the double strike of Miles splint and crutch on the hard packed gravel. However, Tom Miles was not the only man in the 105th in an ill temper, this other being Captain Lord Carravoy, as often ill disposed to the world as was Tom Miles. The subject was the same, the march that they were now enduring, but for Carravoy the subject was his horse, or more accurately, the absence of his treasured mount. For some hours his indignation had been building, in direct proportion to the temperature of his feet and the weariness in his legs. It finally burst, with Royston D'Villiers the recipient.

"Retreat this may be, but we have not been defeated, we are not a rabble, all with us are still in good order."

D'Villiers looked puzzled.

"Yes, Charles, that's true."

"True, yes, so, therefore Officers should be allowed to ride."

"Colonel's orders, Charles. All horses are being used for the wounded. Pulling carts and those travois things that he knows about."

Carravoy's mouth pursed and his brows came together. It was as though D'Villiers had not been listening.

"It's not proper form and damn bad for discipline."

D'Villiers looked away. His own horse was pulling a travois with two wounded men on it and he saw every reason why that should be the case. He changed the subject.

"What's the next town?"

The reply arrived, reluctant and surly.

"Oropesa, as if it will make any difference!"

Thus, for Wellesley's men it continued, in various states of mind, all enduring an exhausting tramp over a dry road rapidly being ground to dust by tens of thousands of feet and hooves and hundreds of artillery wheels, all under a pitiless sun. However, events were now in train, which would at least change the route of their march. At that moment Fray Juan Delica was staring into the terrified eyes of a fellow Man of the Cloth, but him mounted on what was very obviously a very good horse and riding fast and alone in the direction of a known French army. It was the quality of the mount that had attracted the attention of Delica's band, then the saddle and harness and then finally the brand on the animal's right flank: a large N. The well-mounted Friar was doing his best to explain.

"Este es un caballo francés que encontré vagando. Es un callejero, señores."

Riding a French horse found wandering, ex-cavalry or not, Delica was unconvinced regarding the Friar's business; where the horse came from being very secondary. He turned to his two nearest companions.

"Búsqueda de."

The two quickly dismounted and dragged the now utterly petrified man from his horse, to begin the search. Within seconds they discovered a pouch attached to a belt under the cassock. The pouch was cut from the belt and handed up. The Friar now fell to the ground moaning and supplicating, wringing his hands together. Delica gave him but a glance before opening the pouch and extracting three pieces of high quality parchment. The writing was in French and, on discovering this; Delica now gave the cowering Friar a look of utter contempt.

"¿Quién escribió esto?"

The Friar looked up, pleading with both his eyes and hands, but saying nothing. This time Delica shouted.

"¿Quién escribió esto?

Still no reply, but Delica turned to the end of the letter to discover the author and it was clear, 'Le Roi Joseph-Napoleon Buonaparte'. Now, Delica returned to the to the top of the letter and there he was, equally clear, "Marshal General Nicolas Jean de Dieu Soult, Duc de Dalmatie." This was a letter to Soult from the French imposed King of Spain himself, written to co-ordinate French movements. Delica called forward another guerrilla, one who had once been a University Professor, in, seemingly, another age, but this guerrilla could read French. Delica handed over the letter.

"¿Qué dice esto?".

The guerrilla pulled out some spectacles and began to read and translate. After two minutes he spoke, in great detail. Delica looked down at the perspiring Friar.

"¿Dónde está Soult? Dile y yo te prometo una muerte rápida!"

At the sentence of imminent death, albeit mercifully

quick, for revealing the whereabouts of Soult's army, the Friar lowered his face to the ground and set up an appalling wailing. Delica lost patience and he motioned to one of his searchers. The man drew a knife, hauled the Friar's head back using the chin and thrust the point of the knife under it, to the extent that blood began to flow. The result was wild and tearful eyes and one word.

"Plasencia!"

Delica had not finished.

"Cuando?"

The knife was thrust further, producing the same result.

"Lunes."

Delica did the small calculation. Today was Wednesday, Soult was there on Monday. The French could be almost at Naval Moral as they spoke, across the road from Oropesa to Portugal. He had watched the combat of Talavera from the high battlements of the town walls and he was now convinced that only the British could match the French in open battle and inflicting defeats such as that was the only way the French would be expelled from Spain. Yet he also knew what the battle had cost the British and that they were in no shape to fight another so major, casualties and hunger dictated that. Delica did not know where Wellesley was, he may be over the Tagus and safe, but if he was about to use Oropesa as his route back, then he was in great danger of being caught between two French armies, that of Victor and now that of Soult. However, he did know the whereabouts of Cuesta and surely he could be trusted to get the information to Wellesley? Delica looked at his academic, still holding the letter. He threw the leather pouch to him.

"Hacer esto Cuesta en Talavera! Le digo que pase en Wellesley. Vaya con Dios."

A small sack of provisions was thrown across to the man and he departed, in a flurry of dust and loose clothing. Delica looked at his searcher holding the knife.

"Matarlo!"

The knife was thrust upwards and the Friar's eyes rolled for the last time. Delica gave one short look around his guerrilla band.

"A Plascencia."

He led them off at a fast canter. However, as he rode off, leaving the dust to settle on the body of the Friar, events began to unfold which would confirm Delica's deep concern for the safety of the British army, although it began as a minor argument, albeit a very one sided affair. Sir Robert Stapleton Cotton had noticed Captain Lord Templemere remaining with the 14th Light Dragoons as his own 16th rode forward down the road towards Naval Moral. Not one to mince his words, he gave full vent to his fully roused temper, this in the direction of Templemere.

"You Sir! You!"

Templemere instantly turned his head to then be pinned to the spot by an intense stare from his Brigadier.

"You, Sir! You are 16th, are you not?"

Templemere could but nod his head as the focal point of this wave of rage, and then find a small reply.

"Yes Sir. 16th, so I am."

"Then why, Sir, pray, do you indulge yourself here, whilst your squadron rides forward?"

Templemere suddenly felt very diminished as the subject of such a description.

"I have a wound, Sir. Here."

Templemere pointed to his right thigh, the cloth of his uniform somewhat disfigured by the bandage beneath. The reply incensed the cavalry Brigadier even further.

"And how many of us do not?"

The words whirled around Templemere like a vengeful banshee.

"You can sit your horse, can you not?"

Stapleton Cotton did not wait for a reply.

"Get yourself forward, now, this instant. Join your men."

Templemere was by now only too eager to escape the baleful gaze and cutting admonitions of his Brigade Commander and spurred his horse forward, suddenly regarding as a mere irritation the pain this caused in his leg. The last words he heard as he rode on were words of disgust from Stapleton Cotton.

"Wound in his leg. Good God!"

Templemere cantered forward and was soon forced to endure the dust thrown up as he overtook the squadron column. However, it was not too long before he was alongside Tavender, who turned to look at the new arrival.

"Thought you were staying back. That you were having difficulty controlling your mount, what with that cut and all."

Templemere did not look sideways as he made his reply. His temper and indignation at being so recently spoken to in such a manner had been amassing throughout the short journey.

"Changed my mind!"

Tavender smiled and nodded approvingly and, as if to cement his approval, he passed across his flask of brandy. Templemere took a deep pull at the flask and then passed it back, at which point Tavender got down to business.

"You know we are looking for the French? Rumour has it that they are making a raid against our communications back to Portugal, but, in that sort of strength, we can see them off and get out and back."

Templemere looked across.

"Where's back?"

"Truxillo. About two days march after Oropesa, but meanwhile, where are our foe? There's a bridge over the Tagus at Almaraz on this good road. If we get over the Tagus on a good road, then we're pretty much home and dry."

Templemere made no reply, but shifted his weight in the saddle to ease the growing ache in his leg. Just ahead, leading the force of two Squadrons, 200 men, was a Major for whom Templemere had very little time, the Major Johnson of their pursuit of Soult after Oporto, riding beside their Colonel Withers. Johnson had risen through the ranks and had been mentioned in Perry's report to Wellesley after the Regiment's attack on the French rearguard at Salamonde, part of that pursuit after Oporto, back in June. The dislike had grown since then, with Templemere finding Johnson's accent from the Fenlands of East Anglia highly irritating and his uniform being little more than standard issue with badges of rank sewn on. However, Templemere did concede that Johnson knew horseflesh and now rode a captured French mount of evident high pedigree. The two, Johnson and Withers were conversing intently, which discourse continued for the full 30 minutes during which they all continued forward. The pair were not even distracted as they progressed through Naval Moral, which was the usual collection of hovels gathered for sanctuary and spiritual protection around their solid and well-appointed Church. Peasants emerged from the low doors and dingy interiors at the sound of the clattering hooves, yet all they sent in the direction of the passing Dragoons were sullen looks and soon most had turned their backs to return to their dark homes to nurse darker thoughts on the approaching French. Once through the village, Withers turned in his saddle to motion Tavender and Templemere forward. They had halted at a fork in the road.

"We're dividing our force. I'll Tavender's Two Squadron. We'll go left to Almaraz, about 10 miles on. Your Squadron, Templemere, will go with Johnson here, and go right to Casatejada, about 12 miles. Keep your eyes open. The moment you see French, retreat back to here, send a messenger and hold this fork until I return. I'll do the same for you. The French may have reached Almaraz from over the goat tracks."

He turned to Johnson.

"Take yours on."

Johnson motioned for his Squadron to follow and

took the right fork, expecting Templemere to join on. Withers allowed the Squadron to follow Johnson then he diverted the next to follow him and soon all that remained at the fork in the road were hoof prints in the yielding dust. Templemere felt the need to ride beside Johnson, but said nothing and Johnson paid him virtually no attention, instead casting his eyes off to whichever high point may contain a French cavalry picket or even to examine the road in the far distance, when the terrain allowed it. They trotted on for some minutes until Johnson raised his hand and they all halted, the dust from their progress catching up with them on the faint breeze. Johnson rose in his saddle and pulled a telescope from his saddle pocket.

"There! Up there. What's that?"

Templemere sat impassive, now thoroughly irked at being ignored, not having been even consulted once, all the way. Johnson stood up in his stirrups and focused the glass. Throughout the next half minute he sighed in frustration.

"Can't see, can't tell. This rising heat doesn't help. Could be cattle."

He continued his study, but came to no conclusion. Templemere looked contemptuously over, both at his Superior Officer and the inferior telescope that he was using. He drew out his own instrument. The best that money could buy, and thrust it in front of Johnson.

"Try mine."

Johnson lowered his own telescope, examined Templemere's being held before him, then closed his own and put it in his tunic pocket. He took Templemere's, opened and focused it. Soon he made a pronouncement.

"Glad you're here, Fred. This piece of yours does the trick. That's a French vedette!"

He turned to the first rank behind.

"Michael. Up here, please."

The Cornet of Horse walked his mount forward.

"Gallop back to the fork in the road, where we split, and ride after the Colonel. Tell him we've made contact and it looks …………"

He refocused the telescope.

"……… like our French friends are in some force. He'll return and we'll be holding the fork open for him. Go now. All speed."

The Cornet wheeled his horse and galloped off, soon to be lost in his own dust. Johnson returned the telescope, raised his hand, circled it once and then wheeled his own horse around to follow the dust of Cornet Michael Vigurs. His command followed and soon, after a fast trot, they were back almost to the fork in the road, bar 200 yards. Johnson stopped and eased his sabre in the scabbard, which gave Templemere no small qualms of concern.

"Get the men across the road. Two deep. You take the left, I'll come back to the right, after I've had a look from up there."

He pointed to a small hillock and then rode off. Templemere now looked back along the road behind him. He was now in sole command of 100 men, alone with no superior Officer! Luckily, directly in front of him was a Sergeant of Horse, one of Vigurs', and Templemere looked directly at him, not knowing his name, so he motioned with his left arm.

"Take yours off that way. Form a two deep line."

The Sergeant started his own mount to move, but he was not quite clear.

"Facing back up the road, Sir?"

Templemere quickly angered.

"Of course! What else?"

"Sir."

The fifty rode off left, then Templemere motioned to the remainder, Cornet Peterson's Troop, to ride right. The Sergeants and Corporals got them into line and they sat and waited, but not for long. Johnson was returning.

"They're coming down the road. In numbers, 200, 400, hard to tell. So, we have to make a show."

He looked at his men, drawn up on either side.

"With any luck, they'll do as us; be content at having made contact. On the other hand, they may decide that 100 men would be a good bag, if they have us well outnumbered. Time will tell."

Something moved in Templemere's stomach, just below his diaphragm. Johnson sat impassive, staring down the road, whilst Templemere's mind turned somersaults, but he had one major question.

"How long will we have to stay here?"

Johnson sucked in a deep breath.

"Depends! How fast did the Colonel ride on from here? If at our speed, I'd say we need to be here for about 30 minutes. He's got to ride back, remember, and only after Vigurs catches up."

30 minutes! Templemere had bargained for no more than ten! He, too, stared down the road, but with a great deal more anxiety than did his companion. After ten minutes, the French appeared, an Officer first, at the head of what looked like a long column. The Officer raised his arm and the column halted. Within a minute another Officer arrived and joined the first. Johnson sat impassive, using his telescope.

"They're making up their mind about having a go. We will have value to them as prisoners, who can be questioned."

Templemere could barely think. He was a consummate duellist with both sword and pistol, but this was different, the pell-mell of battle. He remembered the confusion of the charge after Oporto, therefore no courage came; a battle was high risk, which his skill with both blade and bullet could not counter.

"What are they waiting for?"

"To see if we have any supports. Making a check around, with their good French telescopes!"

The small humour was totally lost on Templemere in his present state of mind, but then things changed, for the worse. Johnson folded his telescope and grinned at Templemere.

"Aye aye! Here we go."

The reason for his conclusion was obvious. The French were deploying left and right, almost certainly to attack and their extending line, off in both directions, seemed to go on forever.

"400, I'd say. With more behind."

Templemere looked rapidly, several times, from the French to Johnson.

"This is madness! We haven't a hope!"

"Oh, don't say that, Fred. Paget did for twice his number at Sahagun and at Benevente."

Templemere was totally unconvinced.

"It's still madness. We'll all be killed, or wounded and captured."

Johnson leaned over.

"Fred! We have to hold for the Colonel. When you signed up, you knew this could happen. It's what we do and what we have to do!"

Templemere could only mumble a weak reply.

"I didn't sign on. I purchased."

This caused Johnson to laugh.

"Ah well, then, Fred. Not the best use of money that you've ever made! Even us fashionable Lights have to cross blades with the Johnnies from time to time."

There was no reply.

"Right. I'm in front of the right, you of the left. If they charge, so do you. Do not meet them waiting at a standstill! That's crucial. That will be the end of you and of us all. If they charge, so do you. Set an example, Fred. The men will be looking to you."

With that he swung his horse's head to the right and rode the few yards to place himself before Peterson's Troop of 50. Still looking at the French, Templemere did the same, but off to the left and only for a few yards. The moment was heavy with anticipation, nothing being said, the only sound the jingle of head harness as the horses tossed their heads to and fro and the occasional stamp of a hoof. Suddenly, from the French side there sounded a bugle and their whole line walked forward, from about 500 yards off. Templemere heard Johnson shout.

"Draw sabres."

All along their line came the harsh scrape of metal moving across metal and Templemere drew his own sword and then sat watching the French approach. For how long he could not tell, then, inexplicably, the French line halted. Templemere looked harder, barely believing his eyes, then he heard what could only be Ranker banter from behind. He turned around to see that the rest of the 16th had returned and were now forming a second line behind his first and then his eyes was drawn to the right, where the whole of the 14th were extending Johnson's line, ready to hit the French from their left flank, this being onto their bridle hand, where they were most vulnerable. As if to confirm all, Stapleton Cotton was riding to where Johnson was in position. He had brought his whole cavalry Brigade forward. Templemere was in a quandary as to what to do, should he ride over to meet his Brigadier or remain. He decided on the former and rode across to arrive at Johnson at the same time as Stapleton Cotton, but the first words spoken by the Brigadier did much to offend Templemere's sharply honed self-regard.

"Well done, Johnson. You've held them off. Well done."

He then noticed Templemere.

"Wounded hero! Well done also to you, but do you think your hurt is sufficiently minor to allow you to take a message back to Wellesley's headquarters? He's in Oropesa and shouldn't be too difficult to find. Convey my compliments and tell him we have met French cavalry in force."

Something now surfaced in the mind of Templemere, which would allow him a small riposte, however minor, to his evidently somewhat contemptuous Brigadier. Something which, perhaps, his Commanding

Officer had not thought of.

"Where shall I say where we are? Sir."

The last word came very late, but the whole tone was lost on the irascible and pre-occupied Stapleton Cotton. He did not even take the trouble to turn and look at Templemere as he studied what he could see of the French beyond their cavalry line.

"Road fork for Almaraz and Casatejada!"

In thus insouciant manner, Templemere was dismissed, which did nothing to improve his mood.

oOo

For the 105th relief had arrived, albeit no more than a halt to their march and the opportunity to sit in the shade of olive trees out of the fierce sun, this a continuing a torment even in the late afternoon. A building had been noticed but minutes before the order to halt came and so Byford, Saunders and Solomon had gathered all canteens and hurried over, and then hurried back, each canteen full from the family's well. Thus they sat, drinking the cool water, grateful that it helped with their gnawing hunger. No one spoke much, beyond offering others a share of the last of their French hard biscuit, until there came both the sight and sound of rapid movement down the road from Talavera, towards Oropesa. Ten glittering uniforms galloped past at full speed, the radiance of each lessening the further back they were from their magnificently attired leader, but their urgency was very obvious. The group drew a sentient comment from Miles.

"Somethin's up! There's a big worry up top, any money you like! We ain't been on the road for a day an' all's back for another think."

No one replied. The water was too cool and did much to expand the biscuit resting in their stomachs. Then came the order to make camp, conveyed by Ellis.

"No more marchin' today. Seems somethin's

happened as means we goes on no more. Make camp.

Thus, soon, in response, the fires were burning under the olive branches in the dying light and all sat waiting for their share of the porridge made from the horse-oats which Solomon had traded at the farmhouse. Conversation was confined to the hope of supplies arriving from Portugal, for none cared to speculate on the reason for their puzzling halt.

However, next morning it was Lacey who was the first to learn of the importance of the mission carried out by the hurrying Spanish during the previous evening. As the sun climbed to once more quit the Eastern horizon, Donkin called for his Colonels and Senior Majors. Soon, Lacey and O'Hare were sat in a low white building on the outskirts of the Oropesa and Donkin came straight to the point when the last of his Senior Officers arrived.

"Wellesley has received a letter from Cuesta intercepted by guerillas. Soult, supported by Ney, is coming down from the North. What we thought would be no more than a raid by 15,000 now turns out to be 50,000, which is plainly a major effort to cut us off from Portugal. This has been confirmed by our own cavalry meeting the French beyond Naval Moral."

He paused to allow the significance of his words to sink in, then he continued.

"We cannot continue beyond Oropesa on our Westerly route and use the bridge at Almaraz to cross the Tagus, with a force that size menacing our flank. Therefore, the army will be leaving the main road today to march due South and cross the Tagus at Arzobispo. However, if the French do manage to cross the Tagus at Almaraz, then they can still come down upon us and I would not like to predict the outcome in that event. So, to prevent that, the Lights of your Brigade, Lacey, and my whole Brigade, will be joining Crauford's for a forced march over the river at Arzobispo, then along the South bank, to block the bridge at Almaraz from our side and deny it to the French. With that secured, providing Crauford's force arrives in time and has not been beaten to it, the main army is secure to march on to Truxillo, just South of the bridge."

He drew a deep breath.

"Right, if you're involved, prepare your whoever to march this morning with Crauford. I do not need to tell you how important it is to hold that bridge and keep our flank secure. Soult was at Plascencia on Monday, three days ago, and Plascencia's two days march from Almaraz. He may be there now, but the whole population of the place marched out when the French came near and so, reports for Wednesday from the guerrillas say that he is still there. Plundering the place and probably waiting for Ney, coming up behind him."

He paused again to allow comments, but none came, so he continued.

"There's more. The Spanish have abandoned Talavera, leaving our wounded there to fend for themselves. They have forty odd carts to get themselves out and follow us, but many will be on foot. God help them! We will hold at Arzobispo for a day to give them a chance to catch up. Wellesley is taking a chance to give them a chance. He's assuming that Crauford can hold the French back at Almaraz."

He looked around.

"Any questions?"

Lacey immediately spoke up.

"Any chance of extra rations for our men, if they're to undertake a forced march?"

Donkin nodded.

"I do believe that some sort of Spanish ration has been obtained."

With that they dismissed and Lacey and O'Hare immediately paired up. Lacey had one question.

"I want Carr to go with our Brigade's Lights. Do you approve? Officer casualties with the Light Companies of the 24th and 45th were severe. They will need to be combined into a small Battalion and commanded."

O'Hare nodded.

"Yes. That'll be fine. We'll cope."

O'Hare then looked at Lacey.

"I'll find him and give him the good news!"

The Spanish rations arrived at the 105th Light Company on a mule, led by Sergeant Ellis. He began with John Davey's mess.

"Extra rations! Get your haversacks."

Miles was immediately suspicious.

"For what reason?"

Ellis was already dipping a jug into the pannier on one side of the mule.

"We, the Light Company, are joining General Crauford's Light Brigade for a march to a place called Almaraz where we has to hang onto a bridge and keep Johnny on his own side, whilst we sits on the other. But getting there afore him could be a push, so here's your extra."

He held out the jug, not to Miles, but to Byford.

"You, Private Miles, will not be comin' with us, on account of your wound!"

Miles flared up.

"If you think I'm stayin' here, think on. I can march fast as these lads, an' keep up. If I tries and 'as to fall out, then I'll sit there until the rest comes up. But if I get's there, I'm one more gun and no bad leg can spoil my aim!"

Ellis was somewhat startled by the vehemence of Miles' outburst, but he could see that there was some sense in what he said. On this he had to think, but meanwhile Miles had more to say.

"An' if I comes, then it will prevent a murder, 'cos me stuck for days on me own with Nellie Nicholls will surely cause one of us to do the other in!"

Laughter broke out all around with which even Ellis had to join in.

"Right, but if you falls out and dies by the roadside,

that's your affair, not mine!"

Miles stared malevolently at him.

"I wouldn't have it any other way!"

Ellis then held out his jug to pour out Miles' portion of the new rations and the jug was emptied into the haversack, revealing a large, pale orange bean. Miles changed the subject.

"An' these is called what?"

Ellis was by now at the mules' head.

"Spanish calls 'em garbanzos. B'ain't got no English name. 'Cept bean!"

By now he was walking on, but he gave one more simple order.

"Ready to march in one hour."

No sooner had Ellis left, than Captain Drake arrived and all sprang to attention. Drake looked around.

"Major Carr will be commanding the three Light Companies of our Brigade. He'll need a servant."

He had seen the man he wanted.

"That'll be you, Byford."

"Sir."

"That's all. We're marching soon."

With Drake gone, all looked sympathetically at Byford.

"That means you've got to carry his kit, as well as your own."

Byford nodded.

"Could be, but we'll see."

Saunders looked at his friend.

"I'll carry your haversack."

Then Joe Pike spoke up.

"I'll take some out of your pack, if needs be."

Byford smiled.

"Could be. Thanks."

Within the hour, they were formed up on the road, at the head of the much depleted Light Companies of the 24th and 45th. O'Hare came to see them off and shook Carr's hand.

"Good luck, Henry."

Carr nodded and began the march, but O'Hare had something to say to his own men as they passed.

"Good luck, now boys. See you in a few days, all fit and well, but a few pounds lighter after your pleasant walk!"

Almost all raised a smile as they passed their popular Major, but these soon faded as they turned left onto the Arzobispo road and Carr increased the pace for them to catch up with Donkin's 87th and 88th, supported by 270 men of the 60th Rifles These last were in the wake of Crauford's Light Brigade and soon that dour General's complete command had the road all to themselves.

There was little spare time for those remaining. As soon as Crauford's men had cleared the road, the rest of Wellesley force were ordered to form up and begin their own trek to the now only safe crossing of the Tagus at Arzobispo, and before even mid-morning little remained, either in or before Oropesa, to mark the presence of the British army. Soon they were all looking down the ruler straight road that led over the dry plains South, to the bridge at Arzobispo. The road soon became monotonous, merely either slightly up or slightly down, which fact did not escape Toby Halfway, marching beside Jed Deakin with the Colour Party.

"Not too many bends in this road. Not that I'm complainin', but the odd curve might make you feel that you'm getting' somewhere, rather than bein' on some kind of treadmill."

Deakin just looked at his friend and smiled, but Ensign Rushby felt that he could both expand and explain.

"It's a Roman road, Corporal, direct to a Roman bridge, I shouldn't wonder. Talavera had one. Didn't you notice?"

Halfway exhaled a deep breath.

"No Sir. 'Fraid I didn't. We was all a bit occupied

334

with other things, like. Sir."

Rushby did not appreciate the inference, therefore he ploughed on.

"Yes. This whole area was conquered by the Romans. And they left their mark, just as they did on our own country. Roads, bridges and the like. Over two thousand years ago."

Halfway sniffed.

"So, walkin' into other people's country is not somethin' new to our lifetime, so it would seem."

However, before Rushby could expound further the call came to fall out for a rest and the Officers and Other Ranks went their separate ways, Deakin, Halfway, Bennet and the half-Ensign Mulcahy to munch a biscuit and drink some water, Rushby to wait, but not for long, for some coffee made from water boiled quickly on a fire made more intense by the constant working of a pair of bellows. The subject of conversation for the Deakin mess was the same as it had been for the past weeks, started from Bridie.

"Do you think there'll be some supplies come up, at this place we're headin' for, Jed?"

Deakin shook his head wearily. He wished he could be more cheerful, but he couldn't.

"I doubts it, Bridie. Comin' this way, was a change of plan, or so I understands it. That means any supplies meant for our first route has to be diverted. What do you think Henry?"

Henry Nicholls sat forward onto his knees.

"Can't say as I can be any more cheerful than that."

Bridie dropped her gaze down to her own pack and searched in its confines, hoping for a piece of dried fruit, but there was none.

All too soon, for weariness caused by hunger had overtaken them all as they sat in the meagre shade, the bugle sounded to reform on the road and within minutes their march resumed. However, this rest proved to be the only one required, because the low, red roofs of Arzobispo soon appeared on the low horizon and grew steadily with each step. The march had been but seven miles and they entered the town and continued on, down a seemingly endless, wide main street, defined on each side by a long row of terraced buildings, mostly hovels, but some shops and one bar. Few inhabitants came to watch their passing, for they were nothing new on that day; Crauford's men had passed through but two hours before. The army then crossed the low, long bridge, pronounced Roman by Rushby, and on the far side, now South of the Tagus, the order came to make camp. They were remaining there for the night.

Seemingly, within minutes, all around was a scene of domesticity as the Followers joined their men and all rested in the plentiful shade that was available. This included the spiritual section of the 105th, these being Chaplain Albright and his Assistant, Private Sedgwicke. The pair were drinking tea and eating army biscuits, when O'Hare arrived. He was invited by Albright to join them, but he declined, 'Too busy'. He had one simple message.

"Our wounded, those that we had to leave in Talavera, are trying to follow us. The Spanish have abandoned the place and left them to the French. I'm not blaming them, there was nothing anyone could do. So, all our carts are being unloaded and will stay here, hoping for them to catch up. We have to give them a chance. It includes your cart, I'm afraid."

Albright looked at Sedgwicke and then at O'Hare.

"There is no need for any apology, Major. Such is no more than our Christian duty. As Sedgwicke here would agree."

Private Sedgwicke was nothing like so sure, of so definite a conclusion. He would have to carry an extra burden, not all would be left behind, but he had no choice other than to nod his head.

"Yes Sir. Correct."

O'Hare smiled with pleasure at so rapid an agreement.

"The Blessing on you both! I'll see if some of your things can be spread over the men. Pick out what's essential and I'll see what can be done."

With that he departed and Albright began his selection.

"I will need what's required for my own personal hygiene, shaving and washing and so on. And spare clothes, especially small clothes. One perspires so badly in this climate."

He thought some more.

"And eating! There's my cutlery and .... "

He paused.

"Do you think that collapsible table and chair?"

Sedgwicke shook his head.

"I think not Sir. I think they should be sacrificed."

Albright's shoulders fell and he sighed.

"I do suppose that you are right."

Then he looked up, suddenly enlightened.

"What we should do, now, is to unload the cart now and go back. To meet them. We could take some up into the cart, give them a period of rest and then take up another group. Yes. This we will do. Begin now, Private, there is not a moment to lose. We must help, as we are able, to give succour to those in need."

Sedgwicke let out a sigh of his own. He remembered the appalling retreat to Corunna, just that Winter past, when all discipline had been lost and so he was almost certain that the only outcome would be both their mules being killed for food and them joining the wounded on foot, their cart abandoned. However, he held back the thought and stood up to obey the order of his superior.

"Yes Sir. I'll begin now."

It took but minutes to clear the small cart and minutes later they were rolling back over the bridge to soon view the straight road back to Oropesa. The mules trotted on, but with each step Sedgwicke's anxiety grew as he remembered the ravenous gang descending on his then

337

Chaplain, his wife and Sedgwicke himself, to kill their mule for food and dismember the cart for fuel. However, they continued on until they stopped to feed and water the mules, whilst Sedgwicke cleaned the cart and Albright stared down the empty road, hoping for an early sighting. The roofs of Oropesa came into view and still the road remained empty. When they came to the junction with the main trunk road and turned right to take the direction of Talavera, Albright began to have doubts.

"Do you think they could possibly have gone another way, Private?"

"That I doubt, Sir. In all probability, no one has told them that we have turned off the main road. If I'm any judge, that is. They will have begun their journey along this road. To follow us, in their desperation."

Albright nodded, somewhat resignedly.

"Desperation. Yes. They must be. So, continue on."

However, it was but minutes later that a red smudge appeared on the horizon, its outline changing as it shimmered in the heat, but eventually this vague shape came together as a single column on the road. Sedgwicke's anxiety grew with every minute as the scene became clearer. It was a seemingly endless column, with no divisions, a red-coated serpent, filling the road, with a string of wagons at its head. Sedgwicke stopped the cart and allowed them to approach and soon they were within yards of the first wagon, which, to his huge relief, had its right hand horse being led on foot by an Officer of some kind, with a wounded man and a driver on the seat, but the wagon did not stop, so there was only time enough for a brief conversation, begun by the Officer.

"Are you one of the carts, we've been told about?"

Albright nodded.

"Yes, but the rest are not following. They are at Arzobispo."

The Officer nodded.

"As we've been told."

He then released the horse, whilst the wagon rumbled on, and he came over to the pair.

"How far is this place?"

Sedgwicke answered. He had a far better instinct for distance than his superior.

"About twelve miles. Sir. Can I ask how many wounded you have?"

The Officer was clearly a Surgeon who had taken command and was evidently holding the whole affair together. The leading carts rumbled past with their occupancy of wounded, few of whom could even move their heads to look at the new arrival.

"I could get about three thousand out. The rest had to stay."

The Surgeon pointed over his shoulder to the passing carts.

"These are the worst cases who could travel, but there are plenty more almost equally as bad, following on foot."

He looked at the small cart.

"Could you take six, eight, perhaps?"

Albright nodded.

"We'll try."

He nudged Sedgwicke's arm.

"Get down and help."

The Surgeon nodded at Albright's words and said nothing more as the depressing convoy of wagons ground their way past, but, as if that were not disheartening enough, what came next certainly was. A continuous column, the end unseen, seemingly inched its way forward, each man with bloody bandages, many with crude crutches, some with heads bound such that they could not see their way, therefore being led by others, these with their own wounds, but at least able to walk and guide those now blinded. Many were supported by their fellows, but plainly these would not last long, for, all along the road was the heart rending sight of men who had collapsed and could move no more, their prone figures having been pulled out to the roadside. Sedgwicke pointed at the nearest.

"Should we collect such as those, Sir?"

The Surgeon shook his head.

"No. They came with us and took their chance, but it failed. The probability is that they'll not survive anyway. I'll select for you."

With that he stood to watch the stream of wounded passing on foot, looking for those that could benefit most from a rest in the small cart. As they passed he selected six, who made their exhausted way to the cart to climb in, helped by Sedgwicke. The Surgeon looked over to them.

"Any more?"

Sedgwicke made his own judgement.

"I think two more, Sir. Yes."

The two were selected and helped up to join the others, but then Sedgwicke went to Albright who remained sat on the cart.

"Sir. I think that we should not ride. The seat can take two more. We should walk, as the Surgeon is going to."

Albright was somewhat incensed that such an initiative should come from his inferior, but there was no denying the truth in what Sedgwicke said. It was the Christian thing to do, therefore, saying nothing, he climbed down and Sedgwicke called over to the Surgeon, who was busy re-bandaging a wound.

"Two more, Sir. On the seat."

The Surgeon smiled and nodded and soon two more were selected and climbed up. The last looked at Albright.

"God Bless you, Sir. Our thanks to you both, from all here."

The uplifted Cleric nodded an acknowledgement and then stepped back from the cart, as Sedgwicke took down the reins and turned the cart to then guide the team from his position on the ground, beside the right hand mule. As they progressed on, within the column both heard the sounds that distinguished this as a column of wounded, for above the sound of the plodding feet and the cart wheels, could be heard the cries of those wounded in the foot or leg as they did their best to hold their place in the moving mass, but each step was an agony, and many more joined the prone and exhausted figures by the roadside, these who could walk no further.

It was full dark before the wretched column crossed the Tagus over the narrow bridge, for all to collapse on the first piece of vacant ground. Then all the Surgeons that were there with their Regiments, came to them and, by torchlight and lantern-light, administered medical help as best they could, which included more heart-rending amputations. A group of Nuns emerged from a nearby Convent and also did what they could, but the best medicine was to give some food, however little, to those most in need.

oOo

The next dawn found two British forces on the road that followed the South bank of the Tagus; Crauford's about to enter the tiny hamlet of Meza de Ibor, three-quarters of the way to the vital bridge, and Wellesley's main army about to leave Arzobispo and begin their journey to it. All of the latter army now carried extra burdens from the stores unloaded from the wagons which were now full of wounded and it was not long before all came to understand the appalling nature of the road which they were now on. For the 105th, it came when they were required to help haul guns and their limbers up the steep inclines of what was once a road, but had not been maintained for decades. For Stapleton Cotton's cavalry the understanding came when Wellesley gave the order that they were to ride back to Arzobispo and recover the tools that they had abandoned there. A particularly bad part of the road had been reached which would have to be rebuilt and the tools were now needed. Stapleton Cotton sent the 16th under the command of Major Johnson, which included the Squadrons of Templemere and Tavender, and they found that, despite the urgency, they could progress back at no more than a trot; the road was too bad for even a canter. Within sight of the Arzobispo, Johnson called a halt and quickly took in what was happening and made his decision. Not surprisingly, the population of the village were helping themselves to what had been abandoned by the army. Johnson turned to the pair.

"You two. Take dozen men and gallop for the bridge. Stop anyone from crossing."

The pair looked at him in surprise, but Tavender reacted first, to then ride back three ranks and then raise himself in his stirrups.

"First twelve. With me!"

They galloped for the bridge, whilst Johnson took the remaining Dragoons in a wider sweep to the right. The pillagers took a while to notice the charging cavalry, but when they did notice the galloping Troopers it was obvious to them that the new arrivals were not going be too sympathetic to anyone making off with British property, abandoned or not. Within a minute all were running, carrying what they could, but quickly abandoning what was too heavy. The dozen plus Captains were too late to prevent all from crossing the bridge, but many ran along the bank, upstream of the Tagus, carrying what looked like blankets and clothing. Templemere had drawn his sabre and took a swing at a standing peasant, but the man took the blade on the handle of a spade, which shattered the handle but saved the man. When Templemere turned his horse for another attempt, the man was gone and all that remained was the broken spade. Then a bugle sounded recall and the Dragoons quickly regrouped for Johnson to issue his single order, with all Spanish now off over the fields.

"Find the tools."

Tavender and Templemere felt justified in exempting themselves from so mundane a task, but Johnson would have none of it.

"You two! As well. As will I."

For several minutes the Dragoons scoured the area and soon each had at least one navvy tool of some kind: pick, spade or shovel. Johnson gathered his command and led them back, each holding onto their awkward and possibly also heavy burden. Templemere found himself with the point of a heavy and awkward pickaxe lodged across the front of his saddle and he looked around, hoping to order an exchange, but he saw that this was the tool that most had and so he abandoned the idea. However, soon they were riding to the point of constriction, where stood Wellesley himself, watching the ineffectual efforts of some Grenadiers trying to remove a collapsed and rocky bank. The tools were dropped by each Dragoon at the place and a Grenadier then gratefully took it up to put it to good use. Wellesley was both pleased and relieved. The tools were still where they had been abandoned and could now be used to improve what was turning out to be a road that was almost impractical for the movement of an army. His words were brief, but sincere.

"Well done, Johnson."

He then rode off ahead, to find the next obstacle to his army's progress, but progress was a word that could barely be applied to the whole day. On occasions too many to count, the 105th were halted and O'Hare would come to the Company whose turn it was next, to require them to go back or go forward, to haul a gun, limber or wagon up an impossible slope. All were tired and tetchy, even O'Hare, but Carravoy, him most easily roused, certainly was when he looked up to see his own Company marching past, this completely unbeknown to him. He stood up as the Officer leading them marched past.

"Those are my men!"

The Officer was a Captain like himself, but of Engineers.

"Grenadiers are needed. For work up ahead. Orders

from Himself."

Carravoy could only sit and seethe, but most upsetting of all, and for everyone, were the occasions when a wagon of wounded had to be emptied of its suffering burden for them to make their own way up the slope that could only be ascended by their transport if it was empty. Those soldiers not on the hauling ropes took on the mournful task to get the wounded up to where they could once more mount their wagon, to again suffer the jerks and jolts of their vehicle over a road now improved but still too dilapidated for wheeled transport. The one relief that they could all feel was that, in the high hills, the air was cooler and there were some streams to provide clean water. The Noon meal came as a relief and found Deakin leading his Company back from hauling up a gun battery. He sat wearily, but was able to take a long drink from the plentiful water and Bridie then passed him his dinner. He dipped in his spoon and raised it for examination, when his eyebrows came together in puzzlement.

"What're these?"

Bridie looked at him.

"Don't know, but we was given them and that's all there is. An' they takes a great deal of boilin'!"

He looked at her.

"Do the Spanish eat them, or their horses?"

She became irritated.

"It might even be their pigs, but they taste not too bad and do fill you up well enough, though. So there y'are!"

"Interesting colour. Sort of orange."

Deakin put the spoon into his mouth and began to chew. Bridie was not wrong and so the bowl was soon emptied, which was just as well because all too soon the order came to renew the march, but to no great success. Full dark found Wellesley's command still out on the Mesa, with yet another work-party, by lantern-light, using the tools to both widen and repair the road. However, when a report came in that there were several more difficult points still to be passed before the hamlet of Meza de Ibor, Wellesley relented and gave the order to make camp, and so they did, to spend the night out on the Meza, sleeping or dozing to the cry of foxes, owls and wolves, which caused Bridie to inch herself closer to Deakin as they slept under their grey blankets.

However, for Crauford's command there was to be no sleeping. Having cleared the hamlet of Meza de Ibor in daylight, they passed quickly over the last of the collapsed road and away from the poor collection of hovels to then reach the better road that led North to the bridge at Almaraz. This road could be followed in the half dark created by a half moon and so Crauford pushed his men on. During one of the infrequent halts, Crauford took the chance to approach Carr, now sat besides the sleeping figures of Drake, Ellis and Byford. It was not a social visit as Carr immediately discovered as the huge horse loomed up out of the dark, moonlight illuminating the bright points on its harness, and Crauford looked down. He was as blunt as ever.

"What sort of shape are your men in?"

Carr lowered his coffee cup to a point between his knees as he sat a low boulder.

"Not good, Sir. Not after Talavera. It was a hard battle."

Crauford was not impressed.

"Mine marched forty-three miles in twenty-two hours to try and get up in time and play a part."

However, Carr had more to say, on his own subject. He was not in the best of moods.

"And we're starving and have been for two weeks, near as, since leaving Plascencia on our march to Talavera."

Crauford paused for thought. He treated Carr's words as the relaying of simple facts, not a riposte.

"So! Can I use them?"

Carr took a drink from his coffee and chose his words carefully before answering, knowing that this

Crauford is about as sympathetic and understanding as a fox on a hencoop!

"You can, Sir, but they'll serve better if they're given a bit of a rest."

"That applies to us all, Major!"

He paused to change the subject.

"Your men have Bakers."

"Yes Sir, that's correct, but only the Lights of my Regiment."

Crauford returned to his horse.

"I'll bear that in mind. Now, rouse your men."

With that, Crauford adjusted his reins, spurred his horse and rode on, to the rear and presumably Donkin. Carr hauled himself to his feet, to then shake Drake and Ellis awake.

"Get the men formed up. We're moving."

Drake gazed up, sleepily.

"Who was that?"

Carr looked sideways into the dark that had swallowed Crauford.

"Our Commanding Officer. A most genial and accommodating fellow!"

The sarcasm was not lost on Drake, nor Ellis, who moved off to perform his Officer's bidding, but Byford, now roused, took himself to Carr's possessions to pick them up and drape them over his shoulders. The sword he took to Carr to be buckled on, but Carr noticed the extra haversack, his, on Byford's shoulders. He pointed to it.

"Give me that."

"It's not a bother, Sir. There's not much in it, just as for the rest of us."

"All the same, I'll carry it."

The haversack was transferred and Carr walked off to oversee the formation of his men, from all three Regiments. He had noticed Miles since they left Oropesa and could not help but be impressed. He saw him first.

"And how's the leg, Miles?"

Miles immediate reaction was to exaggerate, because such could make him excused from onerous duties, but while he pondered this, Ellis answered.

"He's thrown away his crutch, Sir, but keeps the splint. Bound alongside."

Miles looked daggers at Ellis, but by now Carr was talking.

"So, it's getting better, then, Miles?"

Miles nodded.

"Yes Sir. On the mend."

"Well done, Miles. When this is done, I'll owe you a bottle of something."

With that he walked on, leaving the astonished Miles and his companions silently laughing, but, slowly, Carr was building a grudging affection for his men. He had stood beside them throughout the whole appalling firefight that had been the final act of Talavera, using a Baker rifle himself, and they had maintained their fire discipline throughout the entire close-quarters conflict, for almost half an hour, holding off French veterans at ridiculous odds. Yet now, with many carrying wounds, they were marching and keeping pace with Crauford's famed Lights. Carr walked on, greeting his men and encouraging where he could.

Within mere minutes the march began, at a fearsome pace, North, to the bridge. The sun rose quickly over the clean edged horizon to begin yet another hot, bright day and with the daylight, Crauford called a halt and summoned his Officers to a well appointed farmhouse beside the road, where he wasted no time on introductions.

"If you don't know each other, then make your introductions outside."

With that he spread a map over the sturdy, thick-legged table.

"We'll be there within the hour."

He stabbed his finger on a particular point.

"That's the bridge and my scouting party tell me that there are no French there, at least when they left it, last

347

night. It is three miles South of the town of Almaraz and broken, at least in part. There is passage across for only two men abreast, which makes our job very much easier. There are already fifteen hundred Spanish there, which we did not know about. They'll remain in reserve when we take over."

He paused for breath and to change the subject slightly.

"What Wellesley's counting on, and there is every reason to hope, is that the French will have pillaged every town and village on their way to here, to gain supplies, which will have slowed them up. So, I'm hoping to find the bridge still unoccupied."

He moved his finger.

"There's a ford, just downstream. We have to deny that, also."

He looked up.

"I don't know, but it could be that we will find ourselves in a race, with the Johnnies coming at the bridge from the same distance as ourselves. Be that the case........"

He pointed to Donkin.

"Yours, Colonel, will march straight for the ford. Find it and hold it. Expect no order from me."

Donkin nodded, then Crauford looked at his own three Colonels, each in turn.

"Mine will hold the bridge."

He began to roll up the map.

"Any questions?"

Initially Carr did not dare to speak in the face of so brusque a manner, although he was unsure if he was to be part of Donkin's Brigade, but eventually professionalism held sway.

"I assume that I am with Colonel Donkin, Sir."

By now the map had been handed to an Orderly.

"Assume yes, but I may change my mind!"

"Sir."

"Now. Out! And let's get to the bridge."

The sleeping men were immediately roused and the

march resumed. Soon they were on a bleak, seemingly pitiless, dry upland plateau, devoid of all life, even of the hardy, goat-like Spanish sheep. The road began to dip downwards and Carr assumed that they were moving into the basin of the Tagus drainage system and so it proved. Crauford had placed Carr's Battalion between his own Brigade in the lead, and Donkin's in the rear and, as the gradient gradually steepened into a valley, he could see over the heads of Crauford's men to finally see the bridge off to the right, at the end of the shallow valley they were descending into, which ended at the Tagus. They all assumed the last stretch of road that could be seen in their shallow valley lead onto the vital bridge over the channel that contained the Tagus. Telescopes were immediately raised to bring the bridge into focus. It was Drake who spoke before Carr.

"Deserted! Not one bit of French blue in sight."

Nevertheless, Crauford maintained the pace. Details grew beyond the river of a high bank where the French would appear, also a road running parallel to the river for a short length, after arriving at the river edge to turn left, then right to cross the Tagus, which proved to be down in more of a gorge than a river valley. As they approached nearer, a green uniformed Captain came back to present himself at attention before Carr.

"From General Crauford, Sir. There are no French at the bridge. Please place your men just downstream of the bridge, but set back where you can act as a reserve for both the General and Colonel Donkin."

"We are not crossing the bridge?"

"No Sir."

The Rifles Captain saluted and ran off. Carr turned to Drake.

"Halt the men here. Crauford can march on and Donkin's can come up past us and go downstream to their ford. Then we'll follow and take our own ground."

Drake called a halt and Donkin's Brigade swung off

the road and marched downstream along the summit of their own high bank. Whilst stood waiting, they could hear the Spanish withdrawing, marching behind them, but out of sight beyond a low ridge. With all completed, Carr spoke again, whilst pointing to the highest ground back from the river, covered in small trees.

"Deploy the men along that slope, behind and between the two Brigades. When they are in place, let them sleep. At least this place is not short of shade."

However, it was not long before orders came for changes, in the form of a Major of Crauford's 52nd. On foot, he rapidly climbed the slope to Carr's men.

"Major Carr."

Carr stood up and offered his hand, which the new arrival took.

"Jessop. 52nd. I'm afraid the General has decided that the ford is the weak point, not the bridge. It really is almost useless, so, he wants to hold that with his Rifles, that's his 95th, Donkin's 60th and the Lights of your 105th. The General's Line troops will go down to the ford, but the Lights of the 45th and 24th remain in reserve, up here."

Carr nodded.

"Very good. Leave it with me."

As the Major departed to gather the Companies of the 60th from Donkin, Carr turned to Drake.

"Did you hear that?"

"I did."

"Right get yours over."

Thus for the next half hour, the Companies passed each other in opposite directions, the 52nd and 43rd moving downstream, Donkin's and Carr's Rifle Lights moving upstream to the bridge. Drake's men were not pleased at having to move from so comfortable a spot, but above the bridge proved to be equally tree covered and so they picked the best places to sleep before the 60th arrived. Drake set his pickets and soon was fast asleep himself.

Meanwhile, several miles back, the rest of the 105th

had now passed through Meza de Ibor, but their trials only worsened. Every yard of road had to be fought for if they were not to abandon their guns and the wagons full of wounded. RSM Gibney came to Lacey. Even he was concerned.

"Sir. With respect, Sir, and ah knows that there is not much as can be done, but the men can't take much more of this, Sir. Men are droppin' out, Sir, an' turnin' in same as wounded. Ah tries to get 'em up, but they just lies there, exhausted, like."

Lacey nodded and looked at him with neither anger nor disagreement.

"I know, Sergeant Major and you are right. For the men, there is nothing other than to pull a rope, push a cart, march, or make the road. I know."

He studied Gibney further, but spoke with the utter weariness that he felt himself.

"I know!"

Gibney knew in advance that informing his Colonel would gain no respite for the men, but he did have one question

"Can th'say how much longer, Sir? End of today, or into tomorrow?"

"No, Sergeant Major. I'm afraid I cannot."

Gibney took this as his answer. He took one pace back, saluted, turned and walked off. Within a minute he had a pickaxe in his hands and was joining a work-gang of Number Two Company. After another minute they were joined by O'Hare, him with a shovel in his hands.

"Ah now, move over boys! Now, does it not take an Irishman to show youse all how to make a road!"

Weak laughter came from all within earshot, but the work-gangs had to be changed frequently by rotating the Companies. None could labour for more than one hour, before being overcome by dizziness brought on by lack of food. Wellesley rode back and forth, as gloomy and depressed as anyone, but saying nothing. Encouragement was pointless and, in the circumstances, seemed like deepest sarcasm. The Noon meal came, but it was filled with nothing other than sleep and hot tea. The army inched onwards, such that they could now see the village that was their destination; Mirabette high up on its ridge, on the far side of the same valley that Crauford had recently descended into, but had turned North to the bridge of Almaraz. Finally, onwards but also downwards, into the same dry valley, where there came relief, of sorts, for here was the main road that served the bridge and now no work was required to repair their way. It was now but a task of marching and helping the exhausted and starving horse teams to haul the guns and vehicles up the frequent slopes. Wellesley rode past, now smiling and exchanging pleasantries with his Staff, which was noticed by Deakin as they marched at the head of the 105th column.

"Somethin's cheered him up!"

Halfway watched the Staff party ride on.

"Don't take much, the state we're in."

However, Halfway was only half right. Wellesley now knew that Crauford was holding the bridge at Almaraz and that his own force would next day be safely up in Mirabette, albeit after a steep climb up the ridge. Mirabette was at the top of a deep and impregnable defile that held the road down from this village to Crauford's own force. His army was safe.

At the bridge, safety was far from the minds of Davey, Pike and Saunders as they made their way, hunched down, back into their camp. Each opened their tunic to let fall two or three fish. All around eyes widened with delight, and Davey explained.

"That river's full of 'em."

He paused, for now was the time for a small amount of self-embellishment.

"If you knows where to look!"

Miles was having none of it.

"Gallows bait poacher! Shut your gob and get 'em

352

gutted!"

It was the best meal that they had had in days, weeks! Fish, army biscuits and hot tea, but they felt it prudent to save the orange garbanzos. As the night fell, so sleep claimed them again, but this time a good sleep, undisturbed by the gnawing pangs of hunger. However, they were awakened not by the sounds of 'reveille' but the alarm of 'fall in'. The French had arrived and as their blue and white uniforms took possession of the slopes and banks opposite, Major Jessop again ran around the Rifles' positions and then to Drake's Light Company, whilst Crauford galloped over to Donkin. Breathless from his running and then up Carr's slope, Jessop rested on his sword and drew breath.

"The General wants a demonstration, to show the French that we are here in strength. So, please to form up your men, in full view."

Carr's brows came together.

"In full view! What if M'sieu over there gets his guns up on that high bank? At this range we'll be massacred! Even as we fall back!"

Jessop nodded.

"I think he knows that, but, from the beginning, he wants them to know that we are here in strength. So, please to form your men up and advance them forward."

Carr nodded, his face showing that he was far from happy, but orders were orders. He found a bugler of the 24th, the only one remaining from before Talavera.

"Sound 'form up'."

The notes sounded and the men of the 45th and 24th hurried to form two firing lines. Carr placed himself before the centre and led them forward, but he halted at the first point where he could see the French and they could see him. Immediately to his left were the 43rd, his men had joined onto them perfectly. Perhaps all were a little far back to be perfect for Crauford, but evidently the 43rd Colonel had the same concerns as himself. They stood in place for a good hour, observing the arrival of what was a considerable French force, but it could quickly be seen that they, or at least their General, were not in a warlike mood. Instead, as each French Battalion arrived, so they made camp, felling trees, lighting fires and cooking food. Carr found himself beside the Captain of the Light Company of the 45th, Captain Wood. They had now been stood observing the French for two hours.

"Seems like no battle today, Sir. Or perhaps this is a different kind of warfare, them over there cooking food, in front of us over here starving."

Carr nodded,

"The kind of warfare that preys on the mind, you mean? Could be, but what matters more to me is that he has not brought up his guns onto the top of that bank opposite. From there he could blow us all to Kingdom Come, if we stay standing here, that is."

As if in answer, Jessop arrived again.

"You can stand your men down and pull back. But hold them in readiness, he may try something after he's eaten."

The men immediately behind had heard Jessop and the line dissolved for all to follow their lead and take themselves back into the shade of the trees, where sleep again claimed them. Carr remained alone still watching, still anxious about French guns. As he pondered he did not notice Crauford himself approach from behind. Carr had no time to come to attention, nor salute before Crauford began his questioning.

"Carr. What do you think?"

"Sir?"

"What do you think? You've faced these Johnnies more than anyone here. What do you think!"

Carr drew a deep breath.

"Well, Sir, I have no idea who their General is over there, but I have no doubt that, if we were all Spanish, he'd be over and into us. So, perhaps they're a lot more worried about facing us than we think. Perhaps they now realise, after Maida, Vimeiro, Corunna and now Talavera, that what we deal out is more than they can take. Someone over there knows that any column crossing that ford, would be allowed over, just so far, then a firing line would come over the ridge, where they had been protected from cannon, and send them back, with heavy casualties. Very heavy, with them having their backs to the river."

He looked directly at Crauford.

"I don't see them trying. Sir."

Crauford nodded.

"I'm much of the same opinion. So, we stay, presumably each at our ease, perusing our foes through various telescopes."

Was that humour, Carr thought, but he decided not to take the risk and did not laugh in response.

"Just so, Sir."

Carr felt emboldened.

"But what will force us back is hunger, Sir. We've virtually nothing to eat."

Crauford's face grew thunderous.

"I'm of the same opinion, Major."

With that he mounted his horse and walked it off towards the bridge. Suddenly, Carr felt utterly weary. He turned and walked back to where Byford had a fire and was boiling some garbanzos. He sat and waited for his servant to judge them as edible, but long before that, his head slumped forward and he was fast asleep. Byford took his own share from the cooking-pot, left the remainder and kicked out the fire. If overcooked, the garbanzos turned into an insubstantialdiscernible, tasteless soup.

There was little more cheer to be found within the men of the 105th marching with Wellesley, as Lacey finally led them into Mirabette, their laborious climb completed, but the whole was merely a collection of low novels, even devoid of a Church. Apart from a central square, there was no discernible attempt at a road pattern; it was as though a child's collection of wooden houses had been emptied onto a carpet. The atmosphere was as gloomy and cheerless as a winter's day; in fact, after but a few minutes, it was obvious, that the village had been all but abandoned, bar a few hardy and overly optimistic souls. This was not lost on Toby Halfway.

"I'm sure we've been in more dead-alive holes than this, Jed, but blessed if I can remember when!"

Both in front and from behind, the army poured in, and on through. Staff Officers did their best to allocate buildings, but there were so few that the vast majority of the army were out in the fields and some were even ordered to march the extra six miles to the next village, Jaraceijo. However, veterans that they all were, soon they had fires going to cook what was left of their rations and then the men slept, despite the bright sunlight. Lacey and O'Hare looked out over their now sitting or sleeping command. As light-headed as anyone, Lacey sought the words to sum up their situation.

"All is in disrepair. Boots, equipment and stomachs."

O'Hare looked at him puzzled, but Lacey continued.

"Today's the eighth. We left Talavera on the third. That matches anything on the way to Corunna."

"Bar the cold!"

"Yes, but this weather creates its own problems."

O'Hare took a deep breath, ever the optimist.

"Well, it's done now. If we march out, it's on a good road back to Truxillo, 20, 25 miles."

He smiled at the thought.

"And beyond that, 50 miles is Merida and 30 more Badajoz. Supply wagons can do 30, 40, miles a day, so, I'm hoping that some food may be arriving after two days or so. Merida's a base of some sorts and Badajoz even bigger!"

Lacey nodded and even smiled.

"Well, yes, keep those hopeful facts in mind.

Meanwhile, let's go and see what Bryce has concocted for us."

"No need to speculate. I know exactly. They'll be round and orange!"

Both laughed and walked to their allocated headquarters building.

oOo

For the rest of that day and throughout the night, Wellesley's army was at rest, bar the sentries, mounting a prudent guard. Wellesley's men awoke to no change at all in their situation, but not so Crauford's. Supposedly after a leisurely breakfast, on the French side Battalion after Battalion began to form up on the road back to Almaraz and march off. By Noon the bank opposite was deserted. Crauford came back to Carr's vantage point and watched his green uniformed 95th Rifles cross the bridge to carefully climb the bank and see what was there, or was not. Their reaching the top, to then blatantly stand up looking at the disappearing French, told the whole story, that they were now unopposed. Crauford turned to Carr.

"I have no more need of your men, Major. I cannot feed you. Gather them up and march back to Mirabette."

To Carr's surprise and shock, Crauford held out his hand.

"Good luck, Carr, and thank you for your opinions. I've appreciated your help."

Carr took his hand.

"Thank you, Sir. Pleased to have been of some service."

Crauford nodded and walked away, leaving Carr to instruct Byford to run to Captain Drake at the bridge and bring him and his 105th up directly. Within minutes the men of the three Regiments were formed up and marching off, to immediately ignore the junction with the painful road back to Meza de Ibor, but soon their route was climbing a gentle slope which soon topped a ridge and then they descended into a shallow valley whose far side was a seemingly endless array of steep cliffs, both to the left and right. Carr looked at Drake.

"Is there a road up through that?"

Drake had no answer and so all marched on. The road became steeper and steeper and seemed to disappear directly into the cliff wall before them. Carr called a halt, albeit a brief one, but plainly what they were about to attempt was going to need all of their much reduced strength. After a rest and some water, they began again and now they could see that the road climbed into what was little more than a cleft. They entered and all felt the shock of the chill from cold stone in deep shade. Above them was less that a quarter of the sky that they had been used to, with steep, boulder strewn slopes either side. It was Drake who stated the obvious, using two deep breaths.

"If we'd been pushed back, off the river, we'd have come back to here and that would have been that for the Johnnies."

He took another breath.

"He would have packed up and gone back, tout suite!"

Carr nodded as he laboured with his own climb, but the gradient did lessen and after but 20 minutes more marching, they saw the roofs of Mirabette, then, soon after that, the swarms of Redcoats now calling the village their home. Once in the village Carr took himself off the road and waited for his two Captains of the 45th and 24th to come up. They halted in the tiny square and he shook the hand of both.

"Well done, Gentlemen. We can now only hope, with some justification, perhaps, that things will improve. Good luck to you both."

Both saluted and then they left him to find the campgrounds of their respective Regiments, something that he had to do himself. He sent Ellis and Byford off to do just that, whilst Drake and himself sat on the edge of a horse trough, which somehow continuously poured clean water into itself from a brass spigot. After some time of silence brought on by weariness, Byford returned alone to lead the way for the whole Company. As they passed a fairly shoddy building, with Ellis stood outside, Byford pointed to the door.

"Our Officers are in there, Sir."

Carr and Drake peeled off and Ellis led the Company on to join the rest of the Battalion. The two Officers soon found Lacey in the second of the two downstairs rooms and he stood to greet them.

"Welcome back, you two. I trust all is well."

It was Carr who answered.

"Both well, Sir, thank you, but is there anything to eat?"

Lacey shook his head.

"No! Unless you count those damn orange beans as food. Otherwise, no!"

As a Brigadier and with his Divisional Commander absent at the bridge, Lacey found himself, on the evening of Carr's arrival, summoned to a meeting with Wellesley himself, in a building which fronted onto the square and seemed to serve as a Town Hall. All stood as their Commander entered but he waved them back down onto their crude benches. He looked as haggard and worried as he had been on the road to Meza de Ibor and began by addressing the obvious questions, which he knew they all must harbour.

"First, supplies. I have asked that some be sent from Merida and Badajoz, but it seems that none are there sufficient to our needs, but what little is there will arrive soon, I hope. Our main depot is at Abrantes, but Soult has cut us off from there. Second, why are we remaining here? The answer is both military and political, as ever. Our own Government would wish us to stay to support the Spanish and it is true that by remaining here, in this undeniably strong position, we can threaten central Spain and keep the French very much on edge and persuade them to leave Portugal alone. The Spanish Junta in Seville want us to remain and, as if to emphasise this, they have sent me a present of six fine, white, Andulusian horses. I'm not sure if they intended them for riding or eating, but they arrived this morning."

He paused to allow the faint laughter to die down.

"There is a promise from them of some flour coming up from Truxillo, but we'll believe that when we see it. They are making us promises, which, as we all know by now, will probably count for nothing. The supply situation is not made any easier by the fact that the Spanish army were beaten back from the bridge and ford at Arzobispo. It is now at Meza de Ibor, which we know well and they have taken up a position there as strong as ours here, which is why the Junta want us to remain; from here both armies pose a continuing threat to the French. However, this area was picked clean by the French when they were here and now it has to support two armies. I hope that this is a comfort, Gentlemen, but I have written to the Junta making it clear that, unless supplied, we cannot remain here. Today is the ninth and I have offered eleven more days, that being the 20th. We are either fully supplied or we march back to Badajoz. So!"

His face grew hard.

"The rules of foraging must be relaxed. Any theft remains a capital punishment, but anything outside of an enclosed field or building is fair game. But, warn the men. They will encounter Spanish foraging parties and any injury inflicted on our Allies counts the same as any inflicted on our own."

His shoulders fell and he gave a deep sigh as his face became melancholy.

"I know this is cold comfort, Gentlemen, but this is the game we are in. If there is any benefit from our remaining here, we have to take it. From here we pose a very real and potent threat to the French. Here, we are unassailable and could advance forward either North or East. This will last for eleven days more and then we will know, one way or the other."

With that he reached behind him for his hat and walked up the left side to the door. All stood, but he was soon gone. Lacey returned immediately to O'Hare and Carr, waiting in their allocated building. He came straight to the point.

"For food, we have to forage. Just like the French. There is a Spanish army over at Ibor doing just the same. So, we compete with them, but not violently, we must hope. Allow the men to break all the rules, bar theft. On that Wellesley remains adamant. So, allow them to cut up as many bullets into birdshot as they like, what food there is around here is on the hoof and on the wing!"

Carr was not convinced.

"How long, Sir, and what about desertions from any party we allow out?"

"Eleven days, Henry, and as for desertions, we have to take the chance. We can only hope that the men see things as I do. For a start, where do they go for food? There is nothing out there, this place was picked clean by the French six weeks ago, so the only hope of food rests with remaining with the army. They didn't desert on the way to Coruna and so my faith remains constant for the here and now."

Carr made no reply and so Lacey continued.

"Right. I want all Officers in this building within 30 minutes."

They were assembled within 15 to fill the small space and so Lacey stood on the staircase where he could be both seen and heard. His face was stern and determined.

"You may remember my saying such as this in a place called Bembibre on the way to Coruna. What I said then applies now. Without food, armies fall apart as it did then and it is more than likely that it will again, to us, over the next days. Wellesley wants to hold here for eleven more days and expects the army to hold together. I'll leave any judgement on the likelihood of that to yourselves. After eleven days we are either supplied or we march back to the border. There are eleven days before us, during which we have to hold the 105th together. Over the retreat to Coruna the 105th had a desertion rate as low as The Guards. We held them to The Colours, so what I said then, I say now. First, your men! Not you, them! What we have, we share, equal rations, if nothing that night then you go hungry before they do. If they think for a second that you have extra privilege, morale suffers and then discipline and then we descend into a rabble, as we saw all around us at Coruna. So that's your watchword, Gentlemen, and I mean it. First, your men!"

He paused for effect.

"Dismiss!"

They filed out, any conversation low and mumbled, or if not that, then they were occupied in deep thought. Carravoy, returning to their Grenadier Company with Ameshurst and D'Villiers alongside him gave vent to his aroused anger,

"So, we're to starve, whilst they eat!"

Ameshurst looked at his angry Captain.

"Who are 'they', Sir?"

"The men and the Spanish!"

Ameshurst had his own thoughts.

"Well, Sir. Regarding the men, it may not come to that. Part of a bargain, as it were. If we show that we are playing our part, and receiving no more than them, less even, well, then I feel sure we'll get a fair share of whatever they bring back from foraging. No holding back, as it were. I feel that I can count on their sense of fair play."

Carravoy was unappeased.

"You can believe that if you choose, Lieutenant, but my experience of such as our men tells me very much otherwise."

D'Villiers held his peace. He knew that Ameshurst

362

dwelt in the highest esteem with his men and he could only hope that such also applied to himself with his own men. They came to their camp, but D'Villiers walked on, to his own Section. The least he could do was to ask how they were.

The following day brought news which caused a mixed reaction, both relief and puzzlement, the word being brought to the Grenadier Officers by Ameshurst.

"The French have gone! Left Almaraz and Arzobispo, too. They've gone back behind the Tagus."

This time it was D'Villiers who was unconvinced.

"Well, hooray for that. But it gives even less reason for us to be up here, starving and falling apart!"

So it proved for the following days, which stretched towards a week. The only topic of conversation was supplies and none were forthcoming. If telescopes were used at all, they were used to study their supply road back to Truxillo, but it remained depressingly empty, after a lone delivery of Spanish flour on the eleventh. The road remained empty even of local Spanish going about their daily business. There came more days of increased hunger, with even the betanzos now running out. The conversation amongst the Officers was usually concerned with the deterioration in the men, which was becoming obvious, many were now listless and uncaring, and so standards of appearance and discipline were dropping. Also, the most disturbing reports were of men making off in groups of their own, to find food, from whatever source. Lacey's prediction was coming true, the army was falling apart. The one blessing was that the men were not required to march, which slowed the process of disintegration, and reserves of energy could be found if they were allocated to a foraging party. Hope of food gave energy to tired legs.

On the 15th, however, the situation worsened. The word came first to Drake, who took it to Carr.

"Bad news. A foraging party of the 45th have come back battered and bloody and empty handed. They were a dozen men, sent to escort one of the 'once in a blue moon' flour convoys, and they have been ambushed and roughly handled by a large party of Spanish. Needless to say, they made off with the mules and the flour."

Carr put down the pen with which he was writing a letter to Jane.

"By 'roughly handled' you mean attacked, so that they could take the convoy?"

"Yes, I mean exactly that."

Carr's brows furrowed.

"So, it has finally come down to both armies fighting each other for food."

He pushed the letter to one side and slid the edge of his left thumb between his two front teeth, his normal thinking pose when he was agitated and deeply concerned.

"We have to keep sending out foraging parties. We've five days to go before we may have to attempt a serious march. If the men aren't fed now, we'll never get them on the road!"

Drake had been doing some thinking of his own.

"We send them out in Sections, which for us is 35 men, about. Enough not to look like an aggressive patrol, but enough to take care of themselves."

Carr nodded.

"That's a good notion, but no Officer. They go out with a Sergeant in command. What they will be doing will inevitably be illegal and something which an Officer cannot possibly condone. However, they must come back with something. By hook or by crook."

Drake nodded his agreement.

"Most likely crook! Then what of the Provosts?"

Carr stared straight back at him.

"I don't care! This is where we are. We get something to eat or there will be nothing to mark our presence here bar bleached bones bundled together by red rags. I don't care!"

Drake took the hint and left, to search for Ellis. At

the sight of his Captain, Ellis came to 'Order Arms' and saluted.

"Sir!"

"You've heard."

There was no need to specify the topic.

"Sir."

"Right. Take out Lieutenant Maltby's Section, tomorrow. Ready the whole Section. See what you can find."

He looked fully into the weathered face of the competent veteran.

"No revenge! But defend yourselves and defend whatever you can bring back."

"Yes Sir. Understood, Sir."

Ellis hurried off to the mess area of his best men, Davey, Saunders, Pike and the rest, to spread the word. Soon the whole Section, 41 strong, were opening cartridges and cutting up the lead bullets into as many pieces as their clumsy clasp knives would allow. They slept hungry, but that was now the norm, and, after a dawn breakfast of biscuits and water, Ellis led them out of the camp, with Davey at his side.

"What do you think, John? Where's our best chance of something?"

Davey answered quickly.

"Well, off this ridge for a start. Animals aren't stupid. They needs food and shelter same as us and that's most likely in the lowland. So, I'd say, follow the road downwards, South, then see what the lie of the land is down there."

They walked on, a loose column and, within an hour they were descending off the Mirabette ridge, which took them out of the upland conifers and into deciduous woodland. With the change Davey gave the order to spread out and shoot for birds, of any description and so, in a skirmish line, they pushed through the thin undergrowth and soon the woods were ringing to the sound of musketry as the men tried their luck with whatever large bird they could see. After an hour, Ellis called them in to examine their haul, but it was mostly rooks, crows and squirrels, with one or two game birds, nothing like enough to take back to camp and be judged then as a success. Ellis looked at Davey.

"Keep on?"

Davey nodded.

"What else? There must be some kind of decent animal in these woods: rabbits, hare, deer, boar, or even badger, if they has them in Spain."

Ellis looked appalled.

"Badger!"

Davey was unmoved.

"Yes. Badger. Tastes like pork. You'd be surprised."

Ellis was unconvinced.

"Damn right I would, but we're now some miles from camp and past Noon."

"Agreed. So, we comb these woods some more, but no further, and hope."

For the next hour came the same as those before and the shots continuously rang out. Pike was beside Miles, both with their birdshot gone, so both were now loaded with solid, in the hope of meeting something bigger. It was Pike who heard the rustling in the undergrowth, so he held Miles back.

"Tom. There's something big in the bushes over there."

He pointed and Miles looked at him, then at the bushes indicated. Miles hatched a simple plan.

"You go right, I'll go left, but keep yer bundook pointin' forward. I've already had one bullet."

They advanced slowly and it was Pike who gained the first sight of the animal, its hindquarters, and it was plainly a pig, by the shape of its tail. Pike stopped and cocked his Baker rifle. The pig was still rooting about in the undergrowth, wholly preoccupied, so Pike took sight on where just to the rear of the shoulder would be, although this part was hidden by the screening bushes. He held his breath and fired and all between him and the pig was smoke. When it cleared there was nothing of the pig to be seen and Pike sighed, but only for a moment, for Miles was yelling in triumph.

"Well done, Joe. You got'n, just past the shoulder. Clean kill. Go get Ellis and John. I'll find a good branch what we can sling this fat bugger from, an' then get'n back."

Pike ran over to where he thought Ellis and Davey were and after a few enquiries, he found both.

"John, I've downed a pig. Just over there!"

His words were heard by many others, and all ran over to where Miles had lashed the legs of the animal together and was passing the branch through, ready for it to be carried. However, it was Ellis who first noticed where they were, this being on the very edge of the wood. He peered between the last trees.

"This here's no family animal, more like a boar of some kind, looking for sows and there's the farm. This'n have come in here for that or to root about in the woods. Still, we'll call this a good piece of luck."

He looked again.

"Get this up and let's get gone. Might just be some odd breed as belongs to yon farm."

The nearest four shouldered the branch and they hurried back through the wood. It was a relief when they came to a track, which led in the direction of Mirabette and they took it, all in good spirits, because the pig was a good find and, with all the other kill, their time out had been a major success. The track led to the main road and they hurried along in the last yellow light of full day, the pig prominent in the centre of the their loose column.

It was Davey who saw them first, coming over a slight ridge to their right, the light blue uniforms of Spanish infantry.

"What's this?"

Ellis looked and his face set in a frown.

"How many would you say?"

"Not far short of a hundred."

"And they've seen us and are comin' to see what we've got. And, from what we've heard, it won't be to offer any kind of a bargain."

He looked at his men, who by now had all seen the oncoming Spanish forage party. Miles passed judgment.

"Sod 'em! I'm not givin' up one dead crow to that mangy crew!"

The road was in a slight valley, giving a rising slope on the side opposite that of the Spanish. Ellis gave his orders

"Off the road, left. 50 yards. Single line."

He was obeyed immediately and the single line formed. Ellis stood before them

"Loaded, but hammer down. Fix bayonets."

Within a minute all were loaded, but rifles not cocked for firing and Baker sword bayonets glistened at the end of every weapon. By now the Spanish were crossing the road as a compact group and Ellis watched them approach.

"Byford! Near me."

"Already am, Sergeant. Right behind you."

"Up here, b'side me."

Byford joined him, as the leader of the Spanish foragers, a Sergeant, climbed the slope, grinning widely, but with a total absence of any sincerity or friendship, as though pleased with what he had found and was about to happen. He stopped some 20 yards before Ellis.

"Hola Inglés. Lo has hecho bien, este día."

Ellis spoke sideways to Byford, without taking his eyes off the Spanish before him, all grouped just behind the Sergeant.

"What's he sayin'?"

"Sounds like hello, we've done well."

Ellis smiled and nodded.

"Si!"

The grin died just a little.

"Pensamos que debe compartirla con nosotros."

Grins and laughter arouse from the Spanish and Ellis was aroused.

"What's he say?"

"No idea!"

Ellis took a deep breath. Time to make things clear.

"No!"

The grin died, and then the Sergeant waved his hand in the direction of the pig, on the ground behind the centre rank.

"Este es un cerdo Español. Nos dan algunos. Somos españoles."

Byford did his best.

"It's a Spanish pig. They should have some of it or all of it. I can't be certain."

The reply came not from Ellis, but from Miles stood directly behind.

"Tell 'im where to go, Byfe!"

Ellis said nothing, so Byford again made his best effort.

"No. Todo ello es nuestro."

Ellis spoke sideways.

"What did you say?"

"I told him it was ours. All of it."

Ellis nodded satisfied and stared at the Sergeant, whose face was a blank stare, but from narrowed eyes. That was enough for Ellis. He took a deep breath to shout.

"Make ready!"

All rifles were raised in the air, ready to be lowered into the firing position. Expressions changed amongst the Spanish, even more so with the Sergeant, when Miles came forward to stand beside Byford and lower his rifle and aim directly at him. Things became even more tense when, in the silence, could be heard the load click of Miles pulling back the hammer. Ellis spoke quickly.

"Get control of yourself, Miles. Nothing's happened yet!"

Miles had but one thought on his mind and he did not speak quietly. He wanted the Spanish to hear, if not understand.

"Do you remember that El Navaja guerrilla bastard who wanted us to give him a Baker when we was cut off afore Coruna?"

No one replied, but Miles continued.

"Well, this is his brother. Same family ………….. What's the word, Byfe?"

"Characteristics."

"What he said."

He took another step forward.

"I b'ain't givin' up nothin' to this scavengin' crew of useless shite-auks! As can't face the Frogs unless they'n stood behind two ton of timber!"

He then thought of another insult.

"Then buggers off anyway, to go robbin' our camp. Gutless bastards!"

The Spanish Sergeant was having his own thoughts; he had thoroughly picked up the tone of Miles' words. To approach any closer to these British would mean a firefight, and in that he did not trust his own men. He had been at Talavera and he knew what these very same British were capable of. They were utterly steady under fire, unlike his own, and could manage almost four rounds a minute, whilst his own could just cover two. Also, unlike his own, they were not averse to a bit of bayonet work, after firing a well aimed volley. On top they were obviously ever-ready to die where they stood! A lot of his men would die and it only took one glance to see the malignant face at the far end of the smaller soldier's weapon, to see that he would be the first casualty. However, he stood his ground. He had the advantage of numbers, over two to one, and that may well gain them something. The silence lasted, until broken by

Ellis.

"Zeke! Nat! Pick up the animal."

The three heard the slight commotion behind them as the two heftiest in the Section slung their rifles and picked up the pig. Miles was incensed at the possibility.

"You ain't givin' none of it to these muckrakes. None of it!"

"Shut up Miles!"

Ellis took a deep breath.

"Fall back! Hold your front."

Miles was livid.

"Fall back! I b'ain't takin one step back from this bunch of spineless scrapers!"

Now Ellis was angry.

"You fall back, Miles, or I'll see you on the triangle! Fall back, and no-one gets hurt, nor killed, nor hung. Nor flogged! We've got these stopped. Just fall back and get out of this."

The good sense from Ellis had an effect, also did Byford's hand on Miles' sleeve.

"He's right, Tom. These won't follow. Fall back and let's get some of that pig cooked!"

With his aim at the Sergeant's head not wavering one inch, Miles stepped backwards, alongside Ellis and Byford. The gap grew, because the Spanish did not follow and soon it was well over 100 yards. Ellis looked at his men, holding their line, their rifles still at the 'make ready'.

"Shoulder arms and fall in."

Soon, marching at a rapid pace, they were back on the road and hidden from the Spanish by the intervening trees. Ellis, marching with Davey, gave voice to his thoughts.

"That was close, but that bugger Miles could have started a war!"

Davey laughed.

"Perhaps, but on the other hand he made it very clear that them Spanish were getting nothing from us. Not without killing all round!"

Ellis conceded.

"Perhaps that did make a difference."

Within another hour they were marching through the camp lines to their own Regiment where the pig was quickly butchered and every piece of flesh and offal went into the Light Company's cooking pots, including the trotters. After an hour the stew was cooked, lovingly prepared by Bridie and Nellie and a portion was sent to both of their Captains and to Major Carr. The following morning the leftovers served as breakfast, when Ellis took Shakeshaft's Section out, hoping for the same, but it was not to be. Their haul of crows, rooks and squirrels, joined those of the previous day and that served as the Light Company's evening meal, but at least there had been no confrontation with the Spanish.

The following day, early morning, Crauford's men came up from the bridge, but marched straight through to Jaraicejo. Lacey drew the obvious conclusion as he watched them pass, standing in the shelter of their door.

"He's sending us down the road. This won't last much longer."

O'Hare dropped onto the table the piece of paper he had been reading.

"And something else. He's parading some of us, to take a look, surely that means we are leaving. Nothing's come from the Spanish, nor is likely to. He wants to know what we are capable of, distance on the road each day, would be my guess as to the reason. You can forget our 20 miles!"

Lacey looked inwards from the door.

"A look at ours?"

"More like yours. 105th, 45th and 24th. Also, Stewart's and Kemmis'. Three Brigades."

"When for us?"

"Noon."

"Right. Let's see what we can do."

He took up his sword and went immediately to find Carr, finding him with the Light Company as usual. Within minutes the word was around "Wellesley inspection" and all did their best to clean and polish, although all brick dust had long been used up, months past. When the hour came, the ten Companies of the 105th fell in and marched to their parade ground. Wellesley was perfectly on time and, as he rode past each Company, each gave a very acceptable 'present arms'. He came to the centre, where both Colours were moving in the gentle breeze and where Lacey was stood with O'Hare. Wellesley leaned forward over his saddle horn, a rare smile on his face. He was in a mood for sentiment, perhaps because of feeling relieved, now that the die had been cast.

"Lacey! I trust I find you well."

"Well enough, Sir. Thank you."

Wellesley looked left and right.

"How are your men?"

"Not what they were, Sir, when we left Abrantes."

"Can they march?"

"They can, Sir, and fight, but not as well as we would wish."

Wellesley nodded. What he had thought himself had been confirmed, the harsh reality was evident all over. However, Lacey felt emboldened enough to ask a question of his own.

"So, we are pulling back, Sir?"

"Correct, Lacey. The only question I have now is how many miles can we manage, each day? What do you think?"

Lacey looked squarely at his General as he thought.

"Twelve, Sir. Each day."

"No more?'

"No Sir."

"As I thought, Lacey. Thank you for your opinion. I value it."

He sat back in his saddle.

"Well done, Lacey. I've not forgotten you from Vimeiro. I can have no complaints about your 105th, my old 'Rag and Bone Boys'."

"Thank you, Sir."

Wellesley pulled on his reins to move his horse on, when something caught his eye, the distinctive Drummerboy uniform worn by Patrick Mulcahy. He stopped.

"That a Drummerboy you have holding your Regimental?"

"Yes Sir. That Ensign was killed at Talavera. He took over, just after Mackenzie was killed."

"So he held it up, all through that last damnable episode?"

"Yes Sir."

"And not a waver?"

"No, Sir."

Wellesley smiled.

"So he's doing the job?"

"Well enough, Sir, as you see. His is a Regimental family. His Father was killed at Maida."

"Good enough. Make him an Ensign!"

As Wellesley moved away, Jed Deakin chewed on his shako chinstrap.

"Well I'll be blessed and sent up to Heaven! Up 'till now he's been calling me uncle. Now I've got to call him Sir!"

Halfway chuckled and even Heaviside, stood just in front, grinned as he overheard.

"He shall reward every man according to his works. Matthew 16. Verse 27."

Deakin let out a deep breath.

"Yes Sir. Just so, Sir."

However, back around their campfire, Bridie was anything but impressed, more like totally horrified and blaming Jed.

"How could you let that happen? He'll be stood

right in the centre of the line. He'll be kilt, for sure!"

Deakin felt very much maligned, unjustly, or so he felt.

"What could I do? Neape was knocked over and so they grabbed the nearest, which was him. And I stand in the centre of the line, how much worry do you have for me?"

So pointed a question silenced Bridie and she sat down, head down, shoulders hunched, hands together in her lap. Seeing such a picture of worry and anxiety, Deakin relented.

"Look at the good of it, Bridie. He's an Officer now. An Officer!"

The phrase came into his mind, 'He could die a General', meaning of old age, but she could take that the wrong way. He found other words.

"He could end his days, back home, as a General!"

She looked up.

"Yes. Think on that. 'Tis the boys chance in life. 'Sides, Harry Bennet will look after him. He's as good a Colour Sergeant as any you'd find."

Bridie stood up. She felt like continuing the argument, if only to give release to her feelings, but she knew it was hopeless. Instead she occupied herself with crushing some young acorns, for their next meal. With early afternoon, the order came to prepare for the coming march and in this manner were they occupied until the evening meal, the checking of boots, packs, strapping and crossbelts. Now knowing this, a better mood spread throughout the army, summed up by Tom Miles, now sat examining the livid scar on his leg.

"Too long we bin yer! An' for what? Nothin' these past weeks, ain't seen one Frog, near nor far. Time to clear off and get ourselves back to rights. We've given Johnny a bloody nose. Be happy with that!"

The response from John Davey was simple.

"Shut up and pull up your trousers, afore Bridie or Eirin comes along. Fine sight you looks, patched drawers and all!"

Whilst delivering a highly aggrieved look in the direction of Davey, Miles did as he was told, and resumed the inspection of his kit. That night, Davey was on sentry duty, more to detect likely Spanish raiders, rather than any French, who all knew were now long gone. The Officer of the Watch was Joshua Heaviside, who came to Davey on his rounds and Davey reacted immediately, swinging his bayonetted rifle in the direction of the approaching figure.

"Halt who goes there?"

"Officer of the Watch."

"Advance, Sir, and be recognised."

Heaviside approached and Davey presented arms.

"At ease. Anything?"

"All's well, Sir. Just the sounds of the night. Nothing more."

"He maketh peace in His high places. Job 25. Verse 2."

"Yes Sir. And long may it remain, Sir."

"I doubt that, Corporal."

Heaviside looked at Davey despite the darkness that held them both.

"Hungry?"

"Who isn't, Sir?"

"No indeed. Have some of this."

Davey saw the hand before him, holding what looked like a thin strip of leather. He took it, but Heaviside defined it.

"Dried beef. I learned the technique whilst serving in the Americas. Mrs. Heaviside makes some for me to bring out and this is about the last of it. It's quite good."

With no more words, not even a customary final quote, Heaviside walked on. Davey took a bite, or rather ripped off a section with his teeth and began to chew. It was hard going, but certainly the taste was very acceptable. The piece lasted until he was relieved by George Tucker, as the sun edged over the far horizon and with that dawn the army formed up to march away. In columns of Brigades they stood to, in readiness to take their turn to march forward and out onto the road. The Orders for March stated that the Brigade of Guards were to be first.

Lacey and O'Hare stood at the head of their column with an unhindered view of the road, when the tedium of waiting was broken by a large group of Spanish Officers riding past from the direction of Truxillo. O'Hare read their purpose correctly.

"Last pleading for us to stay."

Lacey gave no reply and Wellesley's reply, although inevitably unheard, was soon made obvious, as the Guards marched onto the road and Lacey's Brigade was ordered to follow. Wellesley had had enough, the Spanish offer, if that was what it was, had fallen on deaf ears. Out on the road, the Guards set a decent pace, as if having a point to make, but they soon slowed when they caught up with Fane's Heavy Cavalry Brigade, the 3rd Dragoon Guards and the 4th Dragoons, these contentedly walking their horses and so the pace slowed. Jaraicejo was utterly lifeless, not even closed and shuttered; both doors and window shutters open at angles which showed their owners had been in too much of a hurry to leave. Halfway noticed the desolation.

"All buggered off. Too many scavengers makin' their lives a misery, both us and the Dons."

Deakin agreed.

"Up in the hills, shouldn't wonder. Best place for their food. And their women!"

The only life was outside the houses, this being Crauford's men and two other Divisions waiting their turn at the roadside, ready to join the long column. Soon they marched on, the automatic rhythm of the march was now controlling their legs, tired as they were. The first night's camp was in the open, but the second was at Truxillo. Here was an area unaffected by war and it showed because, as Deakin in the front right file came to a row of houses, half a loaf of coarse bread was thrust at him and, at later houses, some cheese and an onion. The Spanish people were giving what they could. The comment again came from Halfway.

"They're giving us this, even though we haven't asked and they haven't much. We must look fully starved, more dead than alive!"

"On top, they must think us worth the cost to 'em. These don't look too well set up to me, but still feelin' bound to make some kind of gesture."

He shook his head in both sadness and wonder.

In their night camp they dined on what they had been given, acorns gathered from the nearby woods and any other odd scraps. Carr was sat with the Light Company Officers, as was his habit, and these were also chewing acorn porridge. Drake made the observation.

"I wonder if English acorns taste any better? These are like, well, ..."

He made a face.

".......... nothing comes to mind."

Carr finally managed to swallow a mouthful.

"You can take it from me that I am never going to find out!"

Shakeshaft swallowed a spoonful and spoke up, evidently wholly miserable.

"Is there no food anywhere, throughout the army?"

Carr looked at him.

"From what I can gather, none! We march starving. Either supplies get to us in time, so's we can keep marching, or we fall over at the side of the road and hope that something gets to us before we die, or we just drop down dead and keep it simple."

Drake's brows furrowed.

"We could eat the horses!"

"That means abandoning our guns and neutering our cavalry. He'd never do that. He'll see us flopped down at the roadside, waiting for rescue, before he does that. He has to get his cavalry and guns back to safety, or he has no army to speak of."

Carr reached for the bottle of wine, purchased in the town, took a drink himself and then passed the bottle to Shakeshaft.

"Here. Take the taste away with that."

All took a drink and then Drake looked at Carr.

"Seriously Henry, is it really that desperate?"

Carr took another drink.

"It is, Nat. Touch and go. Between here and Badajoz, I expect the army to fall apart and go off roaming all over in search of food. Just as they did on the way to Coruna."

The night was spent in and around Truxillo, but few slept, because hunger and the effects of poor diet kept many awake. However, veterans as many were, they took comfort from the fact that they were at least resting. The next morning the army resumed its ordeal by marching, but as they left Truxillo there was a long line of its inhabitants either side. As Davey and Saunders, being in the outside files, came to the lines, each was given a cake, a simple affair, mostly plain cake with currants inside and perhaps honey across the top. Some words were spoken as the sweetmeat was passed over, Davey hearing his old woman clearly.

"Gracias pastel."

Davey examined the item and broke it into pieces for distribution, then turned to Byford.

"What she say?"

"Thank you cake."

Davey nodded, but not content.

"Thank you? For what? Could be the French are ready to march back in and we'll have done nothin' to keep 'em away from these good people."

Saunders was listening.

"Don't be so hard on yourself. John. We gave it a bloody good try. Christ, what could be harder than Talavera, and, if the Dons could have given us some food from time to time, we'd have stayed. And the French b'aint here yet!

Without us they could be here already. As 'tis, they'n miles away! Miles!"

There were no 'gracias pastel' for one part of the army, that which had been sent on ahead to meet and guard any supply train coming up from Miajades, some thirty miles distant. Stapleton Cotton's Light Dragoons were far in advance of the infantry; progressing on at a slow trot, slow, in order not to over tax their horses. Templemere and Tavender were in their usual place, behind the leading three, these being their Brigadier, Colonel Withers and Major Johnson. They came in sight of Miajades, when Tavender rose up in his stirrups. He could see between and beyond the three ahead. He turned to his companion.

"Something's coming."

Templemere didn't move.

"A French army? Have they anything to eat?"

By now Stapleton Cotton had raised his hand for the whole column to halt and await the approach of the newcomers, whoever they were, but they soon materialised into a supply train, over 100 fully laden mules. Tavender soon made the observation.

"They aren't French! At least, I know of no French Horse that are dressed in yellow."

However, in saying that, he had missed the point, this being made by Colonel Withers, just ahead.

"This is a supply column, under the escort of Spanish cavalry. Dragoons, if I'm not mistaken. It may be food, of some kind."

Stapleton Cotton, growled his reply, his tone unmistakable for all that could hear.

"Dragoons or not. Those mules are ours, intended for us or not."

He turned to the pair behind him.

"You two. Split the column. Take two files each and get either side of them."

Templemere struggled to understand, but Tavender immediately did and he turned to the Troopers behind.

Heaviside now looked at Carr and posed the important question.

"Do the men know?"

Carr now looked steadily at Heaviside, before replying.

'If we tell them that, and it will sound like a promise, and then there is no food, what then?"

"Then you choose your words carefully, whilst passing on the good word. Make a promise of a better chance of being supplied. That we are entering a land where food should be more plentiful."

He waited for a reply from Carr, but none came, so he continued.

"The men aren't stupid. Just tell them we have high hopes. Nothing more."

However, at that moment, Carr noticed a file of Guards, marching around the camp perimeter, but leaving behind single men at intervals. They were led by a Captain who soon came within earshot of Carr, who was immediately much aggrieved, even insulted. These Guards were forming a picket, with the French a hundred miles away.

"You! What is the purpose of all this?"

The Captain halted and saluted.

"Commander's orders, Sir. To prevent desertions."

Carr reared up at the insult, despite the doubts he had expressed but a minute earlier.

"You take your men to Hell, Sir. There have been no desertions from the 105th, nor will there be!"

The Captain was astonished at the outburst, but it was Heaviside who quelled Carr's temper.

"Easy Henry. He's only following orders. If Wellesley wants it, then it has to be."

Carr looked daggers at the Guards Captain, but said no more and turned his eyes away from the Guards pickets. After a minutes silence and more walking, he returned to the subject.

"So. We just tell them that soon, in fact two days, we will be in a better place where hopes for food can be higher. Is that it?"

"Yes. Give the men hope. This is a good Regiment. You know that and so do I. Give them hope and they will remain."

"Right. We must get that passed around. And hope ourselves!"

"Just so!"

"Very well, Joshua, that is something we can both do."

Silence fell between them, and then Carr had a thought.

"Is this conversation, Joshua, about to be the first between us, that has not included a quote from the Good Book?"

"No. It is not."

Heaviside composed himself.

"Ye shall be sorrowful, but your sorrow shall be turned into joy. John 16. Chapter 20."

Carr smiled.

"Not 'Hope springs eternal, in the human breast?"

Heaviside growled back his very forthright reply.

"I take my inspiration from the only book I read!"

Such finality caused Carr to break off the conversation. In addition and very conveniently, they had reached the tent of Drake, Shakeshaft and Maltby, before Heaviside climbed into his pulpit over the merits of certain texts as sources to inspire the human condition. The two parted company with no more words between them, but agreement had been reached and it was acted upon as orders to Sergeants, who traversed the mess camps of the 105th. Ellis arrived in the camp of Deakin, Davey, Miles et al.

"Word is we can have high hopes of food at Merida, day after tomorrow, if we reaches there."

It was Davey who replied.

"How high?"

By now Ellis was moving on, but there was just an edge of cynicism in his voice.

"Higher than usual!"

With the following dawn, breakfast consisted for most of a dreadful porridge made from stale bread and smashed army biscuits scooped from the bottom of the sacks, this washed down with some kind of coffee made from ground, burnt acorns. That consumed the 105th paraded on the road and resumed their march, behind The Guards. The porridge sustained them for that day and they made their camp in the barren hills, but the slope before them now led down to the Guadiana. All were in better heart, despite their hunger being as severe as at any time, for the word had circulated that, with a good march, they would reach Merida, where chances were higher of some supplies. Thus, was the conversation around the Deakin campfire as they ate the last of their rations. It was Miles who broached the subject, holding up his last crust.

"No more of this tomorrow!"

The reply came from Saunders.

"Perhaps, perhaps not. You've heard the rumour about supplies in this Merida place. One good push and we'll be there tomorrow and that won't be your last crust for the day!"

Miles waved the crust at him.

"So, should I save it?"

Deakin joined in, with a finality that none could argue with.

"Eat it now, better a night's sleep not broke by hunger. Tomorrow we marches with empty stomachs, nothin' new there, but with luck we sleeps tomorrow with full bellies!"

Miles ate the crust and rolled into his blanket. On the morrow all came onto the road with a certain eagerness to complete the last 12 miles and, with the sun well into the West the houses became more frequent; they were reaching Merida. Lacey looked ahead when he heard shouting from the Guards column ahead and it did not take him long to discern what was happening, the Guards had picked up the step and were intent on properly marching into Merida. Lacey's brow furrowed at the next possibility and was determined to avoid it. He turned in his saddle.

"Sar' Major!"

Gibney came running up to reach Lacey.

"Sir!"

"We're entering Merida. Have the men pick up the step. We are not marching in like some defeated rabble!"

Gibney saluted and stood still, but the ranks of four soon reached him.

"Raht lads. Pick up the step. Get th'selves smart! We're no pack of half-arsed Militia. Let 'em know oose come to tahn."

Many came together immediately, but Gibney wanted every foot in the correct rhythm.

"Left ………. left ……….. left, right!"

The marching habit spread back through the 105th and then the whole of Wellesley's army and so it was in this fashion that they entered Merida, to applauding crowds, and their hopes were not dashed, far from it. Not only were there supplies available for purchase in the town, but a British supply train had made the long trek from Lisbon, via Badajoz. Thus, as the day died, pots were bubbling all over the camp full of salt beef, peas and biscuit, whilst, as though that cooking aroma were not enough, Brigade bread ovens were in full production. Again, it was Miles who broached the subject as he consumed his second bowlful.

"Now we'n back in the land of the livin', another pair of boots and socks won't come amiss!"

All around his comrades shook their heads in bewilderment, again it was Saunders who answered, with more than an edge to his voice.

"If it means a full belly, I'll march to Badajoz with straw wrapped round my feet. Carts comin' up loaded with food, suits me a whole lot better than any number full of boots!"

The looks that Miles received from his companions told him that he was very much on his own with that opinion and so he edged over to the cooking pot for yet another helping, this doled out by Nellie Nicholls, who fiercely thumped the ladle into his dish and gave him a look which unequivocally conveyed the fact that full hostilities had been resumed.

However, they were not to reach Badajoz. Orders came the next day, passed on over a substantial lunch at 105th Headquarters. With all thoroughly replete on pork, chicken, peas and potatoes, Lacey reached for the folded paper by his side.

"He's breaking up the army over the three towns. Sherbrook's Division will remain here, Hill's and the Cavalry go on to Badajoz and we will be staying in Montijo a bit further on with Campbell's, where I suspect we can expect a new Divisional Commander and, above all expect a few month's rest."

With that the gathering finished and Carr and Drake walked back together, with Carr in the more thoughtful mood.

"My understanding is, that Wellesley will make no further moves into Spain in conjunction with the Spanish. Too big a risk."

Drake sucked in a deep, well satisfied breath, as much to clear his head somewhat of too much red wine.

"Amen to that!"

"And for another expedition to take place, independent of our allies, there must be some time given to preparation, not least the improvement in our Commissariat."

"Amen to that, also!"

"Right. So. That will take some time. Months perhaps!"

"I consider you to be perfectly correct."

There was a pause.

"I'm going to apply for some leave. I've written to Jane and asked if she agrees, for us to be married, that is, whilst I'm there."

Drake gave out a loud laugh.

"Wonderful! And I see no reason at all why you should not be granted a month or so during which you can stitch things up."

Then, a thought.

"But who will be your Best Man?"

Now it was Carr's turn to laugh.

"I care not! A tiny wedding with none but Jane, myself, a Vicar and the necessary witnesses will suit us fine. But if there is to be any kind of ceremony, then you can write the speech. To be delivered by proxy."

Another thought.

"I'll visit Sophie. I may be there for the birth!"

By now they had reached their tent and within 30 minutes, both were sleeping the sleep of the dead, induced by exhaustion, wine, and a deep satisfaction with their hopes for the future.

The following day, the army, minus Sherbrook's Brigades marched into Montijo to meet a similar reception to that at Merida and the following day, now only in the company of Campbell's men, they settled into what was probably going to be Winter quarters, the Officers in houses, the men in barns, buildings and tents for the less favoured. Carr sent off his request to their acting Divisional General Donkin and eagerly awaited a reply.

However, one morning in their second week, D'Villiers woke and looked across the room to the bed of Carravoy. He sat up.

"You know, Charles. I don't feel too well!"

Carravoy rolled himself out of the bed and sat on the edge, his head in his hands.

"You know, I don't feel too well, either!"

oOo

Chapter Seven

Concerns Martial

"I've done it!"

"Done what, exactly?"

"Written to Jane, telling her that I am applying for leave, which I've said I'm certain will be granted, and when I get home, we'll be married!"

Drake sat back, causing his ancient chair to creak alarmingly, and treated Carr to his 'wearied' look, this used when he suspected that something had been done badly, which could easily have been done much better.

"So that's that then! All done and dusted, orders issued. Much the same as if you were ordering a new pair of boots!"

Carr looked puzzled and not a little surprised.

"That's wrong?"

Drake rocked his head from side to side.

"Well, yes and no. It's just that I have the deepest suspicions that there was nothing in your letter about you desperately looking forward to being man and wife, nothing you want more in this world, undying affection. That sort of thing."

Carr adopted a pained expression.

"I am much maligned! Unjustly! I did, include such as that, perhaps not as much as you would, but it was there! Yes!"

Then came further thought, searching for facts with which to further defend himself.

"Besides, it was written when we were in Mirabete, when things were a bit fraught!"

Drake laughed.

"Oh, I'm sure that will make all the difference! Can't include anything about how much I love you, dear. Bad indigestion caused by Spanish beans!"

The pained expression returned.

"Well, I did say some of that romantic stuff. And, besides the letter's gone off now."

Drake nodded.

"Well, all I can say, is that when the time comes, you need to be well equipped with posies and presents and such as that."

Carr frowned.

"Jane's not one for all that. She's more serious. Intellectual!"

Drake appeared sceptical.

"If so, she's the first I've heard of that doesn't appreciate a few flowers and a present all the way from the sunny Peninsula."

Carr folded his arms, his face pensive.

"Well, we can take care of that, when the time comes. As you say, it will do no harm and will probably do some good."

Suddenly, he leaned forward on the table between them.

"You should apply as well! We won't be moving for months with the political situation as it is between Wellesley and the Don Government. Awaiting events from that would be like watching cold treacle run uphill!"

Drake's face brightened.

"I do believe that you are right. It's got to make sense to try to get to a healthier place than this is proving to be, even back to a cold Autumn in the dear West Country."

"On that subject, how are Shakeshaft and Maltby?"

Drake shook his head.

"Flattened! In no real danger, just flattened. No energy, just, you know, can't cope."

The comment on health was one widely made throughout the whole army, garrisoned at all three towns. A strange, non-fatal but debilitating sickness was adding to the lists of those excused duty. It had certainly struck those now occupying an outlying barn, large enough for 30 souls, which included the messes of Deakin and Davey. Deakin was the most concerned as he returned with sacks of rations.

"Any new today?"

Davey looked up.

"No, just the same. Zeke, Nat and George."

He pointed to the prone figures covered in blankets, lying alongside the rough stonewall. Deakin looked over.

"Least 'tain't like what comes to those servin' in the West Indies. I was there once and it near took the whole Regiment. I was spared, the Surgeon said, perhaps because I was raised on the Somerset marshes."

He became thoughtful.

"On that, it seems to me that those as is bein' took, is those as hails from the towns and cities!"

Davey studied the lock on his Baker rifle.

"You may be right, but then Tom Miles is out of the stews of Bristol. He's alright."

Deakin guffawed.

"What self respectin' disease would have anything to do with him?"

Miles, instantly much aggrieved, looked up from some distance away, where he was strengthening the fixing of a button.

"I heard that!"

Both Deakin and Davey laughed and Deakin reached into the sack of rations.

"You heard that, did you? Then catch this."

A piece of Spanish sausage was thrown across the space, for Miles to catch one handed. Bridie was near, tending the fire in the barn chimney.

"You leave him alone! Sure now, isn't he bein' as good as gold, now, these days. Not a peep out of place, nor a harsh word to anyone!"

Deakin laughed again.

"If not, if t'is like you say, then he must've got the fever!"

Miles looked up again.

"I heard that, too."

Weak laughter came from the three figures under the blankets. However, there was no humour in the simultaneous conversation taking place between Lacey and O'Hare, in the nearby farmhouse.

"I'm thinking of moving us to higher ground. This fever is going through the whole Battalion."

O'Hare nodded.

"Not feeling too clever myself."

He took a long drink of water.

"Guadiana fever, they're calling it. Not deadly, it just brings you down."

He looked at Lacey.

"It's only arisen since we arrived here. If it is to do with the river, then it must be some kind of marsh fever. There's less shelter of any kind up on high ground, but getting us away from the swamps and reed beds and whatnot, can only be to the good."

Lacey studied his good friend.

"Do you feel up to it?"

O'Hare nodded.

"Give me a horse! 'Tis no worse than that damn ague that I get from time to time, since I quit Egypt with the 28th."

Lacey grinned.

"A horse it is. And take Carr with you. Good experience for him."

He grinned as he reached for the nearby bottle and poured out two generous brandies.

Also, at the same time, another even more serious conversation was taking place in Badajoz, in a cramped building inside the walls. It involved little humour, but an atmosphere of contented expectancy was building. The three participants were General Perry, Captain Lord Templemere and Captain Tavender, each now part way through a large glass of brandy. Tavender was well into his explanation as to why they were there.

"Yes General. There is a big question mark over him, two in fact. As I say, the shambles at Casa de Salinas and, second, why did he run from his place at Talavera?"

Perry's eyes sparkled. His mouth curved into a smile and the ringed fingers of his right hand drummed on the table, as he thought.

"So, what you are saying, is that the 105th Lights, with Carr in charge, were holding the Casa when Wellesley was almost captured and that, during the final French attack at Talavera, Carr ran from his place with the 105th."

His face brightened further.

"This has real possibilities. Plainly, the Company under Carr's command were unready when the French arrived. That's the first. The second is why did he leave his men at Talavera at such a critical moment?"

He now placed both hands on the table and drummed both sets of fingers rapidly.

"This has real possibilities. Questions must be asked. After all, our Commanding Officer was almost captured. If our men and Officers cannot put themselves on their full mettle when asked to protect such as him, well, what hope is there? Questions must be asked."

He stared hard at the pair.

"It's our duty!"

Templemere and Tavender smiled in unison, but it was Templemere who replied, him equally enthusiastic at the possibilities.

"So what happens now, Sir?"

Perry already had ideas.

"This fully justifies a letter to The Times, asking just such questions, which I will write. A letter there, linking his name to such events will do him no good at all."

Perry savoured the thought, before continuing.

"He already has a question mark over his conduct; his duel with you, Templemere."

A shadow passed momentarily over the Lord's face at the memory, but the General continued.

"Whatever the outcome, there will be an exchange of facts and opinions and Carr will not come out unsullied. 'Where there's smoke, there's fire.' That sort of thing."

He looked from one to the other, now openly smiling.

"Wellesley was nearly captured and Carr abandoned his men!"

Perry reached for the bottle and poured three more generous measures, but Tavender had not raised the second reason why he was there. He considered this to be the perfect time.

"Sir. I'm going to apply for leave and when I get back I intend to ask for the hand of your daughter, Jane. Do you approve, Sir? Do I have your blessing?"

Perry's face now turned incandescent with joy.

"You most certainly do, and with my sincerest blessing! Go to it, young man. She'll be a fool if she turns you down and she will incur her Father's deepest displeasure if she does!"

He stretched across the table and clinked glasses with Tavender, then the same with Templemere. Between all three there now arouse an atmosphere of deep contentment and anticipation as Perry downed his brandy and then turned towards a half open door, where sat his Secretary.

"Tiptree! Pen and paper. Now!"

The days passed, and a week became two. Those without the fever had recovered from their near starvation of the previous month, but each morning they examined their own condition for signs of the Guadiana ague. By the end of the two weeks, on Lacey's orders, the 105th had been moved higher up the surrounding slopes, these being more windswept with the onset of Autumn, but no-where near the Guadiana marshes. However, with the move, the 105th suffered from the increased exposure and all noticed a marked decline in their creature comforts, for closer to the mountains there existed fewer solid buildings, as O'Hare had predicted. With all now existing in lean-to shelters and both men realising that they were in for a prolonged stay, Jed Deakin and John Davey joined in conversation, Deakin posing the problem.

"Now, if we had animals up here, an' fixin' for 'em to stay the winter, we'd not leave 'em out in all weathers. We'd build shelters, crude and simple, yes, but we'd build. If we didn't, we'd not expect to find so many come Spring!"

Davey nodded, whilst looking around.

"We would, but that's as 'tis back home. There we've stone an' timber. We'd knock up a roundhouse, where the stock could wander in and out. But for us? It'll need a door and a chimney, for the cookin' fire."

Both stood in thought, until Deakin offered his solution.

"We have got timber, woods up above, and there's some stone, these paddock walls, and what we do have is a slope. We dig into the slope, which gives us a back wall, with a slot for a chimney. Then build around that!"

Davey's face brightened.

"Right. And the soil that we digs out is the base for the front, built up with the stone, to hold the roof timbers."

"What about the roof?"

"Oh, whatever! Turf, thatch, a tent! All three! Whatever will serve."

"And the door on the lee side of the wind. Even if t'is only wattle!"

Both nodded, and Deakin continued, looking at Davey.

"You think that'll serve?"

"I do!"

"Right. Tools. That's a job for me."

Within a few more days the Deakin-Davey design was being used all over the hillside, turning the whole area into a Stone Age village, but, with all done, all slept warm and dry as the weather worsened. If a hut proved to be too crowded, then they simply built another. Conditions improved still further with Miles' perpetual wish being granted, that for supplies, which duly arrived, of all types; new uniforms, boots and equipment. Even new Baker rifles for the 105th Light Company, which Ellis issued himself to ensure that the old were collected and not traded, which was the first thought of Miles when he heard of the new that was to come. Ellis was wise to the possibility.

"I wants to see your old up on that cart, Miles. Afore you gets the new."

Miles carefully added his old Baker to the pile in the cart, before presenting himself to Ellis and receiving the new weapon. Ellis looked at him.

"New pattern! A better lock an' riflin'. But, as you can see, all covered in beeswax. Get it clean. Inspection afore lights out."

Miles gave Ellis his best scowl before slinking off, back into the hut, to begin the removal of the dust coloured beeswax. Once inside, Miles had not long sat down, before he had to stand up, accompanied by all the other occupants. Colonel Lacey and Brigadier Donkin had entered their hut, both tall men needing to stoop. Lacey waved them back down and both began to look around.

"Didn't I tell you, Donkin. Warm and weatherproof."

Donkin continued to study, but nodding agreement all the while. Lacey now turned to his men.

"Have you your new rifles, men?"

Davey, as Chosen Man, knew that it was for him to answer.

"Yes Sir. As you probably saw, the old is out on the cart, Sir."

Lacey nodded, whilst looking around at the men of Davey's mess, then he spoke enthusiastically.

"All brand new. And a new pattern!"

Davey gave a brief smile.

"Yes, Sir. So we've been told."

Lacey nodded again and made to leave, but Donkin had his own observation concerning the hut they were in, spoken whilst he studied the roof, admiring branches closely placed over the rafters to hold the thatch.

"You're right, Lacey. Good and solid, both roof and walls. We've no worries with this, if here is our winter quarters."

"No. My thoughts entirely."

Lacey then gave his men a salute and then left, followed by Donkin.

"Resourceful men you have, Lacey."

Lacey turned towards him.

"Yes. All, or at least most, are from the fields of the West Country. A cow byre or even a dwelling such as that, for many is second nature. They could erect one in their sleep."

They walked on, but Donkin was changing the subject.

"We are being re-organised, no surprise there, us having lost Mackenzie."

Lacey turned towards him, listening intently.

"I'm rejoining my 87th as Colonel, and marching back to Lisbon. Wellesley has some scheme going around there. Major General Picton will be taking command of the Third Division. It will have three Brigades, Mackinnon, Lightburn and a Portuguese under Champlemonde. You will be in Mackinnon's with the 74th and my old 88th."

Lacey nodded.

"Thank you, Rufane, I appreciate that but neither Picton, nor Mackinnon are known to me. To you?"

"No, can't help there. Much. Picton has reputation for quick temper and bad language and there was a bit of scandal. He found himself in Court over ordering what some considered the torture of some girl accused of housebreaking, when he was in the West Indies. By all accounts he was lucky to get off. As for Mackinnon, to me unknown, but both are new to this affair. Just come out."

He then looked at Lacey, his face brighter.

"Did I say Wellesley? Well, that's now out of date. The newspapers that came up with the supplies are now calling him Lord Wellington, an award because of Talavera. I assume he's pleased, now that he's been elevated to the Peerage."

Lacey nodded.

"No doubt. One can only hope that he appreciates what it took to turn that battle into the victory that gave him such a boost!"

Donkin did not react to the tone of Lacey's comment, for he had a more serious concern of his own. He reached into the pocket of his tunic and pulled out a newspaper cutting.

"That wasn't all that was of concern to us in the newspapers that arrived recently. There's this."

He passed over the cutting, taken from The Times. It was Perry's letter and Lacey read it quickly, before carefully reading it again. It was not a long letter. Lacey allowed his arm to fall down by his side, his hand still holding the cutting.

"Can I keep this! I need to show it to Carr. That's only fair, in my view."

Donkin nodded.

"Yes, of course. Carr will want to discuss with you how he responds."

He paused.

"On top I have news for Carr, both good and bad. I have granted his request for leave, just about my last decision, in fact, but I suspect that he will not be allowed to go. At least, not just yet. I suspect that there will be some sort of Enquiry. Perhaps even a Court Martial. After all, the French did almost bag our Commanding General!"

Lacey sighed.

"They did! This should be of no surprise, now that the dust has settled on that campaign."

Another sigh.

"May I suggest that we get back down. I now need to see Carr at the soonest."

Donkin immediately turned to descend and they walked together, but not all the way, Donkin soon turned away to his own Headquarters building. Left alone, Lacey became very angry, cursing Perry for the destructive menace that he was but also feeling bemused as to why that obsessed General should still harbour such a hatred of the 105th in general and Carr in particular. Plainly it was unabated since Perry first made his feelings clear before their departure for Southern Italy in 1809.

Once back at their Headquarters, Lacey found O'Hare, seated at a table, drinking what appeared to be some white medicine. He placed the cutting before him.

"Read this."

O'Hare looked up at him as though expecting the onset of some disaster, then he picked up the cutting and began to read. He read it twice, as had Lacey. As he spoke, his anger grew.

"Damn the man! What does he know? He made an utter, and cowardly, shambles of that command he was given at Oporto and now he thinks he can hold Court on the doings of others! Damn the man! Hell's too good for him!"

He looked up at Lacey.

"We have to tell Carr. As soon as possible."

Lacey did not answer; instead he turned to the half open door to their room.

"Bryce!"

A muffled 'Sir' came through the opening.

"Get Major Carr."

Another 'Sir' and then they heard the main front door closing.

"Donkin thinks there'll be an Enquiry. Even a Court Martial."

O'Hare nodded, resignedly.

"I wouldn't bet against it."

O'Hare read the letter again, then passed it to Lacey, who subjected it to another reading. By the time he had finished, Carr was in their room. Lacey handed the letter to him immediately, his face deadly serious, which sight brought a deep frown to Carr's face.

"You'd better read this."

Carr took the cutting and read it, a look of fury growing on his face. Once finished he looked at Lacey, his face writ with the deepest resentment.

"But this just isn't true, Sir. It was all in my report. At the Casa I went to the 87th to advise them to come to the alert. I said so to one of their Captains, Bryant I think he was, and when I came to our Lights, I got them up. And just in time."

He took a deep breath, plainly much agitated. The implications were beginning to fully dawn on him, of what was being said and was now in the public domain.

"As to Talavera, Sir, I left my place to bring the 48th up to us as much as possible. We could not afford a gap too wide to the left of our line, between them and us."

He was now wholly angry and threw the cutting onto the table.

"And they came up to us, Sir, led by their Captain of Grenadiers, Wilson, and, because of that, there was no breakthrough. We held them off!"

Both his Senior Officers were nodding in agreement, but it was Lacey who spoke.

"There are two routes that will respond to this, and you must take both. First, a reply to The Times, although it will take at least a month to get to them and there is no guarantee that they will print it."

"Yes, Sir."

"Second, prepare for an Enquiry. You could demand one!"

He turned to O'Hare.

"What do you think?"

"I think he would be fully within his rights! And let's see what Perry's got. And who's saying it."

Carr was stood gazing at the floor, plainly thinking through his response. Lacey looked at him, his face full of fatherly concern.

"There is a bit of good news. Donkin's granted your leave, to return to England."

This brought Carr away from his own churning thoughts.

"How can I go, Sir? With all this brewing up."

"No, you cannot, but we are getting a new Divisional Commander, one Lieutenant General Picton. When he arrives, I'll speak to him and we'll see how he responds. You will, after all, be one of his Officers who is now much maligned, and unjustly, by someone outside of his Division. He may even, perhaps, have his own opinion of General Perry."

He took a deep breath and then let it out in a quick sigh.

"So now, go and write your letter. Get Drake to proof read. That will do no harm and we'll get Bryce to send it off at the earliest. Take the cutting with you."

Carr picked up the piece of The Times and hurried out, leaving both Senior Officers sat at their table, shaking their heads. Carr did no more than hurry to his own billet, to find Drake reading his own copy of The Times, and the expression on his face made it clear what he was reading. He looked up, horrified, as Carr entered.

"Have you seen this?"

He turned the page so that Carr could see that he was referring to the Letters to the Editor page. Carr waved the cutting before him.

"I have my own copy. Given me by the Colonel."

"What are you going to do?"

"Start by writing a reply. And I'd appreciate your help."

Drake had his own issue to include.

"This damnable scut Perry isn't just castigating you, it's the Regiment as well. We need to include that; a defence of the Regiment! We are the heroes of Maida and Corunna, and favourites of the Prince of Wales. We must include his name in our letter. It'll take more than Perry's got to put a dent in that and, when they fail there, they're more than likely to fail with you."

"Yes, that's good! Now, where's my writing kit?"

oOo

"The General will see you now, Sir."

The Aide-de-Camp, perfectly uniformed, him being a Major in the Grenadier Guards, held open the door for Lacey to rise and walk through. At the opposite end of the room sat a man plainly ill at ease in the ornate chair, which supported him behind his desk, but attempting various postures in order to make himself comfortable. The first impression that Lacey gained was of a tall man, he sat high in the chair, certainly well built and powerful, but his most striking feature was a long and conspicuous nose. However, his mouth and eyes indicated irascibility in the extreme, this confirmed by his first words.

"What the Devil is this all about, Lacey?"

"May I sit down, Sir?"

Picton ignored the question. He had his own spleen to vent.

"This letter in The Times, God rot the pestilential rag, highly critical of one of your men. But it happens all the time! What's so special about this?"

Lacey took a deep breath.

"Three things, Sir. First, the personal courage and competence of my Junior Major has been called into question. Second, also the courage and competence of my Regiment, and, third, the fact that our Commanding General was almost taken. There are lessons to be learnt from that, I feel, Sir."

403

Picton looked long and hard at Lacey.

"So, what do you want me to do? This Carr of yours, he's demanding an Enquiry?"

"Yes Sir."

Picton's face reddened.

"God's wounds, Lacey! Have we not enough to worry ourselves over, without wet nursing the feelings of some young sprat of an Officer?"

Lacey stared back, his gaze unwavering.

"That may be the case, Sir, but the competence of the army in general has been attacked by one of its own, which we should respond to. Also the reasons why we were caught off guard just before Talavera should be explored. Major Carr's personal feelings may be secondary to us, but his reputation is not secondary to him. He wishes to have his say and, when all is said and done, Sir, he has to command men in the field and for that he needs their respect."

Picton stared back hard, but he was clearly thinking.

"If it's that serious Lacey, Wellington nearly in the bag, as it were, and it was your man Carr in command of the men holding this damn Casa place, then perhaps it should be a Court Martial?"

Lacey remained calm

"It may come to that, Sir, post the Enquiry, but I would advance the idea of an Enquiry first to establish the facts and then decide if the matter should then go before a Court Martial."

Picton seized the arms of his chair, plainly running out of patience.

"Still a damn waste of time, in my opinion. A lot of fuss over a narrow squeak. He got bounced by the Frogs! Boo hoo! He's not the first, nor will he be the last, before this business is finally over."

"Yes Sir. Would that were all of the matter, but it isn't. There has been a letter in The Times for all to read.

Lacey now thought it time to perhaps massage the truth.

"From what I hear, Sir, they're making a bit of a joke of it in the Music Halls."

Picton's brows hurried together.

"Which part?"

"Lord Wellington narrowly escaping, Sir. He's being depicted on stage running out of the building with grapeshot hitting his backside, Sir. His brother, prominent in the Government right now, is less than popular. I don't like it, Sir, but it's how these things work."

Picton made yet another change to his bodily arrangements in his chair, than sat very still. A knock on the door possibly interrupted his train of thoughts.

"In!"

The Grenadier Major appeared, carrying a letter. His entrance could not have been better timed to help Lacey.

"Excuse me, Sir, but I could not but help overhearing. This letter arrived today, Sir. From Lord Wellington."

He placed the letter before Picton, who snatched it up, inflicting creases on the smooth page. He read it quickly, before looking back at Lacey.

"He wants an Enquiry."

His face turned thunderous as he stared angrily at Lacey.

"Can this be done in half a day?"

Lacey nodded.

"I'm sure, Sir."

Picton's elbows came onto the desk.

"Your man will need time to build his case, I assume?"

"Yes Sir. Two weeks should be enough. He has already made a start."

Picton sat back with a snorting laugh.

405

"I bet he has, if he's as you describe and as I can imagine. Damn sprat!"

The elbows returned.

"See Major Pengammon here. Set a date for two weeks from today. Here, this place! Damned if I'm going to travel for this pestilential affair."

His head came up at a sharp angle, impatience plain upon his face.

"Now. Good day to you, Lacey."

Lacey came to the attention and punctiliously saluted. The reply was an irritated sweep of Picton's right hand to just above his right eyebrow. Lacey marched out with Pengammon and began the arrangements. The date was set for October 17th.

Carr and Drake were now on their second meeting. The letter produced from their first had now gone, so now they were considering the Enquiry. Drake was holding pencil and paper and doing his best to get some structure into the proceedings.

"Right. La Casa first. Who is there who can say that you tried to bring the 87th to the alert and after that our men?"

Carr's reply was instant.

"Captain Bryant. He said he would go to their Colonel. Also, our Ellis, as soon as I got over to ours, and then there's Hill, who was on picket. I told him to keep a good watch and he said that he didn't like the smoke of the burning huts."

Drake had already written down the three names, when he looked up, suddenly animated.

"The smoke! Yes. That's an issue. Who ordered the huts to be burned?"

"Mackenzie, but he's dead."

"Ordered whom to do it, then?"

"Must've been Lacey. Who then ordered Carravoy! We must call him."

The name was written down, whilst Carr had another think.

"And I told Carravoy as we came across the Alberche that I was going to check on Donkin's Brigade and why. The Johnnies may have been close. As it turns out, they were."

Drake put down the pencil.

"And he saw you go?"

"Yes. I left him to continue on to us and I walked into the woods, to find Donkin."

"God! That's important. It'll go with Bryant's."

His eyebrows rose to their fullest height.

"Anyone else?"

Carr raised his eyebrows.

"Himself? Because we formed a line to oppose the Johnnies, we saved his backside!"

Drake shook his head.

"Forming a good line was too late! The issue is, why were we surprised? And what did you do to prevent it?"

Carr sat back.

"Then I think that's about it."

Drake nodded his head.

"Right, next Talavera. You left our line to bring the 48th up closer."

"Yes. I spoke with their Grenadier Captain. Wilson."

"Who could say that you returned quickly?"

Carr cudgelled his memory, sifting through the images of chaos, carnage, noise, and near panic.

"I said something to Sillery. His guns were firing like mad, but I doubt that he heard."

"All right. But Wilson's the one that matters."

He drew a line under the list of names, but moved the pencil up the page.

"Ours we can call easily, which leaves ……."

He wrote their unit beside each name.

"Bryant, 87th. Wilson 48th . Sillery RHA."

He stood up.

"Off we go to Bryce for letters of attendance, or whatever they're called, to be written up."

They hurried to Battalion Headquarters, where they found Bryce, inevitably at his desk. Bryce looked up.

"Sirs?"

Drake placed the list before him.

"We need a copy of this list for the Colonel and letters to each of these Regiments calling on their Officers to attend the Enquiry. On the 17th."

Bryce read the list and then looked up, his face very anxious.

"You'll be lucky with the 87th, Sir. They marched out last night, for Lisbon."

Drake looked at Carr.

"That's Bryant! He's crucial."

Carr was already at the door.

"They can't have got far!"

He disappeared, then re-appeared.

"Nat! Can I borrow your horse?"

After receiving a brief nod, Carr was gone and within ten minutes his mount was essaying a loping canter down the main trunk to Lisbon. He knew that he could expect the 87th to have covered at least 15 miles if they marched out early last night, and the time now was late morning. After 10 miles he halted at a stream with lush green grass along its bank and allowed his horse 15 minutes to graze and drink, then he re-mounted and resumed his urgent ride forward. Some roofs came into view and he hoped that the 87th would be using it, but no, and his anxiety then increased, centred on the question 'Had they used a different road?'.

Onward through the village and then he saw a dust cloud ahead and hope grew stronger, even more so when he saw the rear of a supply wagon, with Redcoats walking beside it. Coming closer to the wagon, he could see a long column of infantry on the road beyond and so he asked the first soldier he came up to. Salutes were dispensed with.

"Are you the 87th?"

The voice was strongly favoured from Ireland.

"That we are, Sir."

"Is your Colonel with you?"

"Sure enough, Sir. You'll find himself at the head of the column."

At a fast canter, Carr overtook the column, to find the Senior Officers of the 87th riding there. Carr drew level as they turned at the commotion of another mounted Officer coming up from behind. It was Carr who spoke first.

"Sir. If I may, Sir. I'm Major Carr of the 105th. May I have a word, Sir?"

"You certainly may. I'm Colonel Donkin and I know of you. Should we dismount?"

Carr nodded.

"I think it best, Sir."

Both dismounted and walked side by side, but it was Donkin who spoke first.

"I think I know why you are here, Carr. It concerns your Enquiry."

"Yes Sir, and it's this. Before the French surprised us at La Casa, I spoke to one of your Captains advising him to bring your men to the alert, Sir. If he could be witness to that at the Enquiry it would help a lot, Sir. The accusation against me is that I was lax and did nothing with the French potentially so near."

"I can see that, Major, so who was this Officer?"

"Captain Bryant, Sir."

Donkin turned fully towards him.

"I'm afraid he's dead. Killed at La Casa."

Carr felt as though he had been punched and the change that came over him was noticed by Donkin.

"But you came into our camp, did you not?"

Carr was recovering.

"But did Bryant not get to you, Sir, to advise that you come to the alert?"

"No, he did not. The French must have come onto us very soon after. But, as I say, you were in our camp. Did you speak to anyone else?"

Carr screwed up his eyes to picture the scene, and the sequence of events, then came a perfect memory.

"I spoke to a Colour Sergeant, just before I came to Bryant."

Donkin immediately turned to the mounted Officers above him.

"Spence! Get McMichael and O'Finn up here."

The Major reined back his horse and two Colour Sergeants soon appeared and saluted their Colonel, who halted on the road as the column marched by.

"Both of you. I want you to study this Officer and say if you can remember him coming into our camp and speaking to you just before the French attacked us at La Casa. You remember that attack, when we were taken by surprise."

Both nodded and both studied Carr, who turned to fully face each. Both frowned as they thought and then recognition came over the face of one.

"Sir, I do, Sir. Sure, I remember the Major, here. I remember him from this bright green of his facings, Sir. Now, did I not think that he must be from another Irish Regiment? Sir."

"Did you see him speak to Captain Bryant."

"No I did not, Sir. After pointing out Captain Bryant, I went on my way. Until ……"

"Until what?"

"Until Captain Bryant got us up onto the alert, Sir."

"Right, McMichael. Can you sign your name?"

"I can, Sir. I can even write, Sir. Didn't we have a fine Sunday School in our village, now."

Donkin nodded.

"Yes, I'm sure. Now, back to the supply wagon, get pencil and paper and write what you know to be the truth about Major Carr coming into our camp."

McMichael hurried back, whilst Carr gathered his horse and began to follow, but Donkin stopped him.

"This is because of Perry's letter, is it not?"

"Yes, Sir."

"Right. When McMichael has finished. Bring it back to me and I will countersign it. I witnessed nothing of you that day, but my signature will do no harm."

Carr set off to follow McMichael and at the supply cart, he found him already writing. When the letter was finished he did not yet hand it to Carr.

"Sir. I've said that I saw you, but if this is about Captain Bryant, after you left he told us all to come to the alert. We did and that probably saved more than a few lives, Sir. I could add that on, if it'll help, if I've got it right, over what this is all about. There are some of us who can read the papers. Sir."

Carr looked at him gratefully.

"Yes Sergeant. Please to do that."

The sentence was added, the letter signed and then handed to Carr. He had found a half sovereign in his pocket and he offered it to the Sergeant, who instead straightened himself to his full height.

"No need for that, Sir. Right's right!"

Carr, now more than a little ashamed at what he had assumed was expected, returned the coin to his pocket.

"I'm grateful, Colour Sergeant. Thank you."

McMichael reeled off a blistering salute.

"Sir!"

Carr mounted his horse, then rode back to Donkin who added his signature and handed back the letter.

"Good luck, Carr."

"Thank you, Sir."

Carr completed the return journey at an easy trot, in a mood more than content, for it had been a very worthwhile journey. Once back in their billet, the letter was handed to Drake, who read it with increasing glee.

"This is cracking stuff! It proves that you went to the 87th, and they came to the alert, obviously because of your visit."

With a beaming smile, he placed the letter into a folder, which had a label stuck to the front containing the single word 'EVIDENCE'.

"Right. Who next? Wilson and Sillery."

He stood up.

"Time to pester Bryce. Have the letters gone off?"

The answer was in the affirmative and the next time they pestered Bryce the answer was even more encouraging. Replies had been received stating that both would be attending at General Picton's Headquarters and, thus buoyed up, both returned to their billet. The next two days were spent coaching Ellis and Hill and then they came to consider the final witness that both had been subconsciously delaying dealing with. The time came and the trepidatious subject was raised by Drake.

"Carravoy! How do we approach him?"

"Who more like. If we both go, he'll feel badgered, or feel that we're trying to intimidate him, with the pair of us looking at him."

Drake took a deep breath.

"Then it should be me. We're of equal rank. If you go, he'll probably think that you are trying to give him an order, or some such."

Carr nodded.

"I must agree. Because you are right, not because I personally cannot stand the man!"

Drake stood up.

"I think that there is some of that in him, for you!"

"Then I wish you the best of luck and thank you for going."

After a short walk down the narrow Montijo street, Drake entered the correct house to immediately see Private Arthur Binns, Carravoy's and D'Villiers' servant.

"I'd like to see Captain Carravoy."

"Yes Sir. He's upstairs. If you'd like to go straight up, he's in the room to the left. At the top."

Drake made straight for the stairs and followed Binns instructions, to finally reach a closed door. He knocked, to receive an irritated shout.

"Binns! Do not disturb, I'm still not well. Don't you recognise an order!"

"Charles. It's Nat Drake. I need to have a word, if I may."

Silence ensued for almost a minute until the door opened to reveal Carravoy wrapped in a blanket. He may or may not be continuing to suffer from Guadiana fever, but he was plainly unkempt and in a black mood, which was unchanged when he saw Drake.

"About what?"

"About Carr. And this Enquiry."

Carravoy opened the door further, which Drake took as his invitation to come in.

"Where's Royston?"

"Gone up the hill to see his men."

"May I sit?"

Carravoy dismissively flopped his hand in the direction of a chair at the small table, whilst he sat on the bed, from where he looked impatiently at Drake, his eyes surprisingly clear, not as would be expected of a feverish invalid.

"What about Carr?"

"You've heard of the Enquiry coming about that La Casa business. He could come out of it badly."

Carravoy stared back, dismissively.

"We all take our chances."

"Right, Charles, yes, we do, but we have gathered evidence to show that Carr went to the 87th and recommended that they come to the alert and also we have testimony to show that some of them did. In response to his visit, that is."

Concern came to the face of Carravoy, which puzzled Drake but he continued.

"You came across the River Alberche together. With Carr, that is?"

"What of it?"

"He has a recollection of leaving you, saying that he was going to check on Donkin's Brigade. To be certain that they were there and in some state of readiness. He, we, hope that you'll bear witness to that. It'll be a great help."

The expression of concern on Carravoy's face deepened, and Drake frowned at the sight.

"Anything wrong, Charles?"

Carravoy straightened himself on the bed, but ignored the question.

"You say that you have evidence to show that he arrived in their camp? And after, they came to the alert."

"Yes. Well, some did."

"What evidence?"

Drake was further puzzled. Why should he need to know that? He could simply say what he saw happen and let the others do the same. However, in the good cause of recruiting him as an ally, he answered, slightly untruthfully.

"A Colour Sergeant of the 87th saw him there, saw him talking to an Officer of the 87th and those around came to the alert because of Carr's visit. It's all written down and countersigned by his Colonel; Donkin himself."

"Why not the Officer?"

"He's dead!"

There came a period of silence, which puzzled Drake even more. Carravoy was plainly thinking, either trying to recall the conversation at the Alberche, which was good, or something nothing like good, which, in that case, was probably concerned with weighing the odds of Carr being condemned.

"Well, Charles?"

More silence, but not for so long as before.

"Give me time. A day or so. It's all rather vague."

Another excuse came.

"A lot has happened between now and then."

Drake had to concede.

"Well, I hope it comes back and that you can help."

No reaction and so Drake broached the other subject.

"The firing of the huts. Who passed on the order? The smoke gave the French some cover when they advanced. Mackenzie ordered Colonel Lacey to burn them."

"Carr passed on the order."

"And so it was your men who set fire?"

Carravoy angered.

"Of course? Do you think I did it myself?"

"So, who?"

"What is this, Drake? The Enquiry taken early?"

Drake sighed. This had gone badly wrong.

"No Charles. I'm simply trying to help a brother Officer of our Regiment."

Carravoy's face now showed his growing irritation, but the words 'Brother Officer' had some effect.

"It was Ridgway."

Drake stood up.

"Thank you for your time, Charles, and I do hope that you will soon return to full health."

Carravoy remained silent and unmoved, and so Drake continued.

"I'm afraid that you will be called. The conversation that you had with Major Carr could have a vital bearing on the outcome."

He rose and walked to the door.

"I'll see myself out."

The door closed, leaving Carravoy sat on the bed. He remained there for some minutes before reaching for his tunic coat and pulling out a letter. It was from Lucius

Tavender, concerning the forthcoming Enquiry and he read it again, for the tenth time. He had been wrestling with the implications for some time and his eyes dwelt on one salient passage, 'This is our chance to do Carr some real damage. An Enquiry itself is its own condemnation. We have only to throw doubt on what he will say, about either his conduct at La Casa, or at Talavera. We are counting on you to help with this in any way possible.' The last three words stood out even further. The request was obvious, they wanted him to lie, if it furthered their cause, but what was their cause? He greatly disliked Carr, both as a person and as a rival, he had been promoted Brevet Major instead of him after Coruna, but what was motivating Tavender and Templemere? Also Perry; who had written the Times letter? He stood up and poured some water, preparatory to having a shave. He had to pull himself together.

Meanwhile, Drake had arrived back with Carr.

"How far did you get?"

"About as far as the door!"

"Going in or coming out?"

Drake sighed.

"We talked, but, and I quote, "It's all a bit vague".

Carr released sharp breath.

"Why am I not surprised? There is no love lost between us two. I really cannot see him putting himself out on my account. We'll have to get by with what we've got."

oOo

For that morning of the 17th and for this occasion, Picton had adorned himself in his most irritated and irascible expression. He sat behind what had once probably been a teacher's desk, impatiently arranging a pencil, some paper, and a glass of watered down whisky. Most prominent and available for all to see, placed parallel to the top edge, was an Officer's pistol, unloaded, but which he intended to use as a gavel. Interruptions would prolong the affair, stretching his thin patience even further. The room probably was once a school, not the largest room in the small town, but the largest available. The walls were bare, only plasterwork, this being less than half the wall area, because each wall was divided by tall narrow windows, allowing more than sufficient light into the room. The bright beams picked out the motes of dust swirling in the warm air, as the audience and witnesses gathered and hurried to their places. Each was greeted by a baleful stare from Picton, impatient at their lack of urgency, and therefore each quickly took their seat. However, not for long, because a personage entered which caused all present to stand; Lord Wellington himself had entered the room and two Aide-de-Camps immediately required those sitting in the back row, to the right of the aisle, to find alternative seats, their Commander wished to observe from the rear. Picton did not stand, in his eyes he was Chairman of the Enquiry and therefore paramount over all, however, with the entrance of Wellington he had had enough. He picked up the pistol and hammered it twice on the desk.

"The Enquiry will come to order!"

Silence quickly fell, established not only by the thumping of the pistol but also Picton's stoney gaze around the room. He picked up a piece of paper from his desk and began to read from it.

"This is a Court of Enquiry into the conduct of one Major Henry Carr, 105th Foot, The Prince of Wales' Own Wessex Regiment. This being on two counts, firstly, conduct concerning the French attack on La Casa de Salinas prior to the Battle of Talavera and secondly, Major Carr's conduct during one episode of that battle. This Enquiry is at Major Carr's own request. "

He paused.

"I assume that Major Carr is here?"

Carr stood up and came to rigid attention.

"Yes Sir."

That seemed to please Picton, who gave a low growl of approval from somewhere back in his throat, and then moved on.

"Who is presenting the evidence calling Major Carr's conduct into question?"

A voice called out from the doorway and a figure hurried down the aisle.

"I am, Sir."

It was Perry, who had been holding last minute consultations with Templemere and Tavender. Picton looked at him as he hurriedly took his seat.

"And you are?"

"Brigadier General Perry, Sir."

Picton looked at him stonily.

"The letter writer!"

Perry looked more than little taken aback at the bold statement concerning himself, but Picton had moved on before he could respond, this in the form of a procedural thought concerning himself, aside from the main proceedings, now that names were being stated.

"My name is Major General Thomas Picton, Third Division, in case any of you were unaware."

Picton now looking at Carr.

"I assume you will be speaking for yourself?"

Carr stood again.

"Yes Sir."

"Very good. Now General Perry, would you be so good as to begin proceedings?"

Perry stood, remaining facing Picton. He cleared his throat and raised a paper before his chest. Picton noticed that he was smiling.

"On the 28th July of this year, the day before the Battle of Talavera, the forward units of the British army came back across the River Alberche in the face of an overwhelming French advance and took up a position which had the building known as the Casa de Salinas as its centre."

418

Before Perry could continue, Picton raised his hand and looked down to his left.

"Pengammon! Are you taking this down?"

Pengammon looked up from his writing.

"Yes Sir!"

Picton nodded.

"General Perry. Please to continue."

Slightly discomfited by the interruption, Perry raised his prepared statement again, found his place and continued.

"The Regiments placed there, the 88th, the 87th, and the 105th, were surprised by a French attack across the Alberche and routed. This rout almost led to the capture of our Commanding Officer, General Wellesley, as he was then. He was justifiably using the tower of the Casa as an observation post. Major Carr was commanding the immediate Companies of the 105th, which were placed there to defend the Casa. These Companies were not on the alert, but were stood down and preparing food, even though the French could well have been very near. Major Carr did nothing to change that situation and, in consequence, when the French arrived, General Wellesley was almost captured; in fact there were casualties amongst his Staff. Despite knowing that the French could well be near, when he arrived at La Casa, Major Carr did nothing to improve the safety of General Wellesley, nor increase the readiness of his men. It is therefore the duty of this Enquiry to hold him negligent and pass the matter on to a Court Martial."

Picton studied him for a moment.

"What evidence do you have for this?"

"None, Sir, but none is needed. It is a matter of record that all three Regiments were surprised and routed, whilst at ease in their encampments, that General Wellesley was almost taken and that Major Carr was the Officer in command of the immediate area around the Casa. It is also a matter of record that Major Carr's men were the front line before the enemy, yet they were allowed to remain at their ease and in consequence they were routed with significant casualties. His conduct is rightly called into question."

Picton now looked at Carr.

"Major Carr. Do you have a reply?"

Carr stood and only half faced Picton, so that the Court could hear.

"Yes Sir. General Perry is wholly in error. First, that the Alberche was shrouded in smoke, such that our pickets could not see the approaching French, second that I went first to the 87th and strongly advised them to come to the alert, which they did, and thirdly, that I called my own Light Company, at the Casa, to also come to the alert. This just before the French arrived, Sir."

"Very good. Call your first witness."

Carr turned to the audience.

"Sergeant Obediah Hill."

Hill marched forward and was sworn in. Carr looked at him.

"Sergeant. was I the last to cross the Alberche?"

"You were, Sir, with the Light Company. Captain Carravoy was there also."

"Very good, Sergeant. Now, in your own words, describe the situation."

"Well, Sir. I was on picket on our bank. After you and Captain Carravoy had gone on back, the smoke became very thick, so's we could barely see the far bank. The French were in the water and crossing before we saw them. Tens, then hundreds! I ordered our pickets back."

"Very good, Sergeant. And when you came back to our men, what can you remember of their state, when you first saw them?"

"They was up, Sir. On the alert. We, that being me and the pickets, Sir, were able to take shelter behind their line."

"You would say that our men were in a firing line?"

"Close on, Sir."

"Did I say anything to you when I came across the Alberche?"

"Yes Sir. You said keep a good watch. What with the scrub on the far bank they could be up close. They bein' the French, Sir."

"Thank you, Sergeant."

Carr sat, but Picton was leaning forward over his desk.

"When you saw the French, Sergeant, did you not open fire?"

"Some did, Sir, but to stand and make a fight of it, for any sort of time, was suicide. I ordered 'em back."

"Would you say that your firing would have been heard at La Casa."

"Hard to say, Sir. No more than a few fired off."

"How far were you from the river?"

"Again hard to say, Sir, but some distance. It was a long hard run chased by they French skirmishers, I can say that, Sir."

Low laughter was heard which soon finished when Picton raised his head.

"General Perry?"

At the prompt, Perry stood to face Hill.

"Did you exchange any other words with Captain Carr?"

"Yes Sir, he said that the huts had been fired according to orders, Sir."

"And you said what?"

"I didn't like the smoke, Sir."

More laughter as Perry, now finished, took his seat, but Picton was now speaking, hurrying the proceedings along, as Hill stood down.

"Next one, Carr."

"It's not a witness, Sir, but a letter written by a Colour Sergeant of the 87th and countersigned by his Colonel Donkin. The 87th are now on their way to Lisbon. Should Major Pergammon read it out, Sir?"

421

Picton nodded and waved in the direction of Pergammon, who stood to receive the letter. He cleared his throat, studied the page for a second, and began.

"This has been written by Colour Sergeant Liam McMichael of the 87th Foot. He states, as follows."

He cleared his throat again.

"Before the attack by the French that surprised us, Major Carr came into our camp and asked me to point out the nearest Officer. I pointed to Captain Bryant and Major Carr went to him. Minutes later, Major Carr left and Captain Bryant called us to the alert. Very soon after that, the French arrived. We were in a better state because of Major Carr's warning."

Pengammon handed Picton the letter and he studied it for a few seconds and then looked up.

"This shows what, Carr?"

"That I was concerned that we all should be in a state of readiness, Sir. The 87th were stood down when I arrived. The Officer I spoke to was killed in that attack, but he agreed that his men should be in a better state of readiness and the letter proves that he responded to my advice, Sir. That area of the 87th came to the alert, as the Colour Sergeant says."

Carr sat down. Picton looked at Perry, who then stood up to face him.

"I am of the strong opinion that the Court should place very little weight on the word of a member of the ranks. Probably illiterate."

Picton's face descended into a deep frown.

"It is countersigned by his Commanding Officer. He is plainly satisfied with it!"

Perry stared back at Picton.

"That is, of course, for the Court to decide."

Picton snorted.

"At least we agree there!"

Picton transferred his impatient stare to Carr, which Perry took as his signal to sit down.

"Next, Carr."

"Company Sergeant Ellis. Light Company, 105th Foot."

Ellis came forward and stood rigidly to attention, whilst repeating the oath, then he turned to enable Carr to begin.

"Sergeant. Before I arrived back at La Casa what was the position with the Light Company there?"

"We were stood down, Sir. The lads were taking some food."

"And when I came, did I give an order?"

"You did, Sir. You allowed the men to continue to have something to eat, but they were to stay fully equipped and stood in line. Sir."

"Would you say, therefore, that I made changes?"

"Yes Sir."

"To make us better able to repel an attack?"

"Yes Sir."

"Thank you, Sergeant."

Carr sat down as Perry stood up.

"Sergeant. When you say, 'in line', where was that?"

"Right before the house, Sir. In front of the wall."

"Was that the best position in your opinion?"

"I followed orders, Sir, but I'll say that we was in line with the other Companies of the Battalion. Makin' a front, Sir."

Perry immediately sat and Picton looked at Carr. Ellis took both as his signal to go as Carr spoke again.

"Captain Carravoy, please."

Carravoy came forward and stood. As an Officer he was not required to take the Oath and Carr began his questioning immediately.

"Captain. We walked back together part way after crossing the Alberche, did we not?"

Carravoy paused, as though thinking carefully.

"We did. Part way."

"What did we talk about as we walked back?"

Carravoy's face became contemptuous.

"It wasn't a social occasion!"

Carr agreed and smiled.

"No. It was not, but can you tell the Enquiry what our concerns were?"

"That takes no telling! Obviously the French."

Carravoy's hostility towards Carr was becoming evident and Carr felt his own temper rising.

"The French, yes, but anything particular about the French, which you can remember as being of concern to us, at that time?"

"Nothing comes to mind."

"Such as where they were?"

"I'll not have words put into my mouth. Nothing comes to mind, as I have said."

Carr moved on. It was plain that Carravoy was not on his side.

"You hurried on ahead to get to your Grenadiers, causing us to part company."

"Correct."

"Can you recall my saying anything before you went on?"

"No, I had my own concerns."

"You can recall nothing? That I said I would go and check that Colonel Donkin's Brigade was in position?"

"No. As I said I had my own concerns."

Carr gave up the topic and moved on.

"We left the Alberche together, as you have agreed. Were the huts burning?"

"Yes."

"With the smoke blowing down river and across our pickets."

"I did not take the trouble to notice."

"But there was smoke, blowing from the burning huts?"

"Yes."

"When were they fired?"

"Just before my Grenadiers crossed."

"So you would agree that the huts, having just been fired, still had much burning in them, if I can put it that way?"

"I suppose so."

Carr then turned to Picton.

"Sir. It's my opinion that the huts being fired just before we finally crossed, very soon became fully alight and the smoke from them came to its maximum. This coincided with the arrival of the French, Sir, not long after we crossed the Alberche."

Picton looked at him, but made no sign of agreement with Carr.

"Sir. I have no more questions for Captain Carravoy."

Picton moved his gaze.

"General Perry."

Perry stood up, eagerness barely concealed.

"So, Captain. As far as you are concerned, Major Carr here, made no mention of checking on Colonel Donkin's Brigade?"

Carravoy was now in turmoil. He could recall almost every word that he and Carr had exchanged on their way back, because almost all their conversations, each being wholly unpleasant to him, were generally memorable. He had pleaded loss of memory with Carr, but now he was being asked to lie.

"I did not say that. He may have, he may not. I cannot recall. I had my own Grenadiers to worry about."

Perry's shoulders sank slightly. This was setback. He tried a different approach

"So, as far as you are concerned, Carr did not go to the 87th?"

"I have no way of knowing. I hurried on. I was ahead of him."

Perry changed course again.

"What was your impression of the readiness of the 105ᵗʰ when you arrived at your line."

Carravoy was not going to disparage his Regiment.

"The men were cooking, but full equipped. They could have achieved a state of readiness in under a minute."

"Did you pass by the Light Company?"

"Yes. They were the same as my Grenadiers."

"Which was?"

"Fully equipped, but preparing food."

Perry tried one final time.

"When the French attacked, they hit your Light Company first?"

"Yes."

"And they were immediately forced back, being so unprepared?"

"We all were, sooner or later. What happened with the Lights I cannot say. They were at the opposite end of our line to my Grenadiers."

Perry looked directly at Carravoy, more than a little angry, his mouth a thin line. Carravoy was giving evidence neither one way nor the other, so he gave up and turned away, annoyed, even betrayed, in his mind. Carravoy stood his place for a moment, and then returned to his seat. Picton looked at Carr.

"Anything else?"

Carr stood.

"No, Sir."

"Perry?"

Remaining sitting.

"No, Sir."

Picton recovered his single piece of paper.

"I'll pronounce on both cases together. So, now, the next concern. Your conduct at Talavera, Carr."

Carr was still standing, now much encouraged. He thought that, so far, the Enquiry had gone well.

"Yes, Sir, thank you. The point is this, that after the first French attack on the plain proper, the 1ˢᵗ and 2ⁿᵈ KGL,

426

the 83rd and the 61st advanced forward, but were thrown back, in confusion. We were in reserve to these four Regiments. General Mackenzie brought us forward, but the 105th were required to hold a line that previously had been held by three Battalions. We could move neither right nor left. On the left was the biggest concern for there was nothing and would remain so until the 48th arrived. They had been ordered down to fill the gap. That was my position, there on the left. My concern was that they would not come far enough to us and if they did not, then there would be a dangerous gap, which the French could exploit. I hoped to persuade the 48th, when I saw them coming off the Medellin, to come as close to us as possible, to minimise that gap."

Picton nodded.

"Very good. Who do you call?"

"Captain Wilson, Sir. Grenadier Company, 1st 48th."

Wilson came forward from far back in the room and stood erect, awaiting questions. Carr began.

"Captain Wilson. You remember meeting me as you led the 48th onto the plain?"

"I do."

"Please recount to us, what happened."

Wilson took a deep breath.

"You arrived when we were still on our way. You were worried about the gap existing in our line. You asked if I could lead my men as close to yours as possible. I said yes and did so."

"And then? What did I do?"

"You ran back the way you had come."

Carr smiled and sat down. Perry stood at the cue.

"Captain. Describe Major Carr's demeanour when he got to you."

"Demeanour, Sir?"

"How did he appear, to you?"

"Worried, Sir."

"And afraid?"

427

"We all had some of that, Sir."

"And Carr, apologies, Major Carr, ran directly back?"

"Yes. In the direction from which he had come."

"Did you see him regain the end of his line?"

"No Sir. Too much smoke. There was a battery just ahead."

"Thank you."

Wilson looked at Picton to receive the nod to sit down. Carr turned to look back for his next witness.

"Captain Sillery. Royal Horse Artillery."

Sillery came forward to stand the same spot as Wilson. Carr turned towards him.

"Captain. Did you see me running up to meet the 48th?"

"No Sir, I did not."

"So what did you see, of me, at that critical time?"

"I only heard you when you came back, Sir. You said well done and something else that I could not catch."

"Thank you, Captain, that was my next question. Did I regain the left flank of my Battalion?"

"You must have, Sir. It was but yards from my far right gun."

"Thank you, Captain."

Carr turned and sat down. Picton looked at Perry, who stood and approached Sillery.

"Are you sure that it was Carr?"

Sillery looked nonplussed.

"As far as I can be, Sir."

"But he ran behind you, if it was him. You only heard a voice?"

Sillery thought for a moment.

"Yes Sir."

"So, can you be absolutely certain, with all the noise and the distractions that you had, that it was Carr who said, 'Well done'?"

"As certain as I can be, Sir."

428

"Well, Captain, it could really have been anyone, any Officer, could it not, impressed with the way that your battery was conducting itself?"

Sillery stood in silence and did not answer.

"So, you cannot be absolutely certain that Major Carr did return to his men?"

"No Sir, not absolutely, no."

Carr was shocked and he looked at Drake, who was equally ill at ease. Calling Sillery as a witness had done more harm than good. Picton looked over.

"Carr?"

Carr shook his head and Sillery walked back after a wave of dismissal from Picton's hand, then he again looked at Carr, who again shook his head. Picton then continued proceedings.

"General Perry!"

"Captain Lucius Tavender. 16th Light Dragoons."

Tavender strode forward, resplendent and sparkling in his Dragoon uniform. Perry began his questioning, now much encouraged.

"Captain. Where were you during the final French attack?"

"Behind Sillery's battery. Supporting the 105th."

"Please tell us what you saw."

"I saw Major Carr running off to the left."

"Did you see him come back?"

"No. I never saw again on that day!"

Perry began consulting his papers, for no other reason than the fact that he wanted Tavender's final words to dwell with the Court. Meanwhile Carr had recovered and regained a memory. He turned to Drake.

"Get Saunders here. Do it yourself, I'll need Ellis."

Drake stood and within seconds he was gone. Perry turned again to Tavender.

"And Major Carr's demeanour?"

"He looked to me like a scared rabbit!"

There were murmurs around the room as Perry sat down and Carr stood. He needed to create time for Saunders to arrive.

"How many battles have you been in, Captain?"

Tavender looked at Picton.

"Must I answer that, Sir?"

Picton's eyes widened at the question.

"Yes!"

Tavender turned back to Carr.

"Two, as we speak. Vimeiro and this one."

"But this was the first time that you were required to hold a line? I mean at Vimeiro you were part of that, er, less than successful cavalry charge, in which you almost lost your life?"

A pause, as Tavender stared at him angrily, but made no reply.

"So, you are saying, with this non-existent experience as it was at that time, that you can judge a man's state of mind, as he runs off, along his army's front?"

No answer.

"I mean, if a man were running away, actually past you on that occasion, you would be able to see fear in his face, but off to your left, amidst all the noise and smoke and hither and thither, and at a distance, you maintain that you can yet tell a man's state of mind?"

"I believe that one could make some kind of an accurate judgement!"

"Hmmmm. How far back were you, Captain? I could recall Captain Sillery. He would know."

Tavender bridled at the idea that his word would need to be corroborated.

"50 yards. Give or take."

"Thank you Captain. So, in a battle, from 50 yards you are able to come to such a conclusion as that."

Carr positioned himself to squarely face Tavender and speak with a heavy chill in his voice.

"Well. I'll tell you now, Captain, that I was afraid, and yes, terrified, but I was on my way to do my duty as a King's Officer, that being to better fight the French by arranging our line."

Murmurs of approval could be heard, but Picton was now indignant.

"That's for the Court to decide, Carr, not you! Any more questions for this witness?"

Carr turned to face him.

"No Sir, but I would like to call Sergeant Ellis again to help clear up this point, that I did return to my Battalion and was standing with them at the conclusion."

Picton nodded and Ellis came forward again, passing by Tavender without a glance. Pengammon now stood.

"I remind you Sergeant that you are still on Oath."

Ellis looked stonily at him, but replied.

"Yes Sir."

He then turned to face Carr who asked his first question.

"Sergeant. When the French finally fell back, what did the men around you begin to do?"

Ellis thought for a moment. He had fully realised why he had been recalled; to prove that Carr had returned to his men, but what to say? Well, simply answer the question was his first thought.

"They fixed bayonets and began to advance forward, Sir. They wanted at the French."

"And did they?"

"No Sir."

"Who stopped them?"

"You did, Sir."

"Did you see me?"

"Yes Sir. On the end of our Company line."

"Had you not seen me, would you have known it was me?"

431

"Yes Sir. I was your Company Sergeant for two years. I'd know your voice anywhere."

Carr sat down, and Perry stood.

"Sergeant. You say you have served with Major Carr for two years?"

"Yes Sir."

"And over that time you have built up a measure of loyalty towards him?"

"Yes Sir. I've always been happy to be led by him in battle, Sir. Seven, if you counts in the siege at Scilla and crossin' the Douro! Then there was the Retreat on top."

Ellis stared challengingly back at Perry. 'Match that!'

Perry took umbrage at being stared at so pointedly, but continued.

"Loyalty over such a record, could lead you to say just about anything to protect your Officer. Could that not be so?"

Ellis rose up to his full height, above Perry, such that Carr thought for a horrible second that Ellis was about to hit his questioner. Ellis had no great liking for Henry Carr, but he was an Officer who stood with his men, gave good, clear orders and knew the value of training as the best way to keep his men alive.

"If you'm insinuatin' that I could lie, then you can drop that straight away, Sir! I've served under nigh on a dozen Officers and Major Carr here, is as good as any, and better'n most. The truth is the truth and that's what I've said to this Court! It all happened just as I've said."

Perry had involuntarily taken a step back from such a tirade and saw the danger in any more questions. Ellis now clearly had the Court on his side, so Perry turned abruptly and sat down. Picton waved Ellis back to his seat. Carr looked to the rear of the room, but still no Saunders, so he looked at Picton.

"Can I recall Sillery, Sir?"

Picton leaned forward.

"Why?"

"We had several conversations that day, Sir. Perhaps he could recognise my voice."

Picton sat back.

"Denied."

Carr was frantically thinking for something else, when Saunders did enter.

"Then, Sir, may I call Corporal Ezekiel Saunders of the 105th?"

Picton nodded and the giant Saunders came forward, looking more than a little apprehensive. He had no idea why he was there, because it was not Drake who found him, but one of those recruited by Drake to try and find him. Carr began the moment after Saunders had taken the Oath.

"Corporal. You recall the final moments of the Battle of Talavera?"

"Sir."

"Where was I?"

Saunders looked at him, highly puzzled.

"Alongside me, Sir. Working a Baker rifle!"

"How long was I there?"

"Some time, Sir, after you'd come back. Don't know where you went, Sir, but after you came back, it took a while to see 'em off in that final set-to. I took a cartridge off you, the last one I fired. I'd run out."

"Thank you, Corporal."

He looked at Picton.

"That's me finished, Sir."

Picton looked at Perry, fiercely. He wanted no more questions and Perry took the hint and remained seated. Picton, having sat through a good hour, listening to all the witnesses, was now in no good mood. He wanted the affair ended and wasting no more of his valuable time. He sat forward, elbows on the desktop, now prepared to pronounce his judgement exactly as the words came to him. The first were none too gentle.

433

"This is something about nothing! Both affairs. Taking the first point against Major Carr, that of La Casa, I am convinced that he did make an attempt to bring the line to readiness and he cannot be blamed if scrub and smoke and whatnot gave the French the chance to approach our line unseen. On that I have heard sufficient proof."

He sat back, made the sleeves of his tunic more comfortable and then resumed his original posture.

"Regarding the second. Again there is proof that Major Carr's actions were necessary and justified. Perhaps he could have sent a runner to the 48th, but he felt the need to do the job himself and perhaps it's just as well that he did, to co-ordinate with other Officers. Perhaps he was relieved to get away from his line for a while on such a mission, who knows, but that is mere conjecture. Therefore, on the face of it, I can find no proof of any misconduct on the part of Major Carr. He conducted himself as a responsible Officer responding, as he saw it, to a perilous situation in the best way. Therefore, I cannot condemn him there. Either!"

He picked up the pistol and hammered it onto the desk.

"Enquiry closed!"

Carr stood and turned to Drake, who was smiling enough to imperil his face.

"Well done, Henry. Perry and his gang truly seen off."

Carr smiled his agreement, but his voice conveyed no sense of triumph as he shook Drake's hand.

"Thanks for your help."

He then looked at Ellis and Saunders, who were just behind Drake.

"Thank you, men."

He came to the attention and saluted, as did they. Carr then took himself to the back of the room to find Wilson and Sillery. They were both in conversation, which they interrupted as Carr approached.

"I wish to thank you both."

He shook the hand of each, but Sillery spoke first.

"Sorry that I wasn't of much help, Sir. I'd have liked to say more. After all, it was your men and my battery who held the line."

"Think no more of it. You told the truth in answer to what you were asked. You could do no more. You told the truth, unlike some!"

He placed a hand on the arm of each.

"This has taken up too much of your time, but I am in debt to you both. If you ever need my help, it is yours, you have but to ask."

Both smiled broadly at the offer, somewhat surprised, then they saluted and left. Carr, now at the back, stood and waited for Drake to come up to him, so that they could both leave. In the aisle nearby he noticed Picton walking to the door with Pengammon behind, these being passed by a Colonel of Wellington's Staff walking back. As Picton passed, quite close, he looked at Carr, a hard stare, but with no animosity.

"Carr."

Carr came to the attention and saluted.

"Sir."

Picton swept on, followed by Pengammon, who did grin as they passed, but then Drake arrived and so they both left the room. Meanwhile, Perry was standing pleased with himself, a satisfactory result, the Enquiry had run its course and had not been dismissed out of hand. He was gathering his hat and gloves, when Wellington's Aide-de-Camp reached him.

"General Perry."

Perry turned towards the voice, to find himself in the company of a full Colonel, tall, young and resplendent. He was brief and perfunctory.

"I'm Colonel Stapleford, Sir. Lord Wellington wishes to see you tomorrow, at his Headquarters, at eleven."

Perry's face became puzzled.

435

"In Badajoz?"

Stapleford nodded, just before he walked away.

"The same. Sir."

Now Perry was puzzled, also apprehensive. He recalled the last time he had spoken one to one with Wellington and it had been none too pleasant. He put on his hat and gloves, thinking and hoping that this time it would be different. Meanwhile, another meeting was taking place outside, Tavender and Templemere had placed themselves before Carr and Drake, hindering their path. Carr stopped and folded his arms whilst looking from one to the other, for some seconds.

"You wished to see me, for some reason? Captains!"

The use of rank had an effect. Carr was not allowing this to be in any way social, this was military, but it was Templemere who recovered, his voice full of sarcasm.

"We merely wished to congratulate you, Sir, on the verdict just pronounced. I'm sure people will now hold you to be exonerated. That comment about being relieved to leave the line, well, I'm sure it will count for nothing."

Carr again looked from one to the other.

"Those words carry as much truth as those which I just heard in there!"

He stared hard, at each in turn.

"So, if that does conclude your business with me, well, I have none with you. You are both dismissed! Which comes after a salute."

The pair had no choice but to salute, albeit in very desultory fashion and then turn and leave as Carr stood his ground. Stood with Drake, he watched both enter the crowd and they saw Perry join them, then all three disappeared further into the throng, both military and civilian.

"Odious Harpies, each and every corner of that hideous triangle!"

"No argument there, Nat. I can only wonder what I've done to deserve such a depth of dislike."

"Oh, I think I can ascribe some sort of reason to each of them. But to go to these lengths! Templemere, perhaps, what with two duels of sorts, but the other two?"

Carr sighed and nodded.

"The other two! Indeed yes."

Drake looked at his friend.

"Indeed yes, but it's done. You got the verdict."

Carr gave a small laugh.

"Yes, but they've got what they wanted and some of this will stick. A letter to The Times condemning me and also a full Enquiry into my conduct. Such as this will never fully fall away."

Drake looked at him puzzled.

"Only over time! Over time such as this fades from memory and there is a great deal more to come in this Spanish saga; for you to make a name for yourself and for those three clods to cover themselves in incompetence and absurdity."

Now Carr did laugh.

"You do have a good way with words, Nat. You should start a book!"

Drake swayed his head from side to side.

"Perhaps. Perhaps. But now, we have our Leave, mine just granted! Both me and thee! There is nothing to stop us, but the need to pack. Let's get Morrison going."

They both strode off with more than a spring in their step, which could not be applied to Carravoy and D'Villiers, simultaneously making their way through the narrow streets. Carravoy was in black mood and D'Villiers was fairly certain as to why.

"What choice did you have, Charles? We more or less allied ourselves to them, during that evening back in Lisbon, and you carried it through, after a fashion. You showed yourself to be no ally of Carr."

Carravoy looked straight-ahead, almost pushing aside a Montijo resident carrying a basket of fruit.

"I did neither!"

D'Villiers remained silent and waited.

"I neither acted as an ally to their scheme, nor did I support Carr. I made myself neutral."

"What else could you have done?"

"I could have supported a Brother Officer, or I could have used my position to get Carr sent up to a Court Martial. I did neither."

D'Villiers now turned to him, as they walked.

"Then I'd say that you got it about right! You didn't condemn Carr, which would have been a lie anyway and you distanced yourself from this unpleasant scheme and I do think unpleasant, which those three are now cooking up. For their own purposes; revenge, plain dislike, or whatever. Things will be no worse, now, between you and Carr than they were before, and, well, as for the three, in my opinion you'd do well to keep them at arms length. I fear for any future that would be shoulder to shoulder with such as them."

Carravoy felt better. He was right, there had been no real harm done, but he spoke wearily, resignedly.

"Very good, I'll go for that. It's now in the past, let it lie there."

However, one further thought crossed his mind, but he left it unspoken; D'Villiers was growing up!

The following morning, Perry was where he needed to be, but not where he wanted to be. He needed to be in the right place at the right time, but not this, which was for an audience with Wellington. He was stood behind Badajoz church, looking at a large, dignified, grey stone building whose façade was regularly brightened by scarlet and blue uniforms all going in and out of the wide door. His apprehension grew as he mounted the few steps and entered, to be greeted by the ancient and discordant chimes of a large clock, striking eleven. He approached a wide and deep desk, manned by a Major.

"I have an appointment to see Lord Wellington. I am Brigadier Perry."

The Major looked up.

"Indeed you have, Sir. I have been told to send you straight up."

He stood, to be better able to point.

"Up those stairs, Sir, and through the arch that you can see. There is a desk just through there. Say who you are, Sir, and the General's Staff will take it from there."

Perry took two steps backwards, now very apprehensive that the Major did not have any need, even, to consult a list of Wellington's visitors that day. He was plainly very much expected, even arrangements made for dealing with him! Perry climbed the stairs and turned towards the arch, then immediately he could see the desk, smaller than the one in the hall, but manned by equal rank. He came to the desk and noticed a single door, ajar, to the right of it.

"I am Brigadier Perry. I have an appointment ……."

His words were cut off by a shout from inside the room.

"Send him in!"

The Major looked up at Perry and said nothing, but conveying much with a knowing half smile. Perry entered to find Wellington studying papers, a large despatch box open at the end of the desk. There was no other chair and so Perry had to stand. Wellington raised his head and pointed his nose at him, then the high, perfectly arched eyebrows came together in a frown.

"Two things, Perry. Let's begin with the general. You know my army almost fell apart from starvation at Mirabette and Jaraicejo."

Perry nodded.

"Yes, Sir."

"And General George Murray, my Quartermaster General, had placed you in charge of the Badajoz route from Lisbon to my men."

A pause.

"Your responsibility, Perry. What happened?"

Perry found the piercing eyes to be most unpleasant, but he found a reply.

"There were difficulties. Sir?"

Wellington sat back.

"My army starved at Talavera. I blame the Spanish for that. However, as we fell back I sent word that we would be falling back to hold the bridge at Almaraz, sent on the 2nd August."

Wellington sat forward.

"Do you know the date, General, when we finally received some significant supplies from our own Commissariat?"

Perry hands went behind his back, where fingers seized each other.

"27th August, Perry. The 27th ! 25 days, almost a month later!"

Perry untwisted his hand.

"As I say, Sir, There were difficulties."

"What, Perry? Such as? I mean there was food enough in Lisbon, was there not?"

Perry had thought of something, although it was not quite true.

"I received the letter on the 6th, Sir."

Wellington had had enough of this topic.

"You say difficulties. Fine excuse that would be, if I used it as a reason as to why I could not get my army into the field to stop a French invasion."

He warmed to the subject.

"I am no Quartermaster, but I can think, here, now, of a dozen things that could have been done to get supplies up to my men. There were Regiments of cavalry in Lisbon, if nothing else, you could have loaded supplies onto their

440

horses and brought them forward! My army was utterly starving, General!"

"I had not the authority, Sir."

Wellington leaned even further forward.

"Authority Perry! You are a full Brigadier General. Only three ranks below me! And did my request not give you all the authority you needed? To wave under the nose of some obdurate Colonel!"

He sat back.

"My men starved, General, and I hold you responsible, for most, if not all."

A pause.

"Now. This Carr business. What you levelled against him, Perry, was utter stuff! Complete tosh! I got away from La Casa because of Carr's men, not so much the orders he gave them, but the training that he put into them. And as for that rubbish about deserting his post, whilst running along our front to achieve a better conjunction with another Regiment; regarding that, words fail me!"

He sat forward again, elbows on the desk.

"And then, Perry, you write a letter to The Times disparaging one of my Officers and by implication, my army and me!"

A pause.

"For your information, Perry, I have no problem with Major Carr, Colonel Lacey nor any of his 105th. Plainly you have, for reasons I'm sure I would find too tedious to listen to, but my 105th I would put on a par with The Guards for cohesion, discipline and fighting ability!"

He sat back, resignedly, spleen building.

"I've had enough of you, Perry! This has come on top of the shambles you made of that independent command I gave you at Oporto. You're going home! Go home and be a farmer, or some such. You'd do well to think seriously about that, were I you, for I have written to Horse Guards, recommending your removal from the list of active Brigadier Generals. You may, of course, get yourself involved with your local Militia, but I sincerely hope you do not. You may have influence somewhere, but the army that I command and its source of reinforcements, wants nothing more to do, with you!"

He looked at Perry, very briefly, before returning to his papers.

"Dismiss!"

Perry slunk from the room in a daze, only coming to full cognition when the sunlight outside in the Square hit his eyes.

oOo

Chapter Eight

Of Things Marital

Carr sat the narrow cot, which occupied more than half the room in his cabin, with two letters open on the chair before him, reading one, then the other. A third was alongside, but unopened. He was interrupted by Drake opening the door.

"Have we become better sailors? Three days out and I haven't felt the need to visit the lee side once yet."

Carr did not look up.

"No. Just a better voyage, caused by a 'following sea', as I believe the sailors call it."

He moved along the cot to make room.

"These letters that I told you about. What are we going to do?"

Drake looked astonished.

"Do! Why regarding the one from Jane, when you get back, you get married. In an instant! Especially with what she has said about the doings of her Father. Both are pretty much adrift from each other, now, I'd say."

A pause.

"And, from what you tell me about what she has said about you and her, well. I'd say it was now on rails. More than you deserve, in my opinion."

He smiled as he reached across to pick up the more military of the opened two.

"Regarding this from Lacey, stating that we find two more Officers and 70 to 80 more men, well, that's obvious. We go to the Militia and see how many will take the Bounty."

"You think it's that simple? Haul Jane up the aisle and bribe some Wessex Defencibles!"

Drake subsided, considerably.

"Well yes. A quick wedding shouldn't be hard. Just how many guests do you need? Enough to make it look like

443

a wedding and more than half fill the local Church. Using the one that I got hitched in will do. Prior to that you get the Banns read or get a licence, whichever works best. Plainly Jane has no concerns, now that Father's pretty much out of the way. Relations between the two at about the lowest ebb possible."

"And I can count on you to do the Best Man bit?"

"Of course! I've been mulling over various witticisms since you told me that you had, at last, written that fateful letter!"

Carr nodded, smiled and then changed the subject.

"And there's the men. Lacey's counting on us. So's Picton!"

He placed his finger on the unopened letter.

"Every Officer in his Division who has been granted leave has been given one, from him, expecting them all to bring back men. In his letter the Colonel says we lost seventy-six at Talavera, 25 killed, 5 missing and 46 either died of wounds or recovered but no longer fit for service. There are some on this ship with us, are there not?"

"Yes."

Carr's face changed to one of deep concern.

"Can anything be done for them? When we get back."

Drake shook his head.

"What can we do? My people may be able to take a couple, around the estate. It's a scandal, in my view, but what can we do? So many end up as beggars. We could try to get a small pension for them, sometimes it's successful. Wounded at Talavera will help. There will be a local Pensions Board for our area."

He looked at Carr.

"We should give it a go!"

Carr nodded.

"Yes, we should. And see if two or three are fit enough to train the Militia. Perhaps more."

He folded the letters.

"Right. We'll see what we can do when we reach land. In fact there isn't too much we can do about anything until we reach land."

He turned to Drake, changing the subject entirely.

"When we get back, we'll be involved in a wedding and getting around the Militia. And undoubtedly things I haven't thought of. You have some of your pay, I take it."

"Of course. All of it! I have nurseries to furnish and whatnot."

"Right, good. Now, you're dismissed. I've a mind for some more sleep. The motion of the waves and having so little to do, can at any time send me off to the Land of Nod, I'm finding. All I have to do is close my eyes."

"Same here, funny that, but I'll take a turn on the deck. Perhaps to think of a few more embarrassing anecdotes for your post wedding celebrations."

He rose from the cot and left, leaving Carr to himself on the crude structure, unfortunately not quite long enough for a full stretch.

Ten days later both were descending the gangplank at Weymouth, their usual port of both arrival and embarkation, both carrying a large carpet portmanteau. However, both did not leave immediately, instead they assembled their wounded, 23 in all.

"Men. You have your pay?"

Answers to the affirmative came from all.

"Good, if you choose, get yourselves to Taunton, and we'll see what can be done. Both Captain Drake and I will approach the local Pension Board. We make no promises, but we will try."

A Sergeant of Grenadiers stepped forward. He was missing a foot and leaning heavily on his crutch.

"Jem Nicholls, Sir. I'm sure we're all grateful for anything you can do."

Carr nodded.

"See you all at Taunton barracks. We'll do our best."

With that, Carr and Drake took themselves to a local Ostler where two horses were hired and then, with their portmanteaux bouncing behind them, they were soon on the straight road to Dorchester. They did not give a glance to Maiden Castle, off high to their left, and it was with impatience that they found an Inn for the night at Ilminster; so near, yet so far from Taunton. However, their impatience did not prevent some forethought, this coming from Drake.

"We can't just bounce up, out of the dawn! We've had no time to send any word, at all."

Carr rose and left the room.

"I think I know what will serve."

He rummaged in his portmanteau to find paper and pencil, with which he wrote a hasty note, then out to the pump room, where he placed two guinea coins on the bar, with the note beneath and then he looked squarely at the Innkeeper.

"These guineas, if you can get this message to a house in Cheddon Fitzpaine, just beyond Taunton. To get there early next morning."

The Innkeeper placed a large hand over both coins, and then picked up the note.

"My son, Sir. He'll see 'tis done. Does the house have a name?"

"Yes. Fynings Court. It's written on the note."

Carr looked at the Innkeeper steadily and received a steady, trustworthy look back. He nodded to the Innkeeper and returned to his room. Both slept soundly and were only partially wakened at around 4.00 am, by the sound of iron shod hooves on the cobblestones in the yard below their window, this slight wakening caused by the subconscious fear that all infantrymen have of the surprise arrival of enemy cavalry. The sun had just left the horizon as they took the Taunton road, both now in their greatcoats against the late October weather. Carr paid the Turnpike and they made good progress along the good road, soon to cross the

Bristol Turnpike that ran into Taunton itself, but they were going beyond, to the North. The spirits of both rose as the familiar sights of Cheddon Fitzpaine were passed, one by one, to finally take the known and familiar turning for the road that would lead past the longed for gates. They arrived at the ornate construction, already open and both entered to find an already attentive Groom to take their horses. Carr spoke, not looking at the man, but gazing at the imposing Tudor façade of Fynings Court.

"Get these back to the Ostler in Ilminster."

The forehead was knuckled and Carr followed Drake to the door. He was already there when the door opened and Cecily came flying out with all the speed that her condition would allow. Their embrace was fierce but brief, as Drake disengaged himself to examine the now very prominent state of her pregnancy. She was closely followed by Jane, who with much more decorum walked up to Carr, but there the decorum ended, as all four hands were joined, and both looked at each other with a depth of affection that blanked out all other sounds and all other people. Finally, Jane spoke.

"Henry!"

Carr could only mange a choked laugh, such was the tightness in his throat, then he finally managed to bring his vocal cords under control.

"Jane!"

Now she smiled.

"You look terrible, but then you always do when you come back from that dreadful place!"

"Then you need feeding, much and often!"

This last from Lady Constance Fynings, who had been standing nearby, unnoticed in the circumstances and so now she spoke further.

"All is ready! You only have to come inside."

Carr released Jane's hands and he walked over to Lady Constance, to then bring his heels together and bow over her hand.

"Lady Constance. I cannot thank you enough for all that you have done."

"Nonsense! Right's right, you know."

Carr smiled.

"You know, I heard that not so long ago from an Irish Sergeant."

"Well, good for him! Now, inside all of you, this is not the best of weather for such as Cecily."

Servants had long picked up their portmanteaus and so all went inside where they found a large table covered in hot breakfast food. Drake was already at table and stuffing a napkin into the top of his tunic. After engorging themselves, for both men the rest of the day was spent in close company of she who mattered most, each couple never more than arms length from the other. Sat by the fire, Jane raised the subject of their wedding, by tugging at his arm.

"You've a job to do!"

Carr pulled himself out of his half wakeful state.

"And what's that?"

"You must go to the Bishop of Bath and Wells, to get a Licence."

He was now fully awake and more than a little concerned.

"Licence?"

Lady Constance was sat opposite and raised her head from her embroidery.

"Yes. Our local Vicar is refusing to read the Banns."

Carr looked at her, plainly much puzzled, but she answered immediately.

"Yes. On the grounds that you are not resident in this Parish."

Carr sat bolt upright.

"But this is the home barracks of my Regiment! Of course this is my residence. Does he expect me to have the Banns read in a town called Badajoz, on the border?"

"He doesn't see it that way, I'm afraid, and I suspect some influence. Malign influence from some quarter! Did you know that Jane's Father is back in England, having been sent home by Wellington, and with him that odious man Tavender. The latter on leave. He came here asking to see Jane. I threatened to put the dogs on him!"

Carr stared at her, his concern obvious as Lady Constance continued.

"Yes, he did. It's no secret that Jane's Father wishes her to marry this Tavender. Appalling notion! They've been here now for about three days."

Drake was now paying full attention.

"Marry Tavender! Ughh, but God's Truth, that must have been a fast passage!"

Lady Constance turned to him.

"The Tavenders have their own yacht! "

Drake subsided and returned his head to Cecily's shoulder, but Jane was tugging at Carr's arm.

"But it's all right! Lady Constance is a personal friend of the Bishop and the paper is there, now, waiting. You have only to go and collect it."

"Then what?"

Jane looked at Lady Constance, who answered.

"Give it to my Vicar. Fynings Court has its own Church and I've drummed up a Vicar acquaintance of mine. Retired, but not long."

Jane tugged his arm again.

"So there you are. It's all right. No need to worry!"

But Carr did. The destructive influence of General Perry and the scheming of Lucius Tavender were thoroughly uppermost in his mind, borne of the past and supported by recent events. However, at dinner they met the retired Vicar and a more cheerful and jovial man it would be difficult to imagine and he lifted the spirits of all, even those of Carr, which required the most elevation. However, eventually the good wine and the good company and the fact that he could now gaze, to the edge of embarrassment, at Jane as much as he liked, buoyed him up. When the women had withdrawn and the port and nuts were circulating, the Vicar, him being the Reverend James Pendlebury, made things clear.

"Get the Licence to me soonest. That will not be difficult, for I am residing here as long as I'm required. I then, with that authority, enter the forthcoming marriage in the Register, to be completed on the day. That happy day!"

He raised his glass, to find it empty.

"Oh dear, that will never do."

He pointed along the table.

"Captain Drake. The port lies with you."

The port was slid down the table, via Carr and the bucolic Cleric poured himself another measure. The full glass was raised and acknowledged by Drake and Carr. The remaining time over which the three were alone together, was occupied by Carr and Drake forming an attentive audience to the Vicar's stories from Parishes of the past, which pleased both Drake and Carr to be returned, via his cheerful discourse, to the peaceful world of an English Parish. When they rejoined the ladies, they played a few games of backgammon, before retiring and Carr won every time, to find himself condemned by Jane.

"You're too good. You're horrid! I hate you!"

Yet, the two found the time and the space for a quiet moment alone. Little was said, because too much time was spent gazing into the eyes of the other whilst their hands were joined together. However when the servants began their rounds to close down the house, Jane did say one thing.

"What my Father said about you in his letter was terrible! I'm going to write a reply and you'll have to help me write it."

Carr could only nod his thanks before he raised her right hand and kissed it, then each departed to their room.

The following day, Carr was back by Noon from his errand. The paper was handed to the beaming Pendlebury, who read it fully and pronounced all to be well.

"Right! Off to the Fyning's Register of Hatches, Matches and Despatches!"

He then beetled off to the nearest door that led to the Church and Carr looked at Drake, both laughing.

"Right, we've had our lazy day. We must see about the Militia."

He threw Drake his greatcoat.

"We start at the barracks."

Two good horses soon carried then back across the Bristol Turnpike and soon after that, the low, grey, flat walls of Taunton barracks could be seen, up on its slight hill, built and designed as much to keep rebellion out, as brutal soldiery in. They rode through the familiar gate arch, the sturdy gates pinned back, for them both to dismount and hitch their horses to a ring. Drake looked through a window then gazed down the empty Square.

"Not much about!"

"Let's try the Colonel's Office. There may be someone there."

He was correct. An old Sergeant, easily middle-aged, managed to raise himself at the sight of a Major's uniform and salute.

"Sirs. How can I help?"

"We're just back from the Peninsula. The 105th has suffered some casualties and need replacements, so I need to see the Colonel of the Militia. Can you help with that?"

The Sergeant was still standing at an odd angle, plainly from some old wound.

"Please sit, Sergeant."

"Thank you, Sir."

He did, then he opened a drawer to extract a large Register.

"This is the Muster Roll, Sir. As we speak we have a Company of 145. The Colonel is the Honourable Ambrose

Brockenhust, he's our local MP and the Major is St John Slade. They have been in command for about 18 months, Sir, since Colonel Brockenhurst became our MP."

He opened the Register at the correct page, turned it around, and pushed it across to Carr. The pages were well kept with a full entry there for each name, their date of birth, their Parish, their rank in the Militia and the type of Company, Light, Line or Grenadier. There was even a number underlined against each name, choosing from 1, 2, or 3, which were beside each name.

Carr was curious.

"What does this number mean?"

"How good they are at musket drill, Sir."

"Who decides and instructs?"

"I do, Sir."

"Hardly any on three! If that's the best?"

"It is, Sir. I'm sorry to say."

"Why?"

"Not my place to say, Sir."

"But you instruct?"

"I use up all the cartridges allowed me, Sir."

Carr nodded, understandingly. Saying too much could lose him his position. Carr returned to the first subject.

"If all your books are like this, Sergeant, then no-one can have any complaint!"

He looked fully at him.

"You've seen service!"

"Yes Sir. The American Wars. I was lucky to get home, Sir. A lot of the lads didn't."

"No indeed, Sergeant. We can only hope that they ended up with a halfway decent life for themselves. Back over there."

"Yes Sir. And I served with your Colonel Lacey, Sir."

"Oh really. What's your name?"

"Jordan, Sir. Colour Sergeant I was."

Carr smiled.

"When we get back I'll mention you to him."

"Thank you, Sir. But the Militia, Sir, they meet on Saturdays, as Militia they get off work, and Wednesdays, so you've got a bit of luck. They'll be outside the walls at 9 o' clock tomorrow."

"Is there any possibility of my meeting Colonel Brockenhurst today?"

"You'll be lucky with that, Sir. Being an MP and all, he moves about a lot. Staying at various houses of his important acquaintances."

Carr nodded.

"Until tomorrow, then. Meanwhile, can I see all the books of the Militia?"

"Why yes, Sir."

Jordan rose and walked jerkily to a large drawer, from which he drew three ledgers. He brought them over in his arms, then placed each on the desk, after naming each.

"That's the Record of Pay, Sir, that's the Requisitions of Supplies and that is the Record of Training, Sir. What the Militia have done over the past years. A kind of diary."

"How long have you been in charge of these books, Jordan?"

"Six years, Sir. I was lucky to get this job, Sir. My education swung it for me."

"Very well, Jordan, give me some time with them."

"As you say, Sir. You are welcome to use this desk, Sir. About now I take myself off for something to eat."

Carr nodded, but by now he was well into the books, especially the Muster Roll. Drake left him to it and walked out of the Office with Jordan.

"Oh, Sir. I think you should know, Sir, that some of your wounded are now here. That barrack room there, Sir."

Jordan pointed across the square, saluted, and walked on. Drake crossed the square and entered, into a long corridor, this with windows facing onto the square on

453

one side and doors on the other to the individual barrack rooms. He entered the first to find almost a dozen men, sat at the tables, and all rose when they saw him.

"Sit down men. Are you those that shipped back with us from Weymouth?"

It was Sergeant Jem Nicholls who answered, as he had at Weymouth.

"Yes Sir, but not all. Many took their pay and their chances in the towns, Sir. We came on here, rememb'rin' what you said, Sir. That you may be able to help."

Drake studied the dozen. The most visible wounds were to the face, three having lost an eye, two of these with severe facial disfigurements. Three had empty sleeves pinned across their tunics, but he noticed that all could stand.

"How many of you have done the 20 years?"

None raised their hands, meaning none were entitled to the Army Pension,

"How many of you can no longer march?"

Six raised their hands, five with missing limbs but one had a cloth bound around both eyes.

"How many of you can still load a musket?"

Eight of the dozen raised their hands.

"You may be needed to help train the Militia. You'll be paid. Meanwhile, who amongst you can write?"

One raised his hand.

"Good. I want you to write down all your names and what skills you have, gained before they joined the army. Can you do that?"

The man came to the attention.

"I can, Sir."

"Right. I'll see you all tomorrow. Tomorrow we meet the Militia."

He saluted and left, worried on both issues, both the fate of the wounded and quality of the Militia.

oOo

The morning fog was still lapping at the base of the barracks hill as the Militia began to arrive. In clumps of three or four, they strolled up the track to form larger groups across the parade ground, where. Jordan limped around each group, seemingly checking each for uniform, weapon and equipment. Carr and Drake stood back in the shadow of the gatehouse, watching all as it evolved. Stood with them in the gatehouse were four of the wounded from Spain, selected earlier by Drake, who was the first to comment on the arriving Militia.

"They look smart enough."

Carr was unmoved.

"But not tough enough. They look like a bunch of young lads all met up for a jolly."

Suddenly all changed; Jordan was stood in the centre of the square, yelling at the top of his voice.

"Form parade! Form parade!"

In less than a minute all was quiet, still, and orderly, each man at 'ordered arms', their musket grounded beside their right leg. There were even three Officers stood before the first rank, plainly mere boys in their late teens. The change had come about because two Officers, each on a splendid, well groomed horse, were walking their mounts up the track. Jordan was stood waiting at the far end of the parade from where they would arrive and, as the two came within yards of the first rank, he gave his first order.

"Present arms!"

In a smooth and impressive rhythm the whole parade brought their muskets up to the 'present arms', the metal of the barrel just touching their noses. The two riders acknowledged the salute and Jordan gave his next order.

"Shoulder arms."

Again came the smooth movement.

Drake folded his arms.

"All to the good so far."

He looked at Carr.

"What should we do?"

Carr was impassive.

"Wait. I think I know how this is going to work out."

The next hour was spent on musket drill, their muskets swinging impressively through the various positions, and then marching the men around the perimeter of the parade ground, with Jordan in the centre bellowing the orders. After this time, some fifers and drummers arrived and, to their strident music, the whole marched off the parade ground and into the town. Jordan returned to the arch, where Carr asked his questions.

"Will they return?"

"Yes Sir. The Colonel likes them to be seen in the town. Good for recruitment he says."

Carr immediately thought of a more likely, self-aggrandising reason, but did not say it.

"They'll come back for firing drill, Sir, at the butts, that side of the parade ground"

Carr nodded, without looking, then he turned to the four behind.

"Are you sure that you can still load and fire? Like at Vimeiro? You are all unhindered by your wounds?"

All four nodded, but Carr looked at the one with a missing eye.

"Can you?"

The man looked at him.

"Sir, I could do it blindfold!"

Both Carr and Drake grinned and stood waiting, but within an hour the parade returned, the two Officers riding at the head of what was indeed a very smart column.

Carr walked forward.

"Time to introduce ourselves. And this is going to require the height of diplomacy."

Drake sighed.

"Oh dear!"

The two walked out onto the parade ground and awaited their arrival. The two Officers had noticed them immediately and walked their horses over. Carr and Drake came to the attention and saluted.

"Morning, Sir. I am Major Carr, 105th Foot, and this is Captain Drake, Light Company 105th Foot. Just arrived back from Spain."

The two reined in their horses. The more senior was considerably older than the junior, although each immaculately tailored. The former was a good looking and well-built man, not gone to fat, with powerful shoulders, but his face looked sternly on all around, with grim mouth and over-bearing eyes under overly dark brows. Clearly this was a man used to getting his own way. The latter was simply a younger physical version of the former, if more slightly built and wearing the facial expression of someone who counted himself as both a wit and a dandy.

"I have a letter here for you, Sir. From General Picton, our Divisional Commander."

Carr walked forward and handed up the letter. The Colonel's face was already showing some displeasure. As he broke the seal, Carr spoke further.

"Have we the honour of addressing Colonel Brockenhurst and Major Slade?"

Brockenhurst nodded, as he unfolded the letter.

"You have. This is Major Slade."

The last words were delivered with a curt inclination of the head and Slade jerked the butt end of his riding crop at Carr. His face wore a supercilious smile, the expression of one who feels that they have already triumphed in the forthcoming encounter.

"Would you be the Carr that I have just read about in The Times? Who was in charge when his Governor was nearly put in the bag?"

Carr smiled back, a smirk of his own, with raised eyebrows.

"There's only one of me! As far as I know!"

He stared straight at Slade.

"But do watch out for a letter from my intended, assuming that they take the trouble to print it, she writes a good letter, stating that I was wholly exonerated at the resulting Enquiry. On both counts."

Slade sat up straight in his saddle.

"Enquiry!"

"Yes. Demanded by me and granted by General Picton, who conducted the whole thing."

Leaving Slade to make of that fact whatever he wished, Carr then turned his gaze to Brockenhurst.

"I understand, Sir, that your men will now undertake some firing drill?"

Brockenhurst's face became darker, but he did not answer, instead he changed the subject.

"I have a fine body of men here, Major. You'd agree?"

"They look very fine, Sir."

Carr had greatly emphasised the word 'look' and the emphasis was not lost on Brockenhurst.

"They do as I tell 'em, Carr. You can be sure of that. Regarding firing drill, you are correct. That comes next."

"Well, in that case, Sir, seeing as what you have here is no more than a large Company, would you have any objection to my taking the firing drill myself? After all, if some do take the Bounty, out in Spain they will find themselves under the orders of a stranger Officer."

Both Brockenhurst and Slade looked at each other, then back at Carr, but neither spoke. Therefore Carr continued.

"May I remind you, Sir, of something that I am sure you are already aware. It is rate of fire with half Company volleys that is making the difference between us and the French?"

Now Brockenhurst did reply, after a dismissive sharp release of breath.

"Rate of fire! One volley and a bayonet charge is all that's needed!"

Carr drew a deep breath and took one pace back, to ease the angle in his neck.

"With respect, Sir, I beg to differ. General Picton will expect better. At Talavera we stood to the French for over 20 minutes, outnumbered six to one, some say more, in both numbers and time. A bayonet charge against those odds would have lost us the battle. In fact, it was exactly that, which nearly did! However, come the end we won, we stood them off with firepower alone, Sir. They pulled back, when they could take no more."

He allowed the words to sink in.

"Both myself and Captain Carr were there, Sir. The whole time. We saw the same, Sir, at Vimeiro and Coruna."

The significance of those words was not lost either, making it very plain that both Major Carr and Captain Drake were veterans who had faced the French, more then once. At last Brockenhurst spoke, after easing himself petulantly in the saddle.

"Very well. If you must."

Carr saluted and walked to the centre to stand before the short parade of four ranks. He took a deep breath.

"Men! My name is Major Carr of the 105th Foot. I have just come from the battlefield of Talavera. I am hoping that at least 70 of you will take the Bounty and accompany me back out. The Bounty will be 12 guineas. That will see your loved-ones cared for until your pay begins to come back home. The 105th is one of the best Regiments in Wellington's army, the 'Fighting One-Oh-Five' and there is not one man out there who has not double or even triple the Bounty either in his knapsack or lodged with the Purser. The French plunder and rob wherever they go, but when they're dead on the battlefield, what was theirs becomes yours!"

He allowed the words to sink in, before continuing.

"But I speak more of glory than of money. We win against the French! We have the beating of them every time. I've seen it, so has the Captain here. I'm asking you now, to come out, with me, and join the best army that's left these shores since Malborough. We march to glory, boys, sooner or later we will be marching into France, in triumph. So, over the years to come, what will you be saying to your grandchildren? I marched with Wellington across Spain, over the Pyrenees and into France itself. Will you point to the mementoes on the mantelpiece or hanging on the wall? Or will you remember, with shame, the day that you had your chance to join a mighty venture and be part of its triumph, but you backed away, to slink back home, too worried, too frightened, to answer your country's call? We are still in peril, men, we, your countrymen, because given the chance, the French will be over here, marching our streets, plundering our homes and torturing our families to be given food they need, so that they can march on to plunder the next town! So make no mistake, it is good men, first class men, who keep them away, where they belong. Is that you?"

Another pause.

"We are trouncing the French because of our fire power. They have no answer to what we serve out, believe me! A trained soldier should be able to manage three reloads in a minute. Three, after his first discharge. A good one, can manage nearly four. From you, I want three. So, this is what we will do. I will order you to load. You come to the 'make ready' when loaded, then I will say present and fire. After 20 seconds I will order, present, fire, then again after 40, and finally, for the third and last reload, after a minute."

Carr stepped back and looked at Jordan.

"Firing line, Sergeant. Two ranks, facing the butts."

Carr walked to his place as the two lines assembled and he waited until all were in their place.

"Lock on"

460

The rear rank moved smartly enough.

"Order arms."

The muskets came down from all left shoulders.

"Load!"

Suddenly all was frantic activity as Carr looked at his watch. At 25 seconds he saw that about three quarters were at the 'make ready'. He waited until all had their muskets high in the air.

"Present"

The barrels came down to the horizontal.

"Fire!"

The massed muskets crashed out as one and then the reloading began whilst Carr timed the first 20 seconds. At the 20 less than one half were at the 'make ready'.

"Present"

About half managed to level their muskets.

"Fire!

The half fired together, followed by a ragged volley as some latecomers joined on. However, some, even now, did not discharge, but instead came to the 'make ready' to await the next volley. This became steadily worse over the following reloads. At the fourth order to fire, at the end of the minute, barely more than a quarter were able to obey. Carr turned to Jordan.

"Bring out our 105th."

As Jordan did so, Carr marched to the centre.

"For those of you that managed the four – well done! For you that didn't, be aware that by now a French attack column will have marched through your line and you'd be dead, or running from French cavalry. If you've a wish to take the Bounty, then you must improve! You life will depend upon it and those of your comrades either side! If you do choose to come out with me, then you must be better than merely trained, you need to be good!"

By now the four had arrived, albeit limping, and were stood with Carr.

"These men fought at Talavera! They know what it is like to face up to a French column. They looked the Crapauds straight in the eye across twenty yards. They did that and they won! Now they are back home. Wounded, yes, but heroes. And with some money of their own and we are now going to care for them as best we can."

A pause.

"They will now demonstrate the standard needed. I will not time twenty seconds, but order fire when all are at the 'make ready'. Let's see in what time they can manage four reloads. That will mean five bullets sent against the enemy. Captain Drake will give the orders."

Carr again turned to Jordan.

"Get the men either side, Sergeant, where they will be able to see."

Jordan split the line in two and a three deep line was formed either side of the four now stood facing the butts. Carr nodded at Drake.

"Load!"

The four loaded so fast that there was no time for any difference between them to be created, not enough to prevent them all coming together at the 'make ready'.

"Present."

The barrels came down to the horizontal, rapidly as one.

"Fire!"

The muskets barked out and all began their reload. There was not a wasted movement before their muskets were raised almost simultaneously to the vertical again and thus it continued. Such was the total efficiency of each reload that each time they came to the 'make ready' virtually as one. The fifth shot rang out and their muskets fell to the 'order arms'. Carr walked towards the centre, carrying his watch.

"One minute and seven seconds."

He reached the centre.

"Two minutes of that and the French are off and gone. It's more than they can take, I know it because I've seen it!"

He looked carefully at both halves of the Militia.

"I am here for a month, with Captain Drake. We will be here at our Barracks each evening; that's me and my men, to train you and get you up to their standard. If you wish to follow us, out there to Spain, then you will be very welcome to join us here and learn."

With that, Carr and Drake left the parade and walked up to Brockenhurst and Slade. Both were visibly angry, both knew that they had been humiliated, but Carr came straight to the point.

"We can get them up to the rate of fire, Sir, but there are other questions, such as what are they like forming a firing line from column, then forming square? Can they maintain a fire discipline of half-Company volleys?"

Brockenhurst looked down from his horse, with a blank, malignant stare, Slade less so, as he was trying to keep his horse still, after all the noise, but he was plainly equally embarrassed. The training they had been given had been found severely wanting by a serving, front-line Officer.

Carr realised that he would get no answer and so he walked back to the barracks, through the arch and into the Office, where he gathered up the books. Soon Jordan had joined them.

"Sergeant. How often do the men practise firing drill?"

"Each day they come, Sir. On the two days."

"And they fire?"

"Ten each, Sir."

"Get me pencil and paper, if you would be so kind."

Carr reached for the Purchases Ledger and opened it for six months previous. By then the pencil and paper had arrived and Carr began. Over the next hour his face took on a look of deeper and deeper concern. Finally he looked up.

"Sergeant. How many cartridges do you have now, in your magazine?"

"I don't know, Sir. The Colonel takes care of all that, Sir. He has the key."

"The same for flints."

"Yes, Sir."

"When did you last make an issue of cartridges?"

"Last Wednesday, Sir. Thirty to make up the 36 in their boxes."

"And that's the only time you get to go into the magazine?"

"Not me Sir. The Colonel gets some Chosen Men to go in there and bring out the boxes to just inside the arch. Then I makes the issue, Sir."

Carr's face darkened further, then he folded the piece of paper with his calculations and pushed it into his jacket pocket. He looked at Jordan.

"What about rum?"

Jordan laughed.

"That's for me, Sir, when the Colonel orders it."

"Right. Issue yourself a full bottle. Charge it to me!"

oOo

The following week began with Carr and Jane penning the comforting, yet vital letter, which Carr put on the Mail Coach himself, addressed to The Times. Thereafter the following days were fully occupied with substantial meals at Fynings Court, accounts at the barracks and evening fire drill with the Militia, where the wounded of Talavera proved themselves to be invaluable, taking small groups for instruction. At the end of the week, Saturday, the whole line could manage three re-loads in a minute after their first discharge. At the end of that evening, a very pleased Carr and Drake sat down for the evening meal, but before a mouthful was eaten, Jane looked across at both.

"You two! What are you doing on the 22nd November?"

Carr and Drake looked at each other, much perplexed, but it was Drake who replied.

"The date rings no bells, therefore, nothing!"

She smiled, her face a picture of happiness.

"Well, you must keep it free, because on that day, Major Carr, you and I are getting married and you, Captain Drake, are required to attend as the Best Man!"

She beamed at both.

"It is now in the local news sheet and on the Parish notice board."

Whilst Carr looked both overjoyed and astonished at the same time, Drake turned towards him.

"Well there you are, Henry. Orders! Your only choice is but to obey."

However, the announcement had stirred something inside Carr, such that, after the meal, he took Jane into another room and, there alone, he sat her down and knelt before her, taking her hands in his.

"Jane. I know what this will be doing to you. Taking you away from your Father and any family you have, that comes through him. He will disown you!"

He gently squeezed both hands.

"So, are you sure? That one, two, or even five years from now, you will not miss the family that you are leaving behind? Society will judge you by it, that you parted from your family, to marry an almost penniless Infantry Officer, who was the subject of military scandal across the newspapers."

She smiled and gazed down on him before, amazingly, then leaving her chair and kneeling with him on the floor, facing him.

"Henry. The only family I want, is you!"

A pause, whilst her eyes found his.

"And our children. And Nat and Cecily. And Aunt Constance. That's enough family for me. My Father has chosen his path and it is different from mine."

For a long second Carr's face was blank with astonishment, then he smiled, then they both kissed, for a time much longer that convention would tolerate, were anyone there to bear witness and be shocked to any great degree.

The following day, Sunday, an even happier Carr and Drake were at the parade ground and this being Sunday, Brockenhurst and Slade were in attendance. Carr approached Brockenhurst and saluted.

"Sir. Beg to report that your men can now achieve three reloads minute. We have been practising all week."

Whereas Carr expected words or even an expression of satisfaction, instead Brockenhurst's face darkened with displeasure, but Carr continued.

"Sir. Before your march around the town, may we practice going from line to square? As you can see, I have marked out some pegs, which would be the corners of a full battalion square. I want to see how quickly they can take their place as a part of it. Sir."

Brockenhurst said nothing, but gave a curt nod. Carr saluted and jogged over to where Jordan had the Militia in a firing line, two deep.

"Although I'm sure you know, Sergeant, I'm not going to ask. I want to see what happens when the order comes to form square. This number of men will cover only about 20 yards of one side. So you remain standing at one of those pegs and I'll walk the 20 yards from you to mark the end for them."

Jordan saluted.

"Yes Sir."

Carr arrived at his position and turned to the two deep line. He had to shout, for there was now some distance.

"Parade! At the order, 'form square' you form between the Sergeant and myself."

A pause.

"Cavalry! Form square!"

The firing line split raggedly in the middle and the nearest two lines came into position and the furthest jogged behind them to form the third and fourth rank. By that time the front two had fixed bayonets, the first kneeling, the second 'en garde', bayonets thrust forward. Brockenhurst had by now approached.

"There you are, Major. As good as any, I'd say."

Carr looked up.

"With respect, Sir. It's simple, I'll grant you, but too slow. You cannot wait for one half of the firing line to march behind the other. Cavalry could be on them in less than half a minute. I want to teach another drill, Sir, which is quicker. The line must wholly dissolve and then reform as a square. Speed is everything."

It was plain that Brockenhurst would have liked to argue, but Carr must be allowed to try and so he conceded. Permission was given with a sharp nod of his head whilst looking away. Carr saluted and jogged away to stand before the four lines.

"Form line."

The result was the opposite of forming square and soon the Militia were back in a two deep line. Carr spoke to himself, 'Now we start!' Using his twelve wounded veterans, over the next half hour the 145 Militia and their three Officers were pushed, pulled, prodded and punched into position to form a four deep line, at speed, which could form part of a square. Their time improved and then more so, as each learned their position in the four deep line. After achieving the last 'square', which had gone very smoothly, Carr marched over to Brockenhurst.

"Thank you, Sir. As you choose, Sir, I think the men are ready to march off. They have but to shoulder arms and right face."

Brockenhurst pulled himself fully upright in his saddle.

"Thank you, Major, but I think I can work that out for myself."

After the required orders from Major Slade, the whole marched away, to the accompaniment of the fifers and drummers, who all had been stood watching, fascinated, for some time, leaving Carr, Drake and their helpers alone on the parade ground. Carr looked at them all.

"Next we must test them. And I think I know how"

He looked directly at Jordan, waving a hand at his twelve instructors.

"Get these men fed, Sergeant. I think they've earned it."

With that parting, both Carr and Drake walked to the stables, mounted their horses and walked them back along the road to Cheddon Fitzpaine. Drake was bursting to ask and finally he did.

"You think you know how to test them. So? What? How?"

Carr instead brushed his horses mane to one side of her neck.

"Where does Tavender live?"

Drake sat up with such a start that his horse stopped momentarily.

"What!"

Carr turned and looked at him calmly, speaking in the same tone.

"Where does Tavender live? He's here, so I understand, and I could use him and his Yeomanry. So, where does he live?"

"You are surely in jest! You go there and he's likely to challenge you, you arriving unannounced into his very own bailiwick! Are you sure it's so good an idea?"

Carr shrugged.

"Yes, what's the alternative? We need some cavalry. He's a cavalryman with contacts within the local

468

Yeomanry and so I am going to him to require him to help. I could make it an order. It is, will be, a military situation, that being the training of Militia replacements."

"You'll have to forewarn him. You can't just show up and start hammering on his front door."

Carr nodded.

"I know, and that will be done. I'll send him a letter outlining my requirements."

Drake was silenced, but Carr continued.

"So, where? Do you know?"

"Tapleigh Manor. Everyone knows it. Except you, I'd surmise."

"Right. We'll get a letter over there when we get back. Meanwhile, tomorrow afternoon, we get our Militia to fire ten rounds but form square part way through, in the middle of reloading."

The next morning saw Carr coming to the end of an unfamiliar road, which led only to Tapleigh Manor and he entered the gates, having been required to open one side himself. If Fynings Court was neat and well cared for, the garden, even the outer grounds, of Tapleigh Manor were wholly immaculate, as though each leaf and each blade of grass were carefully angled into a pre-ordained place. Gardeners, grooms and servants, all many in number, scurried around the house front or bent themselves assiduously to their duties. The house itself was tall and wide; brickwork scrubbed and perhaps over ornamental to some tastes, but the whole spoke of opulence and extravagance. It was a statement of wealth and influence. As Carr approached the wide, curving double staircase, a groom appeared and took his horse, leaving Carr to choose which set of steps to use. He chose the right, which led him to a wide, black lacquered double doors, which had the high points in the woodwork picked out in gold leaf. He lifted the heavy knocker and struck it twice against the gleaming brass plate. He did not have to wait for more than a count of ten, before an elaborately liveried Footman opened the door.

He said nothing, but did step back to allow Carr to enter, who did not trouble to look around after walking through, but his senses conveyed surroundings of yet more lavishness; statues, paintings, ornaments and tapestries. The Footman took Carr's cloak, whilst he walked to a polished table on which to place his gloves and shako. The Butler then bowed.

"If you'd care to wait, Sir, Captain Tavender is expecting you."

At this point, Carr did look around, but his thoughts were elsewhere; 'So, I am to wait in the hall! Somewhat less than gracious! Still, no matter. Within five minutes I should be gone.' A door opened and what came through it was not one man, but four! Tavender, followed by Brockenhurst, Slade and, worst of all, General Perry. Carr saw the need to adhere to rigid formalities and so he came to the attention and saluted. It was not returned and so Carr counted the regulation ten and then allowed his hand to drop to his side. He saw no reason to not come straight to the point, addressing himself to Tavender.

"Captain Tavender, good day to you. I hope that I am correct in assuming that you have received my request. I hope it can be done, so, what do you think?"

Tavender allowed a silence to hang, which created a contemptuous atmosphere, before replying.

"It could be difficult."

Carr looked directly at Tavender, ignoring the others.

"Difficult! How so?"

"Time and numbers."

Carr dropped his head to one side, quizzically.

"Regarding time, we have almost two weeks. Regarding numbers, I seem to recall that you had quite a Squadron, back in the year six, when we encountered you up in the hills. Have you now lost so many?"

"Yes. Gone out to Spain."

"Well, no matter. I need but a dozen or so. I could mount a dozen grooms and they would do some sort of job, but trained cavalrymen would give the thing that better edge. Surely you can find that number, amongst your existing Yeomanry Militia?"

"It could be difficult."

Carr was beginning to lose patience.

"Captain Tavender. I have made no investigation into the number on the Muster Roll of your Yeomanry, but I'm sure there would be more than a dozen. I carried home a letter from General Picton, requiring me to bring out to the army as many trained Militia as would take the Bounty. I would presume that you did also. The emphasis on trained! Whilst helping me train my men, you also train yours. I'm sure you would not wish your name to be included in my report as being unco-operative, or even oppositional?"

General Perry stepped forward, unable to hold himself back.

"Major Carr! Captain Tavender has given you your answer. Take it with you as you leave!"

However, Tavender now sighed, one of resignation, such as for dealing with something wholly tedious, but inevitable. He was returning to the Peninsula and such a judgement reaching Picton's ears, or even Stapleton-Cotton's could sit very ill with him.

"Oh very well, Carr. It would never do to disappoint your General Picton. You can have your men; I'll pull a few together for next Sunday. How will that suit?"

Carr bowed and began to walk to the table to retrieve his shako and gloves.

"That will do very well. I thank you. Now, if your man could fetch my cloak."

However, at this point, Brockenhurst and Perry stepped forward, the former in the lead.

"Major Carr. I read in the papers of your forthcoming wedding to the daughter of General Perry here."

471

Carr stopped halfway to the table and turned to face Brockenhurst as he continued.

"I'd postpone the arrangements, were I you."

Carr took two paces back towards him, his tone, expression and posture both annoyed and aggressive.

"For what reason?"

"A simple one. Her good Father, General Perry here, utterly opposes the match and I feel that he has the right of it."

Carr stared straight at him, ignoring General Perry.

"My Fiancée has her majority. What she decides to do with her life now rests entirely in her own hands."

Brockenhurst smiled indulgently, as if about to put wise an errant youngster.

"Well, it's this, Carr. You are aware that I am an MP and, in that capacity I can raise all kinds of questions in The House, certainly such as to throw doubt on the legality of your marriage, sufficient to put any possibility of the thing taking place beyond the date when you need to return to Spain."

He allowed the words to sink in and then continued, whilst Carr's face visibly darkened even further.

"The marriage can only take place, if at all, upon your next return, assuming you survive what is next to come in Spain."

Carr advanced forward to but a yard from Brockenhurst, who thought that he was about to be struck, but instead, fortuitously, Carr still had in his pocket the notes he had taken from the Militia ledgers. He took it out and unfolded it.

"Colonel! Your Sergeant of Militia keeps excellent books. And from his Ledgers I have discovered these numbers."

He lifted the paper to chest level and read from it.

"These are my calculations, Sir, bit of maths I'm afraid, but here goes. Each of your men is issued 10 cartridges each day, so, over two days each week, each fires

20 cartridges. With 145 men, that's about 3,000 a week. So, over the past six months, 26 weeks, they will have fired something like 80,000, keeping things simple."

Brockenhurst's face was beginning to show concern.

"Yet, Colonel, over those past six months you have requisitioned 200,000 cartridges. You assemble 145 men on the 52 days over the six months, making about 7540 man/days; I believe that to be the term. 200,000 is enough for each man to have fired almost thirty cartridges. Each day! On each day that you see them. That's more than each man used on the retreat to Coruna, including the battle!"

He allowed those words to sink in.

"Yet your men could not manage three reloads in a minute! And your men are only given ten each time they muster!"

Brockenhurst's face was turning ashen, something that even General Perry noticed, when he was able to take his eyes from the hated Carr, but this abhorred Major was now continuing, in a very light-hearted, but deeply threatening, tone.

"Not that this proves anything conclusive, Sir, but Horse Guards would want to take a look. If they were to be made aware."

His shifted his feet and folded his arms, to then relate a story, wholly fictitious, but conveying the threat very nicely. He spoke in the same jovial manner.

"You know, Sir, I seem to recall a case some while back of ill doings whereby someone in the Militia sold Government cartridges to a manufacturer of sporting gun cartridges. The gunpowder speaks for itself, but the lead balls were melted down and turned into birdshot. The chap was charged with treason, but he escaped the drop, he only got a prison stretch."

Brockenhurst swallowed hard.

"What would happen to him now, at this time, well, what with Wellington's army almost falling apart from starvation for want of carts, mules and supplies, I would guess that they would go through with the full thing. One cold dawn!"

By now Carr's cloak had arrived and he draped it over his arm, whilst the Butler retrieved his gloves and shako. The only sound was Carr's boots on the polished tiles as he turned to the Butler for his gloves and shako.

"Oh yes Sir, just one further thing. I assume that you sit on the local Parish Charity Board, or whatever they call it here, Pension Board or some such. Well, there are twelve wounded men at the barracks, wounded at Talavera. You saw four of them. I would urge you to consider them to be 'deserving poor' at least, or preferably pay them to help train your Militia. Them being fitted with wooden legs and whatnot, would not come amiss either."

Now with all three garments retrieved, he turned to Tavender.

"Well, good day to you, Lucius. So grateful for your help, see you and your Troop this Sunday."

With that he turned and left, his jaw now clenched with anger as he descended the stone steps to his waiting horse, cursing the name of Perry, Brockenhurst and all his associates over what they had just attempted.

The next Sunday dawned true November, intermittent, irritating drizzle falling from a leaden sky, as Carr and Drake awaited the arrival of Tavender and his men. Carr was down the hill out of sight of the Militia, these now assembled in a firing line. They arrived on time with Brockenhurst absent, but Slade was there, accompanying Tavender. There were about 40 Yeoman Troopers and Carr looked past the pair at the assembled men.

"Good turnout, Captain. I'm grateful."

The reply was a curt nod.

"Now, if you could take your men into that dip, out of sight, and then charge whenever you're ready, but let's have no injuries, please, amongst yours or mine. The French will do enough of that when they get out there."

Tavender briefly lifted his hand to his helmet and led his men off the track to the area indicated. Carr mounted his own horse and cantered to the formed line, two deep. At the end of the line he stopped and waited, but not for long. Over the rise came the Yeomanry, a single line, all yelling and waving their heavy cavalry sabres. The shock in the line of infantry was visible, but Carr was shouting.

"Cavalry! Form square!"

The pegs were still in place, but the attempt was a shambles, no line was formed before the Yeomanry were in amongst them, touching many with the flat of their sabres. A trumpet sounded and the horsemen pulled back, while Tavender trotted over to Carr and Drake, a grin of satisfaction on his face.

"Excuse me, Sir, but are these men trained?"

Carr grinned back.

"They are, yes, but first you have to convince them as to why. You have achieved that perfectly. I thank you."

He sat forward in the saddle.

"Now, if you could do it again. In just the same manner."

Tavender swung over his horse's head and led his men away so that soon they were back out of sight. Carr rode over to the now formed up Militia. He raised his voice, his tone stern.

"Now you see why speed matters. You would have been cut to pieces, your square broken and your comrades slaughtered."

He allowed the words to have their impact.

"You must expect cavalry at any time, from any direction and react to that order with lightning speed."

The exercise was repeated, but each time with a better result. The line was formed and the Yeomanry were met with a steady line of bayonets, with muskets at the present in the two ranks behind. The Militia even completed the formation when charged from the rear in the middle of firing drill. Carr and Drake were cock-a-hoop and showed it, not by speech, but by dismounting and saluting their men as Slade led them past for their Sunday street parade. Of Tavender they saw no more, he had led his men away quickly to become the head of the forthcoming parade. Carr gathered his men together, including Sergeant Jordan. All were in very good spirits.

"Well done men. We've all done a good job there."

He grinned at the small collection.

"Now. I'm getting married on the 22nd at Fynings Court Church near Cheddon Fitzpaine. You're all invited, of course. 3 o' clock."

He turned to Jordan.

"Is that bottle used up Sergeant?"

Jordan laughed.

"Yes, Sir."

"Draw two more, for yourself and your comrades here. At my expense."

oOo

The Church of the Fynings Estate lay deep, solid and snug in the slight hollow behind the great house. A sympathetic, but watery sun threw faint patterns of shadow on the light brown gravel of the path and also upon the mid grey of the careful stonework that was the Church. The main path ran from the house, but another took itself off at a different angle, to fall over the slight ridge and then under the wet grey slates of the lych-gate onto the road which marked the end of its run. The shadows were faint, but still, for no wind disturbed the unassailable authority of the ancient chestnut trees that arched, leafless, over all below. All traces of Autumn leaves and horse-chestnuts had been thoroughly removed, by the willing Gardeners. The narrow windows of the Church, reflecting pink from the sky above, remained unblinking, but kindly, awaiting the arrival of the bride to be. Inside, the cheer of the sun was replaced by every possible variety of green, gathered from the grounds and hedges of the Estate and beyond. At their place on the right transept stood Carr and Drake, the former too nervous to sit, the latter doing his best to boost the fragile confidence of his good friend.

"You'll be fine! Just do and say what the good Vicar tells you. You'll be fine."

Carr leaned slightly towards him.

"And not mispronounce the words, or get them in the wrong order, or trip over my sword, or worse still trip up Jane!"

"Now you're being silly! Get a grip and get the thing done. You'd think there was a column of French coming up the aisle."

"That would not concern me half so much."

He looked at Drake.

"You've got the ring?"

"No! I pawned it. Of course I've got the ring!"

Carr did not feel any better, so instead he turned for the tenth time to look back along the aisle. On his side were almost all soldiers from the Militia, on the Bride's side the family of Lady Constance, Cecily Drake and the staff from Fyning's Court. Together they made a good congregation for the small Church. Then Drake had a thought.

"What about your people? Shouldn't they be here?"

Carr took a deep breath as he turned to Drake to answer.

"Yes and no. They're too far North and I'm too much of a black sheep, what with fighting duels scandalously and then getting slammed in the news-sheets. I, we, will get back up there eventually. Seeing Jane will bring them round."

Carr then faced back to the Altar, for another worry had occurred.

"Does the organ work?"

Drake turned to him, now out of patience.

"Dammit, yes! Lady Constance keeps the thing tip top and it's just been given the once over, on her orders!"

He looked up to where the organ was placed, to the left of the Chancel.

"And that chap up there is a first-rate musician. He comes from Wells Cathedral, no less. A personal friend of her Ladyship."

"And what if Perry comes busting in at that point where the Vicar asks if anyone knows of any just impediment, or whatever it is?"

Drake grinned and straightened up.

"Oh, I don't think that's going to happen. You'll see why, when you finally get outside, you and your good Lady!"

Carr turned to Drake with an expression of utter bemusement, but it was at that point that the bucolic Vicar appeared from a side door in the chancel and came forward, beaming, to take his place at the top of the steps down to the transept. Then, the said organ gave a short wheeze and then started up with Bach's Prelude One in C. Carr heard the congregation rise to their feet, but it was Drake who eased himself around sufficiently to look back.

"She's coming down the Aisle."

"Oh Lord!"

"You should turn around and have a look! She'll be here soon."

And so Carr did, and what he saw captured his whole consciousness, for there came a vision from which he could not take his eyes until she came to stand beside him and the Vicar called him to order. Utterly removed from anything like full awareness of his surroundings as he was by the revelation stood beside him, nevertheless, some other, more stubborn, part of his character came to the fore and this carried him through the recitations. At the part where the Vicar asked 'Who brings this woman to this place to be wedded to this man' the booming voice of the Bishop of Bath and Wells gave the short but unequivocal answer.

"I do!"

It was he, unnoticed by Carr that had escorted her down the Aisle. There was some noise, of some sort during the giving of the vows, but the Ceremony was of the briefest and soon Henry Carr and Jane Perry were pronounced 'Man and Wife'. The progress back down the Aisle involved no accidents neither with sword nor uneven flagstone and soon they were out into the light, now somehow brighter than when they had gone in.

However, outside was something astonishing, this being forty Militia, twenty each side of the path to the house, forming an arch with their muskets and bayonets fixed. Sergeants Jordan and Nicholls headed the line with regulation Sergeant's halberds. At that point rice and paper petals came raining in and so the pair embarked onto the path and through the assembled Militia. Many spoke as they past through, simple words came to them, such as "Congratulations, Sir", "Long and happy life together", which moved Carr markedly. Once inside the house, drinks were served and Jane was whisked away by Lady Constance to meet the family who had come so far to see her married. Carr and Drake, stood together, suddenly found themselves approached by the Bishop of Bath of Wells, no less, and a Major of the 40th Foot. Both sprang to attention and saluted, as the Bishop made the introductions.

"Major Carr and Captain Drake, may I introduce Major Aykbourne of the 40th. He performed a little service for us, which turned out to be necessary, although I had hoped that it would not, but I do hope that nothing was heard inside, where you were?"

It was Carr who recovered first.

"Sir?"

"Yes. Our less than civil General Perry arrived, with Captain Tavender and some other Officer, demanding entrance, but your good Militia lads formed line and stood them off. All very legal and proper, them not being invited, and this being a civilian affair on private property in a family Church. They took their leave after being pronounced trespassers by Major Aykbourne here, this authority stemming from her Ladyship herself."

Carr was deeply moved and leaned forward, offering his hand, which the Major took.

"I can only offer my most sincere thanks, Major Aykbourne and hope that there will be no repercussions for you."

"No fear of that, not with Perry involved, doing the complaining! Mine were at Talavera, like yours, but up at the Pajar, off to your right. Part of Kemmis' Brigade in Campbell's Fourth. Both have but scant regard, if any at all, for our General Perry. Ours were reduced to absolute scarecrows because of his lack of competence. You'll find no sympathisers for General Perry in the Fourth Division, from top to bottom, be very assured."

Carr grinned.

"I can only thank you again, for preserving what is mine and my wife's most important day. You must now attend the Wedding Breakfast. I'll see that a place is set for you."

The Bishop leaned over, conspiratorially.

"Already done, Carr. Her Ladyship beat you to it!"

All laughed, as the gong sounded for all to take their places, and so Carr, Jane, the Bishop and Lady Constance greeted their guests before entering the dining hall. The meal was sumptuous and plentiful and the wine flowed. With all now consumed, the speeches began, first with the Bishop, who dwelt inevitably more on the charms of Jane than the virtues of Carr. That done, up rose Nathaniel Drake, very much looking forward to relating the severe embarrassments of Carr, as much as the Bishop had filled his words with anecdotes in favour of Jane. He had not spoken ten words, when a gasp came to him from the far end of the table. All looked to see Drake's wife, Cecily, with a look of utter consternation on her face.

"It's started! It's started!"

Then the pain of the first contraction arrived across her face. For a long moment, no one moved, but then Drake rushed to her side and Lady Constance rushed from the room. Jane followed Drake and Carr stood up.

"Ladies and Gentlemen! I rather think that another happy event is about to overtake this one! Please remain as our guests for as long as you choose and perhaps, who knows, you may be able to hear the happy news concerning this very imminent birth!"

By now, Cecily had been whisked away with Jane in close attendance and Carr followed Drake to the foot of the staircase where both were bid to remain by Lady Constance's maidservant. The local midwife arrived, she being the object of Lady Constance's hurried exit and from then on a very worried and frazzled Drake sat beside Carr on the lower step. Now it was Carr's turn to steady nerves, but all attempts fell on deaf ears. Drake was now an agitated bundle of worries and fears for the worse. They sat there, all through the evening and well into the night, even the small hours, until they heard the doubly welcome cry of an infant. Drake looked at Carr, still worried.

"And Cecily?"

However, at that moment the midwife came down the stairs, looking directly at Drake.

"Up you go, Sir. You have a fine baby girl. Both are doing well"

Drake rose so fast that Carr's attempt to place a congratulatory slap on his shoulder missed entirely, but this was soon forgotten as Jane emerged from the birthing room and held out her hand for them both to finally retire for their much delayed wedding-night.

There was little sleep for any in the household, bar a short catnap through the growing dawn and it was bleary-eyed guests who sat for an early lunch that doubled as breakfast. It was Carr alone, him being accustomed to little sleep, who met the Militia for the evening's training, but he left most of the affair to his instructors, bar informing the men why using half-Company volleys were so important. Come the close of the session, the orders to fire could be left to the three young teenage Officers, which they thoroughly enjoyed.

The following days revolved very much around the infant, especially for Drake. However, Carr and Jane spent all possible time in each other's company. It mattered little what they did, either walking the local lanes or merely talking whilst sat by the fire. All that mattered was that they were within touching distance, each to the other. During the evening, the four, with the baby asleep, took great pleasure in singing around the piano, Cecily played very well and all could hold their place in most choirs, but Carr had only eyes for his dearest Jane.

The leave of both was drawing to a close and only two major events now remained, these being who amongst the Militia would take the Bounty and the Christening of the baby. One afternoon Drake, Cecily and the baby found Carr dozing by the fire, whilst Jane read a book, some embroidery by her side. It was Cecily who spoke.

"I have a request for you both."

Carr opened one eye and Jane lowered her book.

"We want you both to be Godparents."

Jane spoke up immediately.

"We accept!"

Carr looked over at her, but she was continuing.

"Have you decided on the names?"

"Yes. Henrietta Jane Cecily Drake."

The significance of the first was not lost on Carr, who needed to clench his jaw and swallow hard. He managed to choke out one word.

"When?"

"27th The day before you both leave."

"On the 26th we find out who's coming back out with us."

Drake nodded.

"Correct. That also will be an important day."

The day did come, all too quickly, and Carr felt the need to stand before his men on the parade ground and speak a few words. Once again Brockenhurst was absent, but Slade was in the background and remained there. Carr had the men assemble into four ranks, as for a square, and he stood before them.

"Men. You are as trained and capable a Company of soldiers as ever I have seen. I have no hesitation in saying that I would have no qualms at all about commanding you in battle. In fact I would be proud to do so. This is the last time we will see you here, for in two days time Captain Drake and myself will return to Spain. We would like to take you all, but this is now your decision. To make your choice, you are now dismissed and you should go into the barracks and tell Sergeant Jordan of your decision, yes or no. He has the coin, there and then to give you the Bounty, should you do, what I hope you will do, and come out with Captain Drake and myself to meet and defeat your country's enemies."

He allowed the words to hang.

"Thank you and dismiss!"

However, this was not to happen immediately. One of the 'squeaker' Lieutenants, the eldest Ben Quayle stepped forward.

"Men. Three cheers for Major Carr and Captain Drake!"

The cheers rang out and both Carr and Drake lifted their hats in acknowledgment, but, significantly, at the second loud huzza Major Slade turned his horse and left. Now Carr and Drake could only stand and wait. As the men emerged from the arch, having spoken their decision, many spoke both thanks and good wishes to them both. Ben Quayle marched up and spoke, grinning from ear to ear.

"I'm coming with you, Sir, and Joe Underwood."

Carr leaned forward and shook his hand.

"Proud to have you both. Thank you."

Finally the last of the Militia emerged and began their journey home, followed by Sergeant Jordan, who could be seen grinning even in the gathering gloom.

"122 Sir. And two Lieutenants. On top, Corporal Mat Green, as lost an eye, will sign up again, if you're willin', Sir. Says he still has the right, as can still sight along a barrel, Sir."

Carr laughed.

"Tell him any man who stood at Coruna and Talavera will do for me, with one eye or two!"

"I'll add him on then, Sir, so that's 125. Officers and men."

As they returned home, Drake leaned over conspiratorially.

"That's made an awful dent in Brockenhurst's Sunday parade!"

Carr grinned and nodded, but with little mirth.

"Time for home."

The day for the Christening arrived and was to take place in the same family Church as the wedding, the first for decades and therefore much effort was lavished on the ancient font, the wooden lid, the copper and the stonework. The Reverend Pendlebury again officiated and Henrietta howled her indignation as Jane passed her over to the good Vicar and he gently palmed the water onto her infuriated brow.

That night, their last night together, Jane came and stood before Carr, her husband, and looked up at him.

"Do you still have the medallion I gave you before you left for Scilly?"

Carr looked puzzled.

"Yes. I still wear it. You know I do."

She brought her hands from behind her back.

"This is something else. I want you to keep this."

She raised up to his face a small miniature in a silver frame.

"It's me!"

Carr took it and studied it carefully as Jane looked at him.

"I think it flatters me!"

Carr shook his head.

"It does you no justice."

He transferred his fond gaze to her face.

"You could come out with me, you know. I don't want you to, but you could."

She shook her head.

"No, it's best. From what you say, it's just too awful out there. I'd have to stay back in Lisbon anyway and I'd see little more of you there than I see of you now. At least there will be a very good reason for you to come home more often, if I stay here."

Carr nodded.

"One less thing to worry about. No-where is safe, not really. Spain is full of French. One day we could be penned in around Lisbon. Under siege! That would drive me frantic!"

Suddenly something broke within her and she flew into his arms.

"Come back to me!"

He buried his face in her hair.

"It'll take a lot to stop me, neither any sea nor any army. I'll be back. There are just too many reasons why I should."

The following day began with a sombre breakfast then, during the short hours before their departure neither couple; Carr and Jane, nor Drake, Cecily and their baby daughter, were much more than arm's length from each other. Finally came the hour and each Officer carried their baggage to their horse, each standing saddled at the front of the house. Little was said and little was done, beyond a fierce but brief embrace. Tears were held back as Carr and Drake mounted, lifted a last hand in farewell and then left. The ride into Taunton was conducted in silence, each man with his own thoughts, but they were both concerned with

485

the same topics, of loved ones left behind and the sights now around them, of their own country, damp, barren and bleak in late November, but, nevertheless, all the sights of that month carrying the deepest poignancy. They wasted no time, but rode to the head of the column of Militia. Mat Green, of one eye, now made up to Sergeant and with a neat patch over his left eye, yelled the orders, at which signal the fifes and drums stuck up 'Brighton Camp'. The whole then took the road South, through a long avenue of waving handkerchiefs and tearful faces.

oOo

"Is this Christmas Day?"

In response to both the question and to a sharp nudge in his ribs, Byford opened one eye.

"Yes. Or near."

Zeke Saunders drew the horse blanket closer up to his chin.

"Well, I've had one in better places, warmer and a damn sight more easy on the bones."

"Ah, but not one with a better view!"

Saunders dismissed the comment with a guffaw.

"What better view can there be on Christmas Day than a good fire and a table well set?"

Byford chuckled.

"None. I agree."

Saunders looked at his good friend.

"What's the name of this place we'n marchin' to? The next to come."

Byford pronounced the name carefully.

"Theee ooo dad Rodrigoh."

Saunders adjusted his blanket.

"I'll settle for Roger's Town!"

At this point Miles rolled over, next to them.

"Can't you two shut up! They'll have us marchin' again within the hour."

They were all in a long line, the men and Followers of the Messes of Jed Deakin and John Davey, all on a road that was carried by what was no more than a perilous shelf etched into the side of one the mountains of the Sierra De Gata. It was this high point that provided the view, on what was still a clear, although dying day. The temperature was far into freezing, but, on this day, mercifully there was no wind. They were not resting off the road but on it, because there was no space to the side, yet nevertheless they were making good use of the cliff overhang above. In addition, they were also making good use of what had been provided to enable them to make the march, within even the hours of darkness, from Badajoz to the Northern town of Coimbra. All had new greatcoats, boots and trousers and the more astute and veteran, such as these, had obtained thick horse-blankets. Thus they all lay, buried in blankets, of a variety of colours, with a variety of Regimental numbers displayed in the corners.

Supplies were also plentiful, this now evidenced by the arrival of a mule train, with the food for the next four days, although there was little chance of anything perishable going rotten with the temperatures as they were. With this arrival to their particular part of the plateau, came Sergeant Ellis and, as Bridie and Nellie took their rations, Ellis kicked the line of boots to rouse his Company.

"Eat! Then we'n marchin'. 'Twill be into the night. That's orders, to get us out these Godforsaken mountains!"

Within the hour the food had been cooked and, as the men prepared to don their packs and weapons, Ellis fished into his pocket and looked for Davey. He had stayed there to eat, but he wanted nothing to distract anyone from preparing for the march, but now the time had come.

"John. Letter's arrived. Come up with the mules."

He placed the letter in the fingerless-gloved hand of John Davey and moved on, leaving Davey to examine the cover in the fading light. He now turned to Bridie.

"Bridie. Can we get that lantern goin'? Here's a letter. Looks like from Tilly."

At the sound of the momentous name, all preparations ceased everywhere and hands stretched out for their single lantern. A cartridge was broken open and the candle lit in the priming pan of Joe Pike's rifle. By now the letter was in the hands of the 'Mess Reader', this being Byford, and the letter was out and opened well before the yellow light of the lantern fell on it. Byford cleared his throat.

"Dear John and Joe. We are all well and healthy here and hope that you are as well. Molly and Mary have both given birth, Molly had a girl and Mary had a boy. They were only a day from each other and so we call them the twins."

At this point Byford had to stop, all now being drowned out by shouting, cheering and congratulations, Joe Pike subsiding under a welter of back slapping and being jumped upon. Hearing all the joyful commotion, Cyrus Gibney and Captain Heaviside wandered over and when all had subsided, Byford continued.

"Molly has called your new daughter Rachel, this being a good Bible name and Mary has called your new son Thomas, because she quite liked Tom Miles, he always talked good sense and was helpful and sensible."

However, all were looking aghast at Tom Miles who was wearing a very self-satisfied smirk on his weatherbeaten face, but John Davey simply exclaimed one word as he stared hard at the grinning Miles.

"Thomas!"

As the laughter died down, at this point came a quote from Captain Heaviside.

"Let your light shine before others, so that they may see your good works. Matthew 5. Verse 16."

With this now replied to in standard fashion by Jed Deakin, Byford continued.

"Both children are bonny and healthy and will be baptized next week. The Reverend Blackmore said he would do it for free as you are both away fighting the Godless French who killed their own King. The farm is doing well and we have rented some more land. The eggs and chickens are the best for bringing in coin, but we have bought some more cows and the milk is steady coin as well. We sell all in Devizes. Your Mother, John, thinks that we will soon have to spend some money making the cottage bigger, now that the twins are here. We have already made it better, putting in a wooden floor, a good door and a kitchen range which makes all warmer and dry as well. We have all been saying what we would like to happen, but I think two more rooms, one up and one down.

I go to school most days, paid for by the Reverend, and I am learning about all kinds of things, too many to tell you, but my teachers are pleased with me. Give my best wishes to Parson Sedgwicke. I know that it was him that started me with my learning and I am very grateful.

All our love to you both, very much. We miss you terribly and cannot wait for this horrid war to end and to have you back with us. Keep yourselves safe.

Tilly."

Byford, his own voice shaking over the final sentences, lowered the letter in total silence. Many were fighting back tears and others wiped them away, especially Bridie and Nellie. It was left to Heaviside to have the last word before they all formed up to march once more on the frozen road.

"Beloved, we are God's children now, and what we will be has not yet appeared. One John. 3. Verse 2."

oOo

Chapter Nine

The Hills of Busaco

Henry Carr turned once more at the now very familiar corner to undertake yet again the 152 steps down the very familiar street along which he could remember every building as it came. He was just returning from yet another routine inspection of the pickets mounted by the 105th around their sector of the Battalion perimeter, there to protect the small Portuguese town of Trancoso. This was a town they had occupied for so long now, that he could greet by name almost every Portuguese whose regular business it was, to frequent the dry, rutted highway which served as their main street. After reaching the familiar butchers shop, with its grubby sign 'Talhos' above and its habitual trickle of blood managing no more than twelve inches across the hot, parched earth, Carr turned into the welcome shade of their billet, shared, as was habitual, with Nat Drake, and Lieutenants Richard Shakeshaft and Stuart Maltby. He found all three lounging in the downstairs room, a bucket of fresh water on the table, the bucket still wet showing evidence of its trip down the nearby well. Beakers were arranged all around, these also wet, giving evidence of their recent use. Greatly relieved to be inside and duty done, Carr removed his tunic and loosened the cord tie at the top of his shirt.

"God, it's hot!"

On hearing that, Drake pushed across the bucket and a beaker, the latter being eagerly picked up by Carr.

"Any of that wine still going, to give this a bit of a lift?"

A bottle of local white wine appeared around the paper that Richard Shakeshaft was reading and Carr tipped in a measure before filling the beaker to the brim. He took three swallows and then looked at Drake, who was idly looking at nothing.

"What's going round today's rumour mill?"

Drake sat up. At last something to do, if only to converse.

"Us specifically, or the army in general?"

"I'll start with us."

"We're going to attempt another play. Sheridan's 'A Trip to Scarborough' and I've volunteered you for something."

Carr hurried his beaker to the table, the sound waking up Stuart Maltby and some of the mixture slopping onto the wood of the table with the impact.

"Oh God, no. I can't stand it! We've already done 'School for Scandal'. No more, please no more!"

Shakespeare moved his paper to one side.

"Don't you complain! We had to The Rivals whilst you were away!"

The paper moved again to reveal Shakeshaft with an accusing expression.

"And that was before we had to slog our way over the Sierra de Gata, at the summit of which we spent Christmas!"

Carr had every sympathy. They had returned from England to find that Wellington had moved his army North, to defend the 'Northern corridor', this containing Cuidad Rodrigo and Viseu, the latter having the army now concentrated around it, including Mackinnon's Brigade, which the 105th were now part of. He rotated his beaker in the spilt mixture of wine and water. Frustration and boredom was as enervating within him as with anyone.

"Seven months! I marched our new recruits to here last January and here we are, late July. We've practised everything until our boots wore out. The men can move blindfold from closed column to line to defensive square."

He looked at Drake.

"And you must've nearly worn out those new Bakers from exercise in the hills!"

"You exaggerate, but that brings me to the general. Cuidad Rodrigo has surrendered!"

Carr was no longer lounging.

"Just over the border? Crauford's up there with his Lights, at Almeida, just on our side."

Drake nodded.

"Massena and Ney are now on the border."

Carr perked up further.

"May they hurry and cross, if it gets us out of this place."

"Be careful what you wish for. Rumour has it, that he has over 60,000 men, pushing onto 70. Boney made peace with the Austrians late last year and so he's given Massena a sizeable force to come down here and sort us out. Once and for all!"

Silence dwelt for a few moments as those facts were digested, then Carr replied.

"And just over 50,000 is all we can manage. If, and a very big if, you count in the Portuguese."

Drake nodded.

"A very big if. Beresford's been training them up, but what they'll be like in a set-piece, God only knows."

"Anything else to speak of?"

"Not much, other than there's now some different guerrilla chap, one Julian Sanchez, operating up and around here. Mostly over the border, him being Spanish. Bit of a 'cut above', by all accounts."

Carr lifted his head, as if to aid his memory.

"You know he came through our picket line last month. With a crew of vicious looking cut-throats, all mounted on French horses. He showed me a letter from Wellington requesting any British Commander reading the note to supply arms and food and whatnot. I sent him on down to Picton's Headquarters. He must have gone out a different way, because I never saw him again."

He lowered his head.

"And he's on our side! Glad to hear that. The man was an evil scowl sat on top of a malignant block covered in sheepskin."

"Well, there you are! Because, as I understand it, what I've just told you came from him! He's our eyes and ears out there, watching all and reporting it to Wellington."

At that moment, Maltby rose from his chair.

"Must go. Time for school."

Carr's head rose again.

"You mean that thing that Lacey ordered? To keep us all from dying of boredom."

Maltby looked squarely at him, although two ranks his junior.

"Yes. For all our youngsters, Drummerboys and whatnot, and a few more besides. Four buildings down the way, the big building with 'Escola' on the top. Bit of a giveaway really. That's Portuguese for School."

"How long has this been going on?"

"Since late May."

Drake joined in.

"Yes. Since then, but you've been too busy being important. They've started a school for our youngsters."

"They?"

"Yes. Him and Eirin Mulcahy."

A huge grin spread across Carr's face.

"And the very comely Eirin Mulcahy! Well, of course, there's nothing in that, is there, to be speculated upon."

Maltby turned, now very indignant, as he reached the door.

"She was taught to read when we were in Spain last. By Chaplain Prudoe's wife and that Sedgwicke assistant of his. She is very useful and can read quite well."

His sole reply was from long, knowing stares from his three companions, and so he left, indignation undiminished.

Events over the next few hours rapidly created the need for fast horses. The first, to carry one of Sanchez' guerrillas to deliver the message to Wellington that Massena was gathering his men around Cuidad Rodrigo, having recently taken it and the second to deliver a message from Wellington to Picton that he was to move up to Pinhel and support Crauford. The minor message reached Maltby in his schoolhouse, carried by Richard Shakeshaft.

"Sorry Stuart. School's out. We're moving up, in two hours."

Within that time, Picton's whole Division was marching East, Lightburn's in the lead, followed by Mackinnon's and then Champlemonde's Portuguese. Deep within the column, in the centre of Mackinnon's marched the 105th, Chosen Man Davey in an outer rank, marching besides Sergeant Ellis, him marching beside the column.

"What do you know, Ethan?"

"Not much, apart from the common that most knows. The French are up on the border, tens of thousands and they've took Roger's Town. I do know that 'tis only Crauford's as is in their way, so we're on our way up to support. Forced march I'd say. Sleep when we gets there."

Davey looked at him.

"Just ours and Crauford's, now in the way of a whole French invasion!"

Ellis nodded.

"If you can't take a joke you shouldn't have joined."

Davey raised his voice.

"I didn't join! King's Hard Bargain, me!"

"Then you should've let they pheasants run off alive!"

"Bloody useful source of comfort you are."

Ellis chuckled as they hurried on, but it was a good road, mostly gentle hills and yet it was full dark as they entered a dormant Pinhel to be directed into some fields by a member of Picton's Staff. All quickly took off their equipment, rolled themselves into their blankets and slept the few hours until full daylight. After a mid-morning meal, they were re-assembled on the road, where they were required to stand for almost an hour, when they heard the sound of cannon-fire in the far distance. Lacey sat his horse, beside O'Hare.

"How far would you say?"

O'Hare listened to the continuous rumble for a few seconds before answering.

"Eight, nine, miles."

"Then that must be Crauford at Almeida, getting pushed back over the River Coa. Obviously, he can't hold onto the Almeida side. We will either cross to support or he'll be ordered back."

"Cover a retreat more probable! Crauford's will be in no shape to add his to ours, and we'll be one Division against a whole army."

They sat for a further half hour listening to the sound of the combat rising and falling as the wind and heat thermals dictated. Finally, Mackinnon came riding back from his 74th. Over the previous months of idleness, the three had gotten to know each other very well.

"Lacey. O'Hare. We're pulling back and not going up to reinforce. Picton's gone up to the bridge, seen Crauford, but refused to move us up to reinforce. Damn poor, I think, but then it was damn stupid for Crauford to keep his whole Division on the French side of the Coa, with just one narrow bridge to retreat over, so on that score I have some sympathy with Picton. He's leaving Lightburn to shepherd what's left of Crauford's, if and when they get back over, but we're back to Trancoso. I'm on to tell Wallace."

He had barely halted his horse as he passed on the order to the pair, then for him to ride further back to tell the Colonel of the 88th Connaught Rangers. All along the column could be heard the order, 'About turn', and then all began to retrace their steps of the previous day. It was left to Drake to pass comment, marching besides Shakespeare.

"Oh well, it was a pleasant stroll. A quick polonaise to the next village and then a leisurely waltz back!"

However, whilst the 105th settled back into more days of active boredom, this being training and inspections, over the border in Spain hostilities were intensifying, with none more responsible for this than the guerrilla leader Julian Sanchez. Riding at the head of one of his columns at the beginning of yet another August day on the border he had little idea what the day would bring, but it would contain something, either intelligence of French movements, or a chance to ambush a foraging party, or to surprise a French force with a hit and run. His men, 200 strong, were all now adopting a grey/blue uniform, provided by the British, and they had now begun to call themselves the 'Lancers of Castile'. Sanchez, named by his men as 'El Charro', meaning simply 'cavalryman' to any bemused Englishman taking the trouble to translate, had built a formidable force and there were two other similar columns which named him as their 'Comandante' also out roaming the countryside of the Spanish/Portuguese border around Almeida and Pinhel. A fourth was now escorting a mule train over the highest and safest hills carrying muskets and ammunition supplied by the British. Sanchez had higher ambitions than to be the leader of only mounted Guerrillas, he had hopes for his newly formed armed Ordenanza; Militia infantry, would be the basis of a Spanish force that could do more than attack for merely minutes before riding away. These would assault a French outpost for perhaps longer than a day, before melting away into the hills, when French reinforcements approached. He had both plans and ambitions.

That day brought no contact, at least none that Sanchez would risk, but that evening he did pen a despatch to Wellington informing him that the French were massing over the Coa. It would not be long before they moved, with

496

Viseu or even Coimbra as their objective. In this way, up to the end of August he maintained his patrols, harassing and gaining information, whilst tensions built in Wellington's force, not 20 miles away. His Ordenanza were now becoming the best of Light Infantry, trained by the British and able to march at speed and skirmish with any French force, before melting away into the hills, outrunning any French infantry and being careful to avoid French cavalry. They could use Sanchez' 'Lancers of Castile' as a source of information to ensure that none ever came too close. August became September as Massena's army assembled and built up its strength, but what also built was their fear of Sanchez and his men. El Charro' was becoming a legend across the Province of Salamanca.

On the 5th September, two men had their fears confirmed. One was Sergent de Cheval Marcel Lemar, now busy covering himself with the blood smeared body of a comrade, whilst the mounted guerrillas drove off the remaining escort of a convoy of corn brought up with great difficulty over the mountain roads from Plascencia. The other was Colonel Pavetti, stood in consternation in the village square of Nava d'Avel amongst his five Gendarmes escort. Pouring out from every side street and front door came fully armed Ordenanza and so the six Frenchmen had little choice but to stand with their hands high in the air, there to rue Pavatti's decision to ride into the village and enquire directions. Now, several of these evil brigands were advancing on them, each drawing a wickedly pointed and curved knife, such that for Pavatti death was plainly imminent and so he took the only chance he had of saving his life. He took the despatch satchel from his shoulder and waved it in the air.

"Importantes dépêches. Prenez-moi à les Anglais!"

The knives were not used, not on any of them, but one man, certainly their Commander, from the edge of the square, shouted to the knife-carriers.

"Llevarlo a mí."

497

The two nearest seized Pavatti and hauled him in the direction of the Commander, one roughly snatching the satchel from Pavatti's grasp. The Commander took the satchel, opened it to look inside and then uttered a grunt of satisfaction. All six Frenchmen were then stripped of their equipment and then, at bayonet point, forced out of the village and up into the hills, leaving six Gendarme shakoes rolling in the dust.

Two days later Sanchez, at the head of one of his columns, rode into the same Nava d'Avel to find it raised to the ground, every building a smoking ruin, but worst were two mutilated and abused figures hanging from ropes suspended from the nearest tree. His men immediately dismounted to cut them down, whilst Sanchez went to the tree trunk, because pinned to it was a notice, hand written, in large words in Spanish. It said simply that all Ordenanza were to be treated as brigands and rebels and would be executed. By the orders of Marshal Massena. Sanchez carried the notice to the centre of the square and read it out to his men. He had to shout the final sentence; such was the anger the first had aroused. They buried the two men in the Churchyard and then rode on to complete their day's mission. However, over the following days, Sanchez force grew as many more local Spanish and Portuguese came to join, carrying tales of French killings and brutality, meted out to anyone who resisted, no matter how minor. Sanchez now issued his own order; 'Ningún preso!'. Certain death now awaited any Frenchman unfortunate enough to fall into their hands.

It was the exact middle of September when Carr got his particular wish, orders came to move back to the town of Alva, fifteen miles North of Viseu. The French threat was now too great. Most were pleased to leave, bar many of the Followers, which included Bridie Deakin, who looked around as Jed Deakin and the others strapped their equipment onto their packs.

"Ah now, Jed, isn't this a cryin' shame to be leavin' such a place! Haven't we now got this hut fixed up just fine, and now we've got to move on. 'Tis the Lord's pity, so it is!"

Jed had little patience for such complaints.

"Never mind all that wailin' and moanin', get ours packed up and ready to carry. French cavalry could be in here in two hours and they'd just love a portion of the rations we gets sent up these days and then amuse theirselves in God only knows what terrible way. Get yourself and the youngers ready to go. I'd not be surprised if there were orders to fire this place along with all the food that we can't carry or the locals can't take into the hills. Any food we can't take is to be destroyed."

Bridie said no more but hurried to do his bidding and within the hour they were marching down Trancoso High Street to see it no more.

oOo

Whilst the 105th were executing their orders to retreat, the 16th Light Dragoons were executing theirs to move forward, with Tavender and Templemere riding side by side as usual and, as usual, the less experienced enquired of the more so, concerning what they were about to do. The latter gave a brief reply.

"Scouting is what we're about! No combat, that's to be avoided. Find the Johnnies and then ride away!"

Templemere was much relieved.

"Hooray for a good horse!"

However, Tavender was in a teasing mood.

"Unless, of course, they get in behind us. Perfectly possible in these hills, in which case we'd have to cut our way out."

Templemere was suddenly much more apprehensive.

"So, where are we going?"

"Town of Guarda. Nice little place, so I've heard."

499

"How close to the Coa?"

"Oh, 20 miles to the West, give or take."

They rode on, using the good road that led East from Viseu, and, with the Westering sun now throwing their shadows fully before them, they at last came to Guarda. All the way there, coming in the opposite direction, had been displaced Spanish, their column a mixture of refugees, carts and mules, all heavily laden with food and provisions. By Wellington's orders, Massena's route to Westwards from the Coa was to be stripped bare of any sustenance that could support his substantial army. When the 16th reached Guarda, they found it practically deserted, with even those that still remained now preparing to leave, loading carts and animals with their own stores of food. Their last optimism that they would be untroubled by the French, was now thoroughly evaporated. What had finally brought on their decision was the presence of a column of Chavez' Lancers, now occupying many of the buildings and making themselves warm and comfortable. Templemere looked around with distaste at the groups of guerrillas, all grouped around fires, eating, singing and generally in the best of moods.

"Are these brigands the best the Spanish have got?"

Tavender had formed a higher, more professional, opinion of what he saw and felt inclined to put Templemere right.

"I'd back them in a fight. And one of them saved your bacon back at Grijon. Remember?"

There was no time for Templemere to argue, before their Colonel Withers rode up.

"Templemere. Get half a dozen men. I want a picket a mile forward. You'll be in the dark, so keep your ears open. On the other hand, you may be lucky, last night there was a decent moon. You could find anything riding at you; Spanish regular, Chavez Spanish or French Light."

Now with some sympathy, Tavender looked at the worried Templemere.

"You'll need a good Sergeant. I'll pick him and your men."

Half an hour later Templemere was sat his horse, within a copse of fir trees, peering forward into the growing gloom, sat debating within himself whether to send a man forward to form a picket for his picket. His 'good' Sergeant was mounted beside him, staring forward equally intently. Finally, Templemere began to make his decisions.

"Where are the men?"

"100 yards back, Sir. Where we left them."

"I've a mind to hold here."

"Makes sense, Sir. We've a good view forward, but what matters is open ground, so's we can hear, when it gets full dark. The sound'll carry better over open ground, cavalry can't help making a lot of noise, Sir."

Templemere was grateful. That was something that he had not thought of, but he was not going to admit it.

"What about infantry, Sergeant?"

"They make noise, too, Sir. But not as much, and they'll still be way back, Sir. It's cavalry we can expect."

Templemere felt that too much of his ignorance was on display and so he made up his mind.

"Right, we'll both go back to the others, then you bring one man back to here. I'll get you both relieved in two hours."

The Sergeant was now confused.

"Perhaps you should send a man up yourself, Sir, beggin' your pardon, so that I can stay here, to keep the watch."

Templemere had to agree.

"Very good. Keep looking."

The Sergeant sighed, it was ears that mattered now, but at least their arrangements were settled. Templemere rode back and arbitrarily pointed to a Trooper sat by their fire.

"You. Up to join Sergeant Baxter. You'll be relieved in two hours."

He pointed to two more, again arbitrarily.

"Relieved by you after two hours. Any problems, I'll be over here."

He walked to his horse, unbuckled his blanket and sat, miserable, annoyed and alone. Tavender was no-where to be seen, probably snug in some fully furnished, abandoned house. He was not going to sit with the men, even though they had the fire. He dozed, but for how long he had no idea, when he was awoken by a hand on his shoulder. It was the first Trooper sent up to Sergeant Baxter by him less than two hours ago.

"Sir. You'd better come forward. Sergeant Baxter thinks he can hear something."

Templemere allowed his blanket to drop onto the ground as he mounted his horse and then walked him forward the 100 yards to the pine trees.

"What Sergeant?"

"I swear I can hear something, Sir, not too far off."

Templemere listened himself, but could hear nothing of significance.

"I think you may be somewhat overwrought, Sergeant."

Baxter took no notice of the insult, but continued to concentrate.

"There Sir! There's something."

Templemere became irritated, but he knew he had to ask the right question.

"So, what, and how many?"

"Cavalry, Sir. Full squadron, I'd say."

Templemere was now in a quandary. And fearful! He now listened intently himself and discovered that he could faintly hear something that sounded like large pebbles rolling around in large waves, but far distant.

"Right. We ride back to Guarda and tell the Colonel."

Baxter turned towards him.

"Sir! We have to find out who they are! That's our job. We cannot just ride back and say there's a bunch of horsemen coming down the road!"

Templemere was now annoyed.

"And your suggestion, Sergeant, is what?"

The reply was instant.

"Get the men up, Sir, and mounted. Send one back to alert the Colonel. The rest of us challenge this lot and if they're Frogs we ride like Hell out of here. But we have to find out, Sir."

Templemere hesitated, but Baxter was right. He turned to the spare Trooper.

"Get the men up and ready to ride. Send one back to Guarda with the message that cavalry are approaching. Then come back up here to me."

However, Baxter had something to add on.

"And we are trying to find out who!"

The Trooper wheeled his horse and rode back, leaving Baxter and Templemere to listen to the now much more distinct sound of pebbles in the surf. Soon shapes could be seen on the road ahead, but Baxter was not going to wait for any orders. He filled his lungs.

"Halt! Who goes there?"

The sound of hooves on the hard dirt road rapidly fell away, then the reply came back.

"Lancers Castellana! ¿Es usted inglés?"

Templemere was puzzled.

"Who are they?"

"Sanchez' men, Sir. It's what they call themselves. I think they're asking if we're English."

Templemere was much relieved.

"Right! So that's alright, then."

"No Sir. Careful Sir. The Frogs tries that trick, callin' theirselves Spanish. They tried it at Talavera, so I've heard."

Baxter's picket companion returned.

"All done, Sir."

Templemere ignored him, whilst thinking furiously; he was after all the Officer in command, then blessedly an idea arrived. He reasoned that the Spanish language that was required here, really could not be that different from the English and he did know some words of Spanish.

"Uno Officer. Advance."

It was good enough. A lone rider came forward and, whilst little could be seen of his uniform, he spoke sufficient English, even though mixed in with the most obvious of Spanish.

"Buenos noches, Inglese! Uno compania Lancers Castellana. We come de Pinhel."

Templemere was growing in confidence.

"What news?"

The reply came out of the dark, but plainly his command of English was not that good.

"Lo siento, Señor, pero no entiendo. We see the soldados franceses come to here."

This was vital and Templemere knew it.

"When?"

Baxter shouted, "Cuando?" and the accurate reply came back.

"Tres horas. Muchos los soldados franceses."

"Caballeria?"

"No Senor. La infantería"

"I'd say they were alright, Sir. We'd better get that back to the Colonel."

"Agreed. I'll go."

With that Templemere wheeled his horse and spurred it away, leaving Baxter with the Spanish Officer. However, it was the latter who broke the silence of the full dark.

"Venga adelante, si?"

Baxter did not fully understand, but 'yes' seemed appropriate. After three minutes the Spanish column was riding through, with Pearce now in command of the picket and he turned to his companion.

"Harry! Get on back and send up our relief, both, then stand the lads down as've been woke up and get some sleep yourself. I'll stay. I don't like this, but I feels better with Lord Huff-n-Puff now out of the way."

The Trooper smiled in the dark at the use of their nickname for Templemere. Baxter had reasoned that any French infantry would wait for dawn before advancing on a town and he was correct. With the dawn came a French mounted infantry Officer with an infantry column in view, but far back and so, at the sight of both, Baxter retreated back with his two companions to gather the entire picket and ride the mile back to Guarda. Within 15 minutes Guarda was abandoned; the 16th Light Dragoons riding West for the River Mondego, and two columns Spanish 'Lancers de Castilla', taking sidetracks to go up into the hills.

At the same time, Picton's Division were on a leisurely march on the grand trunk to Coimbra, the 105th led by three horsemen; Lacey, O'Hare and their Brigade Commander Henry Mackinnon. It was the latter who dominated the conversation, him considering it to be his duty to keep his Senior Officers informed of the movements of both armies, at least to the extent that he had been made aware.

"This is what I've got from Picton. Wellington's ordered his whole army to retreat, not just pulling back but also pulling in. He wanted to offer battle at a place called Ponte de Murcella but Massena's having none of it. He's over the Mondego and going for Viseu, then perhaps Oporto, hoping to draw us up North and out of the hills. We've no chance of getting across his path, but Wellington knows that Massena daren't leave us in his rear, if it is Oporto he's moving on."

He pulled out a spirit flask, took a drink from it, then offered in round, before continuing.

"So, he's banking on drawing Massena down, him hoping to knock us out and push us back, back down South. On the other hand, Massena may want Coimbra and that's what Wellington believes, so in that case, with Massena now on the North bank of the Mondego, Ponte de Murcella won't serve, he's already around it. So I've heard talk of a ridge called Busaco, about ten miles North-West back from Ponte de Murcella, running up from a place called Penacova. Wellington's ordered all Divisions up to there."

Such a dialogue of high strategy was of no immediate concern to a mere Colonel and a Senior Major, bar the fact that a major battle was imminent, but politeness required some response, this from O'Hare.

"So, a major set-piece is in the offing, Sir?"

"Count on it. Massena's here to deal with us and that means all of his against all of ours."

"Right Sir, but we've marched now for days unmolested. They must know where we are. That's not like the French, with the quality of cavalry that they have."

"Believe it Major, and that's down, not to ours, but to that Spanish chap Julian Sanchez and his Irregulars. If the French want to find out anything, even such as where we are, they have to do it in some force."

It was just such a French reconnaissance force that Julian Sanchez was watching enter a shallow valley, but he was more than a little worried by what he could see. Through his French telescope taken from a long dead French cavalry Colonel, he could see that it was a substantial force; in front were Hussars or perhaps Light Dragoons, supported behind by what were plainly Heavy Dragoons. Their distinctive uniform told all, a green coat with scarlet section at the front and wide white crossbelts, but most significant was the butt of the shortened musket prominent behind each saddle. However, the Hussars looked little better than his own, even worse, many wearing tunics of brown cloth, much the same as a prosperous peasant, but the Heavy Dragoons were the worry, because these could act as infantry, if called upon. The Ingleses cavalry had ridden through, but with these he had made no contact, trusting his own men to know the roads better than any

Ingleses to carry the letter that was already on its way to the Convent of Busaco to inform Wellington of the whereabouts of most units of the French army. Most of these Franceses were up around Viseu struggling with the areas appalling roads, which meant that Wellington would have several days within which to make his own preparations. However, for Sanchez himself, now it was time to do some damage of his own. His own hatred for the invader had grown, as had that of his men, as the tales came to them of French brutality, as narrated by all new recruits. It was this desire for revenge, burning within these newcomers, that continued to swell the numbers of his own forces. In the face of this eagerness he could no longer confine them to merely scouting and searching. If they did not start to hit the French hard, they would begin to question his position as their leader.

His plan was simple. On his side of the valley were his Lancers, just inside the tree line and out of sight. Equally hidden were the Ordenanza infantry on the far side. His Lancers would attack the Hussar squadrons, taking them on their left, bridle hand, but engage very briefly, instead riding straight through, having inflicted some casualties with their lances, but then draw the Hussars up the other side onto the waiting guns of the Ordenanza. The Dragoons, dismounted and fighting as infantry could ruin everything, but he could not cancel and withdraw his men. They wanted their chance at the French and by withdrawing at such a moment, he would lose face as a worthy leader, brave and ready to take risks. He had no choice and so he waited until the Hussars were directly below his men, when he gave the word for a flag to be waved and his Lancers issued silently from the trees. For a full minute they were unnoticed by the Hussars and when they were, it was too late. They turned to meet the oncoming threat, which broke their ranks and then the Lancers were onto them, stabbing once and then riding through to ascend the hill beyond. Many brown shapes now lay stretched on the yellow stubble with riderless horses scattering in panic in all directions. However, the remainder soon recovered and followed, but in no particular formation, to chase his Lancers up the slope. These disappeared into the trees, where the Hussars were met with heavy musket fire, not like the volleys of the Ingleses, but enough to empty even more saddles. The combat continued, with the Hussars attempting to enter the wood, the Ordenanza keeping them out, firing from behind ready prepared barriers. The French Hussars continued to suffer.

This persisted for some minutes, during which Sanchez' anxiety increased. The Dragoons were riding up in support and soon they were dismounted and, in a good skirmish line, they advanced on the Ordenanza. The Hussars withdrew to leave the conflict to the Dragoons, at which point Sanchez ordered a bugle call for retreat, but it did not happen as he wished, for many Ordenanza, carried away with their success, remained to kill yet more Frenchmen and so Sanchez watched, frustrated and helpless. The Dragoons fought their way into the wood to roll up the Ordenanza from their left flank and soon it was all over, the next act being Ordenanza prisoners and wounded being dragged out of the tree-line. An Officer arrived to scream at the terrified Spaniards before each was brutally beaten and clubbed and then the ropes arrived. Each Spaniard was hauled up a tree to kick and convulse until lifeless, even the wounded. Sanchez remained at the edge of the trees with three companions, made the sign of The Cross on himself and then again in the direction of the hanging bodies. Then they mounted and departed as yet more of the French column advanced down the road.

For the 105th, swinging their way down the Main Trunk in the best of spirits, life could not be much improved upon. Rations were regular and plentiful, all waiting for them each day at the end of a march. The only sour note were the looks they received from the locals of the villages that they passed through, and the frequent shouts from the depths of any alleyways or through open windows from inside the houses.

"Ingleses cobardes! Ingleses cobardes!"

Joe Pike, marching on the outside of Tom Miles, heard this more than most and so he enquired, if that was the right term, of his more experienced companion.

"What do you think they're shouting out, Tom?"

"Blessed if I know, boy, but it ain't 'well done' nor 'good luck' to you. Ask Byford, he might know."

Pike turned to Byford in the rank behind, but from him he heard the same as Miles' verdict.

"Can't be sure, Joe, but they're calling us something and it's not a compliment."

The day's march ended at Ponte de Murcella, where they drew their rations and took themselves into the trees to cook, clean, gossip and chide each other, Tom Miles being the usual target for the latter. As usual Patrick Mulcahey arrived for a second feeding, having eaten once with the Officers, but, despite his Ensign's uniform, none stood, nor saluted. He was simply shepherded to a place by his Mother and then given the leftovers from the pot, but he was growing apart from his fellow drummerboys, bar his good friend Henri Rasenne, who often came with him and was usually rewarded with something extra also. However, no one complained because he was a most accomplished fife player and the growing darkness often saw both of Bridie's sons dancing a jig with two of Nellie's daughters, to the sound of Henri's fife and drum, this beaten by Patrick. Where Eirin was, no one knew, but few enquired as they danced and sang until lights-out. The next day, having been fed on bacon, dried fruit and bread rolls they attempted the steep ridge behind the village, moving away from the River Alva to cross the ridge and descend into the steep valley of the Mondego. Penacova was passed through, accompanied this time by different cries, openly shouted, of 'Viva Ingleses!', accompanied by enthusiastic clapping.

"These lot seems happier."

However, Tom Miles was given no time for trading or bartering as they marched on again, up and along the main road towards the town of Luso, with the high Busaco ridge always on their right. After some time they were turned off this main road by a Staff Officer to then climb the ridge itself. The summit was soon gained and they found themselves on a long, bare ridge and perhaps they were at its centre, for it stretched a long and similar distance in both directions, away to their left and to their right. Below was a small hamlet and beyond that a clear and magnificent view to the Northwest. They were stood in admiration on the ridgeline when Ellis came to interrupt their period of sightseeing.

"Get back down, off the ridge. That track we just crossed, a short ways back over, camp either side of that. Here's our place, watching over that dung-pile down there."

He pointed to the hamlet, distinguished from the trees and fields by its dull thatch, but by then all were retiring back to cross the ridge-track and find any spot less steep on the back slope. All that remained on the summit of the 105th were the three Senior Officers, all mounted; Lacey, O'Hare and Carr, but soon they were joined by Mackinnon and Picton himself, with some of his Staff dutiful behind him. They all waited for Picton to speak, which was not long.

"See you've obeyed my orders, Lacey. Good, as ordained by The Peer himself."

The soubriquet 'The Peer', was new to the three, but it must refer to Wellington, then Picton continued.

"He wants us back out of sight, for when Massena arrives, which will be 48 hours or more. We know he's horribly bogged down around Viseu."

All nodded to demonstrate that they were paying attention, as Picton continued again.

"But he'll come, with all his force. This is going to be a big one, meant to drive us back to Lisbon."

510

Again, rapt attention, as this time Picton issued orders as he pointed to the hamlet below.

"That's San Antonio de Cantara. The place is not as big as its name! I want Lights down in there, to keep any nosey Frogs off this slope, but start tomorrow."

He looked directly at Lacey.

"Yours are nearest, Lacey. Tomorrow yours are first in there, then the 74th and 88th."

He turned to Mackinnon.

"What's today?"

"24th, Sir."

Picton nodded.

"Right. Expect them on the 26th. We'll be trying conclusions on the 27th, if I'm any judge!"

With that, he turned his horse and rode on leftwards, towards Busaco, leaving Mackinnon with the three of the 105th.

"Hear that?"

He spoke no more, in order to maintain the silence. There came to them the unmistakable sound of guns in the distance.

"That'll be Crauford's Lights and Pack's Portuguese up at Mortagoa, not two miles in front of Wellington's Headquarters in Busaco Convent. Johnny's already up on our left! He'll be up here with us for the main event, exchanging volleys, a day earlier, on the 26th, is my guess."

Lacey rose in his stirrups to gain a better view of the hamlet below.

"Best get our men in there now then, Sir."

Mackinnon nodded.

"Engage any nosey cavalry and skirmishers and I'll reinforce immediately, but fall back before a serious advance, I've no need to tell ye."

Lacey looked at Carr, who immediately took the hint and needed no further bidding.

"I'll see to it, Sir."

Carr rode back to the road to dismount and hand his horse to Morrison. Nearby were Drake, Maltby, and Shakeshaft, with Ellis close by. The Officer's camp was half on the ridge-track.

"We're to hold that hamlet, San Antonio de whatever, until dusk tomorrow. Get the Company down there."

It was Ellis who voiced a mild objection.

"The lads are just cooking, Sir!"

"Just so! Have the food sent down when it's ready. That's why we bring the Followers along."

Ellis saluted and hurried off, leaving Carr with the three Officers. Morrison found a campstool for Carr to sit and then produced a mug of good coffee. Carr drank from it gratefully, before he realised that the three were watching him intently.

"What?"

It was Drake who explained.

"We thought that you might have some news."

Carr took another drink.

"I have, but I doubt that it's news. There's going to be another set-to. A big one, same as Talavera. Massena's on his way down with just about everything he's got."

However, it was Shakespeare who refused to have his spirits dampened.

"Yes, but not like Talavera. Then we were stuck on a flat plain and very exposed. Here, we're atop a big ridge, bigger than Vimeiro. There, we trounced them after ten minutes, so there's no reason to think we can't do the same here!"

Carr nodded.

"You may be right, Richard, and I hope you are, but perhaps the Frogs will have learned a thing or two since then, and not try us after they've had to climb to the top of a long slope. Perhaps they'll try something different, with us fixed up here."

"Possibly, Sir, but the fact remains; whenever we meet them, we beat them. I have total faith in the men!"

Carr smiled and drank the rest of his coffee.

"I share that with you, Richard. Indeed I do!"

As that conversation finished, so another began, within the Light Company now crossing the ridge-track, to then reach the summit proper and then descend to San Antonio. Miles was the major contributor.

"Now ain't this just fine and dandy, this mornin' we was in that Murcella place, we marches, gets up here, an' we'n not even given the chance to eat our rations. An' on top, there's not even a Frog in sight!"

It was Saunders who, as usual, replied.

"Don't moan. We're going down to a nice village, where we can all eat in a civilised manner, and we'll put you top of the table, with first choice from the knives and forks."

Davey joined in.

"Don't put him there, he might feel obliged to make a speech."

Miles was by now wholly indignant.

"I'm just sayin'! 'Tall seems a bit hurried an' no need for, is all I'm sayin', like."

It was at that point, now descending the slope that they heard the same guns that their Senior Officers had heard not long previously. Ellis was walking nearby.

"There's your answer! The Frogs is pushin' some of ours back. Way over on the left, I grant you, but how far are they away from here?"

There could be no argument. The guns rumbled on, as, in open order, they swished their way through the low but thick gorse and scrub, but some of the Company had an easy route using the steep road that ascended the ridge from the village to the summit. Whilst avoiding some of the larger bushes, Joe Pike became thoughtful.

"They'll have to climb this slope to get at us, won't they, John?"

"That's true, Joe."

"They won't have much fight in them by the time they've climbed all up through here."

Davey looked affectionately at his young companion.

"You know, Joe, you're beginning to talk like an Officer!"

Ellis chuckled nearby.

"That'll be the day!"

It was not long before they came down to the upper buildings of the village, first a cottage and then the Church, this a low building, at right angles to the ridge. They progressed on, past but a handful of dwellings, with Maltby and Shakeshaft in the lead. A very old man and woman emerged from one of the middle hovels to peer terrified from under the awning of their ragged thatch. George Tucker pulled a half sausage from his haversack and thrust it at the old woman. She took it, utterly mystified, before the man managed a croaking "Gracias". Tucker returned to his messmates.

"Seems the least we can do. Seeing as we're soon going to bring the whole bloody place down around their ears!"

His comrades smiled at his generosity, but Shakeshaft was now giving orders.

"Byford and Pike, get further up, along the road, until you get a view that's useful, then mount a picket. The rest of you, find what shelter you can. Apart from those two back there, obviously too old to move, the place looks deserted."

The whole Light Company, now ninety strong since Carr's reinforcements, hurried to claim the best billet, for all knew that they would be spending a night and a day there. Tucker, Solomon, Miles and Davey, all feeling both responsible and protective, entered the home of the old couple, who immediately looked terrified at four huge armed soldiers entering their home, but Davey took charge.

"Whatever you've got in your haversacks, put it on the table. There'll be more rations soon."

This was done and then Davey stood above the food with his hands open in an expansive gesture, moving his palms towards them, clearly meaning, "We give this to you." Both of the couple smiled, then the old women gathered all and took them to the cooking stove, whilst the old man fetched a bottle of wine, displaying an almost toothless, but very definite, grin

Byford and Joe Pike had by now found the spot to mount their picket, merely five minutes beyond, after a short climb out of the depression that held the village. Byford was naturally closed mouthed and reticent, but Joe Pike's innocent questioning often opened him up.

"Another bad battle coming on, in these parts. It doesn't seen right."

Byford turned his gaze from the far distance, his Baker in the crook of his arm.

"How do you mean, Joe?"

"Well, here's a French army marching into Portugal. The people here don't want them, nor those in Spain, so why are they here?"

Byford chuckled at his innocence.

"Well, Joe, the best I can say, is that it has always been so. If someone has more military might than someone else, sooner or later the lesser is invaded by the stronger. It has been like that since time began."

"Is that how that Napoleon thinks?"

"Must do! Not long after their Revolution, he found ways to beat everyone that came at him and so he used those ways to attack and beat them instead, and build an Empire. The temptation was too great. He thought himself invincible and up till now he isn't so far wrong."

Pike looked at him as if to say 'tell me more', so Byford continued.

"I'm not saying he's evil, I mean, from what I read, he's done good things in France, such as education for all and making all equal before the law, but in other people's countries, it's different. He puts his relations on the Throne, like in Spain, even appoints his Generals to rule, and his armies do dreadful things. Remember what we saw in Catanzaro."

Pike nodded. The memory of the slaughtered Italian village after the battle of Maida was always vivid in his mind. Byford continued.

"But we have the beating of them, which makes us an army more powerful than most, and so, when this is done, don't be surprised if we go off and march into other people's countries. We've already done that to India."

Pike was now of a mind to change the subject.

"What will you do when all this is done?"

Byford pulled a face, as if he had no certain answer.

"Stay in the army and see which country we march into!"

He smiled at his own joke, but Joe Pike was thinking.

"You could come and live with me and Mary, on John's smallholding. With them. You could be the local Schoolteacher!"

Now Byford did laugh.

"I doubt that I could assemble the necessary character references. But I do thank you for the offer."

He turned and continued to study the far horizon, deep within his own thoughts, but he did find the time to make a kind suggestion.

"You have a sit down, Joe. Perhaps get some sleep. Who knows what this night and tomorrow is going to bring."

"Thanks, John, but what I might do is run back and see if the food's arrived."

Byford smiled again.

"When are you never hungry? So yes, but be quick. None of our superiors like the idea of a one-man picket. Leave your rifle here."

Joe Pike did as suggested and ran off. At the edge of the village, as luck would have it, he found Solomons at the well.

"Any food yet?"

"No, but soon, is my guess."

Also, as luck would have it, Solomons was correct, for Bridie had just arrived down from their camp with two full cooking pots and three of her children carrying one each, these being Eirin, Kevin and Sinead. They were met by John Davey and all entered the home of the old couple and Bridie, with the children, immediately gained favour by genuflecting at the crucifix on the far wall. Davey looked at her.

"Is there enough for a portion for these two?"

Bridie nodded as she ladled out the stew into the arranged pannikins. Davey fetched two bowls from the shelf and Bridie gave each a portion. Davey looked at the old couple, and went through the motions of eating. The old man cracked again his gap-toothed grin

"Inglese comida!"

Davey grinned back.

"Si! Inglese comida!"

He turned to Bridie.

"We've two up on picket. Joe and Byfe. Some needs to go up."

Eirin immediately volunteered.

"I'll go. I'll take theirs."

She scraped off two of the pannikins into the pot and made for the door, but before touching the handle, she turned to Davey.

"Is Lieutenant Maltby up forward?"

"Yes, but more to the left, with his Section."

Eirin finally left, but Bridie looked at Davey, her face full of concern.

"No good will come of that. Mark my words."

Eirin met Joe coming from the other direction and the food was transferred and he hurried back to Byford.

Eirin looked around, hoping to see her special Lieutenant, but could not, so she wandered over to the far side of the village and asked of a soldier.

"Is Lieutenant Maltby near?"

The soldier pointed.

"That house there."

At this point, her nerve failed her. She could not just walk into the house on no pretext and so, defeated, she returned to her Mother, then all went back up the ridge with the empty cooking-pots.

oOo

That night, all through the watching hours, the picket was manned, each pair remaining alert, held so by the occasional sound of firing from over on the left. The dawn revealed a landscape unchanged, no sign of human life bar one single house on the horizon. The 105th Lights had no cause for complaint, because all had spent a comfortable night and, with the growing daylight, the day became even more pleasant when rations were sent down, consisting of bacon, dried beans, flour and dried Spanish sausage. For the mess of Davey et al, they now had a Spanish cook and the plain army rations were transformed by the old woman into a very tasty and hearty meal. The picket point established by Byford and Pike was regularly changed and all around San Antonio appeared like a relaxed camp during manoeuvres, but tension was in the air, if only evidenced by the frequency that Officers arrived at the look-out points. With the early afternoon Drake ordered a weapons and kit inspection for both Companies, which even Ellis considered to be unnecessary, but it maintained the edge of anxiety, which kept all on the alert. With the arrival of the evening all of Davey's mess were sat at their ease in the cottage, when Saunders gave voice to his concern.

"Come dawn, we'n relieved and then the 74th comes down, vicious Scotch bastards and after them the 88th, even

518

worse. As if that weren't bad enough, right over this place there's goin' to be a God awful battle."

He paused to allow his words to sink in and then give strength to his next.

"We can't leave these two here."

He pointed to the old couple, now sat by their fire. Davey looked at the pair.

"No. You're right, but how do we get them up the hill? They stayed here because they'm too old to move."

Saunders sat forward.

"Same as we got that old dear out of the cellar at Scilla. Remember; the one as chucked a load of Holy Water over our Thomas here, and blessed him with all the Saints. And wanted to adopt him!"

All around grinned and laughed at the memory, except Miles, whose face showed every ounce of his irritation at so embarrassing a subject being brought up, but Saunders was continuing.

"We put her on a chair and carried her out and down to the boat. We could do the same for these two. To get 'em up top."

Davey looked again at the pair.

"Fine. But how do we tell 'em and get them to agree?"

Both looked at Byford, but Davey gave the order.

"That's your job!"

Byford looked both astonished and much put upon, but after studying his much thumbed copy of 'A Treatise on the Portuguese Language', he managed a sentence that made some sense to the two ancients, when he tried it on them.

"Amanhã. Grande batalha. Perigo aqui. Você vem com a gente, até o topo. Cofre."

The old man looked at the old woman and nodded his head, but she buried her face in her much worn apron. However, Miles was curious.

"What did you say?"

"I said, tomorrow, big battle, you come with us, up top. Safe."

Miles nodded himself in the direction of the old two, as if to say, 'yes, yes, the thing to do'.

That night, again, all slept well, despite the rotation of the pickets, but the dawn saw a change in the view forward, because across the whole horizon, from their picket point, many French columns could be seen coming over the hills, marching in their direction. The dawn also brought a change in the occupation of San Antonio, with the Light Company of the 74th descending the long slope from the summit and that of the 105th preparing to move. Outside the cottage, as Two Section marched off, with One Section were two chairs, each with a long pole lashed to the side, and, with the arrival of the kilted 74th Light Infantry, the two ancients were led to the chairs, and each was sat down and tied in. At that point Lieutenant Maltby arrived and took one look.

"What the Hell is all this, Davey?"

Davey sprang to attention, as did all the others, even those manning the poles.

"We thought we'd get these up to safety, Sir, what with the French now arriving and this place soon to be in the middle of a battle. Sir."

Maltby looked at all the preparations, the prepared sedan chairs, the two old ones sat and strapped and the eight members of his Company ready to pick up the poles. He immediately realised that it would be utterly churlish to deny their good intent, but his face remained stern.

"You should have cleared this with me!"

"Yes Sir. Sorry Sir,"

"Very well, but see that they are no bother. I make you responsible for that!"

Davey saluted.

"Yes Sir. Understood Sir."

The journey began. The old man seemed to quite enjoy the trip, but the old woman was evidently much upset

520

at having to leave her home. Once at the top and over the ridge track, they soon came to the camp of Bridie and Nellie to find Jed Deakin there with them. He was as puzzled as Maltby had been angry.

"Where'd you find those two?"

Saunders was nearest.

"In one of they hovels down below. The Scotch are there now, then it'll be the Irish and then the French. We couldn't leave 'em down there. All others is gone from the village, these two was too old to move, so we moved 'em."

Nellie had heard all and answered before Deakin could.

"Set 'em down and I'll see 'em fed."

The chairs descended, the poles were removed and then a bowl of stew was given to each. At this the old woman began crying and seized Nellie's hand, which she pressed to her forehead. The old man tried to comfort her, but he soon became equally upset. Saunders looked at Byford.

"Say something!"

Byford looked amazed that he should be the one who could do anything, but he placed a hand on the shoulder of each.

"Está bem."

Saunders looked at him.

"What'd you say?"

"It's alright."

Saunders looked at the old couple and was pleased to see that the two words had helped. The old woman began eating her stew and the old man already was, but Bridie had her own opinion.

"Tis a crying shame and a sin, so it is, for two such as these to be forced out of their home by a load of maraudin' Devils!"

Jed Deakin had been listening and watching all the while.

521

"You're right there, love, and when I meets the French I'll make sure that they's well aware of your low opinion!"

He then got up and left. The withering look he had just received from Bridie persuaded him that leaving was probably a good idea.

Deakin was making for the ridgeline. Saunders words had told him that the French were arriving and so he went to have a look, as did many others. These included, inevitably, Lacey, O'Hare and Carr and the three immediately began using their telescopes. Lacey asked the simple question of the other two.

"How long?"

It was O'Hare who answered, him not of especially greater experience but one that held a valued opinion.

"Mid afternoon. They'll be here, but not engage, at least not seriously. That's for the morning. They may send a few forward to feel us out."

Picton clearly was of a similar mind as he rode up with Mackinnon, but addressed himself to Lacey.

"Your men been fed, Colonel?"

"Yes Sir. Not two hours ago."

Picton nodded, whilst studying the far distance.

"Right. Get them formed up."

He then looked at Mackinnon.

"I want your Lights on the end of my line. The left. There's a bit of a valley there, making an easier way up."

"Yes Sir, but I only have Lacey's here and the 88th's, who are already over there. The 74th Lights are down in San Antonio. As you ordered, Sir."

Picton's face darkened at having to be reminded of a situation which he had created himself and so he turned to Lacey.

"Yours with the 88th will have to do, Lacey."

With that, Picton pulled over his horse's head and rode back to Champlemonde's Portuguese on his far right;

leaving Mackinnon with the three 105th Officers, but it was Lacey who issued the orders.

"Henry. Get Drake's Lights over beyond the 88th. Go with them, it could well be that you'll have to command both Companies."

Carr hurried off to where the Light Company were camped beyond the back road, with Mackinnon studying Carr's disappearing back. Mackinnon then turned to Lacey.

"That Enquiry business back in October, back in Montijo, any effect on your Major?"

Lacey shook his head.

"None that I've seen. However, knowing him, he'll be fired up by the memory of it, but on the other hand, he's just got married, which may calm him down."

Mackinnon smiled, then his expression changed.

"That damn letter of Perry's. What was the point?"

He drew a deep breath, to almost answer his own question.

"Animosity of some contrivance, but Perry's been dismissed. Did your Major write a reply?"

O'Hare nodded.

"I believe he did, Sir."

"Right, I'll get over there and take a look. On top, a few words from this old curmudgeon may help."

He walked his horse on, towards the 88th, leaving Lacey to then instruct O'Hare.

"Right. Form line."

It was O'Hare who ordered up the Drummers and soon the distinctive roll was calling all the Companies to hurry to their places. Deakin was soon stood besides Rushby, with newly promoted Ensign Mulcahey stood beyond him and it was the latter who gained Deakin's attention. He leaned forward to look at the youngster and saw an excited and eager face beneath the Ensign's shako, slightly too big, which was once worn by the late lamented Neape. All was plainly well with young Patrick, but the 105th remained in line for the rest of the day. However, they remained standing for only a few minutes, before Lacey allowed them to sit, for food and water to repeatedly ease their vigil, yet it was in no way monotonous, as the blue columns, ever clearer and more numerous, gathered on the plain in the distance, barely more than a mile from the summit of their ridge.

Carr and Drake arrived with their men to find Mackinnon already in place at the head of the small valley that was of such concern to Picton. Both approached and saluted, but Mackinnon spoke to Drake.

"Captain. Get your men in skirmish order 100 yards down, to cover that valley."

He then pointed.

"That's the 88th over on your right. I'll get some men from the next Brigade over to cover your left."

Drake saluted and ran over to Ellis to issue the necessary orders. Carr made to follow, but Mackinnnon stopped him.

"A word please, Major."

"Sir?"

Mackinnon dismounted.

"Everything all right with you, Carr, since that Enquiry business?"

Carr immediately became aggrieved, despite his much lower rank.

"Yes Sir. Why shouldn't it be, Sir?"

Mackinnon allowed the challenge to pass.

"That letter in The Times. Did you reply?"

"Yes Sir, we did. Myself and my fiancé, as she was then. She's my wife now."

Mackinnon smiled.

"It would seem that congratulations are in order."

"Thank you Sir. That's very kind."

"Was the letter published?"

"Not during my time back in England, Sir. Since then, I've no way of knowing, until I get a letter from home, Sir."

Mackinnon nodded.

"Now, you'll keep yourself in check, Carr, won't you! This is no time for any daft heroics that you feel are needed to repair any damage that may have been done to your reputation."

Carr remained irritated and replied somewhat stuffily.

"The amount of damage remains to be seen, Sir, but I've no intention of putting my life at risk nor those of the men that I command whilst doing it. Sir."

Mackinnon smiled.

"Just so, Major. Just hold to that thought. It's no individual heroics that'll get us back home and out of here. Just good soldierly technique."

"My thoughts entirely, Sir."

Mackinnon remounted and walked his horse forward, to get over to the next Brigade and keep his promise to Drake.

"Good luck, Carr."

Carr saluted.

"Thank you, Sir."

Both parted and Carr hurried down to check on Drake's dispositions and those of the 88th, barely seen amongst the thick gorse and heather. He came to the far end of his own men to thankfully see an Officer of the 88th at the join of the two Companies. He was a Captain and he immediately came to the attention and saluted.

"Sennet, Sir. 88th."

"Carr, 105th. What say we get the men down out of sight? No point in inviting cannonfire, this far down as we are. I'll do the same with mine."

"Yes Sir. Makes sense. I'll see to it."

Meanwhile, Lacey and O'Hare had remained at the top of their slope, watching the gathering French army. It seemed endless, Brigade after Brigade coming over the far ridge and then descending to add their numbers to those already assembled. O'Hare voiced his thoughts.

"Same size as Talavera?"

"More! Much more. He's here to sort us out. Boney's had enough of bad news from Spain."

He looked along his line.

"See that the men are fed again. My guess is we'll be sleeping in line tonight, making for a restless night. I don't want them hungry on top."

O'Hare was about to reply when they noticed a soldier of the 74th running up the hill, his kilt swinging as he ran and soon his rank of Sergeant could be seen. He paused for a moment to look around, then came up to the pair, these being the only Officers in sight. Breathless from the long, steep climb, he gave his message.

"Sirs. We've seen a large body of French making for the slope over on the left, Sirs."

Lacey looked at him.

"How long since?"

"Just minutes, Sir. I was sent directly up. They'll be at the top in aboot 15 minutes, Sir."

"A column or what?"

"Open order, Sir."

Lacey turned to O'Hare.

"Tirailleurs and Voltiguers! Carr needs warning. Send a runner."

Within five minutes a swift Drummerboy was arriving at Carr's side, where he gave a perfect salute.

"Sir. Message from the Colonel, Sir. French skirmishers are coming your way."

"How long?"

"They was seen from San Antonio about 10 minutes ago, Sir. Must have been seen comin' down their slope, 'tother side of the valley."

Carr smiled at the Drummerboy's deduction.

"Well done. Now get back. You may be needed with your drum!"

The lad saluted and ran off, leaving Carr to descend to his own skirmish line. Ellis saw him coming and realised that there must be a reason.

"Sir?"

"Bring the men to the alert and keep them under some form of cover and out of sight. Some Johnnies are coming up and could be here soon."

Ellis saluted and ran off, and Carr walked over to Captain Sennet.

"They're coming up to try us out. Wait for my order, we could spring a bit of a surprise. When my men come into action, that's your signal."

"Very good, Sir, as you wish, but it does seem that our guests have already arrived."

He pointed down the slope, where French infantry, in skirmishing order were emerging from the even thicker heather and gorse.

"Right, I'll get back to my men."

Carr moved some way to the left, more to the centre of his line. Movement behind caught his eye, a Company of Light Infantry were forming across the slope above. Mackinnon had kept his promise to Drake to send support. They were ready as a reserve. Carr used his small telescope to view the oncoming enemy and soon identified Tirailleurs by their distinctive red collar and shoulder tabs. With them were Voltiguers, their collars and tabs being an equally distinctive yellow and a large and distinctive tassel beside their shakoes. Miles was kneeling nearby.

"Who's comin', Sir?"

"Tirailleurs and Voltiguers, Miles."

"You mean they gamecocks all picked over in red an' they tassel swingin' bastards! Beggin' your pardon, Sir."

"The same, Miles. Could be that they have a few items they'll need relieving of, when this is done."

"There's a lot of truth in that, Sir."

Carr smiled and looked along his line. All were down within the heather and gorse, all in their threes, rifles at the ready, butt resting on the dry, thin soil. He transferred his gaze back to the French, labouring up through the thick covering and the thought occurred to him, 'Good luck to your columns slogging their way up through that! And too far up for artillery support', but then the main task returned fully to mind. He waited until he judged 150 yards, perfect for a Baker, but ineffective for a musket, even the long French Charleville.

"Give fire!"

The trio near him, Davey, Miles and Pike, began, but one at a time, beginning with Davey bringing down an Officer, then Miles and then Pike. French musket balls began to hum past him and so he kept moving. His men were well into their routine, one firing, one reloading and the third watching for the next threat, in this case any Frenchman fixing on them, who then became an immediate target. Carr had trained the 105 Lights himself and they knew their role, to stop the enemy from harassing the main line, not necessarily to defeat them, but to hold them off at a distance. Also, in their 'routine of three' they protected their own lives, fixing on any enemy looking to do them harm.

However, much harm was coming to the French. With their long musket they had to stand to reload, but the Baker, being shorter, could be reloaded from a kneeling position. The elite French skirmishers were suffering, whilst his own men had suffered few casualties, if any. The French line was now further down the slope, not because the French had retired, simply because their leading men had been brought down. It was not long before French bugles blew and all retreated, carrying their many wounded with them. Drake was walking behind his men.

"You've seen them off, boys. The best they've got. Time to rub it in!"

It was already happening; the 105th and then the 88th rose up out of the heather to jeer and catcall after the retreating French, some of whom turned to shake their fist in anger, to then receive the standard English two-fingered salute in return.

Carr noticed some riders above him and a quick look identified them as Picton and Mackinnon, sat there with their Staff. They had ridden over to investigate the sound of firing. Carr now needed new orders and so he climbed the 150 yards to where they were, but he didn't have time to salute before Picton was jumping about in his saddle.

"Damn fine work, Carr! Damn fine! Can't remember the last time I heard of those damn Frog skirmishers being given such a bloody nose! You must have downed almost four dozen!"

He turned to Mackinnon.

"What say you, Mac?"

The 105th's Brigadier gave a Fatherly smile.

"Good technique, Picton. We talked about that a while ago, did we not, Major?"

"Yes Sir. Good technique and a Baker rifle, Sir, but what's possibly more important is that they'll not come marching up here tomorrow with quite so much of their Gallic confidence! As I've heard it, this is a veteran French army."

Picton beamed all over his naturally ill-tempered face, whilst somehow it still retained its irascible edge.

"Just so, Major. As I've heard. Now, hold your men here. They may try again, so hold them here."

He turned again to Mackinnon.

"See they get a rum issue."

He jumped again gleefully in his saddle.

"Ha! Hold that! Frog bastards!"

All the Senior Officers turned their horses, whilst Carr saluted and then descended the slope. His men, and those of the 88th, were already far down the slope, examining French haversacks for food, brandy, general plunder and replenishing their stock of silver buttons from

Officer tunics. Boots also were carefully examined, one pair being spotted by Miles.

"John! This Frog Officer yer. He's about your size an've got a nice pair of cavalry boots!"

It was a happy hour for the 105th Lights, who soon returned to their original positions and began to carefully examine the items that had been found on the French dead and to eat their looted food. Soon after that, as a surprise to them, the rum arrived, from Division stocks. It was doubly a surprise as explained by Miles and the reason why none had touched the looted wine or brandy.

"This is a turn up. Unofficial drinkin' in the front line. That's a floggin' offence!"

With that he seized Joe Pike's mug from him and poured in some water, before the issue.

"Nothin' full strength for you. We don't want to be carryin' you back up the hillside."

Joe Pike grinned and did not argue. He, and they, well knew the impact that strong drink had upon him and happily sipped his watered down portion. Thus, in great contentment sat the 105th Lights, as morning became afternoon, watching events below, although none were in any way belligerent, merely some of the 88th and some of their own, making a last inspection of the French dead. Some of the 88th, passing close, seemed to recognise them and came closer and one, now seen as very familiar, wore an ingratiating grin on his face.

"Well now, boys, we all meet up again. Michael O'Donnell; surely you remember?"

Davey looked up from cutting down his cavalry boots.

"Oh, it's you! Yes, we remember, the one as chiseled us into a wrestling match with the All Irish Champion. Yes, we remember and we found out who he was."

The grin stiffened, just a little.

"Ah, come now, boys. 'Tis all in the spirit of the thing. It would have been a good contest, all the same, would you not have thought?"

Davey was unmoved.

"Aye! With all the odds on your side."

"Well, perhaps we can make it happen all the same, sometime in the future!"

He then noticed the very substantial amount of loot spread around, waiting to be evaluated and shared out amongst the Light Company.

"Sure now, boys, haven't you done powerful well out of the gleanings!"

He allowed his eyes to pass over all.

"Now, don't you think there should be a bit of the share out comin' our way? Now didn't we hold your flank, all through?"

Miles was becoming increasingly irritated. Irish diddykites were a bad memory from his Bristol childhood.

"And didn't we hold yours! And if we've got more, 'tis because we brought down more of 'em!"

Each side now looked coldly at the other, but it was broken by Captain Sennet, seeing his own men idling with those of the 105th, and not where he wanted them.

"O'Donnell and the rest of you. Form up. Now!"

The Irish slunk off, taking no good wishes with them, but the 105th Lights grinned, one to the other. They felt that they had got the best of the exchange and they gave them not a glance as the 88th Lights marched away, up the slope. Within an hour the 74th Lights arrived to take their place, the 88th were now due their turn in San Antonio.

The afternoon wore on with the two Light Companies holding their positions. The Officers of both Regiments grouped together, attempting conversation to relieve the boredom, which was not broken even by the sounds of firing from their left, where they knew the main French strength lay, opposite the Convent. The sounds of conflict also came to them from their own front, from the direction of San Antonio, over to their right. However, with the growing dusk the sounds of both conflicts died away. The last act of the day for them, was the arrival of Mackinnon with the Light Company of the 88th. They had been pushed out of San Antonio by an overwhelming French advance, which had been the source of the sounds of fighting on their right front. Mackinnon went straight to Carr.

"Peer's orders. The army sleeps in position, which means you remain here. Keep a good watch, they'll be up with the dawn to start things off. I'll get some rations sent down."

"Can we cook, Sir?"

"I dinnae see why not. M'sieu knows we're here. Why double the misery?"

Mackinnon was as good as his word, for within half an hour rations arrived on a string of mules; salt beef, beans, peas and bread. Soon cooking fires sprang up, using the thick stems of the gorse and heather as fuel. The Officers dined with their own Companies, but with that done, they congregated together, again for conversation, but, all the while they stared out into the black void beyond them, where could be seen the myriad bivouac fires of the French. Three great masses, each mass a whole Corps, the single largest before their own position, but two more over before Busaco Convent.

oOo

Sedgwicke's cosy dream suddenly took a turn for the worse. He was in an Inn with some of his old friends from Ecumenical College, all sat at a table replete with food, but someone was now pushing him vigorously from the side. He awoke to find that the hand doing the pushing was very real. It belonged to his Chaplain, the Reverend Albright, who was shaking him awake.

"Private!"

Sedgwicke sat up, but not enough to knock his head on the floor of the wagon under which he slept, but his head remained much befuddled.

"Sir?"

"Private, there is about to be a battle."

"Yes Sir."

It now registered with Sedgwicke that all around was pitched dark. The light was coming from the Reverend's candle lantern, but Albright was continuing.

"Should there not be some kind of Service? For the men? Before a battle?"

Sedgwicke rubbed his eyes.

"Yes Sir, if possible, but sometimes circumstances do not allow it, such as this time, Sir. The men went straight into their positions with the coming of darkness."

"So, what can be done? Something should be done."

"Well Sir. The men slept in line. We could simply go along the line and wish them luck, Sir. And the blessings of The Lord."

Even in the poor light, Sedgwicke could see the disgust on Albright's face.

"That's very paltry, Private. Nothing at all adequate for men who may, come this day's end, be stood before their Maker."

"I'm sure that's true, Sir, but the men are in their battle positions. Colonel Lacey, good God Fearing man that he is, would simply not allow any form of distraction, Sir, in the face of the enemy, such as calling the men around for a Service, Sir. That's the way that it is. With respect."

Sedgwicke saw Albright's shoulders slump down, but he conceded.

"Well, yes, and I do suppose that we could say a lot more than just good luck."

Sedgwicke was relieved to hear Albright concede and, despite the unwelcome awakening, could not stop himself from warming to this ignorant but very well intentioned man.

"Yes Sir, we could. We should go now, Sir, and make a start. The Grenadiers are on the right and are just up there, Sir."

'Just up there' was a huge exaggeration, which became very evident when their left the shelter of their cart, for not only was it still full dark, there was a thick fog. Nevertheless, by going up hill, they blundered into the backs of the Grenadiers, already stood to and all eating. They walked to the right and soon came to the end of their line, where stood Captain Carravoy. Albright went straight up to him.

"Good morning, Captain. I thought I would move amongst the men, along the line, that is, and tender my good wishes for them during this coming conflict."

Carravoy could see no objection, nor did he want to find one.

"By all means, Chaplain. I'm sure the men will appreciate it."

"My thanks to you, Captain and may you be the first to receive my best good wishes and hopes that you may safely see the end of this day."

Carravoy saluted.

"My thanks to you, Chaplain."

Thus began the spiritual mission of the good Chaplain Albright and his assistant, Private Sedgwicke, along the two deep firing line of the 105th Foot. All in the line appreciated both the effort and the words that he spoke to them and, in addition, Sedgwicke was universally popular, being frequently greeted by the simple words, 'Hello Old Parson'. Such were the exact words used by Colour Sergeant Jed Deakin when the pair reached the centre of the line, this being the Colour Party. All came to the attention to acknowledge their efforts, even the unfathomably deep Low Church Captain Joshua Heaviside, who made a respectful, even helpful, reply.

"We are not of them who draw back unto perdition; but of them that believe to the saving of the soul. Hebrews 10, Verse 39."

Albright's face lit up, even in the gloom.

"Just so, Captain Heaviside. Be not moved away from the hope of the Gospel."

"No Sir. Colossians 1. Verse 23."

Albright moved on, much uplifted, which was much more than could be said for the Senior Officers of the 105th, these being Lacey and O'Hare, Lacey asking the key question, sourced from his deep concerns.

"Are the pickets out? This fog could not be worse for us, nor better for them."

"Yes they are. Doubled!"

"Good. Then we can do nothing but wait."

Such thoughts were uppermost in the mind of Henry Carr, only with double intensity. He was stood with Captains Drake, Sennet and now Carson of the 74th.

"They'll try here again. This is the easiest ground for a column. With their Lights out in front and now able to come a damn sight nearer with this pestilential fog."

The visibility was down to 20 yards, although the sky above was reasonably bright, but 20 yards visibility completely nullified the long-range advantage of the Baker rifle. Carr made his decision.

"Right. When they come, we'll meet them in two firing lines, a 10-yard gap between back and front. The first gives fire, then files back through, for the second to fire. Then we go to files for the pull-back. That way we slow them up, which is the best we can do. It won't be just Jumping Johnnies this time, but an assault column also, coming up behind."

The three laughed and Carson asked the question.

"Jumping Johnnies Sir?"

"Yes. Voltiguer means 'leaper', or so my educated ranker informs me."

"Right Sir. Jumping Johnny it is."

"Good. At least we've got the names of our foe sorted out. So, as we mean to retreat anyway, we'll start from lower down. 100 yards further down, two lines across."

Within minutes it was done, the 105th first, the 88th in the second, with the 74th split and extending both lines, both further down the valley that cleaved the slope of the main ridge. That done, the same as those in the main line above San Antonio, they could do little but sit and wait. Until Carr had a thought, so he turned to Drake.

"What's above us?"

"The 88th. Minus their Lights, of course."

"Just them?"

"As I understand. I'll go look."

He ran up the hill, soon to disappear into the mist. At that moment came the sound of approaching French, the dum dada dum dada dum dum, came up the hill, distinct, even though suppressed by the fog.

"Stand to! Stand to!"

This came from Ellis, running along the line and immediately all were on their feet and loading their weapons, carefully wiping away any fog damp in the priming pan to make it perfectly dry before tipping in any powder. The minutes stretched out, as the drumming grew louder, then Drake returned.

"Yes. Just the 88th, as infantry that is, but they've heard the drumming and Wallace, their Colonel has readied his men. But, one good thing. The Peer himself is just over and has moved a pair of guns to support us. He must have heard the drumming too."

"Oh fine! Two guns, one battalion! A whole French Division, I don't doubt!"

Every man in Carr's line now stood, peering forward, staring into the mist and wishing for some form of superior eyesight that could give better warning. It came, not as sight, but as sound, that of gaitered legs swishing through the wet gorse and heather. Shapes appeared, vague at first, then more distinct, and the men of the 105th, 88th and 74th subconsciously gripped their weapons a little tighter. Carr was stood at the centre and behind the first line. There were enough targets now, but the French did not seem to have reacted, perhaps not expecting to meet any opposition so soon and so far down. Carr gave his order quickly, whilst the French seemed still unaware. Surprise was never a bad thing.

"Make ready. Present."

He gave time for each man to find a target.

"Fire!"

The muskets crashed out and many shapes fell in the fog before them and then the screaming of the wounded began.

"Fall back!"

All turned to file back through the second line. Carr took charge again, and produced the same result. The French stopped, surprised to find a firing line so far down, but their Officers soon discovered that it was merely a skirmish line and so their advance continued. Carr gave the order to form files of three and soon the French were suffering from the British Lights executing their file drill perfectly and using the fog as cover, but it was they who were retreating and the French who were advancing.

High on the ridge, the main line of the 105th could hear the drumming of their own approaching column, coming up the hill to their immediate front, on the their right of the road up from San Antonio. The 105th were, if anything, in reserve behind the 74th who were immediately at the summit of the slope and close to the road. They all could also hear the thin volleys of Carr's skirmishing line, over to their left, as could Picton and he soon arrived, on a very agitated horse.

"Lacey, get one wing of yours over to aid Wallace. I've sent for both Battalions of the 8th Portuguese on the end of Leith's line, beyond our far right They'll come to your support. Go now. No time to lose. Who knows what's coming up that valley?"

Lacey and O'Hare were stood in the centre of their line and O'Hare immediately offered himself, so that Lacey could remain with The Colours.

"I'll go with half. Carr's already there."

He ran off calling to each Company Captain as he passed and soon one half of the 105th had disappeared into the fog. Picton had gone over to the San Antonio road, because the immediate threat was a French attack directly up it, onto the lowest point of where they were stood; the San Antonio pass. Lacey looked forward into the fog, now thinning, but it remained an advantage for the French. At that point the Portuguese battery, Captain Arentschildt's, at the head of the road, opened fire, their crash drowning out all other sounds and their smoke adding to the mist. Lacey remained with his men and looked behind him.

"Uncase The Colours."

The leather sheaths came off, pulled away by the Ensigns and handed to their Colour Sergeant. The heavy Standards were lifted into their leather holders and set. Ensign Mulcahey had a big grin on his face, which brought a smile to that of Lacey's. Then Lacey's returned his attention to events before him, as from behind him he heard the two battalions of the 8th Portuguese Line passing over in obedience of Picton's orders, using the ridge track just down from the summit. Lacey saw The Colours of the 74th before him raised up and set, then their line advanced forward. The fog was thinning as he saw them bring their muskets to the 'make ready'. The Portuguese guns crashed out again, then the 74th's muskets disappeared as they were lowered to the 'present'. Lacey could see no French, but the 74th opened fire, a volley from each line and then their half-Company volleys began, they had been trained just in the same way as the 105th. He heard the sound of another Battalion volley from the far side of the road over on his right, and then the firefight began, the endless volleys crashing out from the Allied line. The 74th took not one backward step, telling him that this first French attack, in whatever strength it was, had been halted and was most certainly taking punishment, now held up by two Battalions and one battery.

However, for Carr, life was nothing like so simple and life itself was growing more tenuous by the minute. His small force was hugely outnumbered by the oncoming French skirmish screen and so they had no choice but to retreat. The Tirailleurs were causing casualties and the necessary speed of retreat by Carr's men was growing by the minute. Relief of sorts came in the form of a Major of the 88th coming down the hill alone. Introductions were brief before the Major made his suggestion, amidst the buzzing French musket balls.

"Ringwood. 88th."

"Carr. 105th."

"Try to draw them across to their left, across the slope. There's a colossal column, split in two, each a full company wide, coming up. We are above you and, if you can draw them across, we will hit them in the flank. We've got to hope that they will follow in the direction of your fight with their Lights. Perhaps the fog will do the rest and they'll get confused."

Carr did no more than nod, as Ringwood ran back up the slope, then Carr ran along the back of his line.

"Ease right, men. Ease to your right. Draw them over, not up."

His men obeyed and the French skirmishers followed. Carr could not see the column but he was doing as asked, that being to retreat as much across the ridge as up. However, whilst Carr may feel at least satisfied with the movement of his line, serving in it was very much less so. Every muscle in the bodies of many tensed with the anticipated impact of a French ball as they became evermore conscious of the mass of French skirmishers crowding in upon them. No less Nat Drake, very satisfied with the way that his men were behaving amidst the growing desperation of their combat, but Drake himself now needed to use a rifle gathered from a wounded man of his Company, because too many had fallen. He was filing in with two of his men, when the man before gave a scream and fell to the ground clutching his leg, before rising and dragging himself off to the rear, using his weapon as a crutch. This man's weapon had been loaded and he had come the front; the man who had been before him was already back behind Drake. The casualty and Drake's unreadiness, because he was in the process of reloading, left a gap in their line, which a mounted Voltiguer Officer saw and was determined to exploit. He charged at Drake and he, with his ramrod in his hand and no-where useful, saw the danger looming above him, the raised sword and the contorted face. He raised the unloaded weapon to make some effort to defend himself, but a thrust down with the point meant certain death and, with his mind strangely resigned, there came from way back in his consciousness an image of Cecily. The next thing he knew was himself being knocked to the ground by the whirling hind-quarters of a horse, then he sat up, but his men were shouting at him, particularly Byford and Saunders.

"It's alright Mr Drake. We've spun him!"

Drake blinked and looked around to see the French Officer dead on the ground, his chest now curiously concave from the impact of two musket balls. Even though to the rear of their files, the pair had swiftly made themselves loaded and ready. Drake looked at them, grinned and nodded his thanks. He then picked up the rifle and ran back to complete his reload. However, their fallback was now rapid and men were falling regularly, something not unnoticed by Joe Pike as he passed Tom Miles.

"How much longer, Tom?"

Miles had only one answer.

"Just follow your drill, boy, and we'll all get out of this."

Miles now headed the file. He immediately saw a Tirailleur already sighting on him and instinctively he took a large step to his right and knelt down. He knew that he had almost a second between the Frenchman pulling the trigger and the arrival of the ball. The French ball hissed past and Miles sought his own target, ignoring the Frenchman who had just shot at him, with an empty musket he was no immediate threat. Instead he fixed on two opposite, one was priming his musket, the other was returning his ramrod to the guides. He chose the latter, he would soon be a seeking a target. Miles quickly sighted on him and pulled the trigger. The Tirailleur bent double as the half-inch ball hit his stomach and he collapsed. That done, Miles ran back to reload at the rear and give Davey his turn, to then, once more, study all around for any French skirmisher fixing too much upon himself. He needed to look but once at his weapon, as he automatically completed his reload, this to prime the pan. His fingers alone being needed to feel the guides to return his ramrod. Tom Miles was fighting like the veteran he was, but even he could feel the press of overwhelming numbers.

Meanwhile. O'Hare had arrived at the end of the 88th line. He left his Captain's to organise the lines and went straight to Wallace, stood at the 88th's centre. Wallace barely turned to meet him as he studied the oncoming French attack. In turn O'Hare could barely look at Wallace, the oncoming French were such a huge mass, over 10 battalions was O'Hare's first guess.

"Sir. We've been sent over. Half the 105th. Two Portuguese are coming to support, but I don't know where Picton will place them."

Wallace now looked at him.

"You are?"

"Padraigh O'Hare, Sir. 105th."

"Right Major. At the best moment, I'm going to give those Johnnies a full volley into their flank and then give them the bayonet. No sense in setting up a firefight, there's too many. You'll add your men to mine?"

"Yes Sir."

"Thank you. Please to wait for my order."

"Sir."

O'Hare ran back to his first Company.

"Pass the word on, load and fix bayonets."

O'Hare could only stand, wait, and watch the oncoming wave of French. They were no longer in column or battalion formation, this had been much broken up by tramping through the thick gorse and heather, they were simply many large masses of blue uniforms. Carr's firefight was now over on the right, barely heard but it did seem to be drawing the French mass that way as they followed their own skirmishers. They were thankfully tending to their left as much as ascending the hill. Then Wellington's two guns fired from over on the left of Wallace's line, their grapeshot ploughing two lanes through the massed crowd. There could be but minutes to go, when Wallace stepped out before his men. O'Hare turned his head to listen.

"Now, Connaught Rangers, mind what you are going to do, pay attention to what I have so often told you, and when I bring you face to face with those French rascals, drive them down the hill - don't give them the false touch, but push home to the muzzle! I have nothing more to say, and if I had it would be of no use, for in a minute or two there will be such an infernal noise about your ears that you won't be able to hear yourselves".

O'Hare grinned at so paternal a speech, but whatever helped, then let it be so. The groups on the right flank of the French were now up to them and the 88th were taking fire from those on the edge of the French mass as they passed across from left to right. French balls began to buzz over his own command, but then O'Hare drew his own sword as Wallace raised his.

"Make ready."

All along the line, of both Regiments, the muskets were raised in the air. Some French Officers, on the near edge of the blue mass, their faces revealing their deep concern at seeing a long, steady line of Redcoats on their flank, attempted to bring some of their own into position to reply.

"Present."

The musket came down level.

"Fire!"

The full volley, both lines together, crashed out at full volume and the affect on the French, merely 40 yards away, was shattering. They fell in huge swathes as the half-inch balls thudded into and through their ranks. What came next was a howling moan as the 88th surged forward. O'Hare curved his own sword forward, Irish emotion and passion finally getting the better of him

"Charge boys, charge. Into them. Hurrah! Hurrah for the One-Oh-Five. Hurrah for the fighting Rag and Bone Boys!"

He ran forward, followed by his own men yelling insults at the devastated French.

For Carr, the situation was becoming more fraught by the minute as he continued the desperate business of holding the French skirmishers away from the main line and also to draw them across the hillside. His attention was fixed wholly upon his own enemy, greatly outnumbering his own command and these elite French soldiers had become confident enough to crowd up to his own men and reduce the range even further. A reassuring volley of shots crashed out from his files of men, but when the smoke cleared, it seemed to have made little difference. The French were just as numerous and, if anything, closer, but then his total concentration on events before him was interrupted by Ellis.

"Sir. This is as far as we can go, Sir. There's Portugee comin' up behind."

Carr turned and saw, to his huge relief, a long, two deep, brown uniformed firing line, coming across the slope, almost at right angles to the ridgeline. They were advancing at a good pace and soon they were up to Carr's men. Just before they passed through the Portuguese ranks, he took a look back at his own foe, who were now retreating themselves in the face of the advance of two Portuguese battalions. Suddenly, from standing in the midst of mayhem and peril, all was calm and almost quiet, his three Light Companies now standing in groups, as relieved as he was, the Portuguese advancing on.

O'Hare was now in amongst the French, but it was some time before they came to any capable of making any resistance, such had been the affect of the brutal volley. They first had to jump and stamp over the many dead and wounded, but that done, their momentum even increased. First resistance they proved to be wholly feeble, as the maddened Redcoats descended the slope, bayonets levelled against the French, who were still in shock from the terrible volley. O'Hare swept aside a weak attempt to meet him with a bayonet and then cut the man across the neck. Next was a young French Lieutenant, his face contorted in fear and terror, who was kicked to the ground. Then his men were with him, in amongst the more solid French ranks, killing and maiming with bayonets, musket butts and even their boots. All the while, equally terrifying was the eerie moan coming over from the 88th, a chilling background to the sounds and sights of the mayhem created as the Redcoats tore into the French.

A few French stood to attempt resistance and it cost them their lives, for the rest were being driven down the hill and, plainly, they were pushing at the French beyond them, those who had not yet met any British bayonet. These were being pushed back down the hill by their own men from above these attempting to escape the ferocious 105th and the wild 88th. The sense that O'Hare gained was that the whole mass was giving way, being pushed back and down by the frantically battling Redcoats.

"On boys, on! Don't let them stand. Keep at them."

If any heard or did not, it made little difference. The Redcoats stabbed, kicked and stamped their way forward, O'Hare attacked a Fusilier Sergeant, pushing aside his bayonet with his hand guard to then deliver a vicious backhand into the side of his face. After this foe had been despatched, the French seemed to give way further. O'Hare gave himself the time to look over to both sides to see his men, everyone fighting like a demon, moving onward and downward as they pressed on, fighting forward over a carpet of French dead, wounded and dying.

Meanwhile Carr, now somewhat at a loss as to what to do, suddenly found himself surrounded by Picton and his Staff, with the General giving instructions, looking down still somehow disapprovingly from his still skittish horse.

"Good work again, Carr, but now get yours on the end of those Portuguese. If we've got it right, those Frogs that Wallace just saw off will be passing across your front. Make the whoresons feel your fire. Keep 'em moving!"

Carr saluted with his sword and then looked around for anyone with a semblance of authority. He saw Ellis and Fearnley, as nearest, then Drake and Sennet. Carson he could not see for smoke and distance.

"Ned, Sennet! Rally the men. They must follow me. Bring the 74th."

Ellis and Fearnley knew that they were included in the order and soon the 105th Lights were in a group with the 88th behind and the 74th also coming after, or so Carr hoped. He ran forward and soon came to the Portuguese line, who were engaging with the head of the French columns, or so it seemed from the little that he could see. He led his men off to the right and found the end of the Portuguese line, to then place his men piecemeal onto the last file to extend the line further down the hill. The range was less than sixty yards and to each group as they took their place, he spoke the same words.

"There's your target. Fire as fast as you can."

Within minutes the three Companies were all adding their fire to that of the Portuguese who were, Carr noted, hitting the French before them with very disciplined half Company volleys and one look forward told him that the French ranks opposite were beginning to crumble, many now edging away to their left, some even running down the slope.

O'Hare had now noticed that the slope beneath his feet was becoming steeper, but the French were now in full retreat and from his right he heard the incessant crash of disciplined musketry, this being hopefully from the Portuguese that Picton had mentioned. He worried briefly about his own men being hit from the side by this friendly fire, but the fight continued downward, his sword and an 88th bayonet despatching a huge Grenadier. Then, from somewhere came the order to halt, miraculously obeyed amongst the continuing noise and carnage. O'Hare screamed the word several times himself and slowly his men disengaged from the defeated French, all those in front of him now pouring down the hill towards San Antonio as a beaten rabble. French were still running on his right, but the firing from that direction had ceased. He realised that he and his men were now some way down the hill and saw that the 88th were forming a firing line, with his own men complying to extend it to the right, as they had before their charge from way above their slope. All stood breathless and bloody, some slumping to the ground as wounds, unheeded before, now got the better of them at last. Wallace came across to them, hatless, breeches all bloody, one epaulette missing, the other hanging by a thread and a large rent in his tunic. He placed himself before the panting men of the 105th.

"One Hundred and Fifth! I've come to thank you all. I'll not forget you, the 105th, the Rag and Bone Boys, and there'll be a few French rascals tonight who'll remember too, and for the rest of their lives they'll feel the shivers, when called upon to write the numbers 105 or 88!

You're good lads all! And did we not give them one Hell of a towelling!"

A ragged and hoarse cheer arouse from the 105th ranks as Wallace came to O'Hare, offering his hand, which O'Hare took and they exchanged a grip of appalling ferocity.

"Well done, Major, but was that not the most madcap thing you've ever done in your life?"

O'Hare grinned and nodded.

"Can't remember the last time, Sir, and I certainly hope there will not be another."

Both men shared a hearty laugh and leaned forward on each other, the disengaged left hand of each on the right shoulder of the other, in a gesture of relief that bordered on hysteria.

The last of the French were passing across Carr's front, so he judged the fight to now be done.

"Cease fire! Cease fire!"

Fatigue and relief overcame his small command and himself also. For some minutes they stood, catching their breath, with few moving anywhere, most drinking water. Then he saw what he took to be the 88th's holding line retiring back up the slope, clearly because they were coming under fire from some French guns in San Antonio, but then Ellis once again called for his attention.

"Sir. There's another lot coming up this slope!"

Carr turned to look and his heart sank to see that he was indeed right. Two columns were now ascending, each a Company wide with that on the right somewhat in the lead of that on the left. Leading them on foot was a high-ranking Officer, all blue and gold, obvious even at that distance, waving both his sword and hat and shouting at his men. They were heading straight for him. He took a deep breath.

"I can see no skirmishers before them."

He spoke to Ellis again, who was now alongside.

"Then we will be skirmishers for our side. Who have we?"

Both turned to look and find that the 88th Lights had rejoined their Regiment now moving back up the slope, leaving him with the 74th and his own. Looking over on his left, he noticed that some of his own Regiment were on the end of the 88th holding line, their green cuffs and collars very obvious, but there was no time to make any use of that.

"Ned. Carson. Skirmish line across here. Files of three."

Groans came from his own men and the kilted 74th, but the order was obeyed quickly and all formed in their skirmishing formation. Carr placed himself between two files and watched the French advance, now an easier march with the heather and gorse much trampled down. To his right was Davey's file, with him in front, then Miles and then Pike, at five-yard intervals behind.

"Davey. That fancy tailor's dummy at the front. He's yours,"

"Sir."

Davey knelt down, the better to steady his aim, then he checked his sights and priming as Carr judged the distance. The 74th only had muskets and so he would leave their order to fire to Carson. He judged 150 yards.

"Open fire!"

The rifles of the first line barked out and the leading Officer fell, to be almost overtaken by the column, but he seemed to rise again and continue forward, albeit within the column's ranks. Several others had fallen with the Senior Officer, but their bodies were soon covered by the advancing columns. Carr could now see the length of each column back down the hill; the right was three Battalions, the left was four. His men filed back in good order, each man, as he came to the front, sending a bullet into the column, but their advance was unstoppable by so small a force. Two Portuguese Light Companies from the 9th came down to reinforce but if made little difference to the French upward advance.

However, it had not been unnoticed by Picton, riding forward on his even more nervy horse. He saw that the very first column to attack his position half an hour ago still remained stalled on his right and Wallace had removed all living French from his left. However, deeply concerned, he rode back to Mackinnon and Lacey. He had seen the size of the French attack himself.

"There's another coming up and it's yours, Mac! Your 105th in the centre, Lacey. I'll bring the 9th Portuguese up on your right, Mac get their 8th back up to form the left. I'll move Arentschildt's guns at the top of the road to support you, then I'll bring up the Portuguese Thomar Militia from reserve."

With that, he was gone and Lacey and Mackinnon looked at each other, the latter the most worried. The looks they exchanged spoke volumes about their confidence in the Thomar Militia and even the Portuguese, but each said nothing, until Mackinnon looked forward.

"Yours will be the only British in the line, Lacey. Do your best. I'll stand with you!"

Lacey saluted and ran back to his men and once there, was grateful to see Gibney almost immediately, for he was now too much out of breath.

"Sar' Major. Advance the men."

Gibney took a deep breath.

"Paraaade!"

Each musket came beside each right boot.

"Shoulder arms!"

All muskets swung up to right shoulders in unison.

"Forward march."

The single wing of the 105th marched forward, with Lacey in the lead, forward for 100 yards until they could see easily down the slope and to the point where Mackinnon was waiting. Lacey peered forward through the thinning smoke, to see Carr's skirmishers slowly giving ground. Lacey raised his sword and his men halted, then he turned to Heaviside, the nearest Captain.

"Is that Carr, out front? Down there?"

Heaviside nodded, the morning's growth of his beard scraping his collar.

"Yes Sir. I do believe it is."

Lacey nodded, but his attention was drawn to the 8th Portuguese, running back up to form on his left. He wondered how steady they would be after their efforts against the column fought by the 88th, they had already been in one firefight, would they have the stomach for another, probably more severe? However, the two Battalions formed up well enough and set their Colours and then, quickly forming on his right, down came the 9th, also in their brown Portuguese uniforms. Then Lacey looked ahead, to immediately see a problem. The French were in two columns with a gap between them approaching 100 yards and this gap greatly coincided with his own line. The two French columns were heading directly for the Portuguese; his line only slightly overlapped the oncoming right-hand column. Remaining where they were would greatly reduce the impact of their own fire.

Meanwhile, as Lacey pondered, once again Ellis gave Carr the warning.

"Sir. We can't go back up much further. Our line's just behind."

Carr now looked back to see a long line of brown uniforms, then the red of his own, then brown again. The Light Companies of the 9th were already running back to their main line and so his men should also now retire and form on one end of the main line. He chose the shorter of the brown, the right. He called out.

"Fall back. Follow me."

He led his men over, his Lights of the 105th and the 74th, to where the end of the 9th just met the road where Arentschildt's guns were still astride it, but now trained left to meet the oncoming French. Carr then ran along the line, deeply anxious, ensuring a two deep line, but mostly to instruct his Captains. In Drake he has every confidence, but his knew little of Carson.

"Half Company volleys? Do your men know?"

Carson looked at Carr with utter disdain at such a question and Carr was reassured. He ran back to Drake.

"Not long now, but this is getting a mite tedious."

Drake grinned and drew his sword.

Lacey, stood with Mackinnon, needed a rapid decision; would he need to divide his line? Could he leave the two Battalions of 8th Portuguese to deal with the left-hand column and support only the 9th against the right? He had five Companies, the Grenadiers, Nine, Eight, Seven, and Three, the last the Colour Company. British firepower into the flank of both columns could make all the difference. He ran to the centre of Eight, to find its Captain, John Digby.

"John. Yours may have to split if we are to get onto the flanks of both. One of your Sections with the Grenadiers, one with The Colours. But I may bring all ours around onto that right-hand column. I'll be with you to give you the word."

Digby saluted as Lacey ran on, to then find Carravoy.

"Charles, our line may well divide to come onto those two columns. This half I give to you. You will be in command!"

Carravoy theatrically brought his sword up to his chin in acknowledgement and Lacey ran back, and just in time. The French columns were within 200 yards, and Arentschildt's guns opened fire, ploughing lanes through their ranks with grape shot, but the oncoming French ranks stepped over their fallen comrades and came inexorably on.

Lacey and Mackinnon stood together, both with drawn swords, stood before Digby's Eighth Company. Lacey turned around to face his men.

"Half Company volleys. Make Ready."

Along his whole line, the muskets came to the vertical, as did those of the 8th and 9th Portuguese very soon after. The French came on, the left-hand column tending more leftwards, reducing further the effectiveness of any fire from the 105th. He turned to Mackinnon.

"I've a mind to take mine round and onto the flank of that right-hand column. We can do more from there."

Mackinnon shook his head.

"Don't do it Lacey. You break the line and these'll run. As long as we stand, there's a fair chance they'll do too."

He pointed with his thumb towards the 8th Portuguese.

"Those lads have had enough. I see the best we can do is a fighting withdrawal until support arrives. We're not going to do this Lacey, there's too many. I'll need your men solid, here, in the centre."

Lacey took a deep breath. His Brigadier had made his choice, he could do no more now than hope.

"Target right. Present!"

The muskets of the front rank came down as one.

"From you, Heaviside."

The Captain took a deep breath.

"Fire!"

The half Company volley crashed out and then the others rolled on down the line; the firefight had begun. The volume of noise told Lacey that the Portuguese had joined in and he tried to peer through the smoke to gauge the impact, but little could be seen. The noise increased again, meaning the French were returning fire, but no casualties were being inflicted amongst his men, which could only mean that the French were concentrating on the Portuguese. The smoke was hiding all, but there could be no doubt that the drumming from within the columns was growing more distinct within the short space between the Allied volleys. Lacey's 105th continued to fire right, blindly into the smoke, for nothing could be seen of blue uniforms or blue shakoes, but he was becoming more worried. So too was Carr. His French column tramped on, their advance continuing, even though taking severe punishment. Worse, Arentschildt's guns had almost ceased firing; their ammunition becoming exhausted, or so Carr reasoned. He was right, they had been in action since the opening of the battle. Carr was stood at the junction of his 74th and the 9th Portuguese and his anxiety increased as it became clear that they were becoming detached from the 9th. The Portuguese were falling back. Carr gave the inevitable order.

"Edge left. Fall back. Maintain fire."

At the opposite end of the 9th's line stood Carravoy and he, directly opposite the French, could see all too clearly that their oncoming advance was coming ever closer. In addition, it took but one look over to the Portuguese to see that what had once been a regular firing line was now breaking up and giving ground. The 105th were becoming isolated and in great danger, if left facing the French column alone. He, also, gave the inevitable order.

"Fall back. Hold the line. Keep firing."

With perfect discipline, and with control maintained by D'Villiers and Ameshurst, the Grenadiers slowly gave way. It was no different for Lacey on the left of the 105th, because, just as he had feared, the 8th Portuguese were now dissolving to his left. Lacey looked around for Mackinnon, hoping to see him, because some minutes before he had gone to bring up the Thomar Militia. He did return and Lacey looked at him.

"The Militia?"

"Gone! We're on our own. Give ground, Lacey, or we're done!"

Lacey looked across.

"Heaviside! Fall back, but hold the line and maintain fire."

Within less than a minute, Lacey's 105th, now almost alone on the desperate ridge, were taking backward steps. So too were Carr's men, only his was perhaps more

553

rapid. The 9th were offering no resistance to speak of, bar the odd group under the command of a brave Officer.

"Form two ranks. File back."

His men obeyed and it was too soon altogether that one rank filed back through and found themselves looking down at the ridge track, just down over from their position, before they then turned to their front to take their turn. The French were almost over the ridge.

Lacey was of the same mind and ran to the end of his line, to the Colour Company.

"Heaviside! Get The Colours behind our line. The men will hold as they fall back. I leave it to you!"

Heaviside saluted, his face grave, but Lacey left him to it and soon Deakin and Rushby were falling back, both very anxious, but Ensign Mulcahy having to be dragged back by Colour Sergeant Bennet holding onto his epaulette.

Lacey had no idea if support was going to arrive, but the French had at least to be delayed or they could roll up the whole Allied line in whichever direction they chose, probably right, towards Busaco Convent. Mackinnon was still out front and so Lacey ran into the middle of the disintegrating 8th Portuguese Line, where he found their Colours and then an Officer. Lacey knew no Portuguese and so there was only one gesture that he could make, he jammed his sword down into the turf! The Officer looked at the sword, then at Lacey and then his face changed as his jaw clamped together in determination. He turned to his own Colour Company, all edging backwards.

"Retorne, camaradas, retorno. Permanecem com os ingleses.!"

The Colour Party edged back up and a few Officers each brought back a group of men. A ragged firing line was established, but too short to provide a weight of fire. It could do no more than bring down a few more French, whilst the rest marched on. Lacey pulled his sword out of the ground and stood with the Portuguese, he had made up his mind, 'I've asked these lads to stand and die and so they are. The least I can do is to stand and die with them.' His Portuguese line began a stuttering fire, but then came the shattering sound of a full volley, from over on the right.

Carr was busy controlling his retreat, when the next thing he knew was a two-deep Redcoat line arriving from behind his right shoulder. He turned in astonishment to see the Captain of a Light Company, who casually introduced himself.

"Howarth, Sir. Light Company. 9th Foot. 5th Division."

The 9th then halted and poured their first volley into the side of the French column. Their presence announced, they advanced 10 yards, whilst reloading for a second. What looked like a Senior Officer was on horseback before them, waving his hat. The 9th's first volley had damaged the leading French battalion, now very much reduced from the mauling it had received all the way up the slope, and from their long line, which extended someway down the slope, they had also hit the second and third Battalions of the left-hand French column. The second volley was duly delivered with the same shattering effect and the process was repeated twice more as they advanced against what was now the flank of the whole French column. Carr watched, as from somewhere came the command, 'Fix bayonets'. This was also quickly done and then the 9th advanced forward against the French column opposing them, now completely brought to a halt. Then cannon-fire began again from the position of Arentschildt's battery. Carr looked over and saw that another whole battery was alongside Arentschildt's. He turned to his men and called to those he could see.

"Nat! Ellis! Bring the men back. We're finishing this going forward!"

Drake ran off to the 74th, leaving Ellis with his Company.

"Get in line! We're going back!"

Miles was near.

"I've had less up and down than this in a bloody barn dance!"

"You shut up Miles! You just think of all they nice silver Officer buttons there must be, just over yonder!"

The 74th and 105th Light Companies advanced forward, but now against nothing. The nearest French column, once three large Battalions strong, had now reeled sideways and over to crash into the second French column, in order to escape the irresistible advance of the 9th. This was felt by Lacey over on the left as he stood with his Portuguese; the advance of his French column had now shuddered to a halt. The 8th's Officers saw this also and began calling their men forward, such as were remaining and could hear.

"Para a frente. Para a frente. Avanço com o inglês."

Heaviside, whose line still remained closer than any other to the French, saw the column to his right collapse into a rabble, but that to his left still held their ground, despite their comrades from the supporting column now joining their ranks in panic or running back down the hill. A push at this last column, he reasoned, from whoever was still capable, would see this thing ended. He looked behind him at the Colour Company.

"Sarn't Deakin!"

"Sir."

"We are going to advance."

He was not the Senior Captain, but Lacey was elsewhere and Carravoy at the far end. He walked forward to stand before his own Company and raised his sword to shout what his men now knew word for word.

"Let no man's heart fail because of him; thy servant will go and fight with this Philistine. 1 Samuel 17. Verse 32."

He then turned to face the French and curved his sword forward.

"March on boys!"

The wing of the 105th started forward, taking their lead from the Colour Company, with the Colours now returned to the front rank, but just as before Carr's Light Companies, resistance was melting away. The head of the final French column was now the target for Arentschildt's cannon, the Portuguese were rallying before them, a line of red-coats was approaching from their left front and something terrible was coming over from the far left. The column's Commanding Officer, plainly a Senior Officer of very high rank judging by his elaborate uniform, and himself wounded with his arm bound against his body, stood for a moment at the head of his men, him plainly stood in despair, his men had done all they could. Unsupported at the top of a high ridge; the attempt was now hopeless and so he turned and motioned them back. Thus they retired, faces still set towards their foe, taking with them the very first column to attack the ridge, these having been held back all the while by the 74th and the 21st Portuguese. They had now seen the final assault fail and, with this, they also quit the fight and descended the slope.

All along the Allied line came the call to cease-fire and all did. Then came the final sounds of battle, the groans of the wounded and the dying. For the Allies, this was nothing like Talavera, because all their wounded were along the ridgeline, very much unlike those of the French, whose wounded were scattered all across the hillside. However, compared with the tumult of the previous hour the silence was eerie as though the very air had been beaten into frozen submission. Then came the sounds of yet another conflict, seemingly of equal ferocity to theirs just ended, and coming over from their far left.

oOo

Picton galloped up to Lacey and Mackinnon and fiercely reined in his horse.

557

"Lacey! Who've you got that can get over to the Convent and see what's happening? If we're beaten there, I need to know. I'll need all my Staff here, getting us back organised, in case we need to retreat."

Lacey and Mackinnon looked at each other, both puzzled, but then Lacey noticed O'Hare leading his wing of the 105th back up the hill.

"There Sir. My Senior Major, Padraigh O'Hare."

Picton looked at O'Hare, then at Lacey, then he turned to one of his Staff.

"Fenton. Dismount. Give that Major your horse."

Within a minute, the surprised and bemused O'Hare was galloping along the ridge track towards the sound of the guns at the Convent. He covered the near mile after about two minutes to arrive at the junction of his track with another that ran along the foot of the ridge back to San Antonio. It was very obvious that there was, as yet, no conclusion that he could report on, because a full-scale conflict was now in progress. He had arrived at the rear of a formed up Portuguese Brigade of four battalions, these holding the road that led off right to San Antonio, whilst to their left was the edge of a deep, bowl shaped, ravine, the road running on left along its very edge. On the far side of the ravine, on the road, O'Hare could see two more Battalions of Portuguese Infantry, whilst further beyond them were two Battalions of British infantry, all lying down. Just before these last was a lone figure wearing a huge bi-corn hat, fore and aft, and mounted on a huge horse. Where there were no infantry on the road, there were cannon, all firing at maximum rate, their gunners serving their pieces like men possessed.

O'Hare dismounted, tethered his horse and went to the edge of the ravine, there to look down and see masses of French troops, fully covering both sides and in Division strength, one advancing on the Portuguese near him, the other climbing the slope to meet the lone horseman. However, the Division attacking this lone figure was being fiercely resisted by a thick screen of green clad British Riflemen and brown clad Portuguese Cacadores. Consequently, the progress of the French on that side was painfully slow and very costly, judging by the number of prone, blue uniformed bodies littering the slope all the way down to a small hamlet halfway down and many bodies even further below that. The hamlet must be called Sula, because he could see a sign just up the road, pointing down right towards it. O'Hare placed himself at the end of the leftmost of the four Portuguese Battalions and looked downwards. 300 yards below them, the slope was thick with French assault troops in what must also be Division strength, their blue shakoes stretching far back down the hill indicating their large number. O'Hare looked over at the nearest Portuguese to him, a Captain, and received back a confident grin. The guns all across the head of the ravine continued to roar their defiance, inflicting appalling casualties on the densely packed French on either side.

O'Hare looked over to the other conflict which would begin first and, despite the smoke from the guns, he could see that the skirmishers on that side, the Riflemen and the Cacadores, had at last retired to the top of their slope and were spreading either side of the still prone Redcoats. The French, now unopposed, came on and the first of them finally placed a foot on the road at the top. O'Hare became very anxious; they were but 20 yards, or less, from the prone Redcoats. The roar of the cannon blanked all sound, but he saw the lone horseman take off his hat. The Redcoats sprang to their feet and immediately delivered a full volley at what could be little more than ten paces. The French attack, now at the top, crumpled with the impact, then the two flanks of the British Battalions closed in and the French survivors, many still climbing, were trapped within a fearsome semi-circle of fire, but with incredible courage that O'Hare could scarcely credit, the French column continued their attempt to take the summit. O'Hare could see little, because of the smoke, but he knew what was happening inside that semi-circle; death flew over those few yards eight times every second. The French endured the blizzard of musket-fire for less than a minute, before the whole gave way and tumbled back down the slope, many falling away to their left to tumble helpless to the very bottom of the ravine.

The two Battalions of Redcoats charged forward and pushed the whole assault, a whole Division, back down the slope to the hamlet, where they halted. Then came a smaller encore, very similar, just back towards O'Hare on the same side of the ravine as the earlier repulse. What must be a smaller French force was attempting the even steeper head of the ravine and waiting for them was the nearest of the two Portuguese Battalions. They poured one full volley down over the edge to then fix bayonets and charge. Within five minutes, displaying admirable discipline, they had returned back up to resume their place on the road. The clearing smoke enabled O'Hare to see that the Redcoats had remained at Sula and that the skirmishers had run forward to hold the lower edge of the houses. It had taken but minutes, but a full Divisional assault had been thoroughly beaten to pieces by only two Battalions, with some help from a third. Despite the ongoing noise of the cannon, O'Hare took off his hat and cheered, which was taken up by the Portuguese Battalions near him and then the two further along, one recently victorious themselves, supporting the earlier triumphant Redcoats.

O'Hare now knew that, for the French here, there could be nothing other than failure. He was tempted to return with his joyful message but he held his place to observe the final French Division, this on his side of the ravine, now the only target remaining for the merciless cannonade. These were doggedly hauling themselves up the slope immediately below him, opposed by the four Portuguese Battalions waiting at the top. The French eased left, away from the incessant grapeshot but were now within range of the Portuguese. Then came the order.

"Prepare-se."

All muskets came to the vertical.

"Presente."

All were lowered to point down the slope.

"Disparar!"

The half Company volleys began and the French began to take casualties, but did not fall back, the range was just too great. However, any group that did come too close was quickly brought down, but the French continued to attempt the summit with a series of determined assaults at various points, led by Officers of suicidal bravery. However, each time concentrated Portuguese musketry blew away the head of the advance for it to then fall back and, finally, even these individual assaults became less frequent. The Portuguese then began to shout insults down at the French, evidently with much glee and enthusiasm, in between the stuttering musketry and the slackened, but regular cannonfire that still continued

O'Hare was now certain that the French assault at the Convent had been defeated; his side, his army of allies had won, at both points. His final look, from the saddle of his horse, was of a blue rabble milling around at the throat of the ravine, these being the remnants of the main French assault through Sula, but he could see, further back and still in formation, Brigade after Brigade of blue-coated French infantry. He thought to himself, 'They may try here again, but they surely cannot be that stupid. They'll move to get around us, and so we'll move as well. We'll have to!'.

He urged his horse on and soon returned to the pass above San Antonio to see Picton in the centre in deep conversation with two other Generals, one whom O'Hare knew to be General Leith, Commander of the 5th Division, the other he knew to be General Hill, the popular and avuncular Senior Divisional Commander, second only to Wellington. Whilst this significant and nervous conversation continued, Picton's Staff were studying and controlling events, these being to reform his Division.

Picton noticed him from far off and watched him as he approached, his face anxious. O'Hare rode up and saluted, but Picton's answer was one word.

"Well?"

"A complete repulse Sir. We still hold at the Convent."

Picton frowned.

"But I can still hear it all going on!"

"It's petering out Sir. Two French attacks have been held, one utterly defeated, the second with no choice but to give best. They'll soon be pulling back completely. Sir."

It was at that point that the cannonfire did die away, to leave the faint bickering of muskets as the only remaining sound. Picton nodded, but was clearly discomfited that his statement had been so thoroughly rebuffed. Hill, meanwhile, having rode over from his Second Division on the far right where they had not fired a shot, remained thoroughly in high spirits having so recently heard of Picton's and Leith's triumph at the San Antonio pass, and now he was being told of the complete success at the Convent. He beamed down at O'Hare.

"A complete repulse Major, you say?"

O'Hare came to the attention and saluted.

"Yes Sir. Beaten back everywhere. Thoroughly."

Hill grinned at Leith on his right, then Picton on his left, but the latter remained somewhat fractious.

"Anything else to report?"

"Yes Sir. The French still have huge reserves over there."

Picton sat back in his saddle and, whilst pointing down the hill, he looked at Mackinnon, stood silent nearby.

"They still have a Brigade down there, before us, and those that they can rally, of course. What do you think Mackinnon?"

The Scotsman's face showed no emotion as he replied.

"He'll not try here again, Sir. That's for certain."

Now Leith spoke up, whilst Hill nodded agreement.

"He'll try to find some way beyond our flank. How else will he get us off this ridge? There must be roads at both ends that he could use."

Picton nodded his agreement.

"And he'll do it. He's too strong."

He looked around, to almost absentmindedly study his men attending to their own wounded all along their line and also bringing up some French. There were also many burial parties all along his position, as each Battalion interred their own dead.

"Right! Assume that tomorrow we will be falling back. Get all ready."

Picton looked across at Hill and Leith.

"We are agreed? Prepare to fall back?"

Both nodded and spoke no more, but pulled their horses heads over to begin their ride back to their men. Picton gave his final order.

"Mac, I leave you to handle things here. I'll tell Lightburne and Champlemonde."

He pulled on the reins of his horse to turn him away, but Mackinnon had a question.

"What do we do here? About the French wounded? Come nightfall this place could be covered in marauding peasants."

Picton's face was as stone.

"Set pickets for tonight. What else? A strong screen. Come nightime tomorrow this will belong to the Frogs. Let them take care of their own wounded. They were mad enough to try us at the top of a ridge, let them carry the consequences!"

For the rest of the day the survivors spent their time dressing their own minor wounds, eating and carrying the wounded to the Surgeons, who this time, unlike Talavera, had the time to probe for bullets rather than carry out a swift and simple amputation. Lacey allowed both his Majors some rest and both gratefully slept for some hours whilst the preparations for retreat continued and so, for that particular task, Lacey relied on his Captains to prepare their men for marching and for the Reverend Albright to supervise the wounded. Both he and Sedgwicke bustled amongst the rows of injured men, offering water, kind words, and the willingness to fetch anything asked for, but the useful ministrations were carried out by the Followers, all with long experience with wounds of all levels if severity. It was not long before Bridie, Nellie and Eirin had blood up to their elbows as they prepared the wounded for the Surgeon, but Eirin had an extra concern, which she asked of any Light Company member that passed.

"Lieutenant Maltby?"

The first answer was grave.

"He was with Carr. They had it rough."

This depressed her hugely, but the repeat of the question eventually lifted both her face and her spirits to one of open joy and relief.

"He's back over, with Drake."

"Unwounded?"

"Looks so!"

Bridie and Nellie looked at each other and shook their heads.

All those to whom the Surgeon had attended, were carefully carried back down the hill to waiting transport, which then took them into Luso, the pleasant Spa Town, behind The Convent, and just back off the ridge. Just as he had granted rest to his two Majors, the Light Company was also allowed to rest and so picketing duties fell to the Grenadier Company. Either side were the pickets of the 88th and the 74th, but there was little interaction between them as dusk fell. All simply stared forward, studying the French bivouac fires growing more numerous and distinct in the dying light.

Carravoy, with a candle lantern, patrolled the whole of his line and it was not long before he was stood next to D'Villiers. It was their first opportunity for any

564

conversation since the fighting ended, this begun by D'Villiers, staring ahead.

"There are still thousands. Tens of thousands!"

It was a few seconds before Carravoy answered.

"Yes. So, damn lot of good this did. Rumour is, we're pulling out tomorrow. They'll call that a defeat in England. Wellington should have followed it up."

D'Villiers sighed, somewhat exasperated.

"He'd have to be a damn fool to come down off this ridge and attack what Johnny's still got down there. British troops amount to only half of what he still has, so would you trust the Portuguese for an assault? You'd have to!"

Again the long pause, before the unconvinced reply came back.

"All the same. It's us pulling back."

D'Villiers now thought to mention what he very much felt.

"Well, I think our men did damn well today. You saw the numbers that Johnny brought up to take us on and we saw them away, good and thorough, although badly outnumbered."

No reply and so D'Villiers continued.

"And the Portuguese did all right. In defence, that is. I know they were pushed back a little, but not broken."

Again silence.

"The Peer has to hang onto all the force that he has, in the face of an army of that size. No risks. Keep us together as a force that Johnny has to be very wary of. Over at the Convent I hear that two whole Divisions were absolutely wrecked by not much more than a few Battalions of ours. That's given M'sieu something to think about."

Again no reply. D'Villiers could feel that something was seething inside his Captain, but what it was he could not say. And so he waited until it came.

"And what of Carr?"

D'Villiers irritation increased and it showed, a least as much as he dared.

"What of him? If I've got it right, he faced up three times and led his men well. I'd be surprised if that were not noticed."

He paused.

"I'd leave Templemere and Tavender to their schemes, were I you. Whatever bee is buzzing in their bonnets is their affair. I'd leave it as so. None of ours, at least not mine."

He lifted his scabbard in his left hand, prior to walking off.

"But you must decide for yourself, Charles. Now I must be amongst my men. See what's what!"

The 'what's what' turned out to be candle lanterns coming up the hillside. D'Villiers found his Sergeant, Nathan Ridgway, or more like Ridgway found him.

"Sir. There's Frogs comin' up the hill, Sir. Collectin' their wounded. What to do, Sir?"

"Let them up and pull ours further back up until they can be moved. Give them the room. So far, we've acted well towards each other. I, for one, would like to keep it that way. Sometime in the future it could be ours down there. But keep a good watch and don't let them too far up."

"Some of the lads have been carrying their wounded down to them. Sir."

"Turn a blind eye to that, until they make it their main task and do little else. Manning a picket is what we're here for. They are, after all, our enemy down there, and M'sieu is not beyond a little deception."

He watched the lanterns move then stop, as a wounded man was found still alive, then he changed the subject.

"Many Spanish, out plundering?"

"Very few Sir. Hardly any. Probably on account that we're just about in the middle of no-where, Sir."

"Very good, Sergeant. Carry on."

Came the very depth of the darkness at 3.00am the Grenadiers were relieved by Number 4 Company and

566

Carravoy's Grenadiers climbed wearily up the hill to cross the ridge track and sink to the ground for some grateful sleep. They were not woken, for Picton allowed his whole Division to rest, anticipating the arduous march to come, but Wellington's Staff were thoroughly awake and a group arrived at the high rocky outcrop above the San Antonio pass anxious for the dawn and full light. Two remained in their saddles and even stood in their stirrups to gain extra height as they used their telescopes. Lacey, O'Hare and Carr, sat drinking coffee and eating bread rolls, gave both a lazy examination, but it was Carr who spoke.

"Why are they here where we are? All those before us have pulled back. Way back."

O'Hare looked at him and spoke somewhat indulgently

"I think you will find, that this is the highest point of our line, thereby providing the best vantage point to study our friends over yonder."

Carr started another roll as the two galloped off, but within fives minutes Wellington himself arrived to adopt the same pose as his two Staff had earlier, again but yards from the trio. O'Hare looked at Lacey.

"Should we offer him some tea, or something?"

"Seems the right thing to do."

He turned to Bryce.

"Bryce. Get a cup of something to the General, will you?"

Bryce looked rapidly from Lacey, to the coffee pot and then to Wellington. He was required to give a cup of something to the very man himself. It was poured and he carried it over. By now Wellington's own telescope had been collapsed and handed back to an Orderly. He had seen enough, then he looked down at the approaching mug of something black.

"Compliments of Colonel Lacey, Sir."

Wellington took the cup and drank one swallow, before looking over at the three, who immediately sprang to

567

their feet. Wellington actually smiled. He was clearly in a good mood.

"Ah Lacey! How were things over here?"

The use of the past tense clearly meant the battle of the previous day.

"Well enough, Sir. It became a bit anxious at one point, but we saw them away."

"Who did Lacey? Yours or Leith's?"

"Sir?"

"There seems to be a bit of a contretemps between the my two Divisional Commanders as to who did what and unto whom."

"Can't comment, Sir. All I know is, we sent them back down the hill."

Wellington laughed whilst finishing his coffee.

"Too much smoke and hullabaloo, eh?"

Lacey grinned himself, as did Carr and O'Hare.

"Exactly, Sir."

Wellington handed the cup down to Bryce, who held it as though it were some form of treasure, but Wellington now noticed Carr.

"Carr! I hear you did well!"

Carr saluted.

"I did my best, Sir. Tried to do as required."

Wellington was now pulling his horse's head around.

"As do we all, Carr. As do we all."

Bryce was still holding the mug.

"Sir, can I keep this? I'll pay for it."

"You'll not Bryce. The mug's yours."

For all on the ridge, all nine miles of it, the rest of the day was spent in tranquil relaxation, eating, but mostly sleeping, for many still felt the strain of the previous day's exertions. For those with telescopes the movements of the French provided additional diversion. Lacey gave a warning for kit inspection, which was carried out during the mid-afternoon, but there were no defaulters. As all was

568

examined, Miles gave Ellis a challenging stare, the reply to which was a loud sniff. Miles' kit was perfect.

That negotiated, One Section Light Company took it upon themselves to return the old couple to San Antonio. Maltby's permission was gained and the two were chaired back to their home, both exchanging cheery waves with any Redcoat they passed. Their home was much dishevelled, it was the Church that had received cannon hits, but they both looked around seemingly pleased, for nothing had been smashed. Grins and waves were exchanged as they parted and Saunders was the last to leave, at which point the old man noticed five silver buttons and a silver buckle remaining on the table.

Late afternoon the orders came, Picton's Division would be part of the main column under Wellington and would march for Coimbra, Hill would command another and march direct for Lisbon. The explanation was brief, the French were all moving North West, to where a road existed that could by-pass Busaco ridge and so Wellington was taking no risk of being cut of from Lisbon. Therefore, with the arrival of darkness, the army moved off the ridge. Bivouac fires were left burning on the French side and they found their way down the back slope by torchlight and candle lantern. Come the dawn there were no British left on the ridge, bar the 52nd and 43rd of Crauford's victorious Brigade, these remaining on the site of their triumph of the previous day, above the ravine and the small hamlet of Sula. With them was Anson's cavalry Brigade, part of Stapleton-Cottons cavalry Division, including the 16th Light Dragoons and so, through most of the morning, all sat above the ravine and there was not a moment when some telescope, somewhere, was not studying the remaining French force acting as a rearguard half a mile off.

Finally, these last moved even further back and some Officers took it upon themselves to filter down through Sula and examine the French positions. These, inevitably, included Tavender and Templemere, both equally curious, but Sula and beyond proved to be no place at all to boost their relaxed mood, because French dead being stacked up in every yard and corner. It became worse when they heard shouting from some Officers of the 52nd and so they went to investigate and found the source of the commotion to be a large barn. A Captain of the 52nd came towards them, obviously deeply angry.

"Frog bastards! In there and out the back are hundreds of badly wounded French. Too bad to move without carts and so he's left them for the Spanish. They'll be lucky for a quick death."

He took a deep breath to calm himself down.

"So, we, that is the 52nd and 43rd, are going to get them up to the Convent. There's nothing else we can do. Can you ask your Colonel if he can provide some help?"

The pair looked at each other but said nothing in reply, only that Tavender nodded before they turned their horses to return to the heights. Once through Sula, Tavender spoke his thoughts.

"If Johnny's left those behind knowing that we'll look after them, to slow us up, that the worst, lowest, trick I've ever heard of!"

Back on the ridge they found their Colonel Withers and Tavender asked the question.

"Sir. Down there has been found hundreds of badly wounded French, wounded he could not take with him for whatever reason. The infantry have asked for our assistance in bringing them back up to the Convent, Sir."

Withers studied the pair, then gave a terse reply.

"Organise it!"

Then, for some hours the mournful and painful process continued. Some of the French wounded were able to mount horses and were brought up easily, but some had to be carried on stretchers which gave a long, heavy journey. However, there was not one Frenchman who did not breathe his thanks as he was laid onto the ancient flagstones inside the Convent. All had heard of the treatment meted out by the Spanish, of all types and levels, to any captured French. The Nuns bustled about, responding to the need that had been placed upon them.

Finally, all was done and Crauford and Anson came together above the ravine and orders were issued. Within 30 minutes their column marched off, Anson's cavalry in the lead, then came Crauford's Rifles, Cacadores, 43rd and 52nd. As they passed each saluted the fresh, mass graves that held their erstwhile comrades, whilst Spanish peasants moved across the battlefield looking for any saleable souvenirs. The last acts and sounds of the battle of Busaco were the groans of the badly injured French soldiers issuing from the open windows of the Convent.

oOo

Chapter Ten

The Lines of Torres Vedras

The shouts from the alleyways and houses that they passed were disheartening but all too familiar.

"Ingleses cobardes! Ingleses cobardes!"

Luso was being evacuated, all the transport carrying the wounded and supplies had gone in the night and so, mostly unencumbered, Picton's Third Division, second in the long column, marched through the sullen streets with even the windows and doors seemingly morose in the returned fog. The citizens stood and watched, saying nothing, content for the catcalls from behind to convey their feelings. The pace was fast, faster than normal, something not unnoticed by John Davey, marching in the right-hand file of the first rank of the Light Company. Beside him, as usual, was Sergeant Ethan Ellis, and Davey was as mystified as anyone in the long column.

"What do you know, Ethan?"

"Not much, other than what I heard Carr and Drake sayin'. Seems the Frogs have found a road as'll take 'em round the end of that ridge what we've just come off of. There's still a powerful lot of 'em, and so 'tis a race back to Coimbra. After that, God knows. Could be another set-to."

"What if they beats us to it? We all knows they marches faster than us."

"Don't even think on it! This time we has to be fast. Faster!"

With that, all who heard hitched up their kit into a more comfortable position and leaned forward, just slightly, to match the pace.

The road as mentioned in connection with the French was that which linked Aveleira, Boialvo and Sardao, a halfway decent road for any army, which climbed and then descended the passes of the Serra de Carramula. All these names were known to Julian Sanchez, as he watched whilst sat on his horse with his Lancers, the French army pour down the road from the final pass towards Sardao. He cursed the 'Ingles Wellington' for not holding the best of the passes for defence. If Sanchez had more Ordenanza, perhaps better armed, he would have tried himself, but he did not and so now he saw, from his high vantage point, the town of Sardao on his left, the French on his right, and beyond them, where they had come from, the smoke of burning buildings. The French were employing the same methods, which they had used since leaving Cuidad Rodrigo, these being to burn and pillage, and persuade through terror, the surrender of the food and supplies they needed. For this reason did 'El Charro' curse the British. There would be yet more burning and murder before the French were stopped, wherever that was to be.

It would have been useful for 'El Charro', and it would have tempered his feelings towards Wellington, were he attending at the table that lunchtime shared by Mackinnon's Senior Commanders, these being Lacey, Wallace, Champlemonde and their Senior Majors. They were all assembled in what could only be described as an outhouse of an abandoned farm, the farm itself having been wrecked, by whom no-one could tell. Before the food arrived, the question strong in the minds of all was asked and Mackinnon answered the question simply.

"He had no choice. We've not the men to hold the ridge of Carramula same as we held that of Busaco."

He looked at the Commander of his Portuguese Battalion.

"All respect to you Champlemonde, but half our army, more, is Portuguese. Wellington doesn't know yet what you can do. If he detached a force to hold the passes and it was beaten back, being too weak, then he'd be in a helluva fix. That force would probably be lost to him and it would have had to retreat off to the coast. He must keep his army together. Despite so many of his Divisions being smashed, day before yesterday, M'sieu is still immensely strong."

The next question occurred first to O'Hare.

"So where do we stop him?"

Mackinnon's answer was to turn to his Orderly.

"Fraser. Get the map."

The food arrived, but the Orderlies were required to stand waiting, whilst the table was occupied with the map of Southern Portugal. Mackinnon picked up a knife and drew an imaginary line across the wide promontory that had Lisbon at its foot, from the coast across to the estuary of the Tagus.

"Here. Since Talavera he's been building a defensive line across this tongue of land. Redoubts, forts and all sorts. Better roads too. We're back to there and there we'll hold him. He's callin' it The Lines of Torres Vedras."

All saw the strength of the position, but all also saw the length of the retreat that they now had to make. The most optimistic there estimated 100 miles, the most pessimistic 150. With that the map was folded and handed back to be replaced by the food, giving much relief to the servants who had been stood with burning fingers.

"Make good use of this food, Gentlemen, it's the weapon he's chosen to use, to draw the Johnnies deep down into Portugal where they'll sit starvin' unable to get supplies. For us too, we'll be on short commons afore we gets much closer to Lisbon and our supplies. He's given the order that all crops, stores and animals that we cannae take with us on the way down are to be destroyed. All the civilians are to come with us, drivin' the animals an' the supply wagons. As Johnny comes down he'll find himself deeper and deeper in a deep hole, with the cupboard very much bare!"

All looked at each other before they began eating, the same thought, although in different guises, on the mind of each. This was total war that they were part of, using scorched earth and starvation as weapons.

At the same time, total war as it applied to them, at least the rigours of retreat, was uppermost in the mind of Jed Deakin and his good comrades, all sat with their Followers in their own wrecked farmyard, but all were listening to the Good Man Deakin.

"Now listen, Ladies, we'n in for a retreat, not a very hungry one, like last, but 't'as to be quick. We has to get back down to Lisbon, or near enough, afore the French. More urgent, we 'as to win Coimbra afore the French gets in. Once there and through, we'm safe, 'cos the French'll spend days pillagin' the place. So, what sort of shape are you all in?"

Bridie looked at him, she both puzzled and slightly irritated.

"What sort of a question is that? Same shape as we're always in, for any kind of a march."

Deakin was neither appeased nor re-assured.

"But this'll be at a quick pace. Over 20, each day. 'T'as to be."

Nellie was now in the same mood as Bridie.

"What's needed, we'll do. That's how things've always been."

Deakin looked at Henry Nicholls.

"What can we do? What with the burdens and the youngers and all?"

Nellie's husband looked straight back.

"Lighten the load. Unburdened they walk quicker. Lighten the load."

Nellie knew what this meant and looked fiercely at her husband.

"I'm not leavin' but one cookin' pot for those Heathen French. Not one!"

However, whilst they talked about 'lightening the load', Tom Miles, well aware of the future's requirements, had been taking action, this heralded by a loud and disturbing crash from within the barn. Deakin looked over.

"What's he up to?"

This was soon answered as Miles emerged from behind the unhinged and perilous door, pulling some kind of cart.

"Found this! Don't know what it's called, but it has four wheels and moves. This'll help."

Byford had the answer.

"It's a child's toy, a dogcart pulled by a dog or a small pony. It'll take about four infants."

Deakin was not listening, he was examining the wonderful item.

"Good find Tom. This'll fit the bill and perfect."

He pointed at the cart and looked at Nellie and Bridie.

"There! Cleaned up a bit, this'll carry all your pots and pans and whatnot. All you've got to do is pull it."

The two were not listening either, they had already tipped the vehicle onto its side and were brushing it out. The following morning the cart was on its way to Coimbra, but a few hours march away, in the middle of the Followers at the rear of Mackinnon's Division. However, they were unmolested by even the sight of any French, for two reasons, not least, as Deakin predicted, the reason of the French scouring all villages and farms for food, but also the actions of their rearguard, these being Stapleton-Cotton's Cavalry Division, usefully aided by Julian Sanchez Lancers. In this role, Colonel Anson's Light Cavalry Brigade, comprising the 16th Light Dragoons and the 1st Hussars King's German Legion were formed up on a bare ridge, the best place available to make a visible demonstration to deter any French cavalry advance. They were looking back at the burning town of Fornos, many using their telescopes to pick out the detail available from their high perch. Templemere lowered his and looked at Tavender.

"Good Lord! They're slaughtering just about everybody within reach. I know about their edict on the Ordenanza, but this is simply appalling!"

Tavender's reply was flat and laconic.

"Thought you knew! This is warfare Boney style. Live off the land, but there's not much living for any civilians in their path, even those who give them food. They still think that they're holding out, no matter how much they give."

He raised his spy-glass again, but quickly lowered it, the killing and beatings were unabated.

"Especially as us and the civilian Dons who left, have already stripped the place, so now they're taking it out on the poor fools who stayed, instead of getting themselves up into the hills."

Templemere said nothing, but folded his own telescope and carefully placed it in the holder attached to his saddle.

Meanwhile, not so high and far to their right, Julian Sanchez was also observing events with far more aggressive intent. Arranged either side of him were his Lancers, now 500 strong, and both he and they were waiting for the first French to emerge from Fornos. They waited for over an hour, but Sanchez and his men were determined in their patience. The first to emerge was a continuous column of what looked like a mixed force of cavalry, both Light Cavalry and Dragoons, and on their saddles could be seen the results of their depravations of Fornos; fabrics and garments of all kinds and all had suspiciously bulging saddlebags. Sanchez waited. His men were in plain sight, but above the road. He waited but a while longer then walked his horse forward to bring him in advance of his men. Sanchez drew his sword and spoke softly in a wicked hiss.

"Venga, muchachos"

Within seconds he and his men were charging down the slope, for this was to be no ambush, this was an attack to win or to lose, but the result was foregone; the Lancers crashed into the head of the column, many of whom could barely ride from the drink they had consumed. The Lancers rode through and on, attacking further down the column, their lances emptying almost every saddle they came to, the screams of the wounded and dying French adding to the noise of the terrified horses. The French broke and ran, horribly surprised. Some Lancers pursued but not far, their disciplined obedience to bugle calls brought them back. The road was theirs, however temporary, and so now there was just time to despatch the few prisoners, both whole and wounded, this being completed, whilst still remaining up in the saddle, by shots from their heavy British Dragoon pistols. That done, they quickly reformed and took the road upwards that would take them past Anson's men on their ridge. They passed by near enough to hear the cheers and applause of the 16th nearest to them, which were acknowledged by the merest lift of a lance. These were anguished and angry men, who had very mixed opinions about the retreating British. However, Templemere felt moved enough to turn to Tavender.

"My word, but that was smartly done."

Tavender looked at him but said nothing, then he heard the order, 'Form column'. Soon they were following the route of 'El Charro's men, but they did not see them, for the Lancers had soon turned off when they arrived at another potential position for another attack.

oOo

Coimbra was a madhouse as the 105th marched through, the whole in utter turmoil as the population prepared to march South with the army, or float down the Mondego in boats, or take themselves up into the hills. An assiduous forecast would conclude that all the wheeled vehicles would be used for the first possibility and the beasts of burden for the third, but the result would contradict such a conclusion. All the side roads leading off the main highway were jammed with vehicles of all kinds and the main road was choked with carts, carriages, laden people and beasts of burden of every possible shape. The

578

first Allied Division to arrive, these being Spencer's Division including the Guards Brigade had cleared the road, none too gently and so the space occupied by the passing army added to the congestion and panic. From all around came the uproar of shouts, screams, imprecations and bellows of animals, all echoing and bouncing off the walls of the fine buildings. The richer citizens had left during the previous days, obeying their Governments edict to leave and leave nothing behind that could support an advancing army. Those remaining, but now departing, were the poorest, clinging to the fading hope that the French would not arrive and take all that they had. However, the whole Allied army marching through told its own dismal story.

For the 105th there was no alternative, but to close their ranks, lower their heads into their collars and push on through. One incensed citizen stood but a yard from the passing Redcoats yelling at each from a range close enough so that they could smell his breath, yelling what all now knew the meaning of.

"Ingleses cobardes! Ingleses cobardes!"

The Light Company were approaching and Ellis could see Tom Miles slinging his musket onto his shoulder to free at least one of his hands for a blow at their tormentor.

"You hold your place, Miles!"

Miles did as he was ordered and it was Ellis himself who used his musket to shove the man aside. This was no good day for the Allied army, nor the Portuguese civilians, beginning their route to the South. When the 16th Light Dragoons rode in later that morning, they passed first through the lines of the final rearguard, Crauford's Light Brigade. These hard soldiers gave not a glance to the society Light Cavalry passing through. There was only one Brigade that they had any respect for, and this was their own, that which had beaten into pieces a whole French Division by the force of their firepower and the ferocity of their bayonet charge. They now saw themselves as even more of an elite.

Once in Coimbra, any hope that Templemere and Tavender had of any rest and sustenance was quickly dispelled by the mournful sight of the elegant town square littered with all manner of rubbish and abandoned possessions, most of some worth. What none of the Allied soldiers could know, was that there had been a shortage of wheeled transport and all that any of the town's citizens wished to take with them had to be carried on their own shoulders. Many had abandoned the idea before they even began and had left much lying on the stone pavements. The only humans to be seen were Portuguese scavengers, searching the abandoned town for anything of any value, and there was plenty, before they took to the hills and woodland themselves, or slunk off into the holes and cellars of the outskirts.

For the 105th, now out of the town and onto the chausee', the whole day was spent passing a never-ending column of refugees, all carrying whatever they could. However, as the day wore on, more and more possessions could be seen dumped at the roadside as many, especially the old and infirm, gave up the task of carrying such a burden on the seemingly endless trek. Both Deakin and Halfway were moved by the continuous column of misery that they overtook, mile after mile, these refugees having been pushed to the roadside by Spencer's Division to ease the passage of the army, giving them even less room on the good surface of the main chause' South.

"Don't seem like we scored much of a victory back there, Tobe. From what I hear, 'twer easier even than Vimeiro, specially over at the Convent, but now we'n the ones fallin' back, fast as our feet'll carry us."

"You'm not wrong, Jed, like 'tis us as've been beat."

He re-hitched his pack, while he searched for the correct words.

"Outmanoeuvred' I do believe the Generals calls it, and I do believe it sticks to us. The Frogs still has a very

580

powerful army and they got round. So, Nosey might turn to face 'em again if he can find a ridge like Busaco. What you think?"

"Could be, but from what I've heard from Bert Bryce, we'n off to get way down to a bunch of forts an' trenches and whatnot. But we has to get there first."

Halfway's thumb pointed towards the burdened refugees.

"Right, but all the same, the Frogs'll overtake this lot, even after a day or two riflin' through Coimbra. What then?"

Deakin had no answer and hitched his pack and musket into a more comfortable position. Even with the ending of that day, they had not come to the end of the sorrowful column and so, when they drew their rations that were waiting for them, which turned out to be disappointing, much was shared with hungry children, which went some way towards silencing the ongoing cries of "Ingleses cobardes!" What was in many ways worse was the evidence throughout their march of Wellington's 'scorched earth' orders, for all was desolate and forlorn, with neither people nor animals to be seen and all barns and storehouses gaping wide as if in outrage at the thorough removal of their contents from their safekeeping. Most dwellings were wrecked, some thoroughly consumed by fire, their contents scattered and broken apart, all exposed on the ground for any to examine, the sad remains of the individual stories of individual families, that had been gathered and treasured over generations. This was a good time for Portuguese scavengers, who could often be seen, skulking around during both day and night.

Far behind the 105th, the sound of gunfire in the afternoon caused Anson's men to remain in Coimbra, and await developments. The next event was the belligerent Stapleton-Cotton arriving in the town square, conveying his orders around personally to the individual Colonels of Anson's Brigade.

"Withers! Get back out and take a position before the town. Durnfeld's KGL will be with you. Don't think you're alone; De Grey's Heavies and Fane's Lights are off to your left, Slade's Heavies over to your right. When you see any French, when, mark you, pitch into them. Slade's will come in support. The same goes for the KGL, but if any of them go in, you follow!"

Withers, with Johnson, Tavender and Templemere close by, looked blankly back at their Divisional General, whilst Templemere stared at him horrified. Then Withers answered.

"Hit how hard Sir? Enough to stall, then withdraw?"

Stapleton-Cotton was already swinging over his horse's head.

"You've got it! Our job is to make sure that Wellington's gets to Torres Vedras unmolested and intact."

Templemere was appalled! He was being ordered to take part in 100 miles, or more, of rearguard! However, Stapleton-Cotton had one more joyful fact of encouragement.

"We had it easy at Busaco. Our turn now."

With that he was finally gone, followed by Anson and the few Staff of both. Five minutes saw the 16th riding back through the Light Brigade, these now occupying walls and houses and even suffering sporadic cannonfire from some way off. Despite this, they rode on back the way they had come and ten minutes further brought them to a low ridge where Templemere immediately drew out his telescope to train and focus it on any likely point of a French approach. He was much relieved to see no sign, bar the inevitable smoke of burning farms and hamlets. The KGL came up and rode behind to take position on their left. Thus, they sat for almost an hour, peering forward with naked eye, or telescope, expensive or otherwise. The gunfire ceased; presumably the French field-gun battery had now been driven off, perhaps by Fane's Light Dragoons. On the hour Johnson turned to Withers.

"Can the men dismount, Sir, and make a hot drink, at least?"

Templemere was only too pleased to hear the positive reply. It meant a hot drink for him, from their servant, and also, perhaps, it meant that there would be no action that day, as the light faded. Soon after, darkness did reign over them all and Withers ordered a kind of camp, allowing bivouac fires on the reverse slope. His men cooked whatever was in their saddlebags, then they slept, wrapped in their cloaks. Dawn broke over the pair of Captains, both damp and stiff. A hot drink came from their servant, then came Johnson.

"Tavender! Get on watch, just you. I'll inspect your men and send them up. Templemere, inspect yours then stand them ready, but dismounted."

Tavender dragged himself to his horse, held by a Trooper. He forced one stiff leg up into the stirrup and then swung over the other. He decided that he may need a messenger.

"Maguire. With me."

The said Trooper Maguire, much dishevelled, but at least fed, levered himself up from his campfire using his sabre and mounted his horse, to then follow Tavender to the brow of the ridge. The light was not yet sufficient for half a mile beyond the ridge and the pair, Maguire a respectful half a length behind, watched as features emerged from the ever receding horizon. At first they could see only the mundane olive groves and storehouses, static at first, but seemingly closer as the light grew. Then came anxiety followed by definite alarm, because whole columns of French cavalry were riding forward, each little more than 200 yards apart. The first thought that came to Tavender was the totally correct one, that Massena's whole cavalry force, untouched by Busaco, had been sent forward. His next thought was wholly to the point.

583

"Give the alert and then get the Colonel up here. Then find General Anson. Make sure he knows."

Maguire whirled his horse and was gone. Within minutes Withers was up with him and behind came the sounds of the Regiment coming to readiness. Johnson soon arrived also and the discussions began, Johnson speaking first, needing but a second to form his opinion.

"I'd say that was his whole cavalry force, Sir."

Withers lowered his telescope.

"Get the men formed up. I'm not going down there to face them without orders and certainly not alone. Formed up across here, we can certainly give them something to think about and perhaps slow their advance. Then we wait, either for Anson or Stapleton-Cotton."

Johnson at last involved Tavender by simply turning to him.

"See to it."

Leaving his superiors to study developments, Tavender rode back and gave the simple instruction to every Captain he found, then he came to his own Troop and led them forward. Soon the whole of the 16th were formed on the ridge, in full view of the oncoming French and a glance left saw the KGL Hussars formed up also. The French slowed and finally halted and the tension grew. Movement leftwards drew the gaze of all on the ridge, to see Stapleton-Cotton and his whole Staff galloping across the front of the KGL to halt at Colonel Withers. He wasted no time.

"If they stay down there, for the day, then we'll pull back. I'll consider our job done for today. If they move forward, pitch into them and hold them back. Come night, we'll pull back through the town, but if before then, we keep them out. That's crucial. I've got my whole Division now formed, all with the same orders. We are to keep them out of Coimbra."

He looked along the line of the 16th, nodding his head with approval, then he rose in his stirrups, turned to look behind and took a deep breath.

"Are you up for a go at the Johnnies today, boys?"

There was no cheering from the line, but many who heard gave a good reply and many others simply waved their sabres in the air. Stapleton-Cotton turned to Colonel Withers.

"I'm over now to see Slade and his Heavies. Good luck Withers."

With that he was gone, yelling 'Good luck' to all down the 16th's line, which most responded to. However, Anson had remained.

"So, let's hope we all just sit here and them down there, staring at each other."

However, it was not to be. Another study of the French saw an Officers' conference, taking place immediately before them, which then broke up and the French columns again began their advance. Withers raised his telescope whilst obviously addressing Johnson.

"Can you see any Cuirassiers down there?"

Johnson used his own glass to look for the telltale steel breastplates, which meant Heavy Cavalry, perhaps even the famed French Cuirassiers.

"No. All Light. Like us."

Withers snapped his telescope shut.

"Right. We have three columns opposite and four Squadrons of our own. I'll take two against the centre. One and Four. Johnson, you take one against the left, Tavender, one against the right. No heroics, keep your men in hand, we are here to stop, not rout! If mine hits back the centre badly enough, then their two outside will not come on, may even fall back. When I've pushed back the centre far enough, I'll split and come onto the flanks of yours. Good luck to you both."

Both Withers and Johnson immediately wheeled their horses, leaving Tavender to anxiously study his task for a few more seconds, then he turned to ride past One Squadron, this commanded by Templemere.

"Yours are with the Colonel, Fred. You're going against the one immediately below, in our centre. My Squadron's for the one next over. Good luck!"

Shock came over Templemere's face, but Tavender was gone. He rose in his stirrups to better see the wide and dense columns now approaching with evident serious intent, but he had no time for any more pondering, courageous or otherwise. His Colonel had appeared just to his left.

"Draw sabres! Advance walk."

The eerie scrape of steel on brass came to him from all around and then the line advanced. Withers shouted over.

"Keep your men in hand, Templemere, and don't get carried away yourself. We're a rearguard, we stop and hinder."

At that moment the idea of him getting 'carried away' surrounded by French cavalry columns seemed patently absurd, but what did ease his mind were the words 'stop and hinder'. However, Withers had quickened the pace to a trot, then a canter, he was mindful to preserve his horses, not gallop yet. Before them the French were belatedly spreading out to widen their front, but the British were now but yards away. Withers raised his sword.

"Charge!"

All spurred their mounts to full speed and the 16th hit the French line. The sound was like thousands of pebbles being hurled against a wooden fence, the screams of the horses adding another layer of sound. The most damage done to the French was by the heavier and stronger British mounts colliding with their weaker French counterparts and unseating their riders. Templemere's mount was no exception, a shoulder-to-shoulder collision sending the French horse skidding sideways as Templemere blocked the rider's swinging sabre. Then all was noise and a riot of confusion. Where to go next? The choice was made for him, a French Hussar Officer spurred his horse at him and they met stirrup to stirrup, at first exchanging ineffective blows. The confusion of a melee combat always reduced

586

Templemere to near desperation, but this was a single combat one to one and he was no dunce with the blade. From only a yard apart the exchange was rapid and ferocious but first blood was to Templemere, who cut his opponents sword arm and then despatched him with a thrust through his left eye. The sounds of intense combat all around renewed his fear, but a look around revealed more 16th close to him than French Hussars. Then Withers appeared, having cut his way through a group locked in combat, leaving a French Hussar reeling in his saddle.

"Templemere. Get some men and follow me!"

With that he was gone, his sword held aloft and him shouting above the din of horses, men and clashing steel.

"With me, 16th! With me!"

Templemere remained confused, how do you gather men in the middle of this mayhem, but his 'Good Sergeant' Baxter was nearby.

"Sir! We've got to follow the Colonel."

Templemere looked at him, still yet confused and so Baxter advised again.

"Just follow him, Sir, shouting for some lads!"

At that moment Baxter himself was attacked, but he leant into his attacker, moving inside the swinging sabre to then punch the bellguard of his sabre into the face of his opponent, who then fell senseless to the ground. Templemere was nonplussed at the sight of so easy a despatch, but Baxter was moving.

"Come on, Sir."

He was off, yelling for support and gathering men. The centre column had been pushed back and Withers was keeping his promise of support to Tavender. With him, 40 to 50 men cannoned into the side of Tavender's opposing column and, again, most of the damage was done by their horses crashing violently into the side of the French mounts, who then saw fit to carry their riders off and away. Templemere had no time to exchange more than a few blows before, from somewhere on the British ridge, a bugle sounded recall. The 16th inflicted a few more hits and slashes on the retreating French before disengaging and then leisurely returning to their former position.

The recall had been sounded by Stapleton-Cotton, remaining on the ridge and now well content with what had been done. The 16th reformed, at least those that were whole, for many were helping back wounded comrades. Anson rode up to Withers.

"Well done, Withers, but what's the time? How much daylight left?"

Withers reached for the chain in his waistcoat, but withdrew it empty. His brow furrowed.

"One of those bastards has relieved me of my watch!"

Anson could not help but laugh.

"I'll buy you two more."

He looked at Johnson.

"Can you help?"

Johnson could, and he hauled out a plain steel timepiece.

"Pushing up towards three, Sir. Plenty more time yet."

Withers was still studying his severed chain, mightily aggrieved, but now mindful of his men.

"Allow the men a drink."

He thrust the chain away.

"This isn't done yet."

Johnson turned his horse to obey the order, leaving Tavender, him binding a cut, in the company of Withers and Anson, the latter now giving his judgement.

"He'll re-form and reinforce. Likely to bring up some Heavies, if he's got any."

He turned to Withers.

"Get yourself a drink, and sending one up for me would be much appreciated."

Withers turned to Tavender.

"See to it!"

588

Tavender did nothing himself to achieve compliance, other than ordering a Trooper in his command to do his Colonel's bidding. His cut now doctored, he felt able to ride over to see his fellow Captain and friend of circumstance to find Lord Templemere dismounted and examining his sword.

"Lord Fred. Pleased to see you in one piece!"

Templemere looked up, but his face still showed the shock of close combat, his eyes wide, his mouth turned down.

"Will that be it, do you think?"

Tavender shook his head.

"Not by a long shot. Expect another. Get a drink, then get yourself ready."

He dismounted himself, as Templemere continued to worry at the notch in his sabre.

"Don't worry about that, Fred. The armourer will take care of it, this evening, when we're back and out of it."

Templemere returned a blank stare, somewhere between hope and disbelief, then some coffee arrived, one mug only, but he was in no mood to share with anyone, even Tavender. Templemere growled an order, as much to vent his own feelings as to provide Tavender with a hot drink.

"Get another, damn you!"

Another soon arrived, Templemere added some brandy, and the pair stood together drinking and watching the French. Their wounded and dead had now been retrieved so that all that remained on the field between both sides was the detritus of combat, mostly shakoes and Hussar busbies. Thus, it was gone Noon before formed-up French cavalry re-appeared and came forward again, this time at a trot. This time there was to be no leisurely advance. Anson and Withers used their telescopes together and spoke the word together.

"Heavies!"

The action required to stop such as Heavy Cavalry was one of shock, not hit and disrupt, but Light Dragoons would be unlikely to match such as Cuirassiers in such an action. However, an attempt had to be made. Anson folded his telescope.

"Right, we stay here and use the slope. That'll give us some push against them, us charging downhill."

Withers nodded.

"Same again! That's their Heavies in the centre. Lights either side. I'll take two Squadrons against the centre, one either side."

Almost as soon as the words were uttered the French changed formation, the columns breaking out, in good time, to form continuous lines with the Cuirassiers prominent in the centre.

He turned to Johnson.

"Sound 'stand to'."

The bugles sounded out what now seemed to be wholly mournful notes and the 16th mounted and formed up behind their Officers. Anson turned to Withers.

"We could use some Lancers against those Cuirassiers. What's happened to those Spanish brigands, El Charro's bunch of cut-throats?"

Withers shook his head.

"Wish I could say, Sir."

"Wish I could say what would be a good outcome from this, come 30 minutes from now."

"Yes Sir, but we'll do our best."

The sound of the oncoming French grew by the second, coming on at a canter as had their British opponents earlier, to then accelerate into a gallop for the final yards. Anson watched all carefully, precise timing was needed if they were to meet shock with shock, yet not to sacrifice the advantage of the slope. The time was near, he raised his sabre, and again came the eerie scrape.

"Trot. Canter."

Then, after barely seconds.

"Charge!"

The 16th sprang forward to crash into the oncoming wall of Heavy cavalry, but a wall was the apt metaphor. Merely a few penetrated the French ranks, where they had to fight like Demons to preserve their skin, one of these being Templemere, whose good mount had carried him between two Cuirassiers and, once there, he was assailed from all sides. Luckily another Trooper came through the gap that he had made and, side-by-side they defended themselves, each the flank of the other. The combat itself was almost all between the front ranks, the 16th using the height of their position to stand in their stirrups and deliver crashing blows down onto the helmets of their opponents, but the outcome was inevitable. Rank upon rank of French cavalry were ascending the slope and, like a phalanx of old, they were pushing back the lighter and less numerous British. For Templemere and his Trooper companion, life within the French ranks was, besides extremely perilous, a blur of steel helmets, flashing swords, shining breastplates and angry, moustachioed faces behind thick brass chinstraps. He was defending himself well, but, outnumbered, could not land any kind of blow on any opponent. Then, above the din of combat he heard the notes to retire. His companion whirled his horse around twice, to make room and then spurred himself out, Templemere then following through the gap, breathless and in shock from what he had just endured. He was almost on the ridge when he finally came to notice the gash in his right sleeve. He anxiously pulled up his cuff to see but a graze, then, absurdly, he thanked his tailor for insisting on the thicker cloth of superior quality.

All of the 16th were pulling back, most in headlong flight. This was not to be a regroup over the ridge; this was now headlong flight to get back to the safety of Coimbra. At a gallop all rode down the rear of their ridge which was now impossible to hold, and all were grateful that their superior mounts took them away from the French. Templemere, in the midst of several Troopers felt the need to look back, to see to his relief that the French were now some way behind, still advancing, but at a steady canter. He felt able to slow his mount, as did those around and at a steady canter of their own they came to the outskirts of Coimbra, where, remaining as rearguard were Crauford's Light Brigade, their redcoats forming a beacon of safety as they rode through the entrances of the roads and alleyways and into the suburbs. There they heard the rallying bugle call and all stopped, but all remained anxious for what may follow.

However, they were soon re-assured, not least being a full field-gun battery opening fire upon the oncoming French. Templemere's duty as an Officer now prevailed and so he walked his horse back to the position of the infantry to gauge events, but there he was doubly re-assured, for the French had stopped. Stapleton-Cotton had sent back a message to Crauford detailing what was likely to happen and indeed now had, and the French Commander, General Sainte-Croix, did not relish the thought of combat with the dreadful British infantry, all secure behind walls and other useful enclosures, and also filling the doors and windows of prominent buildings. He had been present at Vimeiro and had more respect for British infantry than many of his fellow French Commanders and therefore saw no point in sustaining heavy casualties to no avail, attempting to take a town that would be theirs anyway, come the next day. In addition, more British field-guns opened up, the French began to take casualties and so it was not long before the whole long line of French cavalry turned their horses and withdrew out of range. Anson now rode up amongst his men, anxious that the French may bring up their own field-guns to batter the infantry, at that moment secure behind solid stonework. It was their role to prevent that, if they could.

"Rally and form up. We're going back out."

His men did as requested, although many were wounded and they were all mixed in with the KGL Hussars, but they followed Anson back out through the lines of the Crauford's men. Then, weary, bruised and bleeding, six or seven hundred yards beyond, they re-gathered as individual Regiments and formed a sentry line, to then send pickets some more hundreds of yards further out. Half a mile beyond, the French did the same and thus it remained until darkness. With the full dark, came the message which was passed around in a whisper, this to Templemere from Major Johnson.

"Crauford's pulling back. We're to follow, now. Stapleton-Cotton wants us way past Coimbra before dawn."

Templemere frowned into the dark in his direction.

"What about sleep and food?"

The answer was a funny noise, like a sharp exhaling of breath.

"For your horse, perhaps!"

Then he was gone.

oOo

For the men of Picton's Division, many miles ahead and now clear of refugees, the morning had been one of little more than a leisurely walk, albeit at marching pace, through the pleasant Portuguese countryside, all enjoying the dry and warm October weather. The one depressing feature was any march through a farming area with its abandoned farms and villages, the burnt crop fields and the grassy fields with no animals of any description. With the Noon break, all Messes handed over their food to their cooks and a good meal was prepared and all ate heartily. There was no concern in any of them caused by the possibility of having to eek out rations. To end the privations of the previous days, a supply column had met them that morning, albeit with nothing like full rations, but they had every confidence that there would be another waiting sometime tomorrow. However, there had been carts laden with spare boots and trousers. For the Deakin and Davey messes the one glum spot was a downcast Eirin

593

Mulcahy, but all, including her Mother, thought it best to leave her alone.

"Ah, sure, is she not amongst the lovelorn? Missing her Lieutenant and their time together at school!"

However, for the men of the 16th Light Dragoons the retreat was anything but a pleasant journey through peaceful country with plenty to eat. Concerns for creating an effective rearguard across a wide area and also the paucity of supplies, now caused Stapleton-Cotton to split his command, sending De Greys Dragoons by a more Westerly route, and Slade and Anson's men more Easterly, to cross the River Mondego at the ford of the village of Alciada, this almost part of the city, just over a mile from Coimbra, now deserted and wrecked, not by any soldiery but by Portuguese scavengers. There, for them, the coin fell on tails, because all the way to the ford from Coimbra, the last Troop in the column, this being Tavender's, had only to look back from any form of vantage point to see the bulk of the French cavalry. Those which they had held off the previous day, were now following them. As the 16th, the last in the cavalry column, came up to the ford they passed Anson, Slade and Stapleton-Cotton, all plainly anxious, this unease confirmed by the fact that a dozen of Anson's KGL Hussars had been sent back the other way to report on the French. Anson followed the 16th through the shallow waters to catch up with Withers and they had not splashed through the final yards of the ford before Anson was pointing at a slope topped with an olive grove.

"Form yours up there! The KGL will remain where you see them. Expect to be in action."

'Where you see them' was directly across the road out of the ford, about 100 yards back from the water. Templemere took this to be a sign that action was imminent, this thoroughly confirmed by the sight of Slade's only Heavy cavalry, his 1st Dragoons, dismounted, carbines at the ready and divided between the upstream and downstream banks of the river. He had barely time to take this in before

594

the dozen scouting KGL came galloping back to plunge into the ford and allow their horses to cross in a series of giant leaps, the water being too deep to trot or canter. Then the French appeared, first in the form of gilded Officers, their cavalry uniforms even more magnificent than most of their General Staff. However, Anson, still beside Withers, did not allow his telescope to dwell on the eye-catching sight, instead he was focused on the cavalry behind, who very likely would soon be their first opponents.

"I see Lights, Withers. You agree?"

Withers lowered his glass.

"I do!"

"Right! The KGL will hit them when they have one Squadron out of the water. That'll make enough of a mess to block the rest. The Dragoon with their carbines will stop them spreading too far off the ford. The KGL may well be forced back, then you will charge again with half yours. The other half in reserve. Clear?"

"Sir!"

"Right. Get organised."

Withers first took a glance at the French before ascending the slope, to see no movement as yet. By the time he had arrived at the top he had made his decision.

"Johnson. Take two Squadrons, Somers-Cocks' and Mortimor's. The KGL will go in first, then pull back for you, or more like be forced back. I'll hold with Tavender's and Templemere's as a reserve."

Johnson saluted briefly before pulling his horse over and riding to the two Squadrons nearest the ford, these being the pair selected by Withers, who was now free to trot over to Tavender and Templemere, the pair now sat conveniently together.

"You're in reserve, under my command. Watch me. When I go forward, you follow."

Anxiety resurfaced in Templemere.

"Against what. Sir?"

Withers was highly irritated, this not least stemming from Stapleton-Cotton, who, in Withers opinion, had been far too leisurely in quitting Coimbra. He should, Withers felt, have pushed his men on at a much faster pace to leave behind the oncoming French, whose infantry were lodged in Coimbra and would be for some time, gathering plunder. He took it out on Templemere.

"The French, damn you! The French that I will be riding at and expecting you to follow. Preventing them from crossing the ford, or has that objective escaped you!"

The charged air that remained after the outburst seemed to crackle, before Withers continued.

"Now! Ready your men and watch for me."

Much chastened, this including even Tavender, the pair returned to their Squadrons, each passing their Troop Commanders and giving the simple order.

"Watch the Colonel. When he goes in, so do we."

However, the tone of voice employed by Tavender conveyed much more confidence in the outcome of their efforts than that issuing from Templemere.

Meanwhile, there was little pause for extra thought, because the French were now into the water, a continuous column that stretched back even along the road. Those to the sides explored the depth of the water and some went too far and found themselves partly detached from their mount, now taken to swimming. Others, also on the edges, soon found themselves under fire from the Dragoons and thus the width of the French attack was limited to the width of the ford, but it was still 60 to 70 yards wide, almost the width of a whole Squadron, Johnson counting 50 men across. All Officers who could, were studying events intensely, none more so than Johnson sat before his wing of the 16th and also studying Anson, now before the KGL. The timing had to be perfect. 60 men out of the ford would not, even if broken, create enough of a barrier against their oncoming comrades, but significantly over 100 could probably create enough resistance to hold a bridgehead on the British bank for the rest of their column to exploit and cross over in force.

The first French were now over halfway across the ford as the KGL started forward, but the French Commander also knew his business and immediately accelerated his men. He wanted the 100 out of the water to hold the shock of the inevitable charge and it seemed to both Johnson and Withers that he had succeeded. The KGL themselves accelerated over the final yards and the shock was appalling to all who could only observe; the shouts of the men, the screaming of the horses and the raised sabres rising and then slashing downwards. But the French had their bridgehead, they now held enough of the bank and were far enough up from the ford for many of those following to squeeze past and get onto dry ground. They were arriving in force and their threat was very real.

Withers raised his sword and charged forward to take head on those that were spreading out onto his side. The collision, when it came, was equally sickening, but the French were in no formation and the solid line of the 16th, two and three horses deep, crashed into them. Then it was a matter of push between the horses, whilst their riders, sat above them and trapped by their legs, hacked at each other. The French advance was halted, so also was their progress against the KGL, the 16th coming in from the flank had made the difference. The leading French Squadrons were forced back into the water, to become a confusion of kicking and screaming horses with unseated riders doing their best to escape the flashing hooves. A bugle sounded and the French cavalrymen turned their horses and returned, whilst those who had been involved, but survived the recent combat, came back over to their safe bank as best they could, some swimming, some wading and some being dragged over by returning horses. The Dragoon skirmishers continued their bickering fire and some survivors fell to float downstream, but the action was done and soon there were none alive left in the Mondego, this now stained pink downstream of the ford.

The 16th and KGL helped their own wounded out of the water. The KGL had suffered most and Templemere, more concerned over such issues, counted four dead, all now laid out on the bank and several wounded. His own 16th needed to help but two wounded. The only sound now was of the waters rushing across the shallows, in deep contrast to the sounds of combat but minutes before. Even the Dragoons had now ceased their pot-shots as the French. Anson, Slade and Stapleton-Cotton came together on the road, all plainly relieved to have held the ford, but the mass of French cavalry, still threatening on the far bank, was plain for all to see. This gave concern to all, but their fears were slightly allayed by what they could hear coming for Coimbra, where all that was fragile was being smashed and all that could be eaten or sold later was taken. In addition many fires throughout the town were started and the smoke began to reach them, its acrid smell coming to them on the breeze. The three Commanders parted company and Anson rode up to Withers.

"They'll not try again, at least not today, and if I'm any judge Johnny will be in Coimbra for days, wrecking and plundering. Their infantry won't leave such rich pickings and these cavalry won't want to get detached too far in front by chasing us some more. Which is now our worry, of sorts. Remaining here much longer could mean us losing touch with ours, infantry, I mean."

Withers nodded but said nothing.

"So, stand your 16th down. We're leaving as soon as it's full dark."

"Maintain a watch on the ford Sir?"

"What else? But ready yourselves for a hard march."

For the remains of the day little happened and so Withers allowed his men to rest by Troop and so Templemere, both his Troops given their orders, found a tree, wrapped himself in his cloak and slept beneath its branches. Despite the activity all around of preparing for the forthcoming march, he slept soundly. The French disappeared to the comfort of their own bivouac fires, maintaining only a picket on the far bank, but the intervening river prevented any trade. The only life that crossed the ford were the last of the inhabitants from Coimbra, either the scavengers or the desperate, who had finally had their merest hopes shattered by the marauding conscripts of two fresh French Battalions who had been on half rations for weeks. These last refugees were indeed desperate and in despair, carrying nothing, for they had been stripped of all by the French cavalry that they had to pass through.

With the gathering dusk, Withers came to Templemere.

"Seeing as yours weren't engaged this morning, yours have the job of lighting fires at the waters edge, so that we can see any Johnnies sneaking up. We'll build the fires up again before we leave. So, set your men to it."

Templemere was now much puzzled and at a loss.

"What do I use for fuel, Sir?"

Withers pointed to the substantial group of houses on their bank, the major part of Alciada.

"Whatever's in those, get it out. Rip all apart if you have to. Whatever will burn; doors, windows, floorboards. Ceiling beams if you can. And furniture, of course."

With that he rode off to take his own rest, leaving Templemere to find his two Cornets of Horse and issue orders. Soon his whole Squadron were into the houses and soon after that combustibles of all descriptions were out and being piled into three heaps at the waters edge. Templemere, with his more privileged background, was somewhat of a connoisseur of furniture and many pieces that had been dragged out were obviously quality, evidently a family heirloom from over the centuries, but even these were soon in splinters from the Farriers' axes and soon

599

recognisable only as fuel for the fires. One piece was a musical instrument of spinet size, which was played upon most proficiently by a Trooper, a scenario which Templemere found to be most macabre, before it also was smashed and the pieces tossed onto the fires. With the deepening darkness the light from the fires danced on the tumbling rapids of the ford and over onto the far bank, revealing merely the half dozen French picquets. With the full dark, the fires were rebuilt and Stapleton-Cotton's cavalry rearguard took their leave, walking their horses quietly so as to make no sound that could be heard above the rushing waters of the ford. They left four graves by the roadside and a dozen French bodies at the waters' edge. If they were buried or not was an issue for their foe.

oOo

Bridie and Nellie were in a very good mood. They had been four days on the road and another two would see them in camp at this place 'The Lines' and, now that they were so much nearer to Lisbon, full rations had arrived. The dogcart found by Tom Miles had been a real blessing, taking much of the weight that would normally be around their shoulders and it was now cleaned, greased and working as new. In fact, on the subject of Tom Miles, relations were at a better low-ebb, because Tom Miles being an expert wood carver, had made Nellie a new wooden spoon when her old one broke. He had carved it out of a table-leg found on the road, the left-overs from some minor looting. In addition, the pair being cooks for Light Infantrymen, these all being good shots with the excellent Baker Rifle, their meals were regularly augmented with rabbits and hares taken during the march, which was much to the good, as rations had dwindled during the previous days, but not down to 'starvation'. In fact, it was this general subject of cooking which had added to the happiness of both, for they were now cooking in the proper kitchen of a well-appointed house.

This house was deserted, as were all the towns and villages that they had passed through, but the 105th being a Regiment favoured by Wellington for its good order and discipline, was allowed into the said towns and villages to bivouac, whilst less disciplined and less trusted Battalions regarding looting and plunder, were required to camp far away, in the bare fields and woodland. The final blessing was that this kitchen had a plentiful and varied stock of herbs and spices all around on the shelves and drying racks. Bridie tasted the stew and pronounced it good and Nellie gave her dough-cakes a final prod. Nellie looked at her three girls, Sally, Trudie and Violet, sat warm and content by the fire, playing with their rag-dolls.

"Youse three. Go around the house, now, and get the men to come. 'Tis all now ready."

The three girls scuttled off, leaving their three dolls sat on the bench, propped one against the other, which cause both women to smile. Soon, heavier footfalls could be heard coming nearer and each man stood his turn to receive the stew, the peas and generous doughcake. There was little conversation, for there were few real concerns, because the leisurely pace of the march had given ample opportunity for repairs and maintenance of their boots and kit, and there was little to complain about, despite the fact that they were retreating. Such issues were the concerns of Generals. The most common topic was that of their destination and most of the questions were directed at Jed Deakin, him being the most senior and therefore most likely to hear any rumour or even news. Most worried about his creature comforts was Tom Miles.

"What's this place like, then, Jed? The Lines. Villages or open fields? Have you heard?"

Jed Deakin allowed himself the time to fully chew his mouthful, before forming an answer and speaking somewhat indulgently.

"Well, Tom. I can say, that all is but twenty miles or so from Lisbon and so I should say, this bein' the capital of this Portugal, that there'll be plenty of buildings of one sort and another existing all around."

He looked at John Byford sat quietly in the corner, the acknowledged academic.

"Would I be right in sayin' such a thing, John?"

Byford looked up, surprised at having been brought into the conversation.

"Yes, Sergeant, I'd say that you would be. The area around most large cities is usually well populated and they obviously must live in buildings, usually well appointed."

Deakin nodded and returned to Tom Miles.

"There you are Tom. So I daresay that we'll be able to find you your very own shed or stable somewer'".

From around came the additions, 'Plenty far off', 'An' he can bloody well stay there', but there was no offence anywhere. All was more than well with the two Messes headed up by Jed Deakin and John Davey. The meal consumed, all the men went outside to smoke and sing and generally while away the last of the day with memories and experiences. The children, too, went outside to play, then came the last to be fed, Ensign Patrick Mulcahey and his Drummerboy companion Henri Rasenne. These were given a bowl and they took themselves outside to join the men. That left Bridie, Nellie and Eirin to clear away the plates and pots of the meal and it was at this point that Eirin burst into tears. Bridie and Nellie stopped everything to look at each other and then at Eirin. She was Bridie's eldest daughter and so it was her Mother who spoke.

"So what ails you?"

Eirin collapsed into a chair and brought her apron up to her face. After four or five shoulder heaving sobs, she lowered it, to speak in gasps, her face running with tears.

"Ma! I'm going to have a baby!"

Nellie dropped her spoon and Bridie her tin pannikin, but it was Bridie who spoke, her voice flat and serious.

"How many have you missed?"

602

"Four!"

"Stand up!"

Eirin obediently stood and Bridie went over to her to kneel and reach under her skirt to feel her lower abdomen. The telltale curve was there. Bridie's own head and shoulders fell with her own despair. Seeing her friend so brought down kindled a measure of resentment in Nellie towards Eirin.

"No need to ask who the Father is. Have you told him?"

This brought yet more floods of tears from Eirin and it was some moments before she could say anything and when it did, it came between deep sobs.

"Yes."

Nellie again.

"And he said what?"

The apron was raised and the sobbing began again, louder than ever. Nellie was losing patience.

"Get a hold of yourself now. You think you're the first! What did he say?"

The apron was lowered, then used to wipe away the flood of moisture that had issued from her eyes, nose and mouth.

"He said, 'Are you sure I'm the Father?'"

Nellie's spoon was picked up and thrown violently into the cooking pot, then she stood, arms akimbo, her face set in anger. Bridie, however, rose and took Eirin into her arms, then she looked at Nellie.

"Get Jed in. He'll know what's best."

Nellie departed and came back in with Deakin, his face serious; he had picked up the storm signals from Nellie.

"What's up?"

Bridie looked at him directly, but spoke quietly.

"Eirin's pregnant."

Deakin's jaw clamped together and his face took on a deep frown.

"Maltby?"

603

Both Bridie and Eirin nodded.

"And he's said what?"

It was Bridie who answered.

"That it may not be his."

Deakin released a long hiss of breath, saying nothing, but his face conveyed all the anger he felt. Bridie looked pleadingly at him.

"Jed. What can we do?"

Deakin rubbed his face with his left hand, whilst he thought.

"Well, there's one good thing. At least we're not on some retreat and we'll be at this Torres Vedras place for some while, but then we'll be back out on campaign. That's my guess, and that's when real troubles will start."

He paused, while the vital question came into his head.

"How far gone?"

"Three months is our best guess."

"Well, we'll not be six stayin' down around Lisbon. We'll be pushin' the Johnnies back up country soon enough is my guess, after they've sat and starved. The question for us is where will she be during her final months, then givin' birth and her time after that, with a babe and all."

"What can you do, Jed?"

Deakin's face set hard.

"Talk to Maltby. This b'ain't the first I've heard of; Officers fathering childs in the Followers, an' I've a fair idea of what to say. I should get something out of him and then we'll go from there."

He looked at Eirin, but when he spoke, it was with little sympathy.

"Thought you had more sense of how things are, Eirin. He'll not marry you, never would of. What we might get him to do is to see that you'm cared for."

With that said, his tone became warmer.

"Whatever, girl, you've got us. All of us. We'll see you through it."

Bridie put her arm around her daughter and smiled, but Eirin was up and had flung her arms around Deakin and was sobbing again.

"Oh Uncle Jed!"

Deakin nodded, patted her head and then gently detached himself.

"Right. Meanwhile do what your Mother and Aunt Nellie tells you. They're your best help now."

Deakin took himself outside and sat amongst his friends, his face grim and telling its own story of trouble. His friend Halfway was sat beside him.

"What's all that about?"

"Eirin's pregnant."

"Maltby?"

Deakin nodded once and depression fell immediately upon the once cheerful group.

That night brought misery of a different kind to the cavalry rearguard. At Midnight, it began to rain, not heavily, merely a steady, soaking continuum of slanting droplets, falling unseen from a black sky. These created the only sounds, as they fell on metal helmets and saturated cloaks, this mixed with the sound of the horses hooves churning through the soft mud of the disappearing road. None spoke, each too concerned with the arrangement of their collar, or the hem of their cloak, points at which the rain could reach their uniform and soak their skin, for it had also become cold. October was asserting itself, even in Portugal.

Templemere allowed his hands to remain on the pommel of his saddle, the reins slack, as his horse made his own way, instinctively following the mount in front. The 16th was in one continuous column of four, many half asleep in the saddle. Templemere drew his cloak tighter, grateful that he had spent the extra money on the best boat cloak that Bond Street could provide. When dawn eventually came, this fact because they could now see the rain descending from a slate grey sky, which, at least, was no longer an all encompassing black. Yet the dawn raised no spirits, because they all knew that this day would only bring what the previous had, a full scale charge onto their pursuing French counterparts, to drive them back, at least far enough for their Brigade, now only Anson's, to resume their retreat. Templemere, in his misery, was seriously thinking of resigning his Commission. The cold, the hunger, the squalor and the danger were all taking their toll.

Perhaps less depressed, Tavender, in the light of dawn, received orders from Johnson.

"Hold here with five men. When you see them, let us know. And how many! Not just that they are back up with us!"

Tavender halted his mount to wait for Sergeant Baxter.

"Baxter! You and four men. With me!"

Tavender waited whilst Baxter called out four names, then they waited until the column had fully passed, the last being the wounded from the skirmishing of the previous days, these having inevitably fallen behind. Some were able to support themselves; others had comrades beside them, holding them upright in the saddle. With the passing of the last, Tavender and his picket remained alone on the churned up road and he took a look at his surroundings. The road was in a well-defined but shallow valley; their road in the centre, but the light was not yet good enough to see to the far end where the French would enter.

"Baxter, take two up there. I'll take two up opposite. Send a man if you see anything."

The picket split and the two parties of three splashed their way up the sodden opposing slopes and there they waited as the day gained strength. Tavender reached for his brandy flask from his saddlebag and took a long pull. It was immediately returned, with no thought of offering it to his equally chilled and wet companions, a non-gesture which did not go unnoticed, each raising their eyes skyward to the other. They managed some compensation, however, one tearing in half a strip of dried beef and both sat chewing, that at least partially taking their mind off the steady rain. It was one of these two who noticed activity from the far side of the valley.

"Sir! There's a lad coming over."

Tavender lowered his telescope from studying the far end of the valley, to look over and see the approaching Trooper.

"Mackleson. Go and see what he wants."

The said Trooper swung over his horse and trotted down to meet his companion and soon the shout came up.

"Sarn't Baxter can see them. Sir."

Tavender swung over his own horse.

"With me."

The remaining Trooper followed and Baxter took his cue to also descend from his side and all met on the road. Tavender addressed Baxter.

"Can you see how many?"

"Not yet Sir. Only that there's a column of some sorts. Could be just a reconnaissance, Sir. Could be the main column."

"Right, we have to find out. Back up to the tree line so's we can see more from the side. Head on tells us very little."

Baxter was instantly concerned.

"Sir. These are good Frog cavalry, Sir. They're most likely to send scouts ahead along the tree line to see if any of them Spanish lancers is waitin' up ahead. They'll have learnt their lesson, Sir."

Baxter was too likely to be correct to justify any argument.

"Possibly, Sergeant. So, take a man along the tree line for 200 yards or so, but my prediction is that we'll see them, then they'll see us and we'll both ride back to report. No fighting. I'm sure that they are as wet, cold and sick of this as we are."

"I do hope you're right, Sir."

607

Tavender detected insolence in Baxter's tone, even if there was none intended.

"That's enough from you, Sergeant! You have your orders."

Baxter nodded and spurred his horse away.

"Jim!"

A Trooper spurred his horse and the two rode off to take a shallower angle as they climbed the slope, which would place them further along the tree line than Tavender, who rode straight up to a better vantage point and extract his telescope. The French cavalry emerged into the valley and from his angled position he could make a better judgment of the length of the column. He was estimating numbers when one of his companions pointed along the tree line.

"Sir. Sarn't Baxter is comin' back, Sir, and he seems in a hurry. His sabre's out, Sir."

A pause.

"There's some in pink followin' up behind."

Tavender snapped his telescope shut and looked for himself, but by then Baxter was but yards away.

"Strong picket on their way Sir. We've got to go!"

Baxter and his companion galloped past and the four soon followed. A glance back revealed pink uniformed cavalry emerging from the trees in pursuit, but the six had enough of a start and, on superior horses, galloped off to gain the road about half a mile on. Nothing more was said and, within fifteen minutes they came to their Brigade, drawn up at the head of another valley with one flank on the tree line, the other on a group of rocks. It was a perfect position. Whilst his men rode to their Regiment, Tavender went to Anson and saluted.

"A strong column, Sir, about a mile behind us."

Anson frowned.

"Strong! How strong?"

"I could not tell with any great accuracy, Sir. We were forced back by a patrol in strength before we could take a good look, but I think I saw one Brigade of horse, at least, with infantry some way behind."

Anson nodded.

"How far back?"

"Significant, Sir. Perhaps a mile."

"Good enough Captain. Now, back to your men. Give your Colonel my compliments and ask him to join me here."

Tavender delivered his Brigadier's compliments and Withers met with Anson and Durnfeld of the KGL. Anson was brief.

"We've got to hit them. They're too close. We've got to knock them back, at least until tomorrow, when we do it again. After that we should be in The Lines."

He turned to Withers.

"Your Captain tells me he can see infantry, Withers. And how many cavalry, we'll see in a short while. He says one Brigade."

The two Colonels departed and rode to the head of their men. The rain had eased but was still falling and so Withers was forced to give an unwelcome order.

"Cloaks off and rolled."

No one could fight whilst wearing a cavalry cloak and so, all along the line, including the KGL, cloaks were pulled off, rolled and stored behind their saddles. The sign was obvious to all, that today would see a combat much as that of the previous day. Meanwhile Officers were employing their telescopes to see the French force becoming clearer at their end of the valley and then they watched them deploy. Withers rode along his line to find Tavender and then study the French himself, this now possible with the naked eye.

"Seems you are half right, Lucius. There are two Brigades, I'd say."

Tavender was not comforted by the half compliment

"What will he do, Sir, General Anson, I mean?"

"Hold here and then hit them as we did at Fornos and yesterday. What worked once should do so again."

There was little comfort either in the mind of Captain Templemere, as the French deployed to equal their front, him sat before his own Squadron, his own thoughts and fears building significantly. The French came on, multi-coloured uniforms defining the various Regiments comprising their line, the pink most prominent amongst the blue and maroon. Telescopes revealed the tossing pelisse cloaks of the Hussars and the bobbing tassels beside almost every busby and so it was with relief that all concluded them to be Light Cavalry. Withers noticed Anson drawing his sabre.

"Draw sabres!"

The now familiar eerie scrape sounded from all along the line, from both the 16th and the KGL, for the French were but 500 yards away. Anson rose in his stirrups, sensing the unease behind him. All could now see by how many they were outnumbered.

"Steady lads! Steady. Let them come on."

He turned in his saddle.

"These know that we can best them, boys. We saw them off yesterday and we'll do the same now. Don't get carried away and listen for the bugle."

The French front matched their own, but his was only two deep, whilst that of the French was four, at least. He was as irritated as any at this useless skirmishing, but this was his allotted task, therefore he would hit them at the full gallop. He raised his sword.

"Charge!"

He spurred his horse forward and the whole line sprang forward to achieve full gallop within seconds. The yelling Troopers, the waving sabres and the horses at full pelt caused many in the French line to slow almost to a halt, which was totally fateful. The 16th and KGL crashed into the French line with no less a fearful shock than any of the actions before and such was the impact that the first two

610

French lines were forced back onto the third. Then it became a fight as much between horses as men, and soon the weaker French gave best, turning to escape the dominant British mounts. Templemere, as trapped as anyone in the melee, exchanged wholly ineffective blows with a Hussar at maximum sword length, but then the Hussar's mount decided that enough was enough and turned, enabling Templemere to stab the man in the back. He fell and his horse careered off to the side.

All along the line, the French were giving way, especially against the ferocious KGL, and soon all were retreating back in flight. With superb discipline, Anson's men reformed their line and cantered on, pushing the French before them. The race lasted but half a mile before the French split to reveal at least a Brigade of infantry, drawn up in four squares to receive them. Anson had kept his Bugler close and he now touched him with the end of his sabre, the signal to order withdraw. The notes sounded and his men halted to quickly turn and ride back, leaving Anson alone, facing the French infantry just within musket range, but no fire came. He studied them for a short while, before bringing his sword up and across his face in salute. Some could say that it was a mocking gesture, but it was returned by an infantry Officer sat on his horse between two of the squares, which made it a gesture of respect from both. Anson then turned and rode back to follow his men, very content with a job well done and at little cost, this being no more than a handful of wounded throughout his whole Brigade. There were French dead stretched across the wet turf, but none of his own. Withers and Durnfeld were waiting for him and he was characteristically brief.

"Back on the road. Now!"

His two Regiments quickly formed up and joined him on the dark brown strip of rutted soil that doubled as a road. Then the rain came on harder.

Although marching in bright sunshine some 20 miles ahead, the mood in the Light Company of the 105th was dark. All by now had heard of Eirin's condition and all knew who was responsible and with no word as to what was to happen next, all drew their own conclusions. Inevitably, they were of the worst, because Lieutenant Maltby was an Officer and Eirin merely a Follower. That she was to be abandoned to her fate, used and discarded, was the general conclusion. Most incensed, inevitably, were the men of the Messes of Davey and Deakin, but it was those of the former who marched within One Section of the Light Company, this commanded by the Officer in question, Lieutenant Stuart Maltby. He was in his place, marching alongside his men and it was not long into the morning before Zeke Saunders, marching close but behind, thought of something significant to say, pointed, but sufficiently anonymous.

"Who was that Officer, Byfe, what we saved back at Busy Co?"

Private John Byford, having no idea what his good friend had in mind, did no more than answer the question.

"Captain Drake. We brought down a French Officer who was, well, about to suffer him great harm."

Saunders sniffed.

"Captain Drake, wer' it? I've a memory that it wer' another, and if it was this 'un I've in mind, then I'm of the opinion that we shouldn't have bothered. This man bein' of the sort that you'd want to do no favours for."

Byford caught on immediately.

"When you say 'no favours', in fact you mean not aiding that someone out of any form of difficulty! If you had the choice."

"You've got my meanin' entirely."

John Davey was not slow to pick up on what was being constructed.

"This 'other' you'm referin' to, you mean he weren't no good sort of comrade? Even though an Officer!"

Saunders continued, as much uncaring of the consequences as emboldened.

"No, he was worse. This 'un. He dabbled amongst the Followers. The girls it wer'! Now that's bad."

"The girls you say? In the Followers? Now he must be some piece of work!"

Davey paused, but all knew there was more coming.

"A man should pick up on the things that he does. What happens from it, like. An Officer 'specially. 'Specially if it means someone's whole life gets all changed around and sent down the drain."

It was Tom Miles who had the last words, each carefully spoken, their threat little hidden.

"You'm right there, John. The finish of such can be 'specially dire! Like if such a man were to cross your sights in the middle of some set to, well, you'd not be too sorry after you'd pulled the trigger sort of by instinct, like. One of them things!"

There was no further sound other than that of marching feet. All four were astute enough to realise the benefit of saying no more and allowing their words to remain large within the space of silence. For Lieutenant Stuart Maltby each word registered its impact and each gave cause for some thought, but, him feeling thoroughly secure as an Officer of King George, it registered as being of no great significance.

In fact, with the day's march done and himself, Carr, Drake, and Shakeshaft now snug in yet another good billet, what had been said on the march had been all but forgotten, as Nat Drake pulled the cork from a very decent bottle of wine. As he poured the contents equally into the four beakers, it was Maltby who asked the question.

"Should not all of that, wine and such, I mean, have been destroyed, as The Peer ordered, along with any food?"

Drake grinned and looked at him.

"True, Stuart, very true, but have you not noticed some of our more enterprising refugees carting along all kinds of supplies and setting up a stall at the end of each day. Most enterprising, most laudable and most convenient for us, I'd say, for those of us who appreciate a fine bottle."

He held it up to the candle light.

"Such as this. One we've not had before. Now, a toast."

All picked up their beaker.

"To The Lines and comfort and security to us all!"

The toast was repeated and Morrison brought in the food, in plentiful quantity, stewed pork, peas, potatoes and new baked bread. With each plate full, the conversation was resumed, as usual by Nat Drake.

"So, in The Lines tomorrow. What's the prognosis for what comes next?"

Carr swallowed his mouthful.

"Rest and comfort will suit me."

"Militarily, I mean."

Richard Shakeshaft, usually the most belligerent of the four assembled, spoke of his hopes.

"I want them to take a crack at us! Give us a chance to deliver another Busaco. Behind trenches and redoubts or not, wherever we are, it doesn't matter."

Maltby was more thoughtful.

"My betting is that he didn't lose a fifth of his army, a dreadful mauling though we gave those he sent up. He's still a lot left, of a veteran army."

He rested his forearms on the edge of the table, knife and fork erect.

"And don't forget. Half our army is Portuguese!"

Drake tilted his head to one side in thought.

"True, but they did pretty well, is my impression. A bit mixed with us above San Antonio, but at The Convent they did as well as any of ours, that's what I've heard it. You may be too harsh in your judgement. They're coming on is my impression. Unlike the Spanish!"

All gave a short laugh and then Carr spoke.

"For me, I'd rather sit in some billet and let them starve. For those that he sent up that hill, their defeat was crushing, but without that ridge, who knows? Boney tells his Marshals to send forward Tirailleurs to soften you up, then a column with guns either side. Then cavalry. All that we got, pretty much, were the columns. That's all he could get up that ridge against us."

He paused.

"If he can mount a full attack, on good ground, it'll be another Talavera, and I'd prefer to sit in boredom than have the excitement of another like that!"

He blew out his cheeks.

"Time to count our blessings, I think!"

He turned his head.

"Morrison, another bottle. Do we have one?"

Morrison was standing by.

"Oh yes Sir. Several!"

Before inserting a mouthful, Drake looked at Maltby.

"Once in The Lines is school back on?"

Maltby nodded.

"Colonel's orders."

"With the charming assistance of Eirin Mulcahy?"

"Anything's possible!"

Not 20 yards further down the road another meal was being assembled, but the atmosphere was far less convivial, although the rations were plentiful. Eirin was in better spirits but still morose, yet the unburdening of her secret had lifted her somewhat and the pledged support of all around had given her some comfort. Jed Deakin was sat with his 'wife', Bridie, and she was studying him carefully.

"What are you going to say, Jed?"

To whom was obvious and Deakin stretched his mouth over his face in thought.

"'Twill need careful handlin', that's for sure, tacklin' an Officer over such."

He turned to look at her with a kindly smile, one just for her.

"But I'll get it done and I'll get something. Don't you worry, we'll see her cared for, one way or another."

Bridie put down her plate and curled her arms around his neck. Then she kissed his bristly cheek and rubbed it with the palm of her right hand.

"Tonight you has a shave!"

Deakin allowed his eyebrows to lift a full inch!

20 miles further back down the road all was anything but convivial. Templemere and Tavender sat in the remains of a hovel, which now was not even that, now that half the roof had collapsed after a fire caused by Portuguese looters. The building, if such an exaggeration could be applied, was part of what remained of the neat village of Aloentre, but was now an assemblage of wrecked cottages, many destroyed by fire, most without a roof. The only comfort for the 16th was that some rations had been waiting at the end of the day and the pair's Servant, Trooper Ted Robinson, had a stew of salt beef, peas and potatoes boiling over a large fire, large for cooking but barely adequate to provide any warmth. The pair sat huddled and wrapped in their cavalry cloaks, both sat on a crude bench under the only part of the roof that remained. Their horses were tethered in the open area of the house walls, this conforming to Withers orders, that mounts were to be no more that 10 yards from any bivouac. At last Robinson judged the tough meat to be edible enough for those with good teeth and so a bowl of the stew was handed to each along with two biscuits, although not Army, these had the Navy stamp in the centre. With Robinson departed, conversation could begin, first from Templemere.

"I'm thinking of resigning my Commission!"

Tavender looked at him and swallowed, prematurely, making this difficult, before he spoke.

"Not what you expected, eh?"

Templemere had not taken a mouthful of the gristly meat.

"This is little more than perpetual misery. On top, we are the Rearguard, outnumbered and under assault, day after day. And the Army's falling apart. You saw those two Royal Dragoons hanging from a tree in Leiria. Caught looting. Royal Dragoons!"

Tavender dropped his piece of meat back into the bowl. The foppish, complaining nature of his companion, when it arose, always irritated him.

"We are fighting the French. Fred! They are the best led, the best equipped and the best trained army in Europe. They have crushed everyone, except us. It's only us, led by The Peer, who've given them any trouble. What did you think it was going to be like? A jolly Foxhunt with some society acquaintances?"

He allowed his words to sink in, then he changed his tone somewhat.

"We are on campaign! And retreating, what's more. You get looting on any retreat, but one more day, probably, and we'll be in The Lines, which are pre-prepared defences. A whole chain of strongpoints and redoubts, so I've heard. Once behind that and manned by our good infantry, damn fine infantry, I think you'll find that life will pick up, somewhat, in fact I'd say considerably. Now, eat your stew. Some of it will be edible."

Templemere selected a piece and began to chew, but at that point, not four yards away, Tavender's horse staled onto the rotten straw that had once been the flooring. Templemere dropped his spoon into his bowl and lay himself down on the floor, his cloak brought tight about him

Predictably it was a disturbed night. Sleep was interrupted either by one of the mounts moving around or the heavy showers, these carried by the wind blowing in under the edge of the shattered roof. With the dawn, Robinson arrived with some coffee and rolls just as the final note of Reveille died away. Each sat up, keeping their cloaks close gathered, then Johnson arrived, attempting to be cheerful.

"Up you get, Gentlemen. Let's see if we cannot see them off, this last day. Keep them far enough back for us to ride in triumph into these 'Lines' that we've heard so much about."

The pair did their best to grin a reply to their superior Officer, but it came across more as the rictus grin from a pair of corpses. However, the Regiment was awakening and preparing for the rigours of the day and they could do nothing other than follow suit. Both stood and stretched, pushing out stiffened limbs, then Tavender walked forward.

"Right. Tackle up and saddle up!"

As a good horseman, he saw to his own bridle and saddle and Templemere, somewhat reluctantly, followed in his direction to do the same. That done they led their mounts out of the hovel to immediately encounter Somers-Cocks, the Captain of Two Squadron.

"Morning, you two. Dry day for once. And we've been given some guns, a whole Field Battery. They came up in the night. Bit of a lift, what?"

His cheerfulness depressed both and the best reply that they could manage was each to raise his left hand, then Johnson found them again.

"Get to your Squadrons, we're pulling back. Anson wants a better position for today's Society Ball."

The thought of almost certain combat, yet again, did nothing to raise their spirits, but soon, at the head of their men, they were on the road beyond the village, awaiting the order to move. This came and lasted but a minute, for then came panic, beginning with Anson riding fast along their column, halting at Withers.

"Where are the guns?"

Withers looked astonished.

"Up front, Sir. Surely?"

"They are not. Where did they camp, last night?"

"Back down in Alcoentre, the far side is my guess. I saw them move through myself, last night, led by one of your Staff."

Anson's face grew desperately worried, even fearful.

"Whose is your last Squadron?"

"Somers-Cocks. Three."

"Whose is this?"

He was pointing at the Troopers immediately behind Withers.

"Templemere's. One."

"Right. I'm sending Somers-Cocks back to get them and this in reserve. Send these after me!"

He galloped off and Withers turned to Templemere.

"You heard your orders. Back to the village. If you are called into action, keep your men together. Four ranks."

Templemere felt his stomach jump as he saluted and rode back the way they had come, his men wheeling into position behind him. This being a dry day, visibility was adequate and soon they were close behind Somer-Cocks squadron cantering through the village, with its nearby bridge over a river as its reason for being. Templemere decided that his place was with his Commander and so he galloped along Two Squadron's ranks to join Anson and Somers-Cocks, then his stomach did tie itself in knots. The Field Battery had been established, wrongly, far back from the 16th's bivouac of the previous night and they were frantically limbering up their guns. The cause for their haste was a whole Regiment of French Light Cavalry approaching the village from the far side, but they were not yet at the bridge, which was the only point where they could be held and allow the guns to escape. Anson lost no time and pointed at Somers-Cocks.

"Get yours down there! Jam the bridge. Forget formation, get down there!"

Somers-Cocks drew his sabre and turned to the his men, standing in his stirrups as he did so, the better to make himself heard.

"With me!"

He galloped forward and his Squadron followed. The next minute was one of great anxiety for both Anson and Templemere. Who would win the race to the bridge? If the French got over in strength then the battery was lost. Two Squadron hurtled down the slope and past the Battery who had at least put their horses into harness, but no team was hitched to any limber nor any limber to any gun. The French were over, perhaps twenty, when Two Squadron crashed into them, Somers-Cocks in the lead. Anson watched all through his telescope, anxiously chewing his lower lip, but, after much subconscious punishment of that part of his mouth, finally he was content that the bridge was now thoroughly jammed with men and horses. He turned to Templemere.

"Get yours down there, just off the road, to the right. Give the guns room to get back, using the road."

He used his telescope again, giving Templemere excuse for delay.

"Hold formation up the slope. Three deep line. You making a threat may be enough to cover Somers-Cocks coming back."

Templemere certainly hoped so as he rode back to give his orders to his two Cornets of Horse. Within a minute his Squadron was trotting down to form a line three deep, off the road, but threatening the exit of the bridge. On the bridge continued the cavalry equivalent of a rugby maul, but the French were being held. Then there were sighs of relief all round as the Gunners mounted both their gun-limbers and horses and were now whipping their teams into a frenzied gallop to escape. Anson turned to his Bugler.

"Sound Recall."

The notes sounded out and Somers-Cocks' men detached themselves, but the French did not follow. Three

Squadron rode back past Templemere's and then Somers-Cocks, on his own initiative, drew up his men behind Two Squadron, a solid line in support of Templemere. Sergeant Baxter was sat just behind the said Captain.

"Sir, we should draw sabres if we're to make those Johnnies think we're going to charge."

Templemere whirled around and suddenly realised that his men were just sat, as if on parade. He took a deep breath.

"Draw sabres!"

There came the scrape of steel on brass and all sat with their sabres at the ready. Again there was relief all around as the French made no further attempt to cross the bridge. Recall was sounded again and both Squadrons quickly formed on the road and trotted back, following the guns. Templemere and Somers-Cocks were together as they rode past Anson, him still studying the French.

"Well done you two! We'll make cavalry Commanders of you yet."

Templemere felt a small lifting of his spirits, but not much, as his stomach settled back into its normal state of hunger.

Merely a few miles down the road they found the Rearguard halted and reinforced, not just by the Field Battery just rescued, but also by the 'Heavies' of Slade's Brigade, the 1st Royal Dragoons. Withers, as the Senior Colonel had allowed the whole Brigade to dismount and make themselves a hot drink and so, following the guns, it was into a cheerful encampment that the two Squadrons of the 16th rode to rejoin their Regiment. Half an hour later Anson re-appeared from his studying of the French and within minutes all fires were extinguished and his enlarged Brigade was back on the road, the guns in the lead, then the Royals, then the 16th with the KGL 1st Hussars bringing up the rear. They rode on through the morning and on past Noon and Templemere often heard shouts and bugle calls from the KGL behind, for him to turn and see KGL

Squadrons returning back up to re-join their column. The only possible conclusion was that they had, once more ridden back to meet the oncoming French, who must be near and in close pursuit.

It was late afternoon when Templemere saw Wellington and his Staff ride down the column, to meet with Anson, who was again controlling events at the rear. After but a few minutes Wellington rode back, with Anson at his side and then the Brigade swung off the road, both to left and right, with the guns nearest to the road on the left centre, then the KGL beyond them on the far left flank. The 1st Dragoons formed on the opposite side of the road, the 16th furthest out on the far right. Within minutes, Withers was riding to meet each of his Squadron Commanders. He stopped at Templemere.

"The Peer wants a final riposte to the French, here. All ours are not quite yet within The Lines and will be entering through the night. He wants us to hit them once more to keep them off for the rest of the day and probably into the morning, when we will enter. With the Royals in the centre this will be easier than of late. Four ranks. We'll go straight into the charge, Anson seems to think it the most effective. Good luck."

Templemere had been hoping that the bridge affair at Alcoentre, rescuing the battery, had been the last of this God-awful rearguard business, but plainly it was not to be. He called wearily over his shoulder to the first of his Cornets.

"Form four ranks."

He heard the shuffling and movement of the horses behind him as his men formed up, which made their line shorter, but the Brigade still covered the whole of their position, again at the head of a valley. A chill wind came from the East and he wished he could don his good cloak, but they were on the alert and must remain as so. When the French arrived, the pink uniforms were missing, instead it was a bottle green that stood out amongst the more common blues and maroons, but their intent was obvious, they were going to attack with the same vigour as during any engagement of the past retreat. There were two Brigades of them and one quickly formed across the valley for the second to then also form up across, but much further back than previously. That far back, the second would not be able to support the first when the two forces first clashed and this dawned on Templemere but any further significance escaped him. Whatever, his thoughts on French cavalry tactics were, they were immediately thrust aside as the Field Battery opened fire with what must be round shot, judging by the gouts of earth thrown up before the first French Brigade. The range was adjusted and some men and horses fell, but mostly, at maximum range, the heavy balls merely ploughed into the saturated earth and remained buried.

The French came on at a good canter and, very oddly, the second line followed, but at a trot and thus, the gap between them increased. From the centre of the 16th came the familiar, but no less stomach tightening sound of sabres being drawn. Templemere's Squadron copied and so there was no need to give an order, but his own, now usual, deep anxiety had increased. How many more of these could he survive? The odds were shortening. The French came on and the situation was so familiar that almost every man in the line could give the order at the correct time. The cannons fired once more, but the range was wholly wrong and it did no damage at all, but there was no time to dwell on that. Anson had his sabre in the air and had spurred his horse forward. Templemere, by now almost shaking with fear, did the same, as did his men, only this time accompanied by a ferocious yell, as they spurred their horses into the gallop. The gap closed rapidly, but at 30 yards the French whirled their horses around and began galloping back. To many, Anson, Withers, Johnson and even Tavender this was not good, in fact deeply worrying, the French must have some scheme. All called to their men, and all along the line such could be heard repeatedly above the galloping hooves.

"Hold steady, boys. Keep the line! Listen for the bugle."

However, to such as Templemere the sight of French backs and horses tails came as a source of huge relief, an emotion soon replaced by the need for revenge, the wish for dire vengeance to be visited upon those who had reduced him to such a state of terror. He spurred his horse into yet more speed which stretched out the distance between himself and his own men 'holding steady' and reduced the gap between himself and the French. Then he was in the French line, at enough range to stab at an exposed French back, but then he was nudged sideways by a French Hussar on his left and his horse lost momentum and fell back.

Then came the huge surprise. With admirable control and discipline the second French line opened to create gaps that the first line rode through, to then turn to follow. The second came on to meet the British. Templemere, because he was somewhat advanced from his own line, found himself surrounded by French because they met the British line someway behind him. He was alone, but not being fiercely attacked such as to threaten his life. They were merely fending off his blows, which completely distracted him, enabling one Hussar to seize his bridle and pull his horse out of the fight on the French side. He was now surrounded by four maroon uniformed Hussars, all with their sabres menacing him and a fifth still holding his bridle. He tugged at it uselessly, moving only the Trooper's arm, not his own horse. He shouted something, but he knew not what, his mind was so far detached from his actions. All five, including him, came to a halt. He was a prisoner, this now confirmed by the individual Hussar to his right front menacing him with his sword and speaking.

"Ne vous se rendent, monsieur?"

He had no choice, either surrender or be killed. He nodded his head and the group began to move and canter back, leaving the conflict behind them, which seemed to be lessening. Once amongst many French cavalry, his head still whirling, his mind disbelieving and in fragments, they halted and one of the Hussars, who was plainly an Officer, dismounted and came to stand by his right knee and hold out his hand.

"Votre sabre, Monsieur, s'il vous plait."

Templemere allowed the very fine and expensive blade to dangle from his wrist and the Officer detached the loop of cord to take the sword. Once in his hand, the Frenchman swished the sword to and fro, an expression of approval growing on his face.

"Mes compliments, Monsieur. Un très bon blade."

Templemere was both annoyed and distraught at the same time, his very fine blade, the best that Wilkinsons could supply and which had seen him safely out of many a duel, was to be his no more. What was more, two Troopers were now rifling through his saddlebags and a third was unbuckling his very fine cloak. Surrendering his sword was a necessary act, but to lose his valuable cloak was simply being plundered. He reached back to save the cloak at least, but the Trooper had only one strap left to run through and have the cloak almost for himself. Templemere managed to get one hand on it.

"I need that!"

The Officer now intervened, his voice sharp and angry.

"Laissez le!"

The Trooper released the cloak immediately and Templemere gathered the cloak to his waist, but the Officer was now speaking to him.

"Vous devez maintenant démonter."

The gesture downwards with his free hand provided all the translation needed and Templemere dismounted, to find that he was a head taller than the Officer, who now gestured for Templemere to follow.

"Suivez-moi."

Templemere followed the Officer, him carrying and further examining Templemere's sword, with two Hussars either side, each with drawn sabres. The last Templemere saw of his fine horse and saddle, was of both being examined by another Hussar Officer. He was led back several hundred yards to a small cottage and taken up to the door, but not through it. The Officer turned to his escort.

"Lui tenir ici."

A Trooper pushed Templemere against the wall, whilst the Officer went inside. Templemere, his ability to register his surroundings returning, saw three other British prisoners being marched past, two KGL and one of his own Regiment, but they did not look up and he did not call out.

Meanwhile, back at the British position, all was now peaceful and all three Regiments had returned back to their positions to simply mount picket, whilst the remainder rested and cooked their rations. It was at this point that Templemere was missed by one of his Cornets, Nathaniel Vigurs, who then approached Withers, now dismounted and following his horse, which was being led back to the tethering lines, whilst Withers carefully removed his gloves.

"Have you seen Captain Templemere, Sir?"

The final glove came off.

"No."

Vigurs became worried and it showed.

"I have enquired of Sergeant Baxter, Sir, who told me that he last saw Captain Templemere out in front, amongst the French."

"Have you checked the wounded?"

"Yes Sir. He isn't there."

Withers stopped, plainly somewhat irritated.

"Then post him missing!"

He paused, to give himself time to think.

"Then, for the time being, we need a new Squadron Commander. Which of you two is senior, yourself or Peterson?"

"I believe that I am, Sir. By three months."

"Right. You're Brevet, until a new Captain arrives or a new Cornet, I would assume, if you are confirmed."

He walked on, but Brevet Captain Vigurs had an additional concern.

"Who takes over my Troop, Sir?"

"Who's your Senior Sergeant?"

"Sergeant Baxter, Sir. A good man."

"Indeed he is. Put him in charge, pro tem."

Vigurs saluted and marched off, to first find Cornet Peterson and tell him the news and then Sergeant Baxter. This NCO worthy departed from his new Squadron Commander with a smile on his face and a spring in his step, which took him straight to his messmates.

"Seems we've lost Lord Huff-n-Puff!"

He sat down on a convenient ration box, smiling broadly.

"Where's the French brandy?"

The flask was handed over and Baxter pulled out the stopper and raised the flask in the direction of the French.

"My best to you, Sir. May the French take to you as well as we did!"

He drank deeply, whilst all around laughed, then he passed the flask on.

At the time of the toast, the said Lord Huff-n-Puff was being ushered into the cottage where was sat a very elaborately uniformed Officer, with much gold braid and decorations, extending from his waist to the top of his high collar, these hiding almost all of the blue of his standard French uniform. This evidently high ranking Frenchman turned to one of the many Staff behind him.

"Une chaise pour cet Officier!"

A chair was brought forward and Templemere was motioned to sit, which he did, still clutching his precious cloak. Two Troopers stood behind him. Now down on the same level, this gave him the chance to examine his host, something that the said Officer seemed to be doing to him. In the silence, Templemere gained the impression of a man of handsome features, perhaps early fifties, but plainly at ease in his role and with clear eyes that told of a very capable intellect. He was sat forward, his chin supported by his hands folded together, his elbows on the table. He spoke good English, but with a thick French accent.

"I am Marshal Andre Massena. To whom do I have the honour of speaking?"

Templemere drew himself more erect. If this was to be a matter of status, he could compare as well as any French Field Officer.

"Captain Lord Frederick Masefield Templemere. 16th Light Dragoons. At your service."

Massena smiled, mostly at the last three words.

"I am sorry for you in your present situation, Lord Templemere, mais c'est la guerre? Non?"

Templemere nodded agreement, but said nothing, so Massena continued.

"You are an Officer, Captain and as such, you will be treated well. If you agree to give your Parole, you will be moved quickly back to England. We have no wish to detain such as you."

Templemere sat up further, now very interested, as Massena continued.

"If you accept your Parole for the duration of the hostilities between our two countries, then this can be arranged very quickly."

Templemere nodded and began to speak, but Massena interrupted by holding up his hand.

"But first, before this can happen, there are some things which I wish to know. Things tres petite, of no real consequence and I will know sooner or later in any case, but

628

I would prefer sooner, as you can imagine. But the speed of your Parole will depend on this."

Templemere nodded again. He was indeed very interested, because, if he gave his Parole, then he was out of this war for good and out of it honourably. He had served, but been taken prisoner in combat and he would be honour bound not to return. In this case as described, he could have given his Parole at that moment, but native cunning told him not to be too enthusiastic.

"I'll help. If I am enabled, as a British Officer."

Massena smiled and nodded.

"Just so, Captain. First, your army at Busaco. How big?"

Tenplemere had no problem with this, this was past history, but he would not be too detailed.

"Forty to fifty thousand, give or take."

"How many were engaged?"

Templemere sat back.

"That I could not say. I am cavalry and was held in reserve. We didn't draw sabre once. I saw nothing."

"But you can give me some idea. Half? Quarter? What?"

"Say a quarter."

Massena sat back and turned to look at one of his evidently more Senior Officers, this one tall, younger than Massena and with a fierce gaze, which never left Templemere. His uniform had gold embroidery of less coverage than Massena's but far greater intricacy. Massena spoke directly to him.

"Ils nous ont battus avec mais un quart de leur force, Reynier!"

Reynier's countenance became even fiercer, as though he would wish to pounce on Templemere there and then, but he said nothing. Massena then turned to another Marshall, him older and his face somewhat kindlier, but he carried an indisputable air of authority.

"Ney?"

Marshall Ney's face somehow saddened before he spoke.

"Nos hommes ne pouvaient pas faire face à la vitesse de leurs tirs. Pas pendant cinq minutes."

Massena turned back to Templemere, his face pleasant and his tone ingratiating.

"Marshall Ney has just paid your men a high compliment, Captain."

Templemere allowed himself a slight smirk.

"Oh really! What did he say?"

"He said that our men could not stand before the strength of your fire. Not for five minutes, even!"

The smirk became wider.

"We train them for exactly that, Sir."

"How many reloads each minute?"

"Some can manage close to four."

Massena turned back to his two Marshals, to regard each quickly, saying nothing, but giving the pair a look which said 'There! Now isn't that something?' He returned to Templemere, but this time his face was serious and his voice had a hard edge. The time for social niceties was over.

"Captain. I have offered you a quick Parole and my offer stands, but I need to know the object of your Wellington's retreat. Does he mean to offer battle further South or what? Why has he gone so far South, so quickly, giving up so much territory?"

Templemere had long realised that to give Massena the information that he wanted, in the detail that he wanted was at least dishonourable, perhaps even treasonable, but he very much wanted out of this detestable war and away from the fear, the deprivation and the squalor. He reasoned that Massena would be finding out sooner or later and that no-one could know who had revealed what all in the British army now knew. Other prisoners could well be speaking what they knew as well as he, at that moment. If he was awkward and reticent, he could expect months in a French prison before arriving home. It was not worth the risk. He sat forward.

"We are retreating into what we are calling The Lines. They are called that, but it is really a series of forts and redoubts. Trenches too, I should imagine."

Massena sat forward, seemingly surprised.

"How far from here?"

"My Regiment will be in sometime tomorrow."

Massena sat back, even more surprised. Ney now spoke.

"Il importe que son infanterie est déjà en."

Massena answered whilst still regarding Templemere.

"Oui."

"Cela signifie un siège."

Massena did not reply, but now sat forward, staring straight at Templemere. He was plainly highly displeased and not a little anxious over what he had heard.

"So! Your grand General Wellington means to sit behind piles of earth!"

Templemere sat back, inwardly content. The die had been cast.

"It would appear so."

"Are they extensive? These Lines?"

"I can only say that they have been being constructed since the battle of Talavera."

A dark shadow passed over Massena's face and remained there.

"So, the thinking amongst your army is, that these Lines will hold you all?"

"Yes."

"Do they run from the Tagus to the sea?"

"I can only assume so. I have seen no maps."

"One final thing, and then you are on your way. Have you lost many men while you retreated back?"

"That I cannot say. My Regiment suffered some losses. You are probably in a better position to judge that, rather than I, who only encountered your cavalry."

"Have you been fed and supplied?"

"Yes."

"Well?"

"I'd say so."

Massena sat back, plainly he had heard enough. He looked at the two Trooper escorts behind Templemere.

"Le sortir!"

One of the Troopers took a step forward and Templemere was pulled up by a rough hand under his armpit. Massena then turned to an Officer stood by the door.

"Le Jean! Voir à sa Libération Conditionnelle."

Le Jean followed Templemere and his escort out of the door. He was marched to another building and pushed inside, where he saw his three fellow captives sat at a table, each with a bowl and spoon and a lump of very coarse bread. All were eating, or more accurately drinking, for the bowl contained thin gruel. Templemere found a place at the table as far from the three as he could and sat, when a bowl and bread of the same was placed in front of him. He picked up the spoon and fished through the scum of fat on the surface, to find nothing and so dropped the spoon back in the bowl. This was noticed by one of the 16th.

"Begging your pardon, Captain, but if you don't want that, may you pass it up to us?"

With a look of distaste on his face Templemere pushed the bowl and the bread up the table. The Trooper reached for it.

"Thank you kindly, Captain."

The Trooper then broke the bread into three and poured an equal measure of the gruel into each bowl. He continued eating and the other member of the 16th looked down the table.

"Have they granted you Parole, Sir?"

Templemere felt like replying 'None of your business', but self-interest prevailed, these may be travelling companions for a while and he may be dependant on them during that time.

"Yes. They have."

The Trooper nodded.

"Well, good luck to you with that, Sir. 'Tis a nice thought to be goin' home out of this. We'n for a French prison for as long as it all lasts."

Templemere nodded and arranged his cloak across his lap, then he closed his eyes in the hope of sleep, but none came, other than a fitful doze. After an unknown period, he opened his eyes, because Le Jean had returned with a piece of parchment that was evidently his Parole. This document Le Jean placed in front of him, then came pen and ink. He pointed to the foot of the page.

"Il signe."

However, before signing Templemere scanned the page. It was in poorly constructed English but the meaning was clear enough. He signed and, with that done Le Jean hauled him to his feet, leaving the paper on the table. Templemere saw in the gloom that his three fellow prisoners were now sleeping on the floor and that was the last he saw of them as Le Jean pushed him to the door. Once outside the pushing continued, only this time towards a small cart, in which were some wounded French Officers and a wounded English Trooper. Le Jean pointed at the interior.

"Monter dans le wagon."

Templemere reached up with one hand for a rope that would enable him to haul himself up, but as he did so Le Jean seized the cloak that was now only held under Templemere's left arm. Templemere, now halfway up, came back down to the ground.

"That's mine. I need it!"

Le Jean pushed him back, his face and voice full of contempt. The cloak was now secure under his arm.

"Vous n'avez aucun honneur! Vous avez trahi vos camarades!"

Le Jean pointed again.

"Monter dans le wagon."

Le Jean now had his hand on the hilt of his sword and so Templemere got in. The Trooper in the cart pulled down the back canvas and the cart rolled forward. Templemere was fortunate that in the darkness he could not see the expressions of his fellow travelling companions, who had heard and understood every word. He sat in the wagon glumly, seeing only five sets of white eyes, staring forward through the darkness.

oOo

Close to the town of Torres Vedras, Lacey was stood on a bank of earth overlooking the road that led past the first of the earthworks that they had seen had so far of The Lines. In his hand was a newly opened letter and on the road were his men, this last a very pleasing sight, all were marching well and easily, which told the story that all were well fed, healthy and strong. However, concerning the contents of the letter, these he was not so sure about, once he had read them. He looked at O'Hare.

"Staff have been busy, since we left Coimbra."

O'Hare looked at him.

"Wellington's re-organised again. Seems that he's just received another Brigade, but they're new from Walcheren, so must be considered to not be in the best of health and therefore suspect. They've been given to Erskine and we've been added. As a stiffener I shouldn't wonder. So, we're no longer with Picton's 3rd, we're now in Spencer's 1st, in the Brigade of General Erskine, with the 1st 50th , the 1st 92nd and some of the 60th Rifles. More introductions to be made."

He lowered the letter.

"I'll miss Mackinnon and Wallace, but there it is."

O'Hare nodded.

"But perhaps not so much Picton!"

Both laughed, before Lacey continued.

"However, one good result from prompt Staffwork is that we know where we need to be straight away, where we need to be with Erskine. We have not been required to march somewhere else with Picton and then march back. Our place is about ten miles further on from here, perhaps a bit less. Somewhere called Sobral. Good Staffwork, certainly. See, I've even been given a map!"

He pulled a neatly folded map from his pocket and pointed to the place on the map for O'Hare to take a look. That done he took out his watch.

"How long since the last rest?"

O'Hare knew immediately.

"One hour and one half."

"Right. Rest now for 15 minutes, then push them on and we'll be there for the evening meal and in camp."

He studied his men some more, even waving at some.

"What's the date?"

This O'Hare also knew.

"10th October. In the year ten!"

After the rest, his men rose up easily to reform on the road and three more hours of steady marching past well tended farms and countryside brought them to a large village, the largest since Torres Vedras. Lacey decided that they had arrived.

"Sobral may well be that village there. If this map's correct."

He pointed towards a group of white buildings tumbling haphazardly forward down the hillside from its summit, on which was perched the village church. At the rear was a deep valley, almost a ravine.

"Best get the men into bivouac and await Erskine's wishes. It would seem that this is his part of what we're now calling 'The Lines'."

Excellent Staffwork was again apparent from the fact that supply wagons were waiting for them at the entrance to the village, with several members of the Royal Wagon Train, led by a Sergeant. Lacey rode up to him.

"Is this Sobral, Sergeant?"

The Sergeant replied in a very distinctive East End accent.

"Yes Sir. Sobral, Sir."

"And your supplies are for?"

"General Erskine's Brigade Sir."

"Well, we are the 105th of General Erskine's Brigade. Are we included in your orders?"

The Sergeant did not need to consult any papers.

"Yes Sir. You and the 50th, the 92nd and a Company of Rifles."

"Very good, we'll take our share when we're in camp."

The Sergeant saluted.

"Very good, Sir, I'll get the wagons open and ready."

Lacey slapped his gloved hands on his saddle pommel in contentment. All was exceedingly well. He looked back at O'Hare.

"Right. In the absence of anything to the contrary, we'll put the Lights into Sobral, Carr in command, the rest to bivouac in these fields here, down in this valley. Make camp and get fed. We'll take that farmhouse, there, alongside the hill with the semaphore mast. Get Bryce onto it. Carr should take a look at the French side, from this Sobral."

Within the hour the pervading sound in the camp of the 105th was that of crackling cooking fires, their smoke filling the air as much as the chatter of the men and Followers. Half a mile away, Carr and Drake were stood leaning on a wall on the far side of Sobral, looking down the slope whose main feature was the main road that ran North. Each was eating their own bread roll filled with salt-pork and they were sharing a bottle of local wine. However, the road was not empty, it was the main road from the North and was almost full of the refugees from Coimbra and all parts between. The orders had been strict and thoroughly enforced; no single item of food nor animal was to remain to succour the French. People were to move also, for they could be tortured to reveal hidden stores or killed if they revealed nothing and these refugees looked what they were, sad creatures torn from their homes, destitute, ragged and exhausted. Within their number, and looking far from identifiable from the throng, were Portuguese and Spanish Ordenanza, distinguishable only by the fact that they were carrying a musket and there were various equipment straps about their persons. The pitiable column trudged past, then Drake levered himself off the wall.

"There's some of ours coming. Cavalry!"

Carr reached into his pocket for his small glass, extended it and focused.

"Yes, Cavalry, and they look as beat up and knocked about as those they are travelling with."

Drake borrowed the glass,

"They must be our cavalry rearguard. They look all in, even from this distance. Can't we give them some food or something?"

Carr stood staring forward.

"I daresay we can. Our fellow Brigade Regiments have yet to come up from Lisbon. They've just landed and so won't be here until tomorrow. I'm sure we can give them something, if it's only dried meat and biscuits. I'll see to it."

He walked back through the village, leaving Drake to await their arrival, who then went down to the road, which brought him closer to the procession of misery that was the refugee column. They were also half starved and in need of food, but the responsibility of the Portuguese Government, or so he reasoned. He did not have long to wait, before the leading Officers of the cavalry arrived.

Drake came to the attention and saluted, trying to be welcoming and cheerful.

"Captain Drake, Sir. Light Company, 105th Foot. You've reached The Lines, Sir."

Stapleton-Cotton and Anson reined in their horses, Stapleton-Cotton looking first up at the buildings of Sobral.

"So this is The Lines, Captain?"

"Yes Sir, the start of it."

Stapleton-Cotton nodded and brushed some dirt from his sleeve, as Drake continued.

"Sir, I can't say if this will be of any use to you, simply that we are but one Battalion and we have supplies for three. As we speak, my Major is trying to organise a rations issue for you, Sir. Should you wish it."

For the first time for days both Stapleton-Cotton and Anson managed broad grins.

"We most certainly do wish it, Captain. We have had next to nothing by way of supplies since we left Coimbra. We are very grateful. Your Major is?"

"Major Carr, Sir, and the supply wagons are just up the hill, Sir, just beyond the crossroads."

"Very good, Captain, and my compliments to you."

Drake saluted as the column continued past, 16th in the lead, then KGL, Artillery and 1st Dragoons. He was not there to see Tavender ride past, he was by then back up at his wall to finish his bread, pork and wine.

Carr, meanwhile, was busy applying his signature to a document given to him by the Sergeant of the Royal Wagon Train, him having continuously pleaded his case.

"You see how it is, Sir. These was meant for General Erskine's Brigade and it should be his signature I get if I am to hand 'em over to someone else, Sir. To show that I did at least get to the right place, Sir."

Carr handed back the paper and pencil.

"I understand perfectly, Sergeant. Now please get your wagons up to the crossroads. There's a whole column of cavalry now approaching who have been our rearguard for the past week or so. They are undoubtedly starving and so I think we should give them something, don't you, especially as two-thirds of our Brigade are yet to arrive and so what you have here is going begging. As it were."

The Sergeant stuffed the precious paper into his pocket and saluted.

"Yes Sir. We'll just get these up a ways, then, Sir."

He called to his fellow Waggoners and the horses were walked forward, just in time to meet the head of the cavalry column. Stapleton-Cotton rode his horse up to Carr, whilst Anson turned to Withers and organised the issue. Carr saluted as Stapleton-Cotton looked down, both hands on the pommel of his saddle.

"I understand that I have you to thank for this, Major."

"These supplies are going spare, Sir, and I don't doubt that you've not been too well provisioned over the past days."

"You'll get no argument from me on that score. You are Major Carr, I take it?"

"Yes Sir."

"I've about 1400 men, Major. Will these suffice?"

"Well, about that, Sir. There are enough for two battalions, who have not yet arrived."

"Very good, but where is your Regiment?"

"In the valley, Sir, the other side of the village. There are good areas beyond them to camp for the night."

"Our cup overfloweth, Major. I bid you good evening."

Stapleton-Cotton brought his riding crop to the peak of his shako and moved on. Meanwhile Withers had bade his men dismount and for the Mess Leaders to walk past the supply wagons to be given a portion of the food and then move on. The issue was rapidly made and the 16th passed by. It was then that Carr noticed Tavender and each acknowledged the other with a curt nod of the head, but Carr felt obliged to walk forward. Tavender looked utterly

639

done in, which fact became more apparent as Carr came nearer.

"Lucius."

Tavender leaned both forearms wearily onto the pommel of his saddle.

"Carr."

The animosity between the two was plain, but, as far as Carr was concerned, Tavender was a fellow Officer who always tried to do his duty. He should be credited with that and therefore he had a duty towards him.

"You look as though something to eat would not come amiss."

Tavender nodded, but his reply was curt.

"You'd be right."

Carr turned to the nearest Waggoner.

"What do you have that can be given to this Officer this instant?"

The man came to the attention.

"We have some bread and sausage, Sir. Bread baked yesterday."

"Fetch a portion of each. And whose is that bottle of wine?"

Carr pointed to a bottle of red wine beneath the wagon.

"Ours, Sir."

"Then I'm sure you can see your way clear to share a glass with this Officer here."

Within a minute half a loaf and some sausage appeared, followed by a beaker of the wine. Tavender did not dismount, placing the food on the front of his saddle and holding the beaker in one hand. He did not look grateful, but politeness required that he say something, but it was spoken in an utterly flat tone.

"My thanks."

Both rank and salute were omitted, but Carr felt that duty had been done towards an Officer in need. He was about to leave, when he had a thought.

"Lord Fred. What of him?"

Tavender took a drink of the wine, before lowering the beaker.

"Posted missing. Yesterday."

"A prisoner?"

Tavender nodded.

"Most likely, but could be dead. We had no opportunity to examine the field."

He finished the wine and tossed the beaker onto the nearest supply wagon. Saying no more, he rode on, his face of stone and not one backward glance at Carr, who stood watching until the figure was absorbed into the crowd, then he spoke softly to himself.

"So, no change, not even now, when I try to get you the food that you need. You try to ruin me at an Enquiry and do your best to wreck my wedding. With me and thee there really is not much point!"

oOo

Whilst the British were being supplied and thoroughly, the French were being thoroughly denied, at that very moment, in the form of a supply column being driven away by the men of Julian Sanchez' Lancers, albeit that the pack-mules carried only sacks of flour, tubs of fat and sacks of beans, all very suspect. The Lancers had ridden out of the trees as one disciplined line, quickly overwhelming both the escort and the Waggoners and those who died in the short but honest combat were the lucky ones. Now, every French Waggoner and Dragoon taken prisoner was dead at the side of the road, with a deep axe wound in the back of his head, whilst their two Officers hung lifeless and eyeless from two nearby trees.

With the dawn came General Spencer and General Erskine himself to find the 105th. Both rode first into, then through, the camp to discover Lacey and O'Hare outside their farmhouse, taking breakfast in the sunshine. These

641

stood up at the arrival of their Divisional and Brigade Commanders, but the two cordially strode forward, offering their hands in a very open and civil manner, but Spencer had rather bad news as he turned to Lacey.

"Good to have yours with us, Lacey, but your men will have to move back to where the rest of the Brigade are. They arrived last night. Sobral is outside The Lines. Do you have any in there?"

"Yes Sir. My Light Company."

"Good. Keep them there. I'll send the rest of the Brigade's Lights in with them. Meanwhile move your men the other side of this sharp looking hill, Monte Agraca, I do believe it's called."

He pointed, but it was fairly obvious. On top was the semaphore mast noticed by Lacey and all around were earthwork redoubts.

"The Lines start beyond there so remaining here you are outside. Get beyond and restore your camp. You won't be in any earthwork; the Peer's got Spanish and Portuguese for that. Our job is to ready ourselves to march to meet any threat. He's improved the roads as much as thrown up all those mud pies!"

As they all laughed, the pair returned to their horses and mounted.

"Right. Must be off to the others. Good luck Lacey! O'Hare!"

Within two hours, the 105th had moved the other side of Monte Agraca and the 105th Lights found themselves sharing the buildings of Sobral with the Lights of the 50th, the 92nd and the 60th Rifles. However relations were immediately much less than cordial, as some men of the 50th moved in beside the mess of John Davey who, up until then had had a large house all to themselves. A highly belligerent Midlander Corporal saw the 105th men and immediately vented his spleen.

"We hear tell that you lot give our rations away last night!"

All the men of Davey's mess turned towards him, but, unsurprisingly, it was Tom Miles who answered.

"And you think we gave that order!"

"I'm not saying that, but what I do know is that you've been fed and we haven't. And I see that's a fine cooking pot you've got going there. Very fine and very full!"

The men of Davey's mess looked at each other, but Miles remained belligerent.

"'T'as been plenty of times we've been on the wrong end of a deal like this. Many a time. Was you on The Retreat? 'Cos that was real hunger! Not just missin' a day's rations."

There was only one 'Retreat' that could be referred to in such terms, the retreat to Coruna, but the Midlander did not give an inch.

"Yes we bloody well was! Bentinck's Brigade. And up above the village come the battle."

Miles was somewhat taken aback, but at that moment Ellis came in, alerted by the noise of the argument and well aware of the subject and the protagonist of the 105th.

"Give these lads what you can. There'll be another supply for us all, come Noon."

He paused to look at each 105th in the room, particularly Miles.

"Besides. Remember that second column we took on at Vimeero? They Grenadiers. Well, we was on one side and these boys was on the other."

He allowed that to sink in.

"Give what you can!"

That was enough. All in the room reached for their haversacks, bar Miles, him still with something to say, it being disobedience serious enough to see him charged and flogged, but his ill mood did not allow him to hold anything back.

"An' just how much is left in your haversack, Sergeant?"

Ellis opened his own rations haversack, thrust in his fist to pull up the bottom and turn it inside out, for nothing to fall out bar some biscuit crumbs. He much more enjoyed the complete defeat of Miles to putting him on a Charge.

"Nothing! I gave the lot to their Light Company Sergeant!"

Miles had no choice now but to reach into his own haversack, extract the contents and place them in the waiting sack of the Midlander Corporal, who was clearly of a character not dissimilar to Miles' own. He was not finished.

"And who are you?"

That question Miles understood perfectly. He was not being asked his name by way of social introduction.

"The One Hundred and Fifth! Like it says there!"

He pointed to the steel badge where his crossbelts joined, but a grin came over the Midlander's face.

"Ah, the Rag and Bone Boys!"

Miles was close to hitting the Corporal, but Ellis was watching every move and Miles had his own riposte. He had read the number 50 on the Corporal's badge.

"So, you've heard of us! Well, we 'aven't 'eard nuthin about you, an' no reason why we should. Fiftieth is it! An' what do they call you, like?"

The Corporal straightened up and there was some pride in his reply.

"The Dirty Half Hundredth."

Now it was Miles' turn to grin.

"Dirty for why? Dirty deeds an' goin's on?"

The Corporal raised the cuff of his sleeve.

"Dirty 'cos our facings is black. Like that."

A fight was very near, especially with Miles so thoroughly involved. Ellis stepped in.

"Enough!"

He looked at the Corporal.

"We've given all we have. There's no more, and a supply wagon will be up come Noon. Best you get back and eat what you've been given, if you're sayin' that you'm all that hungry."

The Corporal looked around the room and nodded his thanks to all, as did his companions, but for Miles he reserved a malignant scowl, but they did leave and Davey then shared out the hot stew. No-one spoke again of their loss, because it was of no real concern, all now being well fed.

However, one particular concern was uppermost in the mind of Jed Deakin as he climbed the hill that led out of the deep valley between Sobral and Monte Agraca. As a Colour Sergeant he had some licence to come and go as he pleased and today was the day he would confront Lieutenant Maltby, who was away from the main 105th camp and in Sobral with his Section of the Light Company. Once into the village and when he eventually came to the buildings occupied by the 105th Lights, the first Officer he found was Captain Drake, out in the street. He sprang to the attention and peeled off an immaculate salute.

"Beggin' your pardon, Sir, but I was hopin' to see Lieutenant Maltby. 'Tis a private matter, Sir. I'd be much obliged if he could give me some time."

Drake, cheery as usual and being asked by their highly respected Colour Sergeant, replied in the affirmative.

"Yes Sergeant. I'm sure he'll speak with you. Would you like to come inside?"

"Beggin' your pardon, Sir, but I think that this is a matter best dealt with in the open."

Drake's face clouded somewhat, but he managed a smile as he mounted the first step into the building.

"As you choose, Colour Sergeant. I'll just ask him to come out and see you."

Drake disappeared as Deakin rehearsed again what he was about to say. He knew how delicate the matter was, that he, a ranker, would be confronting a Commissioned

Officer over his conduct. Within a minute Maltby emerged and Deakin repeated his immaculate salute, but Maltby spoke first.

"Yes Sergeant. What is it?"

"Beggin' your pardon, Sir, and thank you for your time, but I think it best that we walk off aways, off from here, Sir."

Deakin took a pace along the road and was much relieved to see that Maltby was following him. When they were side by side, Deakin began.

"It concerns Eirin Mulcahy, Sir. You know of her condition, Sir. An' your name's been mentioned."

Maltby stopped and looked hard at Deakin.

"This is no concern of mine. How do I know that I am the Father?"

They were in an open space and so Deakin answered.

"You can say that, Sir, but if you've 'been there', if I can put it like that, then you may well be, Sir. The Father, that is. And Eirin Mulcahy's no easy wench, Sir."

Maltby said nothing and so Deakin continued, relieved that at least there would be no argument over that point, at least not at this stage.

"We all knows that marriage is out of the question, Sir, but there is the question of responsibility. She's a good girl and I served with her Father, till he was killed at Maida, and I took over the family. She should be provided for, in some way, Sir. Her and the child."

Maltby's head jutted forward.

"But I deny that I am the Father. Why should I be responsible for any 'providing for', as you put it? And inevitably at some cost to myself. In addition, she's a Follower. Don't they march with their Regiment, even though pregnant and giving birth as and when, during the campaign?"

Deakin nodded.

"They do, Sir, and like as not half the babes do not come to full term or dies within six month, or the Mother herself dies. That very thing happened in our Mess. Joe Pike's wife lost her baby on the retreat to Corunna. She couldn't hold it to full term, what with the cold and the hunger. And this new campaign, what's coming, will be in the Winter, what's also coming. I wouldn't give much for her chances, Sir, if we'n forced into another Winter retreat."

Maltby was unmoved.

"That's our lot. For all of us."

Deakin twisted his face into a pained expression.

"Well now, Sir, lookin' on it that way could be a mistake and may I say that I have come across this before and I've seen both a good and a bad outcome, dependin' on what's done next."

He paused.

"May I speak plainly, Sir?"

Maltby nodded.

"Well, as the philosophers say, Sir, 'tis not what the truth is, that counts, 'tis what men believe to be the truth and all in your Section believe you to be the Father. The next point is that you go into battle with these men at your back and all around you. Could be this very day. All has deep feelings for Eirin as one of their own, and they knows what the future may well hold for her. If we has to take her with us when she comes close to her time, she won't be able to keep up, Sir, and she'll get left behind. Then she's just an unmarried Mother, like as not, to end up a pauper in some gutter somewhere, both her and the child finally took with consumption or somesuch."

Maltby interrupted.

"Why should all this land on me?"

Deakin ignored the question and continued with his theme.

"She's safer if we can leave her somewhere and be cared for. Your men will hold you in very poor regard if you does nothin'. And here's the point for you, Sir. Who knows what can happen in a battle? All your men is killers, Sir, it be their job, to single out one man and put'n down. Blow his head off! They does it time after time. They aren't the lads who stands in a firin' line, and just gets off their ten into the smoke. They's all ready to kill individual men, as they sees it."

Maltby shot up straight.

"Are you threatening me, Sergeant?"

Deakin took a deep breath.

"No Sir, not at all, I'm just trying to tell you how things are and, like I say, I've seen both, a good and a bad. As your men see it, if you do nothing for Eirin, then you'm just a dishonourable scoundrel, as've used one of their own and then cast her aside when she comes with child. You can see the danger for yourself in that, Sir, and I do tell 'ee, Sir, that 'tis real!"

Suddenly, what Maltby had heard on the march from his men, some days back, now came to mind. Those words, spoken by men such as those of his Section, as Deakin had described them, provided threat enough. He paused for thought, a space which Deakin allowed him.

"What would they have me do? Set her up in a house in England? I have no resources for such as that."

"No Sir, not that. She'll still be in no good state, Sir, alone with a child and unsupported. She could pass herself off as a widow, husband killed in the wars, but she'd still be alone and all short of coin. No one expects you to see her and the child set up for life, but, for your own reputation, Sir, amongst your men, you needs to do something, if only by way of acknowledgement, like, to show you'm prepared to help pick up the pieces."

"So what would you have me do? What was a 'good' in your experience?"

"Well Sir, the first worry is going on campaign in her condition, which will just get worse and harder when we pushes the Frogs back up, as we surely will. At some point we'd have to leave her behind somewhere and that's when it

648

could all go wrong, like I've described. To cope with that, and this is what I'd call a good outcome, Sir, most Convents in these parts will take in expectant Mothers and care for them, even into the child's first years. How they treats the Mother, as a skivvy or as someone to be given a bit more care, depends on the contribution made to the Convent's coffers. They expects some payment, in fairness. 'Twill not be much, but that's where you come in, Sir, and the lads as knows Eirin will chip in too, Sir."

"And when the child grows up?"

"Too far into the future, Sir. What matters to us all, me and those as knows Eirin, is that she's cared for during her time and after, when the child is still too small to walk and do any carin' for itself. After that time, I'd say 'tis likely she'll become a Follower, Sir, and become the wife of some lad as'll care for her. As I cares for my Bridie and hers, even though none of they four is mine, Sir."

Maltby folded his arms and considered for a few seconds.

"What sort of figure did you have in mind, Sergeant, that will persuade a Convent to take her in and treat her above and beyond that of a mere scullery maid?"

"In my experience, Sir, to get enough, I'd say you needs to put in a month's Officer's pay."

Maltby was unmoved, which encouraged Deakin. It would seem that for Maltby, such a sum was not too great a sacrifice. Then Maltby spoke with a level voice.

"Nine pounds and fifteen shillings!"

"If you made it a clear ten pounds, Sir, I'm sure that'll do the job."

"And some of yours will also contribute?"

"Yes Sir, as'll probably bring it up to fifteen or so. That's the figure I has in mind."

"French plunder!"

"There be no other source, Sir, not for the likes of such as us."

"So, ten pounds from me?"

"Yes Sir, then you'm free and clear, but when the time comes for Eirin to go, a bit of concern and good wishes for her afore she goes, into her confinement like, would not come amiss, Sir. Not only with her. There's her Mother for one."

Maltby nodded.

"You'll tell my men? What I have agreed to do."

"I will, Sir, within this very hour."

With no more said, Maltby spun on his heel and walked off. Deakin looked at his receding back.

"I'll be in touch then, Sir. When the time comes."

Maltby raised his left hand from his sword hilt in some kind of acknowledgment, but said nothing more. Deakin waited for a respectful distance to come between them and then followed. After some enquiries, he entered a building that was on the very edge of the town, to immediately come upon the perfect man for his purpose, John Davey. The respect between the two men was absolute, but Deakin said but one brief statement.

"Maltby will help us get Eirin into a Convent. So he has said. He'll throw in one month's pay, which will do it, what with ours thrown in. Tell the lads."

Davey nodded and Deakin left the room and the building. Simultaneously, Maltby was entering the room reserved for the Light Company Officers of Erskine's Brigade. His entrance caused Drake to look up.

"Hello Stuart. Your business all squared away? Nothing serious, I hope."

Maltby smiled dismissively and shook his head.

"No. Nothing serious and all now dealt with."

Then a Major of the 50th burst in, dusty and breathless from his short ride.

"Sobral's to be given up. Everyone to pull back to the redoubts! Orders from Division."

oOo

The dawn of the following day had fully broken, as the Light Companies of Erskine's Brigade trooped back into Sobral, from the orders of their Commander in Chief, no less. Drake was not alone in his complaint.

"So what was the point of that, Spencer pulling us out for the night and The Peer putting us back in?"

Carr still remained the commanding Major of the four Light Companies and he had no answer, other than to say that there was no answer.

"Bad mistake! Staff mistake! Miscalculation, who can say? My worry is that we've lost a night to get the place fortified. We'll be attacked, be certain. Massena will want to try us out."

He pushed open the door of what had, yesterday evening, been the Officers' billet.

"Just get around, will you, Nat, and make sure that where we all were yesterday evening is where we all are now. I want no distractions from arguments about who's now got what and shouldn't have. With all settled, get the place Johnny proof, or as much as. He'll want this place and he'll get it. We're outside The Lines, so our job is to make him pay a price, but a low one ourselves."

Drake dumped his portmanteau which he had carried across the valley himself and quickly left to tour the buildings and the yards that were held by the 105th Lights. Maltby's Section was one of the first he came to, holding their own billet houses, but also a paddock that had probably been a pig-sty, but all the animals had long since been taken into The Lines. Nevertheless, the unpleasant evidence of their occupation was being shovelled over the wall by as many of the men as could be furnished with shovels. Drake was happy with the way the windows of the billets had been narrowed, but not the paddock. He found Chosen Man Davey.

"Where's Lieutenant Maltby?"

Davey leaned on his shovel.

"I think he's upstairs, Sir, watching down the road."

Drake nodded and then studied the walls around.

"I want loopholes in the walls of the pigsty house and the stones of that wall behind brought to this one in front and dropped over to act as a glacis slope that will deflect any cannon-shot."

Davey was not happy. A pile of stones at the front of the wall would make it easier to climb over, but this was an order.

"Yes Sir. I'll see it's done. When we've cleared this muck away."

Drake left to enter the building and climb the stairs to where the floor divided into two rooms. In one, Maltby was at the window, which provided the best view down the road. He turned briefly when Drake entered the room to quickly turn back and resume his watch forward.

"Hello, Sir. All quiet so far."

Drake came to the window.

"Have you any men out forward? As an advanced picket?"

Maltby pointed out the window.

"Yes Sir. Three hundred yards out, in that clump of trees, Pike and Miles."

Drake nodded.

"Good. Keep your Section at it. Carr's certain that Johnny will arrive sometime today."

Three hundred yards forward, the objects of their conversation were busy cutting branches.

"Get these piled here, Joe. You can bet that some Frog Officer has got his telescope on this here place and it can be no bad thing if they can't see us."

Joe Pike added a well-leafed branch to the top of a bush, adding it to many others and nodded his satisfaction.

"That do, Tom?"

Miles now sitting himself behind it, provided an answer.

"Right. Let's start on that sausage and biscuit. What've we got to drink?"

"Some white wine."

"White wine! Watered down for you!"

Miles did the watering down, whilst Pike divided the food. Soon both were eating and drinking contentedly, but Pike was plainly the more relaxed of the two and perhaps the most distracted by his own thoughts. The subject on his mind dwelt very much within his own painful experience.

"It's a bad thing with Eirin."

Miles was busy peering between branches.

"'Sright, but 'tis not unknown. Young Officers meddlin' with the girls of the Followers. Young wives too!"

"Do you think she ever thought he'd marry her?"

Miles emitted a sharp breath.

"Who can say? Young girl like that. Who knows what hopes they keeps within 'em."

"She's not so young. Seventeen, goin' on eighteen."

"Young enough to think it'll all come up roses."

"Still, Tom, according to Jed, Maltby's putting up, so as she goes into a Convent."

Miles spat to one side.

"I'll believe that when it happens! And only then!"

Always looking forward, suddenly he tensed.

"Johnny's on his way, boy. I'll stay a while more, but get back to Drake or Carr."

"And say what?"

"The French is comin'. Enough to fill a racetrack!"

Puzzled, Joe Pike left the trees to sprint back and found both Officers together. He spoke the exact words to his Captain, who grinned at the description.

"And whose judgement is that?"

"Tom Miles Sir."

Drake looked at Carr.

"That'll do for me!"

"And me. Order stand to."

Within minutes, all tools and shovels were discarded and the men of Erskine's Light Companies were

653

donning their crossbelts and equipment and carrying their weapons to their prepared positions. Flints were checked and also cartridges, for ease of extraction from their box. The men of Maltby's Section saw Tom Miles scurrying back and Drake questioned him when he had scrambled over the paddock wall.

"How far behind, Miles?"

"'Bout 200 yards, Sir. Comin' on slow, feelin' their way, like."

"How many?"

"Hundreds, Sir. Quite a crowd."

"A column behind?"

"Couldn't say, Sir. They's too dense."

However, from the upstairs window, Carr could and, being stood alone, he spoke to himself.

"No column, but there's many more than we can hold back."

Behind him he had a messenger for each Company, plus John Byford and he turned to address the Company messengers first.

"Tell your Captains, I leave it to them to decide when to fall back. We rally on the far side of the ravine, but all retire at the sound of 'Retreat'. Got that?"

Four 'Yes Sirs' came back, not quite in unison, but they saluted and ran off.

"Byford! Back to the redoubts. Tell the Colonel or General Erskine what's happening."

As Byford clattered down the stairs, Carr returned to his window, to see the first of the French skirmishers enveloping the trees used by Pike and Miles. Carr ran down to Drake's Light Company, who were to the left of the road, with the 60th on the opposite side, also armed with Baker rifles. Creating the rest of the line, to the left of Drake were the 50th, and the 92nd formed the far left. The road came through Carr's right centre, the ravine being behind the 50th. Carr found Davey at the stonewall and was brutally brief.

"Him on the horse!"

"Sir."

Davey looked forward to see the leading Officer, encouraging his men on, so many of them and so compacted, that they did almost form a column. Davey set his sights for 150 yards, then the order came from his Company Captain.

"Load!"

Davey pulled out one of the soft leather patches that were sometimes used to wrap the ball, so that it would better grip the barrel rifling of a Baker. Instead of ramming down the ball still in the paper, he tipped in the powder and wrapped up the ball, before squeezing it into the muzzle. It went down snugly and so he rammed all down tight and waited. Drake was behind and gave his order, which caused many to chuckle.

"Fire when you think you'll hit something!"

Davey was content. He knelt down at the wall, rested his Baker between two stones that he had placed there himself and took aim. He held his breath, took final sight and squeezed the trigger. The rifle went off with its sharp bark. Davey had been the first to fire and so he was enveloped in smoke, but the cries of satisfaction from his messmates told him that his aim had been true, the most loud and gleeful coming from Tom Miles.

"You gott'n, John! You gott'n."

The smoke cleared and Davey could see the Officer slumped over his horse, this now being held by a Tirailleur, whilst the Officer was taken down to lie very still on the turf. Then, at that point, the whole British line opened fire for all to be enveloped in smoke. The one man who could see best was Carr, now returned upstairs and above the smoke, but of one thing he was determined and again he spoke it aloud

"Not one man, if I can help it. This is just theatre to show the Frogs that whatever they get, they'll have to fight for. And pay a price!"

However, 'Bugle Bates' was close, which fact Carr had forgotten.

"The lads'll appreciate that, Sir."

Carr turned to see him, a little surprised, but he may as well make use of his presence.

"Get to that window to the left. When the Frogs are 50 yards up to the 50th and 92nd, I want to know."

"Sir."

Bates went to the window and watched. He knew what Carr was thinking, that the 50th and 92nd, armed only with Brown Bess muskets, would be the first to fail to hold the French at a safe distance. Carr added within himself that he did not want his own 105th and the 60th to be in any danger of being cut off from the ravine. He was once more studying his own front when Erskine arrived.

"What have you got, Carr?"

"See for yourself, Sir. Reconnaissance in strength, with more behind."

Erskine peered forward through the window.

"Right, but you've got almost a whole wing in here. Hold them. Don't give best easily, but come back to the other side when you judge best. I'll have the guns ready in support."

With that he was gone, before Carr could reply. He now looked forward for himself to see that the French were fighting very cleverly, not walking forward, but kneeling to fire, or even lying down, thus their casualties were few, but they were exerting little pressure on the British. This went on for some minutes, until another French Officer arrived, him on foot and he began shouting and gesticulating towards the village. With that, the whole French line stood and began to advance. They were met by a volley from the village, but the dense smoke now lingering from the ongoing conflict spoiled the aim of almost all and only a handful of unlucky French were felled. Carr grew anxious.

"What have you got, Bates?"

"There's too many to stop, Sir, and they're up close."

"Right. Sound off."

Bates, stood at his open window, sounded 'Retreat'. Almost immediately the British fire fell away and Carr decided it was time to leave.

"Come on, Bates."

The two descended the stairs and ran out of the front door to find the streets full of running Redcoats. He ran over to look for the 60th Rifles beyond the road and they were also pulling back to safety. However, some, very well trained, perhaps too well, were filing back in their threes, following their fallback drill. Carr ran over.

"Forget filing back. Out! Get out the village. Get to the far side of the ravine."

All the 60th were now running back and Carr turned to look back down the main street to see the first French arriving. Musket balls whistled above him as he finally passed the last buildings and he was one of the last to descend into the ravine but he had time to help a man of the 105th, hit in the leg. Now supported, the man could hobble faster and they soon reached their two deep line, only 50 yards from the top of the slope. The line was solid and well formed, with the slope so steep that the second line could fire over the heads of the first.

It was not long before the first of the French emerged from the nearest buildings of Sobral. Carr scrambled up the rest of the slope to reach the semaphore mast whose arms were working maniacally. There he found Erskine and Spencer, with Wellington himself but a little way off. Carr saluted, but said nothing, until Spencer turned to him.

"Think they'll cross, Carr?"

Carr had no hesitation.

"No Sir, they'll not. I feel these are too well led."

Spencer looked down at him.

"Too well led!"

"Yes Sir. They came on carefully, feeling their way. They've got the village, which was what they want."

Each minute that passed gave weight to Carr's opinion. The French formed a line, but remained close to the walls of Sobral. Spencer smacked his right fist into his left palm.

"You're right, Carr, but these Frogs can have some grapeshot anyway."

He turned to an Officer close behind him.

"Buckley!"

Buckley hurried off and within three minutes the first gun from the many redoubts around them fired. However, at that first gun the French hurried back behind the stonework of Sobral and the remaining Agraca redoubts loosed off their guns against an empty space, but Spencer smiled as the grapeshot splattered against the white walls of Sobral, leaving pock marks that revealed the dark stone beneath.

"No matter. Now they know this will be no easy nut to crack!"

"Do I pull my men back, Sir?"

"No. Hold them here. My guess is that Johnny's not done. He'll try with a full column before this day's out."

If his men were to remain there, Carr thought it only right that he remain with them, and so he descended the short length of slope to find Drake.

"Spencer wants us still out here. I can't see Johnny trying anything more this day, but he thinks they will. Give it an hour and then let the men sit and eat."

Drake nodded.

"Very good."

"I'll get around to the other Captains. I'd say we're here until dark."

The men of the four Light Companies sat the comfortable slope and ate their food, all emptying their haversacks, confident that more would arrive with the

658

falling night. Tom Davey and Ellis sat together in the growing gloom.

"Not much longer, Sarn't."

"No. Us sat here is a plain waste, but some poor buggers will be gettin' a night duty to put a barrier across that road. That's for sure."

He pointed to the only road linking Sobral with Monte Agraca, running around the head of the separating valley. Davey looked at him, then he heard footfalls behind him and turned to see Drake, but he had come for Ellis.

"We're pulling back to our camp, Sergeant. I leave that to you. I'm going around the other Companies."

Ellis stood up with Davey.

"Sir."

Then, with Drake gone, Ellis spoke to Davey.

"Get 'em out of here, John. Sharpish! We don't want to be about when some Officer decides to start some building work."

The retreat of the 105th Light Company was indeed very rapid, almost precipitate, and those with the awareness of their escape, including Davey and Ellis, sat gratefully around their messfires to partake gratefully of the saltfish stew that Bridie and Nellie had prepared. After the routine cleaning and inspection of their equipment and weapons, all sat talking and waiting for 'lights out'. The one departure from the routine was Jed Deakin doing the rounds with a spare haversack making the collection for Eirin. There was little in the way of coin but much that had been gleaned from French Officer's uniforms. He came to Tom Miles.

"You put in?"

Miles looked up, meeting the challenge.

"Yes. Twice."

"What?"

"All the buttons what I got. There b'ain't no more."

"No coin?"

"Not 'till payday. Like the rest."

Eirin had heard and seen all and managed a slight smile, then the sickness took hold of her once again.

Dawn found that Ellis' prediction of nightime barrier building had been false, but the sounds of fighting from over on their left were enough for all to don their equipment and once more check their weapons. Lacey and O'Hare took themselves forward to the semaphore station atop the mount. There they found Erskine and Spencer and it was the latter who spoke first.

"Yours ready, Lacey?"

"Sir."

Spencer nodded.

"That over to the left, which we can hear, is Cole's Division being tried out, but the Peer is most worried about Sobral over there. If Johnny tries anything serious, it'll be against us."

Lacey turned to him, frowning.

"Then we'll be called forward, Sir."

"Probably, yes, but you'll not be alone. He's brought down from the North the whole of both Picton's and Campbell's Divisions to support myself and Cole. Here!"

The last word was thoroughly emphasised, but Lacey felt relief. There would be no prolonged rearguard for his men and he was also relieved, for their sake, to see the Company of the 60th busy gathering anything that could be included in a barrier which they were building on the road, over to Lacey's right, between the stone walls that girded the road. Spencer and Erskine, meanwhile, were busy with their telescopes, studying Sobral, Erskine giving the running commentary.

"All I can see is a few heads bobbing about. Nothing serious at all."

Spencer was nothing like as sanguine.

"He'll try, though. He's got to. He has to push us out of here and then pierce The Lines to get us back to the sea. He can't sit out there. It's him that's under siege. Not us."

Erskine lowered his telescope and looked at him.

"How so?"

"Every Portuguese and Spanish out there, Regular, Guerrilla and Ordenanza have pulled in behind him. Nothing's getting through to him. Two weeks and they'll be starving!"

He was still looking through his telescope when suddenly he tensed.

"There! Look there, the windows of that place with the green shutters."

Erskine drew out his telescope and focused.

"What I can see is a whole tailor's shop of splendid uniforms at each window."

Spencer lowered his telescope and snapped it shut.

"That's Massena! Come to take a look. I'm off to The Peer. If Massena's here, it must be us."

With that he was gone, leaving Erskine with Lacey and O'Hare.

"This afternoon or tomorrow, Lacey. I'll need your Lights to support the 60th at that barricade."

With that, he was gone, leaving the two stood together. All the while O'Hare had been using his own telescope.

"I think we can discount today."

Lacey looked at him, and spoke, evidently much puzzled.

"Why?"

"Can you see any guns? I can't. He'll not try that road without artillery support and that means getting guns through and into Sobral. If he does choose here, that'll take the rest of today."

He looked over to the barrier, now almost complete.

"Sending anything over that ravine or down that road is madness! Even without that barrier, the road's worse. With all the guns we've got up here, half of his men,

661

more, will be knocked over before they reach that barrier. It's nearly half a mile from the village!"

He sighed, half in sadness, but said no more as Lacey replied.

"I'm sure you're right, but we'll hold the men in readiness."

O'Hare began walking back.

"Agreed. Kit off, but none to stray."

O'Hare was right and for the rest of the day the Officers of the two armies regarded each other through telescopes, both accurate and expensive or otherwise. With the growing darkness, the mess of John Davey witnessed the Light Company of the 50th moving forward to the slope under the Semaphore Station, which sight Tom Miles could not resist.

"Don't you go sleepin' on the job, now boys. I'd not like to see any of you on the triangle!"

Despite their battle record together, there was no love lost between the 50th and the 105th and a curt reply came out of the dark.

"Sod you and sod off!"

However, then came a more pointed reply.

"Least mounting picket gets us out of manning that barrier! We're on the slope before that mast, that's us occupied. The 60th's already at the barrier, so, when they comes off, the next nearest is you!"

The brutal accuracy of the reply silenced Miles. He sat back down.

"He's right! Lovely job that'll be, with a whole French army comin' down that road."

He rolled himself in his blanket, touched his Baker rifle in the dark to reassure himself and fell immediately to sleep. Thus he could not hear what the 50th could, all through the night came the sounds of French guns being moved up and walls demolished to provide firing positions. Miles was the first to be woken by Ellis.

"Form up. Now! Bring what food you can."

Within ten minutes the Light Company were formed on the road, in fours, with Carr and Drake at their head. They marched forward through the chill, but growing dawn until, 200 yards before their ridge, the barrier became clear, with the still resting figures of the green uniformed 60th gathered on the British side. The order came back from Drake.

"Halt! Rest and eat. Breakfast time."

The 105th Light fell out and then sat or rested against the walls that bordered the road, drinking cold, very weak tea and eating biscuits, sausage and salty dried fish, which needed the tea to wash it down. Drake and Carr continued forward to find the commanding Captain of the 60th, but he found them, walking back to meet them. On seeing Carr, he saluted.

"Morning, Sir."

Carr knew most of his Officers from their time together in their shared billet in Sobral.

"Morning. Shepherd, isn't it?"

"Yes Sir."

"How many have you?"

"Sixty-two, Sir."

"And what do you suggest at that barrier?"

"Four ranks, Sir. Take position, fire, fall back, reload, then back into firing position."

"A spread of 15 at the barrier each time."

"Just so, Sir."

"They'll send a column down the road, after giving us a taste of round shot. I'd put mine in advance of your barrier, to get onto their flanks, but I fear we'd be dreadfully exposed."

"You're right, Sir, you would be, but if I may say, Sir, our job is to give them the barrier, but only after we've broken them up in taking it. Then reinforcements will finally push them back."

Carr nodded. His own thinking remained what it had been in Sobral, to minimise casualties.

"My thoughts entirely, Captain. Draw them onto the redoubts and a waiting firing line."

He looked behind him. The only sheltered area was before and after the barrier, on the road itself at the head of the ravine, as it ran between two low banks surmounted by the walls. He turned back to Shepherd.

"When it looks like bayonet work, fall back, past mine. We'll be 30 yards back and we'll give them a few volleys as they come over your furniture there. Then it'll be up to our supports."

Shepherd smiled and nodded.

"As you say, Sir."

Carr leaned forward offering his hand.

"Good luck, Shepherd."

"Thank you, Sir."

Drake offered his hand also and they exchanged the same words, then the two walked back to their men.

"Right, let's get ready. One Section each side, ready to close after these 60th have gone through. What time have you got?"

Drake pulled out his ornate watch.

"Just gone seven. Ten past."

Almost the same words were being spoken behind them, on the ridge. Wellington himself was bringing forward the 105th as Lacey spoke to O'Hare, the former with his watch in his hand.

"Ten past. Must be soon now."

Wellington now approached the pair.

"Pleased to see it's yours, Lacey."

Lacey could not quite bring himself to answer with similar words. He was not at all pleased that it was his Battalion once again in the way of a French column.

"You can depend on us, Sir."

"That I know, Lacey, but there's support if you need it. The 50th will be on your left."

Both men saluted as Wellington rode to the Semaphore Station, then Lacey looked for Spencer or Erskine, to see neither.

"He's placed behind the ridge, out of harms way. Good, but there's no one to call us forward, at the right time. Even The Peer's gone. I'll not wait. Best get yourself up there and give us the signal."

'Up there' was the top of the ridge, where all could be seen and so O'Hare trotted forward until he could see the barrier, almost hidden within the stone walls. He barely had time to take in the scene before the French guns opened fire, all concentrating on the barrier. Then the guns in the redoubts doubled the noise when the French column emerged from Sobral onto the road and their roundshot began to damage the leading French Battalions. However, in order to do any damage to the barrier, first the French guns had to lower the walls beside the road before it and so the 105th Lights, 30 yards back, found themselves being showered in dislodged stone, some dangerously large. The Section most exposed was Maltby's, under the wall to the right, because being there they were more in the line of fire from the village than Shakeshaft's. Men were being injured, but if the Section raised themselves to fall back, this would mean even more casualties. Drake called out.

"Stuart. Get yours over behind Richard's. All lie down."

Hearing Drake's order, One Section rolled over the road to the opposite side and, thus, they endured some minutes of bombardment, all prone on the damp earth, watching for any large lumps of masonry that came bowling down towards them. Shepherd's men were sheltered from the flying stones by their barrier, but the 105th had to endure what came, all lying prone within the angle of the wall and road, some lying on others in some places. John Davey and his Captain, Stuart Maltby, found themselves side by side, but any amount of camaraderie was plainly absent on the face of John Davey and also by the flat tone of his voice in his reply to Maltby.

"I'd prefer the French column to arrive, Davey. Would you not?"

"As you say, Sir."

Nothing more was said for the remaining minutes, then the French bombardment stopped, their own column was now too near and then, but a minute after, the 60th began their volleys, only 15 men at a time, but it was almost continuous, although barely heard as the British guns behind fired at maximum speed. With no more pieces of wall coming their way, Carr looked back.

"As you were. Each side. Get the wounded back."

There were several, most with head wounds from the flying stonework, but each Section now crouched and waited on both sides of the road. On the ridge, O'Hare needed no telescope to see that the column was taking heavy punishment from the Rifles at the barrier, with no let up from the Monte Agraca redoubts. However, there was no halt to their progress, it was merely slowed. What worried him most was the size of the attack, three Battalions, a whole Brigade had been sent forward out of Sobral.

Carr and Drake both looked forward to watch the continuous round of Riflemen falling back a short way to reload and then await another turn at the barrier. The minutes ticked by and then there was cannon support from only two Agraca redoubts, these far over to their left, because the French were now masked by the 105th and 60th from the redoubts in line with the road, but still there came the non-stop sound of the defence of the barrier. Then a whistle sounded and all the 60th turned to run back. Carr looked back at his crouching men.

"Up! Stand up. Make ready."

All checked their flints and priming as the 60th ran past.

"Now!"

All ran into the road to form a three deep line, all standing at the 'make ready'.

"Present."

Carr waited through the dreadful seconds before any French began to climb the barrier. Then shakoes appeared, then heads and then white cross belts.

"Front rank. Fire!"

Thus it began, Drake counting the ten seconds needed between each rank's volley to give time for the reload. Many French fell as they continued to come over the barrier, but it was being demolished from the far side and then the whole column came on, now reformed, easily striding over the remains. Drake allowed one more volley, which felled many in the French front rank.

"Back! Fall back."

As the barrier was abandoned, so O'Hare signalled the 105th to come forward, stood patient in their two deep line. In the centre, Lacey turned to his men, his sword half aloft.

"The 105th will advance."

Also in the centre, Colour Sergeant Deakin remained dubious.

"One more turn at Shy at the Cockerel! All the fun of the Fair."

Equally sceptical was Toby Halfway, stood immediately behind.

"Aye! But at this Fair the cockerel can shy back!"

However, at this moment Captain Heaviside turned to inspire his men in his customary fashion.

"The wicked flee when no one pursues, but the righteous are bold as a lion. Proverbs 28. One."

All in the Colour Company grinned as Lacey led them forward, the smoke from the conflict at the barrier issuing gently back over the ridge towards them. Over on the road, also issuing back, but vigorously, Carr was met by General Erskine, him pointing over with his right arm.

"Form on the right of your 105th, Carr. Over there. When they come over the ridge."

The 60th were already on their way and so Carr stopped and pointed after them with his sword.

"Follow the 60th. Form on our Grenadiers!"

Now unmolested by any French fire, they ran to meet their own Battalion now arriving. Leading all, the first Officer Drake met was Carravoy, Captain of the Grenadiers, at their place on the right of the line.

"Hello, Charles! This is a bit of a turn up. Us on the right, up alongside yours!"

Carravoy gave but a glance past his sword as he led his men forward, but Carr, last to make the journey, took the time to take a look at the majestic double line of his own Regiment, muskets all at the 'make ready', both Colours standing out straight and clear in the steady breeze. Thus inspired, he felt the need to bring his sword up in salute to The Colours, which was returned by Lacey, advancing but yards in front.

Stood where he was, Carr could see that his 105th, were not alone, for over the higher part of the ridge came what he took to be the 50th, their black Regimental Colour providing the obvious proof. Appearing on the left of the 105th, they provided an equally intimidating sight. Now seeing both British Regiments now before them, the French gunners lifted their aim and soon round shot was ploughing the earth before and parting the air above, but the range was too far for accuracy and, besides, round shot gave no anxiety to veterans such as the 50th and the 105th. What anxiety there was existed in the minds of the oncoming French, these being the battalions of Menard's Brigade who, at Busaco, had observed and absorbed only too clearly what happened when an unsupported column met a British line, in that case, Crauford's Light Brigade. The sight of the long line of the 105th, with the 50th in support, by itself halted all progress on the road. Their hesitancy was not lost on Lacey, nor the reason why.

"We're going right up to them, boys! Right into their faces!"

He led his men to within 40 yards of the first of the French, who were trying to deploy into line. Lacey then gave his flanking Companies time to lap around the French column, which they did.

"Volley by ranks. Present."

All muskets came down level.

"Fire!"

The whole first rank fired with an appalling crash. Lacey allowed the smoke to thoroughly clear before repeating with the second rank, then, in the smoke he gave his final order.

"Fix bayonets!"

There was a frustrating delay of seconds, but not a period that the thoroughly disordered French column could use. Lacey raised his sword.

"At double time. Advance!"

The whole line moved forward, at a jog or a quick walk and, at this sight, the numbed survivors of the French column turned and ran. Lacey was the first onto the remains of the barrier.

"On! Keep on boys. Don't let them stand."

Lacey had seen that the final Battalion of the three was still intact and knew that the remnants of the first two must not be allowed to rally on them. He shouted at the top of his voice, a repeat taken up by O'Hare and his Captains.

"Follow close. Don't let them stand."

The double time advance had become a run, yet no British bayonet was used. If the third French Battalion made any attempt at resistance, it was not felt by the 105th, because it was swept up in the rout, as the whole French force fell back and divided itself into the streets and alleys of Sobral. Still at the front, but breathless, Lacey was grateful to see Bugle Bates, who had remained close to his Colonel. Lacey was worried, Sobral must be full of French and their guns were still there, in fact he looked over to see some of his men engaging with those very gunners on the edge of the village in hand to hand combat.

"Sound recall!"

Bates took a much needed deep breath of his own and the notes sounded out. Lacey now had enough breath of his own to shout his order, which was repeated all down his line.

"Retire. Double time. Reform on the ridge."

Like a wave receding from a sea wall, his men fell back, to turn and run back along the road and across the ravine, to reform on the ridge. The whole had not taken fifteen minutes. Lacey stood panting amongst his breathless men, but, although in full view of the French, they came under no fire. Spencer himself now came down, on foot.

"Well done Lacey."

He turned to the reformed ranks.

"Well done, 105th!"

There were a few cheers in reply, but Spencer had turned back to Lacey.

"Get your men back over the ridge, Lacey. I'd say that's that, for us around here!"

oOo

Four miles to the East, General Crauford was stood atop the parapet of Redoubt 120, acknowledging the end of the combat at Sobral by the sound of the cannonfire dying away, whilst massaging upwards his own irascible mood caused by the continued inactivity at his section of The Lines. On either side Portuguese gunners polished the barrels of their new pieces, checked touchholes for cleanliness and chipped rust from roundshot. Beside him stood Colonel Beckwith of the 43rd, one of the two Line Battalions of his Brigade. Crauford raised his telescope for the 25th time to examine the doings of the French opposite, but all that could be seen were a few French picquets, most almost a mile away, leaning on fence posts or against the trees and the walls of buildings. He turned to Beckwith.

"Who was it, that the Frogs just tried conclusions with?"

"I believe Spencer's, Sir. Probably at Sobral."

Crauford grunted, his ill mood in no way reduced.

"Would that they should try us here."

Beckwith fully appreciated his Brigadier's taste for action and his hatred of inactivity, but he remained silent. Crauford raised his telescope yet again, but this time it seemed to Beckwith that Crauford saw something, evidenced by his very careful focusing of his instrument.

"What's this?"

He passed the telescope to Beckwith.

"What do you make of that group, coming along the main road, our left centre?"

Beckwith did his own focusing, then made his own judgement.

"They've left the road and are coming towards us, Sir, and, if pressed for an opinion, I'd say that it is Massena himself and his whole Staff. And alone, Sir, no troops anywhere, of any sort. He must have come to take a look, at us and what we're about."

Crauford seized back the telescope and studied the group for himself. With the distance now reducing he could clearly see the elaborate uniforms of all in the group, identifying them as definitely Generals and Staff. The group continued to approach and therefore it was not long before Crauford began to feel much affronted by the impertinence of their continued approach to his Lines. He looked down at the Officer commanding the redoubt.

"Give them a gun!"

He pointed at the group that were the target, now within plain sight. The orders were given and promptly obeyed. The Officer sighted the gun himself and himself took the lintstock. A last look, a blow on the ember to make it glow and the end was applied. The gun crashed out and recoiled back. All was smoke but Crauford already had his telescope up and ready. What he saw was not the arrival of the shot, but the leading Officer in the group had stopped and was raising his hat, to plainly acknowledge that he had trespassed too far. This man turned his horse, as did the rest of his entourage and rode back. Crauford grunted his satisfaction.

"That, Beckwith, may be the most important shot of this whole damn war!"

oOo

Chapter Eleven
Leaving The Lines

"How many is that?"

"What?"

"Deserters come in this week?"

Drake looked at his logbook. They had been ordered to keep a record of all events opposite Sobral.

"Seven."

"Most last night?"

672

"Yes. The three you saw."

Carr lowered his telescope from his daily study of Sobral.

"Nothing new that I can see."

He closed the telescope and looked down at the log, displayed on the parapet before Drake.

"I think they're starving over there. Seems to me that it is they who are the besieged, rather than we. Those last night looked half dead!"

Then a thought.

"Were they regular French, or conscripts from conquered countries? I didn't notice."

"Regular! Two were Voltiguers."

Carr raised his eyebrows and screwed his mouth sideways.

"Elite! Seems that things are getting a mite desperate for our near neighbours."

He yawned.

"Right. I'm for some sleep. Night picket must be about the most tedious of all possible duties, I am of the strongest opinion. Who has Sentry after you, come this dingy dawn?"

"Stuart."

"Very good, but tell him to keep a good watch. Spencer wants to know what Johnny's up to, but how we're supposed to know, escapes me. Nothing's happened this past week. I'd say things have just about finished here, between us and them, fighting wise I mean."

"I hope you're right, in fact I'm sure you're right, but we keep a good watch and we keep the log."

Carr's voice contained but slight sarcasm.

"Most assiduous! But more time here, snug within The Lines, would not come amiss in any form. Sleep, food and good conversation. Present company excepted, of course."

"Of course! I've never counted myself as any form of raconteur. Well, not of the best, at least."

Drake looked up.

"However, I do hope that you are not fleecing too many at backgammon?"

Carr shook his head.

"No. Small stakes and no doubling dice. Purely social only."

"Have you written?"

"Yes. Twice."

With that he was gone, to cross over with Stuart Maltby in the communication trench. Salutes were exchanged and the pair walked on, each to their own destination. Drake now stood up to face the newly arrived Maltby.

"There's your spyglass and there's your log. I'm for sleep."

Behind and also alongside, Sergeants and Corporals were organising the men for the change of Watch and soon all were settled, the men sitting and eating what was a second breakfast of apples, dried fish and biscuits. However, they had little time for more than a few mouthfuls before Erskine and Spencer arrived and all sprang to their feet. However, Spencer waved them back down and took the log.

"Three last night, Erskine. Three. And there'll be more, in greater number, I'll lay a bet on it."

Erskine nodded.

"No doubt. And from what we hear, the Ordenanza and El Charro's crew are in behind them tight as a drum. Nothing's getting in. Or out! On top, I'll wager they arrived with damn all, what with Wellington ordering all destroyed on the way down or carried back."

Spencer nodded himself as he looked across at the silent Sobral, but with no telescope, for he was still holding the log.

"Yes, but he's fortified all that over yonder, blocked off doors, windows and what have you, but that finished days ago."

674

He placed the log on the parapet beside Maltby and turned away.

"Yes. All we can do is observe developments, but that can wait until after breakfast. You'll join me?"

"I will."

With that the pair departed, leaving Maltby with thoughts of his own, mostly concerning Eirin Mulcahy and the words of Jed Deakin, these having been spoken but four days ago. The two subjects of his thoughts were some way back over the ridge, sat around their own mess fire, but it was Deakin who was surprised enough to comment on the thickness of his waist, as he buckled on his equipment.

"I think I've put on weight!"

John Davey was the nearest.

"No bad thing. Be glad. A bit of extra will keep you going when we're ordered out of here to go chasing Johnny again."

Zeke Saunders was buckling on his own equipment.

"And the further off that is, that better I like it. Full sleep and a full belly, regular like, you can't have too much of, is how I sees it."

However, the one anxious face was that of Bridie, even as she concentrated on preparing food for the Noon meal.

"Jed. What about the Convent for Eirin, here? 'Specially if there's now talk of us movin' out and back up country."

Eirin looked up from studying the ground between her feet to look at Deakin, but said nothing while Deakin answered.

"I'm on my way now, to see Parson and the Reverend Albright. Such askin' by Men of the Cloth at a Convent is more likely to get a better result, I'm thinking."

Bridie smiled up at her 'Army Husband' and Deakin smiled back, to then place his reassuring hand on Eirin's head as he walked past her. A five-minute walk through the tent lines brought him to the small cart of

Reverend Albright, where the senior of the Spiritual Pair was reading a book, and the junior going about his duties as servant. Deakin cleared is throat and the two looked up, but Deakin addressed Albright.

"Excuse me, Sir, beggin' your pardon, but I've come to ask a favour, if you've no objection."

Albright lowered his book and Sedgwicke lowered his dishcloth.

"Yes Sergeant? Deakin, is it not?"

Deakin nodded.

"Yes Sir. Colour Sergeant."

"Then tell me, Colour Sergeant, what is it that you want of us?"

Deakin cleared his throat again.

"Well Sir, I don't know how much of this you know, but one of our Mess, in the Followers, Eirin Mulcahy, my step-daughter and my wife's eldest, well, she's in the family way, Sir, four, five, months gone. If we has to march out on a new campaign, which is very likely, and with a Winter comin' on, then I don't give much for the chances of her, nor the babe. 'Specially if it comes to a retreat, which is the most of what has happened so far in this war. So, Sir........."

Albright held up his hand for Deakin to stop.

"Is she married?"

"No Sir."

Albright looked at Sedgwicke.

"Did you know about this?"

Sedgwicke nodded.

"Yes Sir, I did. A very nice girl of good family."

Albright started upright in his chair. The gesture was clear, 'So why is she pregnant?'. However, he returned to Deakin.

"Go on, Sergeant. In what way do you want us to become involved?"

"Well, Sir, I was comin' to that. You see, the Father, as we believe him to be, is willin' to put up a month's pay and the lads've all chipped in to raise about 15 pounds, all told, which we hope will get her into a Convent for the child to be born and then grow up some. For 'em both to be looked after, Sir, and then to come back with us, Sir, when they'n able."

He paused to gauge the reaction on Albright's face, but it was blank, so he continued.

"Well, you can see now where you come in, Sir. We was thinkin' that a man such as yourself, goin' to a Convent and doin' of the askin' would be much more likely to get agreement, rather than the likes of us knockin' on their door and askin' the same, Sir."

The Reverend threw his book onto the small table.

"And this Convent is where?"

"There's a big one at Mafra, Sir. About ten miles back, as the crow flies."

Albright frowned.

"And who is the Father?"

Deakin took a deep breath.

"An Officer, Sir. But I can't say no more than that."

The frown did not disappear.

"And does he acknowledge himself to be the Father."

"Well, yes and no, Sir. He accepts that he could be."

Thoughts now entered Albright's head regarding the character of the said Eirin, placing huge significance on the words, 'could be'. However, he did not pursue the idea, at least he would not do so with Deakin now present. He folded his hands over his generous stomach.

"I will think on this, Sergeant. I have a concern that, if an Officer is involved, whose side should I take, regarding who speaks truthfully, and to what extent should I allow myself to become involved? Clearly there has been some sinful behaviour."

He immediately noted the concern on Deakin's face.

"However, I will give you an answer Colour Sergeant, before this day is ended. Please now allow me to think this over."

Deakin's face darkened as he came to the attention and saluted.

"Sir!"

He executed a smart and thorough 'about turn', including a stamp of his right boot, which certainly conveyed his anger to Sedgwicke, if not to Albright, and then marched away. Sedgwicke, for his part was deeply concerned and upset. He knew the Mulcahy family well and had found no flaw in any and he had taught Eirin to read himself. They were of the best of the Followers, good, kind, solid and reliable, who had certainly been nothing other than generous and welcoming to him. In addition, this was particularly so of Jed Deakin when Sedgwicke had been condemned into the Army after stealing his Bishop's silver to pay for drink. He had been a rock of support for someone as utterly unfit for soldiering as ex-Reverend Percival Sedgwicke. All sorts of emotions played within him, not least the kindness and sympathy that Jed Deakin had shown him over the five years he had been in the Army. All the events from the past welled up emotions strong enough to cause him to speak out exactly as he felt.

"Sir, we must help! It is both our Christian duty to help those who fall, but repent, and also Eirin being an expectant Mother following an army during a Winter campaign creates a huge risk to both herself and the child. That is a major concern. It seems that finance has been found for this, Sir, and all that we are being asked to do is to make the request of a Mother Superior. To use our good offices and position to bring this about, Sir, to a satisfactory outcome."

Albright was somewhat shocked by this outburst from his inferior, but there was logic in Sedgwicke's words, yet he returned to his own suspicions.

"This Eirin. Is she of good character? Nothing that could be termed slatternly?"

Sedgwicke angered.

"No Sir, absolutely not. It is my opinion that she is a good girl who has been led astray. Used, in fact."

"Is the Father known?"

"I can only speak from rumour, but from what I hear, the Father is Lieutenant Stuart Maltby, of our own Light Company, Sir."

"And he denies that he is the Father?"

"Not in so many words. He insinuates that the child may have a different Father to himself, which, in my opinion is a shocking slander, designed to deflect responsibility from himself."

The 'Sirs' were becoming less frequent. They were now speaking as equals and Sedgwicke was at least the intellectual equal of his military superior. He continued.

"And Colour Sergeant Deakin is as good a man as you'll find anywhere. He made himself responsible for the family when Eirin's Father was killed in Sicily, which is why it is he that has come to us asking for help. And you may recall how well Eirin behaved amongst the wounded during Talavera. She, herself, should be given some credit for that."

Albright was moved, but not convinced.

"And it is Lieutenant Maltby who is contributing to the fifteen pounds?"

"Yes. And, as I see it, that is sufficient acknowledgment to dispel any fears we may have of supporting the least trustworthy party in this."

The 'we', in this case was plainly singular, applying solely to Albright, yet Sedgwicke spoke further.

"And, as has been said, the requirement upon ourselves is merely to pay a visit to the nearest Convent, to help out this unfortunate girl. For us to act as forgiving and Christian men!"

Albright looked at Sedgwicke, with no little concern showing on his fleshy face.

"It will be Catholic. I know your views on such."

Sedgwicke knew that he was winning, but he remained stern.

"I will pray for forgiveness, but, surely, in a cause such as this ....?"

Albright was no longer listening as he retrieved his book.

"Very well. Inform Deakin that we will do as he requests."

Then a thought, as he searched for his place within the pages.

"What's the hospitality like, in a Catholic Convent, do you think?"

Sedgwicke was already on his way.

"Oh, of the best, Sir. Of that I am sure. Especially to one of High Church, such as yourself. I'm sure that they will make allowances for us being English and having broken with the Pope!"

Deakin had not long sat down by the fire, sat in a pose which thoroughly conveyed the anger that he felt towards Albright, many times mumbling, "The likes of them and the likes of us."

All the Followers around had heard him tell of Albright's reluctance and were equally cast down. Finally, Deakin spoke himself.

"We'll just have to get Eirin there ourselves. Then they can see her. I'll go with her and, when they see her, they'll not say no!"

At that point Sedgwicke arrived and Deakin stood, more in anticipation than in greeting, but Sedgwicke spoke first.

"He'll go! I persuaded him. It didn't take much, so he'll go and ask on your behalf."

Several huge hands descended on Sedgwicke's back and shoulders, such that he was grateful for Nellie ushering him to one of the few chairs that they had around the fire.

"Good man that y'are, Parson darlin', now sit you down and soon as sayin' we'll get you some tea and a dough cake."

Sedgwicke sat, plainly the hero of the hour and the sheer warmth and good will directed at him from the small camp around, lifted his spirits more than at any time that he could remember from his years in the army, especially when Bridie continued to refill his mug with the strong tea.

oOo

Julian Sanchez allowed the corn to run through his fingers into the French shako. It smelt mouldy and looked it, in fact it must be, the damp of the mould causing the grains to form clumps that remained within his fingers. The French foraging party must have found this in a poorly made clamp in the ground, yet they had brought it anyway, which proved how desperate they were for food. The remains of the foraging party were all knelt at the side of the road, the men silently awaiting their fate and hoping that it would be quick, whilst the Officer alone was shouting and holding up a despatch wallet, which he had taken from within his coat. Sanchez tipped the corn onto the ground, then pointed at the Officer.

"Llevarlo a mí."

The Officer was hauled to his feet and brought over to Sanchez, at whom he immediately began shouting, several times.

"Je suis un très important service de messagerie!"

He knew that his life was in the uttermost peril and his importance as a Courier was all that could keep him alive. His terror was not helped when Sanchez nodded to his men guarding the French captives and one walked along the row removing French shakoes, for the next to deliver a

681

massive blow on the back of the head of each with a hatchet.

"Je suis un très important service de messagerie."

Sanchez made another gesture to his nearest man and the Officer received a vicious punch onto his mouth. Sanchez now had the pouch and he withdrew a single document of one single page. A study of top and bottom revealed that the sender was Massena and the intended recipient was a General Eble. He scanned the body of the letter, but could gather only two words, 'Tagus' and 'Santarem'. He looked around for their French translator.

"Dónde está Michel".

The reply came back.

"Él está muerto."

Sanchez became deeply angry that a good friend and valued member of his band had been killed in the skirmish. He had wanted to ask the Frenchman why a Courier should be part of a foraging party, but that was now put aside. He punched the French Officer in the face, at which point the even more terrified man fell to his knees, to repeat his standard plea.

"Je suis un très important service de messagerie."

Sanchez returned the unintelligible letter into its case and turned to one of his Lieutenants.

"Haz esta carta y este desgraciado a Wellington. Esto es muy importante. Ir por el mar de Vimeiro."

The Lieutenant took the case and hauled the Frenchman to his feet. He hit him several times around his head as he was pulled to a horse, but the gesture to the Frenchman that he should mount instead of preparing himself to be killed did much to change his state of mind.

"Merci, M'sieu. Merci!"

Sanchez spat in the man's direction, but shouted at his escort.

"Ponerse en marcha. Con rapidez!"

The small party escorting the Officer hurried away, leaving only the question of what to do with the few sacks of mouldy grain, still on the mules. Sanchez pointed at it.

"Tomar esto para alimentar a los chanchos!"

His men grinned, at least their capture would be put to some use, feeding their pigs.

The following day, late afternoon, the consequences of the capture became to known to Lacey, when Spencer arrived, as usual with Erskine.

"Lacey. How soon could your men move, if needs be?"

Lacey's brows came together; he was puzzled.

"Two hours, Sir. A little more, if they need to be issued their own rations."

Spencer nodded.

"Good. That's reassuring."

He looked across at Sobral before continuing.

"The Peer's received a captured despatch, which came down by boat this morning. Sanchez' men intercepted it. Massena's trying to build a pontoon bridge over the Tagus at Santarem, about 40 miles up river. If he gets his men over, he'll be in an area untouched by any army and there they'll get supplies. Right now they're starving, of that we're certain."

He smacked his riding crop against his boot, but his face betrayed his anxiety.

"He may pull out, overnight, if he gets that pontoon built. The Peer may go straight at them, now, as they are. We'd go straight through those over there, but we've little idea what he's got further up country. They may be in better shape and able to fight a defensive battle against our advance. It's a nice decision and I'm glad that it's one that I do not have to take. It could be that remaining here and allowing the units opposite us to fall apart from starvation may be the better bet. Then advance forward."

Hunger to any degree was far from the mind of the Reverend Albright as they caught their first sight of the

Convent at Mafra. The journey had been most pleasant, along good roads and through well-kept villages where, in each, there were stalls to sell food and other luxuries to the billeted British and Portuguese. Albright had required Sedgwicke to stop in almost everyone and now the sun was descending to join the Western horizon. Sedgwicke hurried the two mules on and the Convent grew larger, but not in any detail, for there were none, save the Crucifix over the gnarled double door, both seemingly too small in proportion to both the length and height of the high white wall, it being all of weathered, but clean, plasterwork. Sedgwicke halted the wagon in a dip of the road, which now hid them from the walls.

"Best robe up, now Sir."

Albright nodded. The reason was obvious, because to appear as a Priest of any kind would guarantee entrance, at least. It took half an hour to don and arrange all the vestments, but eventually it was done and Albright decided to walk the short way as would Sedgwicke, leading the mules. They approached and Albright knocked on the small window set in the door at head height. It opened immediately and Albright spoke.

"Can we speak to your Mother Superior?"

A disembodied voice came back, in a tone that conveyed ill temper.

"¿Qué?"

Sedgwicke stepped forward, alongside the confused Albright.

¿Hablas inglés?

A reply came back.

"Espere un momento."

Nothing more, but at least the 'speaking window' remained open. After some minutes, conversation was resumed, and this time constructively.

"I speak English. What is it that you want?"

Albright stepped forward, now realising that some persuasion was required.

"I am a Vicar of the Anglican Church serving with the British Army. May I speak to your Mother Superior, please, on an important matter?"

The 'speaking window' closed, but the door soon opened, swinging easily back on colossal, yet noiseless, hinges. This revealed a deep arch, at the end of which was a sizeable courtyard, but stood immediately before them was a single Nun, wearing a pure white cloak over the black habit that extended over her head. She stood motionless, her hands buried within her clothing.

"My name is Sister Consuela. I am English. I joined the Carmelite Order long ago. You can make your request to me."

Albright advanced two paces forward, but something made him stop. Sister Consuela remained still as a statue.

"I do feel that this may be a matter best decided upon by your Mother Superior."

She remained unmoved.

"You may ask of me."

Albright advanced merely two more paces.

"We have a woman now with child, some way advanced, whom we feel will be in need of care during her confinement and whilst the child is small. Our understanding is that, for a contribution to your necessary expenses, you may take in such a woman and provide that form of care within the walls of your most devout institution."

The reply was instant.

"Is she married?"

Albright was stunned, both by the brevity and finality of the question, but Sedgwicke had very much anticipated this and was ready with an immediate answer.

"Yes! The girl is Irish Catholic, but the ceremony was not according to the Canons of your Catholic Church."

Sedgwicke smiled.

"More an army ceremony, which happens quite often and commonly in the circumstances of army life."

There was no reaction, at least none to the small humour, but the reply was equally brief and brooked no argument.

"If the girl is to be cared for within these walls, then the union from which this child has sprung must be blessed and sanctified by the Catholic Church. In a Catholic Church!"

Albright remained wholly nonplussed by the requirement and its implications, but Sedgwicke pressed on.

"This can be done. The husband and wife can appear, as you desire, and what you require will take place to your satisfaction, I am sure."

Such unequivocal answers to equally explicit requirements seemed to satisfy the Sister.

"Very well. And you say that you can make a financial offering to us to help with their provision?"

Albright had by now recovered. He was not now required to speak any untruth or even half-truth.

"Yes, Fifteen English pounds."

There came a curt nod of her head.

"Then let it be so."

Albright continued, now much recovered and buoyed up by her agreement.

"Is there somewhere that we can say a prayer together to thank our Dear Lord for leading you into such an act of charity?"

Her eyes warmed by the faintest amount.

"Yes, but I can allow you no further into our Convent. Please follow the wall around towards the town and you will find the entrance to the Chapel of Our Lady, which is available for the people of the town. I will meet you there."

There was no further movement from her and neither Albright nor Sedgwicke could think of anything further, apart from Albright waving his hand to his right as he faced her.

"That way?"

"Yes."

Both bowed awkwardly, then turned and left, for the full wooden door to be closed, with no other sound than the slight bump of the heavy wood closing together. Albright set off, with Sedgwicke quickly catching up, but the former was less than happy.

"That was an outright lie, Private, that you just spoke in there. She and the Father are not married. This you well know."

Sedgwicke was unrepentant. These were Catholics after all, always over fussy with everything that involved their inflexible Dogma.

"Well Sir, going by my experience in the Army, the word 'marriage' is as broad you want it to be. A man and a woman can stand together and each hold the end of a piece of rope for them to be 'married' in the eyes of their comrades and they are treated as so. And they act as so! It may not be a Church wedding, but it holds together as a union that I cannot see our Dear Saviour looking too unfavourably upon."

Albright turned to Sedgwicke, now somewhat incensed.

"But there is no husband! Is there?"

"No Sir. And for that I shall do penance. However, it is clear that without the ceremony she would be denied entrance."

Albright now raised his voice.

"And a husband!"

Sedgwicke was wholly dismissive.

"Oh I'm sure we can manage that, Sir. For such as Eirin Mulcahy."

"Wholly irregular, Private. We have been deceitful."

"Yes Sir, but me, not you. Be of clear conscience yourself."

They came to the corner of the Convent and turned to see the overhanging porch of the Church door and the profile of the Crucifix above it. Once beneath both, a small individual door was open in the main double doors and in they went, Albright first. Sedgwicke took a deep breath and stepped inside, but the powerful smell of incense still assaulted his nostrils. However, the impact of this was as nothing compared to the sight of the Altar, at which Sister Consuela was kneeling. The whole was an ornate confection of gold and silver all before a backdrop of heavy pure white cloth. It was as though the designer had been given the whole cargo of a treasure ship from the Americas and been determined to use every item; any that were unused on the Altar had been added to the central statue of the Virgin Mary holding the Baby Jesus, both radiant in silver, gold leaf, gold accoutrements and diamonds. Sedgwicke could approach no further, but all that was required was for Albright to continue and kneel beside the praying figure of Sister Consuela. Sedgwicke felt himself superfluous as the two knelt together and so he took himself outside to suck in lungfuls of the clean air and gratefully speak his own simple prayers. Eventually, Albright came out, alone.

"I have arranged the date for the day after tomorrow. At 12 o' clock. We must now return and see what can be arranged."

The journey back was faster than that of coming out, but Albright still took the opportunity to indulge in one or two delicacies from the stalls that continued to line the road in each village. When they finally returned to the camp of the 105th, day had almost become full night. Once their cart and mules were safely separated, one from the other, Albright came to Sedgwicke.

"I want no further part of this. I have thanked our Good Lord for the charitable deed of the Nuns, but my role halts here. This smacks of pure expediency. Nothing to do with the love of two good people, each for the other, to be blessed within our Mother Church. This now lies with you!"

Sedgwicke saluted.

"Yes Sir. I'll go now."

With that he turned and hurried to the camp of Deakin and Davey. When he arrived they had finished their evening meal and were sat talking or mending kit. However, with the arrival of Sedgwicke, everything stopped, but none asked the question. All awaited Sedgwicke's pronouncement.

"The Convent will take her, but they have made conditions."

No response, all remained silent to hear what came next and so he continued.

"She must be married, in their Church at 12 o' clock, the day after tomorrow. That done to their satisfaction, they will take her in."

Silence remained. Deakin looked at Davey, Bridie at Nellie, Eirin looked at everyone. Eventually it was Nellie who spoke.

"She needs a husband! Any man'll do, long as he stands beside her and says the right words. What difference will it make, with her spending a year, nearly, there in that Convent? What happens after that, well, the Good Lord only knows."

She was looking at her husband, Henry Nicholls, but he was as puzzled as anyone.

"Who've we got that's single?"

He looked first at their two newcomers, Tucker and Solomon.

"You two married?"

Both nodded vigorously. He then looked a little nearer.

"Zeke? Tom?"

It was Saunders who answered.

"We're both too old and he's too ugly."

Miles said nothing, plainly in agreement with at least one of the descriptions, but Saunders smiled gently at Eirin, now plainly fearful and worried.

"Why she's still but a slip of a girl. Eighteen?"

Eirin nodded, but then Saunders looked at the one figure who, so far, had said nothing.

"Byford! How old are you?"

Byford took a deep breath and spoke very softly.

"Twenty-two."

"Say again!"

This time louder.

"Twenty-two."

"Perfect!"

A look of utter horror came across Byford's face, this delivered in Saunders direction.

"I do think that we should ask Eirin about this."

However, Nellie answered quickly.

"Sure now, what for? All she needs is a man, there at the Altar, ready to say the right stuff!"

Bridie was in tears and went over to put her arms around her eldest daughter, but now it was Deakin who spoke.

"You're right, John, but will you do it?"

Byford took a deep breath.

"Yes, if it'll keep her safe. We all remember what happened to Mary, begging your pardon, Joe."

Joe Pike nodded acknowledgment as Byford turned to Eirin. He chose his words and phrased them together very carefully.

"Eirin. Would it be alright with you, if it is I who speaks the vows with you? In this Church."

Eirin looked at him and saw nothing but sympathy, even in the poor light of the fire. She nodded.

"Yes."

Deakin clapped his hands together and then rubbed his palms together.

"Right, that's that. Tomorrow, you're off to the Colonel. To get permission. First thing."

First thing, even before breakfast, found Byford standing at the attention outside the tent of Colonel Lacey, with RSM Gibney beside him. Both stood waiting, Gibney looking down at Byford, him looking straight ahead.

"So, tha' wants to marry Eirin Mulcahy?"

"Yes, Sergeant Major."

"Ah'm hearin' that she's with child."

"That's correct Sergeant Major."

"'Appens as tha's the Father?"

"No, Sergeant Major."

"But tha' still wants this?"

"Yes Sergeant Major. It happens all the time, in a Regiment such as ours. As I'm sure you're aware."

"True! Raht, in tha' goes."

Gibney held open the tent flap and Byford marched forward. Within two minutes he was out and he nodded in Gibney's direction as he walked away. Then Bert Bryce emerged.

"Sar' Major. The Colonel would like a moment of your time."

Gibney marched in and saluted.

"Sir."

Lacey looked up.

"What's all this about young Byford marrying Eirin Mulcahy? They've never been seen walking out together. Even!"

"No Sir, but she's expectin'. Sir."

"And Byford's doing the decent thing, even though he tells me he's not the Father. So, who is? Do we know? There's been no violence upon her, has there?"

"No Sir. Ah'd've heard."

"So who knows the full story? Colour Sergeant Deakin took on the family. Get him in here."

Within minutes Deakin was saluting in front of his Colonel simultaneously with Gibney. Alongside Lacey was

Major O'Hare who had meanwhile been summoned. Lacey sat forward, elbows on his desk, his chin in his hands.

"Now then, Colour Sergeant. We want to know the full story, as you see it. I'm sure we can help."

Deakin took a deep breath and within five minutes all the details had been spoken, from when Eirin helped at the school in the time before Busaco, then on to why Byford had just asked permission to be married. Lacey sat back, saddened and looked at O'Hare.

"Get Maltby in here."

He looked at the two Sergeants.

"Dismiss!"

They saluted, spun on their heels and left. Within minutes O'Hare had returned with Maltby. O'Hare resumed his seat, but Maltby was left standing. This time, Lacey leant back.

"Stuart. I've just had one of your Section, Private Byford, in here asking permission to marry Eirin Mulcahy so that a Convent will take her in and look after her for the birth of her child and the time after."

He paused.

"But I'm hearing that you are the Father!"

Maltby shifted awkwardly.

"I could be, Sir."

"Could be! And what do the men believe?"

"That I am, Sir."

"And you made an agreement with Colour Sergeant Deakin that you would give a month's pay to ease her passage into this Convent at Mafra?"

"Sir."

"Have you done that?"

"No Sir."

"And why not?"

Maltby took a deep breath.

"Because I do not feel it to be certain that I am the Father, Sir."

"Which means you think that Eirin Mulcahy could be of easy virtue?"

Maltby shifted awkwardly but said nothing. Lacey sat forward.

"Let me explain something to you, Lieutenant. The men believe you to be the Father and they know that you have made a commitment towards her care. If you break that and abandon this girl, things could go very hard with you, very hard indeed!"

"Yes Sir. Sergeant Deakin explained all that to me, Sir. In Sobral, some time back."

Lacey raised his voice.

"And he has the absolute right of it!"

He sat back.

"Do you have the ten pounds?"

"Not yet, Sir. Not until payday."

"You know that they need the money tomorrow?"

"No, Sir."

"But you did not find out?"

"No Sir."

Lacey turned to O'Hare, as he pulled out his own wallet.

"O'Hare!"

With a face of stone, O'Hare found his own wallet and pulled out a five-pound note, to then place it on top of that produced by Lacey, who pushed the notes forward, both issued by Drummonds Bank

"You take these, now, to the Purser and get them exchanged into Escudos. Come pay day we will expect back, what, O'Hare?"

"Ten guineas!"

Lacey paused.

"I'm of a mind to require you to take the money to Sergeant Deakin yourself, but I'll not embarrass you to that extent. Give it instead to RSM Gibney. Clear?"

Maltby picked up the money.

"Yes Sir. Very clear."

Lacey now stood up.

"And one further thing, Lieutenant. Our Followers are not there for your amusement. They are vital to what we do, in fact without them, we could well fall apart."

He turned to O'Hare.

"You'd agree."

"I would. I'd go further, if I could find the words!"

Maltby saluted and left. Within an hour, Gibney was at the fireside of Jed Deakin, with a purse full of Portuguese Escudos, which he handed to Deakin.

"From Maltby. Ten pounds worth."

Deakin took the money.

"Thanks Cyrus. You'll take some tea?"

"Ah will that!"

He sat on a box and took the tea. Eirin and Byford were sat together. He looked at them.

"Hast tha' a ring?"

The couple looked at each other, then back at Gibney for Byford to shake his head. Gibney reached into his pocket.

"Then take this. 'Tis an earring. Dohn't ask how ah come by it, but ah'm thinkin' that it should fit."

He handed it over to Byford.

"Don't try it yet, That'll be bad luck, tha' knows."

Bridie had listened to all and came over to kiss Gibney on the cheek, avoiding the swooping whiskers.

"No need for that, Missus! Just a drop more tea!"

His cup was refilled, twice over.

Before the next dawn, Byford was despatched to march over to the Convent with Zeke Saunders. Proprieties were to be observed, the Groom was not to see the Bride before the ceremony. Long before Albright was awake and could object, Sedgwicke arrived with the cart and in climbed Eirin, her Mother Bridie, her Aunt Nellie and Jed Deakin. He carried the purse now bulging with Escudos, he himself having sold the battlefield booty in the villages around. It was a sombre group that sat in the cart, but all managed a warm smile in Eirin's direction. Deakin patted her on the knee.

"It's worked out, Eirin. 'Tis all for the best. You and Byford may want to cleave together, when all is done. He's a good man, and educated! I've heard nothing bad said against him. Never. You could do a lot worse!"

The result was a single tear and so Deakin shut up.

The Convent Church was arrived at, Sedgwicke tethered the mules and the group entered to find Byford and Saunders waiting inside, stood before a solemn Priest, him with huge hands folded across his chest, this overhung by a hooked nose which held apart two deep set and very dark eyes. Two nuns stood by, one being Sister Consuela. Deakin led Eirin down the aisle to stand beside Byford and, whilst he took a long look at her, she but glanced up at him. With the raising of one of the hands to describe the sign of the Cross, the Ceremony began. Deakin and Saunders understood not one word, Byford a little more, because the Service was all in Latin. Sister Consuela provided the necessary prompts, for Deakin to himself 'the man who brings this woman here to be married' and Saunders to produce the ring, which fitted very well. Both Bridie and Nellie cried silently. With the final 'In nomine Patris, et Filii, et Spiritus Sancti, Amen,' the ceremony ended and the Priest disappeared out the front door. Deakin handed the money over to Sister Consuela, then the five congregation, himself, Saunders, Sedgwicke, Bridie and Nellie walked back to the main door as used by the Priest, leaving Byford and Eirin standing awkwardly at the Altar. Byford, however, smiled, which Eirin faintly responded to, then he took both her hands and they kissed briefly, for Sister Consuela to come forward and try to usher Eirin out through a side door, but Eirin ran to the four stood at the back and embraced her Mother, then Nellie and then Deakin. That done, she took herself to the side door where stood Sister Consuela and passed through, leaving the six, now including Byford, standing there alone. The whole affair had taken little more than fifteen minutes. Deakin waved them out, his voice resigned and sad.

"Away and back!"

oOo

"I can't see this doing anything to ease their state of mind!"

All three, Lacey, Erskine and Spencer were staring out into the darkness at the myriad French bivouac fires, whilst behind them, in full swing, were the celebrations for Guy Fawkes Night. Bonfires were burning merrily all along the British positions and Congreve rockets, condemned as useless by Wellington, were being put to a more celebratory purpose. As another rocket burst high above them, a servant arrived with three glasses of rum punch and each toasted the other in the light of the nearest bonfire. Erskine looked Heavenward, concerned for a falling rocket shaft, but none came.

"It won't be long now!"

His words required no further explanation. All three, in common with almost all other Senior Officers had spent the past days studying the French lines through their telescopes, mostly observing foraging parties leaving and returning, almost certainly they concluded, empty handed. However, the memories of the past days were soon dissipated by the goings on behind them, of much merriment, where fiddles, squeeze-boxes, fifes and penny-whistles were all blasting out popular tunes that the men and their Followers could dance, or at least, sing to. Wellington himself could be seen riding amongst his men, enjoying an evening away from the pressing concerns of when, or how, to attack Massena.

However, with the following day, all returned to their duties, either major for Wellington and his Staff, or minor for those manning The Lines. Telescopes were re-employed, especially at Sobral, where O'Hare and Lacey scanned the far distance, each requiring all that they could see to be logged by Colonel's Secretary, Sergeant Herbert Bryce. O'Hare touched Lacey on the shoulder.

"What's that? On the ridge to our slight right front? By the clump of trees in line with that far mountain."

Lacey adjusted his own instrument.

"Looks like cavalry. But rumour has it that Massena's sent all his cavalry and guns back up North. He can't feed the horses."

He studied the scene through his telescope further.

"I'll bet that to be Spanish irregulars. El Charro's brigands. If it is, they're now coming mighty close to the main French army. Their confidence must be growing."

He turned to Sergeant Bryce.

"Get that in the log and make sure that a copy gets to General Spencer."

He drew out his watch and consulted the time.

"When we're done here, that is."

O'Hare was still on the original subject.

"They can have every confidence, because if what you say about his cavalry and guns is true, then they are the only ones out there with horses fit for any purpose."

He paused.

"There's more! I swear I can see French running back, and ………………… Look, there's smoke coming from that nearby building. Farm or whatever. They've just driven back a foraging party and now they're burning the buildings that the French are using for shelter."

He now turned around.

"Got that Bryce?"

Bryce put down his army biscuit and picked up his pencil.

"Sir!"

Noon arrived on the 6th November to the sound of poles being hammered into the ground at the top of the slope beneath the Semaphore Station atop Mount Agraca, and to the British left of the remains of the barricade, this now held by Number Six Company. It was Maltby's Section

697

who were doing the hammering and relations between this particular Lieutenant and his men were now much more convivial, in this particular case between himself and Joe Pike.

"What are these for, Sir?"

"We're going to hang food on them, Pike. In full view of the French. To tempt a few more to desert."

"Yes Sir. Makes sense, Sir."

However, it made little sense to Tom Miles, overhearing all with Zeke Saunders, Miles holding the pole, Saunders smiting the top with a large mallet.

"Won't do nothin' bar give food for the birds. Hanging loaves of bread out in the middle of nowhere!"

Saunders gave a last mighty blow.

"Ah now, Thomas, that could be just where you are wrong. Clumps of birds are more obvious than a loaf and lots of birds means food. That's what the French will see."

Miles gave a dismissive guffaw.

"You think our Officers has got enough sense to work that out?"

Saunders looked directly at him

"If they have or not, that's what'll happen. They'm comin over in droves now, so, better as prisoners than some more that we has to fight our way through."

He picked up another pole and moved away about 12 feet.

"Here. Hold this."

Miles did as he was told and Saunders raised the mallet to strike yet more blows, the sound of which, unbeknown to anyone on the British side, reached the ears of French sentries in Sobral. Their curiosity held their attention to what was happening and so, when the food arrived at the top of the poles, and then some birds as Miles had predicted, their stomachs pained them even more.

The evening sentry watch was to be held by Maltby's Section taking the first two hours, but they were accompanied by Captain Drake and also a whole array of lanterns along the top of their position to guide in any French. Drake had taught his NCOs what he hoped was the correct French to challenge any French deserters and he now stood, content in his optimism, studying the buildings of Sobral as they disappeared into the growing dusk. He walked back behind the row of lanterns, now lit and throwing their yellow light onto the faces and uniforms of his men. There he sat and pondered, 'Do I eat my sausage, or drink some wine?'

It was not long after full dark when there came a hoarse shout from out of the darkness, subdued, but enough to be heard.

"M'sieu! M'sieu. Es-tu là?"

None of his men answered, as ordered. The deserters were to be tempted closer. The next words did indeed sound closer.

"Rosbifs! Rosbifs! Es-tu là?"

Miles rose up, incensed.

"Rosbifs! I'll give that bastard 'rosbif' with my bayonet through his backside!"

Davey turned to him.

"Shut up! We do this properly."

Davey stood up and spoke the first French of his life.

"Déposez vos armes et de se presenter."

The reply came out of the dark.

"Nous n'avons pas d'armes."

Davey spoke the second phrase he had been taught, having understood not one syllable of the reply.

"S'avancer lentement."

All Davey's comrades were stood at the ready, bayonets fixed, and almost immediately a large group of French soldiers walked slowly into the lamplight, as ordered. Drake came running over.

"Continuer à marcher!"

The French did as ordered and walked on, all the while menaced by British bayonets, but soon they were over the parapet and into the shallow trench. There waited more men of One Section, including Tucker and Solomon, all holding either a haversack of biscuits, or lumps of bread or dried fish. Seeing the sacks, plainly offering food, all the French rushed forward to plunge in their hands and extract whatever the haversack contained. Then they fell to their knees or sat, voraciously consuming whatever they had found. The sight was moving, even to the likes of Tom Miles and Zeke Saunders, both speaking simultaneously.

"Poor bastards!"

Even in the poor light of the lanterns, it could be seen that the French soldiers were utterly destitute, not just by the way that their wolfed down their food, but by their ragged uniforms and haggard faces. Some were even barefoot and several were obviously ill, coughing and choking between mouthfuls. Many of the watching British, veterans who could remember the privations of their own desperate retreats, offered their new prisoners a drink of rum or wine and the responsive thanks were profuse and continuous. The French could have sat there forever, or so it seemed, but they had to be marched back. Drake came into the trench and began gesturing with his sword, something that was quickly copied by his men, in their case gesturing with their bayonets and repeating his words.

"Venez. Rapide."

The French rose and all those who could reach, took another dip into the haversacks as they passed by. With all gone, the watch was resumed. One more group of deserters arrived before the watch was changed and One Section then filed back, subdued in some ways to see men, whom they did respect but would never admit to, in such appalling circumstances. However, in other ways they were buoyed up and the reason was obvious, these starving and diseased French would make little resistance in any coming conflict.

It would seem that much the same conclusion was arriving in the minds of Wellington and his Staff, conveyed as usual to Lacey by Erskine, some days later after the number of French deserters had topped two thousand, to that date, 13th November.

"They can't stay much longer, but Wellington's not going at them, he's going to let them pull out, as thcy choose, then push them back up and see where they make a stand. Then tackle them there."

Lacey nodded.

"The longer they stay, the fewer there'll be!"

"Exactly! Massena's army is falling apart by the day. You've seen the state of the deserters coming in. I'm amazed he's hanging on as he is. The man must be as stubborn as a mule!"

"And his men are paying the price."

"Yes, but it will lower the price we'll have to pay to kick them back into Spain."

Erskine paused to take a long look over at Sobral.

"There's one worry! This pontoon bridge. All the prisoners speak of it. If he gets it built and gets over the Tagus then it's a different kettle of fish altogether. The Peer's got Portuguese guarding every bridge over the Tagus up as far as Abrantes, 100 miles up. He'll not get over anywhere that will allow him to hang on to Portugal, unless that pontoon gets built. At Santarem, so we are informed."

Lacey said nothing, waiting for more. It soon came.

"He's sent over Fane, with 1500 Portuguese, some Cacadores Rifles and a few guns. And a Rocket Troop. Apparently Sanchez is over there to give some help, although what they'll do from the wrong side of the river is anyone's guess."

Exactly that question was being pondered at that moment by the same General Fane and Julian Sanchez, both well mounted and sitting their horses within a clump of trees that hid them both from Santarem opposite, but did provide a good view. From across the river, the sound of hammering reached their ears, telling of urgent activity. Both men were using good telescopes, but it was Fane who was speaking, entirely to his own Staff, most of whom were

701

English, the rest Portuguese. Fane was pointing, using his telescope for added emphasis.

"There, alongside that large grey building, there's some kind of dockyard."

His Staff all raised their own telescopes, whilst Fane continued to speak.

"I believe I can see boats, or at least pontoons. What say you?"

All the telescopes began to bob up and down with the nodding of heads in agreement before they were lowered. His Senior Colonel then spoke.

"Yes, Sir Henry. That's how it appears to me."

General Fane folded his arms over his broad chest, while his pleasant face became troubled. He looked at Sanchez, and then spoke, through an interpreter.

"What to do? Any suggestions?"

Sanchez had seen all he needed to and his answer came, in full detail from the interpreter.

"Use your guns and rockets from here. Fire until you have nothing left. Do what damage you can."

Fane nodded. There was little that could be disagreed with, but the interpreter was speaking further, in response to more from Sanchez.

"El Charro says that just being here will be enough. Even if they build what is needed, they know they cannot set the bridge over the river with us here. If they do that, we will throw them back as they come over. It will be over a narrow bridge, impossible against an enemy already waiting. We have only to show them that we are here."

Fane nodded again.

"Can anything be done from the French side? Do you have contacts over there? The more we worry them, from whichever direction, the more likely they are to give up the idea."

For some minutes Sanchez studied the far bank with his telescope, then he lowered it and spoke. The interpreter passed it on.

"My men have some French grenades. I will send some over and, if they can throw them from the downstream side, then they will."

Sanchez spoke further.

"But it will add little to what we are trying to do, to show the French that they cannot cross on their little bridge of boats. Better to parade your men, and mine, to make them think that there is a large force over here."

Fane looked across at Santarem and then turned to the interpreter.

"Tell Senor Sanchez that I agree. There can be no point in risking his men to no real gain. Keep them all on this side. My men are not yet all here, but they will be tomorrow."

All withdrew from the copse to make camp, whilst Fane's command arrived throughout the day. However, during the night, Sanchez' men built good fires and danced and sang around them well into the small hours, which convinced all under Fane's command that the French could not fail to realise that an enemy force was now opposite them, on the far bank. However, lanterns could still be seen illuminating the French dockyard.

Fane waited until full daylight to make his target as clear as possible in the November gloom, when he gave his orders.

"Parade the men in a single line, then we'll appear as a larger force. Tell Captains Pearce and Morgan that they can open fire at their leisure."

The Staff Officer rode off and Fane continued to study the far French bank. It seemed to him that the more of his men who came into view, the more French appeared on the far bank to study them. Then the first British gun crashed out, to be followed by the first rocket. The ball passed over and the rocket hit the large grey building to the right of the target. If the aim was adjusted it was difficult to tell, for approximately one in five rockets hit the dockyard and about four out of five for the cannonballs. The most effective was the single howitzer which sent spluttering shells through a very high arc to land accurately amongst the boats and pontoons This started some fires, but they were quickly put out and all the while the Portuguese Regiments and Cacadores cheered wildly, whilst El Charro's men sat their horses silently, looking stoically on.

At Noon all ammunition had been used up and the men were allowed to stand down by Companies and cook their meal. Through telescopes the French were observed to be scurrying about throughout the afternoon, but then night fell. With the dawn, Fane and Sanchez sat in the same small copse, when a Staff Officer approached.

"Parade the men, Sir?"

"No."

He looked at his Officer.

"Tell me, Vickery, what can you hear?"

Vickery lifted his head.

"Why nothing, Sir."

"Exactly, Vickery. No more hammering. The French have stopped."

Both men grinned at each other, but Sanchez merely looked at both.

"Muchas gracias, General Fane. Dios está con nosotros."

With that, he swung his horse's head over and was gone, his men following him in neat sections of four.

Fane watched him go and then turned to Vickery.

"I think a few earthworks about here would not come amiss, Vickery. Our palisades from these trees. The more obvious the better. I feel we could be here for some time, at least the foreseeable future".

On the evening of the same day, Carr, O'Hare and Lacey were summoned to General Erskine's Headquarters, a nearby farmhouse, but inside they found not just Erskine, but Spencer and Wellington himself. Their Commander looked thin and care-worn but he spoke with a smile on his face, addressing the three together.

"I'm fearful that the French are pulling out, now, as we speak, in fact I'm convinced of it, but I want us after them, right on their heels. I need to know if they are still holding on, pulling out, or even gone."

He looked directly at Lacey.

"Sobral is a key position, Lacey. At your first suspicion that it's deserted you get some of your men over there to take a look."

The order was brief and brutal and Lacey knew the risk, especially as his was a Line Battalion, not raised for a purpose such as this.

"Beg pardon, Sir, but would this not be a job better undertaken by some Rifles, or even Cacadores?"

"It would, Lacey, but they may well be out doing just the same before their own positions. Crauford's especially. So, Lacey, it's yours and I'm leaving the timing up to you."

The statement brooked no further argument and so the three saluted and left. As they walked back, Lacey turned to Carr.

"A job for you, I'm afraid Henry. You're ex-Light Company, making you best suited. You'd best choose your men and get them ready."

Once at their lines Carr wasted no time but took himself immediately to One Section, where he found those he most sought and he waved them back down onto their chairs and boxes when they immediately stood as he entered their camp.

"A reconnaissance party is going to be needed during a morning, very soon, to go over to Sobral and take a look. We need to know if the French are still there or gone, or whatever. I need six men, ready each morning starting tomorrow, so that's you Davey, Miles, Pike, Saunders, Byford."

Then he pointed at random because he knew no other names. The finger chose Solomon.

"You! We start tomorrow, making ourselves ready. Dawn's at seven, so meet me at 6.30, at the barrier."

He turned to go, but Miles had now stood up, very, very concerned.

"Beg pardon, Sir, but we're Redcoats, and that'll mean we stands out, full and clear, as we walks across."

Carr now faced Miles, standing with his right thumb in his waist band, his left on his sword hilt.

"Yes Miles, that is what we are being ordered to do! Ordered!"

Miles was incensed by the whole idea and his comrades were very fearful for him, but he pressed on.

"Sir! If the Frogs is on the alert, then we'll all be knocked over, Sir. The whole lot of us!"

However, before Miles could receive the inevitable rebuke, Davey now stood, which perhaps saved Miles a punishment.

"Sir, if I may suggest, Sir, that we all wears our greatcoats. In the half dark of first light, grey is as good as Rifles' green. Sir."

Carr grinned and nodded.

"There you are, Miles. Now you can be sure that all will be well."

Meanwhile Sergeant Ellis had newly arrived and to him Carr spoke his last words.

"You come, too, Sergeant. In case I get knocked over, as Miles here puts it. These will explain."

Carr departed and then Ellis looked at Davey

"What's this?"

However, it was Miles who answered his question.

"Carr wants a forlorn hope to wander over to Sobral as and when he fancies, and ask the Johnnies if they'n about to take their leave. And our ex-poacher here, has just made it all alright by sayin' that we only has to wear our nice grey greatcoats for to make ourselves invisible!"

Ellis sat down, somewhat in shock. He had wandered in hoping for a cup of tea and now he was part of a mission to creep up to the French lines. The tea arrived, but he did not notice, even when it was put into his hand.

There was an equal amount of concern in the tent of Colonel Lacey, sat with Major O'Hare.

"I don't like this, Padraigh. Not one bit. The Peer'll be content to sacrifice some men, if it proves that the French are still holding their positions. As will become obvious when they open fire on those whom we've sent over to spark them up!"

O'Hare poured two glasses of whiskey.

"Yes! So, if the French are there and do open fire, then we must be in support to make them put their heads back down. Carr must have the Light Company up behind him, and the whole Battalion within range. A few volleys across will give Carr a better chance to fall back, but it will need the French to open fire too soon, if they're to get a chance to run!"

Lacey took a swallow and then sighed. He fully realised the possibilities.

"Yes. But nevertheless, I'll get Erskine to stand to the gunners in our nearest redoubts. Some grapeshot flying across will do no harm at all."

The following morning was nothing like a dawn; a thick fog had arisen during the night. As Carr left his tent, he found Lacey waiting.

"With this fog, Henry, you have to go over. Now."

"Yes Sir. I expected it. My men should now be waiting at the barrier."

"Advance with caution. The rest of the Light Company are in immediate support and the rest of the Battalion behind them, on our slope."

"Thank you, Sir, but best I get on. I said 6.30 and I should not be late."

Lacey nodded.

"Good luck, Henry!"

"Thank you, Sir."

He hurried on, but was still the last to arrive at the barrier to find the seven stood waiting, stood at 'order arms' as Ellis had commanded and it was Ellis who saluted, but said nothing. Any kind of 'good morning' seemed wholly inappropriate, but it was Carr who spoke.

"Seems you've got your wish, Davey. A decent fog!"

"Yes Sir. Someone must be in favour, Sir."

Carr nodded, but he did not hear Miles mumble to Saunders

"But it ain't us!"

"Right. Over we go."

'Over' meant to climb the stonewall to the left of the barrier and then spread out onto the lower reaches of the slope below the Semaphore Station. Now opposite Sobral and in the ravine, they descended slightly further before tackling the upward slope. Behind and to their left, they could see their own Light Company formed up, but the fog hid the whole Battalion further behind. Carr spoke to them all.

"Right. Spread out, but still keep in sight. Ellis, alongside me. Load now."

They did as ordered, loading their weapons before taking position, but before parting company with Davey, Miles spoke his own fears.

"This bloody fog means they'll only see us when we'n closer to their own lines. At least if we're seen 100 yards away, we've half a chance of buggerin' off!"

Davey wiped his hand across his face.

"If you hears a shot, we just turns and runs anyway. For what comes after, what's that, at least we'll still be alive."

By now Miles had moved on, but each then spoke to the other.

"Well, good luck."

Now in position, they climbed the slope. For a minute nothing could be seen of Sobral through the fog, but then the blank sides of the houses came through the mist. Davey instinctively dropped to one knee and listened. The silence was absolute; all he could hear was his own breathing. He looked over to his left to see Miles in the same pose, but to his right, Ellis was moving forward. He rose and did the same, and the details of the buildings became clearer; door latches, rusting hinges and windows turned into firing slits. He chose the nearest gap between the immediate buildings; it was a narrow alley and he went to the entrance, to stop again. Again silence. He crept forward, then he heard a shout, the unmistakable voice of Miles.

"Bastard!"

However, there was no shot and there came no other sound, then he heard footfalls, which he decided must be Miles, running in his direction along the outside of the houses. He returned to the entrance of the alley, just as Miles passed.

"Dummies! The Frogs've rigged up dummy sentries."

The last words were almost inaudible as he ran to where Carr had last been seen.

"The Frogs've all buggered off!"

Miles found Carr at a house door, within another alley. Carr was deciding whether to enter the building, when Miles arrived.

"Sir. I'm sure they've gone, Sir. We can see dummy sentries all along the wall of some kind of square, just up over."

Carr gave a heavy sigh of relief.

"Right. Thank you, Miles. Now run back. Find Captain Drake and tell him to bring the Company forward. Then go back and tell the Colonel."

Miles, without thinking came to 'order arms', saluted and then ran off. The first soldier that he came to in the ravine was Lieutenant Shakeshaft, advancing slowly, sword in hand.

"Sir! They've gone, Sir, an' Major Carr wants the Company brought up, Sir, to join him."

"Sobral's empty?"

"Yes Sir, an' I'm to go on to the Colonel, Sir. If you could tell Captain Drake that, Sir, what Major Carr wants."

Shakeshaft nodded.

"Yes. Very good. Get on your way."

Meanwhile, Carr, now with Ellis in close attendance, was easing his way into Sobral, building by building, but the further they went, the greater the evidence that the French had, indeed, gone. However, Ellis was doubly uneasy.

"They've either gone, or are tempting us further in."

The 'Sir' was not added as he cast his eyes everywhere, whilst Carr fixed his on what was ahead, each sign of desolation being revealed slowly in the mist that hung between the buildings. However, the further forward they crept, the clearer it was that Sobral had been abandoned. The village was an utter ruin, the streets littered with rubbish and wreckage, not one piece of wood remaining to form a door or window frame, both gaped wide as though in horror at their naked stonework. Most telling was the fact that the streets had been taken over by animals, abandoned cats and dogs roamed the streets and ragged black crows landed and then flew off, disappointed to find that what looked like food was merely a piece of rubbish.

Carr straightened, then did Ellis, as both became less tense. They did not even look around as footfalls sounded behind them and Shakeshaft brought his men up, but Carr remained cautious.

"Hold yours here, Richard. Myself and the Sergeant will go on alone and take a better look."

He moved forward.

"Take up holding positions. Watch for our return."

Carr and Ellis continued on, careful to remain quiet as they picked their way through the debris. Ellis was coming to his own conclusions.

"Looks like Johnny picked this place clean, Sir, takin' anything that would make a fire, even."

Carr did not answer, he was looking for the building that had been their Officers' billet when they had first arrived at The Lines, this being on the very edge of the French side of Sobral, where they had mounted a rearguard when they first occupied the village. Then he saw the building, in a very much sorrier state than when they had left it. They crossed the wide street, each looking sideways more than forwards and they entered the doorless opening. There were no stairs anymore and so Ellis had to heave Carr up to the higher level. He went cautiously to a window and peered out. The fog lay even thicker on the open fields, so he could see nothing. Carr sighed and descended using the exterior ancient stone steps that led down from the upper floor. He then returned to what had been the main door.

"Sergeant!"

Ellis came quickly out.

"Sir?"

"We have to go forward. Somewhat further. We have to see if the French remain in any way close."

Ellis looked at him, his expression somewhere between shock and amazement.

"Further, Sir?"

"Yes. Half a mile. Are you able to judge that, walking through fog such as this?"

Ellis nodded, his face remaining very anxious. Here was another almost suicidal order from this same over zealous Officer. He was not going to hold his peace while being asked to walk blithely into such danger.

"Yes Sir, I can. But if there are French roamin' about in this fog and they comes onto us. What then?"

Carr acknowledged the sense of Ellis' concern.

"Wearing our greatcoats we look much the same as any Frenchman. We only have to leave our shakoes behind, they are much too different."

Ellis took off his shako and placed it on the wall. Then he took off his pack, opened it and fished inside, to take out a soft forage cap, definitely not British issue.

"That's French, Sergeant."

"Yes Sir. Theirs is better than ours."

"Like most other things!"

"Yes Sir."

"Do you have one for me?"

"No Sir. 'Fraid not, Sir."

Carr conceded and placed his shako alongside that of Ellis.

"Right. Half a mile. That will be enough."

He started forward and Ellis joined him, the pair walking side by side.

"We has to be careful, Sir. Fog can deaden sound, so we may come up onto them at short distance."

Carr nodded.

"Understood Sergeant. Proceed with caution."

After three minutes Ellis decided that caution was in short supply. The pace was too quick for his liking and the swish of their boots through the uncropped grass did nothing to ease his mind. However, they progressed on, seeing nothing and hearing nothing, but both stared forward until their eyes ached. On and on, until Ellis held up his arm, perhaps because his hearing was that much better, but both stopped. Then Carr heard what Ellis had, hooves somewhere in the murk, but Carr urged him forward.

"Keep walking, we'll look less suspicious, as though going about our business."

At this point Ellis subconscious asserted itself.

"I'd say that was about half a mile, Sir."

The hoof beats grew louder, then a vague shape resembling a horse and rider loomed up in the fog, but it passed on. Both men let out a long, deep breath as the silence returned. They moved on but a few more yards, and then they encountered a squatting figure, just on the edge of the fog. It was too obvious what he was doing and so they hurried away, but Ellis muttered.

"Oh My Lord! We'n in their latrine!"

Then again he held up his hand.

"Up ahead, Sir. That's fires, bivouac fires. The French is cooking."

Carr peered forward and could just make out the glow himself, then he heard the sound of men talking, just about discernible as French.

"That'll do! Well done Sergeant. Time to return."

Ellis needed no further encouragement, but turned back as his Major did. They hurried back, at a far quicker pace than their cautious progress outward. The relief of both was palpable and genuine, as they at last saw the buildings of Sobral. Luckily they turned in the right direction to bring them back to their shakoes, which they picked up without stopping as they both hurried back to the British side of the village, where Shakeshaft had positioned his men. Shakeshaft was stood out in the road.

"Sir. You've been some time, Sir. You had us worried."

"We went further to take a look, which was valuable. Pull your men back, Richard. Johnny's only half a mile beyond. It's not for us to hold this with a single Company. If Erskine wants it, he'll put in what's needed, a whole Brigade."

They all walked back through the now thinning fog and soon the whole Battalion was back at their messfires, enjoying a good breakfast, all save Lacey, O'Hare and Erskine, all looking sombrely at Sobral whilst the semaphore arms above them whirled their discovery around The Lines. O'Hare and Lacey stood silent awaiting Erskine's verdict on what next to do. It was not long in coming.

"I'll not move forward! Not from here, with the Frogs still in view. Not without orders. That's The Peer's decision now."

At 11.00 The Peer did arrive, to find the three still in place.

"So they've gone. The Sixth Division saw no sentries and the Light Division found a lot of dummies opposite them. They discovered that at about 10.00 when the fog cleared. How's it here?"

It was Spencer who answered.

"Yes Sir. We found out just the same a while before, not that it makes much difference."

He took a deep breath.

"However, one of my Majors went further forward and says he found them about half a mile beyond the village, Sir. They were cooking, Sir."

Wellington sat upright in his saddle.

"Were they moving, or what? Leaving some behind as a rearguard?"

"Impossible to say, Sir. The fog was still too thick, but he's convinced the French were still at camp. Cooking, as I said."

Wellington sat back.

"What Major was that?"

"Carr, Sir."

Wellington lifted his head, and nodded.

"Ah! Right."

He looked across at Sobral.

"Erskine, get some cavalry in there. I want to know if they're still where Carr saw them. When this fog finally does clear."

Half an hour later Carr was at the barrier with Number Four Company, quietly studying the heartbreaking sight that was Sobral. He heard a soldier come up behind him.

"Sir. There's some cavalry coming down."

Carr levered himself off the wall and turned to see a Troop of Light Dragoons on the road descending from the ridge. The fog had now gone, but after a minute his spirits sank and he spoke softly to himself.

"Tavender! It had to be."

The Troop of 16th Light Dragoons trotted up and halted before Carr, where Tavender had reined his own horse to a halt.

"Lucius. Good afternoon. I'll guide you in. Take you to the best place, where you can watch, unobserved."

Tavender's face remained cold and expressionless.

"No need. We can find our own way."

Carr bridled immediately.

"I have my orders, Captain, to guide you through. I cannot be certain you'd get to the best place and we don't want any of yours springing out in front of the French like some kind of a jack-in-the-box, now do we?"

"I'm told the French have gone!"

"Perhaps yes, but perhaps no. Therefore, I will lead you forward. Captain!"

The mention of rank spoke volumes and Carr walked forward through the remains of the barrier, followed by Tavender, who remained just behind, too far for any conversation. Within ten minutes they were at the far end of the main street, looking at the wreck of their Officer's erstwhile billet. Carr was brooking no argument.

"Keep your horses back here. That building gives you the best view, those stones steps are your only way up. Let's go there now, me and you. Now that I'm here, I may as well get another look, for my return."

Tavender turned to Sergeant Baxter.

"Sergeant, we dismount here. Get the horses tethered and the men into some kind of shelter. They can light a fire and cook."

Carr turned slightly.

"They won't find a single stick left in the place that'll give any kind of fire, but good luck anyway."

He looked up at Tavender, still mounted.

"Now. Shall we?"

Tavender dismounted, gave his reins to Baxter and then followed Carr over the wide street. Carr held up his arm for Tavender to stop as Carr peered around the stones steps. He then placed his foot on the first and began to ascend.

"All's well."

He mounted the steps and Tavender followed, whilst looking across to the distant fields. Once at the window both used their telescopes, but Carr gave the verdict.

"Still there, as per this morning, but I'd say fewer. It seems that they are on the move and this is the last of them. If they continue to take their leave of us, then Erskine wants to know, so send back a messenger, in fact send one every half hour. This is critical."

He paused.

"You are clear?"

Tavender nodded, but then Carr stood facing him, for some long moments, looking directly into his eyes. It was time for some plain speaking,

"I'm told that you arrived uninvited at my wedding! Never had you down as that much of a bad loser. You could have wrecked Jane's day entirely. If you'd all got into the Church!"

Tavender gave no answer. He knew that this was ground for an argument on which he was certain to lose. Carr waited, whilst Tavender stared back, but, when nothing came, he moved on.

"It would seem, Lucius, that there exists some kind of issue between us. If there is, then it needs to be resolved. One way or the other."

Tavender met his gaze.

"You mean a duel?"

"It may come to that, but it would ruin us both for the Army. You know Wellington's orders about duelling."

"If not that, then what? Some kind of brawl?"

"I'll meet you in the ring, if needs be."

"It should be an honourable and properly conducted duel, Carr, but judging by what I hear from Templemere, any kind of contest with you, ends up as a brawl fit only for the gutter."

Carr was not drawn, but his temper did surface.

"Templemere found out, as you will, if you choose, that when I'm in a fight, I fight! I'm an Infantry Officer, Tavender, and that's how it has to be when you're stood toe to toe and you want to stay alive! So, he has no cause for complaint, he knew who he was taking on."

He paused.

"So, if you consider that there is something between us that needs to be settled, let me know. Spain's a big place, we can find somewhere, but we'd need to be alone. No Seconds, none of the ritual. Just a fight! Me and thee! Right up close!"

He paused, but then spoke in a quieter tone.

"On the other hand, you may see fit to consign all to the past, and keep it there, whatever it is that's stuck in your throat. That'll suit me just as well, I'm a married man now and I want to get home and spend a life with my family."

He turned for the door, but half turned as he walked on.

"I've no problem with you as a more than halfway decent Officer."

With that he left and hurried back through the streets now crowded with 16th Troopers. Somehow he felt very much at peace.

oOo

Carr was dozing contentedly in Jane's arms, when the arms suddenly became very masculine and violent and he awoke to find Captain Lord Carravoy bending over him, shaking him awake.

"Henry, we're moving forward."

717

"Charles! Thought I'd gone to Heaven, then I woke up sure I'd died, to find myself in the Other Place!"

Carravoy ignored the sarcasm.

"The Peer's sending the whole of Spencer's forward, around Sobral."

Carr sat up and reached for his sword.

"And the French beyond Sobral?"

"Gone. A message has come back from Tavender."

"Tavender! Then it must be true!"

Carravoy ignored that sarcasm as well.

"Spencer is sending the whole of Erskine's down the road."

Carr stood to buckle on his sword.

"Who told you this?"

"Major O'Hare, who sent me to wake you."

"Right, so Wellington's finally decided to push onto the French, even though they began their retreat yesterday! We've been on a one hour alert for God knows how many days and so now we're finally going to use it."

"So it would seem."

Carr nodded, but did not leave the billet just yet. Instead he took the time to face him.

"Charles! I've never properly thanked you for telling it straight at that enquiry. You played a straight bat and I'm grateful."

Carr held out his hand and Carravoy took it, but only briefly. Although his face was blank, he did nod an acknowledgment. Carr said no more and hurried out to see the whole of the 105th assembled on the road and what he took to be the whole of the 16th Light Dragoons ahead on the same road but disappearing over the ridge to Sobral. Luckily he soon saw O'Hare.

"I'm told we're moving up. At last."

O'Hare nodded.

"Don't be critical Henry. When you move an army, you need to know where. He's only just found out, according to Erskine, which road Massena's on. He's up for Santarem."

"And we're going through Sobral?"

"Yes. Our column straight through, the 50th across the fields to our right, the 92nd to our left."

"The Rifles?"

"Already through and beyond Sobral. As a screen."

"Where do you want me?"

"Up ahead, with the Grenadiers."

Carr immediately thought, 'I haven't seen Carravoy in months, now twice in one day', but this he did not utter, instead he was more concerned with his creature comforts.

"Right, I'll get my pack and greatcoat."

He ran back into the billet to see Morrison packing up.

"You've heard we're moving?"

"Yes Sir."

"Before I did, it would seem."

"You were fast asleep, Sir. Talking about someone called Jane."

Carr could not prevent himself from grinning.

"My wife, Morrison. But enough of that, where's my pack and greatcoat?"

"On the back of the door you just came through, Sir."

Carr peered behind him to see both.

"Right, yes, well done Morrison. Carry on."

"Yes Sir."

Carr had to run to the head of the 105th's column, which was already moving, and there he found Carravoy and D'Villiers. Whilst buttoning his greatcoat, he turned in greeting.

"Gentlemen. Some events, at last."

"Sir."

The greeting came from D'Villiers, but Carravoy said and did nothing. They marched on in silence; Carr speculating on the days ahead, Carravoy and D'Villiers in shock and wonderment at the state of Sobral, even though, as though from the sky above, some of the citizens had returned and had begun the process of clearing up, even repair. It did both Grenadier Officers good to pass the sorry final house and begin the straight road that led Northeast, enabling them to see their brother Battalions on either side, the 50th and the 92nd. Carr was, as usual, thinking military, concluding that there must be good going over the bare fields, because both were keeping pace with the 105th on the easy road. Half a mile on, which confirmed Carr's reconnaissance, they began to find the detritus of the French retreat, mostly plundered but abandoned items that were either too big or too heavy to carry. It was at the very first hamlet that they came to, Valverde, that it began, the horrors of following a retreating French army. Here, and also on the road after, the 105th encountered dead French soldiers, stragglers picked off and murdered, each with a deep axe wound in their head. When they came up to the next village, Carnota, there were some lucky French still alive, these lucky enough to have been overtaken and captured by the single Company of the 60th Rifles. They had been guarded by them until the main column came up and then the Riflemen hurried away to catch up with their comrades now far ahead.

However, in Carnota it was worse, for here the French had found civilians who had made the appalling mistake of returning to their homes, thinking the French were now very much elsewhere. All were dead and many showed the unmistakable signs of torture, obviously inflicted to reveal the whereabouts of food. Here a rest was granted, but many buildings could not be used for any form of shelter for they contained the noisome remains of whole families, their bodies revealing the obvious way that they had been killed, either by a bayonet thrust or their skulls smashed with a heavy musket butt. Whilst the few French prisoners, all near to death, pleaded for food, not one scrap

720

was given. Erskine came to Lacey, as it was his Division that was now all around the village.

"What to do?"

The subject was obvious. Lacey replied, his face grim and ashen.

"Mass grave and mark it to give any left from this tragic place somewhere to mourn? Or put them all in one house and burn it down."

"That's quickest. We are in pursuit, after all."

He paused.

"There'll be more, Lacey. You know that."

"Sir. I heard of the same from Major Carr, when we were in Sicily. He was still a Captain then."

"Can I leave it with you?"

Lacey nodded.

"You can, I'll get Carr onto it."

Carr was as livid as anyone at what they had found and simply gave Carravoy the direct order, so that when they marched out of the village, it was through the acrid smoke of a fierce house fire on the furthest edge. Now on the road, no-one felt any sympathy for the murdered French frequently found at the roadside, each with the telltale axe wound in the back of their head. Many took the trouble to spit in their direction.

Sedgwicke and Albright rode their cart, placed between the rear of the 105th column and the Followers, Albright staring at the boards between his feet, mumbling unintelligibly. Sedgwicke looked at him with some concern, the cause of his depression was obvious, but all he could do was explain what they had seen, in the forlorn hope that it would help.

"We're following a defeated and starving army, Sir. 'Twas ever thus."

Albright barely lifted his head.

"But it's utterly medieval, Private. These are men from our own European civilisation, this is something from another age, from another ……. another……….. way of doing things! These are all God's Creatures, made in God's Own Image."

"You are right, Sir, but as I say, we are following starving and desperate men. The French live off the land, Sir, they don't get supplied as we do. If civilians cannot provide them with the sustenance they need, then, well, they take revenge. Even if they gave, the French still think they're holding back."

Sedgwicke hoped that his explanation would help, but he knew that it was unlikely, especially as he also knew that, inevitably, more was to come, possibly worse. The road they were taking had obviously been used by the French, for it was strewn, not only with abandoned plunder and equipment, but also with the bodies of mules and horses, dead from want of forage. French dead also added to the charnel house they passed through, all with their heads misshapen, speaking the story that they were stragglers who had finally lain down to die, but had been despatched by the local peasants using a large rock. Flocks of crows helped themselves to the dead flesh, both human and animal. Every house and hamlet was destroyed to the point of obliteration, each no more than a collection of wreckage along the way.

It was no better in the next large village, Alenquer, set deep within its river valley. The 16th Light Dragoons, in the lead, had passed straight through, as had The Rifles, leaving Erskine's Brigade to arrive in the near dark, which was beneficial considering the sights that awaited them there. All around were the dead of two nations; French murdered swiftly, some beaten to death, and with them many murdered Portuguese, most thrown into the deep river bed. Amazingly, in some alleyways were some French soldiers, more dead than alive, which had probably saved them, being too starving and ill to move, they more resembled corpses. These were thrown unceremoniously onto mules, which ended the life of several, but those who survived were laid out before the Town Hall, where Medical Orderlies did just enough to keep them alive, making the attempt if they had a reasonable chance of surviving. The dead civilians were gathered, including those in the river and brought also to the Town Square to be laid out alongside the dying or recovering French. Sedgwicke could not keep Albright away from the harrowing sights, and so, after their evening meal, the Battalion Chaplain toured the rows of dead, his arm raised and outstretched to throw forward the weak and yellow light of the lantern he carried. As he moved he recited in mixed up fashion whichever lines of whichever prayers came to mind. He returned to their cart and immediately found their bottle of rum, intended for warming purposes, but he used it to drink himself into a stupor. With the morning he remained in a catatonic state, unable to rise or walk. Now very anxious, Sedgwicke hurried into the main camp to encounter Major O'Hare.

"Sir, I need your help, please. It's Chaplain Albright, I fear that he has suffered some kind of breakdown, Sir. Caused by the dreadful things that we have seen on our way here."

O'Hare frowned.

"What sort of state is he in now, Sedgwicke? Is he still alive?"

Sedgwicke nodded.

"He is, Sir, yes, but he drank a whole bottle of rum last night, but he's more than ill from just that, Sir."

"You say! Well, we're moving out in half an hour, so get him into that cart of yours, get him fed if you can and then hope for the best. What else?"

O'Hare moved on, he had more urgent business, leaving Sedgwicke, in truth, still stood unknowing as to what to do. However, luck was with him when he saw Colour Sergeant Deakin in the distance and so Sedgwicke ran over, but, with him now so breathless, Deakin spoke first.

"Hello Old Parson, what's bidding you into a run?"

Sedgwicke took a deep breath.

"It's Chaplain Albright. He's suffered a kind of mental collapse. Almost certainly from what we saw here yesterday."

Deakin frowned.

"And what we're likely to see today! Where is he?"

"By our cart."

"Mental collapse you say. Right. There's nothing for it, but to get him into his cart and get him on the road, with the rest of us. Then pray that the Good Lord will come to his aid."

He looked around to see the strongest, Saunders and Solomon.

"Zeke. Nat. Go with Parson here. The Chaplain's in a bad way and needs loadin' into his cart. Be sharp, we'll be marchin' in a few minutes. Best take George there, too."

Sedgwicke was immediately off, followed by the three. They found Albright slumped against a wheel, making inroads into another bottle. Without ceremony, Sedgwicke pulled it out of his hand, just as the three pulled him upright, if not to his feet. Then, with Solomon in the cart to take his arms, he was hauled in, then his legs were bent up and the tailgate closed. Saunders took the bottle from Sedgwicke, took a long pull and then passed it to Solomon, who did the same and then passed it to George Tucker, who imitated the other two before returning it. As they turned to leave, it was Saunders who spoke his thanks, of sorts.

"Handy job that, Parson. If you've got any more like that, come to us first."

With that, Sedgwicke quickly threw into the cart their few camp possessions and harnessed the mules. From the cart there came not a sound, not even as he whipped on the mules to join the end of the 105th column. The square was a sorry sight, the only cause for optimism being the few Portuguese who had come down from the hills, these now preparing the dead for burial. Of the French wounded there was nothing to be seen. Sedgwicke spoke a small prayer and then set the mules for the hill that led out of the town.

Crauford's Light Division had arrived into Alenquer at the dead of night and had then moved on after a brief rest. They were to be Wellington's advance guard and were out on the single road to Santarem long before Spencer's Division. However, furthest up the road, even beyond them, were the 16th Light Dragoons, on the road but often forced off, such was the clutter and jumble of corpses, abandoned vehicles, some wrecked, and a multiplicity of rubbish. The bodies were now mostly dead Frenchmen, their animals having expired soon after being required to become beasts of burden beyond Sobral. The 16th had ridden through the night to try to make contact and now all the 16th Troopers rode in subdued silence, not just from lack of sleep, but mostly because all had memories too fresh and too harsh for any form of comradely chatter. They had seen Alenquer, but the next settlement, Azambuja, entered at dawn, had been even worse, because of the many dead civilians and the almost complete despoliation of what had been a peaceful and well-appointed town. Now, mid-morning, the 16th were taking their turn as the leading Regiment of Anson's Cavalry Brigade, with the 1st Hussars KGL immediately behind. Anson rode at the head of the column, with Colonel Withers and Major Johnson in close attendance. Tavender's Squadron led the Regiment and so he was close behind. After two hours riding, Johnson dropped back.

"Lucius. All the signs are that we are catching up with the French. Not least that we are overtaking many that are more alive than dead. Now we're coming up to stragglers who simply haven't been able to keep up, rather than not move at all. Expect yours to be in action first."

Tavender nodded.

"Thank you, Sir."

However his thoughts were much less than charitable. 'What was the point of that? I'm still on the

725

same road, still behind you!'. However, he was wrong. Within five minutes a party of scouts returned and soon after Johnson turned in his saddle.

"Lucius! Take yours off to the right. Keep a close line, but pitch into whatever you see. Vigurs is going off to the left with One."

Tavender raised his arm and then pointed right, for his Squadron to climb the slope above the road and reach a point of vantage where he could see that the road ahead was indeed populated by French, not a dense column, but more a collection of very mobile marauders and stragglers. Over to his left, beyond the road, was a hamlet of some kind, but Tavender's duty lay with the loose group on the road, immediately to his front. He turned in his saddle.

"Four lines. Hit the road in echelon."

He waited until the lines were formed, each Troop in two lines, each behind the other. Each line would turn to attack the road at a point just beyond the one before, thus each half Troop would come into action slightly after their predecessor. Tavender had chosen his tactics perfectly; they cantered down the slope and overwhelmed the few French on 300 yards of road without a shot being fired. The French beyond took to their heels, running off the road into the fields and trees. Several of Tavender's men quickly dismounted and were now disarming the French, which merely involved removing their bayonet from its scabbard; they had thrown down their musket themselves. Tavender made a quick count, 24 or so. A good haul. He looked for one of his Cornets and found one.

"Smythe! Hold your Troop here, to secure the road. I'm going back with Almond's and the prisoners."

A salute was the reply and the task began of shepherding the prisoners back down the road, each pleadingly shouting 'Alimentaire', whilst pointing into their open mouths, but the reply was, as often as not, 'Shut yer gob, French bastard!'; the sights of Azanbuja were still vivid in all memories. The French were forced into a faster pace as the 16th trotted behind and alongside and soon they came to Anson and Withers, both obviously in the best of moods. Withers rose up in his stirrups.

"Well done, Lucius. How many is that?"

"Two dozen, Sir. About."

He expected more congratulations, but instead came a shock and the reason for the good humour of both.

"Sergeant Baxter has just bagged over 50. With just five men! Surprised what must have been an outpost, all with stacked arms and busy cooking. Came onto them in those buildings over yonder."

He pointed with his thumb in the direction of the hamlet, then he sat back in his saddle, still beaming, Anson the same.

"That's 80, nearly. We must now be up to them, if they're now holding together like the group that Baxter surprised."

Tavender smiled in reply. It rankled slightly that he had been very much outdone by a Sergeant, but that was the luck of it and, really, he was too tired to care. What he really wanted was a dry stable and a few hours sleep.

After the Noon meal, Tavender got his wish, brought about by the advance finally coming to a halt. He rejoined Smyth's Troop still securing the road by riding back up to the point with Almond's and, once rejoined, he gave his orders, at the same time using his telescope and indicating his choice of Cornet by pointing at Almond.

"See that small hill, half a mile up, with a group of bushes? Get up there with six men and see what you can see. At the gallop, find out quickly! The French are now thicker on the ground."

Within a minute, Almond and six men were galloping for the hill and after less than ten they were galloping back, because the bushes on the hill had erupted musket fire. Almond came straight to Tavender, but he held up his hand before Almond could speak.

"Yes, Edward, it would seem you have found the French. Our advance is at an end. Ride back now to General Anson."

The first that Colonel Lacey knew that the French had been found was when General Spencer rode up to him at the head of Erskine's column, Lacey there with O'Hare and Carr, the latter now mounted on a spare cavalry horse.

"Lacey! Crauford's Light is now sat looking at a French Division in front of the next town, supposedly Cartaxo, although what's left of it is anyone's guess. He's over to the left and minded to attack, but feels that he is outnumbered, so I'm giving him all the Light Companies of Erskine's Brigade. Your Major Carr here can take command. It's urgent, but isn't everything that involves Crauford. So, I'll ride on and get the rest moving."

Lacey turned to Carr.

"Get our Lights moving right away, Henry. Expect the 50th and 92nd soon after. Good Luck."

Carr saluted and turned his horse to canter back down the 105th column. In their place as the rearmost Company in the 105th column, the Light Company marched on and their first rank of Davey, Miles, Pike and Saunders saw Carr approaching. Miles was the first to voice the thoughts of all.

"This doesn't look good."

Carr reined in his horse and dismounted and they saw him talking to Drake and Maltby and then the latter came back to talk to Ellis.

"We're going ahead to join Crauford facing some French. Just us. The Lights of the 50th and 92nd will be following. We are ordered at the double."

Ellis turned to face the men.

"At the double!"

He led off, following Carr, Drake and Maltby up ahead, all at a jogging pace and soon they had passed all the 105th and then swung off the road to the left, onto heathland covered in short gorse and heather. Soon, they came to a low ridge and, once over, they could see Crauford's command, six strong Battalions, a battery of field-guns and the 16th Light Dragoons. Beyond, by about half a mile and drawn up before a town was what could be taken for a whole French Division. Carr halted his men and looked at the French.

"There's more there than Crauford has. We have to wait for the 50th and 92nd, and meanwhile perhaps Crauford will come over and find us and tell what he wants."

The last words were wholly true as Crauford galloped over, with three Staff. Once up to Carr he fiercely reined in his customary huge horse.

"Ah! Carr, it's you. So, how many are you?"

Carr saluted.

"Three Companies, Sir, about 240 men."

"Very good. Now, you see that farm out there, just about closer to us than it is to them?"

Carr looked to where Crauford was pointing. The farm was obvious on the flat heath.

"Yes Sir."

"Get up there and hold it. Take it, if the Crapauds are in residence. I don't want that on my flank full of Johnnies when we go forward."

"Do you know if there are any French in there, Sir?"

"I don't, but whoever is running things over there would be a damn fool if there wasn't."

He looked behind.

"Will your others be up soon?"

"Yes Sir. I'll move on as soon as they arrive, which should not be too long ."

"Very good."

With no further word, he turned his horse and spurred him back to his main command. Carr meanwhile took the time to study his objective, speaking to Drake as he used his telescope.

"That farm's a large affair. Barns, paddocks and walls all around, besides the house itself."

He refocused his telescope on the French line beyond.

"And I wonder why he's grouped all his cavalry on this side, in line with the farm."

However, he had no time to answer his own question before Maltby spoke.

"The 50th and 92nd are here, Sir."

Carr turned to see the two Company columns, the 92nd all kilted men. When their men halted, their Captains ran forward, that of the 50th arriving first.

"Bright. Sir. 50th Foot"

Him of the 92nd soon arrived.

"MacConagle, Sir. 92nd Highland."

All shook hands, and then Carr pointed to the farm.

"General Crauford wants us to take that, but almost certainly there's French in there, probably Tirailleurs and Voltiguers. Most of the buildings and paddocks are to the left of the main house. They'll be your objective, Bright. The 105th will go for the main house and the area close either side. MacConagle, hold yours in reserve, but give me a runner. I'll send him to let you know if you're to come up in support or cover a retreat."

He turned back to Bright.

"Your men understand advancing in file order?"

Bright nodded.

"Yes Sir. Files of three."

Carr nodded.

"Good. Position your men. If Johnny's in there, it'll be straight in with the bayonet. No hanging around outside trading volleys. Save our shot for driving them back from the walls!"

The two saluted then returned to their men. Meanwhile, the 105th Lights had been standing idle, studying the French in the far distance and it was Saunders who first came to his own conclusion.

"I'd say they was the one's as did for that town we came through this mornin'. More'n likely."

Byford, applying logic, came to the same conclusion.

"If they are the rearguard and I'd say they must be, then they were the last out or close and must be responsible for some of it, if not all."

Miles spat.

"I thought that what we saw at that Catanzaro place in Sicily was a one off, but this crew! That's how they goes about their business!"

It had been a grim march since leaving Azambuja, all carrying the sight of dead civilians, killed by bayonet thrust, often in the back, or a crushing musket butt. However, the worst image that they carried with them was the picture of children crying beside their dead parents. As a following Battalion, they had to take their turn with clearing the houses, again laying out the dead in the town square, in the hope that returning Portuguese would conduct a proper burial. Nat Solomon, him of the East End, understood the feud and lived by it, and he spoke what many felt.

"There has to be a reckoning with this lot. Has to be."

Those that heard, checked their priming pans and the touch-hole, then they checked that their 'rifle sword' came easily out of its scabbard. Then came the order, 'Files of three' and they broke ranks to re-assemble in their files, a five-yard gap between each. Carr could be seen at the join of the two Companies and their own Officers were stood before them. The order came down the ranks.

"Load!"

All did so and came to Order Arms.

"Fix bayonets!"

There came the slight rattle of the Baker 'sword' meeting the 'bayonet bar' alongside the muzzle, then back to Order Arms. Carr looked back to see the 92nd in two lines and so, satisfied, he drew his sword and waved his men forward. It was a 600 yard advance and all felt the eyes of waiting French upon them. Below, their feet brushed through the low gorse and heather, whilst above, a flock of crows circled, cawing for reasons that none below knew nor really cared to think about.

The details of the farm became clear, three large barns on the left, each with a loft and stone walled paddocks before and to the side. The main house had one central door and several windows to each side and along the top floor. Skylights were also in the roof. Carr gripped his sword and his men subconsciously flexed their hands on the wood of their weapons, now held across their chests. At 200 yards, Carr checked for movement at the farm, but saw none, the same at 150, but at 100 it came. First, French shakoes appearing everywhere and then came the volley. Balls buzzed and sang to the side and above, then came many grunts and cries of pain. Drake heard the cries from behind, from his own men, not least "Joe's down!", "And George." Drake pressed on, leading his men, but Nat Solomon had halted to reach down to George Tucker, but Ellis saw it.

"Leave him! Get forward. You want to wait here for another dose!"

Solomon renewed his grip on his rifle and regained his place.

Carr knew that the French would be reloaded in 20 seconds, and so expect another after that, but before it came, get to the wall through the smoke. He raised his sword.

"Charge! Charge, boys, charge. Over and into them!"

However, the French had another rank and this volley sang and buzzed amongst them, but, in the lingering smoke, the French aim was poor. Saunders went straight at the main door with a vicious shoulder charge. It buckled, but held, but not for long, when another shove from his massive frame and the boots of others saw it collapse back into the room. Four Baker rifles came to the present in the doorway and fired, and then Saunders and the three with him were in and going straight forward. The next four, as they had been drilled fired to either side then joined the melee inside. Saunders and Solomon engaged a Voltiguer each and it would have made no difference if the French were resisting or trying to surrender. Saunders thrust his bayonet through the eye-socket of his opponent so fiercely that the bayonet came out of the back of his skull and pinned him to the wall. Solomon took his opponent in the throat and then finished him by swinging the butt of his rifle up into the man's temple. Then on, with the others, all fighting like maddened demons in the gloom of the farmhouse interior, fighting from room to room, floor to floor.

Carr came to the wall to find a moustachioed Voltiguer staring at him from the other side. He knocked the bayonet thrust aside, and smashed the bell guard of his sword into the man's face. Then he climbed, using the footholds in the mercifully rough wall. Once on top he jumped down, landing both feet on the crawling figure of his erstwhile opponent. His men were with him, but he wanted no headlong charge over the walls and fences.

"Keep the line, boys. Keep the line. Hold together!"

He concentrated on defending himself, leaving the combat to his men following. He wanted the time to look and discover, he was convinced that this was more than just an outlying farm to the French. A Voltiguer came at him, the tassel alongside his helmet swinging wide. Carr deflected the bayonet and delivered a vicious left hook into the man's face, then a bayonet from a man of the 50th thrust forward and the Voltiguer fell. Carr looked over to his left, to see that the Lights of the 50th were fighting their way forward, both from the front and from the flank. Then firing intensified before him, not a volley, but a spluttering increase in volume.

Drake was content with the progress of Maltby's Company, but what of Shakeshaft's? He looked to that side and immediately saw Sergeant Ellis.

"Ellis! With me."

Drake trusted Shakeshaft the least to not to get carried away in the fighting, him being easily the most aggressive of the Light Company Officers. They both ran across to the right to find that this Lieutenant was now stood with his Section, looking at a large barn, the building furthest back from the farmhouse. It had a very large door and a smaller loft door above. All along the sides were ventilation slits, too high to merely stand at, but a box or a barrel beneath made each a perfect firing slit. The space between was very open. Drake was immediately worried, but he had no choice.

"We have to take it, Richard."

"Yes Sir, we do."

Ellis was pleased with this small amount of caution, that Shakeshaft was thinking before committing, but what came next raised Shakeshaft in his estimation considerably.

"I've an idea, Sir."

"From you, then."

Shakeshaft turned to Ellis.

"Everyone loaded in a firing line, but, when we go forward, you keep five with you. Do it now."

Ellis ran along the line of men and soon all were loaded and facing the barn, rifles at the 'make ready'. The tempting target of a firing line, although well over 100 yards away, was too much for many in the barn and bullets whipped and buzzed around them from men using the ventilation slits. A man dropped his rifle and fell to his knees, clutching his shoulder. Shakeshaft came to Ellis at the end of the line.

"Your five take care of anything appearing in that loft."

Then he looked along his line.

"Present!"

All barrels came level.

"Fire!"

The line erupted with smoke and noise.

"Reload and fix bayonets!"

This was done within 30 seconds, and during it Drake realised Shakeshaft's purpose. The space between them and the barn was now filled with smoke, drifting forward on the gentle breeze. Shakeshaft filled his lungs.

"At them, boys, at them. It's our turn now!"

Led by Drake and Shakeshaft, the line sprang forward, but Ellis held his group together, him watching the loft opening. As they finally emerged from the smoke of their own volley, Ellis saw four blue-coated figures crouching in that space. He brought up his own rifle to immediately fire and his target toppled back into the barn. His five others downed two of the remaining three and the last, his aim spoiled by what had happened to his comrades fired and disappeared. Two of Ellis' men began to reload.

"Bugger that! This is Brummagen work now!"

The two dropped their torn cartridges and followed Ellis into the barn, 'Brummagen' outstretched at the end of their weapons. They found the barn practically cleared, even the loft, because the French had run out through the back door and now Shakeshaft and his men were pouring after them, Captain Drake visibly encouraging them on. Ellis was instantly worried.

"He doesn't know what's out there!"

He ran forward, now at the rear of the Section, to find both Officers leading Two Section across a paddock chasing the French, who were now scaling its back wall. This was manned by French, but both Officers had it right, because keeping close to the running French prevented those behind the wall from firing. Despite being breathless, Drake was shouting.

"Take the wall, men. Push them back from it!"

Many of his men were still loaded and they stopped before the wall to put a bullet into the back of a fleeing Frenchman, or into the head of one stood behind it. Then it was butts and bayonets across the wall, amidst curses, shouts and cries of agony, but the British had the advantage.

It was soon plain that the French, having starved for over a month, had not the strength to sustain a prolonged hand-to-hand over the narrow wall. In addition, the ground in the paddock was higher than that outside and, also, the British were taller than the nimble Voltiguers, thus they were fighting from above whilst the French were fighting from below. After but a short but intense fight, the survivors of the French defence were running back, however, onto more reinforcements. There were more French in the field beyond the farm and all were now advancing forward. Shakeshaft took a deep breath.

"Not loaded, step back and reload. Loaded. Present!"

Around half his men trained their rifles over the wall.

"Fire!"

The rifles crashed out and smoke obscured all. Stood back from the wall, Drake looked left and was much relieved to see that many of Maltby's Section had emerged from the farm to man their paddock walls. Together, they could all now mount some form of effective resistance to the oncoming counter-attack.

Meanwhile, on the left of the farmhouse Carr assessed his situation. He knew that French resistance was stiffening, but not so much that a push from a whole Company would not clear the farm. His nearest men were holding a line by manning the walls and fences, but they were mainly 50th using the less accurate Brown Bess musket. It seemed to him that the number of French putting up resistance were almost as numerous as when they first attacked, so they must be receiving reinforcements, but there was nothing organised about their defence. He decided; 'We can take this place!' so he looked for his runner, the kilted Scotsman of the 92nd.

"Get back to your Captain. Tell him to come forward at his best speed."

The man saluted and ran off, then Carr looked to his right, to see that Drake's Company were now manning paddock walls on their edge of the farm. There was nothing beyond them, but Carr had a final barn in front of him. Then he turned when he heard shouts and yells in an undeniably Scottish nature coming from behind him, to see the Lights of the 92nd vaulting the walls and fences. He decided that their momentum must not be lost, so he waited until they were almost level with his own men and then he stood.

"Forward, boys, forward. Come on the Dirty Half Hundredth. That barn and it's done!"

The 50th, now with the men of the 92nd beside them all rose up, climbed the last wall and sprang forward. They were met by a spluttering fire but their charge was irresistible. MacConagle led his men straight into the barn, Bright around the far side and Carr took a mixture of 50th and a few 105th around his side. There was a final wall running across their path from the back of the barn but it was lightly manned. The few French there quickly fled and Carr took his men up to the rough stonework.

"Reload and hold here. No further!"

He peered through the thinning smoke and knew that he had given the correct order. A strong Company of Voltiguers, now reinforced by the retreating French, were forming a firing line 100 yards beyond, but beyond them there was more, but it was difficult to see at ground level. He ran into the barn and climbed the rough wooden steps to the loft floor, stepping on a dead Frenchman as he did so. Once at the top he used a ventilation slit to look through to the French and saw the reason for their holding beyond the farm. The French line was covering a battery of six field-guns, all positioned to enfilade any advance by the British, in this case Crauford. He ran out of the barn and over to his own 105th, where he found John Davey.

"Davey! Gather as many of ours as you can and get into that barn. Our rifles can do some damage from there. Go for the artillery. Tell either Captain Bright or Captain

MacConagle to get their men down to these walls to replace yours. But, if you see them turning one of those guns on you, get out. Clear?"

Davey saluted.

"Sir!"

"Next, who's our best runner?"

"Private Miles, Sir. None faster."

"Where is he?"

"There, Sir."

Davey pointed to an almost maniacal figure, firing and reloading at absolute maximum speed. Carr allowed him his final shot.

"Miles!"

Tom Miles turned to the direction of the sound, his ill temper at being interrupted very evident on his face, but this changed when he saw that he was being called by his Regiment's Junior Major. He jogged up to Carr and saluted and Carr wasted no time.

"Get over to General Crauford at your best speed. Tell him that we have taken the barn, but the French have six field-guns behind it. With reinforcements and some cavalry we can capture them. What orders does he have for us?"

One half of Miles' mind was absorbing the message; the other was calculating the possibility that a messenger to someone of such high rank, usually received a coin.

"Yes Sir. Go now, Sir?"

Carr nodded and Miles was gone, running out through the paddock gates. Once past the farmhouse, however, he saw the wounded of the first French volley being tended to by George Fearnley, now that the fighting had died down somewhat. One was Joe Pike and Miles ran over despite the order of 'best speed'.

"Is he dead?"

Fearnley did not look up.

"No, but 'tis bad. He's only still with us, 'cos the ball hit a cross strap as took some of the speed, but 'tis still in there."

"Can you get it out, like you did for me?"

"No Tom! This is a Surgeon's job. All I can do is halt the bleeding some."

"What about George Tucker?"

"Gone! Right through the chest."

Miles reached down to touch Joe Pike's head, although the boy was barely conscious.

"You hang on, now, Joe. You'll be fine. We'll get you back to the Surgeon and he'll fix you up. Course he will!"

A final pat of his head and then Miles was gone, running to the group of Officers that he could see some distance up the slight slope. Miles settled into an efficient loping run, his rifle slung over his chest. Within minutes he was up to the group, all high ranking Generals and Staff. He unslung his rifle and came to 'order arms', then he began his message.

"Beg pardon, Sirs, but I have a message for General Crauford, from my Major Carr."

One of those at the fore of the group eased his horse out of the group. Miles recognised him as General Wellington himself.

"You can deliver your message to me, Private."

Miles took a deep breath, he was still slightly winded from his run.

"We have taken the farm, Sir, but there's still plenty of French on the other side and six field-guns, what we can't see from here. Major Carr says that we can take the guns if he gets some reinforcements and some cavalry. Sir. He wants some orders, Sir."

However, there was no coin, instead Wellington turned to General Crauford.

"There you are, Crauford. How fortunate it was that I put a stop to your advance. Those guns would have cost you dearly."

Crauford sat his horse, with the same expression on his face as though he had swallowed a wasp!

"Which is why I sent forward to take the farm, first. Sir."

At that moment came the sound of a single cannonshot.

"Seems as though M'sieu is now using those guns on the men you sent over."

Without waiting for any reply, Wellington returned to Miles.

"Who is your Officer?"

"Major Carr, Sir."

"Good. Tell Major Carr that he is to withdraw, with no delay. There will be cavalry to cover his retreat."

Miles saluted and turned to leave, but Spencer stopped him.

"Private!"

Miles turned to face him and found a coin being tossed his way, which he caught and instantly pocketed, then he began his run back, but the delay had enabled him to hear Wellington order Anson to lead the 16th Light Dragoons over to cover Carr's retreat.

Miles, now running downhill, soon arrived at the farm to find Carr where he had left him.

"Sir. This from General Wellington, Sir. We are to pull back with no delay. Cavalry will cover us, Sir."

Carr's jaw clamped together with anger, but he gave his orders.

"Get over to Captain Drake and Lieutenant Shakeshaft. Tell them to pull back and assemble on the other side of the farm."

Miles saluted and ran off, but he did not find Captain Drake, instead Drake found Carr.

"What news?"

"We're to pull back! Orders from Wellington himself. All this has been for nothing!"

Another cannonshot hit the barn and passed out through the near wall, sending a shower of brick and plaster into the paddock below.

"You get these back. Reform beyond the farmhouse. Keep them together, what with Frog cavalry so near, but we'll get some of our own so I've been told. I'll see to the 50th and 92nd over on the left."

Carr ran over, giving his orders to anyone in authority, Sergeants included. All on that side fired one more shot at the French, as much to make smoke as to cause damage, and soon the farmhouse and all its buildings were evacuated. Carr's three Companies were assembled together at the front of the farmhouse, but he was worried about cavalry, despite seeing the 16th some 300 yards away to the left. Once their men had assembled, Drake, Bright and MacConagle had run over to him. He gave his orders.

"Get the men in three columns, closed up. Johnny may send some cavalry round the far side."

He waved in the direction of Shakeshaft's barn.

"Carry the wounded in the centre."

"And the dead?"

This question from MacConagle.

"Them too!"

The three ran off to form up their men, leaving Carr to look back at the farm. He could see no French re-occupying the buildings, but he could see his own dead, where they had fallen from the first French volley, but now being picked up. 'All for nothing' again entered his mind. Then he turned to make sure that the line of their retreat angled back towards the protective cavalry, stood drawn up on the slope. However, they were not molested and, as Carr passed the group of Colonel Withers, Major Johnson and their Captains, including Tavender, Carr brought his sword up in salute and thanks. All dutifully returned the gesture.

Inside the three columns the wounded were being carried on blankets, including Joe Pike. The 105th had five wounded, but Joe Pike was the worst and so George Fearnley was in close attendance. None spoke, instead they fretted at the slow speed, but there was one item of comfort, this being the sight of their own 105th drawn up on the ridge. The three Companies parted when back on the ridge to join their own Regiments, where Carr hurried further on to meet Lacey, who had but one question.

"Casualties?"

"Three dead, Sir, and five wounded. One badly."

Lacey turned to O'Hare, him still mounted.

"Get Pearce up here. Tell him it's urgent."

O'Hare galloped off and, within minutes, Pearce and his wagon were hastening to the front. Pearce jumped down and quickly examined the wounded. He gave quick instructions to his two Orderlies for the other four, but then stopped at Joe Pike. John Davey and Tom Miles, now dismissed from the columns, hurried over as Pike's tunic was pulled open to reveal the hole in his chest, merely inches below his heart, and still issuing blood. Davey saw all and his face fell.

"What do you think, Sir?"

Pearce ignored him, instead he looked up at the Orderly stood with him.

"I'll operate immediately. The ball has to come out and while there's still good daylight. Get my instruments."

The Orderly ran off and Davey spoke again.

"Can we help, Sir?"

"Yes. Hold him down, but he looks beyond knowing, to me."

The Orderly returned and the instrument roll was thrown open. Even though Pike was semi-conscious the leather gag was inserted into his mouth and then Davey and Miles pinned down his shoulders. Pearce went straight to Pike's tunic and shirt to examine the holes and nodded, plainly satisfied, all edges came perfectly together. That done and the blood wiped away, Pearce began to open the wound. Pike writhed at the pain and Miles was encouraged.

"He can feel something! That's good, isn't it, Sir?"

Pearce ignored him, he was skilfully parting both ribs and flesh, whilst the Orderly wiped away the fresh blood. Pearce was speaking to himself, relating what he had found.

"Two cracked ribs! But how far in is the ball?"

He cut deeper, the Orderly doing his best with the flowing blood. Then Pearce selected a redactor and adjusted it to fit between the two ribs. The redactor was inserted and the screw applied for Pike to writhe again and the two ribs to ease apart, as he spoke half to himself, by way of encouragement.

"Good job these ribs are half gone through!"

Pearce picked up his probe and began to use it. Pike writhed even more, but, after a minute's searching, Pearce extracted the ball, a bloody object between the bloody jaws of his probe.

"Right! Sew him up and bandage him up."

Davey watched Pearce quickly inserting the stitches.

"Can we keep him with us, Sir? In our Mess. Our Followers will care for him."

"That I do not doubt, but temporary, until I can establish an Infirmary of some kind. Then he's best there, where I can keep an eye on him."

Miles now spoke.

"So what are his chances, Sir?"

Pearce shook his head and waved his hands dismissively.

"I do not know if the ball pierced his lung. If not, it still may be bruised and that could cause an infection. If none of those, it's up to him!"

The afternoon was now turning into evening as the 105th made camp for the night and Joe Pike was carried back to Nellie and Bridie who both ran towards them when they saw a figure in a blanket. When they discovered that it was Joe Pike, ashen faced and his tunic still open to reveal bloody bandages, their consternation intensified, each gripping a section of their apron to their faces as he was carried to where their fire was being kindled by Toby Halfway. Joe was laid on the ground and a rolled up horse-blanket placed under his head. Bridie looked at Deakin, she most concerned for her brother-in-law, her younger sister's husband.

"Jed! What do you think?"

Deakin could not bring himself to say what he truly felt.

"He's young and he's strong. There's got to be hope."

"Do you think we can get him to eat?"

"Come tomorrow, you might get some soup into him, right now let him rest."

The words did nothing to ease her deepest worries and so the apron wringing continued. Meanwhile, Zeke Saunders was ripping up a spare shirt, French, found in an Officer's portmanteau in Azambuja.

"Those bandages will need changin' afore long."

oOo

With the dawn, Lacey and O'Hare walked the short stretch to the ridgeline to join Erskine and the Colonels of the 50th and the 92nd, Peterson and Rundle respectively. The three were looking down at the farm and the fields beyond, all now empty.

"Johnny took himself off, soon as it got dark. That's Cartaxo, we now know."

Lacey looked at him

"Is he holding it?"

"Can't tell for sure, I've not been told, but it seems not. He's going right back into Santarem, is the received wisdom."

He took a last look through his telescope.

"Right, get your men up in columns. Line abreast. Rundle, yours can have the road."

Within half an hour the three Battalions of Erskine's Brigade were line abreast on the ridge and Erskine waved them forward. Being in the centre the 105th passed closest to the graves of their dead, new brown earth prominent on the ridge, including George Tucker's and, as they passed, most of the Light Company gave a small fingered salute in that direction. The farm was now a blackened shell; the French had fired it before they left, but all eyes were now on the buildings of Cartaxo, all growing larger as the distance lessened, but they marched straight in. Crauford's Rifles had entered during the night to find the town abandoned, scoured for anything useful by the French, but not wrecked; the French had passed through and on too quickly. Thus, it was to the sounds of Rifle Regiment bugle calls to 'form up' that the 105th arrived at the first houses of Cartaxo, and there they halted to give the 95th space on the streets to form their marching columns. Almost incredibly, seeming to emerge from out of the ground, civilians began to be seen, all hurrying to what had been their dwellings before the French arrived.

Erskine, Lacey, Rundle and Peterson had been riding together before the 92nd on the road and, when they halted, Spencer arrived at a canter, showing some urgency.

"Crauford's for pushing on and taking a look at Santarem, about six miles on. I've no orders, but I'm minded to support, so, keep yours in column and follow Crauford out."

With that he spurred forward his horse and rode back down the main road, passing the 92nd still waiting in column. Erskine looked at his three Colonels.

"Right! 50th first through, then the 105th, then yours, Rundle."

He rose up in his saddle, but then sat back down with a sigh, plainly worried, but he did not explain at that moment.

"Lacey, you've had Brigade command, keep with me. I'm for staying close to Crauford."

For Lacey, that was sufficient explanation, Erskine was apprehensive that Crauford's natural aggression would take him into some form of conflict, in which Erskine may be required to become involved, if only to support him and his men. When alone, Erskine spoke further.

"It may be that we'll need to urge caution, Lacey. Spencer did not say so, but, as we speak, we are unsupported. We have only Pack's Portuguese and Anson's cavalry with us. Wellington's called out Cole and Leith from The Lines, but they are two marches away."

Lacey raised his eyebrows.

"What do we know of the French, Sir?"

"Practically nothing! They may be holding in Santarem, or they may not."

"They're still starving, Sir."

"Yes, and that's what Crauford thinks, so he's convinced they'll pass on through and keep pulling back. Wellington thinks that, too, but I prefer caution."

They had to canter to catch up with Crauford's Brigade, now effectively a Division, comprising his six strong Battalions and a field-gun battery. High on its hill, Santarem became visible and, when in telescope distance, its medieval walls could then be made out, ringing the town. However, it was not these formidable defences that most concerned Lacey. After three miles, he began to notice the nature of the country that they were riding through. Their road had become a raised causeway and on either side he now saw more and more marsh grass, ponds, rhynes and dykes. The countryside before Santarem was little better than marshland, in many ways a more effective defence than any walls or redoubts. Lacey turned to Erskine.

"Sir, I'm of the strong opinion that the only way up to those walls is along this causeway! All around is very wet."

Erskine turned to him.

"Marshland, you think?"

"I do, Sir. I've seen a lot in Somerset, where we come from, and it's just like this!"

"Perhaps Crauford thinks the same. Look he's stopped."

The six Battalions ahead were spreading left and right. The pair maintained their walking pace on the road and soon came up to see why they had halted. The causeway was now a long bridge that crossed a muddy river and the swamps that half formed its banks. French piquets were at the far end, being studied by Crauford, who was the furthest forward, his horse actually stood on the first boards of the bridge. He was peering ahead, using no telescope, but chewing his lower lip to aid his concentration. Erskine rode closest.

"Afternoon, Crauford. What do you think?"

Crauford merely glanced behind.

"Erskine!"

He chewed his lip some more.

"He's not holding here. I'm convinced! He'll pass on through, leaving us stuck here worrying about a bit of wet! And a few starving Rearguard!"

Erskine pulled out his own telescope and made a quick study, lingering at one stage.

"I would urge caution, I really would. Massena may have his whole army in there, supplied and recovering. On top, take a look at that knoll, more like a ridge, at the end of the road after the bridge. He's getting guns onto it!"

At this point, Crauford did extract his own instrument and quickly focus it. Lacey did the same, to see a high, elongated knoll, where the straight road after the bridge was forced to turn left. Any guns on its summit would completely dominate that section of road that ran arrow straight before it. However, Crauford snapped his instrument shut.

"Rearguards have guns! It's not unknown."

It was plain that Crauford was about to order some form of attack over the bridge and down the causeway, when Wellington arrived. All saluted and waited, whilst he went alongside Crauford, him looking with ill-temper at his Commander in Chief, who knew full well what Crauford was intending, but Wellington spoke what Crauford did not want to hear, at least at that moment.

"We'll try a demonstration. Tomorrow, to try them out. Massena should not stay there, he'll starve, it's almost as bad as camping before The Lines. But we'll see, tomorrow, when Leith and Cole are closer, should things go wrong."

He was evidently in a good mood and looked around, to fix on Lacey.

"What do you think, Lacey?"

Lacey was thunderstruck at being asked such a question, but he had an opinion and he spoke it.

"He has guns on that knoll, Sir, directly ahead, and any force attempting that causeway will be damnably mauled. Also, if he does have his full force in the town and they come out to meet any of ours, outnumbering them, then ours will be stuck with this river and swamp at their backs and only this bridge as a sure retreat. Sir."

"I agree! "

He turned to Crauford and grinned. It was plain that, at that moment, Crauford dwelt firmly in the 'bad books' of his Commander in Chief.

"There you are Crauford. Never a good idea to be over a river with your single retreat being just one bridge!"

Whilst Erskine looked admiringly at Lacey and Crauford looked daggers at being reminded of the Coa, Wellington rose in his stirrups to look right and left.

"So! What we will do is this. Crauford, when good light arrives tomorrow, see if you can get around that knoll to the right, close to the Tagus. I'll send Pack left, to see how far he can get forward up there. Erskine, you have the bridge here. If Crauford and Pack can get far enough forward, M'sieu will not risk those guns being cut off and they'll clear that knoll. Then you go."

He took one further look and then swung his horse's head back around.

"See you all on the morrow."

All saluted as he left, then Erskine looked at Crauford, still as frustrated as ever.

"Will you take yours into position? Now?"

Crauford nodded and began shouting orders, for his command to begin the difficult march down the bank of the River Mayor towards the main Tagus. Soon, there was only Spencer's Brigade at the bridge and he looked at Lacey.

"We'll spend the night on this road. We don't want to lose any men down some boghole!"

However, he had more to say.

"Your Lights have Bakers, yes?"

Lacey nodded.

"Right, yours up to the bridge, now. We'll need them to engage those picquets come daylight."

Lacey trotted his horse back past the 50th, to then bring his own men forward. Evil looks were exchanged with the men of the 50th, especially when Miles saw his protagonist from Sobral, but nothing was said. Respect and deference demanded it, because the 50th fully appreciated that the 105th would be the vanguard of any attack. Now in position, all three Battalions camped on the road. There was no local fuel to be had, but all had a few sticks of kindling with them and so a fire was started and some hot stew made. Miles and Davey heated their pot, now only two-thirds full, there being just the two of them. Whilst eating the hot food they sat with Saunders, Solomon and Byford. Saunders looked up at Davey.

"You heard any more about Joe?"

"Not a thing. They took us quick through that last place, but it all looked in good shape, well enough, so my guess is that he's in some kind of infirmary set up there. Good thing."

Byford looked up.

"If we move forward, he'll be sent back to Lisbon in a convoy. If we stay here, then he'll stay also. That's how it works."

Saunders nodded.

"Good thing too. Them base hospitals is no more than a few breaths away from the morgue. God awful places! Back in that Cartaxo, the women is there, and that's bound to help."

All nodded agreement and then set about the final tasks of the day, checking their weapons and equipment. At the throat of the bridge, Carr was standing alone, his telescope unused with the dark near full, but he was staring ahead at the close groups of bivouac fires that could be seen on the knoll. Only 500 yards away in the dark, the grey of the bridge guided his sight towards the fires, before it disappeared into the darkness.

"This is not good!"

The whole Battalion, all ranks, spent the night on the road, the only shelter available being that given to Albright and Sedgwicke by their small cart, but even Albright, inside the cart, was woken by the heavy rain that came on at Midnight and Sedgwicke found himself woken by sodden blankets as the rainwater ran off the causeway. The whole Brigade awoke to the misery of the running water and so most simply sat, with their blankets over their heads and shoulders. Thankfully, the rain ceased, but the dawn soon followed and their remaining precious kindling, warmed their food to begin the day, which came reluctantly, the grey clouds that had disgorged rain through the night, lingering still, to threaten yet more rain. However, the rain did hold off and Carr stood again at the end of the bridge, using the naked eye, waiting until the growing light would reveal the French sentries. When it came, there was plainly more than a few picquets. The French had seen their arrival and instead, at the edge of the swamp, there was a whole skirmish line. Drake was nearby.

"Right Nat. Get them up. Slow and certain firing. All to use the leather patch."

Drake ran back to where his Light Company were gathered and passed on Carr's instructions. Soon they were all in a firing line at the edge of the swamp and soon all began firing, slow and deliberate, as Carr had instructed, over the 150 yard distance. French bullets came in return, but did little damage to the kneeling Light Infantrymen. What damage they were doing to the French was impossible to tell, but Drake and Carr, kneeling in a ditch, were more interested in the French guns. Drake lowered his telescope.

"Why aren't they using their guns?"

"Who knows? They want to wait for us to get onto that causeway, or they may be conserving ammunition. They may be short, they lost a lot of draught animals and couldn't get it back from The Lines. Who knows?"

Drake crouched down and waited.

"Shouldn't we be hearing about the doings of Pack and Crauford either side?"

Carr nodded and sat back on a folded blanket himself.

"We should and a lot of it, if Johnny is to be persuaded to get his guns off that knoll."

Back along the causeway, the 105th waited, arranged either side as Lacey ordered. He did not want a solid column stood waiting to tempt the French artillery into action. The Grenadiers were the leading Company and would be first over the bridge. Their three Officers stood nervously, Carravoy, D'Villiers and Ameshurst, all three staring along the bare, straight, open road, all flexing their fingers on the handles of their swords. The minutes became half an hour and then one hour. The bickering fire some 200 yards before them seemed to slacken, as though both sides saw it as becoming increasingly pointless. Lacey and O'Hare were stood on the road just up ahead of them, with Erskine, when suddenly a galloping horseman arrived, plainly an Aide-de-Camp. He dismounted, went up to Erskine and saluted. The three Grenadiers were close enough to hear and listened intently.

"The attack's off, Sir. General Wellington's orders. General Crauford crossed the Mayor, but the ground's too bad after that rain to get any further forward. They exchanged some fire, but that's all."

Erskine leaned forward.

"And Pack?"

"Much the same, Sir. They also crossed the Mayor upstream, but could not get their guns forward."

"So what orders?"

It began to rain again.

"None Sir. Other than to call off the attack."

Erskine pulled up his greatcoat collar.

"I'm obliged to you Major, I'm sure!"

The Aide-de-Camp saluted, remounted and rode off.

"Tell your men to cease fire, Lacey."

The order was given, but Erskine had more to say.

"So we spend another night here!"

"Yes Sir. We must maintain contact. We've no choice."

Erskine nodded.

"Allow the men some food. It must be near Noon."

The relief throughout the 105th was palpable, beginning with the three Grenadier Officers, who grinned at each other almost in embarrassment and then the two Lieutenants walked back to their Sections. Carravoy remained and took a long pull at his spirit flask as the noise of the news spreading came to him from the column, all plainly joyous.

At Noon, the height of the day saw Crauford return, his men behind him in a very long line that stretched back into the mist along the riverbank. Predictably, Crauford was in no good mood.

"Last night's rain did for us!"

He took a pull at his own brandy flask and, to the surprise of all, passed it to Erskine.

"What orders have you?"

Erskine passed on the flask.

"None! Other than not to attack."

"Well I have! To maintain contact along the river. Me and Pack."

"That's what we've been doing!"

"Then it's our job now. I'd get yours back to Cartaxo. You can support from there and, judging by this lot, that'll be your winter quarters. Get in there and claim it. No one will move you. This year's over!"

oOo

Carr awoke from his comfortable cot in the corner, again enjoying the grateful thought that he did not have to sleep fully clothed. He sat up, swung his legs off the bed and reached for his shirt and breeches. With the latter he was immediately dissatisfied and so, in his indignation, he yelled at the door leading to the next room.

"Morrison! Did I not ask that these be washed?"

Henry Morrison knew immediately that the subject was the Major's breeches.

"You did, Sir, but your others has a hole that needs mendin'. In an important place, Sir. 'Twill be done for tomorrow."

Carr sniffed, somewhat put out, but then he transferred his attention and studied Drake, sat at the table.

"You read that letter any more and you'll wear out the words!"

Drake returned an aggrieved frown.

"And how many times have you read Jane's last letter?"

Carr smiled, knowing that he had no defence against the accusation, then he noticed that Drake was holding a small tuft of blond hair in his right hand, tied with a thin pink ribbon.

"When we get home Henrietta may well be a brunette! Their hair colour can change as they get older, so my Mother remarked, once."

Drake turned to him, ignoring the subject.

"Have you heard anything about your request for leave? Nothing's come back for me."

At that moment Shakeshaft entered the room and went immediately to his own kit and possessions, speaking over his shoulder.

"Johnny's quitting Santarem and heading up North. Things are happening."

By now Carr was fully dressed and stood at the table with Drake.

"How'd you know!"

"I've a friend in the Horse Artillery. They've been told to prepare for campaign."

Drake looked glumly at Carr.

"Seems the Generals have decided that Winter's ending early."

He released a heavy sigh.

"Bang goes our chance of England."

Carr looked sympathetically at his friend, his own feelings much less than buoyed up, but he understood the weight of circumstance.

"Never mind, at least we're still getting letters from home. It was always a long shot. Johnny's been too close these past three months, just up the road. Not releasing Officers can be no surprise."

Drake nodded as he returned both the letter and the lock of hair to their envelope and placed it carefully down into the inside pocket of his tunic.

The next morning Ethan Ellis was pushing open the door of Deakin's and Davey's billet to immediately feel the warmth of the room inside. The first soldier he saw was Private Byford.

"Where's John?"

"Out the back, Sergeant, making another hurdle."

"Here's a letter."

Ellis threw the letter in Byford's direction and then carried on through to the backyard, to find Davey sat with Zeke Saunders, Davey using a mattock to tamp down the last of the hurdle's woven packing.

"Good hurdle makings they grows around here, Zeke. This for the uprights is hard and takes a good point and the withies bends around fair easy. Don't need no soakin'."

Saunders was busy assembling a chair.

"Yes. So you keep sayin' time after time. You've turned this place into a Gloucester small-holding!"

"Nothin' wrong in that!"

Ellis came forward to look down at Davey.

"We're movin' out! We're going forward, probably today. Johnny's shiftin' an' going on up North. He's been seen leavin' Santarem, an' Nosey'll have us followin' close. Be certain."

Davey stood up and tested the hurdle for rigidity, but Ellis continued.

"So, get yours ready to move come afternoon. You've eaten?"

"We have."

"Right. Good. Get all packed up, then ready for an inspection. That's orders afore we leaves. Where's Jed?"

"Next room. With the families."

Ellis re-entered the house from the backyard and turned into the next room to find all very much in celebratory mood. Deakin sat at a table with Bridie, Nellie and Byford, all grinning widely, but Ellis had no time for such frivolity.

"Jed! You heard?"

"What"

"The Frogs is quittin' Santarem. We're to be on the road come the afternoon."

All three immediately stood up and busied themselves with their preparations and Ellis looked at Byford, remembering the letter.

"That word from Eirin?"

"Yes. It's a boy! And both are doing well. Eirin wrote the letter herself."

Ellis grunted approval, but then the Portuguese occupants of the house came into the room, husband and wife, both late in years. Ellis looked again at Byford.

"You'd best tell these that we'm on our way!"

Byford delved into his pocket for the necessary volume and began his composing, but the look of consternation on the face of both husband and wife, showed that they had picked up themselves on just what was now happening. Ellis stood for a moment at the door.

"Inspection two hours!"

At the required hour, One Section was paraded in two ranks at the edge of the road, with Ellis waiting to begin his inspection, stood before all. He saw the old man and woman come out of their door and go up to Davey who was, as a Chosen Man, at the end of the rank. The old man placed one hand on Davey's chest and looked full into his face.

"Nunca te olvidare inglés soldados. Nunca!"

The old man patted Davey twice on the chest.

"Mucho gracias. Que Dios esté con todos vosotros. Adios!"

The pair then went back to stand on the path to their house. Ellis looked at Byford, stood in the rank behind.

"What he say?"

"Something about not forgetting English soldiers. Thanks. God be with us. Good-bye."

Ellis nodded, then his face became concerned, even emotional. He looked at Davey.

"What can we leave these two? As a memento, sort of. What've you got spare?"

Ellis was as veteran as could be and had spent most of his years in the ranks. He knew that every Mess kept spares to replace what could be lost, for which they could be deducted pay. Ellis turned his gaze to Miles to give him a knowing look, whilst Miles simply looked annoyed, but he did let down his pack and delved into its depths, to bring out a 105th crossbelt badge, nicely polished. Ellis nodded, content.

"Give it to the old man."

After a frosty look towards Ellis, Miles went across to the old couple and held out the badge. The old man hesitated and so Byford spoke up.

"Para você. Para lembrar."

The old man grinned and took the badge, before handing it to his wife, who studied it carefully, then the two went to stand in the doorway of their home, both now studying the badge.

Satisfied, Ellis went to the first rank for the inspection. He ignored Davey and instead placed himself squarely before the soldier stood next to him. Ellis reached forward to grasp one of the crossbelts on the man's chest, the one that supported the cartridge pouch. He ignored the evil look he got from Tom Miles, in his place as the next one along the rank.

"Surprised they didn't give you a new one back at the hospital. Fine sight you look on inspection wearing one with a bullet hole!"

He reached inside his own haversack. He had evidently anticipated Joe Pike needing a new one.

"Here, get this on you before Maltby arrives. An' get the pouch shone up!"

oOo

Footnotes.

At the Battle of Talavera, the heroic conduct of Mackenzie's Brigade, 2/24th 2nd Warwickshire, 2/31st Huntingdonshire, 1/45th Nottinghamshire, was unheralded at the time for the simple reason that their Divisional Commander, this being Mackenzie, had been killed, and therefore no written report was given to Wellesley which could be included in his report on the battle. The 2/24th suffered 343 casualties out of a complement of 783. It was left to Sir Charles Oman in his History of the Peninsular War decades later to put anything in writing to correct the balance which until then had been almost all in the favour of the 48th Northumberland, heroic as their own efforts had been during the crisis. I have tried my best to add to that correction.

I have taken a liberty with the conversation between Miles, Ellis and a member the 50th Queen's Own when they meet in Sobral. In my book 'Close to the Colours', at the battle of Coruna the 105th are in the place of the 50th above Elvina and also in the place of the 50th at the battle of Vimeiro.

The incident with Captain Drake at the beginning of the Battle of Busaco is taken from what happened to Ensign Robert Blakeney of the 28th Foot, The Gloucesters. During the retreat to Coruna, the Light Company of the 28th were sent back over the half demolished bridge at Betanzos, the Engineers having failed to blow it up. They were attacked by Heavy Dragoons, one targeting Blakeney. He had only a light infantry sabre with which to defend himself and the Dragoon raised his heavy sabre for the fatal blow. Instead what came down onto Blakeney was the French Dragoon, now dead. From behind came the cry from a man named Oates, "Mr. Blakeney, we've spun him!"

Printed in Great Britain
by Amazon